Publication Number 24

Duke University Commonwealth-Studies Center

Economic Enquiry
in Australia

Duke University Commonwealth-Studies Center Publications

Economic Enquiry in Australia

Craufurd D. W. Goodwin

Published for the
Duke University Commonwealth-Studies Center
Duke University Press, Durham, N. C.
1966

Printed in the United States of America
by Kingsport Press, Inc., Kingsport, Tennessee

To N. V. G.

Foreword

There are fashions in the social sciences, among them economics, just as in many other of man's activities. Utility functions shift and with them demand schedules. In the realm of inorganic science, interest in its evolution has increased appreciably in recent years. In the realm of economics, by contrast, the corresponding subjective utility function seems to have shifted downward. Today some, though by no means all, economists seem to believe the purchase price of knowledge of the development of economics and its application to be too high in terms of opportunity-foregone to warrant their giving it much attention. Presumably they believe modern economics to be very superior to its predecessors, and they suppose there still remains too much to be learned to justify a review of ancient folly and its impact. Perhaps also they suppose that a branch of economics concentrating on economic cooperation among interacting individuals is endowed with a very wide rather than a relatively narrow range of problem-solving power.

Are these inferred propositions tenable? Did the economists of yesterday do so badly? Do those of today do as well as has been implied? Is there something useful to be learned from study of the role of a developing social science in a developing society? Professor Goodwin's book prompts these questions anew, though quite convincing answers have already been given.

Yesterday's economists did not do so badly, George Stigler finds; nor is "perfection yet the signature" of the modern economist. "Modern economists at their best can write somewhat better reports," though they "usually write inferior ones." Here Stigler is referring to the report of a Royal Commission appointed by Queen Victoria in 1837 to inquire into the condition of the unemployed hand-loom weavers and put forward corrective solutions; and he adds that the work of the classical economists on such questions as those relating to money and banking was of the same high order.

Why did the classical economists do so well? It was not because their technical apparatus was superior to that of today's economists. After all, great progress has been made in economic science in the last hundred years. It was, as Stigler suggests, because the classical economists focused their apparatus upon issues posed by concrete problems. The problems under analysis channelled the discussion, fitting it to the peculiarities of these problems, and when necessary curbed the economists' "striving for generality." This early concern with serious problems also produced a second effect. It inverted a principle made concrete by Gresham; interest in great problems displaced that in small problems.[1] After all, England was too poor in economists to waste their time upon minor matters, thus setting an example that might well be followed in present-day Africa and Asia.

Much, perhaps all, of the world today still bears a strong resemblance to the world of the classical economists. It is vastly richer, of course, in goods and services. In some regions it is well enough endowed with economists to permit many of them to behave as J. von Neumann observed some mathematicians to do; they may transform ideas emerging out of empirics into ideas with lives of their own and thus make of political economy a kind of *l'économie pour l'économie*. Yet man's world remains a world of problems, not "one world" with quite similar problems, but a collection of small worlds each afflicted with its own particular problems. What is set down in leading American textbooks, therefore, is of quite limited use to administrators and others confronted by particular problems in particular worlds; the textbooks have little to say of concrete problems, and what they do say usually is not made highly relevant to any one of these worlds. "Principles," even when highly generalizable at an abstract level, must be subjected to the discipline of real problems before their application can contribute much in the form of

1. This and the preceding paragraph are based upon Stigler's *Five Lectures on Economic Problems* (New York, 1950), pp. 34–36.

concrete solutions; and visiting economists, if they would succeed, must allow for the dearth of relevant information in the countries to which they minister as well as for unique elements in the socio-economic environments with which they have to deal.[2] Even so, given the continuing discipline of problems in search of solutions, visiting as well as indigenous economists can make the modern analytical apparatus yield workable solutions.

Professor Goodwin's new study of the development of economic science in Australia lends support to Stigler's findings and to Seers's wise counsel. While the migrants settling in Australia brought with them a considerable if uneven acquaintance with received and non-received economics of British provenance, they had to constrain their application of this imported body of generalities within confines imposed by the problems under analysis. It is not surprising, therefore, that though Australians produced no all-encompassing systems of Walrasian genre, they did produce much competent discussion, and, in the area of inter-economy relations and macro-economics, analyses of a high and sometimes path-breaking order. Failure of the antipodal world to appreciate the worth of these contributions largely reflects the absence in the nineteenth century and even in the early twentieth century of that vast infrastructure of international communication which today places at the disposal of the economist in Montreal exposition of a theory formulated in Sydney only several months earlier. Parochialism of economic thought need dog the economist no more, however space-bound be the problems which he is called upon to solve.

Professor Goodwin's illuminating study may be fruitfully compared with his earlier study of the development of economic science in Canada. In both countries we find the same problems emerging and persisting, problems much more typical of newly and sparsely settled countries than of the densely populated, village-studded lands of present-day Asia: what to do about trade, protection, and industrialization; how optimize land settle-

2. See Dudley Seers, "The Limitations of the Special Case," *Bulletin of the Institute of Economics and Statistics,* Oxford, XXV (May, 1963), 77–98, and "Why Visiting Economists Fail," *Journal of Political Economy,* LXX (August, 1962), 325–38; M. Bronfenbrenner, "Balm for the Visiting Economist," *ibid.,* LXXI (June, 1963), 293–97.

ment; how meet the money, tax, and fiscal needs of a young economy; how resolve the problem of transport, so crucial and strategic in the economic development of every extensive land mass; how define the economic role of the state; how cope with population shortage and release economies of scale; and so on. There are differences too. More interest was manifest in social evolutionary theory in Australia than in Canada and there was greater concern with labor problems, since the pattern of population distribution and the inflow of trade-unionists made for the early development of an Australian trade-union movement. Coping with a shortage of university economics teachers seems to have presented greater difficulties in distant Australia than in Canada which could draw more easily upon the mother country as well as upon its neighbor to the south, a neighbor whose potentially ominous presence incidentally fed Canada's unifying nationalism.

Professor Goodwin's study draws attention finally to many factors which condition the international diffusion of social science theory and practice. Correlated to this is his evidence of the interaction between the development of economic ideas and their application and the development of an emerging national economy in form and character. Even his description of representative samples of Australian pamphlet and related literature contributes to our understanding, for this literature, however pedestrian or worse, often kept discussion alive in an age when modern media of communication were not available.

One is tempted in an introduction to draw attention to choice bits. This temptation must be resisted. Even by readers had happiness and satisfaction best be earned.

The Commonwealth-Studies Center is concerned with the encouragement of research, and specific theories or interpretations of Commonwealth affairs appearing in these publications do not constitute an expression of the view of the Center or of the Carnegie Corporation, which has furnished financial support to the Center. The respective authors of the several publications are responsible for the conclusions expressed in them.

JOSEPH J. SPENGLER

Introductory Statement

The past two centuries have witnessed an international flow of ideas unmatched at least since the Hellenistic and Roman periods. The great colonizing nations of Europe have sent forth social philosophies and practical expertise in community organization together with their capital, labor, and entrepreneurs. Throughout the British Empire, until the middle of the nineteenth century, compulsion played the major role in the transplantation of institutions and of thought. Embryonic parliaments, systems of law, revenue devices, monetary forms, and land regulations were established under the close scrutiny of colonial authorities. After mid-century, the passage of ideas and of institutions became more complex. British influence remained predominant through continued economic and political ties and an uninterrupted flow of immigrants and cultural media. With independence, however, colonists became more selective in making adoptions and accepting inspiration. The influence of North American experience increased steadily through publications from the United States, visits abroad by colonists, and arrival of American immigrants. Continental ideas were introduced directly by European settlers and second-hand by English-speaking writers. By the second half of the nineteenth century, British colonies had developed a diverse cultural heritage and had begun to produce their own intellectuals capable of distinctive creative thought.

This book is an essay both in economic history and in the history of economic doctrines. It proposes to shed light on the process of economic development and to trace the modification and advance of ideas in a new environment. The study focuses on enquiry into aspects of the Australian economy from early days of settlement until the onset of the Great Depression in

1929, by which time the continent had begun to achieve cultural autonomy as well as political union and independence. During this period an idea system was transmitted from the relatively advanced civilizations of Europe and America to the primitive surroundings of the Southern Hemisphere. Australians imported and adapted economic theory and analytical techniques as they sought to understand and to control the functioning of their economy. This study is rooted fundamentally in a belief that a full explanation of economic development requires an analysis of factors that are not susceptible to statistical treatment. Economic ideas, as a strong force driving men to action, constitute one of the most powerful of these factors.

Economic ideas were only a part of the intellectual equipment, cultural heritage, attitudes, and beliefs settlers brought with them to the new world, and in some respects these ideas were as inappropriate as plum pudding at a southern Christmas. But Australians selected, modified, and operated fundamentally within the structure taken from abroad. The nineteenth century was a time of active intellectual ferment as well as of rapid colonization, and even imitation required close attention to outside developments. The distinctive feature of British settlement in Australia was less the need for extensive adjustment of social forms to the new environment than the relative lack of complications encountered in bestowing old-country institutions on the new.

It was possible for Australians to take from foreign countries and apply locally some types of economic thought more easily than others. Fundamental issues in monetary, commercial, population, and transport policy had been discussed fully in older lands, and contemporary pronouncements from abroad were merely interpreted for local controversies. The basic question of the correct role for government in the economy had long held the attention both of mercantilist and classical economists, and this dispute was taken directly from the old world to the new. In some matters, other countries had little to contribute to discussions of Australian economic policy. For example, both British and American intellectuals were fascinated by land disposal and settlement, but their lack of familiarity with the distinctive character of the Australian pastoral economy and their personal prejudices based on long residence in a different environment limited the usefulness of their comments. In considerations of labor regulation and welfare legislation, Australians usually were in advance of other countries and could receive guidance only on matters of principle. Certain basic dissimilarities between the societies and economies of Australia and of Great Britain, in particular the different conceptions of democracy and the contrasting factor scarcities, limited the simple transplantation of all economic ideas from the mother country to the colony.

The raw materials of this study are books, pamphlets, lectures, debates, articles, and public documents prepared by residents of the Australian continent. A few of the works examined claim places in the history of economic analysis, but these are not the center of attention here.[1] The principle objective is to identify the presence of ideas and methods of enquiry rather than to assess the relative importance of individual contributors. Unfortunately, limitation of space has prevented inclusion of extensive background material describing in detail the economic conditions and political controversies in which economic ideas were discussed. Social, economic, and political histories of the country should be used in conjunction with this work.

In order to trace the development of economic ideas in a society where professional social scientists had only begun to appear, more attention has been given to purely polemical literature than is customary in studies of the history of economic doctrine. It was not possible to canvass all relevant materials; the large number of subject areas and the lengthy time span under examination necessitated rough sampling of less valuable items with concentration on few. In some instances little-known pamphleteers may seem to have been given more prominence than their place in history warrants. This has been necessary in some cases because of the wish to select authors for the quality of their thoughts as

1. Professor J. A. La Nauze has provided detailed discussions of three outstanding Australian economists, W. E. Hearn, W. S. Jevons, and David Syme in *Political Economy in Australia: Historical Studies* (Melbourne, 1949).

well as for their reputations, and in others because of the need to focus on representative works in a very large literature. The unusual appearance of some of the materials examined accounts for occasional peculiarities in footnote form. The designation "n.p., n.d." indicates that place and date of publication are not known. Extensive quotations have been provided throughout the text so as to give the flavor of writings which, for the most part, will be unavailable in the original to a majority of readers. Obvious typographical errors in the originals have been corrected. Some repetition of references was necessary because of the treatment of distinct topics in separate chapters.

Three potentially fertile sources of data—newspapers, manuscripts, and parliamentary debates—were not examined systematically, in part because of their relatively ephemeral character but mainly because of the prohibitive labor. One unfortunate result of this necessary but regrettable exclusion may be an apparent overemphasis on separately published literary material which was often no more important than some leader and correspondence columns and legislative discussion. Heavy dependence generally upon eccentricities in manufacture and preservation of all printed material is recognized.

It is hoped that gaps and distortions in this account may stimulate others to remedy the errors and omissions. The broad-brush approach which has been used, covering a time span of more than a century, was adopted with the conviction that in intellectual history it is better sometimes to have a vision of the forest before examining all of the trees.

This study was begun in the summer of 1960 with assistance from the Duke University Commonwealth-Studies Center which generously made possible six months of research in Australia and the same amount of time in Great Britain. I am grateful to the Australian National University for an appointment as Honorary Research Fellow in 1960–61 and for the use of facilities in Canberra. The Canada Council kindly provided a summer research grant in 1962 to facilitate completion of the manuscript, and the Duke University Council on Research has provided for manuscript typing. My debts to colleagues and friends in Australia,

England, Canada, and the United States are numerous. In particular, Professor John A. La Nauze read all of the manuscript and offered sage advice; Professors Percy Partridge and W. D. Borrie, and Dr. R. T. Appleyard read selected chapters. Professors S. J. and N. G. Butlin gave valuable guidance. I thank them all sincerely and absolve them from the unwitting errors of an inquisitive outsider. The National Library of Australia, the Mitchell Library, Sydney, and the Library of the Royal Commonwealth Society, London, were unfailingly helpful and courteous. Mr. and Mrs. William Musgrave of Epsom, Surrey, provided exceptionally gracious and generous hospitality and access to the personal papers of Sir Anthony Musgrave. The editors of the *Economic Record*, the *Journal of Transport History* and the *Journal of the History of Ideas* have kindly granted permission to reproduce portions of articles by me in these journals. Finally, I must pay special tribute to Professor J. J. Spengler who inspired and guided the project, and to my wife, Nancy, who gave both essential encouragement and tireless assistance.

Contents

Part One
Theory and Policy

Part Two
The Science of Enquiry

Part One

Theory and Policy

International Commerce: I. Protection

Economists in Australia remained preoccupied throughout the period under study, as they did in Europe and America, with questions of international trade. During the first half of the nineteenth century, discussion was restricted in scope by limitations on legislative independence, and during the twentieth century debate was characterized predominantly by tedious repetition. However, in the second half of the nineteenth century, tariffs were the single most controversial economic issue, and writings during these years receive greatest attention here. From the beginning sides were drawn up over the issue of protection to specific industries, and arguments developed by advocates and critics of high tariffs are examined in separate chapters.

Agricultural Tariffs for Colonial Development

The first tariff in the Australian colonies was imposed in 1800, and customs duties became established thereafter as an important revenue source for government.[1] With the exception of certain luxuries, British goods were excluded from colonial tariffs and received preference in this way. Even before 1823, when creation of a nominee Legislative Council brought the earliest vestige of representative government, a few colonists saw in tariffs a potential tool for national development. W. C. Wentworth in 1819 condemned duties on Australian products entering other British possessions such as the Cape of Good Hope and India. He said:

1. A detailed account of early Australian tariff history is: John A. La Nauze, "Australian Tariffs and Imperial Control," *Economic Record*, XXIV (1948), 218–34.

"It can hardly be credited that the veriest sciolist in political economy could have been guilty of such a palpable deviation from its fundamental principles; but it is still more unaccountable, that a succession of governors should have pertinaciously adhered to a system of finance so absurd and monstrous."[2] He deplored also in Australia itself "the present unnatural efforts of the colonists in the establishment of various manufactories, particularly those of cloth and hats."[3] However, despite these protestations in defense of free trade, Wentworth gave unqualified support to an openly protectionist plan for "imposition of so high a duty on the importation of spirits from abroad, as would amount to a prohibition." In "a hasty survey of the advantages" of this proposed restriction, Wentworth set forth the germ of arguments developed repeatedly and in great detail much later in the colonies. He explained:

It would afford employment, and thus impart fresh health and vigor to the agricultural body, debilitated by long suffering and disease; it would place the means of the colonists on a level with their wants, and by creating a good and sufficient medium of circulation in the place of the present worthless currency, would give rise to other channels of industry, and to the speedy establishment of an export trade. It is the only possible way of insuring the colony against the calamitous effects which have hitherto been invariably attendant on the inundations of the river Hawkesbury; it would lessen the injurious preponderancy of the government in the market, by creating a great competition for the purchase of grain, and would thus prevent the arbitrary imposition on this, the principal production of the colonists, of a maximum that is frequently beneath its just value, and it would improve the morals of the present and of future generations.[4]

Wentworth concluded his appeal for favored treatment to distillers and their agricultural suppliers in the same righteous tone used in succeeding years by his protectionist descendants. He maintained: "With these irresistible arguments in favour of this measure, it must be evident that the cause of justice and morality

2. W. C. Wentworth, *A Statistical, Historical, and Political Description of the Colony of New South Wales, and Its Dependent Settlements in Van Diemen's Land* (London, 1819), p. 290.
   3. *Ibid.*, pp. 189–90.
   4. *Ibid.*, pp. 265–66.

would be violated by any further unnecessary delay in its adoption."[5]

Domestic distillation, accompanied by a modified form of agricultural subsidy, remained the objective of colonial protectionists throughout the 1820's. Support came principally from actual and prospective grain producers who wished a buoyant and steady market for their products without the threatened disruptions of periodic foreign importations. Commissioner Bigge, following his mission of investigation, recommended in 1823 special treatment for producers of spirits and also duties on tobacco "with a view to encourage the domestic growth of that article."[6] In Van Diemen's Land, the Hobart *Colonial Advocate* defended mercantilist techniques in general and suggested that protective tariffs were necessary not only to acclimatize domestic industries to new problems of production but also to condition recent immigrants and develop tastes for unfamiliar products. In particular, it was argued, Tasmanians needed special encouragement to acquire a preference for the home-made product over imported rum.

If then it were possible to convince the consumers of ardent spirits, that whiskey was the least destructive to their constitution, and it must be equally pleasant to the taste, there might be some little chance of our distillers coping with the West India Planters on the principles of "Free Trade;" but until that is the case, the produce of Colonial distillation must be in a measure forced into the market by a strong protecting duty upon *all* Foreign and English spirits.[7]

James Atkinson in New South Wales prepared an elaborate case to show that distilleries could become the backbone of Australian agriculture by permitting crop rotation, diversification, and improved efficiency. Distillers might provide markets for produce of a farming yeomanry and reduce economic fluctuations by allowing for export (during depressions) of alternative products

5. *Ibid.*
6. *Report of the Commissioner of Inquiry, on the State of Agriculture and Trade in the Colony of New South Wales* (London, 1823), pp. 32 and 59.
7. "The Custom's Duties," *Colonial Advocate, and Tasmanian Monthly Review and Register,* April 1, 1828, p. 89. See also "Colonial Policy," *ibid.,* May 1, 1828, 113–17.

to grain.[8] After colonial distillation had finally become established in the 1830's, its prohibition was contemplated again. Accordingly, the infant "vine growers" combined and formed a predecessor of later special interest tariff lobbies.[9]

In addition to self-interest, a powerful motive behind early requests for tariff protection was the desire to create a viable balanced economy through commercial restriction, one of the few devices open to colonial governments. Protectionist arguments in the colonies usually were strongly mercantilist in tone and lacked the concern for consumer sovereignty and for freedom of private business enterprise present in contemporary debate in Britain. One spokesman in New South Wales in 1830, after reflecting upon the vital role of the state in a colonial economy, concluded— "I much fear, if we are not fostered and guided by the assistance of the government, and are left to the slow course of time, to force us into a knowledge of our own interest, that the Colony will long languish and be retarded in its prosperity."[10]

During the depression of the 1840's, high tariffs on agricultural products were suggested as a means of restoring lagging prosperity. In 1842 the possibility of independent action by the New South Wales government increased when two-thirds of the Legislative Council were made elective. Protectionists argued that if the home market could be reserved for domestic farm producers a minimum income at least would be guaranteed to the primary sector. One resident of New South Wales claimed: "A duty of 1s. per bushel on wheat, and on other grain in proportion, would fully accomplish all that is required; and if the grain should continue to come in, yield £33,000 per annum to our revenue; if not, our greater and better purpose would be answered."[11] A West Australian advised the local Agricultural and Horticultural

8. James Atkinson, *On the Expediency and Necessity of Encouraging Distilling and Brewing from Grain in New South Wales* (2nd ed.; Sydney, 1829).
9. "Vine Growers—Distillation," *Votes and Proceedings of the Legislative Council of New South Wales*, 1839.
10. John Jamison, *Report of the Agricultural and Horticultural Society of New South Wales, for 1830, by the President* (Sydney, n. d.), pp. 64–65.
11. "State and Prospects of New South Wales.—'Jasoniana,'" *New South Wales Magazine*, 1843, p. 317. See also "Legislative Council-Prospects of the Colony," *ibid.*, pp. 509–19.

Society to secure prohibition of agricultural dumping and thereby "obtain for its producers such legislative protection as will save them from being obliged to gamble upon the chances of accidental importation."[12]

In the depths of depression even some ardent free traders came close to endorsing high tariffs. Archibald Michie, commenting on the collapse of wool prices, expressed regret that laissez faire resulted in dependence on a single export staple. He recalled from the writings of Francis Bacon that humans everywhere tend to imitate and need special encouragement to change modes of behavior. In the colonies where government gave little guidance to private initiative, he observed, several years of hardship had been required to persuade pastoralists that boiling sheep for tallow was profitable when wool prices were low. Only after unnecessary delay had those "who came to scoff, remained to boil." As soon as profitability had once been proved and illustrated publicly, even "tolerably stout old ladies and gentlemen felt almost nervous about trusting themselves with a quiet stroll, in the neighbourhood of a sheep boiling establishment."[13] Michie was led by his reading of Bacon combined with observation of colonial circumstances almost, but not quite, as far along the road to infant industry protection as was John Rae in Canada.[14]

One enthusiast of assistance to colonial agriculture examined British experience with Corn Laws and discovered:

that under the operation of the Corn Laws the price of wheat is infinitely more steady than in the freest possible state of the trade. In the one case the fluctuations never reach 400 per cent., while in the other they range from 250 to 5500!—a rather startling truth to the supporters of a theory which, brought into operation, would ruin and degrade the whole British empire.[15]

12. *Journal of the Agricultural & Horticultural Society of Western Australia*, I (1842), Appendix, p. v.
13. "Mr. Michie's Lecture on the Expediency of Establishing a Society for the Advancement of the Arts, Agriculture, and Commerce of the Colony," *Sydney Morning Herald*, June 4, 1844.
14. John Rae, *Statement of Some New Principles on the Subject of Political Economy* (Boston, 1834).
15. A Pythagorean [Francis Campbell], *An Abstract of all the Corn Laws, which have been Passed from Time to Time, for the Regulation of the Export and Import of Corn, &c., &c., and for the Encouragement of Agriculture, Compiled from Various Sources* (Sydney, 1844), pp. 55–56.

This author decided, as did other Australians, that local corn laws for the colonies had become vital just at the time they were being abolished in the mother country. He concluded: "It has always appeared to me that Agriculture must either be encouraged by some legislative protection, or we shall be obliged at last to go back to the mast and the acorns, the beans and the lentils of the golden age, without the advantage of its simplicity and innocence."[16]

The culmination of protectionist activity in the 1840's was a customs bill which passed the New South Wales Legislative Council in 1843 but was disallowed by Imperial authorities. A gradual return of prosperity helped reduce sentiment in favor of higher tariffs, and the clear evidence of British adherence to free trade in repeal of the Corn Laws intimidated hesitant protectionists. A few staunch advocates did remain; for example, in New South Wales, James Martin repeated the plea that national development could not take place without an industrial sector supported by government, and he cited the English writer John Barnard Byles for authority. Martin summarized his critique of laissez faire thus: "The transparent error of the free traders consists in the assumption, that under their system all persons will be fully employed. If such were the fact, then probably it would be a sound principle generally to buy in the cheapest market. But the fact is far otherwise."[17] Writing as he was on the brink of the gold rush Martin, for a few years, was as one crying in the wilderness.

Self-Government and Gold

The Australian Colonies Government Act of 1850 made possible the introduction of modified responsible government in

16. *Ibid.*, pp. 3–4. Additional manifestations of support for agricultural protection in the 1840's are described in Michael Roe, *Society and Thought in Eastern Australia, 1835–1851*, Thesis Submitted for the degree of Doctor of Philosophy in the Australian National University, 1960, pp. 129–30, 149, and 320–21.

17. James Martin, *Speech Delivered in the Legislative Council, on Tuesday, the 2nd Day of July, 1850, on Moving the Second Reading of a Bill to Abolish all Duties on Brandy and Spirits Distilled in the Colony of New South Wales, from Grapes and Grain of Colonial Growth* (Sydney, 1850), p. 13.

all the older colonies during the 1850's. Legislatures were given freedom to determine their own commercial policies, with a single prohibition on discrimination among foreign countries. The discovery of gold in 1851 created complicated problems to test this new-found independence. Protection did not become a major issue until later years of the decade when decline in the yield of surface metal posed difficulties of adjustment for thousands of unemployed miners.

In New South Wales, in contrast to Victoria, a relatively diversified economy and smaller proportionate impact of gold discoveries prevented the protectionist movement from becoming dominant. But in Sydney considerable agitation did take place. After a public meeting in 1857, representatives of a "League for the Protection of Australian Industry" petitioned the Legislative Assembly for diversification of the economy through "state encouragement." They claimed that the current "general depression of business" and "want of employment" were "all traceable to the excessive importation of such foreign commodities as we are perfectly well able to produce ouselves, and the abstraction of our circulating capital for the payment of them."[18] Ironically, one of the committee's delegates was, in the tradition of Bastiat, a candle-maker.

James Norton, a vocal protectionist in the New South Wales Legislative Council, could muster a variety of convincing arguments in support of trade restriction. He emphasized the need to provide increasing employment for a rapidly growing population, and he noted social economies generated by protected manufacturing industry. Norton doubted that a staples-producing economy could either employ the sons of graziers and miners or provide the new nation with capable leaders. He explained:

It is the bane of the colony that it presents no means of employing the educated of the rising generation. To provide for its population by the raising and sale of raw produce would perpetuate a condition fatal to its future national character. It is by the varied arts of manufacture that science is called into operation and a demand created for

18. "Colonial Industry. (Petition for Protection to.)," *Votes and Proceedings of the Legislative Assembly of New South Wales,* 1857.

the exercise of scientific and mental pursuits. Until that period, in its history, shall have arrived, her sons must exchange their school and college studies for the barbarous pursuits of the grazier. Never will the colony be in a condition to supply its great national councils until its wants are provided for from within. Never will the fortunes necessary for the maintenance of gentlemen of high breeding be realized until the genius of the people is directed to the manufacture and construction of things which are essential to the existence of a cultivated state of society. Until the accomplishment of this object, the accumulations of wealth required for the support of gentlemen, who can afford to devote their time and talents to the interest of their country can never take place.[19]

Norton made effective use of protectionist authorities, particularly J. B. Byles and John Stuart Mill in discussions of infant industries. He admired tariff policies of the United States, and he referred his audience enthusiastically to "the works of Mr. Daniel Webster and Mr. Henry Clay."[20]

W. B. Allen, another vocal protectionist, emphasised the relativity of economic principles used to bolster free trade. "I look upon it as extremely doubtful, whether any system of political economy can be laid down that will in detail meet the circumstances of all, so long as the nations themselves are so dissimilar."[21] Australia, he said, must adopt a vigorous national policy if it wished to grow diversified, independent, and strong like the United States. Anticipating protectionists later in the century he maintained that high tariffs could bring benefits to everyone, including consumers, and losses to none. "If I pay the shoemaker and all others extra for their articles, I get it back from the shoemaker and all others who pay extra for mine. Thus in the end I am nothing out of pocket, whilst we all get constant employment at a fair remuneration, and are richer as a nation by the difference between the export value of the raw material on which we labour,

19. James Norton, *Government and Taxation of the Colony* (Sydney, 1856), p. 10. A similar exposition is contained in J. Norton, *Free Trade and Protection* (Sydney, 1857).

20. James Norton, *Facts for the Protectionists* (Sydney, 1857), p. 8, and *The Condition of the Colony of New South Wales* (Sydney, 1860), pp. 5–6 and 14. A collection of Norton's writings was published as *Australian Essays on Subjects Political, Moral, and Religious* (London, 1857).

21. *Lecture on Protection, Political Economy Proper for New South Wales* (Sydney, n. d.), p. 3.

and the price we must pay did we purchase the foreign manufacture."[22]

In the New South Wales Legislative Assembly, Henry Parkes gave support temporarily in the late 1850's to proposals for protection. Parkes read widely in the literature of economics, and a report of a Select Committee on the Condition of the Working Classes of the Metropolis, of which he was chairman, set forth cogent arguments for a restrictive policy. He emphasized the need to provide stable employment for city dwellers, and he outlined the infant industry argument of Mill, possibly influenced by a reading in the original of John Rae.[23] Parkes quoted at length from Richard Jones to show that colonies should pursue an independent course in economic policy, and he maintained that prevailing circumstances dictated an immediate increase of tariff rates.

We have the authority of eminent economists in support of raising revenue in a new country by the imposition of duties that would tend to foster manufacturing enterprise, and such encouragement to our own people, within well considered limits, would not be inconsistent with practical freedom in our commercial intercourse with the World, while no nation affords us an example of the establishment of manufactures without such encouragement. But it is respectfully submitted that we are not to follow blindly the course of other countries, but to be guided in our economical arrangements by such principles as are most applicable in the peculiar circumstances of our own.[24]

Parkes' enthusiasm for protection did not last long under the personal attack, while in Britain, of such authorities as Mill and Cobden, and he became known again by the mid-1860's as a prominent champion of free trade.

Protectionist sentiment in New South Wales was so strong by

22. *Ibid.*, pp. 14–15.
23. J. A. La Nauze, " 'That Fatal, That Mischievous Passage,' Henry Parkes and Protection, 1859–66," *Australian Quarterly*, XIX (1947), No. 2, pp. 52–61, and *Political Economy in Australia: Historical Studies*, p. 15 n. A review article in Parkes' newspaper, the *Empire*, entitled "Economics in the Sandwich Islands" may have referred to some of Rae's obscure later writings. *Empire*, February 4, 1853, p. 1914.
24. "Report from the Select Committee on the Condition of the Working Classes of the Metropolis; together with the Proceedings of the Committee, Minutes of Evidence, and Appendix," *Votes and Proceedings of the Legislative Assembly of New South Wales*, 1859–60, p. 11. See also T. A. Coghlan, *Labour and Industry in Australia* (London, 1918), pp. 702–3.

1862 that a petition praying that government "by every possible means, encourage the Colonial Manufactures" attracted 3,666 signatures.[25] A select committee in 1862 examined the health of the economy, and deplored the high level of unemployment it discovered. The committee condemned dumping by foreign suppliers in the colonies, a practice described as "the free importation of inferior goods, particularly the system of consignments, which are generally sold at auction for much less than the first cost of manufacturing." Committee members considered the infant industry argument carefully, and after hearing plaintive appeals from witnesses for at least "incidental protection," recommended an immediate alteration of the tariff "to encourage the manufactures and cultivation of the Colony."[26] Of fourteen petitions submitted to the Legislative Assembly in 1863–64 dealing with commercial policy, nine favored "protective duties;" only two were opposed directly to protection; and three were equivocal.[27]

In Victoria, protection came to be viewed in the 1850's as an appropriate panacea for a number of pressing problems. During the gold-boom years early in the decade, farmers, beset by soaring costs and enraged with the loss of customers to importers, appealed for preservation of the home market for domestic producers. Led by the Geelong *Advertiser*, farmers repeated arguments, now familiar, for assistance to raw material producers.[28] Later in the 1850's demands for protection became more complex. Farmers complained still of their hardships but were joined by spokesmen for miners faced with declining gold yields and barriers both economic and institutional to appropriation of the land. Return to the old country was a desperate last resort for the unemployed miners, and the only alternative seemed creation of employment—generating industries in the towns. A tract in

25. "Petition. Colonial Manufactures. (Encouragement of)," *Votes and Proceedings of the Legislative Assembly of New South Wales*, 1861–62.

26. "Progress Report from the Select Committee on the State of Manufactures and Agriculture in the Colony; together with the Proceedings of the Committee, and Minutes of Evidence," *Votes and Proceedings of the Legislative Assembly of New South Wales*, 1862, pp. 3, 9, 23, and 25.

27. *Votes and Proceedings of the Legislative Assembly of New South Wales*, 1863–64.

28. W. T. Charles, "The Victorian Protection Movement," *Victorian Historical Magazine*, XIV (1931), 7–23.

1856 by H. L. Lindsay, a civil engineer and surveyor attracted by gold to Victoria from Ireland, illustrates a combination of these two protectionist motivations. Lindsay recommended government assistance to farmers through subsidized irrigation, free land, and the introduction of new crops, and he also proposed moderate infant industry tariffs to afford occupation for non-farm labor in use of "the produce of this colony which might be manufactured at home . . . with protective duties on foreign articles of a similar kind, to balance our want of coal."[29]

Several Victorian protectionists began to inject into economic arguments for tariffs a note of aggressive nationalism and neomercantilism. William Bryson, another civil engineer, saw industrial protection as a vital step toward achievement of colonial greatness. "Manufactures would open an healthy outlet for colonial industry, invention, and enterprise for the present and future generations. And while the production of raw materials gives employment to only a few in the lowest order of labor, manufactures would require a division of skilled labor, and diffuse benefits among the general population."[30] Bryson believed that Australia could not count forever on British beneficence, and he expressed concern over the threat of transport interruption by Russia during the Crimean War. He urged rapid attainment of economic autonomy—"in time of war dependence on such importations must reduce us to great straights, and panics, and severe loss, and possibly even to plague and famine."[31] As attainment of national greatness became the declared aim of protectionists, the example of United States economic growth was admired often. Writings of American economists, particularly Henry Clay and Friedrich List, were cited regularly and were even reprinted.[32]

29. H. Lill Lindsay, *The Industrial Resources of Victoria with Practical Suggestions on Agriculture, Employment of Labour, Water Supply, &c.* (Melbourne, 1856), p. 49.
30. William E. Bryson, "On the Resources of Victoria, and their Development," *Transactions of the Philosophical Institute of Victoria*, IV (1859), 142.
31. *Ibid.*, p. 144. Similar appeals for the development of Victorian industry were: Cincinnatus, *The Best Plan to Improve the Affairs of the Colony* (Melbourne, 1860); and Charles Mayes, *Essay on the Manufactures more Immediately Required for the Economical Development of the Resources of the Colony, with Special Reference to those Manufactures the Raw Materials of Which are the Produce of Victoria* (Melbourne, 1861).
32. George Ward Cole, a prominent Melbourne merchant and member of the

The disastrous Irish famine of the 1840's was selected usually by protectionists as a typical example of catastrophic results of free trade in the British Empire, a particularly vivid illustration for the many recent immigrants from Ireland. Considerable latent republicanism and transplanted Irish nationalism lay beneath the surface of demands for protection in Victoria. Settlers from the old country demanded repetition in the colonies of American economic success and not of what they considered the shameless exploitation of Irish peasants by English landlords. For example, William Robinson warned in 1860: "If duties be not imposed on foreign goods for the purpose of employing a higher percentage of the labor power of this country at farming, mining and manufacturing pursuits, the people of Victoria, like the inhabitants of Ireland, may find, when gold becomes scarce, the much puffed-up theory of free trade like Franklin's whistle."[33]

By the end of the 1850's effective propaganda from protectionists had caused knowledge of the case for high tariffs to become widely known in Victoria. A legislative committee called to investigate the question received extensive testimony from many witnesses and was presented with a variety of arguments both

Legislative Council, extracted and published from List's *National System of Political Economy* portions which "contain much to instruct those who have made Victoria their home." Cole was convinced that "A careful perusal of the extracts from 'List' will shew clearly the necessity of a careful revision of the tariff, not with a view of fostering any particular branch of manufacture, but a comprehensive scheme that would foster every branch of manufacturing industry, and give security to those who would embark their capital in manufacturing enterprise." G. W. Cole, *Protection as a National System Suited for Victoria: being Extracts from List's National System of Political Economy* (Melbourne, 1860), p. iii. Cole published selections from speeches by Henry Clay in a pamphlet entitled *How a Protective Tariff Worked in America: To the Editor of the Age* (Melbourne, 1861). Cole repeated his protectionist arguments ten years later in: *A Policy of Action, in Employment for the People* (Melbourne, 1871). A biographical sketch of Cole is contained in the *Australian Pictorial Almanac* (Sydney, 1880), p. 40.

33. William Robinson, *Protection to Native Industry: A Lecture Delivered at the Melbourne Mechanics' Institute, on Monday, 27th November, 1860, in Support of the Views Advocated by Those who are in Favor of a System of Protection to Native Industry* (Melbourne, 1888), p. 5. Robinson gave a graphic portrayal of the horrors which would result from continued free trade. "In addition to some forty or fifty thousand mothers who are anxious to have employment found for their children at some branch of industry we have eighty or ninety thousand children who must become hewers of wood or occupiers of gaols, reformatories, and brothels if the State does not impose taxes upon articles manufactured and breadstuffs grown in foreign countries, for the purpose of enlarging the circle of employment here." *Ibid.*, p. 16.

reasonable and fallacious. Victorians testified that, in addition to increasing employment and developing infant industries, protection would create a valuable pool of skilled labor, improve the level of economic stability, attract immigrants and foreign capital, prevent dumping, and eliminate leakage from the monetary circulation. One manufacturer who objected to protection in principle was asked sternly by the committee: "You are aware that McCulloch, and all the political economists, recommend in the exceptional case we are in, as a young colony; or, if they do not recommend, they say, that duties may be levied to foster native industry?"[34] The committee concluded that for an "advantageous re-adjustment of the Tariff . . . the condition and interests of the industrial classes of the Colony should receive primary consideration."[35]

In 1860 David Syme assumed control of the influential Melbourne *Age*, and through a steady stream of editorials, manifestos, letters, pamphlets, and articles, made protectionist arguments commonplace to the Victorian public.[36] During the 1860's protection became associated firmly in the minds of voters with radical nationalism, aggressive colonial self-assertion, and opposition to monopoly and tight imperial control.

Diversification of a Staples Economy

Throughout the 1860's and 1870's, protectionist arguments, already familiar by the end of the 1850's, were repeated often in all the colonies. The final and bitter failure in 1863–64 of attempts to bring about intercolonial tariff co-operation gave free rein to provincialism,[37] and in New South Wales signs of official interest

34. "Progress Report from the Select Committee upon the Tariff; together with the Proceedings of the Committee and the Minutes of Evidence," *Votes and Proceedings of the Legislative Assembly of Victoria*, 1859–60, p. 126 and *passim*.
35. *Ibid.* Graham Berry set forth a summary of contemporary protectionist arguments in a letter to the Melbourne *Age*, 7 June, 1859, reprinted in C. M. H. Clark, *Select Documents in Australian History 1851–1900* (Sydney, 1955), pp. 260–62.
36. Syme's contributions and his place in the controversies surrounding commercial policy are described by Professor La Nauze, *Political Economy in Australia: Historical Studies*, pp. 122–24.
37. Cephas Daniel Allin, *A History of the Tariff Relations of the Australian Colonies* (Minneapolis, 1918), *passim*.

in trade restriction appeared. During a recession which began in
1864, Saul Samuel, the colonial treasurer, proposed a system of
high revenue tariffs with a measure of "incidental protection"
similar to that introduced in Canada a few years earlier by
Alexander Galt. Samuel cited McCulloch to show the reasonableness of such action, and after describing the beneficial effects in
Canada, concluded: "That was the result of Mr. Galt's experience
in Canada; and I think we require nothing more to show the
fairness and justice of the proposition I have now submitted."[38]
The New South Wales tariff imposed in 1866 did include relatively high ad valorem duties and inspired protectionists in the
legislature to form a special committee to state their case more
fully. This committee deplored the existence of unemployment
"to an extent never before experienced in this city" and recommended as an appropriate antidote a tariff of twenty per cent
on imported goods manufactured of wood or of leather.[39] The
suggestion was not accepted, partly because of vigorous opposition from Henry Parkes, now a convinced free trader.[40] After
this date and until the 1880's protection did not gain any
measure of respectability or support in New South Wales, and the
occasional advocate often felt compelled even to write under a
pseudonym.[41] Archibald Forsyth, a Sydney rope manufacturer,
was exceptional in his outspoken and often expressed appeals
for higher tariffs.[42]

In Victoria protection gained strength and favor just as it de-

38. James Thomson, ed., *The Financial Statements of the Colonial Treasurers
of New South Wales* . . . (Sydney, 1881), p. 150.
39. "Report from the Select Committee on the Unemployed; together with the
Proceedings of the Committee, and Minutes of Evidence," *Votes and Proceedings
of the Legislative Assembly of New South Wales*, 1866.
40. T. A. Coghlan, *Labour and Industry in Australia*, pp. 1137–39.
41. For example: Patriot, *Letters on Free Trade v. Protection and Encouragement to Native Industries* (Sydney, 1877). The author emphasized the contrast
between United States prosperity and Irish poverty but without hope of the
enthusiastic reception for this comparison customary in Victoria.
42. Archibald Forsyth, *Free, Fair, and Protected Trade: Which is the Best for
England, New South Wales and Australia?* (Sydney, 1885); *Protection or Free
Trade* (Sydney, n. d.); *The Lines on Which a Federal Tariff Should be Based*
(Sydney, n. d.); "Relations between Capital and Labour Examined," *Aus-
tralian Economist*, I (1888–90), 99–103. Forsyth was attacked often by New
South Wales free traders because he was one of the few articulate local targets.
See Edward Pulsford, *Free Trade and Protection: An Answer to Mr. Forsyth's
Pamphlet* (Sydney, 1885).

clined in New South Wales. Melbourne in the 1860's did not have as powerful or established a merchant class favoring low tariffs as did Sydney, nor did it have a free trade tribune of Henry Parkes' stature. Victoria did, however, experience a proportionately greater impact from gold discoveries, and it inherited as a result a larger share of social problems. Melbourne received a steady flow of ambitious and energetic immigrants from the United States and from Britain—particularly from Ireland—who were not responsive to resigned statements that unemployment was inevitable or that national development should be left unencumbered to take place "naturally." Settlers, who before their gold fever had been skilled laborers, demanded in the 1860's employment in their old trades which, they maintained, could be created in new surroundings by a beneficent government.[43] A select committee in 1864–65 examined the experience of the distilling, brewing, and tobacco industries, the only ones which hitherto had received favored treatment under colonial tariffs, and optimistically it "arrived at the conclusion that the imposition of these duties has led largely to the investment of capital, the employment of labor, and a decrease in the cost to consumers of the articles manufactured."[44] Thus, practical evidence was added to the often proclaimed theoretical arguments for increased protection.

In 1866, after a campaign in which city artisans led by Syme and the *Age* joined displaced gold miners and even some farmers, the Victorian Legislature passed the McCulloch tariff, the first openly-avowed protectionist program in the colonies.[45] The tariff, in fact, was only mildly protectionist of selected articles and was compared to Galt's Canadian "incidental" protection.[46] But the

43. Alfred Deakin reminisced about the excitement of commercial policy controversies during this period in, *The Crisis in Victorian Politics, 1879–1881: A Personal Retrospect*, edited by J. A. La Nauze and R. M. Crawford (Melbourne, 1957), p. 2.
44. "Report from the Select Committee upon Manufactures; together with the Proceedings of the Committee, and Minutes of Evidence," *Votes and Proceedings of the Legislative Assembly of Victoria*, 1864–65, p. iii.
45. T. A. Coghlan, *Labour and Industry in Australia*, pp. 1137–39.
46. *Age*, January 10, 1866. J. Beaufort Hurlbert, a relatively obscure Canadian protectionist propagandist, was even cited as authority. *Ibid.*, January 25, 1866. See my *Canadian Economic Thought* (Durham, 1961), pp. 46–47. In the early 1870's the ideas of an equally obscure American protectionist disciple of Henry

protection issue was discussed thoroughly as part of the complex conflict of class interest surrounding the election. Tariffs were identified by the *Age* as the policy of "the people" with support from groups similar to those behind the British Anti-Corn Law League. Free trade, on the other hand, was said to find advocates in "the friends of squatterdom," "the Melbourne Club and the banks."[47]

After Victoria had once embarked definitely on a protectionist course it became increasingly more difficult to turn back. Within ten years, from 1864 to 1874, employment in manufacturing quadrupled, from approximately seven thousand to twenty-eight thousand, and a solid body of voters with a special interest in high tariffs was created.[48] During the same period New South Wales became committed firmly to free trade, and rivalry between the two colonies over commercial policy grew intense. A reversal of legislation by Victoria would have required a painful admission of past error and recognition of the greater wisdom of a competitive neighbor. Moreover, protectionists in Victoria were emboldened by their initial success in the 1860's and they intensified pleas for still higher rates. They drew comparisons between conditions before and after 1866, and invariably they found the latter more satisfactory. For example, James Mirams in 1873 compared the period 1859–65 with 1866–72, and he discovered that as a result of protection all aspects of daily life had improved, even to a reduction in the numbers of "criminals executed" and "suicides committed." He concluded:

Free-trade is no doubt a beautiful theory, but, like many another, it is perfectly unworkable in practice. There can be no doubt that the idea of men of all classes, of all countries, and of all colours, exchanging the fruits of their soil, the products of their skill, and the results of their genius, perfectly untrammelled, without customs duties or restrictions of any sort is a grand idea, suitable for an Utopian age, and for that only. Unfortunately, or fortunately, we live in an age

Clay, the Rev. Calvin Colton, were influential in the Democratic Association of Victoria. Henry Mayer, *Marx, Engels and Australia* (Melbourne, 1964), pp. 12–13.

47. *Age*, October 14, 1865; November 7, 1865; January 16, 1866; January 30, 1866; March 5, 1866; and April 21, 1866 when the *Age* declares it has "fought and won . . . the fiscal battle."

48. T. A. Coghlan, *Labour and Industry in Australia*, p. 1153.

when all such Utopian ideas have to give place to the practical; when fancies have to make way for figures; when theories have to bow to facts, and when the ideal has to submit to the real.[49]

Throughout the 1860's and 1870's Victorians continued to debate protection as a question of high principle. David Syme, by this time a remarkably successful and astute journalist and the most influential advocate of tariffs, had become also an economist of considerable international reputation.[50] He laid great stress on Mill's infant industry argument and on the wisdom of a community encouraging economic enterprise which would yield general social benefits.[51] Probably influenced by Syme, Francis Gould Smith, a native Australian who called himself "Professor of Political Economy," published in 1877 a lengthy catalog of contemporary protectionist arguments, authorities, and relevant historical experiences, the result of "calm and unprejudiced and fully matured researches." He explained that until 1852 he had himself been a convinced free trader; then:

I had my senses whetted on the goldfields of Victoria, in political discussions with men of MANY NATIONS, including the Americans. I now gave myself up to study the cause—for I saw the effects—of our depression in earlier days. . . . From the above-named study of our political condition (which I have continued to this present hour, December, 1876, during which period I have read the history of every civilised nation on the globe) I have arrived at the juncture that a most unflinching and uncompromising system of strict protection to all native industries—not only to those now existing in our midst, but to all those we can develop from the natural resources of each of our colonies—is imperatively demanded.[52]

49. James Mirams, *A Generation of Victorian Politics: Personal Records* (n.p., n.d.), p. 34.
50. J. A. La Nauze, *Political Economy in Australia: Historical Studies*, pp. 98–138.
51. David Syme, *Outlines of an Industrial Science* (London, 1876), pp. 185–87.
52. Francis Gould Smith, *The Australian Protectionist* (Melbourne, 1877), pp. 3, 5, and 6. Smith recounted at a later date in more detail: "My knowledge of the people and governments of foreign nations is based on education and the friction of society in general, including many years on the goldfields of New South Wales and Victoria, before and after the Ballarat disturbances, at which I was present, being at that time the principal 'furnisher' of slabs and all necessaries essential in the sinking of shafts. . . ." *Danger Ahead! Anti Imperial Federation of Australasia* (Melbourne, 1889), p. 1.

Smith was able to cite mercantilist arguments by Tooke, Mun, Child, and Gee, infant industry arguments of classical economists, protectionist popularizations by Byles, and statements on American policy by Henry Clay and Alexander Hamilton. He selected carefully examples from history to show that national development had always taken place through the fostering hand of government.

Relatively sophisticated writers such as Syme and Smith were not the only proponents of protection. Radicals on the lunatic fringe also came to endorse high tariffs and to condemn laissez faire, not so much as part of a constructive program as a form of social protest. John Ebenezer Goodwin, a representative writer of this type, remarked "What political economists say of the natural laws of freedom and the eternal truths of free trade, is effete twaddle and vapid word-wasting."[53]

Widespread enthusiasm for protection posed difficult problems of conscience for some Victorian politicians. Although they themselves favored free trade they sided with protectionists in other economic debates, particularly over land reform. They recognized, moreover, that outright rejection of protection could be tantamount to political suicide and might destroy their influence on all policy matters. Charles Gavan Duffy, an expatriate Irish leader who had emigrated to Melbourne, wrote to John Stuart Mill in 1866 for a solution to this dilemma. Mill formulated a rationale for acceptance by free traders of protective policies which was adopted subsequently by a number of prominent Victorian statesmen. He said:

If an Australian politician wishes to be in the Assembly for the sake of questions which he thinks much more important, for the time being, than that of protection, I should hold him justified in saying to a constituency, "I think protection altogether a mistake, but since it is a *sine qua non* with you, and the opposite is not a *sine qua non* with me, if you elect me I will not oppose it." If he conscientiously thought that the strong feeling of the public in its favour gave them a right, or made it expedient to have it practically tried, I should not think him wrong in promising to support it; though it is not a thing

53. John Ebenezer Goodwin, *Scientific Legislation* . . . (Melbourne, 1878), p. 51.

I should lightly or willingly do. He might even, for adequate public reasons, consent to join a protectionist ministry, but only on condition that protection should be an open question, and that he should be at liberty to speak his mind publicly on the subject.[54]

Charles H. Pearson, an outspoken free trader while a student at Oxford, was willing in Victoria to accept Mill's advice and to embrace protection for the sake of his primary interests, land and educational reform.[55] Alfred Deakin described thus his own conversion from doctrinaire laissez faire to protection:

In 1879 the Free Trade cause was out of court and hopeless. The only question was of higher or lower protective duties, and it was far less uncongenial to consent to increases of ten per cent or fifteen per cent than to have been ranged against the whole of the Liberal programme with which in other respects he was strongly in sympathy. In my own case their was no difficulty at all when I was once satisfied that state interference if wise was beneficial. Disputes as to the particular levies to be made upon imports were evidently to be determined according to the merits of each case. The one remanet of my Free Trade teachings was a conviction that while Protection was judicious the undue or unnecessary increase of duties tended towards monopoly and was to be resisted on that score.[56]

Henry Bournes Higgins, distinguished jurist and prize-winner in political economy under Hearn at the University of Melbourne, was converted to protection in large measure by a dislike of free traders.[57]

The debate over protection in Victoria dragged on into the 1880's. The *Age*, assisted by a few tireless publicists such as James Mirams, continued to issue polemical tirades which consisted more and more of almost meaningless comparisons between

54. Letter to C. Gavan Duffy, 2nd October, 1866, in Hugh S. R. Elliot, ed., *The Letters of John Stuart Mill* (London, 1910), II, 67.
55. "He [Pearson] did not care to tilt against windmills, any more than to build houses on sand." William Stebbing, ed., *Charles Henry Pearson, Fellow of Oriel and Education Minister in Victoria: Memorials by Himself, his Wife, and his Friends* (London, 1900), p. 252; and see also J. M. Tregenza, *The Life and Work of C. H. Pearson, 1830–1894*. Thesis Submitted for the degree of Doctor of Philosophy in the Australian National University, 1959, pp. 31–32, 215, and 287–88.
56. Alfred Deakin, *The Crisis in Victorian Politics, 1879–1881: A Personal Retrospect*, edited by J. A. La Nauze and R. M. Crawford (Melbourne, 1957), p. 6.
57. Nettie Palmer, *Henry Bournes Higgins: A Memoir* (London, 1931), p. 126.

Victoria and New South Wales favorable to the former.[58] A Royal
Commission with Mirams as chairman was appointed in 1881
to take stock of past protection, the initial plan in 1866 having
been to continue tariffs only for a fifteen year infancy period.
Replies to questions put by commissioners to the 548 witnesses
reveal the effectiveness of protectionist propaganda. Spokesmen
for the "mining, agricultural and pastoral, mercantile, and manufacturing classes" were able to explain that tariffs made possible
stable full employment, diversified domestic industry, increased
competition, and improved local working conditions. Farmers,
witnesses observed, gained through strengthened internal markets. To hesitant suggestions that protection might now be
dropped with the end of industrial infancy, the commission retorted that, for the time, dangers of speculative dumping were
too great.

Protection at this point might perhaps be supposed to cease, having
completed its work; but the Victorian manufacturers, in order to
maintain their position in the outside market, must feel assured of
the home trade. Without the duties levied on the articles they manufacture, the Victorian market would, in their opinion, be subject to
periodical disturbances, in consequence of inundations of goods sent
out as speculative shipments. The rates of duty at present in force
steady the market, and speculators have little inducement to make
Victoria the field of their operations.[59]

In the smaller colonies, although controversies over commercial policy were often dissimilar in significance and scope, the
same arguments for protection were used as in New South Wales
and Victoria. Protectionist propaganda from Victoria had considerable impact on other colonies, while at the same time aggra-
vations of Victorian provincialism generated demands for
retaliation.[60] In Tasmania a legislative committee reported in

58. For example: *Protection in Victoria versus Free-Trade in New South Wales*,
reprinted from the *Age*, March-April, 1887 (Melbourne, n. d.); and James
Mirams, *The Progress of Victoria* (London, 1883).

59. "Tariff. Report of the Royal Commission; together with Appendices, and
Minutes of Evidence," *Papers Presented to the Parliament of Victoria*, 1883, Report, p. lxxvi. See also "Tariff. Minutes of the Proceedings of the Royal Commission, 1881–1883," *ibid.*, 1884.

60. B. R. Wise, *Industrial Freedom: A Study in Politics* (Melbourne, 1892),
pp. 58–59.

1868 that "either by means of a Bonus in each case, or by special provision for the protection . . . many latent resources may be developed which would tend to encourage a spirit of enterprise, enlarge the operations of the Agriculturist, and employ a large number of the young people of the Colony, for whom at present no remunerative employment can be secured."[61] Later other Tasmanian protectionists repeated pleas for tariff walls, for the benefit of both manufacturers and farmers.[62] These presentations, however, generally were undistinguished, and one Launceston protectionist was moved to observe regretfully in 1885: "It is unfortunate for the subject that we have no one in the colony who has had advantages of education, leisure, research to take up the question, and more unfortunate still that the Press of the Colony, without exception, holds the strongest free trade views."[63]

A few early South Australians recommended tariff protection in hopes of naturalizing new domestic industries, and by 1880 the case for high tariffs had received full expression.[64] However, not many prominent persons took a positive stand on the tariff, and in general, as Coghlan remarked, "A sort of fiscal indecision was typical of the attitude of South Australia during the whole period."[65] Protectionist conversions in Victoria and in Canada were watched carefully, as was also "the natural shrewdness of the Americans, who would never persist in a policy injurious to themselves."[66] Infant industry arguments of Mill and other economists were collected and interpreted to show that South Australia needed barriers even against her larger colonial neighbors.[67] By the mid-1880's there was evidence of growing support

61. "Report of Select Committee on Colonial Manufactures," *Journals of the House of Assembly of Tasmania*, 1868, p. 3.

62. For example: *Tasmanian Interests in the Proposed Reciprocity Treaty* (Hobart, 1885); and J. W. Cheek, *Protection: as it Affects the Farming Industry of Tasmania* (Launceston, 1888).

63. Thomas Hogarth, *Protection to Colonial Industries: Being a Reprint of a Series of Letters which Appeared in the "Launceston Examiner" August and September, 1885* (Launceston, 1886), p. 6.

64. Samuel Davenport, *Some New Industries for South Australia, Silkworms, Mulberry, Olives, Tobacco, Etc.*, (Adelaide, 1864); and remarks by Governor Sir Anthony Musgrave appended to John Fairfax Conigrave, *South Australian Manufactures and Industries* (Adelaide, 1875), p. 21.

65. T. A. Coghlan, *Labour and Industry in Australia*, p. 1159.

66. *Protection or Free Trade* (Adelaide, 1880), p. 9.

67. The anonymous author of one tract announced modestly that he had

for protection in South Australia and also in the other less populous colonies.[68]

For colonists who were uncertain about the ultimate wisdom or intellectual respectability of protectionism, John Stuart Mill's exposition in his *Principles of Political Economy* [69] of the case for infant industry tariffs was both a comfort and a reassurance. In almost every extensive defense of restrictive tariffs, Mill was certain to be cited at first or second hand, and in many presentations his statements were fundamental to the argument.[70] Mill himself, however, was far from happy with this result. On being informed in 1865 of the impact of his writings in the colonies, he wrote to a correspondent in Victoria a clarifying letter which was published later in a Melbourne newspaper. Mill explained:

It is a great compliment to me that my supposed opinions should have had the influence you ascribe to them in Australia. But there seems to have been a considerable degree of misunderstanding about what they are. . . . I never for a moment thought of recommending or countenancing, in a new colony more than elsewhere, a general protective policy, or a system of duties on imported commodities,

---

"merely endeavoured to collate some of the arguments of others in favor of Protection into a more concise and popular form than they are to be met with in technical works on Political Economy." He added, "The scarcity of Protectionist literature of any kind, in both our private and public libraries, induces the hope that the present imperfect effort may at least lead some who have hitherto blindly accepted Free-trade traditions as infallible, to investigate a little more critically, the respective merits of the two fiscal systems of Protection and Free-trade." *The Advantages of Protection* (Port Adelaide, 1883), p. 1.

68. In South Australia one of twenty-two protectionist petitions for "Alteration of Customs Tariff" in 1884 bore 2,315 signatures, *Proceedings of the Parliament of South Australia*, 1884. The West Australian Tariff Commission in the 1880's maintained repeatedly that one of their aims was "to foster all local industries" by "levying larger imposts on certain manufactured goods—when it is thought such may be successfully produced within the Colony." "Report of the Tariff Commission," *Votes and Proceedings of the Legislative Council of Western Australia*, 1882, and 1887–88.

69. J. S. Mill, *Principles of Political Economy* (4th ed.; London, 1857), II, 512.

70. J. K. Brown, a representative protectionist writer in Melbourne, labeled Mill "the most profound thinker of this, or indeed of any age," and Brown was pleased to assure his audience that "We do not undervalue the beneficial operation of abstract philosophical principles in forming our opinions, or in regulating our conduct." *Our Fiscal Policy: Being an Earnest Expostulation Addressed to Freetraders and Protectionists Alike* (Melbourne, 1875), p. 7. The great weight attached by colonists to Mill's dicta was attested by Waldemar Bannow, *Australasia's Future: How to Shape It* (Melbourne, 1890), p. 9.

such as that which has recently passed the representative assembly of your colony.[71]

In 1868, in a letter published later in Sydney, Mill complained to G. K. Holden that his careful distinction between a selective infant industry tariff and an inclusive protective system continued to be ignored. Mill wrote dejectedly:

. . . I confess that I almost despair of this general understanding being ever practically established. I find that in Australia, protection is not advocated in this form or for this purpose, but that the vulgarest and most exploded fallacies are revived in its support. As far as I can perceive, those who contend for protection in Australia mean it to be as permanent as any other legislative arrangements; and hold to all the false theories on the subject, of which Europe is rapidly ridding itself, and which are declining even in America. In such a state of opinion as this I should resist, with my utmost strength, any protection whatever, because it is far easier to withstand these false and pernicious doctrines before they have been carried into practice to any serious extent, than after powerful protected interests have been allowed to grow up under their influence.[72]

The example of Australian misuse of his theoretical statements and the actual adoption by Victoria of broad and high protective duties led Mill even to revise his position regarding commercial policy. He wrote:

These considerations have greatly shaken the opinion I expressed in my book; and though I still think that the introduction of a foreign industry is often worth a sacrifice, and that a temporary protecting duty, if it was sure to remain temporary, would probably be the best

71. Letter to Henry Soden, in Hugh S. R. Elliot, *The Letters of John Stuart Mill* (London, 1910), II, 27. In a letter to F. Milnes Edge in 1866 Mill admitted that his infant industry argument was employed "in the Australian colonies, erroneously in my opinion, but certainly with more plausibility than can be the case in the United States, for Australia really is a new country whose capabilities for carrying on manufactures cannot yet be said to have been tested. . . ." *Ibid.*, p. 58.

72. *Ibid.*, p. 117, and see also p. 154. Mill wrote to Archibald Michie in 1868: "I need not say how glad I should be to believe that the Victorian Protectionists are Protectionists only within the limits of my excepted case, *i.e.* that they only wish for temporary Protection to try the experiment of naturalising foreign branches of industry. Unfortunately the writings I have seen on their side of the question—I admit that they are not numerous—make no reservation of the kind, but advocate the general theory of Protection on the old ignorant grounds, and support it by the old stock fallacies, and refer to the stupidest authorities— British, American, and Continental—as a sanction for it." *Ibid.*, p. 149.

shape in which that sacrifice can be made, I am inclined to believe that it is safer to make it by an annual grant from the public treasury, which is not nearly so likely to be continued indefinitely, to prop up an industry which has not so thriven as to be able to dispense with it.[73]

A letter from Mill to E. W. Stafford vigorously condemning protection was published in the 1870's by the Free Trade League of Victoria, but to little avail.[74]

Labor, Depression, and Federation

The incessant debate between Victoria and New South Wales over the virtues of their conflicting commercial policies still remained inconclusive by the 1880's.[75] However, significant changes occurred in the circumstances of the protectionist movement during the later years of the 1880's and in the 1890's. First, onset of the greatest depression in half a century reduced employment and government revenues and gave support to calls for protection as a practical solution to both these problems. Second, high tariffs came to be viewed sympathetically in all the colonies by an appreciable portion of the growing labor movement, with the result that protection lost some of its characteristic identification with wealth and with narrow special interests.[76] Third, a mounting sentiment in favor of colonial federation acted to restrain both extreme protectionism and doctrinaire free trade. In early approaches to intercolonial co-operation, notably in 1870, statesmen had found fiscal incompatability to be the main stumbling block and they were anxious to avoid this difficulty in future.[77]

73. *Ibid.*, p. 149, and see also letter to A. M Francis of Brisbane, Queensland, *ibid.*, pp. 200–202.
74. "John Stuart Mill on Protection," in *Free Trade Papers Addressed to the People of Victoria to the End of 1876* (Melbourne, 1877).
75. Even an unbiased American observer in 1888 could see no clear case either for protection or for free trade on the basis of the Australian experience. Fred. Perry Powers, "The Australian Tariff Experiment," *Quarterly Journal of Economics*, III (1888–89), 87–98.
76. F. Picard, "Henry George and the Labour Split of 1891," *Historical Studies Australia and New Zealand*, VI (1953–55), 45–63; and Gordon Greenwood, ed., *Australia: A Social and Political History* (Sydney, 1955), p. 156.
77. "Intercolonial Conference, 1870," *Proceedings of the Parliament of South Australia*, 1870–71.

One of the principal results of these three changes in the background of commercial policy controversy was that protectionism gained strength in all the colonies in addition to Victoria. As B. R. Wise, a prominent free trader, explained in 1892, the British Corn Law protection of early in the century, sustained by the self-interest of a relatively few land owners and overthrown ultimately by the more numerous middle class, was superceded now by protection to manufactures supported in large measure by newly enfranchised industrial workers.[78]

Protectionists in New South Wales began to attract a sizable body of support for the first time in 1885, and they won a general election in 1891.[79] The influence of successful Victorian protectionists was substantial during this period, and arguments in New South Wales were similar to those used earlier in the neighboring colony. Much emphasis was placed on the prevalence of depressions under free trade, on allegedly spectacular progress made by avowedly protectionist countries, and on pronouncements by such authors of "celebrated works on political economy" as J. B. Byles.[80] Adoption of protection by radical leaders was illustrated in contributions to the Sydney *Bulletin*, where writers condemned regularly works of classical economists, Henry George for his free trade advocacy, and local free traders such as Edward Pulsford and Bernard Ringrose (called usually by the *Bulletin* "Ringnose") Wise.[81] The *Bulletin* differed from protectionist manufacturers by insisting that wage increases should always accompany higher tariffs.[82]

Of considerable significance, the *Bulletin* articulated a new

78. B. R. Wise, *Industrial Freedom: A Study in Politics* (Melbourne, 1892), p. 8.

79. The early years of success for New South Wales protectionists are described in: Barbara Atkins, "Antecedents of the N. S. W. Protection Party, 1881–1891: The Protection and Political Reform League," *Royal Australian Historical Society Journal and Proceedings*, XLIV (1958), 239–58. See also Robin Gollan, *Radical and Working Class Politics: A Study of Eastern Australia, 1850–1910* (Melbourne, 1960), p. 95.

80. For example: Henry Dwyer, *Pauperism in New South Wales: Its Cause and Cure* (Sydney, 1887); and C. O. Waldow, *The Present Depression in Trade: Its Cause and Remedy* (Sydney, 1887).

81. "The Progress of Protection," *Bulletin*, VII (1886), No. 354, p. 4; "The Fruits of Free Trade," *ibid.*, No. 355, p. 5; and "Protection and Land Nationalisation," *ibid.*, VIII (1888), No. 419, p. 4.

82. "Protection and Wages," *Bulletin*, III (1886), No. 151, pp. 3–4.

argument that protection was an essential tool for maintenance of a white Australia. Only with tariff walls, it insisted, could white workers be sheltered from the sweated labor of the dreaded "Chow." "We will slowly learn," the journal warned, "and we trust before it is too late to profit by the lesson, that Protection is something more than a means of conserving the local market to the local trader. That it is also a necessity of national existence."[83] The *Bulletin* endorsed the fallacious argument that multilateral trade was possible only between nations with similar living standards, and it claimed that Australia would always need import restriction so long as it faced the menace of a poverty-stricken Asia: "Protection is not a sacrifice in any sense of the term, and it is not for a time but for the best part of an eternity. It will end, and there will be universal Freetrade, when all the nations of the earth have attained to practically the same standard of civilisation."[84]

Under the pressure of depression both radicals and conservatives flocked to the protectionist cause. The poet and solicitor A. B. "Banjo" Paterson attempted to refute Bastiat and Adam Smith on the ground that tariffs alone would "give our industries a start on some other basis than that of cheap labor."[85] E. W. O'Sullivan, journalist and prominent labor leader, cited the "celebrated writers" Henry Carey and Friedrich List to show that protection was essential for maintenance of high wages. He described a succession of similar periods in history when state intervention clearly had been necessary, and he concluded that "nearly all the great practical statesmen of the world—the master minds of the human race and the leaders of men—have been protectionists."[86] In reply to disciples of classical political economy, O'Sullivan said: "What, then, is the value of the theories of philosophers and economists when compared with the successful practical achievements of the master minds of civilisation?"[87] In contrast to O'Sullivan in all respects except views on commercial

83. "Protection—a National Necessity," *Bulletin*, IX (1888), No. 433, p. 4; and see also "Some Georgian Fallacies," *ibid.*, X (1889), No. 474, p. 4.
84. "Watering the Tree of Protection," *Bulletin*, XIII (1894), No. 727, p. 6.
85. A. B. Paterson, *Australia for the Australians* (Sydney, 1889), p. 31.
86. E. W. O'Sullivan, *Protection or Stagnation; Which?* (Sydney, 1897), p. 21.
87. *Ibid.*

policy, Arthur Duckworth, an insurance executive and active amateur economist, approved use of protection with arguments from Tooke, List, and Roscher.[88] In addition to spokesmen for labor and manufacturing, landowners in the 1890's also gave support to a policy of high duties, both as protection for agricultural products and as an alternative revenue source to projected taxes on land rents.[89]

In Victoria little remained to be said for protection during the 1880's and 1890's. Nevertheless, the *Age* sustained a steady flow of propaganda to its weary audience, emphasizing during the depression the "selfish" character of free trade and how Britain was attempting finally to destroy colonial industry and to reduce Australia, like Ireland and India, to a role as hewer and drawer.[90] As tariff rates continued to rise, one protectionist leader-writer for the *Age* exclaimed with satisfaction—"we possess a more scientific Protection than ever we had before," and for clarification he explained: "The economic basis on which Protection rests involves a study of more than mere wealth-getting. It reaches up to the highest social functions of the race."[91] In Victoria as in New South Wales, farmers joined other mendicant economic sectors during the 1890's in pleading for government assistance.[92] After a substantial increase of tariff rates had been approved in 1892, a Board of Inquiry in 1894 reported with alarm that levels of restriction at last seemed "excessive." The Board indicated that although the protection principle was accepted widely, voters retained a limited tolerance for extreme imposts.[93]

88. A. Duckworth, "Notes on Tariff Restrictions," *Australian Economist*, II (1890–93), 229–33.

89. A. W. Martin, "Free Trade and Protectionist Parties in New South Wales," *Historical Studies Australia and New Zealand*, VI (1953–55), 315–23; and W. Pember Reeves, "Protective Tariffs in Australia and New Zealand," *Economic Journal*, IX (1899), 36–44.

90. *The Protectionist's Handbook. Being a Discussion on the Nature and Operation of the Laws of Trade, Reprinted from the Age* (Melbourne, 1895).

91. Benjamin Hoare, *Twenty-Five Years of Protection: How it has Helped Victoria* (Melbourne, 1896), p. 3.

92. W. A. M'Comas, "The Depression in the Wheat Industry and Its Remedy," *Bankers' Magazine and Journal of the Bankers' Institute of Australasia*, VI (1892–93), 902–5.

93. "First Report of the Board Appointed by His Excellency, the Governor in Council to Inquire into the Effect of the Fiscal System of Victoria upon Industry and Production; Upon the Employment of the people; Upon the Condition and Extension of Agricultural, Mining, and other Producing Interests; and

In the smaller colonies the idea of protection during depression had powerful appeal as a solution to unemployment and falling government revenue. A Tasmanian legislative committee in 1889 went so far as to ask advice on how to proceed with commercial restriction from the noted Victorian protectionist James Mirams.[94] R. M. Johnston, Tasmanian Government Statistician, argued that tariffs were a legitimate developmental and antidepression measure, and he cited the American writer Henry Hoyt for authority. Johnston applied the hedonistic principle to commercial policy thus:

> It is the conditions of the various countries which determine *means* to ends. In one country the *means* is Protection, in the other Free Trade; but the *end* in both cases is the same, viz., *the best available mode of supplying the greatest amount of satisfactions to each individual(including local employment to the rising generation) with the least expenditure of individual effort.*[95]

South Australian legislators, although under increasing pressure from distressed industries, remained equivocal.[96] A select committee reported in 1890: "Your committee, whilst not wishing to under-value the necessity existing in every young country for true self-reliance, are compelled to place into prominence the fact that assistance from time to time must necessarily be given by a State to its producers in order to establish and foster new industries"[97] A Western Australian Commission in 1893 refused on principle to recommend out-and-out protection, but at least

---

upon Exports and Imports," *Papers Presented to the Parliament of Victoria*, 1894; and "Second Report . . . ," *ibid.*, 1895–96.

94. "Customs Tariff: Report from the Select Committee, with Minutes of Proceedings and Evidence," *Journals and Printed Papers of the Parliament of Tasmania*, 1889.

95. R. M. Johnston, "Root Matters in Social and Economic Problems. (Is the Poverty of the Masses a Necessary Concomitant of Increased Accumulation of Wealth in the Aggregate?)," *Papers and Proceedings of the Royal Society of Tasmania*, 1889, p. 168; and repeated in "Observations on Current Social and Economic Problems," *Report of the Second Meeting of the Australasian Association for the Advancement of Science held at Melbourne*, 1890, pp. 143–44.

96. "Petition for Protection of Local Manufactures," [2,390 signatures], *Proceedings of the Parliament of South Australia*, 1887.

97. "Report of the Select Committee of the House of Assembly on Bonuses for Agricultural, Dairying, Fruit, and Wine Industries; together with Minutes of Proceedings, Evidence, and Appendices," *Proceedings of the Parliament of South Australia*, 1890, p. v.

for one market it proposed exclusion of "the very lowest classes of goods" on the ground that for these "ample local competition" existed.[98]

The Commonwealth and "New" Protection

At Federation in 1900, debate over commercial policy shifted from the states to the federal Parliament. Protectionists responded immediately to this new challenge and adapted their arguments to the wider sphere. An "Intercolonial Protectionist Conference" was held at Sydney in 1900, and it concluded that high tariffs were vital for creation of a viable Commonwealth. The balanced growth of the United States and Canada were described from "history and common observation," and the dangers in Asiatic competition were emphasized. Agriculturalists were warned particularly that—"a tariff any way approximating the English free-trade one, which was the ideal aimed at by their opponents, demanded a stiff land tax, and perhaps an income tax, to make up the shortage in revenue, and consequently the writing down of their capital (their landed asset) by hundreds of thousands of pounds."[99] The President of the New South Wales Chamber of Manufacturers cited Henry Clay and Archibald Forsyth to prove that protection should be a "permanent policy."[100] Sir William Lyne, Commonwealth Minister of Trade and Customs, termed Sir John A. Macdonald, father of the Canadian protectionist "National Policy," "the greatest of all the sons of Canada."[101] The Melbourne *Age* resurrected significant passages from Mill, List, Carey, and even from Alfred De Lissa's precocious formulation of an international trade multiplier.[102]

98. "Report of the Commission Appointed to Inquire into the Operation of the Existing Customs Tariff of the Colony," *Minutes and Votes and Proceedings of the Parliament of Western Australia*, 1893.
99. *Report of the Intercolonial Protectionist Conference held in Sydney, N. S. W., April 18th to 26th* (Sydney, n.d.), p. 7.
100. Charles E. Ludowici, *Farmers and Manufacturers under Federation* (Sydney, 1900).
101. The Hon. Sir William Lyne, *Imperial Reciprocity* (Sydney, n.d.), p. 3.
102. *A White Man's Land. Australia for the Australians. Free Trade a Failure. Victoria and New South Wales Compared* (Melbourne, 1901), pp. 79–80 and *passim*. See also below Chapter 14.

Protectionists kept their case before the public in submissions to Parliament and through issuance of propaganda.[103] Benjamin Hoare, an *Age* journalist and leader of the Protectionist Association of Victoria, compiled a volume of protectionist argument "to warn others off the quicksands and shallows of fallacy which were a sometime lure and somewhat of a danger to me." Hoare was ecstatic over Carey, List, and Byles; he approved Mill, Carlyle, and Ruskin; and he noted that when he himself had been "half caught by the fascinations of some of the Cobdenic theories" then "the profounder reasonings of the German School of economists came as a corrective."[104] Hoare devoted a chapter of this tedious book to the studies of Schmoller, Knies, and his employer David Syme, the disciple of German historicism in Australia.

The most significant feature of tariff discussions after Federation was an unqualified assurance by protectionists that gains from high tariffs would be shared by all social classes.[105] Tariff advocates promised that under a proposed "new" protection workers would benefit as much through higher wages as would capitalists from greater profits. Increased gains of labor had been used to justify colonial protection for some years, particularly the high rates in Victoria, and part of the labor movement had been willing to endorse protection for industrial encouragement as early as the 1870's. But throughout the colonial period an influential proportion of labor spokesmen refused consistently to accept this device which they feared would merely take from workers through higher prices and give to employers greater profits. It came to be believed after formation of the Commonwealth that at last, with establishment of machinery for wages arbitration, tariff concessions to manufacturers could be made

103. Protectionists testified at length before the Royal Commission on the "Bonuses for Manufactures Bill." See "Report; together with the Proceedings, Minutes of Evidence, and Appendices," *Papers Presented to the Parliament of the Commonwealth of Australia*, 1904.

104. Benjamin Hoare, *Preferential Trade. A Study of its Esoteric Meaning* (Melbourne, 1904), p. 4. A favorable review of this work was: *Imperial Review* (Melbourne, n.d.), No. 41, pp. 2–4.

105. W. K. Hancock, *Australia* (New York, 1930), pp. 82–86; Gordon Greenwood, ed., *Australia: A Social and Political History* (Sydney, 1955), pp. 216–20; and for a contemporary account, Victor S. Clark, "Australian Economic Problems: II. The Tariff," *Quarterly Journal of Economics*, XXII (1907–8), 576–601.

conditional strictly upon division of the spoils with workers. After 1900, insistent pressure from labor spokesmen and a desire of Prime Minister Deakin to construct a broad and permanent base for tariffs led to formulation on this basis of an official program.[106] The infant industry and employment arguments for tariffs were replaced by a less reasonable but more appealing argument that through tariffs foreign suppliers could be forced to pay for higher returns to all Australians.

The flexible Melbourne *Age* endorsed the change of emphasis to new protection and insisted merely that "the old protection" of special favors to manufacturers was still "necessary to the new." The paper said: "We have seen that it is quite possible for tariff protection to the manufacturer to exist without any similar safeguard to the worker. But it is impossible to give any validity to a statutory wage or to the standards of unions unless as a precedent condition the manufacturing producer is placed beyond the competition of the foreign sweater."[107] New protection was given application in 1906 when a Royal Commission reported that high tariffs on imported agricultural implements were necessary to permit payment of adequate wages to Australian workers in that industry.[108] The principle was embodied then in legislation by the Excise Tariff Act of 1906, the Customs Tariff Act of 1906, and the Australian Industries Preservation Act of 1906. A summary government report stated: "The 'old' Protection contented itself with making good wages possible. The 'new' protection seeks to make them actual."[109] Prime Minister Deakin explained to an audience at Ballarat:

New protection, as you know, seeks to secure fair conditions to all those employed in industries which receive the care of the State. I now use the word "care" in a wider sense than "protection," because we propose that the new protection shall not be limited to "protected" industries. They have, perhaps, the first claim, but we desire to es-

---

106. William G. Spence, *Australia's Awakening* (Sydney, 1909), p. 411.
107. *A Wages Question. How Freetrade Injures the Worker. A Series of Articles and Some Letters Reprinted from "The Age"* (Melbourne, 1904), p. 21.
108. "Report of the Royal Commission on Customs and Excise Tariffs," *Papers Presented to the Parliament of the Commonwealth of Australia*, 1906.
109. "New Protection—Explanatory Memorandum in Regard to," *Papers Presented to the Parliament of the Commonwealth of Australia*, 1907–8, p. 1.

tablish fair conditions in all industries in Australia whether subject to fiscal protection or not. (Cheers)[110]

By a clever association of manufacturing with labor interests, protectionists guaranteed broad-based support for their program. Although all workers and raw-material producers did not welcome protection wholeheartedly, most were willing to partake of tariff revenues and were grateful for relief from threats of direct taxation. The formal machinery of new protection was declared *ultra vires* in 1907, but the principle of tariffs designed to raise together wages, profits, and revenue became a widely accepted part of Connonwealth policy.[111] A tariff revision in 1907–8 was openly protectionist and received wide labor support.

Despite high levels of wartime protection, both natural and legislative, protectionists after World War I resumed the flow of tariff propaganda. Ambrose Pratt, the idolatrous biographer of David Syme, prepared a "Tariff Handbook" embodying old and often repeated arguments bolstered by contributions from Meredith Atkinson of Melbourne University and R. F. Irvine at Sydney. Irvine concluded: "I believe that List's argument still holds good."[112] The tariff of 1920–21 gave protectionists most of their requests.

After protection had become established firmly as accepted Commonwealth policy, some Australians attempted to devise a truly "scientific" or "optimum" tariff which would reflect more than merely the pressures of party politics. Concern was not with the virtues of protection, but rather with methods of implementation.[113] In the early years of the Commonwealth, a Royal Commission considered means of devising an ideal tariff (1904–7), and an Interstate Commission reached "conclusions" on the question

110. *Prime Minister Deakin at Ballarat. Fiscal Policy, Trade Proposals, New Protection, Financial Agreement, State Debts, Postal Reforms, Defence, National Expansion* (Ballarat, n.d.), p. 12.

111. "New Protection Memorandum Relating to the Proposed Amendment of the Constitution," *Papers Presented to the Parliament of the Commonwealth of Australia,* 1908. King O'Malley, an emotional but influential labor leader, was a particularly strong supporter of protection to limit competition of Asian with Australian labor. Dorothy Catts, *King O'Malley: Man and Statesman* (Sydney, 1957).

112. Ambrose Pratt, ed., *The Australian Tariff Handbook 1919* (Sydney, 1919), p. 26. A later example of manufacturing propaganda was J. Hume Cook, *The Australian Tariff Problem, Protection versus Free Trade* (Melbourne, 1925).

113. See for example, Alfred McLennan, *The Other Way Round* (Perth, 1908), p. 37.

in 1913–15. But these bodies, like their predecessors in the nineteenth century, became in fact little more than fora for exposition of the old conflicting views. Commission members were not trained in economic analysis, and witnesses were openly self-interested. Impartiality and objectivity were not possible or expected, and neither Parliament nor the public gave their reports serious attention. In 1921 an effort was made to remedy the situation by establishment of a Tariff Board composed of representatives from government, manufacturers, importers, and after 1923 primary producers. This body was designed to achieve rationality in detailed discussions of commercial policy, to guard the public from exploitation, and to advise Parliament and the Minister for Trade and Customs on all matters related to the tariff.[114] The Board possessed no direct executive authority, but with co-operation of the government created in effect "a system of administrative as well as legislative Protection."[115] The Board "always looked upon its functions as being to carry out, not to question, the settled policy of protection," but it brought about substantial tariff increases particularly through activities under antidumping legislation of 1921.[116] In the latter half of the 1920's, the Tariff Board gave some evidence of uncertainty and disillusionment with the basic wisdom of protectionist policies, particularly as criticism from university economists increased and the economic climate generally began to worsen.[117]

The 1929 Tariff Enquiry

At the end of the period under investigation, a committee of economists in universities, government, and business submitted

114. The activities of the Tariff Board up to 1927 are described in detail in R. C. Mills, "The Tariff Board of Australia," *Economic Record*, III (1927), 52–81.
115. *Ibid.*, p. 76.
116. *Ibid.*, p. 79.
117. R. C. Mills, *ibid.*, pp. 80–81, and "Tariff Board Report on Agricultural Implements," *Economic Record*, II (1926), 43–50, where Mills said of the Board: "Were it not so strongly entrenched in Australian public policy, and so well buttressed by private interest, Protection might well ask to be saved from its friends." p. 50. F. C. Benham, " 'The Australian Tariff and the Standard of Living': A Reply," *Economic Record*, II (1926), 20–42. W. K. Hancock, *Australia* (New York, 1930), p. 102. Gordon Greenwood, ed., *Australia: A Social and Political History* (Sydney, 1955), pp. 310–14. Colin Clark, *Australian Hopes and Fears* (London, 1958), p. 156.

to the federal prime minister a report on *The Australian Tariff*, which constituted the most significant Australian contribution to the literature of commercial policy to that date. J. B. Brigden, D. B. Copland, E. C. Dyason, L. F. Giblin, and C. H. Wickens prepared this study as "a free gift to the Australian people" in response to an expressed belief by Prime Minister Bruce that "It is not enough for us to affirm confidently that protection is the only policy for Australia; we should be intelligently and fully informed as to every aspect of its operation; we should be able to assess its benefits and its costs, not in general terms but with all possible exactitude."[118] The authors discovered after eighteen months of investigations that, despite inadequacy of data and uncertainty about some methods of anaylsis, they were "able to reach agreement on all the principal issues."

The tariff enquiry had its beginnings in an article by J. B. Brigden in 1925 entitled "The Australian Tariff and the Standard of Living."[119] Brigden's basic thesis, uncertain and incomplete in details, was that the tariff could be a useful and valuable tool for altering patterns of income distribution and for maintaining long-run levels of worker income. Brigden was unable to convince some free-trade economists by his arguments, and especially not F. C. Benham.[120] However, he did gain many influential converts, including, in most respects, the other authors of the 1929 report. An important distinction which arose in the controversy over the Brigden hypothesis was between native Australian economists who believed intuitively in the merit of tariffs and observers from abroad who remained to be convinced by closely reasoned argument.

The purpose of the tariff enquiry was twofold: to assess historically the "effects of tariff policy upon national prosperity," and to prescribe "principles which should guide the application of a tariff policy in Australia."[121] This represented one of the earliest attempts by a group of professional economists anywhere

118. *The Australian Tariff: An Economic Enquiry* (2nd ed.; Melbourne, 1929), pp. vii and xi–xiii.
119. *Economic Record*, I (1925), 29–46. The tariff literature in and on Australia during and after the 1920's has been examined carefully in A. J. Reitsma, *Trade Protection in Australia* (Leiden, 1960).
120. See below pp. 566–67.
121. *The Australian Tariff: An Economic Enquiry*, p. 1.

in the world to estimate systematically and in precise terms the benefits and costs of an actual tariff policy, and the result was a landmark for other countries as well as for Australia. The authors were compelled to pioneer both in compilation of relevant statistical evidence and in formulation of analytical tools. They examined critically arguments for and against tariffs, separated much fact from fiction, and gave precision to many emotional and sentimental claims. The conclusions of the enquiry were the most unusual feature of the report; having studied carefully arguments for free trade and having discounted heavily the importance of the infant industry and short-term full employment effects of tariffs, the authors concluded nevertheless strongly in favor of protection as it had developed in Australia. They considered the tariff, if imposed judiciously, an important and valuable tool of statecraft. "We think the tariff may be likened to a powerful drug, with excellent tonic properties, but with reactions on the body politic which make it dangerous in the hands of the unskilled and the uninformed."[122]

The authors listed as "costs of protection" the out-of-pocket expenses paid by consumers through excessive prices for favored goods. They estimated the distribution and incidence of these costs throughout the population and concluded that in general "9 per cent of the present price-level is due to protection."[123] The authors did not attempt to estimate the indirect costs of trade restriction through distortion of the patterns of resource allocation and consumer expenditure, and for this reason their totals contained an unknown error of underestimate. No calculation was made of the loss in consumer satisfaction which resulted from less-than-ideal purchases, or of the potentially depressing long-run impact on national income of encouraging less efficient productive sectors instead of more efficient ones.

The tariff report gave an unusual set of weights to alleged benefits from protection. It summarized its position thus: "The chief benefits that may be derived from a limited application of

122. *Ibid.*, p. 99.
123. *Ibid.*, p. 68. Almost forty years earlier, in 1893, Matthew Macfie had made an estimate of "costs of protection to Victoria" from a freetrader's viewpoint. He arrived at a total of £5 18s. per capita per annum, not including "indirect loss" from distortions. "Australia under Protection," *Economic Journal*, III (1893), 297–307.

protection may be summarized as (i) the establishment of infant industries, (ii) the relief that may be afforded from the pressure of increasing population on inferior soils, and (iii) the advantages of stability and diversity of production."[124] Unlike most earlier defenders of tariffs, the authors discounted the first and last of these benefits and rested their case heavily on the second, the ability of protection to provide employment for a growing population. Protection in the Australian case of advanced staple production, they argued, could alone make possible full employment and continuous economic growth. The report continued— "It seems certain that without the tariff we could not have offered the same field for immigration, and would not have been able to maintain our growth of population." Furthermore, "it appears very unlikely that under Free Trade conditions any form of alternative production could have been found to take the place of protected industry which would give the same national income as at present."[125]

As Professor Jacob Viner pointed out in a critique of *The Australian Tariff* in 1929, these conclusions rested on at least two basic assumptions which were not specified and probably were accepted intuitively and tacitly by all the authors.[126] The first of these was that per capita income of workers rather than of all the population was the correct goal of economic growth. The second was that Australian staple industries were limited fundamentally from profitable continued expansion by geography and conditions in world markets. These assumptions, both of which had a long tradition in Australian social thought, were tied closely together as the basis for the policy recommendations of the report. The authors believed that staple production currently made use of the major portion of arable land in Australia, and that more intensive use would lead quickly to diminishing returns. This pessimistic belief was supported by the writings of Professor Griffith Taylor and other geographers.[127] The clear im-

124. *Ibid.*, pp. 30–31.
125. *Ibid.*, pp. 84 and 87.
126. "The Australian Tariff (Review Article)," *Economic Record*, V (1929), 306–15.
127. Thomas Griffith Taylor, *Australia in its Physiographic and Economic Aspects* (Oxford, 1911), and later editions; *The Australian Environment* (Melbourne, 1918); and *The Resources of Australia* (Honolulu, 1927).

plication of the position was that government should encourage labor-intensive industry in order to prevent a wage decline. Population growth was regarded as inevitable on the Australian continent, and manufacturing industry was viewed as the most satisfactory means of allaying the Ricardian nemesis of declining income for the increasing factor. As Viner explained emphatically, these assumptions might be accepted as valid for purposes of argument, but failure to state their hypothetical character in the enquiry cast doubt on the value of the report. If primary industries should in fact remain (as a result of technological improvements) the best source of jobs in the Australian economy, or if the incomes of landlords and capitalists should after all be given equal consideration with those of wage earners, or if additional exports of raw materials would not saturate world markets and worsen terms of trade, the report could no longer provide such strong support for tariffs. Viner concluded: "I am not convinced that the authors have successfully established their central thesis, even on the basis of their statement as to what Australia regards as desirable objectives for itself. I must admit, however, that they have made out a stronger case for their position than I would have supposed possible before reading their report, and I not only regard their investigation as well worth the great amount of effort which it must have cost, but deserving further extension and refinement."[128]

The major achievement of the tariff enquiry was provision of a sharp stimulus to economists in Australia and in the rest of the world to re-examine carefully and with an open mind the policy issues of international trade, a field which had remained relatively dormant since John Stuart Mill.[129]

128. *Op. cit.*, p. 314.
129. A. J. Reitsma, *op. cit., passim*; and W. S. Kelly, "The Tariff Enquiry, 1928," *Economic Record*, XXXVI (1960), 151–55.
The basic contention of the authors of the tariff enquiry, that it was possible theoretically for Australia to gain from a policy of protection, was disputed in 1938 by Professor Karl L. Anderson, "Protection and the Historical Situation: Australia," *Quarterly Journal of Economics*, LIII (1938), 86–104. Mrs. Marion Crawford Samuelson illustrated in 1939 that by diverting trade Australia could in fact gain theoretically by improving her terms of trade and receiving compensation from substitute production. "The Australian Case for Protection Reëxamined," *ibid.*, LIV (1939), 143–49. Professor Anderson recanted, *ibid.*, pp. 149–51.

2

International Commerce: II. Free Trade

Defense of Orthodoxy

Expositions of benefits from free trade in the colonies were inspired usually by proposals for protection. The British Colonial Office consistently opposed local tariff restriction as being inimical to imperial policy, and while the colonies gained a measure of legislative independence during the first half of the nineteenth century, the mother country itself moved from policies of mercantilism to free trade. By the 1840's, during the period when an element of representative government was granted the dependencies, laissez faire, justified by appeals to principles of classical economics, triumphed in Britain. In commercial policy controversies, supporters in the colonies of free trade came to be identified with the wishes of authority, and often they believed themselves that they were necessarily on the side of justice and moral rectitude. Generally, free-traders acted as if laissez faire were essentially right and natural; its virtues, like those of biblical commandments, needed exposition principally after transgression.

Mildly protective agricultural tariff bills of the 1840's, one of which was passed by the Legislative Council of New South Wales, were the first serious incitement to free-traders. Commercial policy had been judged before according to canons of political economy,[1] but now pointed analyses were carried out. Several periodicals in particular acted as media for the defense of free trade, notably the Sydney *Morning Herald* and the

1. For example, "The Revenue and Expenditure—in a Letter to Mr. Secretary Stanley," *New South Wales Magazine*, I (1833), 136–46.

Launceston *Examiner*.[2] The *New South Wales Magazine* proposed that the motto on the banner of all colonies should be "Free Trade and Laissez-faire" and it explained how agricultural protection caused direct economic loss:

the faster flour was brought to them from South America, or any where else, so long *as they could pay for it*, the greater would be the amount of available labour, the greater would be the amount of money let loose by the capitalist in return for that labour, and the greater consequently, would be (according to Malthus and Macculloch [sic]), the productive energies of the people—to augment which is obviously a primary object in *colonization*.[3]

The Sydney *Weekly Register* adopted the high moral tone characteristic of the free-trade movement and exclaimed that protective duties, and particularly those of Van Diemen's Land, were "opposed to all existing theories of economy, and are condemned by the experience of every nation in Europe."[4] The paper ridiculed attempts to justify protection by arrogant appeals to theory such as the following:

Such an article [protectionist] from the pen of a professing political economist of the present day is calculated to make an impression similar to that which would be caused by a philosophical lecture proving that the earth is circumscribed by the horizon, or bounded by the pillars of Hercules.

Educated men of every political creed have, at least theoretically, long since abandoned protective duties as mischievous and defenceless.[5]

Colonists were told that special conditions in Australia were no excuse for departure from a strict economic code. "Why, if the principles of sound political economy are of easy applicability any where, it is in a new country, where there are no established

2. Michael Roe, *Society and Thought in Eastern Australia, 1835–1851*, Thesis Submitted for the degree of Doctor of Philosophy in the Australian National University, 1960, pp. 61, 74, and 129–32; and Cephas Daniel Allin, *A History of the Tariff Relations of the Australian Colonies* (Minneapolis, 1918), p. 23.
3. Q. E. D., "An Enquiry into the Causes of the Former Prosperity and Present State of the Colony of New South Wales," *New South Wales Magazine*, 1843, p. 401.
4. "Import Duties in Van Dieman's Land," *Weekly Register of Politics, Facts, and General Literature*, I (1843), 314; and also "The Prorogation.—Defeat of the Proposed Bread Tax.—Retrospect," *ibid.*, pp. 345–46.
5. "The Political Register. Protective Duties," *ibid.*, III (1844), 253.

interests and powerful factions to oppose them."[6] The *Weekly Register* endorsed doctrinaire laissez faire as emphatically as any Manchester liberal. It said:

> The truth is legislators have nothing to do with commerce but to provide that justice may be done between buyer and seller, exporter and importer, and after this to let it alone. Nature and Providence will regulate the rest. The slightest interference beyond the enforcement of *justice* disarranges the whole system and inflicts injury on all immediately concerned, and through them on the whole community to which they belong.[7]

Several prominent immigrant intellectuals were particularly zealous in defense of doctrinaire free trade. When it seemed that protectionist heresy might triumph in the 1840's, the Reverend Henry Carmichael scheduled evangelical lectures on political economy.[8] Robert Lowe brought fresh to New South Wales in 1842 the spirit of British liberalism, and with recent experience in the Oxford Union he became the natural champion of the free-trade gospel.[9] In the Legislative Council and from his newspaper the *Atlas*, Lowe relayed the message of Cobden and Peel. A parliamentary committee of which he was chairman reported in 1844, two years before British Corn Law repeal, that proposed Australian duties were both inappropriate and untimely and that "those doctrines of protection which spring from national and commercial rivalry, are inapplicable to parts of the same empire."[10] Lowe cited often both English and French classical economists—Smith, Ricardo, Quesnay, and Say—to establish the orthodoxy of his position.[11]

Several factors contributed to the development in many Australians of a strong allegiance to laissez faire: effective demon-

---

6. *Ibid.*, p. 254.
7. *Ibid.* On another occasion the journal insisted: "There is no principle in political economy more completely established than that of free trade." "Corn Laws," *ibid.*, II (1844), 503.
8. Henry Carmichael, "Duty on Foreign Wheat," *Sydney Morning Herald*, April 3, 1844, and *ibid.*, April 29, 1844.
9. S. Elliott Napier, "Robert Lowe and his Associations with Australia," *Royal Australian Historical Society Journal and Proceedings*, XVIII (1932), 1–31.
10. "Report from the Select Committee on the Council's Corn Petitions," *Votes and Proceedings of the Legislative Council of New South Wales*, 1844, p. 2.
11. e.g. *Atlas*, January 18, 1845, p. 86; May 17, 1845, p. 289; and August 30, 1845, p. 472.

stration of allocative efficiency present in a free-market economy, identification of economic freedom with political liberty, and appreciation of the "natural justice" in income distribution according to productive contribution. For many colonists free trade became an article of faith based on a mixture of sentiment, intellectual conviction, and self-interest. James Barnard was representative when he assured Tasmanians in 1849 that "It is by free and open competition alone that extravagant prices and exorbitant profits are restrained, and that the public are supplied with commodities as cheap as the producer can afford to sell them."[12] Disbelievers were instructed with such parables as Bastiat's petition of the candle-makers against the rays of the sun.[13]

During the gold rush, while the economic role of the state grew rapidly, worried free-traders restated repeatedly the case for laissez faire. Chambers of commerce led by two outstanding merchant intellectuals, William Westgarth in Melbourne and Thomas Daniel Chapman in Hobart, proclaimed often the virtues of free trade.[14] One Victorian, after citing Smith and Mill and recounting instances of governmental inefficiency during the Crimean War, concluded:

In a word, if Government would allow men to form their contracts at their own discretion, and would not disturb the ordinary operations of the market by its interference as a dealer; but if it would direct its attention to the best and quickest and most certain means of enforcing these contracts, and of preventing any individual from doing injury to public rights, it would save itself a great deal of unnecessary and disagreeable labour, and the interests of society would be much more efficiently served.[15]

12. James Barnard, "Statistics of Van Dieman's Land for 1844–1846 . . . ," *Tasmanian Journal of Natural Science, Agriculture, Statistics, &c.,* III (1849), 447.
13. "Random Readings: Economic Fallacies, from M. Bastiat's 'Sophismes Economiques' . . . ," *Australasian,* I (Melbourne, 1850–51), 476–78.
14. Cephas Daniel Allin, *A History of the Tariff Relations of the Australian Colonies* (Minneapolis, 1918), pp. 41–42.
15. "State Interference," *Melbourne Monthly Magazine of Original Colonial Literature,* I (1855), 82. For a similar statement in Sydney see "School of Arts. Literature of Working Men. Substance of a Lecture Delivered to the Members by W. G. Pennington, Esq.," *The Operative: A Journal of Progress in the Interest of the Working Classes,* I (1854), No. 2, pp. 12–13. Free-trade arguments were employed prominently by writers opposed to "government banking." See "Report

Regarding the difficulties of agriculture during the 1850's, N. L. Kentish remarked cautiously: "I venture an opinion that it is the true policy of Victoria to *promote agriculture* throughout her vast territory *by every legitimate means*; of which, in her present circumstances, import or customs duties is *not* one, but would be suicidal and unjustifiable in the highest degree."[16] James Aikenhead, proprietor of the Launceston *Examiner,* believed that to arrest acceptance of misguided protectionist policies, widespread familiarity with economic principles should accompany democracy. In 1856 he published for Tasmanians a series of lectures on political economy presented earlier to the Launceston Mechanics' Institute, and derived substantially from works by McCulloch and Mill with references to Senior, Ricardo, Smith, Malthus, Storch, Child, Quesnay, and Elihu Burritt, "the American blacksmith." Aikenhead described a glorious path forward through history from the dark ages of mercantilism to the enlightenment of free trade. He praised the role of merchants in human society, listed the benefits of international specialization, and said of government: "it is simply an arbiter selected and empowered to keep the peace."[17]

Except for one brief period of flirtation with protection, Henry Parkes was for almost half a century the most influential advocate of free trade. Before and after his "terrible error" of endorsing protection in the late 1850's, he preached the doctrine of the Manchester free-traders whose wisdom he imbibed from the prophet himself "one cold winter's night with Richard Cobden."[18] In his newspaper, the *Empire,* Parkes proclaimed the principles of political economy, and what he considered was their corollary—commercial laissez faire. He explained in 1854:

Political economy, in every department, has its laws which cannot be restricted or aided without damage, just as much as the physical

from the Select Committee of the Legislative Council on Government Banking; together with the Proceedings of the Committee, and Minutes of Evidence," *Votes and Proceedings of the Legislative Council of Victoria,* 1853–54, particularly questions numbered: 72, 253, 395, 535.

16. N. L. Kentish, *Question of Questions: Just Shewing, How to "Speed the Plough" in Victoria* . . . (Melbourne, 1855), p. 11.

17. J. Aikenhead, *Principles of Political Economy* (Tasmania, 1846), p. 33 and *passim.*

18. J. A. La Nauze, " 'That Fatal, That Mischievous Passage,' Henry Parkes and Protection, 1859–66," *Australian Quarterly,* XIX (1947), No. 2, pp. 59–60.

growth of man. There are certain principles inherent in human nature, and in the modes of its action and association, which resist interference, and avenge themselves for every coercion or restraint. A human law to foster them, by special privileges, would be as fatal to their healthy development as would be an attempt to overrule them. The modern acknowledgement of the Free Trade principle, is a concession to the opinion we have expressed.[19]

Parkes published in his journal unbroken columns from Adam Smith and McCulloch (that "enlightened authority upon commercial subjects") to support his position, and he termed James Martin, a prominent protectionist, "an advocate of the doctrine of scarcity." He called the restrictive United States President Millard Fillmore "probably the last of that by-gone School of Political Economists likely to fill that important office."[20] To dissatisfied farmers, Parkes said: "it will be found that, not encouragement to agriculture, but the leaving it and all other industrial operations alone, are the true dictates of a rational, generous, and enlightened policy."[21] On one occasion in 1855, Parkes read aloud selections out of J. S. Mill's *Principles of Political Economy* from his seat in the Legislative Council, and he informed his colleagues that the implication of Mill's words was that "the time had arrived when the broad principles of free-trade which had been so successful in the mother-country, and which were rapidly gaining ground in all the countries of a commercial standing, should be adopted in this colony to the fullest extent."[22]

When it became apparent in the 1850's that protection had some reasonable hope of gaining legislative success, free-traders reacted vigorously. Treasurers of New South Wales, among others, affirmed repeatedly their faith in the teachings of political economy and in laissez faire. For example, Stuart Alexander Donaldson in his financial statement of 1856 read to the legislators

19. "The Balance of Industrial Interests," *Empire*, January 27, 1854, p. 2.
20. "The Great Interests," *Empire*, I (1851), No. 85, p. 350; "Mr. James Martin," *ibid.*, No. 190, p. 78; "Commercial Record: Speculation and Monopoly," *ibid.*, pp. 78–79; Mercator, "Original Correspondence: The Impolicy of an Export Gold Duty," *Empire*, October 9, 1852, p. 1495; and "President Fillmore's Advocacy of a Protective Policy for the United States," *ibid.*, April 2, 1853, p. 2122.
21. "Population and Production," *ibid.*, September 6, 1851, p. 127. See also "The Purposes and Principles of Taxation," *ibid.*, July 14, 1852, p. 1194.
22. Henry Parkes, *Speeches on Various Occasions Connected with the Public Affairs of New South Wales 1848–1874* (Melbourne, 1876), p. 54.

Adam Smith's canons of taxation, and he observed: "All these maxims may be applied according to the peculiar state of a country, and are in a great respect applicable to all."[23] Donaldson urged strict adherence to fiscal orthodoxy in New South Wales because "the eyes of the financiers of Europe—the eyes of the Ricardos and the Rothschilds—will be upon the financial arrangements of the colony."[24] Geoffrey Eager, colonial treasurer in 1863, explained carefully that tariff increases he proposed were designed strictly for revenue; concerning management of the public debt, he recounted to Parliament "what M'Culloch says on that point" in order to "make a colonial application of the English principle."[25] By 1874 Treasurer George Alfred Lloyd could report with pride that the free-trade policy of New South Wales "has not only attracted the attention of the neighbouring Colonies, but the mother-country and the United States have in their leading journals and in their Houses of Legislature expressed their appreciation of the wisdom displayed by this Parliament in releasing commerce from its fetters as far as possible, and reducing the tariff to as few articles as is consistent with a due regard to the revenue which must be obtained from the imposition of Customs duties."[26]

Free Trade Success in N. S. W. and Failure in Victoria

Depression in the early 1860's generated sufficient protectionist sympathy to give Sydney free-traders brief cause for alarm.[27] A New South Wales Free Trade Association was formed in 1863 for dissemination of propaganda, and the secretary, Frederick A. Bell, published a turgid tract with arguments of classical econ-

23. James Thomson, ed., *The Financial Statements of the Colonial Treasurers of New South Wales* . . . (Sydney, 1881), p. 9.
24. *Ibid.*, p. 13.
25. *Ibid.*, p. 122.
26. *Ibid.*, p. 312.
27. After a commercial policy debate at the Sydney Mechanics' School of Arts in 1860, "the division took place, and the Protectionists were defeated by a majority of seven." "The Institutes' Chronicle," *Month: A Literary and Critical Journal* (Sydney, 1860), p. 45.

omists which refuted protection. Bell elaborated Smith's four maxims of taxation, and Turgot's "seven reasons." He summarized also writings by Storch ("the talented and enlightened preceptor of the late Emperor of Russia"), Mill, Ricardo, Say, Whately, and Bastiat. Bell decried in petulant tones alleged inattention of legislators to the classics of economics.

The opinions of all the great writers on political economy are to be found in the library of our Legislature, but of what use are they to addlepated men, who consider that no question, motion, or inquiry is too absurd to occupy the time of Parliament, and to annoy and harass the Executive by every nonsensical and expensive return they can devise, which they have not the ability to use when placed before them, whilst subjects of the most vital importance to the community lie entirely dormant from want of men to grapple them?[28]

New South Wales free-traders in the 1860's came to accept as their spokesman the indefatigeable Henry Parkes. At Albury in 1866, Parkes expressed his opposition to a strong state in society in terms which would have sounded timely even a century later. He said: "A Government in a young country should interfere as little as possible with the operations of industry, and avoid all action savouring of a paternal and patronising Government; the very perfection of free and good government consisted in letting people alone to do the best within the reach of their own capabilities for themselves. They had an example of paternal Government in Russia, but that was not what was wanted here."[29] In a speech to the Legislative Assembly in 1873, Parkes defended his support for free trade by describing the experience of other countries. Britain, he insisted, had stagnated under mercantilism and had flourished under free trade. "As the activity of her people had been relieved from all impediments, the commerce of the people had more and more expanded."[30] Parkes cited Amassa Walker and David A. Wells to show that the United States had thrived because of its extensive foreign trade and in spite of

28. Frederick A. Bell, *Industry and Commerce Relieved and Increased by Means of Free Trade and Direct Taxation*, first published in the Sydney *Empire* in 1863 (Sydney, 1866), p. 39.
29. Henry Parkes, *Speeches on Various Occasions Connected with the Public Affairs of New South Wales 1848–1874* (Melbourne, 1876), pp. 207–8.
30. *Ibid.*, p. 391.

high tariffs. Protection "only encouraged a sickly growth, subject to artificial fluctuations, and which sooner or later must perish and inflict serious consequences or collateral injuries upon the country."[31]

In Victoria, where protectionists gained strongest support in Australia, free-traders found pressing need to elaborate their case. A Free Trade and Financial Reform League was founded during the 1850's and published both appropriate utterances of local free-traders and propaganda by well-known writers such as Bastiat.[32] Archibald Michie, a prominent politician, was a particularly influential free-trade spokesman and was often the target of protectionist attacks. In 1860 Michie attempted to nip high tariff legislation in the bud with a scathing denunciation of protectionism. Against John Stuart Mill's infant industry argument Michie cited James Mill, and he revealed considerable insight by detecting the strong emotional appeal of protection. He said:

I suspect many attendants at meetings hardly know what protection means. "Protection to native industry" has a sentimental sound about it. We all like to be taken care of, and the expression savours of that, so that you have only to start the word "protection" at some meetings, and you catch a large portion of the audience at once, who are for protecting everything and everybody, even to the "unprotected female," made immortal by *Punch*.[33]

As alternatives to protection Michie called for long-run growth policies of increased immigration and a government bank.[34]

Throughout the 1860's a few brave free-traders sustained op-

31. *Ibid.*, pp. 393–98.
32. Some of the free trade tracts issued by the League during the 1850's and 1860's were titled: *Protection only Taxation in Disguise; Robbery by Law (Adapted from Bastiat); How Robinson Crusoe Protected Himself. Adapted from the French of Frederick Bastiat; The Fallacies of Protection. Abundance or Scarcity? Adapted from the French of M. Bastiat;* Edward Langton, Secretary of the League, *A Lecture on Free Trade, June 9, 1865; Free Trade at Vancouver Island; Dr. Guthrie on Free Trade; Nine Months' Experience of Protection in Victoria; Mr. Higinbotham on Protection; What Will Protection Do for the Labourer?; What Effect has the Tariff on the Working Miner?*
33. Archibald Michie, *Victoria Suffering a Recovery: A Lecture* (Melbourne, 1860), p. 9.
34. An earlier but less convincing indictment of protectionism in Victoria was: Financier, *Our Financial System, Indirect versus Direct Taxation: or the Ways and Means. Addressed to the People of Victoria* (Melbourne, 1858).

position to the ascendant protectionists in Victoria. William Westgarth, a Melbourne merchant who moved to Britain in the 1850's, paraphrased for the colonies in 1861 the writings of Bastiat; he remarked: "say the Victoria advocates, in a struggling young colony many vocations require protection. Perhaps they do; but in such a country of all others, can the other vocations afford to pay for it?"[35] The Melbourne *Argus* replied to polemics in the *Age* by claiming that protection in Victoria would lead either to "rupture and disunion" as in the United States, or to "impenetrable functionarism which hangs like a cloud over the civilization of the Muscovite."[36]

Melbourne University was a stronghold of laissez faire.[37] W. E. Hearn, both in his economic writings and on the hustings, proclaimed the wisdom of unrestricted commerce. In his *Plutology* Hearn observed: "Impediments to the development of exchange can never increase but must always diminish wealth."[38] He condemned indirect taxation in all forms:

It interferes with the free action either of labour or of some of its aids. It presents an artificial obstacle to the attainment of the desired object; and not unfrequently this obstacle is much greater than the actual amount of the tax would seem to indicate. The spontaneous course of industry is thus disturbed, and various industrial derangements follow.[39]

Hearn was overly optimistic when, only three years before introduction of an extensive protectionist program in Victoria, he

35. William Westgarth, *Australia: Its Rise, Progress, and Present Condition* (Edinburgh, 1861), p. 84.

36. *Free Trade versus Protection: being a Series of Papers Illustrative of What Protection has Done for "The United States of America" and for "Russia," and of What Free Trade has Done for "Switzerland,"* reprinted from *"the Argus"* (Melbourne, 1864), p. 1.

37. Ernest Scott, *A History of the University of Melbourne* (Melbourne, 1936), p. 30. Ironically, Richard Windeyer, first graduate of Sydney University, announced in 1860 that in New South Wales "All the University men are protectionists." J. A. La Nauze, " 'That Fatal, That Mischievous Passage,' Henry Parkes and Protection," *loc. cit.*, p. 57.

38. William Edward Hearn, *Plutology: or the Theory of the Efforts to Satisfy Human Wants* (Melbourne, 1863), pp. 265–66. See also J. A. La Nauze, *Political Economy in Australia: Historical Studies*, pp. 78–79; and D. B. Copland, *W. E. Hearn: First Australian Economist* (Melbourne, 1935), pp. 40–44 and 68–75.

39. *Plutology*, p. 431. This comment from Hearn was noted and used as support by other free traders. See, for example, William Ritchie, *Letters on Fiscal and Land Law Reform* (Tasmania, 1884), p. 22.

wrote: "There is now little risk at least in any Anglican country that the old extravagancies of state-action will be revived."[40] In the 1870's Hearn was treasurer and J. S. Elkington, his successor in the chair of political economy, was a council member of the Free Trade League of Victoria.[41] The influence of Hearn on political economy at Melbourne University remained strong even after his departure into law, and the institution was regarded as a breeding ground of free-traders. An annual silver medal for proficiency in political economy was accepted in 1881–82 from the Cobden Club,[42] and prominent alumni, such as Alexander Sutherland and Bruce Smith, were outstanding opponents of high tariffs.[43]

Several distinguished Victorian intellectuals and public figures were ardent supporters of laissez faire. R. Murray Smith, a vocal free trader at Oxford in the 1850's, settled in Melbourne as a prosperous merchant and remained unshaken in his doctrinaire conviction. For almost half a century, Murray Smith tirelessly cited Adam Smith, Mill, Cairnes, and other economists in opposition to protection.[44] However, S. M. Ingham recounts: "As was

40. *Plutology*, p. 442.
41. Considering the luminous literary talent boasted by this League the quality of its publications was disappointing. The following selection from a tract entitled "The Miner and his Mate" is illustrative.
"Tom.—So we all thought, Jem, when the gold had fallen off to half some twelve years ago . . . fresh trades were the thing to save us, but we should have looked below the surface, mate. There's the sun sailing round us, and don't we all fancy that its moving, and we are standing still; but its the earth for all that's going around, and so we must look beyond our noses and see the effects.
Jem.—That's political economy, Tom.
Tom.—Economy, or no economy, it's sense, Jem."
"The Miner and his Mate," in *Free Trade Papers Addressed to the People of Victoria to the end of 1876* (Melbourne, 1877), p. 3. Other tracts were entitled: "What is the Cost of Protection?," "How Can we Promote Native Industry?," "What Are We to Do With Our Children?," "How Victoria Had her Nose Cut off to Improve her Face," "Prices and Protection," "The Three Tariffs," "What has Nature Done for Us in Victoria?," "Machinery and its Results," "The Farmer and his Wife," "John Stuart Mill on Protection," and "Protectionist Tactics in Victoria."
42. *Melbourne University Calendar*, 1881–82, pp. 235–36.
43. Alexander Sutherland, "The Effects of Protection on the Imports of Australia," *Report of the Fourth Meeting of the Australasian Association for the Advancement of Science held at Hobart, 1892*; pp. 520–24; and Bruce Smith, *Liberty and Liberalism* (Melbourne, 1887).
44. For example, R. Murray Smith, "The Victorian Tariff," *Victorian Review*, I (1879), 94–104. In 1891 Murray Smith reminded protectionists of their promises in 1865 that high tariffs would be only temporary, as prescribed by John Stuart Mill. *The Tariffs of Victoria: An Address Delivered before the Free Trade Democratic Association of Victoria* (Melbourne, 1891).

to be expected, Murray Smith's political career was one of singular isolation. An embarrassment to the Conservatives to whose party he belonged, he generally sat in a remote corner of the House."[45] Charles H. Pearson, Murray Smith's close friend and free-trade associate at Oxford, remained nominally in favor of low tariffs, but he allied himself with protectionists in order to achieve other ends. He said: "I am myself a Freetrader. But because I am a Freetrader, I do not think that Freetrade is always and at all times the one question of the day."[46]

Tariff controversies of the late 1870's and early 1880's in Victoria brought forth articulate protagonists on both sides. James Smith translated and summarized portions of writings by Physiocrats to illustrate the vital interests of agriculturalists in maintaining a free economy. He wrote:

Survey it in what light we will, the earth is, as Dr. Quesnay says, "the unique source of riches," the purveyor of our food, clothing and fuel; of the timber, clay and stone with which we build our habitations; of the iron out of which we fashion the implements of tillage, in the first instance, and our machinery as civilisation advances, in the second; and of the innumerable raw materials which we work up in our manufactures, or employ in the ornamental arts of life.

What, then, is the duty of the State towards agriculture in a country like our own, for example? Clearly to remove every impediment to its successful practice.[47]

Local merchants, and even the redoubtable William Westgarth, who was still writing about Australian problems from Britain, helped to spread the gospel and used again such hoary authorities as Adam Smith's maxims of taxation.[48]

45. S. M. Ingham, "Political Parties in the Victorian Legislative Assembly, 1880–1900," *Historical Studies Australia and New Zealand*, IV (1949–51), 247.

46. Charles H. Pearson, *Political Opinions on Some Subjects of the Day: Being Extracts from a Lecture and Speeches* (Melbourne, 1877), p. 6. See also J. M. Tregenza, *The Life and Work of C. H. Pearson, 1830–1894*, Thesis Submitted for the degree of Doctor of Philosophy in the Australian National University, 1959, pp. 94 and 277–78, and above p. 21.

47. James Smith, "The Farmers and Protection," *Victorian Review*, I (1879), 184; and also "The Abolition of Labour," *ibid.*, I (1880), 349–62.

48. W. Jardine Smith, " 'Liberal' Finance in Victoria," *Victorian Review*, I (1880), 444–68; Hugh R. Reid, *A Customs Union for Australasia;* and H. R. Hogg, *Intercolonial Free Trade in Australia* (papers read at the Conference of Delegates from the Australasian Chambers of Commerce and Manufactures; Melbourne, 1883); and William Westgarth, "Practical Commerce *versus* Theoretical

Whereas free-traders in Victoria lost hope progressively as the popularity of protection increased, their counterparts in New South Wales gained confidence steadily. George Reid, political rival of Henry Parkes and his successor as premier, won a Cobden Club medal for *Five Free Trade Essays* in which he set forth the customary combination of carefully selected examples from history and extracts from writers such as McCulloch and David A. Wells.[49] George Lacy, an immigrant journalist, related laissez faire to the preservation of basic democracy and social welfare. He urged free-traders in 1879 to maintain vigilance at all times because "Protection, with the same sort of peculiar magnetism which causes suicides, murders, railway-accidents, and other calamities, to follow in each other's wake, is spreading from one community to another."[50] Edward Pratt, a resident of Cooma, used McCulloch's translation of Storch to illustrate the selfishness of protection. He considered the fact disgraceful "that these dogmas should in the present enlightened age survive and flourish even amongst people of the same race with Cobden and Peel."[51] Pratt believed that widespread ignorance of fundamental truths in political economy explained the permanence of trade restrictions. Misunderstanding persisted, nurtured by protected interests, even though "the general principles which underlie foreign trade . . . can be demonstrated to the satisfaction of any intelligent child."[52]

In the less populous Australian colonies commercial policy was not as controversial a topic as in Victoria and New South Wales, in part because the possibility was never as great of establishing viable domestic manufacturing industries by protection. Occasionally free-traders did proclaim publicly their faith, but usually

---

Political Economy, VI. Free Trade *versus* Protection: An Essay towards a Conclusive Deductive Argument," *Chamber of Commerce Journal*, II (1883), 358–60.

49. George H. Reid, *Five Free Trade Essays* (Melbourne, 1875); and Reid's *Protection or Free Trade? Speech in Favour of Free Trade Delivered at a Public Discussion with David Buchanan, Esq., M. P. . . .* (Sydney, 1880).

50. George Lacy, "Free Trade and Protection," *Australian*, III (1879–80), 532; "State Socialism, a Warning," *ibid.*, V (1881–82), 92–101; and *Law and Liberty* (London, 1888), *passim*.

51. Edward Pratt, "The Balance of Trade," *Melbourne Review*, VII (1882), 374.

52. *Ibid.*, pp. 374–75.

in relation to another policy issue such as land taxation or state banking and without the missionary fervor evidenced in the larger colonies.[53] Revenue tariffs having some measure of "incidental protection" were passed in all the smaller colonies, but were not extreme enough to enrage either free-traders or their opponents.

Challenge of Depression and "Protection-all-around"

During the last two decades of the nineteenth century, declining incomes and popularization of the principle that rewards from high tariffs could be shared between workers and employers gave new strength to the protectionist movement. In response to this serious challenge, free-traders in all the colonies accelerated their literary output. Low tariffs were pictured as the ultimate goal of mankind, difficult of attainment mainly because of human avarice and ignorance.[54] Bankers, merchants, and landowners made every effort to prove that protection was "the bleeding and leeching of the body politic."[55] Some free-traders portrayed tariff reduction as a necessary prelude to intercolonial reciprocity or federation; one South Australian predicted that under a customs union "Australasia will then grow like a mushroom, both in wealth and population" while another remarked "we could write by

53. For example, "Report of the Select Committee of the House of Assembly, Appointed to Report on the Question of Taxation; together with Minutes of Evidence and Appendix," *Proceedings of the Parliament of South Australia*, 1858; Theodore Bartley, *The Present Financial Crisis in Tasmania* . . . (Launceston, 1872); and William Ritchie, *Letters on Fiscal and Land Law Reform* (Tasmania, 1884).

54. See for example, "Henry George on Protection, and his Critic," *Australian Magazine*, 1886, pp. 254–59; and J. Reid, "Agricultural Protection," *Sydney Quarterly Magazine*, 1887, pp. 65–71.

55. D. Brown, *Wealth and Wages in New South Wales: An Examination of the Income of the Community, its Source and its Application* (Sydney, 1891), p. 30; also E. Jowett, "Free-Trade v. Protection," *Journal of the Bankers' Institute of Australasia*, II (1887–88), 406–15; W. J. Curry, "Imports, Exports, and our National Wealth under Protection," *ibid.*, IV (1890–91), 125–33; F. T. Hickford, "Adam Smith," *ibid.*, IX (1895–96), 12–13; Alexander W. Johnston, *Strikes, Labour Questions, and Other Economic Difficulties: A Short Treatise of Political Economy* (London, 1895); *Tariff Reform: Victoria's True Policy, the Most Work, the Best Wages, the Highest Values* (Melbourne, 1895); William Bateman, *Australian Produce: the Best Means of Realising Thereon* (Melbourne, 1897).

the hour on the advantages to be gained."[56] Familiar selections
from classical economists were resurrected yet once more, particularly from Bastiat who by this time, through his homely
parables and analogies, had retained popularity in the colonies
for fully half a century.[57]

Australian free-traders received some support in the 1890's
from British economic liberals who had their interest aroused in
colonial matters by dramatic financial collapses and by the
apparent threat to British investments from a profligate government. Charles Fairfield launched a scathing attack on all aspects
of Australian state enterprise and blamed restriction and distortion of private activity for the current disasters.[58] Matthew Macfie, from experience in the colonies, assured readers of the
Economic Journal that despite appearances "the more intelligent
classes" in Australia were "uniformly free traders."[59] Robert Giffen in a very balanced analysis concluded that, in general,
protection had not affected the colonies substantially one way or
another.[60]

In the 1880's several outstanding new expositors of economic
liberalism came forth, notably Edward Pulsford and B. R. Wise
in New South Wales.[61] Pulsford, a merchant from Hull in England, settled at Sydney in 1884 and became active immediately

56. "Report of the Royal Commission on Intercolonial Free Trade; together
with Minutes of Proceedings, Evidence, Appendices, Etc.," *Proceedings of the
Parliament of South Australia*, 1891, pp. xxviii and xxx; and also J. T. Walker, "The
Federation of British Australasia; a Sketch from a Political and an Economic Point
of View," abstract, *Report of the Seventh Meeting of the Australasian Association
for the Advancement of Science held at Sydney, 1898*, pp. 904–7.

57. C. McKay Smith, *Trade Depression and Wasted Resources: with some Remarks on Popular Government in New South Wales* (Sydney, 1887), *Free Trade
and its Influence on National Prosperity* (Townsville, 1888), and *Capital, Labour
and Taxation: Some Pleas for Common Sense* (Sydney, 1894); and Edward
Davies, *Capital: The Friend and Ally of Wage-Earners and the Mainspring of
Commerce: Extracts and Notes by a Wage-Earner for more than half a Century*
(Melbourne, 1896).

58. Charles Fairfield, "State Socialism in the Antipodes," in Thomas MacKay,
ed., *A Plea for Liberty: An Argument Against Socialism and Socialistic Legislation* (London, 1892), pp. 124–72.

59. Matthew Macfie, "Australia under Protection," *Economic Journal*, III
(1893), 298.

60. Robert Giffen, "Protection for Manufactures in New Countries," *Economic
Journal*, VIII (1898), 3–16.

61. The account of a free trade gathering at Sydney in 1889 illustrates the
dominance at this date of Pulsford and Wise aided still by Reid and Parkes.
*Report of the Proceedings and Public Meetings of the First Annual Conference
of the Free Trade and Liberal Association of New South Wales* (Sydney, 1889).

as a journalist and member of parliament. In 1885 he was appointed secretary of the newly formed Free Trade Association of New South Wales, and without delay he began a stream of pamphlets, books, articles, and addresses which flowed steadily for more than thirty years. Pulsford was thoroughly convinced of the rectitude of his liberal position, and he believed that mere statistical description of relative conditions and progress rates in protected and unprotected nations would demonstrate successfully the value of free trade. Pulsford was one of the first Australian writers to use Michael Mulhall's statistics of the colonies, and he collected and published data from many other sources.[62] He defended Timothy Coghlan vigorously from Victorian critics and advocated increased expenditures on statistical services in New South Wales.[63] He digested and interpreted a variety of statistical publications for his own writings, and he cautioned the public against attaching undue significance to the movements of economic variables such as "national capital" which were subject to wide fluctuations for relatively unimportant reasons and which concealed more significant changes in income.[64] Able to captivate a sophisticated audience, Pulsford could also write for the masses, including both farmers and city workers. For example, he recounted with moving eloquence in 1887:

some young girl, well-known to some of you, may shortly find herself compelled to teach music to provide bread for herself and for an invalid mother. She has saved £50, and she knows that this is the value of a good piano; but stop, protection steps in and says: "My dear girl, you must foster native industry by paying an extra £15; you cannot have this piano under £65." Yes, that is the way. Protection is a cheat and an impostor. . . . When once a wild beast has tasted blood, he

62. Edward Pulsford, *Free Trade and Protection: An Answer to Mr. Forsyth's Pamphlet* (Sydney, 1885), and *Freedom in New South Wales versus Oppression in Victoria: a Reply to the "Age" Articles* (Sydney, 1887).

63. Edward Pulsford, *New South Wales' Statistics and Victorian Critics* (Sydney, 1889).

64. Edward Pulsford, *Notes on Capital and Finance in Australasia* (Sydney, 1892); *The Rise, Progress, and Present Position of Trade and Commerce in New South Wales* (Sydney, 1892); "An Australian Lesson," *Nineteenth Century,* XXIV (1888), 393–409; "A Lesson from Australia," *ibid.,* LXV (1909), 471–79; and "The Beneficial Influence of a Free Trade Policy upon the Colony of New South Wales, having a Special Regard to her Industries," in *Prize Essays on Free Trade and Protection* (London, 1887).

will be as likely to forego the indulgence as will the protectionist to forego the privilege of collecting taxation for his own purposes.[65]

Pulsford maintained always that free trade was the only route to colonial federation and imperial unity.[66] He was recognized widely outside Australia for his consistent and missionary defense of free trade, particularly through his book *Commerce and the Empire*.[67]

Bernard Ringrose Wise was the most distinguished intellectual in the New South Wales free-trade movement. As a student at Oxford between 1880 and 1882, he studied under Arnold Toynbee and became proficient both in history and economics. He was concerned deeply about the influence being gained by protectionists over the labor movement, and after his return to New South Wales, he set out to reverse this development through strenuous activity both in parliament and in the press. For example, during one lengthy discourse in 1884, he called forth pronouncements of Cobden, Ricardo, Mill, Brassey, and Giffen, and he assured Australian workers that: "Neither Free Trade nor Protection can directly raise Wages, but Free Trade benefits the Workman indirectly by increasing the fund from which Wages are paid, and strengthening the Workman in claiming his share. Free Trade, however, does directly steady Wages and reduce prices."[68] Wise attempted the difficult task of disassociat-

65. Edward Pulsford, *Protection: its Inconsistency, Absurdity and Injustice, versus Free Trade: its Simplicity, Truth and Power* (Sydney, 1887), and also *The Blessings of Taxation* (Sydney, 1886), and *An Address to the Farmers of New South Wales* (Sydney, n.d.). Pulsford was editor of the federal free trade newspaper *Our Country*, Sydney, 1900–1901.
66. Edward Pulsford, "Commercial Federation of the Colonies, and Commercial Relations between the Colonies and the Mother Country," in *Report of the Proceedings of the Australasian Commercial Congress held at Melbourne, 1888* (Melbourne, 1889); and paper presented to an International Free Trade Congress at London, see *Report of the Proceedings* (London, 1908).
67. Melbourne, 1903, and second edition, London, 1917. Favorable reviews were by H. O. Meredith, *Economic Journal*, XX (1910), 405–7; Edwin Cannan, *ibid.*, XXVII (1918), 91–92; A. L. Bishop, *American Economic Review*, VIII (1918), 155; and George O. Virtue, *Journal of Political Economy*, XXVII (1919), 414–15.
68. B. R. Wise, *The Influence of Free Trade on Wages; or Why Working Men Should be Free Traders* (Sydney, 1884), p. i. Wise reported that this tract was initiated as a joint publication with Toynbee, was revised after the latter's death, was sent to the Cobden Club for publication where the manuscript was lost, and was rewritten for a third time in 1884. *Industrial Freedom: A Study in Politics* (Melbourne, 1892), pp. v–vi. He dedicated the pamphlet to "the Memory of

ing the principle of free trade from a wider philosophy of laissez faire. He argued that advocacy of low tariffs in no way implied condemnation of trade unionism, industrial arbitration, or aggressive developmental policies of government. In contrast to many protectionists who promised immediate higher wages, Wise was careful only to advise modestly that on such matters "Free Trade is neutral." He insisted, rather, that all restrictions on trade did cause "a waste of our national resources," and that "the larger portion of the community can never be 'protected.' "[69] As Wise himself recognized increasingly, however, a steadily diminishing number of Australians considered that they were in that unprotected "larger portion" of society.

In 1892 Wise published an elaborate and sophisticated discussion of commercial policy in the colonies entitled *Industrial Freedom: A Study in Politics*. This book began as a revision of his 1884 pamphlet and developed as an extended "tribute to Toynbee's memory." Wise discussed the effects of tariffs on economic development in Australia, Europe, and America, and he concluded that beneficial results of restrictions had never been proved. He maintained that the claims of List, Hoyt, and other "nationalist economists" that economic welfare required a restraining hand of government on the consumer were unreasonable. Wise observed that protection had been introduced in all countries either in wartime or in depression as an emergency measure to redistribute income and to increase employment. In every instance government had done both jobs badly. He wrote regretfully that in Australia the revival of protection had been largely due to the following causes, viz.:

1. To the fact that Free Trade writers have directed their chief attention to the effect of the policy in increasing wealth, instead of considering its effect on wages.
2. To the discredit which has attached to Free Trade through being associated with unpopular or aristocratic parties.

Arnold Toynbee, who Suggested this Work and Gave to it all its Value by his Teaching and Criticism."

69. B. R. Wise, *The Position of the Liberal Party* (Sydney, 1888), pp. 23–24, and "The Revival of Commercial Restrictions," *Australian Economist*, I (1888–90), 139–43.

3. To the idea that Free Trade is identical with a general policy of "laissez faire."

4. To the idea that Free Traders are indifferent to the evils of the competitive system.

5. To the prevailing discontent with existing social and industrial conditions.[70]

Wise was generally charitable and reasonably dispassionate towards individual protectionist adversaries, except for an occasional reference to "the morbid and diseased mind" of List or to the corrupt motives of Wharton in endowing at the University of Pennsylvania a professorship of economics for the protectionist economist Simon Nelson Patten. From experience in the colonies Wise remarked particularly that protection tended to nurture depravity in a democratic system: "the cost of a Protective tariff is beyond what can be measured in mere money, because it weakens the fibre of national life, by giving rise to political and social evils, which must be counted as of graver consequence than any economic loss."[71] He dealt sympathetically and in detail with Mill's infant industry argument, admitting that bounties but not tariffs might be used to encourage innovation.[72] Wise cited with approval the work of his fellow Australian free-traders, and he used extensively writings by Frank Taussig and William Graham Sumner, who were "too little known in England and Australia." *Industrial Freedom* was a perceptive analysis of the politics as well as the theory of commercial policy, and it was all the more unusual, as he said, because it was written "at intervals during the rare and busy leisure of an active professional and public life." The book obtained for Wise an international reputation as an able defender of free trade.[73]

In Victoria, Max Hirsch, a merchant who settled in Melbourne during 1890, joined R. Murray Smith as an outstanding doctrinaire champion of free trade. Hirsch usually linked demands for

70. B. R. Wise, *Industrial Freedom: A Study in Politics* (Melbourne, 1892), pp. 16–17.

71. *Ibid.*, p. 328.

72. *Ibid.*, p. 345.

73. Favorable reviews were by David Kinley of the University of Wisconsin, *Annals of the American Academy of Political and Social Science*, III (1892–93), 160–62; and L. L. Price, *Economic Journal*, II (1892), 676–81.

tariff reform with proposals for a single tax on land, and he may have been responsible in part for driving some traditionally free-trade landowners into the protectionist camp. For example, the following declaration by Hirsch could only have brought discomfort to landed proprietors:

a system of free trade, the removal of the veil which hides from workers the fact that they pay the bulk of all taxes, will teach workers the true theory of taxation, will cause them to place taxation where it belongs, on the rental value of land, on the value, which is not created by any one individual, but by the community as a whole, and which therefore belongs to the community.[74]

Like Pulsford in New South Wales, Hirsch was an indefatigable publicist, and he used every available platform to plead the case for free trade.[75]

Free-traders in the colonies greeted the Commonwealth in 1900 as a triumph over protection, and they issued a barrage of propaganda for permanent low tariffs.[76] However, they were able only momentarily to arrest the movement towards widespread protection led by Deakin and supported eventually by all parties. Despite revived tariff discussions in the 1920's, it became apparent that a few university economists were almost the only remaining vocal free-traders.[77]

74. Max Hirsch, *Protection in Victoria* (Melbourne, 1891), p. 29, and *The Fiscal Superstition* (Melbourne, n.d.).
75. Hirsch was the influential secretary of a Victorian Board of Inquiry on Unemployment which attributed a multitude of sins to protection. See "Report of the Board of Inquiry on Unemployment," *Papers Presented to the Parliament of Victoria*, 1900. To a free trade gathering in London Hirsch listed no less than fifteen distinct arguments why free trade was preferable to protection. *Report of the Proceedings of the Free Trade Congress* (London, 1908), pp. 171–220. See also articles by Hirsch in the free-trade organ *Our Country*.
76. For example: W. H. Renwick, *An Exposure of "Age" Statistics* (Melbourne, 1901); William Bateman, *Protection in the Commonwealth, How it Burdens the Primary Producer; also a Comparison with the Argentine Republic* (Melbourne, 1902); *Free Trade and Tariff Reform* (Sydney, n.d.) [a collection of essays by G. H. Reid, Bruce Smith, W. H. Renwick, Max Hirsch, and others, shortly after Federation].
77. For example, F. C. Benham, "'The Australian Tariff and the Standard of Living': a Reply," *Economic Record*, II (1926), 20–42; F. C. Benham, "The Australian Tariff and the Standard of Living: a Restatement," *ibid.*, III (1927), 239–48; Edward Shann, *Bond or Free? Occasional Economic Essays* (Sydney, 1930), p. 55. R. C. Mills questioned many aspects of protection in "The Tariff Board of Australia," abstract, *Report of the Eighteenth Meeting of the Australasian Association for the Advancement of Science held at Perth*, 1926, p. 599; and in *Economic Record*, III (1927), 52–81.

3

Land Disposal and Taxation: I. The Wakefield System and Homestead Settlement

Three great land controversies shook the Australian colonies during the nineteenth century. The issues in dispute were: the virtues of Edward Gibbon Wakefield's schemes for systematic colonization; the desirability of small-scale homestead settlement; and the justice of state confiscation of an "unearned increment" in land values, either through nationalization or taxation. Discussion of economic factors in these controversies centered around a fundamental question of the relationship land should have to other productive factors in an economy. Although the writings of foreign economists had substantial impact on discussion, the colonies could receive little guidance in answering questions directly from the experience of other countries. Formation of satisfactory land policy was a challenge which Australia, like other new countries in the nineteenth century, had to meet on its own. The three land controversies overlapped in time and in argument, but for convenience they are examined here in separate sections.

The Wakefield System and the "Sufficient Price"

New South Wales was founded as a penal settlement, and for two decades it remained little more than a penitentiary. By 1808 fewer than one thousand persons out of a population of ten thousand lived as farmers on a mere one hundred thousand acres granted by the colonial governors without system and according to "no precise rule."[1] During the administration of

1. Stephen H. Roberts, *History of Australian Land Settlement* (1788–1920) (Melbourne, 1924), pp. 17 and 25.

Governor Macquarie (1809–21) the potential usefulness of Australia to Britain as a supplier of raw wool became apparent, and government began to provide land to staple producers, both free immigrants and ex-convicts. During the 1820's colonists and British officials suggested the desirability of replacing the haphazard granting system with land sales; Governor Macquarie, W. C. Wentworth, and Commissioner Bigge all advocated sale at prices between five and ten shillings per acre.[2] An experiment to combine land sales with free grants began in 1824 and ended in 1826 only when it appeared that a land price would stunt colonial growth.

Edward Gibbon Wakefield wrote his ficticious *Letter from Sydney* from Newgate Prison in 1829. It contained the first expression of his thoughts on land policy, and very rapidly he gained substantial influence over colonial policy. Wakefield's theory evolved during the subsequent thirty years and generated an almost continuous storm of criticism and of praise. Because Wakefield himself never set foot in Australia and the development of his ideas has been described carefully elsewhere,[3] these matters will not receive attention here. However, Wakefield's writings did have a direct impact on Australian thought, and colonial reactions to this British prescription for land policy will be examined below.

Wakefield's plan seemed particularly appropriate for Australian conditions. He complained fundamentally about the lack of system in British colonization: inefficient administration, inadequate surveys, and general governmental disinterest and lethargy. To such demands for improvements in public administration most colonists found they could murmur "Amen."[4] But

2. *Ibid.*, pp. 35–36; *Report of the Commissioner of Inquiry, on the State of Agriculture and Trade in the Colony of New South Wales* (London, 1823), pp. 49 and 91; W. C. Wentworth, *A Statistical, Historical, and Political Description of the Colony of New South Wales, and its Dependent Settlements in Van Diemen's Land* (London, 1819), p. 392.

3. Stephen H. Roberts, *op. cit.*, pp. 73–148; R. C. Mills, *The Colonization of Australia, 1829–1842* (London, 1915); Klaus E. Knorr, *British Colonial Theories 1570–1850* (Toronto, 1944), pp. 269–315; and Paul Bloomfield, *Edward Gibbon Wakefield* (London, 1961).

4. R. C. Mills has described the reception given by colonists to Wakefield's *Letter* in 1829 in "Gibbon Wakefield's 'Letter from Sydney,'" *Royal Australian Historical Society Journal and Proceedings*, XV (1929), 121–42. K. Buckley has pro-

Wakefield suggested also two policy principles which brought him many enemies in the colonies and only a few supporters. He recommended first that land be not granted but sold at a price "sufficient" to discourage undesirable dispersion of settlers and to sustain a landless labor force, and second, that proceeds from land sales be used to defray the costs of bringing immigrants to the new country. The combination of labor and land in correct proportions which would result under his system, Wakefield insisted, would attract surplus capital and men of substance from the old country. Wakefield was certain that an optimum relationship between all factors of production might be determined scientifically, and that an excess supply of land was quite as injurious as a deficiency. He believed that economic development would take place most rapidly where productive factors were "concentrated," and he expressed a personal aversion to the primitive social forms of a frontier economy.

The Australian colonies seemed to provide every indication of the need for a high land price for the dual purpose of restricting settlement and subsidizing immigration. Many of the early problems of development stemmed from the evils Wakefield attacked, particularly excessive diffusion and a shortage of hired labor. In Western Australia, Roberts reports, "the Swan River settlement had amply proved the folly of large grants and dispersion of settlement," while in Tasmania "Waste and confusion, monopoly and distress made the island a happy hunting-ground for the Wakefield theorists."[5] During the 1820's the Australian Agricultural Company and the Van Diemen's Land Company indicated the constructive role that private capital might play if only it could be persuaded to migrate.[6]

Wakefield's opponents conceded that he had diagnosed colonial diseases correctly, but they insisted that his remedies were unsatisfactory. Restrictive use of productive land, the colonies' distinctive resource, they argued, would simply discourage pro-

---

vided a thorough discussion of attitudes toward Wakefield's ideas in New South Wales over a longer period in "E. G. Wakefield and the Alienation of Crown Land in N. S. Wales to 1847," *Economic Record*, XXXIV (1957), 80–96.

5. *Op. cit.*, pp. 45 and 50.
6. *Ibid.*, pp. 51–70.

spective settlers. Capital extracted by a high land price, they continued, could be employed more effectively within the colonies than on subsidized immigration. Colonial critics concluded that Wakefield's dislike of a frontier economy was based more on snobbish prejudice than on economic analysis and could be defended only as personal taste.

Although experiments were made with land sales in the 1820's, sales did not supersede land grants completely until the Ripon regulations of 1831. The influence of Wakefield's ideas then became evident in all the colonies during the 1830's and 1840's, and particularly in South Australia where settlement was established avowedly on his principles.[7] John Dunmore Lang, cleric, politician, journalist, and promoter, was one of the earliest colonists to provide a careful defense of Wakefield's proposals. In 1833 Lang, in the same way as Wakefield, outlined to a Sydney audience the complementary needs of the colonies and the mother country, a shortage of capital and labor in one and superabundance in the other. Australia's great problem, he maintained, was to lure immigrants from going to Canada, and the only hope was assisted passages. He asked:

how is such a population to be attracted to our shores? We can not expect it should find its way to us spontaneously, or that Great Britain should send it out to us by taxing the nation for that purpose; for Canada is so much nearer home than this Colony and the passage thither is so much cheaper than to New South Wales, that whether the emigrant pays his own passage or has it paid for him by the Government, Canada will undoubtedly be resorted to by the great majority of free emigrants. If it is therefore an object of vast importance to this Colony to obtain a large agricultural population in the way of immigration . . . it follows that the Colony must in one shape or other pay for their importation, by affording them in the first instance at least a gratuitous passage.[8]

Lang claimed that a minimum land price was the only practicable means of raising necessary immigration revenue. He reported:

7. Stephen H. Roberts, *op. cit.*, pp. 131–40; and Douglas Pike, *Paradise of Dissent, South Australia, 1829–1857* (Melbourne, 1957), pp. 74–95.
8. John Dunmore Lang, *Emigration; Considered Chiefly in Reference to the Practicability and Expediency of Importing and of Settling Throughout the Territory of New South Wales, A Numerous, Industrious and Virtuous Agricultural Population* (Sydney, 1833), pp. 6–7.

There are differences of opinion among intelligent persons throughout the Colony; 1st. as to the propriety of selling land at all; 2nd. as to the propriety of fixing a minimum price, in the event of its being disposed of by sale; and 3d. as to the propriety of fixing that minimum at five shillings an acre. For my own part, I feel perfectly satisfied with the Government Regulation as it stands. I am decidedly of opinion that land ought to be disposed of by sale only, and not by grant, that there ought to be a minimum price in all cases, and that that price ought in no instance to be less than five shillings an acre.[9]

Lang recommended that immigrants of substance who were prepared to pay their own passage should be granted special concessions.

Critics of Wakefield soon became more vocal than defenders. Specific complaints were with the two proposals for subsidized immigration and a high land price. It can be doubted whether many early colonists pondered seriously or even read works by the systematic colonizers. But the term "Wakefield system" quickly became common currency, and colonists identified the author in general terms with land restriction and assisted migration. Objection to the Wakefield system was in part to the principle of government collection of revenue from one group for questionable community benefit. Land purchasers in particular resented use of their resources for importation of labor from which they would not necessarily derive direct advantage. Residents of New South Wales suspected that Wakefieldians wished high land prices in other colonies, especially to permit continued experimentation in South Australia.[10]

Despite their obvious self-interest in the matter colonists were able to ground resistance to Wakefield on well-established economic principles. They argued first that withdrawal from colonial circulation of the proceeds of land sales to spend abroad on immigrant transport exerted a depressing effect on the domestic economy. Thomas Bannister, Sheriff of Van Diemen's Land, ac-

9. *Ibid.*, p. 9.
10. Opposition of the Sydney *Herald* to the Wakefield system is described in Michael Roe, *Society and Thought in Eastern Australia, 1835–1851*, Thesis Submitted for the degree of Doctor of Philosophy in the Australian National University, 1960, pp. 42–137. K. Buckley has observed that the natural support for Wakefield's ideas from wealthy landowners in New South Wales was largely removed because with large-scale agriculture "access by workers to land in New South Wales was effectively restricted before Wakefield's views became important." *Op. cit.*, p. 85.

cepted the desirability of land sales in 1833, but he insisted that if the land fund were used to bring in pauper immigrants the restrictive result of the cash outflow would discourage a corresponding number of prosperous prospective immigrants. He wrote:

> With respect to the sale of lands, I think there be no question, but that that measure is one of great wisdom, provided, the proceeds be laid out for Colonial purposes, and the only way this can be done with advantage to the Colony is, that these proceeds be credited to the local Government, and expended in the Colony, to meet the expences of the Government, in lieu of taxation, in fact, to give all the waste lands to the local Government for the benefit of the Colony, in the place of sending these monies out of the Colony, and introducing through them a pauper population into it; it may be said that such a system would prevent the flowing of population to the Colony, and that it would work injuriously to the mother country, by not drawing off a portion of its people. I submit, as under it, the Colony could but be wealthy and prosperous, and never as under the system pursued elsewhere, losing its very life blood in a great portion of its capital being constantly withdrawn from circulation, by being sent away, and receiving in exchange but a pauper population, that the inducement to persons in England to emigrate, would be so great, that emigration would set towards it, much more rapidly, than under the present system, of what might not unfairly be termed a forced emigration.[11]

A writer in Sydney during 1838 preferred complete cessation of land sales to the continued deflationary reduction in the money supply caused by outflow of the land fund. He maintained:

> The sooner, then, this branch of our revenue diminishes, though people may acquire less land, the better for trade and the general interests of the Colony. During the last two years the produce of the land sales thus locked up in the coffers of the treasury, and not returning into circulation, has been equal to more than *one-third* of the whole revenue of the Colony in each year from all sources—which, under such a system (as to the appropriation of the receipts), is more than a young Colony like this can bear. It is out of all proportion to the extent of our circulating medium, which it absorbs perpetually. . . .[12]

11. Thomas Bannister, *A Letter on Colonial Labour, and on the Sale of Lands in Austral-Asia Addressed to the Right Honourable the Secretary of State for the Colonies* (Hobart Town, 1833), p. 15.
12. *Australian Magazine*, I (1838), 56.

William Bland in 1842 reiterated what was in effect a mercantilist argument, that any reduction in the domestic circulating
medium was a national calamity. He recommended that all public
levies and loans, even those raised abroad, be spent internally.
He insisted:

the application to Immigration purposes, of any fund raised on the
lands of this Colony, either here or elsewhere, is wrong in principle;
such funds being required in this country for works of necessity—
roads, bridges, tanks, school-houses, places of public worship,—both
with regard to a due economy of labour, as well as to the health and
progressive moral and religious well-being of its inhabitants. . . .[13]

An anonymous critic in 1842 pointed out that if subsidized
immigration would bring highest yields to colonial capital, local
entrepreneurs voluntarily would support such a project. The
1840's were a period when liberals in Britain proclaimed loudly
ways in which commercial free trade facilitated optimum allocation of resources, and colonists were able to apply these arguments to conditions in their own land and labor markets. Expenditure of the land fund on sponsored passages, this critic
continued, resulted in misuse of scarce colonial purchasing power,
and thereby retarded growth.

If the waste lands of this Colony are sold in England, and the
proceeds expended on Emigration to this Colony, those funds are expended on the mere importation of labour, at a time when additional
capital is required for the employment of that labour on its arrival—
if the waste lands are sold here, &c., in addition to the above objection,
capital is exported from that part of the Empire where it is the most
wanted, to that where it the most abounds—while such system compels
the former part of the Empire to vest capital without the possibility
of any timely return, and interferes, as far as the effects of its operation extend, with the most profitable and safe mode of investing
capital, which the latter could adopt.[14]

Protests against collection of a land fund through high land prices
and against expenditure of this fund outside the colonies had

13. William Bland, *Objections to the Project of His Excellency Sir George
Gipps, for Raising a Loan to be Secured on the Ordinary Revenue of the Colony
. . .* (Sydney, 1842), p. 8.
14. *Expenditure of the Land-Fund of New South Wales in the Colony, and
Principally on Public Works; as a Means of Promoting and Supporting Immigra-
tion* (Sydney, 1842), pp. 3–4.

strong roots in colonists' pocketbooks. Nevertheless, their objections gained strength and respectability from appeals both to mercantilist arguments against reductions of the money supply and to classical expositions of gains from laissez faire.

The second basic objection to the Wakefield system of land settlement, after its alleged misuse of colonial capital, was to the restriction of land use. John Lhotsky, writing in Sydney in 1835, presented an argument which seemed common sense to most immigrants, that the only reasonable policy in a new country was for each settler to be given "just so much soil as he wanted." He recommended free grants of land on the basis of ability to use property effectively, and he concluded "it is a fact reserved for the elucidation of a deep political economist and philosopher, why the British Government (and a land of British origin the United States), have alone departed from the principle of granting land."[15] T. Potter MacQueen, a prominent early settler, conceded that public land should be sold, but he pointed out that while forced concentration might be appropriate for an agricultural economy it was ruinous in a pastoral one:

in a country depending on its *natural* grasses and herbage, a much larger portion of land is required for pastoral purposes than where artificial grasses and clovers can be produced. This can only be obviated by surveying and selecting large portions of land, dividing them into blocks of two or four square miles (1280 or 2560 acres) securing a regular supply of water to each, and then by affixing a fair, *but not excessive*, price, either induce the neighbouring Settler to purchase, or present a ready investment for the excited energies and industry of the newly-arrived Emigrant.[16]

Colonists were able to demonstrate effectively that the Wakefield system prevented most efficient use of national resources with regard to the market for land and the labor and capital markets. Employment of land proceeds for subsidized immigration, they pointed out, increased capital costs and reduced labor costs arti-

15. [John Lhotsky], *Illustrations of the Present State and Future Prospects of the Colony of New South Wales, by an Impartial Observer* (Sydney, 1835), p. 24. Similar reasoning was expressed by N. L. Kentish in *The Political Economy of New South Wales . . .* (Sydney, 1838).

16. T. Potter MacQueen, *Australia as She Is & as She May Be* (London, 1840), p. 30.

ficially; the Wakefield "sufficient" price rendered marginal land a scarce productive factor where, in an unrestricted market, it should have been a free good.

Prescriptions for the Wakefield system were not followed explicitly in any of the Australian colonies. There was no scientific search for a sufficient price, and governments made no rigorous commitment of a fixed portion of land proceeds for assisted immigration. British authorities as well as colonists were uneasy about translating Wakefield's theories into practice. For example, when Governor Bourke wrote to Lord Glenelg, Secretary of State for the Colonies, concerning the settlement at Port Phillip in 1835, he began:

> Admitting, as every reasonable person must, that a certain degree of concentration is necessary for the advancement of wealth and civilization, and that it enables Government to become at once efficient and economical, I cannot avoid perceiving the peculiarities which, in this Colony, render it impolitic, and even impossible to restrain dispersion within limits that would be expedient elsewhere.[17]

Glenelg replied in essential agreement. He wrote:

> New South Wales is, therefore, not only marked out by nature for a pastoral country, but for a country of which the pasturage must, from the quality of the soil, inevitably separate the shepherds and herdsmen, and all their associates in labor, very widely from the general seat of Government, and from each other. The principle of counteracting dispersion, when reduced to practice, must unavoidably, be narrowed within the limits which these physical peculiarities of the Colony dictate, and require.[18]

Particularly during the 1830's both governors and the governed felt confusion and mixed sentiments about the Wakefield system. Roberts concluded:

> the practical results of some of the mangled parts of Wakefield's theory—a price but not a "sufficient price," emigration but not a wholly systematic emigration, concentration but not Wakefield's labor concentration—far exceeded the importance of the doctrine as a whole.

---

17. Bourke to Glenelg, October 10, 1835, "Despatches on the Subject of the Settlements at Port Phillip and Twofold Bay," *Minutes and Proceedings of the Legislative Council of New South Wales*, 1836, p. 588.
18. Glenelg to Bourke, April 13, 1836, *ibid.*, p. 589.

And it was because of this practical trend, due more to the author than the theory, more to its misconception than its understanding, that the ideas were so epoch-making for Australia.[19]

Throughout the 1830's the majority of Australian writers resisted the Wakefield system in a desultory fashion while land policy varied and vacillated in response to special problems of particular areas and changes in opinion of colonial authorities. In 1840, however, new regulations of the Colonial Land and Emigration Commissioners increased the dosage of systematic colonization and stiffened opposition substantially. The price of Crown land in New South Wales was raised drastically from twelve to twenty shillings per acre, and land sales almost ceased. In 1842 the policy was extended when a British act of parliament specified that after January, 1843, public land in all the Australian colonies could be disposed of only at auction with a minimum price of £1 per acre. From 1843 until early in the 1850's when responsible government brought the colonies control of their own land policy, criticism of the Wakefield system was sustained at a high pitch. Sir George Gipps, Governor of New South Wales, opposed many features of the arrangements, but the instrument of their enforcement bore much of the blame.[20] Agitation was strengthened by depressed wool markets during this period, but the restrictive character of the high land price is indicated by the total yield from land sales between 1839 and 1851 of a mere £370,000.[12]

During 1843, as the combined effects of diminishing wool receipts and artificial land prices were experienced in the colonies, a new journal, the short-lived *New South Wales Magazine*, volunteered a series of sensible comments on the situation. It listed ways in which Australians themselves had contributed to the crisis by "speculation" and "over-action," but it concluded that the inevitable collapse had been worsened by the sudden and unwarranted increase in land values. A contributor explained:

19. *Op. cit.*, p. 93.
20. R. C. Mills, *The Colonization of Australia* (1829–42) (London, 1915), pp. 294–96; and George Nadel, *Australia's Colonial Culture* (Melbourne, 1957), p. 11.
21. S. H. Roberts, *op. cit.*, pp. 101–9.

This price is so exorbitantly above the average productive value of such land, that its enactment has put a stop to the land-sales, and consequently to the importation of labour. The non-importation of labour, and the extravagant price of land, have again operated to the discouragement of the immigration of capitalists; this again has deprived our settlers of a market for their surplus stock; and thus all the evils of our own mismanagement have been made worse and worse by the mismanagement of our rulers.[22]

The magazine claimed that "land-shark" Wakefield, by dictating too high a land price, had in fact stopped funds going to subsidized paupers and at the same time had destroyed the colonies' attractiveness for self-supporting immigrants as compared to America.[23] A writer in the *New South Wales Magazine,* who called himself appropriately "Q. E. D.," cited Malthus and McCulloch to prove by classical economic reasoning that "Free Trade and Laissez Faire" were best for all segments of a colonial economy including the land market. Productive factors in the absence of restrictions would yield maximum returns. He wrote:

> The essential elements of colonial wealth appear to be Land, Capital, Labour, and Population . . . the more these are brought into a state of productive activity—to act and re-act on each other, the "greater will be the prosperity of the greater number" of the people. Just as these elements are fairly applied, or misapplied, or are present in true or false proportions, so the results will either be prosperous activity comparable perhaps to chemical action in the phial of the Alchymist, or there may be stagnation only.[24]

Government determination of land prices at levels twice as great as would have prevailed in a free market, it was argued, was "exactly as if wages had been raised 100 per cent, or as if a tax of 100 per cent had been laid also on all other articles sold in the colony." To relieve the colony from depression, land should be granted freely to "*bona fide* settlers," or at least should be permitted to find its own price in an open market. "The exorbitant price set upon land subsequently; great reflux of capital; and

22. "The Affairs of New South Wales: II," *New South Wales Magazine,* 1843, p. 248.
23. Jasoniana, "State and Prospects of New South Wales," *ibid.,* pp. 299–322.
24. Q. E. D., "An Enquiry into the Causes of the Former Prosperity and Present State of the Colony of New South Wales," *ibid.,* p. 400.

prostration of the colony, might well support objections to almost any price, but the essential principle to be insisted on is, that the upset price at auction should in no case exceed the average price obtained for land at ordinary sales."[25] Q. E. D. concluded by contrasting unfavorably on economic grounds the Wakefield system with the long-established practice of convict transportation.

Let those "rigidly righteous" compare the working of the Transportation System with the Emigration System of Wakefield, by considering their respective effects in this colony, and they will find they have produced fruits of very different qualities. The former had the effect of reforming the criminal by opening before him the straight and narrow path leading to prosperity;—the latter the broad path to ruin, by its tendency to impoverish and degrade the educated class of immigrants, in some cases even to the condition of felons.[26]

One writer in the *New South Wales Magazine* pointed to the special difficulty of taking first steps in colonial growth and of breaking the vicious circle of undevelopment. The Wakefield theory was fallacious, he argued, because proceeds of land sales could not provide funds to import labor until land first had been rendered valuable by the presence of the labor which it was planned to attract. He suggested that British systematic colonizers had erred fundamentally by not distinguishing near-valueless unsettled waste land in new countries from the scarce and productive land which held the attention of classical rent theorists.

In reading about Wakefield's principle in England then, it never occurs to us that the general waste lands of our colony, are scarcely worth the smallest upset price, which can be put upon them; that, as agricultural operations can never be remunerative until we have markets and mouths for our surplus food, capitalists can never . . . venture to give a pound or even five shillings an acre for the lands of this colony.[27]

The only solution to the problem of growth, this writer concluded, was for colonial land to be granted without charge.

All critics of Wakefield did not condemn out of hand the fundamental desirability of systematic colonization. One author praised

25. *Ibid.*, p. 403.
26. *Ibid.*, p. 408.
27. "What is to Become of the Colony?," *New South Wales Magazine*, 1843, p. 619.

the practice of company settlement and described how firms, incorporated in Britain with grants of Australian land in the manner of the Australian Agricultural and Van Diemen's Land companies, could benefit both stock-holders and colonists by using British capital to attract immigrants and, ultimately, render valuable the company land holdings.[28]

Many of the most articulate opponents of the Wakefield system were from the "squatter" class of large pastoralists who dwelled and grazed their sheep on extensive tracts of Crown lands by license and not by right of ownership. To the landowners' complaints in general of capital export and resource misallocation, squatters added specific objections to systematic colonizers' plans for settlement of sheep stations by "a sturdy yeomanry." Squatters recognized that under Wakefield's proposals they would be expected not only to help pay for immigration by purchase of part of their runs, but also to provide homesteads for settlers from property which they had come to regard virtually as their own, and at least as essential to their livelihood. Gideon Scott Lang, a leader among the squatters, formulated a convincing statement of opposition to systematic colonization. He argued that if maximum economic growth was to be obtained settlers had to make full use of available natural resources. Pioneer squatters, the adventurous risk-bearing entrepreneurial element in the colony, should be given every encouragement to expand, including absolute possession of all land they rendered productive. He explained:

There is only one *natural limit* to the extension of stock over the Continent of New Holland, and that lies in the quantity of land capable of depasturing it; to cause this stock to occupy the land *productively* as it extends, a certain amount of Capital is required and much labour and hardship must be encountered; in the limited number of parties possessed of the requisite capital, and of energy and self-denial to undergo the hardships and deprivations necessarily endured by the first occupiers of a wild and uninhabited country, lies the only necessary *artificial limit* to the naturally rapid increase of stock, and the extension of the Colony.

28. "National Emigration and Colonization," *New South Wales Magazine*, 1843, pp. 583–88.

There are two sources from which the necessary capital can be derived, from the immigration of capitalists, and from the profits of capital already invested in the colony; the supply from these sources depends, not upon the demand, or rather the scope for its investment which is unlimited, but upon the degree of encouragement to invest afforded by the returns; the Government, therefore, in order to induce the largest number of capitalists to invest in the Colony, *so that the productive extension of stock, may, as nearly as possible keep pace with its natural rate of increase,* should afford every facility to the Capitalist in first settling, ample security for his money while investing it, liberty of action and full scope for enterprise and exertion, and lastly, *absolute certainty of reaping the full fruit of his labours,* all which will enable him to obtain at the smallest risk, the largest profits which the circumstances of the case will admit.[29]

Lang insisted that premature attempts to force new countries into enterprise other than staple production resulted in capital loss. He subscribed to a stage theory of development in contrast to Wakefield's belief that the society of an old country could with profit be transplanted in miniature to a new one. On this difference in principle Lang's objections to Wakefield's policy rested. In contrast to Wakefield's plea for balanced growth with plentiful labor and land restriction Lang wrote:

Until the land is fully occupied, and while the immigration of Capitalists continues, Capital will be invested in such employments as will yield the largest profit with the exertion of the least skill, and the capital and labor of the Colonies will therefore be directed to the production of raw material for exportation, such as wool and tallow, from New Holland, tobacco and cotton, from the United States, and hides and copper ore, from South America.

No more labor should be imported than can be employed by sheep and cattle, because while there is room for them to increase they will continue to absorb the whole Capital in the Colony, and the surplus would not find subsistence from the want of Capital to employ them.[30]

Lang repeated familiar colonial arguments against export of capital and added that in new countries, because profits were almost always reinvested, government levies inevitably restricted capital accumulation. He explained:

29. Gideon Scott Lang, *Land and Labour in Australia* . . . (Melbourne, 1845), p. 11.
30. *Ibid.,* p. 102.

even though paid out of profits and consequently not so immediate in its effects as if paid out of capital, any sum withdrawn from the Settlers to be expended out of the Colony, will act as a check upon its progress, not only by withdrawing capital without giving a return in exchangeable value, thus deranging the monetary affairs of the country, but because the capital in this or any other Colony is so limited, in proportion to the scope for its investment afforded by the unlimited extent of waste land, that all profit becomes capital and is invested as soon as it is realized, and the exportation of profit is therefore equivalent to the exportation of so much capital actually in use.[31]

Lang emphasized that frontier wasteland in Australia, when first settled, had no value in exchange, and all subsequent produce was attributable to the squatter's efforts alone. "To make Waste Land produce and be of value a certain amount of labour and capital is required, and from the application of this capital and labour arises its value, whose amount is that for which the produce forms an adequate return."[32] Systematic colonizers, Lang asserted, believed erroneously that in new countries as in old a distinction could usefully be drawn between returns to land and to labor. "In a Colony the settler has the expenditure of both Landlord and Tenant, and is therefore entitled to the profits of both, different however both in amount and proportion from the Rent and Farmer's profit in Britain."[33] Lang calculated in considerable detail the potential revenues and expenditures of a hypothetical squatter, and he concluded "There is sufficient encouragement for the immigration of the capitalist for whom the country is adapted but *no surplus profit.*"[34] During the 1840's, while pastoralists boiled sheep for tallow in their desperation over drought and falling prices, Lang's powerful arguments were reiterated fervently.[35]

In 1842 Robert Lowe, a brilliant young Oxford graduate, who later as Lord Sherbrooke was destined for a distinguished career in British politics, arrived in Sydney and entered the thick of

31. *Ibid.,* p. 14.
32. *Ibid.,* p. 20.
33. *Ibid.,* p. 21.
34. *Ibid.,* p. 99.
35. See for example, "Report from the Select Committee on Immigration, with Appendix and Minutes of Evidence," *Votes and Proceedings of the Legislative Council of New South Wales,* 1843; and Charles Griffith, *The Present State and Prospects of the Port Phillip District of New South Wales* (Dublin, 1845).

controversy over the Wakefield system.[36] Lowe was fresh from debates on tariff legislation in Britain, and he found it simple to shift arguments from defense of free trade in corn to support for free trade in colonial land. He was first appointed to the Legislative Council, and later stood successfully for election. In 1844 he founded the *Atlas* newspaper and through this medium attacked repeatedly the Wakefield system. During the violent disputes of the 1840's, Lowe had few challengers as the most competent master of economic analysis.

In the first issues of the *Atlas*, Lowe set forth clearly his views on land policy which amounted to a doctrinaire application of Ricardian and Malthusian economic principles to colonial conditions. He stated the following "Theorem" with no less than twenty-three distinct and carefully listed arguments in support: "It is better to grant the waste lands of the Crown in fee simple at once, subject to a rent proportionable to their different values and uses, than to sell them."[37] He insisted that all economic resources should be put to work as quickly as possible, and that an immigration fund was undesirable because it would be "recklessly spent" by government. Furthermore, "England needs emigration even more than the colonies need immigration," and therefore the mother country should be required to pay the migration bill. A high land price, Lowe insisted, checked "the influx of capital," encouraged speculation, placed scarce purchasing power in the hands of an untrustworthy government, and required continuation of a leasing system which discouraged land improvements and capital accumulation. From an interpretation of Ricardian rent theory and in anticipation of Henry George, Lowe suggested that government revenue be raised by rent on public land which would amount to a tax on unimproved land values; he noted: "the objection of M'Culloch to taxes on rent, that you cannot distinguish between that which is paid for the powers of the soil, and that which is paid as interest on capital spent on improvements, does not apply to the rent of waste lands, on

36. S. Elliott Napier, "Robert Lowe and his Associations with Australia," *Royal Australian Historical Society Journal and Proceedings*, XVIII (1932), 1–31.
37. Robert Lowe, "Occupation of Crown Lands.—Rent Better than Sale," *Atlas*, December 7, 1844, p. 15.

which no improvement has been made." Lowe cited ample authority for the derivation of government revenue from land rent —"[James] Mill, in the first volume of his History of India, and in his Political Economy, and also Mr. Ricardo, and Adam Smith, are favourable to this plan of raising a revenue . . . it is believed that there is no authority against it."[38] Lowe presented the most reasonable case for continuation of the system of squatters' licenses.

Lowe called for unrestricted disposal of public lands "as soon as Government sees that land will be *bona fide* and profitably occupied," and he pointed without valid evidence to alleged liberality and success of Candian policy. He remarked: "to a wise and far-sighted Government, the price it obtains is entirely a secondary and trivial consideration—the main and principal object being so to distribute the Public Land as to ensure the greatest good to the community."[39] He maintained that land in a new country should be treated as a free good.

Estimated by the law of political economy, which regulates the price of an article according to the ratio of demand and supply, land is, and for ages must be, in this vast uninhabited continent, a drug, a thing of very small exchangeable value; but, placed in the hands of monopolizing government, it becomes the most costly of commodities—the absolute ownership of which, including the mineral treasures it contains, cannot be purchased at any price, and a qualified ownership only at one absolutely ruinous.[40]

Lowe described an improbable imaginary conversation between David Ricardo and J. B. Say ("the great French political economist") to show that restriction of land in the colonies was similar to imposition of a tax on pastoral operations; the British consumer paid for this folly, he maintained, by an increase in wool prices. The result, he predicted, could even be calamitous for the Empire.

By taxing the raw material of British manufacture which is produced in Australia, the government of Australia enhances the price of that material to the manufacturer, and thus obliges him to employ a larger capital than he otherwise would, to produce his woolen goods, and

38. *Ibid.*
39. "The Alienation of Waste Lands," *Atlas,* March 8, 1845, p. 169.
40. "Government Monopoly of Land," *Atlas,* February 15, 1845, p. 133.

to demand a larger price for his goods when produced, from the consumer, in order to repay the extra capital so employed, and the profit which he has a right to look for from it. The effect, then, of the Squatting Regulations is, like that of all taxes on raw material, to increase the price of the manufactured goods, and thus, by rendering Great Britain less able to cope with her Continental rivals, to cripple her energies and curtail her commerce.[41]

The *Atlas* (with Lowe as editor) was extremely abusive both of Wakefield personally and of the low state of economic science in the colonies. The paper remarked in disgust: "Political economy, it would appear, has not crossed the line, except in the odious and spurious shape of the Wakefieldian theory." An *Atlas* "poet" wrote:

> To mock, to thwart, to baffle still,
> From what is good, to work out ill;
> Has Gibbon Wakefield tried his skill
>   Since before Newgate knew him;
> Abduction there had lodged him fast,
> But his deductions that surpassed,
> And young Australia's hopes did blast
>   When Russell listened to him.[42]

Hearings of parliamentary committees were a popular forum for informed discussion of land policy, and they helped to reveal the state of contemporary thinking. In 1843 testimony before a committee of the New South Wales Legislative Council indicated widespread concern about a recent increase in land prices. The committee deplored the action and it repeated arguments for a free land market in particular, and for laissez faire in general. The report said in part:

The value of land, of course, can only be determined by the return it gives; and must depend altogether upon population, labour, and capital. If it is capable of producing nothing, it is worth nothing; if it produces a certain profit, it is worth a certain price; and that price, be it great or small, must always be proportionate to the profit it yields. This is the criterion whereby value is to be ascertained. As it is diversified in quality so must it vary in value; and therefore your

41. "The English Side of the Squatting Question," *Atlas*, May 17, 1845, p. 289.
42. "Gibbon Wakefield," *Atlas*, May 31, 1845, p. 314.

Committee cannot consider that a uniform fixed price is at all applicable to this Colony.[43]

As had its predecessors, the committee expressed dismay at the loss of capital to the colony as a result of expenditures abroad of proceeds from land sales—"capital and labour, as elements of colonization, should exist in a new country in proportion to each other; and it was a fatal mistake to send the one *out* of the country, in order to bring the other *in*." The committee indicated, however, that opposition to the Wakefield system was not united in all its conclusions. Squatters complained only that crown lands were not made freely available for pastoral operations, while spokesmen for landless immigrants condemned land restriction but objected also to the contention of squatters that Australia should remain for the forseeable future a pastoral rather than an agricultural economy. The 1843 committee expressed concern for the landless in guarded terms:

These extensive tracts . . . great as are their natural capabilities, are now appropriated to pastoral pursuits alone; and your Committee, though sensible that, while a demand exists for the increase of stock, grazing must be one of the most profitable pursuits in a community, which can command extensive pastures, feel bound to remark, that it is an occupation of all others, the least calculated to develop the energies of industry—the active powers of the human mind—or the real resources of a country; and that they are consequently the last of all, to which a civilised community, or a fertile soil, should be *totally* abandoned.[44]

Another New South Wales committee in 1847, with Robert Lowe as chairman, repeated again arguments for free trade in land and concluded in a more theoretical tone that the British government by adopting the Wakefield system had repudiated "the doctrine of supply and demand" "in utter defiance of the principles of political economy."[45]

In 1847, opposition to the Wakefield system was reduced dras-

43. "Report from the Select Committee on the Crown Land Sales Act, with Minutes of Evidence and Appendix," *Votes and Proceedings of the Legislative Council of New South Wales*, 1843, p. 2.
44. *Ibid.*, pp. 1 and 3.
45. "Report from the Select Committee on the Minimum Upset Price of Land, with Minutes of Evidence," *Votes and Proceedings of the Legislative Council of New South Wales*, 1847.

tically. A British order-in-council gave to the squatters security of possession without purchase of lands they held by lease and thereby removed squatter concern with land sales and price.[46] Criticism of land restriction and high prices hereafter came principally from spokesmen for would-be agricultural settlers.[47] As soon as squatters lost their position in the eyes of Robert Lowe as victims of harsh imperial policy, he switched allegiance to "the popular party" and aimed his fire still at the Wakefield system but also at all large land-holders, including his old allies the squatters. In a select committee report in 1849, Lowe accused squatters of profiteering under the new regulations: "the only persons who wish to perpetuate the present price are those who have the same interest in it as the smuggler has in a high rate of duty. Free trade ruins the smuggler—cheap land destroys squatting."[48] Applications of the restrictive Wakefield system to prospective new farmers combined with its relaxation for squatters, Lowe maintained, had the effect of placing a discriminatory tax on agriculture as opposed to pastoral operations: "the prohibitory price only exposes those who have paid for land to an unfair competition with those who have not."[49] Lowe argued that paradoxical effects of the Australian variant of the Wakefield system were economic stagnation and a market value for land even below what it would have been in the absence of government supports. "It is thus that the outraged laws of political economy have avenged themselves, and the greediness of the Government

46. See S. H. Roberts, *op. cit.*, p. 186.
47. Distinctive working class objections to the Wakefield system were voiced before 1847 but were submerged beneath the squatters' powerful opposition. See, for example, *The Citizen: A Weekly Paper of Politics, Literature, Science and the Arts* (Sydney), October 3 and 10, 1846.
48. "Report from the Select Committee on Crown Lands, with Appendix and Minutes of Evidence," *Votes and Proceedings of the Legislative Council of New South Wales*, 1849, p. 2.
49. *Ibid.*, p. 4. Sir James Stephen in 1856 used the same analogy as Lowe to explain the squatters' change of heart toward the Wakefield system. He said: "the squatter . . . like his counterpart the English smuggler, fattens as the demands of the Government upon the fair trader grow excessive. Because people could not buy farms at twenty shillings an acre, the squatter seized upon tracts as large as parishes, hundreds, and counties, at nothing at all per acre. . . . The squatocracy, being indirectly indebted to Mr. Wakefield's theory both for that sonorous name and for the possessions to which it refers, acknowledge and revere in him their patron saint." "Colonization as a Branch of Social Economy," reprinted in Paul Knaplund, *James Stephen and the British Colonial System 1813–1847* (Madison, Wisconsin, 1953), pp. 295–96.

in demanding more for its lands than they are worth, has resulted in depreciating all land, alienated or not, far below its natural value."[50]

Direct criticism of the Wakefield system continued into the 1850's, but was combined more and more with demands for agricultural as opposed to pastoral development. One anonymous author proposed in 1848 that the evils detected by Wakefield in colonization policy—absence of system and excessive dispersion—could be overcome more effectively than with a "sufficient price" by offering a fixed quantity of "land script" to every new immigrant who could either demand waste land for his own use or sell the certificates to other settlers on an open market receiving thereby remuneration for his passage. Through this device additions to the supply of both new landholders and landless labor would be regulated "automatically;" land would be permitted to find its own market price; and scarce capital would not be extracted from the colony. The author wrote:

> when there is a demand for labour in a colony, it is evidence of the existence of unemployed capital; if, then, as much waste land as is necessary be bartered for as much labour as is required to employ the unemployed capital, the true and perfect balance between waste land, labour, and capital will have been attained; because the waste land will have been applied in the only way in which it can be made valuable, namely, to the introduction of labour; capital will be employed in the way in which it can be best invested; and labour will have been introduced to that extent only which would lead to its being sufficiently remunerated.[51]

This author argued that land in colonies was the abundant resource and ought to be employed to the full in development schemes. The Wakefield system proposed land sales for the extraction from settlers of capital—one scarce factor—for the importation of the other scarce factor, labor. A more sensible alternative, he claimed, was his method of using plentiful land to attract both capital and labor. In addition to its economic rationale, however, the scheme had social overtones; it was designed to

50. "Report from the Select Committee on Crown Lands," 1849, *loc. cit.*, p. 6.

51. *Direct Remission Advocated: Being a Consideration of the Connexion between Waste Lands of Colonies and Emigration* (Sydney, 1848), p. 15.

encourage in the colonies growth of small farming and immigration of modest capitalists with funds at least sufficient to pay for their own sea passage. The Wakefield system, to which this plan was a reaction, was designed to perpetuate a distinction in the new world between workers and employers and was intended to replenish the supply of colonial workers from the British poor. It was inevitable that Wakefield's scheme should have greater appeal to the governing class in Britain than to hopeful new settlers in the colonies.

Familiar arguments for liberal land disposal in opposition to the Wakefield system were repeated throughout the nineteenth century with emphasis on the contentions that capital extracted from the colonies by a land fund had depressing effects on the economy, and that colonial resources should be left unrestricted to find their most productive occupation.[52] For example, in 1857 William Stanley Jevons, living in Sydney and employed at the new mint, indicated once again how the Wakefield system interfered with crucial colonial markets, was inconsistent with classical political economy, and by encouraging urbanization discouraged "the agricultural, pastoral or mining interests, which are evidently the original source of the wealth and general prosperity of all colonists."[53]

George Wyndham, a wealthy landowner, cited McCulloch, Adam Smith, and the Scriptures in criticism of Wakefield and in support of his belief that free grants were "the natural mode of acquiring property in land in a country where land lies waste." He insisted that "to demand a money payment, ere a man shall occupy waste land is to erect a barrier between man and God's gift—in defiance of God and His command to man 'to subdue the earth.' "[54] In South Australia, Wakefield was blamed for all

52. "How is Immigration to be Paid for in Future?," *Australia Felix Monthly Magazine*, October, 1849, pp. 155–62; William Bland, *Letter to His Excellency Sir Charles Augustus Fitzroy, Governor-in-Chief of New South Wales* (Sydney, 1850), pp. 7–9; Samuel Sidney, *The Three Colonies of Australia* (London, 1853), pp. 92–104; *The Letters of "American," on the Projected Railroads, and the Public Lands of Tasmania* (Hobart, 1856), p. 33.
53. [W. S. Jevons], "Comparison of the Land and Railway Policy of New South Wales," *Empire* (Sydney), April 8, 1857; and see J. A. La Nauze, *Political Economy in Australia: Historical Studies*, p. 40.
54. George Wyndham, *On the Land Policy of New South Wales* (West Maitland, 1866), p. 2. See also, for a similar denunciation of Wakefield, *Coalition between the Squatters and Free Selectors* (Sydney, n.d.), pp. 4–5.

manner of disasters,[55] and throughout the colonies frustrated land-seekers cursed his ideas long after systematic colonizers had lost all influence over Australian policies. In 1909 W. G. Spence attributed the strong and early growth of the Australian labor movement to the success of Wakefield's disciples in keeping workers from the land.[56]

After 1847 several spokesmen for the newly secure squatters executed a complete reversal of principle and came forth in vigorous defense of the Wakefield system. Under new land regulations squatters were made curators of public lands by lease, and it became to their advantage to defend a high land price, thereby lessening the quantity of land demanded for agricultural use and sustaining the supply of landless labor. In 1861 Colin Campbell explained to a gathering of miners at Ararat the beauty of Wakefield's theory, from the squatter's viewpoint, emphasizing the important part played by pastoralists in Australian development. He said:

> Suppose, then, that land is supplied in sufficient quantity, and at a sufficient price, to meet all legitimate demands, the wants of the purchasing class will be provided for. But there remains another class carrying on pastoral pursuits as Crown tenants, who have been placed advisedly, and by the authority of the supreme Government, in that position in order that the public domain might be turned to a profitable account until it became wanted for sale at a sufficient price.[57]

Wakefield was cited for authority throughout the century on a variety of matters other than the land price. Alexander Stuart, colonial treasurer of New South Wales, applauded the "great wisdom" of "Mr. Wakefield's system" in 1877 when justifying expenditures on public works from proceeds of land sales.[58] Sir Charles Nicholson from New South Wales and Anthony Forster from South Australia both paid tribute to Wakefield as the pioneer

55. See for example S. Newland (Late Treasurer), *Our Waste Lands* (Adelaide, 1888).
56. W. G. Spence, *Australia's Awakening* (Sydney, 1909), p. 14.
57. Colin Campbell, *The Land Question: A Lecture delivered at the Ararat Mechanics' Institute* (Ararat, 1861), p. 11. A similar contemporary brief but full exposition of the Wakefield system was "Wakefield and Colonization," *Victorian Monthly Magazine,* I (1859), 221–30.
58. James Thomson, ed., *The Financial Statements of the Colonial Treasurers of New South Wales* (Sydney, 1881), p. 364.

of colonial economic planning.[59] The battle for Wakefield's system was fought and lost between 1830 and 1847. The influence of his ideas remained, but in fragmented and indirect form. The great land controversies after responsible government were not over the land price but over the fundamental rights of propertyless colonists to gain small agricultural holdings on the frontier.

Homesteads for the Yeomanry

During the first half of the nineteenth century, some colonists hoped for duplication in Australia of the American homestead system and encouragement of a hardy independent frontier landowner class. W. C. Wentworth proposed in 1819 that surveyed farms of one hundred and sixty acres be auctioned to new settlers on easy terms "as in America," and he cited writings of "Messrs. Birkbeck and Fearon" as evidence.[60] John Dunmore Lang, both by word and by deed, sought development of homestead agriculture as a complement to large-scale pastoral operations, and he worked all of his life for creation of "an industrious and contented peasantry."[61] During the depressed early 1840's, a Mutual Protection Association in Sydney aimed at making small farmers out of unemployed town laborers.[62] The farms and land regulations of the Canadian colonies were viewed with particular envy.[63] But this ferment had little effect before 1850; and sheep-raising

59. Sir Charles Nicholson, "The Principles which Ought to Regulate the Determination of the Political and Municipal Boundaries and Divisions of the Colonies," *Proceedings of the Royal Colonial Institute,* XII (1880–81), 318; and Anthony Forster, *South Australia: Its Progress and Prosperity* (London, 1866).
60. W. C. Wentworth, *A Statistical, Historical, and Political Description of the Colony of New South Wales* (London, 1819), pp. 391–92 and 421–23.
61. J. D. Lang, *An Historical and Statistical Account of New South Wales* (London, 1837), I, 398–400; and Lang's other works *passim.*
62. Gordon Greenwood, ed., *Australia: A Social and Political History* (Sydney, 1955), p. 58. A few pastoralists also looked to homestead settlement as a possible solution to their economic problems. K. Buckley, *op. cit.,* pp. 93–96.
63. "Systematic Colonization," *Weekly Register of Politics, Facts, and General Literature* (Sydney), June 15, 1844 [a report of a debate in the Canadian Parliament]; "Regulations for the Disposal of Lands in British North America," *ibid.,* December 14, 1844 [an extract from McCulloch's *Dictionary of Commerce*]; and speech of Henry Parkes to the Legislative Assembly of New South Wales, 1861, in Henry Parkes, *Speeches on Various Occasions Connected with the Public Affairs of New South Wales 1848–1874* (Melbourne, 1876), p. 140.

continued to hold a commanding position as the crucial staple industry. Discontent with the growth of large estates had to be directed against the British government far away in London, and was confused with opposition to the high land price of the Wakefield system. Advocates of small holdings faced serious charges that their reform would injure the only possible major export trade and would lead to major diseconomies of small-scale production.

During the 1850's the land situation changed drastically. The colonies obtained rights to formulate their own economic policies and at the same time found themselves faced with a challenge from thousands of new immigrants, lured by gold fields but overflowing into all segments of the economy. Pressure for alteration of land regulations to facilitate small-scale settlement increased steadily, particularly after decline in yields from alluvial mining. Some older settlers were concerned about effects on society of a growing body of itinerant miners, and called for transformation of "diggers" into farmers. Other colonists feared that, unless alternative attractions were provided, Australia would lose her footloose new citizens. When returns from surface gold panning began to disappear and mining came to consist more and more of company operations with hired labor, independent spirits among the miners themselves looked for freedom on their own land if not on their own claims. At least while the gold boom lasted advocates of homestead farming seemed assured by high prices of agricultural products of some success for their schemes.

During the first period of acute labor shortage in 1851, the Sydney *Empire*, edited by Henry Parkes, suggested that a variant of the Wakefield system of subsidized immigration might relieve the current emergency. The paper said:

The principle first propounded by the promoters of the colonization movement of 1830—that of applying the proceeds of the sale of waste lands in new countries towards the introduction into them of a labouring population—has received the sanction of the most profound and enlightened investigators of economical science.[64]

64. "The Natural Immigration Fund," *Empire*, November 21, 1851, p. 386.

By 1854, however, after labor had poured into the colonies voluntarily in search of gold, the *Empire* came to the conclusion that the "Canadian system" of awarding small grants to bona fide settlers was, after all, best for Australia. Canadian regulations, it was said, had "been reduced, as near as human practice will admit, to the principle of political economy, that land is of no value without population."[65]

Mining made its earliest and greatest impact on Victoria and stimulated there the most insistent demands for land reform. In 1853 an anonymous writer in Melbourne implored the British government to establish a satisfactory pattern of homestead settlement before abandoning the colony to a responsible legislature.[66] N. L. Kentish, long an opponent of the Wakefield system, warned in 1855 at the height of the gold boom that unless special precautions were taken quickly, agriculture, faced with high costs and short labor, would decline beyond recovery. He recommended as an immediate practical reform that the government enable "all persons who will *guarantee* to cultivate the soil, to become possessed of farms, as freeholders, and even as lessees, upon *liberal, easy,* and even seductive *terms*."[67] H. L. Lindsay, an immigrant Irish surveyor who used "Adam Smith's arguments on the Wealth of Nations . . . as a standard guide . . . in writing on the *Political Economy* of Victoria," concluded that the colony was passing currently through its pastoral stage of development and required only moderate encouragement to move into the agricultural stage. Land dispersal alone was necessary for the transformation:

the labor at the gold fields which is not productive of national capital, is retarding the progress of that kind of labor which is itself the capital; but this difficulty can be obviated by the selling, or letting, of lands in small quantities, so that every man, who would desire it, might have his own farm, and his settled homestead.[68]

65. "The Land System of Canada," *Empire*, May 20, 1854, p. 4.
66. Aristides, *The Approaching Crisis of Britain and Australia: With a Way to Escape the Ruin it Threatens* (Melbourne, 1853).
67. N. L. Kentish, *Question of Questions: Just Shewing How, to "Speed the Plough" in Victoria, and to Convert Scarcity and High Prices of Food, into Cheapness and Abundance, with Prosperity to the Agriculturist* (Melbourne, 1855), p. 11.
68. H. Lill Lindsay, *The Industrial Resources of Victoria, with Practical Sug-*

Increasingly, land reformers came to realize that more fundamental legislative change might be needed than mere alteration
of the regulations for disposal of unalienated crown lands. Frederick Vines, in a radical tract during 1856, pointed to large blocks
of arable land already in the hands of pastoralists as the primary
hurdle to advancing homestead settlement. He explained:

The sold but uncultivated land is for the most part of the best description, some of it from its quality and richness, others from being
in the convenient vicinity of inhabited parts; yet for the most part
the holders of it can neither sell it, nor lease or let it, on terms at the
same time profitable to themselves and those who take it. Few are
able to buy because of the price demanded, and because of the uncertain and unsettled state of the land laws; few will take leases because they wish not to give the advantage of their industry and money
to enhance the value of another's property. Here then is a damaging
obstacle to the foundation and progress of a nation's wealth—agriculture, and the establishment of a free and independent yeomanry.[69]

Vines considered that a system of leases, by discouraging improvements, discriminated against agriculture in a new country.
Land sales at auction, moreover, fostered speculative monopoly
and retarded growth even more. He implied that the sheep
industry of Australia had succeeded only by default through the
presence of institutional arrangements which effectively had eliminated agricultural competition. He charged:

to the present land laws is mainly attributable the misapplication
and misdirection of industry and capital which has caused excessive
useless importations, ruinous competition in trade, ruinous building
speculations, the unhealthy crowding of population in towns, and the
commercial panics, insolvencies which have been experienced, energies, industry, and opportunities wasted, demoralization and poverty
generated, driving people from the colony in disgust, sending the
profits on industry, the profits on accumulated deposits of the diggers,
and a vast deal of money in a variety of other ways out of the country
to support absentee proprietors, or to purchase edible commodities at
a much more expensive rate than that at which they could be
produced here from the soil.[70]

gestions on Agriculture, Employment of Labor, Water Supply, &c., &c. (Melbourne, 1856), pp. 1 and 26.
    69. Frederick Vines, *The Cue to Prosperity: or, Our Lands, and How to Get
at Them* (Melbourne, 1856), p. 18.
    70. *Ibid.*, p. 25.

Vines drew analogies of principle from experience on the gold fields. Idle land like an unused claim, he insisted, should be thrown open to actual entrepreneurs. He expressed faith in the possibility of agricultural cooperation—"a system of cultivation by partnership and associated labor, similar to what is customary upon the diggings." Remembering informal practices of selecting and registering mining claims, Vines called for uncomplicated disposal of homesteads.

The opportunity to "select land" at a "fixed price" and on settled, understood, and definite terms and conditions—similar to the plan followed by the Americans—secures the immense advantage of bringing the most suitable land into cultivation first, without permitting or creating monopolies or preferences, every man is served in his turn upon the principle of "First come, first served". . . .[71]

Vines endorsed and reprinted a report of the Melbourne Chamber of Commerce in 1855 recommending "Land at a *low price, and easy terms of payment,* with the view of attracting and retaining capital in the colony."[72]

Agitation in the colonies led to vigorous political campaigning for homesteads by "free selection." Activity culminated in several dramatic manifestos and popular conventions.[73] Henry Parkes observed in 1859 that the single most important cause of distress to the working people of Sydney suggested by witnesses before his select committee was "mal-administration of the public lands."[74]

By 1858 governments of all the colonies, under pressure from an enlarged franchise which included numerous unemployed miners influenced strongly by American precedent, contemplated seriously methods of encouraging homestead settlement. An early action taken was the Real Property Act of 1858 in South Australia,

71. *Ibid.,* pp. 30 and 33.
72. *Ibid.,* p. 57. A similar tract on land reform is reprinted in C. M. H. Clark, *Select Documents in Australian History 1851–1900,* pp. 103–4.
73. See for example, *Victorian Convention. Resolutions, Proceedings, and Documents of the Victorian Convention, Assembled in Melbourne, July 15 to August 6, 1857* (Melbourne, 1857); and *Manifesto of the Land League of New South Wales, 26 April, 1859* (Sydney, n.d.), and reprinted in C. M. H. Clark, *Select Documents in Australian History 1851–1900,* p. 58 f.
74. "Report from the Select Committee on the Condition of the Working Classes of the Metropolis; together with the Proceedings of the Committee, Minutes of Evidence, and Appendix," *Votes and Proceedings of the Legislative Assembly of New South Wales,* 1859–60, pp. 10–11.

a technical improvement in land registration devised by the Registrar-General, Robert Torrens, son of the economist Colonel Torrens, to make land transfer similar to exchange of marine
property.[75] Torrens was inspired by a statement of John Stuart
Mill that "To make land as easily transferable as stock would be
one of the greatest economical improvements which could be
bestowed on a country."[76] He was particularly anxious to render
land a readily marketable commodity suitable as security for bank
loans.[77] J. T. Walker attested in 1888 to Torrens' success in this
respect.

The community is . . . greatly indebted to Torrens' Act . . . by
which dealings in land are so facilitated that the banks have not
hesitated to consider land mortgages as good security for temporary
advances, and, for a limited portion of advances, practically for a term,
although nominally otherwise . . . it must not be forgotten that to
banking assistance, in the first place, the pastoral and agricultural
interests owe much of their wonderful development.[78]

The Torrens system ultimately was adopted in all the Australasian
colonies and in a number of other countries.[79]

In 1860 legislation was introduced for the first time in both
Victoria and New South Wales to stimulate small-scale land
utilization. Land reform measures which followed in all the colonies were vacillating, complicated, and on the whole unsuccessful in achieving their declared purpose.[80] It has been argued that
in New South Wales land reform failed in part because pieces of

75. S. H. Roberts, *op. cit.*, pp. 218–19 and 222–23; and T. A. Coghlan, *Labour
and Industry in Australia*, pp. 649–67.
76. Robert R. Torrens, *A Handy Book on the Real Property Act of South
Australia* (Adelaide, circa 1863), p. 11.
77. Robert R. Torrens, *Project for the Establishment of a South Australian
Land Bank . . .* (Adelaide, 1858).
78. J. T. Walker, "Some Remarks on Australasian Banks and on Banking as a
Factor in the Progress of Australasia," *Australian Economic Association Papers*
(Melbourne, 1888), No. 4, p. 35.
79. See for example "Registrar-General's Report: South Australia," *Journals of
the House of Assembly of Tasmania*, 1861.
80. Dealing with the land legislation of New South Wales after the gold rushes
Coghlan remarked: "All this legislation had little success in effecting the purpose of its authors, and at the end of the period the industrious yeoman was as
conspicuous by his absence as he was at the beginning, in spite of the sale of
some 5,000,000 acres of land, the greater portion of which was parted with by
the colony in the fond belief that it would be occupied for purposes of tillage."
Labour and Industry in Australia, p. 979.

legislation were not viewed as a form of "social engineering designed to put small settlers on the land; but rather . . . were designed to attack the privileges of the squatters in accordance with the liberal ideals of laissez-faire and equality of opportunity."[81] The land laws of 1862 in Victoria, designed by Charles Gavan Duffy specifically to encourage small farming, resulted in a mere one hundred selectors obtaining title to almost one million acres of public land.[82] Pastoralists, threatened by the approach of selectors, devised numerous ingenious ways of safeguarding their property against what they termed the "cocky farmers."

It is significant for this study that homestead legislation in the colonies did not stimulate valuable analytical discussion or consideration of economic principles. Absence of inquiry was partly the result of confusion of issues, and partly of the openly redistributive character of measures. Land reform was defended on grounds of social justice rather than with pleas for more productive use of resources. Occasionally squatters presented a case for defense of large holdings, but their arguments too were generally without distinction. The kernel of their argument was usually the growth theory of Adam Smith, that an economy must pass through a pastoral stage of development before coming to agriculture. For example, William Macredie, Secretary of the Pastoral Association of Victoria, talked of the function "pastoral tenants of the Crown" performed as custodians of the greatest national resource.[83] Samuel Cook, inspired by a prize of one hundred guineas, outlined in 1870 the unsuccessful homestead policy of New South Wales and argued that should small farms in fact be created Australia would never be able to make the best use of its bountiful endowment. He called for a land policy "based upon more enlightened views of political economy and good government," and he explained, using McCulloch, that capital was wasted when agriculture was forced artificially. Australia should wait for larger supplies of labor and for greater accumulations

81. D. W. A. Baker, "The Origins of Robertson's Land Acts," *Historical Studies Australia and New Zealand*, VIII (1957–59), 179.
82. S. H. Roberts, *op. cit.*, p. 240. Gavan Duffy explained his land policy in *The Land Law of Victoria (Australia)* (London, 1862).
83. William Macredie, *Land Question Considered with Reference to Pastoral Occupation in Victoria* (Melbourne, 1867).

of capital before encouraging farming. Where tools were expensive, labor was scarce, and land was abundant, large-scale pastoral operations alone permitted optimum combination of the productive factors available. He wrote:

Labour is the first element, but capital is the second, and must be combined with the first; and the small proportion which our labour and capital bear to our land (which is the third great requisite of production) indicates the large field we have for enterprise; but it is as impossible for labour to endure without capital as for capital to increase without labour. Therefore we must have regard to these conditions in alienating our public lands, and in the application of the revenue derived from them to the purposes of immigration, we must seek to preserve the proper relations between those two great elements which are necessary to make productive the national estate.[84]

George Ranken, an astute contemporary critic of land policy in New South Wales with the pseudonym "Capricornus," condemned in 1875 doctrinaire advocacy both of free selection and of squatting monopoly.[85] He blamed the sharp cleavage of opinion for Australia's slow growth rate. He explained:

These principles have been adopted by two opposing schools of economy. The first points to the production of wealth as the true and only criterion for the right use of the soil, and follows the old teachers in their dogmas, propounded under the emphatic titles of Capital and Rent. By their theory, the human population has no claim of right in the land, but takes its place incidentally as supplying labour for the use of capitalists, or as buyers of marketable produce. The modern school takes a different position. The distribution of wealth is by its teachers rated as of equal importance with its production, and they hold that the earth should be used for the residence and support of the human family, a view of the matter which their opponents entirely ignore.

In the colonisation of Australia, no attempt has been made to regulate or reconcile these conflicting theories, but systems based on each have been planted in extremely antagonistic forms, sometimes side by side, sometimes the newer tenure over-riding and displacing

84. Samuel Cook, *The "Wagga Wagga Advertiser" Prize Essay on the Future Land Policy of New South Wales* (Sydney, 1870), p. 10.
85. Ranken was appointed Royal Commissioner to investigate the land laws of New South Wales in 1883. He collected abundant evidence of the failure of free selection, but he was not able to provide a workable alternative. See S. H. Roberts, *op. cit.*, p. 230.

the earlier, but almost always in the position so that the success of the one involves injury to the other. The fruit of this pernicious legislation is found in the division, of every community in the southern continent and islands into two powerful bodies, the squatting and the freehold interests, each of which seeks to destroy the other.[86]

Ranken emphasised correctly that the root of the squatter-selector controversy was an irreconcilable argument. Pastoralists insisted on optimum allocation of resources as the only justifiable criterion for land policy, while farmers appealed to the social benefits of citizen settlement. Dominance of the controversy by partisan and unreasonable disputants prevented serious and objective analysis.

86. George Ranken ("Capricornus"), *The Squatting System of Australia* (Edinburgh, 1875), p. 4; and see also his *Bush Essays* (Edinburgh, 1872), and the following reprinted articles from the *Sydney Morning Herald* in 1876: *Colonisation in 1876* and *Homestead Settlement: Grazing, Past, Present and Future.*

4

Land Disposal and Taxation: II. Nationalization and Taxation

Serious attempts to settle small farmers on the land were made in the colonies during the 1860's, but either from faulty legislation or insurmountable economic barriers results were disappointing. Having failed thus to obtain through encouragement of private enterprise the comfortable homesteads they desired, reformers bent their efforts to what seemed the next best alternatives, expropriation of privately owned land or income from it and use of public land in common. Two specific reforms were proposed: perpetual government ownership with Crown lease, and continued private property with heavy taxation. Both schemes were defended with dicta of economists from other countries and were discussed often as matters of principle.

Land Nationalization

The practice of leasing government land had a long history in Australia as the pastoral squatting system. Thought was given to modifying this system for small-scale farming operations at an early date, and George Higinbotham reported in 1875 that plans for an experiment in leasing for agricultural purposes were abandoned in Victoria during the 1850's only after J. S. Mill had condemned the undertaking in a letter to the Melbourne press.[1]

Land nationalization as a panacea evolved less as a protest of radicals than as a program of middle-class liberals. It was viewed as a method whereby the state could control society to preserve

1. James Mirams, *The Land Question in Victoria* (Melbourne, 1882), pp. 28–29.

an independent peasantry in the face of pressures from aggressive entrepreneurs for monopoly and concentration. Economic development, land nationalizers hoped, would bring government gains from appreciation of land values and would permit full and equitable compensation of expropriated land-owners. Unlike later land taxers, land nationalizers made few charges that landlords were guilty of rapacious social exploitation.

In Melbourne during the 1870's, where land hunger and frustration with government policies were intense, a Land Reform League dedicated to land nationalization flourished. The League advocated cessation of Crown land sales, repurchase of land already alienated, and "gradual abolition of all indirect taxes whatever. The revenue of the state to be derived solely from the rentals of land."[2] The League followed closely reform discussions in Britain and reprinted publications which seemed to provide arguments for its platform, including extracts from Spencer's *Social Statics*, Mill's *Principles of Political Economy*, and Carlyle's *Chartism* and *Past and Present*. Impatience was expressed with the reluctance of other reformers to approve land nationalization, and it was noted with pride that Australia through squatting provisions had pioneered the system. In a League review of recent periodical literature, the author observed:

Perhaps, owing to the absence of personal experience of the facility with which the Government can assume the functions of the Landlord, there is a weakness in most of the notices, as to the rectification of the existing system. In the colonies, where we have the double system in full operation, it seems only to require to exhibit the monstrous injustice of the custom of absolute sale to enable the leasing arrangement to be extended over the whole of the Crown lands.[3]

Land nationalization received support in other colonies during the 1870's. A Tasmanian writer contended that only a state leasing system could make available property to worthy settlers without capital and could allow government to limit the size of

2. *Land (Tenure) Reform League Tract No. 5.* (Melbourne, 1872), p. 1. The history of the Land Tenure Reform League, of which W. H. Gresham was the leader, is described in Henry Mayer, *Marx, Engels and Australia* (Melbourne, 1964), esp. pp. 25–29.
3. *Selections from Mill's Political Economy: Land Reform League Tract No. 3* (Melbourne, 1871), p. 2.

holdings. If leases were long-term and rents were based upon unimproved values, government revenue would be steady and growing while tenants would not be inhibited from making improvements. He insisted:

> by leasing in lieu of selling, or giving away, they [the government] would be in receipt of a perpetual and increasing revenue; at the same time the public estate would increase in value, and afford a far more safe and valuable security than the fluctuating revenue from the sale of lands, or from the receipt of custom duties. And here we would ask, what right has the present or any government to sell the land, which we assert is not only the property of the present generation, but also of those in all time to come.[4]

In Sydney land nationalization was endorsed by a Lands Settlement League. Robert Barbour M. P., President, cited Mill and Spencer at length on the unearned increment in land values and implored the colonial government to introduce state leasing as the sure road to justice and prosperity.

> Let us throw open the lands so as to bring the profitable employment of them within the reach of all; let us encourage people in crowds to settle permanently thereon to draft the surplus population of towns, enabling them to be producers in the country and thereby to increase and cheapen the necessaries of life.
>
> I shall only add that I sincerely believe that all this can be done by stopping alienation and substituting a universal leasing of our public estate.[5]

Mounting evidence of concentration in land ownership as a result of unsuccessful settlement legislation inspired land nationalizers to frantic propaganda. One spokesman wrote in 1879:

> The possession of land is the chief foundation of all wealth, and although the land will no doubt eventually accumulate in few hands (unless indeed the Government should always hold the position of

---

4. "Public Lands," *Quadrilateral* (Hobart), 1874, p. 51. A short-lived Land Reform League was founded at Kapunda, South Australia, in 1872. Henry Mayer, *op. cit.*, p. 29.

5. Robert Barbour, *The Land Question, Leasing not Selling, or Homes for All* (Sydney, 1879), p. 37. Charles Fairfield reported in 1892 "An unfortunate expression of the late Professor Fawcett's to the effect that he 'viewed with alarm the rapid alienation of the public domain in Australasia,' is constantly quoted by the advocates of 'bottling up' the nation's patrimony." "State Socialism in the Antipodes," in Thomas MacKay, ed., *A Plea for Liberty* (London, 1892), p. 146 n.

landlord), it is a pity that this great inequality should be precipitated by forcing the lands indiscriminately into the market, with the proved futile idea that, because there are many *buyers*, therefore there will be many *holders.*[6]

A customary appeal of land nationalizers was to principles of social morality. Land was said to be the common property of humanity to be held perpetually in community. Henry Edmunds stated: "as a matter of right, for the better and more convenient meeting of the general requirements of man, we propose that our common powers and possessions be organized and applied direct to the good of the people, under management responsible to them."[7]

Land nationalizers often used historical description to substantiate their contention that communal ownership of property would reduce social problems. W. E. Hearn, in his book *The Aryan Household,* described from history how primitive tribes had viewed land as a common possession of the state and how this tradition had been modified but not destroyed on its spread through Europe and Asia.[8] Land nationalizers took this account to be sufficient justification for a prohibition against private alienation. J. Reid declared in 1879: "Nothing can be much more different in appearance, than the present land systems of India, and the squatting system of the Australian Colonies, and yet they both proceed on the same assumption, namely, that ownership of land is vested, in the first place in the state, and not in the individual."[9] Reid asked a question which for him required no answer: "As a remedy for the difficulties that have already made themselves felt, and as a preventive of the possible dangers of the future, might it not be advisable to discontinue the alienation of Crown lands, substituting for sales an equitable system of leases?"[10] Other writers also were influenced by Hearn's anthropological work; one observed in 1879: "All the Aryan races, as

6. A. W. Bucknell, "Our Land Regulations," *Australian,* II (1879), 189.
7. Henry W. Sanderson Edmunds, "Social Science," *Sydney Quarterly Magazine,* 1883, p. 265.
8. London, 1879 (first published in Melbourne, 1878), pp. 212–58, 372–80, and 411–29.
9. J. Reid, "Early Aryan Land Laws," *Australian,* II (1879), 291. See also J. Reid, "The Indian Land System," *ibid.,* III (1879–80), 26–33.
10. J. Reid, "The Tenure of Land," *Victorian Review,* 1881, p. 600.

far as we know, without exception, have made the holding of
land depend on rendering good service in some form or other to
the state. Feudal tenures, which have been so much misrepre-
sented, are only one of the forms in which this principle has been
applied."[11] Urquhart MacPherson examined the experience of
classical Greece, Rome, and early Britain and discovered that
oppressive land monopoly had been the cause of all their down-
falls. He warned that implications for Australia were clear:
"Agrarian usurpation, and the misuse of the power of wealth,
blur the historic page of ancient Greece and Rome; and the analogy between the course of events in those countries and our own
is sufficiently striking to arrest attention."[12]

J. W. Thompson in 1888 explained the important role of amateur historians in the land nationalization movement and expressed a hope that their influence on policy might increase. He
said:

I know that many have studied the history of Europe with the special
object of gaining the knowledge of what to adopt and what to avoid
while assisting to establish equitable laws in a new country; and the
land being the primary feature, land in relation to man their principal
study. They have learned from their researches that it is impossible
to establish a sound foundation for a country's welfare unless the crown
act as the only ground landlord. But, although, up to the present time
the party who have studied the subject feel themselves too weak to
successfully oppose the influence of capital, yet I trust that they will
deem that the time has now arrived for them to act in accordance with
their convictions.[13]

David Syme, influential editor of the Melbourne *Age*, was
vocal in condemnation of ineffective attempts to encourage home-
steading in the colonies.[14] He was fascinated by the peculiar
behavior of property values in land, and the manner of their
increase. Unlike many other land reformers, he was concerned
more about reducing incomes of large land-owners than about
providing for small farmers. He wrote:

11. "The Economic Aspect of Feudalism," *Australian*, II (1879), 446.
12. Urquhart MacPherson, "Land Monopoly, Ancient and Modern," *Victorian Review*, 1880, p. 732.
13. J. W. Thompson, *An Appeal to Patriotism. The Land Question. Alienation, the Very Rich and the Very Poor. Leasing Policy, Justice to All* (Brisbane, 1888), p. 4.
14. David Syme, *Outlines of an Industrial Science* (London, 1876), pp. 65–67.

The owners of land in all countries enjoy immense advantages over every other class in the community. Everything that benefits the public brings an advantage to them. Land is the natural deposit bank into which all the savings of the community gravitate. If population increases, there is an increased demand for land. If wealth increases, land commands a higher price in the market. The owners' profit is not a reward for their own efforts, but a penalty imposed on the public by their increasing wants and necessities. It is not the owner, but the would-be owner, who creates the profit; not those who have, but those who have not.[15]

Syme maintained that land-owners gained rewards at the expense of others in the community.

It is a well-known economic fact that the price of land rises, not in the ratio of the increase in profits and interest, but in an inverse ratio. As wealth increases, profits and interest have a downward tendency, while the price of land has an upward tendency; and thus the land-owning class are benefited by the general prosperity of the community, which they have done nothing to promote.[16]

Syme favored a system of government land ownership with rentals to farmers and confiscation of increases in rent. "It would seem to be the duty of the Government . . . to absolutely stop the sale of any more land, and to utilize what is left in such a manner that the State may reap the full advantage of any future increment in its value."[17]

Tacit support for land nationalization came from some colonial authors who, while reluctant to sanction the method itself, were impressed nevertheless by arguments used in its defense. For example, the special character of land rent and property values was acknowledged by R. Savage who argued that increased income attributable to expenditures on public works belonged rightfully to the state. He wrote:

land-owners have derived full benefit from the fourteen millions [spent on railway construction], for which they pay no interest, nor are they in any way responsible for the principal. This fact offers a glaring instance of the injustice of the claim of holders of land in fee simple, whether in large or small quantity, to enjoy for themselves

15. David Syme, "On the Increment in the Value of Land in Melbourne," *Melbourne Review*, IV (1879), 231–32.
16. *Ibid.*, p. 232.
17. *Ibid.*, p. 234.

and transmit to their posterity what J. S. Mill only of late discovered
the importance of, namely, the unearned increment in rent and
value.[18]

Savage concluded that in general "The increment in the value of
land should have been saved for the public, and this would have
yielded an ample revenue for all purposes of government."[19] The
existence of an element of land values created by the community
was accepted widely, and was cited by Henry Gyles Turner in
1880 as justification for bank loans on real estate. He said: "in a
new country like Victoria, the often-quoted 'unearned increment'
in the value of real property offers a certain margin of security to
the lender, which can always be relied upon in the long run."[20]

Government leases for agricultural purposes were accepted in
principle by a few colonial political leaders, but with few exceptions, they were not successful when introduced in practice.[21]
Land nationalization leagues remained active throughout the
1880's but with a steadily increasing emphasis on dogma and
without the freshness and hope which had characterized beginnings of the movement. Members, it seemed, had less and less
real faith, after decades of disappointments, in the chances of
replacing landlords and of creating a landed peasantry, and they
began to turn to other panaceas. The South Australian Land Nationalization Association was particularly energetic during the
1880's, and published fifteen thousand copies of its "Manifesto,"
including selections from Spencer and Mill. William Patrick,
secretary, announced "All interested (and who are not?) are
invited to assist the Society in establishing Branches all over the
colony." However, he continued plaintively "everything published by the Society is distributed gratuitously, and considerable

18. R. Savage, "The Incidence of Taxation and Expenditure of Public Money,"
Melbourne Review, II (1877), 199–200.
19. *Ibid.*, p. 203.
20. Henry G. Turner, "Victorian Banking Considered in Relation to National
Development," *Australasian Insurance and Banking Record*, IV (1880), 403.
21. See for example James Mirams, *The Land Question in Victoria* (Melbourne,
1882), pp. 28–29. In Queensland an unsuccessful experiment with leased farms
was undertaken during the 1880's under the direction of a zealous reformer,
Henry Dutton. Equally unsuccessful co-operative labor colonies were introduced
as emergency measures in the 1890's. S. H. Roberts, *op. cit.*, pp. 301–4, 330–34,
and 383.

expense is incurred in advertising, &c."[22] During the closing years of interest in land nationalization, the influence of land reform schemes of Emile de Laveleye in France was evident in South Australia.[23]

One of the most able and energetic land nationalizers in the colonies was A. J. Ogilvy, a land-owner living near Richmond in Tasmania. Ogilvy was both leader of the Tasmanian land reformers and vice president of the international Land Nationalisation Society. Alfred Russel Wallace, president of the larger body, praised Ogilvy's self-sacrifice for the cause: "It says much for his freedom from prejudice and independence of thought, that under these conditions he has arrived at conclusions which are practically identical with those of English land nationalisers as to the evil results of private property in land."[24] Ogilvy viewed his own role of land-owner as that of an exemplary would-be martyr. In fact, under the arrangements he proposed of full compensation to property holders, his sacrifice would have been limited. He defended his continued personal ownership of private property thus:

I can serve the good cause better in a number of ways by staying in than by going out—amongst other ways, by affording one standing example of a landlord pleading for land nationalisation and offering his own land, or so much of it as may be wanted as the first to be taken for the purpose at its actual value, as may be decided, on whatever system may be adopted.[25]

Ogilvy was one of the few Australian land-reformers whose works were read outside the colonies. He accepted an orthodox version of land nationalization principles, and held as an article of faith the proposition that access to land for all citizens was

22. *The Manifesto of the South Australian Land Nationalization Society* (Adelaide, 1884), p. 2.
23. *Ibid.,* and W. H. Bundey, *Land Reform and Land Taxation* . . . (Adelaide, 1889), p. 36.
24. "Introductory Note" to A. J. Ogilvy, *The Third Factor of Production and Other Essays* (London, 1898), p. vii. See also William G. Spence, *Australia's Awakening* (Sydney, 1909), p. 368; M. D. McRae, "Some Aspects of the Origins of the Tasmanian Labour Party," *Tasmanian Historical Research Association: Papers and Proceedings,* II (1954), 21–27; Percy R. Meggy, "Land Monopoly in Australia," *Review of Reviews for Australia,* 1906, pp. 459–61.
25. A. J. Ogilvy, *The Third Factor of Production and Other Essays,* p. 99.

vital to social well-being. He was a founder of the Tasmanian
Land Nationalization Society in 1887 which advocated four major
measures: cessation of public land sales, progressive repurchase
of private property at market values, reservation to the state of all
mineral rights, and taxation of "the unearned increment" on lands
not yet repossessed.[26] Wallace claimed that Ogilvy's most substantial contribution to the movement internationally was refutation, on the basis of experience in Tasmania, of "one of the com-
monest fallacies of our opponents—that large farms lead to better
cultivation and higher production than small farms or peasant-
holdings." Ogilvy explained rather unconvincingly that "owing
to the inevitable working of the law of self-interest . . . the large
owner or large tenant will often cultivate his land badly, or even
leave much of it uncultivated, *because he obtains the largest net
returns by doing so.*"[27]

Land nationalization died as a practical proposition in the
colonies during the 1880's. By this time even the most staunch
reformers lost hope of repossessing land for use as government-
owned small farms and grew receptive to plans for confiscating
income while leaving property in private hands. Moreover, it
became painfully evident during the 1880's that government land
ownership could have effects on the public purse in two directions. A steady decline in world prices for Australian exports
accompanied by climatic hardships made discussion of compensation for an unearned decrement in land values more relevant
than confiscation of an increment. As property values and rents
fell, expropriation lost its appeal.[28] During the 1890's the land
nationalization issue was raised only occasionally and usually as
a delaying tactic by opponents of schemes for land taxation who
preferred the principle of full compensation.[29] A few half-hearted
schemes for leasing unused crown lands, a small concession to

26. A. J. O., *The Land* (Hobart, 1887), p. 22. This pamphlet was published
also in Adelaide in 1887.
27. *The Third Factor of Production and Other Essays*, p. viii and pp. 55–123.
28. Charles H. Pearson in 1893 predicted disaster for any foolhardy colonial
government which nationalized land and then experienced declining product
markets. *National Life and Character: A Forecast* (London, 1893), pp. 174–76.
29. See for example, A. Forsyth, *On Land Taxation and Nationalisation* (Sydney, 1890); and W. O. Strangeward, "The Single Tax Proposal," *Bankers' Magazine and Journal of the Bankers' Institute of Australasia*, IX (1895–96), 106–7.

land nationalization doctrine, were introduced after 1890 in several states, but without conspicuous success.[30]

A Tax on Land

Classical economists led by the Physiocrats in France and by David Ricardo in England examined in detail the behavior of returns to land. Ricardo observed that while capital and labor tended to increase in quantity over time, land remained in fixed supply; in a free market, with constant technology, payments per unit to land rose more rapidly than did those to other factors. The obvious policy implications of Ricardian long-run rent theory were that the share of national income accruing to land-owners would grow steadily and should with justice be regulated by the state. Pronouncements of classical economists on land theory and policy were well known in the colonies; for example, a Victorian Royal Commission in the 1860's comforted itself by affirming that "The right of the State to interfere with private property for public purposes is clearly stated by J. S. Mill...."[31]

W. E. Hearn, writing in Melbourne in 1863, maintained that, although Australian experience with the sequence of settlement was similar in some ways to that observed in America by Henry Carey—from less productive to more productive land—Ricardo's rent theory remained valid in all situations. Hearn suggested that the high cost and scarcity of capital in the colonies had induced settlers on farms to cultivate open and sandy soils before proceeding to more fertile wooded areas, and gold-miners to undertake first "surfacings and shallow sinkings" before deep shafts. By this illustration of the significance for resource exploitation of capital costs, Hearn reconciled effectively the principles of Carey with those of Ricardo. He wrote:

When a man then has the power of choice between two natural agents, whether land or any other kind, of which one is intrinsically

30. S. H. Roberts, *op. cit.*, pp. 383–85.
31. "Report of the Royal Mining Commission Appointed to Enquire into the Condition and Prospects of the Gold Fields of Victoria," *Papers Presented to Both Houses of the Parliament of Victoria*, 1862–63, p. 20.

more potent than the other, if the means at his disposal enable him to use with advantage the superior agent, he will use it accordingly; but not otherwise. If his means be inadequate for its use, the inferior agent becomes for him at that time the superior. When the principle is thus stated, a reconciliation seems possible between the hostile schools of Ricardo and Carey. Mr. Ricardo's theory, indeed, is rather partially true than absolutely false. It was constructed solely in reference to countries long previously settled, and well supplied with all the aids to production; and its author had not that familiarity with a different state of facts which only residence in a new country still in course of settlement can give. Mr. Mill declares that the Ricardian theory does not and never was intended to apply to a new country; an admission however which quite destroys its value as a general law. But on the other hand the two propositions which according to Mr. Mill are all that the Ricardian theory really involves, may well be accepted by those who concur generally in Mr. Carey's view.[32]

W. H. Irvine and John Winthrop Hackett, both lecturers in political economy at Melbourne University, followed Hearn's lead and published defenses of Ricardian theory. Hackett remarked: "If indeed the theory of rent, and with it the theory of the unearned increment, be a delusion, it is high time to declare the whole science has been miswritten, that exchange is an absurdity, values unmanageable, and above all that free trade must be given up as a puerile deception."[33] Firm establishment of the classical tradition at Melbourne and extensive use of Hearn's *Plutology* as an economics text in universities throughout the colonies help to explain the prevailing absence of criticism of Ricardian theory.

Australia did not appear early in the nineteenth century to be a country where classical fears of rising land rents would take strong root. Population was settled in a thin fringe around an almost empty continent, and land shortage accompanied by monopoly exploitation seemed anything but an immediate problem. The possibility of a redistributive government levy on land was considered infrequently before 1870 and even then with mixed motives. Henry Melville in Van Diemen's Land [34] and Goderich

32. William Edward Hearn, *Plutology* (London, 1864), pp. 113–14.
33. John Winthrop Hackett, "Our Land Policy," *Melbourne Review*, II (1877), 369; and W. H. Irvine, "Prof. Bonamy Price on the Doctrine of Rent," *Victorian Review*, X (1884), 217–29.
34. Henry Melville, *The History of the Island of Van Diemen's Land, from the year 1824 to 1835 Inclusive* (London, 1835); Herbert Heaton, "The Taxation

in the Colonial Office suggested a land tax as early as the 1830's, and Thomas Bartlett, a military surgeon who visited the colonies, proposed in 1843 that a land tax be imposed both to penalize owners of "all uncultivated and unoccupied lands, which are not only a complete dead weight, but exercise a very pernicious influence on the toiling colonist" and to capture from land-owners the increment in land values attributable to "the unremitting assiduity of the hard working population."[35] A writer in the Sydney *Weekly Register* in 1844 quoted Adam Smith, Sir James Steuart, James Mill, and Archbishop Whately in support of a similar proposal.[36] A Melbourne author in 1855 suggested that a land tax be used to equalize the burden of public expenditures among all citizens by taking from land-owners what they had gained through the gold-induced inflation. He said: "A land-tax, to sustain the general expenditure, might be put upon all lands, whether lying unproductive, in the hands of land-jobbers, or productive, in the hands of agriculturists and squatters."[37] The Land League of New South Wales in 1859 listed as its sixth demand after free selection and sale by auction, "The Taxation of all alienated land."[38] A legislative committee under the chairmanship of Henry Parkes reported at the same time: "any equitable reform of our fiscal system should include the introduction of the principles of direct taxation, based on the well-known axioms of Paley and Adam Smith—that the burden should be borne in just proportion to the ability to bear it, and the advantages enjoyed for which it is imposed."[39] Early proposals for land taxation were not confined to urban radicals. George

of Unimproved Value of Land in Australia," *Quarterly Journal of Economics,* XXIX (1924–25), 415; and S. H. Roberts, *op. cit.,* pp. 96–97.

35. Thomas Bartlett, *New Holland: Its Colonization, Productions, and Resources, with Observations on the Relations Subsisting with Great Britain* (London, 1843), p. 115.

36. "The Political Register: The District Corporations," *Weekly Register of Politics, Facts, and General Literature,* January 20, 1844; and "The Squatters' Parliamentary Agent," *ibid.,* September 21, 1844.

37. "Financial Prospects," *Melbourne Monthly Magazine of Original Colonial Literature,* I (1855), 311.

38. John Black, *Manifesto of the Land League of New South Wales* (Sydney, 1859), p. 9.

39. "Report from the Select Committee on the Condition of the Working Classes of the Metropolis; together with the Proceedings of the Committee, Minutes of Evidence, and Appendix," *Votes and Proceedings of the Legislative Assembly of New South Wales,* 1859–60, p. 12.

Wyndham, a prominent pastoralist, sought to legitimize squatting tenure by providing that "occupation and the payment of the land-tax" should be "the basis of ownership" for unsettled lands.[40]

By the 1870's supporters of a land tax in the colonies hoped for three results from the reform: provision of revenues to replace customs duties and thereby facilitate free trade, discouragement of large or idle land holdings, and appropriation for the state of all increases in rent and value attributable to community growth. Individual proponents looked to one or several of these results, but the arguments for each are examined separately here.

Defense of land taxation on grounds of its potential revenue-producing importance for free trade was essentially pragmatic. Discussion of principle was confined mainly to cataloging the virtues of unrestricted international commerce. Customs duties were regarded as unjust, and yet it was recognized that government revenues had to be gathered. Levies on land seemed the best alternative expedient. As early as 1855, Henry Parkes read to the Legislative Council of New South Wales extracts from works by John Stuart Mill to show that indirect taxes such as tariffs were "opposed to sound principles of political economy."[41] A land tax, on the other hand, would obviate the tariff and incidentally stimulate cultivation. Parkes stressed the success of American land taxes; it was reported:

Such a tax he had no doubt would work as beneficially in this colony as a similar tax had worked in the United States of America. Apart from the question of revenue this kind of direct taxation would prove most beneficial to the colony, by preventing that system of speculation in land which had been described by Earl Grey as a system most disastrous to the settlement of young countries. A land tax would prove most beneficial by forcing land into cultivation and general use, and so stimulating improvement that would react in enhancing the value of all classes of property. Such had been the result of a land tax

40. George Wyndham, *On the Land Policy of New South Wales* (West Maitland, 1866), p. 4.
41. Mill himself wrote to F. Sinnett of Melbourne in 1857 that although "in principle" he was "quite in favour of considering all land as the property of the state, and its rent as a fund for defraying the public expenses" the antipathy of Anglo-Saxon immigrants toward a leasing system and the high administrative cost of land taxation should dissuade any colonial government from attempting to capture land rent. Hugh S. R. Elliot, *The Letters of John Stuart Mill* (London, 1910), I, 198–99.

in the United States, and he did not see why a similar result should not follow here.[42]

John Pow, writing in Melbourne during 1858, maintained that direct taxation, in contrast to tariffs, alone conformed to "the social and political economy which God, as the lawgiver of the Jews, promulgated, through Moses, to that race." He explained, rather obscurely, that "Direct taxation requires property to pay its equitable proportion for the protection it enjoys; while the trader, operative, and laborer, only pay in proportion to the protection they require, in following peacefully their lawful callings."[43] Frederick A. Bell, Secretary of the New South Wales Free Trade Association, provided in 1866 a list of extracts from "eminent political economists" in support of low tariffs and land taxation, including selections from works by Mill, Say, Bastiat, Storch, McCulloch, and the Physiocrats. He examined Smith's four maxims of taxation, and he discussed Turgot's "seven reasons" why direct taxes should be preferred to indirect taxes.[44] Saul Samuel, Treasurer of New South Wales in 1865, quoted Mill, McCulloch, and Fawcett on the dangers of direct taxation restricting capital and savings; [45] but by 1870, he was willing to take this chance rather than accept the possibility of higher tariffs. He said:

As property does not contribute its proper proportion to the State, and as we have already gone for revenue to that source which bears upon those who have no property, I think it is but right that we should look now to those who are deriving large incomes from that source to augment the revenue.[46]

David Syme, a staunch protectionist and land nationalizer, approved a land tax to penalize speculators holding idle property

42. Henry Parkes, *Speeches on Various Occasions Connected with the Public Affairs of New South Wales 1848–1874* (Melbourne, 1876), pp. 54 and 68.
43. Financier [John Pow], *Our Financial System. Indirect versus Direct Taxation: or the Ways and Means. Addressed to the People of Victoria* (Melbourne, 1858), pp. 5 and 7.
44. Frederick A. Bell, *Industry and Commerce Relieved and Increased by Means of Free Trade and Direct Taxation* (Sydney, 1866), pp. 13, 16–17, 29, and 59–60.
45. James Thomson, ed., *The Financial Statements of the Colonial Treasurers of New South Wales* (Sydney, 1881), pp. 145–46.
46. *Ibid.*, p. 254.

and to provide revenue in place of customs duties. Unlike free-traders, however, Syme expected tariff revenues to disappear under protection because of extremely high rather than low rates.[47]

B. R. Wise recounted in 1982 how colonial governments which held free-trade sympathies traditionally met stiff opposition when they used direct taxation to gather revenue and how they welcomed all arguments which strengthened their policy position. He wrote:

Direct taxation must always be a matter of difficulty in young and sparsely settled countries. If land is taxed, the cry is raised that the development of the country is being retarded; if realised wealth is taxed, the Government is denounced for discouraging the investment of foreign capital. And whether the taxes are levied on land or personality, it must always be difficult in a young country, where local and personal feelings run so high, either in friendship or enmity, to obtain satisfactory assessments without incurring the charge of favouritism or needlessly exposing private affairs.[48]

Reformers who lost faith in the efficacy of land nationalization as a means of encouraging yeoman settlement turned in many cases to taxation.[49] J. J. Casey, a member of the Victorian Legislative Assembly, argued in 1877 that the desire of immigrants for private property and the competing attractions of other new countries ruled out the feasibility of government homestead leasing. He wrote:

Whatever may be said in favour of the leasing system in theory, practical observations show that an Englishman will go, even at some inconvenience and disadvantage to himself, where he can obtain a freehold, rather than remain where he cannot. What is to be done then, it is said, to obtain for the State the increment of the improved value of the land—if leasing cannot be adopted? The answer is obvious: Taxation.[50]

47. David Syme, "On the Increment in the Value of Land in Melbourne," *Melbourne Review*, IV (1879), 235–36.
48. B. R. Wise, *Industrial Freedom: A Study in Politics* (Melbourne, 1892), p. 62.
49. William Pember Reeves declared that Australian land taxation had always been designed primarily to break up large "latifundia." See his "Land Taxes in Australasia," Presidential Address to the Economic Science and Statistical Section of the British Association for the Advancement of Science, *Economic Journal*, XXI (1911), 513–26.
50. James Joseph Casey, "The Land Systems of South Australia and Victoria Compared," *Melbourne Review*, II (1877), 18.

Casey believed that a land tax would serve two immediate purposes: "firstly, to obtain for the State a share of the increment of its improving value, and secondly, to induce the holders of land to use it in a manner that would be most beneficial to the public." Like many nationalizers, Casey's primary aim was encouragement to small farmers rather than income redistribution. He emphasized: "The confiscation of the property of the rich because they are rich, is as wicked as it is foolish, and happily finds no sympathy with the average Englishman. The taxation of land, to promote its cultivation or secure its being held by the many instead of the few, is a legitimate exercise of legislative authority."[51]

Charles H. Pearson was one of the most articulate and influential advocates of land taxation during the 1870's. A British liberal of considerable reputation before he came to the colonies, Pearson brought many of his ideas on land policy directly from the old world.[52] He arrived in Australia in 1864 convinced of the vital importance of small farms for healthy social development, his conviction based partly on the economic ground that an economy of large estates was not viable permanently, but also on an intense dislike of large plantation ownership as a social institution. He wrote in 1877:

Land differs from other property in several important respects. It cannot be produced or extended at pleasure; its subdivision among the working class tends to make them independent and prosperous; its concentration in a few hands disturbs the political balance and throws power into the hands of a minority . . . the State is directly interested in the distribution of land. It needs the yeomanry as an element in natural life; it needs population to feed its railways, to supply its factories, to make it powerful and respected by its neighbours.[53]

Dissatisfaction with crowded conditions in Europe was one reason for Pearson's own migration, and he settled first on a small

---

51. *Ibid.*, pp. 20 and 21. A similar defense of the principle of land taxation was contained in Henry John Wrixon, *Self-Government in Victoria: Its Present Condition and the Questions it has to Deal With* (Melbourne, 1876).

52. For several years a distinguished Oxford historian, Pearson moved to a farm in Australia, lectured for a year in history and political economy at Melbourne University, and became Victorian Minister of Education. See William Stebbing, ed., *Charles Henry Pearson* (London, 1900).

53. Charles H. Pearson, "On Property in Land," *Melbourne Review*, II (1877), 144–45.

holding in South Australia.[54] He regarded government land policy
pre-eminently as a tool for limiting the size of individual holdings. He sympathized in principle with Cliffe Leslie who had
proposed that in Britain estates be restricted to a maximum size
through forced sales of any amount of land above a certain limit
at each succession of property. However, he did not fail to observe that "Professor Cliffe Leslie had the United Kingdom in his
view when he wrote, rather than Australia." Pearson recognized
that the regulations embodied in Cliffe Leslie's scheme could be
evaded easily in the colonies, and that random forced sale might
result in serious inequity. He explained:

An only son, succeeding to an unencumbered estate of a hundred
thousand acres, and obliged to sell sixty thousand, could surely arrange
a collusive sale, by which he might keep possession of the original
estate. Then as regards the compulsory sale of encumbered land at
the deaths of the head of the family, this, in Australia, would I think
prove ruinous in bad years. Fluctuations of value are so great in a new
country, where there is not as large a reserve of capital as in England,
that land thrown suddenly on the market in time of drought or of an
European war, would often, I fear, go for one-half or one-third its
value.[55]

In Australia, Pearson maintained, an appropriate reform to encourage small farms would be a land tax designed through
discriminatory rates to restrict the growth of extensive holdings.[56]
Large land-owners would be required to pay higher rates than
would small ones.

   Pearson campaigned for a seat in the Victorian parliament in
1877 with a platform of progressive taxation on estates larger than
six hundred and forty acres.[57] He proposed also that land-owners

54. J. M. Tregenza, *The Life and Work of C. H. Pearson, 1830–1894*, Thesis
Submitted for the degree of Doctor of Philosophy in the Australian National
University, 1959, pp. 31–32, 133, and 148.
   55. Charles H. Pearson, "On Property in Land," *Melbourne Review*, II (1877),
144.
   56. Pearson suggested that Australia had much to learn from ancient Rome,
where land monopoly had brought final disaster. He wrote: "Those who wish to
consult the working of a system very like our Victorian land law, will find
Mommsen's or Merivale's account of the agrarian laws of T. Gracchus very
interesting. The Graccan system was finally destroyed by the abolition of the
residence clause, and by license to alienate." *Ibid.*, p. 143 n.
   57. In his political speeches Pearson acknowledged his obligation to Cliffe
Leslie's ideas and to proposals of other colonial politicians. Charles H. Pearson,
*Political Opinions on Some Subjects of the Day: Being Extracts from a Lecture
and Speeches* (Melbourne, 1877), p. 3.

be required to value their own property with knowledge that the state could purchase at any time at the self-assessed price. He was supported in Melbourne by a National Reform League, and to some extent by other groups,[58] including the Liberal party led by Graham Berry. Pearson pointed out to the free-trader that "if he assist to carry a land tax, he will have established the one great measure which must be achieved before a thorough-going reform of the present tariff can be even thought of."[59] But Pearson hoped at the same time not to offend protectionists, many of whom endorsed land reform, and he added carefully: "I consider myself bound not to offer any factious opposition to their financial policy, so long as the issue between Protection and Freetrade is not the great question of the day."[60] Pearson remained for many years a vocal and respected advocate of "bursting-up" large estates, even though he achieved little direct success. In 1880 he reiterated his position thus:

I can scarcely exaggerate the importance I attach to the subdivision of land in equitable proportions among a people. I think the system of large estates fraught with every possible evil and danger; bad for production, bad for national strength; and certain to engender a bitter class-feeling in all ranks; dangerous in the rich to democratic equality, and among the poor menacing the institution of property.[61]

Pearson had several sympathizers who, although agreeing with the principle of land taxation, disliked the element of conscious discrimination inherent in tax progression. John Winthrop Hackett repeated familiar arguments for development of "a numerous yeomanry" and concluded: "In short, if we are to allow the people, without question, to continue to crowd into populous places, the individual, in some respects, must expect decay, while the race itself, as it will miss many aids, must expect a slower advance."[62] Hackett, with Pearson, approved a land tax, but he warned that it must never exceed the level of real economic rent. "If such a tax would touch anything more than a special profit

58. J. M. Tregenza, *op. cit.*, pp. 287–88 and 354.
59. *Ibid.*, p. 7.
60. *Ibid.*
61. Charles H. Pearson, "The Liberal Programme," *Victorian Review*, I (1880), 527.
62. John Winthrop Hackett, "Our Land Policy," *Melbourne Review*, II (1877), 367.

accruing over and above the proper profit of the capital and labour sunk directly in the soil, words would be weak to denounce it in adequate terms."⁶³ Hackett opposed penalizing large landowners and insisted: "what is chiefly to be relied on is the high probability that these large estates if left to themselves will fall to pieces naturally."⁶⁴ He was confident that, under favorable circumstances and appropriate legislation, the Australian settlement pattern would follow that of the United States.

Edward Langton, an enthusiastic free-trade member of the Victorian parliament, supported a land tax on grounds similar to those of Hackett. After consulting "a famous canon of Adam Smith" which "still remains as the embodiment of the only principle on which, consistently with justice, taxation can be based," Langton observed: "That every man ought to contribute towards the cost of government in proportion to the revenue he enjoys under its protection, is a proposition as self-evident as it is sound."⁶⁵ Langton expressly condemned Pearson's plan for progressive land taxation, and reported: "Although great names have been cited as giving countenance and approval to this bursting-up scheme, scarcely an economist of note, however liberal or even radical his tendencies, can be found to sanction it."⁶⁶ Langton found special comfort in noting disapproval by Bright, Fawcett, and John Stuart Mill of schemes similar to that proposed by Pearson.

Henry George's *Progress and Poverty* was published in the United States in 1879 and was serialized in a Sydney newspaper during the same year. It was soon recognized by Australian reformers as a significant and valuable work. Catherine Spence regarded George's proposed single tax on land rent as a desirable alternative either to nationalization or to Pearson's progressive taxation. She explained that George "believes, and I believe with him, that this high tax will do more towards a fairer distribution of the good things of this good world than any other thing could

63. *Ibid.*, p. 368.
64. *Ibid.*, p. 376.
65. Edward Langton, "On Taxation in Victoria," *Melbourne Review*, II (1877), 222.
66. *Ibid.*, p. 231.

do, however benevolently it might be devised."[67] Throughout the 1880's, however, the influence of John Stuart Mill and other British liberals remained at least as great as that of George, and reformers were able still to present a case for land taxation without even mentioning *Progress and Poverty*.[68]

For many supporters of land reform the distinction between different proposals was always obscure, and the appeal to them of taxation or nationalization was emotional and humanitarian rather than theoretical and intellectual. One representative South Australian in 1883 combined the works of Mill with those of George and Wallace in what he termed "this new LAND GOSPEL." The description of his conversion to a "religion" of land reform is illuminating. He said:

> The writings of T. Spenc[e] were the first to attract my careful consideration to this important subject. I then studied the works of Herbert Spencer, George, Wallace, and other eminent political economists, who have recently given to the world the results of their investigations. I have felt while reading the testimonies of eyewitnesses to the misery, distress and pauperism that exist even at this moment in centres of population in Great Britain, Ireland, and Italy, &c., my heart grew sick and sad.[69]

Frederick Cornell in 1883 defended Henry George from a New Zealand critic, but failed himself to distinguish principles of land taxation from those of land nationalization. He said: "Mr. A. R. Wallace, who has since published a very interesting and able treatise on 'Land Nationalisation,' agrees with Mr. George in his main proposition, but offers much fuller working details of his scheme, which includes provision for full compensation to existing landowners and their immediate heirs."[70] Cornell concluded

67. C. H. Spence, "A Californian Political Economist," *Victorian Review*, IV (1881), 145.

68. William Ritchie, an energetic reformer in Launceston, quoted at length from Hearn's work, and cited Mill and Smith, but not George. Henry Edmunds leaned almost exclusively on Cliffe Leslie. William Ritchie, *Letters on Fiscal and Land Law Reform* (Launceston, 1884), and *Letters on the Decay of Agriculture* (Launceston, 1885); and Henry W. S. Edmunds, "Land, Labour and Capital. Salus Populi Suprema Lex," *Sydney Quarterly Magazine*, 1885, pp. 37–49.

69. A South Australian, *Land Nationalisation, Based upon the Principles Laid Down by George in "PROGRESS AND POVERTY," Wallace, "Occupying Ownership," J. S. Mill, and Others* (Kooringa, 1883), p. 1.

70. F. Cornell, "Progress and Poverty: A Defense," *Victorian Review*, VIII (1883), 620–21.

by misinterpreting George and assuming that Pearson's progressive rates, regardless of rent levels, would be a fundamental feature of the single tax.[71]

Doctrinaire land nationalizers in the 1880's made extensive use of George's writings in addition to their longstanding British and French authorities. Land proposals generally became more and more a mixture of arguments for nationalization and taxation with confusion between distinct schools of thought and evidence of simple faith in the possibility of social improvement through any type of property reform.[72] An enthusiast in Sydney explained during 1884 that opponents of "the new gospel" could be divided into the "timid," the "ignorant," and the "unscrupulous."[73] The Physiocrats, or "French School" as they were often called, were given respected places beside George and Wallace in the firmament of saints.[74]

Discussion of land reform even penetrated the universities; in Adelaide questions about "the unearned increment" were placed on examinations, and in Sydney the first lecturer in political economy declared: "I esteem land to be the common pivot upon which the societies of the world turn. The relations of a people to it will generally explain the relations, both political and social, in which they stand to others of their own race. The monopoly, as I have said, hangs like a fetter about the loins of labour

71. Land reform doctrine in this period, although confused, moved in two directions across the Pacific. William Westgarth, a Melbourne merchant in Britain, advised the London Chamber of Commerce in 1883 to sanction confiscation of "the unearned increment" by municipalities in England. William Westgarth, " 'The Unearned Increment' of Value in Real Estate," *Chamber of Commerce Journal*, II (1883), 95–96.

72. See for example: *The Manifesto of the South Australian Land Nationalization Society* (Adelaide, 1884), p. 2; Percy R. Meggy, "Land Nationalisation—What is it?," *Sydney Quarterly Magazine*, 1889, pp. 311–16; James Ashton, *The Great Land Question!* (Narandera, 1894). Some cautious reformers expressed despair at the possibility of any genuine improvement ever being achieved. See T. C. Aldrich, "The Land Laws of New South Wales," *Victorian Review*, VIII (1883), 490–507.

73. Judex, "Henry George and Some of his Critics," *Sydney Quarterly Magazine*, 1884, pp. 317–30.

74. E. W. Foxall, "The Principles of Taxation," *Australian Economist*, I (1888–90), 42–46; John Hurst, "A Tax on Unearned Increase in Economic Rent," *ibid.*, III (1893–94), 304–7; Percy R. Meggy, "Henry George and his Predecessors," *Sydney Quarterly Magazine*, 1890, pp. 51–62; and *New South Wales Parliamentary Debates*, 1895, p. 377.

wherever it is permitted."[75] But academic study of land policy was not confined to universities. Waldemar Bannow, "a Victorian pioneer of 1853," rejected George and cited Fawcett and Mill in a call for taxation exclusively of idle property. To certify his knowledge and to prove his good faith, Bannow explained:

I have spent at least eighty Sunday afternoons on the Queen's wharf, filled to combustion point almost by all the talking gas let loose there. Besides this, I have attended, at a low computation, at least four hundred meetings, lectures, &c., in the city and suburbs, and the time employed at the Public Library, if added together, would total up to several months, studying the while social and economical questions of all kinds.[76]

The influence of Henry George reached a peak in Australia during the late 1880's and early 1890's, a period of falling prices and mounting unemployment. Growth of a distinct labor movement over these years indicated that workers were coming to accept the inevitability of their status as urban wage-earners, and preferred a program designed to bring increased income rather than renewed futile attempts at homestead settlement. Creation of a yeomanry remained an avowed goal of statesmen, but landless voters became progressively more skeptical about their chances of land ownership and more enthusiastic about the prospect of confiscating an "unearned increment."[77]

Single tax leagues were formed throughout the colonies in the 1880's. They were made up of farmers, city workers, and business and professional persons. They were inspired by hard times, and their target was the supposed opulent and profiteering land-owner whom they blamed for all ills but who ironically by this time existed more in imagination than in fact. Unlike land-

75. *Adelaide University Calendar,* 1885, p. xcix; and Alexander C. Wylie, "The Relations between Capital and Labour," *Victorian Review,* XII (1885), 377.
76. Waldemar Bannow, *Australasia's Future: How to Shape it* (Melbourne, 1890), pp. 4, 6, and 9.
77. L. G. Churchward, "The American Influence on the Australian Labour Movement," *Historical Studies Australia and New Zealand,* V (1951–53), 258–77; Vance Palmer, *The Legend of the Nineties* (Melbourne, 1954), pp. 74–76; and Gordon Greenwood, ed., *Australia: A Social and Political History* (Sydney, 1955), pp. 158–60.

reformers of the 1870's and early 1880's, the leagues were concerned less with theoretical detail and historical precedent than
with the principle of action. Members often understood only
faintly the nature and implications of the panacea they endorsed
except that it stood for rebellion against an economic system
which in their eyes had been proved unsatisfactory. A trade-
union congress in 1888 gave the single tax unqualified approval,
and a visit by Henry George himself in 1890 afforded drama and
extra stimulus to the movement.[78]

In Tasmania, beginning in 1886, a group led by F. W. Piesse
waged a vigorous campaign for the single tax on the ground that
"the Landowners, who, without cost or labour on their part, get
from the State *at a special expense to it, a special benefit, should*
make, *out of the added value* they thus receive, *a special contribution* towards the cost of that benefit."[79] A. J. Ogilvy, a member
of the Tasmanian organization, contended that depressions were
a result of under-consumption by land-owners, and he proposed
that the single tax be used to redistribute purchasing power and
increase community demand.[80] Ogilvy was concerned more about
transferring quickly land rents from property owners to workers
than about specific means of doing so, and he was willing to
sanction, in addition to land taxation, aggressive collective bargaining, land nationalization, and an income tax.[81]

Confiscation of the unearned increment was defended in Syd-
ney by such prominent men as the poet and solicitor, A. B.
("Banjo") Paterson, and the politicians B. R. Wise and George
Reid. Paterson, like C. H. Pearson a few years before, proposed

78. Vance Palmer, *The Legend of the Nineties*, pp. 136–67; and Henry George,
Jr., *The Life of Henry George* (London, 1900), pp. 529–38.
79. F. W. Piesse, *State Improved* (*Or, Unimproved Capital*), *Value of Land,
A Catechism* (Hobart, 1887), p. 8; and *A Letter to the Members of the Legislature of Tasmania, being a Plea for the Imposition of a Tax Upon the Unimproved Value of Land* (Hobart, 1886); "Real and Personal Estates Duty
Proposals: Petitions for Amendment," *Journals and Printed Papers of the Parliament of Tasmania*, 1886; and see Percy R. Meggy, "Land Monopoly in Australia," *Review of Reviews for Australia*, 1906, pp. 459–61.
80. A. J. O., *The Cause of a Crisis* (Hobart, 1894); and see below pp. 251–54.
81. A. J. Ogilvy, "Can Strikes Really Improve the Condition of the Masses?,"
Papers and Proceedings of the Royal Society of Tasmania, 1890, pp. 202–7, and
Labour v. Capital (Hobart, 1895). Ogilvy was refuted by R. M. Johnston in
"General Increase of Wages Falls upon Consumers of Products, and in No Way
Encroaches upon Rent or Profits of Capitalists," *Papers and Proceedings of the
Royal Society of Tasmania*, 1890, pp. 208–31.

self-assessment of land values with periodic government purchases to insure taxpayer honesty. In this way, he insisted, idle holdings could be eliminated and the Treasury would "amass a huge revenue of Government."[82] Colonists did not, as might have been expected, divide over a land tax according to their views on commercial policy, and Wise, a noted free-trader, joined Paterson, a staunch protectionist, in supporting levies on "the State-earned increment of land."[83] The movement also contained overzealous as well as these cautious members. T. O'Reilly proclaimed that a land levy would bring back "those ancient obligations of chivalry" and would restore the glories of feudalism.[84] Arthur Griffith of the Sydney Grammar School compared the work of George to that of religious reformers and Marx; in his mind, at least, land policies had become merged in a wider vision of social reconstruction. Griffith wrote:

> Wycliffe and Luther dared to leave the dusty ruts of conventional thought and to scandalize respectable Society by telling the people that their kings were but men, their priests but liars, and their gods but idols—so to-day Karl Marx and Henry George have horrified the bovine understanding of that worthy creature, the "right-thinking person," by telling him that Gold is not God, that Humanity is more sacred than Property, and that there is a higher religion than the "Law of Supply and Demand;" and the workers of the world have welcomed the new gospel as earnestly and hopefully as did the peasants of Saxony or the burghers of Leyden.[85]

One writer who called himself "Cinderella" defended George from "the small beer of school political economics" and excepted John Stuart Mill as "the Henry George of his generation."[86]

82. A. B. Paterson, *Australia for the Australians* (Sydney, 1889), pp. 24–31.
83. B. R. Wise, "What Parliament Can Do for Labour," *Sydney Quarterly Magazine*, 1891, pp. 220–37, and "Land Betterment Taxation versus Land Property Taxation," *Cosmos Magazine*, I (1895), 383–88.
84. T. O'Reilly, *The People's Heritage: A History of English Land Tenure* (Sydney, 1891), p. 65.
85. Arthur Griffith, *The Labor Platform: An Exposition* (Sydney, 1893), p. 1. Another account of land reform as part of a wider social revolution is Alexander W. Johnston, *Strikes, Labour Questions, and Other Economic Difficulties: A Short Treatise of Political Economy* (London, 1895).
86. Cinderella, *A Manual of Political Economy for Free Men* (Sydney, 1890), and *Money versus Wealth, or the Origin of Interest Clearly Explained by a Pupil of Henry George & John Ruskin* (Sydney, 1890). Cinderella may have been Hugh Gilmore; see Harry S. Taylor, *Tucker Prize Essay on the Single Tax* (Adelaide, 1892), pp. 26 and 39.

A main reason why the single tax lost popularity quickly after an initial flurry of excited interest was conflict on the one hand with principles of indirect taxation and tariff protection and on the other with special interests of landowning free-traders. As indicated above, many free-traders viewed with approval a land tax for the revenue it would provide in place of customs duties and because of the sanction of revered classical economists. However, many influential free-traders were themselves large land-owners, and they could not help but look coldly on proposals for rent confiscation. The first annual conference of the Free Trade and Liberal Association of New South Wales in 1889 closed deliberations with "cheers for the chairman, the secretary, the Queen, and Henry George," but still it was unwilling to endorse unreservedly the single tax.[87] Protectionists might have accepted willingly the single tax on their platform as an additional expression of frustration with a staples-producing economy had not George condemned so explicitly their tariff program. Conflict between single taxers and protectionists over commercial policy led to a serious split within the young New South Wales Labour Party in 1891.[88] A land tax was placed on this party's platform in the 1890's, but without strict adherence to Georgian doctrine and leaving room for such goals as high tariffs.[89]

Discussion of land taxation in the Sydney *Bulletin* during the 1880's and 1890's reflected in exaggerated form the rapid rise and decline of enthusiasm for Georgian principles. In 1885 one contributor to the *Bulletin* spoke of George and Jesus Christ in the same breath and identified the existing land system as the only barrier to the reign of true Christianity on earth.[90] Subscribers were urged to buy works by George for six pence or a shilling "from almost any considerable bookseller."[91] Land systems of other countries were described with suggestions as to how single

87. *Report of the Proceedings and Public Meetings of the First Annual Conference of the Free Trade and Liberal Association of New South Wales* (Sydney, 1889), pp. 69–84 and 117.
88. F. Picard, "Henry George and the Labour Split of 1891," *Historical Studies Australia and New Zealand*, VI (1953–55), 45–63.
89. W. G. Spence, *Australia's Awakening* (Sydney, 1909), pp. 411 and 597–630.
90. William Webster, "Lay Sermon on the Land," *Bulletin*, II (1885), No. 86, p. 22.
91. "Appropriation of Rent," *ibid.*, II (1885), No. 89, p. 3.

tax reform should be enacted there.[92] Readers were advised to reject the pessimistic teachings of Malthus, Annie Besant, or Charles Bradlaugh, and to study Henry George and Christ as proper guides to "the millenium." Phrenological practitioners even observed (with the aid of an illustration) that George was "the man with the brainpan resembling in altitude and capacity the dome of St. Paul's Cathedral."[93] However, toward the end of 1885, the *Bulletin* found that it faced the same disturbing conflict worrying other supporters of George; although his single tax was an admirable protest measure, he opposed tariff protection, a redistributive device favored by the editors and an increasing number of subscribers.[94] The dilemma became acute for the *Bulletin* with publication of George's doctrinaire *Protection or Free Trade* (1886);[95] the *Bulletin* faced the contradiction and jettisoned George and the single tax in favor of high tariffs and radical socialism.[96] George was grouped with Darwin and Shakespeare as a writer who "finding a number of isolated facts which had been collected but not arranged by his predecessors, dovetails them together, and by that means constructs a symmetrical theory in which each of the formerly unclassified truths finds its fitting place." But he was condemned for ignoring the vital importance of an aggressive national policy.[97] During George's visit to the colonies in 1890, the *Bulletin* reviewed *Das Kapital* by Marx and remarked: "had the Single-taxer read it, and the people of Australia read and mastered it, they would give Mr. H. George a short shrift; and would, instead of having him lecturing to them, give him more useful work to do."[98] George's Australian tour was reported in tones of heavy ridicule.[99] In subsequent

92. "The Land Movement in Scotland," *ibid.*, II (1885), No. 91, p. 3; and "The Plutocrat in Power," *ibid.*, II (1885), No. 93, p. 3.
93. "The Millenium," *ibid.*, II (1885), No. 100, pp. 3–4; and "Land," *ibid.*, III (1885), No. 123, p. 3.
94. "A Trio of Anomalies," *ibid.*, III (1885), No. 130, p. 3.
95. "George's New Book," *ibid.*, III (1885), No. 134, p. 3; "Land Taxation—Its Justice and Advantages," *ibid.*, IV (1886), No. 164, pp. 3–4.
96. "Protection and Land Nationalisation," *ibid.*, VIII (1888), No. 419, p. 4.
97. "Some Georgian Fallacies," *ibid.*, X (1889), No. 474, p. 4.
98. A. G. Yewen, "The Single Tax and Socialism," *ibid.*, XI (1890–91), No. 522, p. 5.
99. "Henry George," *ibid.*, XI (1890–91), No. 526, p. 4; "The End of a Liason," *ibid.*, No. 530, p. 6; "The Descent of George," *ibid.*, No. 533, p. 4; "Henry George's Latest Speech," *ibid.*, No. 535, pp. 4–5; "The Taming of George," *ibid.*, No. 539, p. 5.

years, land reform was discussed by writers in the *Bulletin*, but the single tax received consistent criticism and little support.[100]

In South Australia, the writings of Henry George achieved such a peak of popularity that in 1892 C. Tucker, mayor of Port Adelaide, was moved to award a twenty guinea prize for an essay on the single tax. The winner, Harry S. Taylor, deplored "blind and unreasoning worship . . . to the bright genius of the Californian seer" but modified Georgian dogma only enough to permit simultaneous approval of socialist principles. In South Australia as in the other colonies, radicalism increased during the 1890's, and characteristically Taylor railed against what he considered the conservative "Mill-Fawcett" school of political economy.[101] J. Medway Day set forth a physiocratic argument that "the earth is the SOURCE OF ALL WEALTH," and that "the real basis of all landownership, as it is called, is force." Day seemed willing to sanction the single tax only as a tentative move on route to "a purely communistic state of society." He wrote:

> The first step in the march of progress is, therefore, to secure for the community that which under the competitive system is created by the community.
> In this first step the individualist and the socialist—though the terms, if intended to indicate opposites, are absurd—may join. For having put an end to this private taxation of industry, both the individualist and the socialist will have a fair field.[102]

Variants of the single tax became a regular part of radical reform programs in South Australia.[103]

By 1890, the year of Henry George's visit, the single tax was much discussed in Melbourne and formed a part of many radical reform demands.[104] Land taxation was a favorite debating topic

---

100. See for example, "Single-tax alias Confiscation," *ibid.*, XI (1890–91), No. 613, p. 6; "Land Tax v. Single Tax," *ibid.*, XIII (1893–94), No. 710, p. 4; and "Max Hirsch's Superstition," *ibid.*, XVI (1895), No. 786, p. 7.
101. Harry S. Taylor, *Tucker Prize Essay on the Single Tax* (Adelaide, 1892).
102. J. Medway Day, *Political Economy in a Nutshell for Young Men and Women* (Adelaide, 1893), p. 38.
103. See for example, "Final Report of the Select Committee of the Legislative Council on the Unemployed Problem; together with Minutes of Proceedings and Appendices," *Parliamentary Papers of South Australia*, 1894, p. 5; and John Law, *Imperial Credit* (Adelaide, 1899), pp. 39–40.
104. For example, a selection from Henry George's writings was included in

even in such conservative strongholds as the Bankers' Institute.[105] The most energetic Victorian single-taxer was Max Hirsch, a German merchant with a penchant for economic theorizing who visited Sydney in 1879 and after a stay in Ceylon returned to settle in Melbourne. In the words of the *Bankers' Magazine* in 1895:

Some brief years back, Hirsch was a giddy youth, chiefly remarkable for the ease with which he executed the "military valse," then exotic in this country. Then he went to Ceylon's isle, and it was a kind of John Baptist's wilderness to him, where he studied the "black art" as interpreted by John Stuart Mill; thence he came by ordinary routes to Victoria, and was duly announced as a new star in the constellation "Politicus."[106]

Hirsch entered the single tax controversy soon after his arrival in 1890.[107] Thenceforth he turned out a stream of carefully prepared books, pamphlets, public addresses, and other items of propaganda.[108] Hirsch gathered together and elaborated all available arguments for the single tax, and he listed benefits which he believed would ensue, including: elimination of land speculation; reduction in house rent; increase in wages through expansion of effective demand, stimulation of production, and full employment; equalization of per capita income and social classes; control of monopolies; free trade through abolition of all other taxes; regeneration of family life and the dignity of man; repopulation of the countryside; and generally improvement in social justice.[109] He answered specific objections to the single tax

---

a typical collection of readings prepared for workers. *The Labour Question* (Melbourne, 1890), pp. 34–38.

105. Charles Rennick, "Henry George and his Utopia," *Journal of the Bankers' Institute of Australasia*, IV (1890–91), 168–79 and 252–59; James Ashton, "Henry George and his Utopia. A Reply to Mr. Rennick," *ibid.*, pp. 297–303; Beta, "Henry George and his Utopia," *ibid.*, pp. 354–57; James Ashton, "Henry George and his Utopia. Reply to Mr. Rennick's Rejoinder," *ibid.*, pp. 527–31.

106. "Editor's Notes," *Bankers' Magazine and Journal of the Bankers' Institute of Australasia*, VIII (1894–95), 801–2.

107. Max Hirsch, "The Single Tax," *Journal of the Bankers' Institute of Australasia*, IV (1890–91), 336–54, "Progress and Poverty: An Open Letter to Mr. Charles Rennick," *ibid.*, pp. 522–27, and *Protection in Victoria* (Melbourne, 1891), p. 29.

108. Some of Hirsch's more important works were: *The Fiscal Superstition* (Melbourne, 1895), *Economic Principles* (Melbourne, 1896), *Democracy versus Socialism* (London, 1901, and 2nd ed.; London, 1924), *The Problem of Wealth and Other Essays: Memorial Volume* (Melbourne, 1911).

109. *Democracy versus Socialism* (London, 1924), pp. 396–413.

of such formidable critics as H. M. Hyndman, J. A. Hobson, Edward Atkinson, and Francis Walker.[110]

Hirsch saw that one of the principal obstacles on the path to success for the single tax was the competing attractiveness of other panaceas, and he devoted a substantial part of his energies to attacking arguments for protection, trade unions, and socialism. In this direction he fought an uphill fight; his rigid interpretations of Henry George's writings brought support from doctrinaires, but his absolute rejection of all other reforms alienated both workers and the middle-class.[111] Hirsch presented his case clearly and reasonably, but his personal dogmatism must have done as much to injure as to strengthen the cause. He continued his campaign for the single tax long after all hope for its implementation had been lost, right up to his death in 1909.[112]

During the 1880's some variants of the single tax gave hope of being introduced as leagues were formed and such influential journals as the *Bulletin* and William Lane's *Worker* and *Boomerang* in Queensland came to its side. In the 1890's, however, the movement died as a powerful political force. Charles Fairfield, writing in England in 1892, reported with good reason that by this time radical land-reformers in Australia had become "politically, about as influential and important a body, as, let us say, the Swedenborgians in this country."[113] Nevertheless, following in the tradition of the classical rent-theorists, Henry George made

110. *Ibid.*, pp. 403–51.
111. Exaggerated assessments of Hirsch's influence are contained in prefaces to *Democracy versus Socialism* (London, 1924), and *The Problem of Wealth and other Essays* (Melbourne, 1911). *The Bankers' Magazine and Journal of the Bankers' Institute of Australasia* observed in 1895 that Hirsch's efforts to link free trade land-owners with urban single taxers were "as amusing as the attempted alliance between a cat and a mouse." VIII (1894–95), 801. Sidney Ball wrote in a review of *Democracy versus Socialism*: "Mr. Hirsch does not do much more than add to the original statement an examination of the principal objections that have been brought against the ethics and economics of the Single Tax. . . . The discussion certainly tends to be in the air, and the argument is for the most part too general—even for economic reasoning. Mr. Hirsch, however, is at home in the literature of the subject, and writes with the full force of conviction." *Economic Journal*, XI (1901), 550–51.
112. Max Hirsch's last work for the single tax seems to have been "The Limit of State Action," *Report of the Twelfth Meeting of the Australasian Association for the Advancement of Science held at Brisbane*, 1909, pp. 527–31.
113. Charles Fairfield, "State Socialism at the Antipodes," in Thomas MacKay, ed., *A Plea for Liberty: An Argument Against Socialism and Socialistic Legislation* (London, 1892), p. 137.

a distinct contribution to Australian social thought. Most colonial reformers became discouraged quickly about the feasibility of achieving the grandiose goals promised for the single tax,[114] but George left behind important new converts to the fundamental principle of land taxation. These included, in addition to those already mentioned, W. M. Hughes, W. A. Holman, Henry Bournes Higgins, King O'Malley, G. S. Beeby, and A. B. Piddington.[115] Even where his principles were misunderstood or condemned George stimulated discussion and inquiry. E. W. Foxall wrote in an obituary of George in 1898:

nearly twenty years after the publication of "Progress and Poverty"— there are men who profess its principles, without in the least comprehending them, and who therefore propose and advocate measures in the name of Henry George, in direct opposition to his teachings; while, on the other hand, there are those who can hardly mention the man's name without foaming at the mouth, who, without knowing it are striving their utmost to accomplish the very reforms which Henry George aimed at.[116]

Demands for taxation of unimproved land values were inserted automatically in most radical programs in the 1890's and afterward. Although it is difficult to assess the impact of ideas on legislation, it is significant that property taxes designed both to yield revenue and to penalize large and idle estates were introduced in South Australia as early as 1884 and in other colonies during the next few years.[117] The Commonwealth imposed a land

114. See for example, Ebenezer, *A Plea for Democracy: or the Land for the People, a Treatise on the Political and Economic Conditions of New South Wales* (Sydney, 1896); and Waldemar Bannow, *The Colony of Victoria Socially and Materially* (Melbourne, 1896).

115. Speech of W. M. Hughes, *Parliamentary Debates of New South Wales*, 1895, pp. 375–79; and speech by A. B. Piddington, *ibid.*, pp. 583–84; L. F. Fitzhardinge, "W. M. Hughes in New South Wales Politics, 1890–1900," *Royal Australian Historical Society Journal and Proceedings*, XXXVII (1951), 145–68; H. V. Evatt, *Australian Labour Leader: The Story of W. A. Holman and the Labour Movement* (Sydney, 1945), pp. 21 and 41–42; Nettie Palmer, *Henry Bournes Higgins: A Memoir* (London, 1931), p. 126; Dorothy Catts, *King O'Malley: Man and Statesman* (Sydney, 1957).

116. E. W. Foxall, "Henry George," *Australian Economist*, VI (1898), 13–14.

117. Arguments for land taxation were contained in: *Report of the Commonwealth Labour Conference held at Trades Hall, Sydney, 1902* (Brisbane, 1902), p. 3; Argyle McCallum, *The Social Unrest of the Present Day and What Causes it* (Yass, ca. 1906); Surplus Wealth Tax League, *Political Economy in its Relation to the Urgent Demands of the Present Period* (Camperdown, 1910), p. 5; Alexander W. Johnston, *Law and Liberty* (Sydney, 1910), p. vii; Fred Saidy, *Workers' College Teaching: the Law of Cause and Effect: Economics and Political Science* (Wollongong, 1929).

tax in 1910 and prohibited private ownership of land in the Commonwealth Territory at least partly from consciousness of a potential future unearned increment.[118] As late as 1925, a Commonwealth Royal Commission was appointed to inquire into methods of assessing "unimproved" land values; the concept that a portion of land prices was attributable to community growth had become an accepted part of social doctrine.[119]

Opposition to Land Reform

A fundamental assumption underlying land reform proposals in the colonies was that in a new country returns attributable to land, the relatively abundant and productive factor, were unusually high. Reformers failed to recognize that because of the very abundance of natural resources, the other factors—capital and labor—and not land, tended to receive the highest rewards. The ready availability of land made possible a high per capita income in the colonies but resulted also in a low marginal productivity and small relative factor share. Land-owners often did have large personal incomes but usually because of shrewd entrepreneurship or substantial holdings of equipment and stock. One proof of the low real rent on land was the difficulty encountered by absentee colonial landlords, unlike their counterparts in the old world, in leaving properties in the hands of tenants with expectation of high returns. Critics had constantly to remind advocates of schemes for confiscation of allegedly extortionate receipts by landlords that their objection was really against unequal personal income distribution rather than the presence of economic rent. Moreover, land-reformers seldom recognized that if a government levy exceeded the real rent level it would disturb the optimum allocation of resources.

118. Dorothy Catts, *King O'Malley: Man and Statesman,* p. 182.
119. "Report of the Royal Commission on the Method for Determining the Unimproved Value of Land Held under Crown Leases; together with Appendices," *Papers Presented to the Parliament of the Commonwealth of Australia,* 1925; Discussions of land tax legislation are contained in: Herbert Heaton, "The Taxation of Unimproved Value of Land in Australia," *Quarterly Journal of Economics,* XXIX (1924–25), 410–49; S. H. Roberts, *op. cit.,* pp. 380–84; Gordon Greenwood, ed., *Australia: A Social and Political History* (Sydney, 1955), pp. 177–78; and Colin Clark, *Australian Hopes and Fears* (London, 1958), p. 164.

Two early treasurers of New South Wales became aware of problems posed by a land tax in new countries when they pondered alternate methods of raising government revenue. Geoffrey Eager in 1863 observed that neither property nor general incomes constituted a satisfactory tax base as they were both subject to wide fluctuations and because in "all new countries the land, although it may be occupied to a considerable extent, yields but a small return."[120] Saul Samuel in 1865 estimated that the total real income attributable to land was less than one and one-half million pounds, and a reasonable tax on this amount, he argued, would barely be worth collecting. A land tax, he added, might discourage settlement, and "In this country, perhaps more than any country in the world (though there are other colonies in the same position as ourselves), it should be the policy of the Government to encourage the acquisition of property."[121] To buttress his position Samuel read to the colonial legislature from works by McCulloch, Mill, and Fawcett.

Arguments that a land tax would be both unjust and injurious economically were voiced regularly in the 1860's, and 1870's, particularly during periods when it seemed that such a tax might actually be imposed. An alarmed Tasmanian in 1872 quoted Adam Smith and McCulloch on the virtues of unfettered industry and condemned a proposed land tax thus:

Such a proposal to impose upon property . . . additional taxation, and at the same time exempt that portion of the community who in great measure occasion the necessity for additional revenue from any contribution towards it, is opposed to every principle of equity and political expediency, and appears to me would be introducing a large instalment of "French Communism" amongst us.[122]

In the political confusion of Victoria during the late 1870's, radical land reform seemed an imminent possibility. In particular, Charles H. Pearson's insistent pleas for progressive land taxation to encourage small farmers at the expense of large

120. James Thomson, ed., *The Financial Statements of the Colonial Treasurers of New South Wales* (Sydney, 1881), p. 114.
121. *Ibid.*, p. 145.
122. Theodore Bartley, *The Present Financial Crisis in Tasmania . . .* (Launceston, 1872), p. 34.

land-owners generated vigorous controversy. J. S. Elkington, Pearson's successor in history and political economy at Melbourne University, launched a scathing attack on his proposals. Elkington argued that Pearson had abandoned economic reality for sentimentalism by proposing creation of a farming yeomanry at the present stage of colonial growth. Few people were on the land, he insisted, simply because less and less labor was required for efficient agriculture.[123] He observed: "with the progress of civilization the numerical proportion of agriculturists to the whole community of labourers *decreases* by rapid strides; in addition to which, the agricultural returns leave no room for doubt that the agricultural products of the soil have as steadily *increased*, and that they are now absolutely greater than at any former period in history."[124] Elkington raised two questions which were particularly embarrassing to land-reformers. First, he asked, if gains from land ownership were to be confiscated, should not owners be compensated as well for losses:

If the lucky owner of land which has acquired enormous value merely by the progress of society is to forfeit so much of his advantage as accrues from that cause, it seems to follow that the unlucky owner of land which by the same process—the progress of society—has become enormously reduced in value ought to have the deficit made up to him.[125]

And second, Elkington queried, what distinguished in theory and therefore singled out for confiscation the "unearned increment" of land from increases in the value of other forms of property?

Catherine Spence in South Australia agreed with Elkington's description of increasing economies of scale and decreasing labor intensity of contemporary agriculture. She too reminded Pearson of the penalties imposed by the unseen hand on all

123. J. S. Elkington, "An Historical Glance at the Land Question," *Melbourne Review*, II (1877), 247–48. Elkington suggested that Tiberius Gracchus was a predecessor of Pearson in attempting unsuccessfully to reverse the progress of agricultural depopulation in ancient Rome. R. M. Johnston formulated a similar argument against sympathizers of yeoman settlement in "Notes on the Natural Limits to Occupation on the Land," *Papers and Proceedings of the Royal Society of Tasmania*, 1892, pp. 1–8.
124. "An Historical Glance at the Land Question," p. 242.
125. *Ibid.*, p. 260.

colonies which experimented with uneconomic operations. Immigration would decline, she predicted, and capital would move to more favorable environments. She explained:

Capital is a beneficent genius, but she is shy, and can easily take wings and fly from land to land; and if by over-taxation of the wealthy we make the colonies distasteful to those whose present interests are so strongly bound up in their prosperity, they and their property—all but their land greatly reduced in value by their absence—would take their departure for a newer or an older country, and the loss would be ours rather than theirs.[126]

Miss Spence expressed understandable concern about the dangers of tax evasion under Pearson's progressive taxation scheme, and she declared that following his reasoning concentration of wealth not merely of land should be discouraged by government policy. She recommended as an alternative measure a graduated succession duty; she explained:

It is just, because it is through the sufferance and protection of an orderly government that the property, whether real or personal, has been acquired, and that the heir, who may be weak in body or feeble in mind, comes into peaceable possession of any portion of it; it is scarcely felt because it is taken from unearned money before it has been received; it is the most cheaply collected and the most difficult to evade of any description of tax.[127]

Miss Spence was an intellectual disciple of J. S. Mill, and like Mill, but unlike Pearson, she took care to insure that proposed community action, unless absolutely necessary, would not interfere with either optimum economic allocation or accumulation.

Proposals for land taxation, even when not progressive, raised storms of criticism grounded usually in self-interest but based often on interpretation of classical economic theory. John Winthrop Hackett in 1877 claimed that a tax which had been suggested for absentee land-owners would contract the margin of cultivation, discourage capital imports, and limit domestic investment. He cited Ricardo, McCulloch, and Senior to show that

126. C. H. Spence, "Graduated Succession Duties," *Melbourne Review*, II (1877), 445.
127. *Ibid.*, p. 446.

in a young country such a tax would seriously restrict growth. He suggested:

To a property tax no doubt we shall one day come; but what is true of an old and settled country, where it is likely most fortunes are held, not that they may fructify but that they may be spent, may not obtain in all places. Here the case greatly differs. Owing to the high rate of interest, most part of all large incomes assume the shape of capital. A tax, therefore, of this complexion at the present time might be not so much a tax on property as a tax on investments and their profits. These at least we must take care not to touch. To tax them would be tantamount to lessening the current rate of interest offered for investment in the country.[128]

Pronouncements by classical economists were used extensively as evidence against proposed land taxes. Prideaux Selby laid special stress on Adam Smith's first maxim of taxation which stated that an equitable tax would be levied in proportion to the incomes of those taxed. He used also Bastiat's *Harmonies of Political Economy* to illustrate that penalties on the colony's great staple industries were "suicidal." He exclaimed: "If the labouring classes could only be brought to see that their true interest lies in fostering capital, and causing it to increase more rapidly than their own numbers, we should have fewer contests; less waste of energy and of *life* in grasping at the unattainable; and a higher standard of comfort and happiness. . . ."[129] Classical economic doctrine, and particularly Smith's four maxims of taxation, remained the most popular weapon against land reform.[130] One brave critic, however, dared to use a technique of land nationalizers against their own policies. He argued that an examination of history showed not that traditionally the state had controlled land, but that government should maintain strict laissez faire. "Arbitrary restrictions, therefore, on the alienation

128. John Winthrop Hackett, "Should Absentees be Taxed?," *Melbourne Review*, II (1877), 86.
129. Prideaux Selby, "Thoughts on Taxation," *Melbourne Review*, III (1878), 218.
130. See for example: W. Jardine Smith, "'Liberal' Finance in Victoria," *Victorian Review*, I (1880), 444–68; C. Wesley Caddy, "The Education of the Educated," *Melbourne Review*, V (1880), 432–39; and W. Campbell, *Farewell Address to the Electors of the North-West Province* (Melbourne, 1882).

of land are evidently absurd if we argue from first principles alone, and we know from history that they have been invariably injurious in practice." He concluded: "Looking at the question thus, we are forced to the conclusion that our safest plan is to give absolute ownership to the cultivator to do as he wishes as with his own property. If we restrict the power of sale we simply repeat the blunders of the Spartan laws, which were inoperative and finally destructive."[131]

Criticism of Henry George followed closely the favorable reception of his writings in the colonies. Samuel Rinder replied to Catherine Spence's early praise of George with arguments against a land tax, and he emphasized in particular that the single tax, by penalizing industry, would diminish the wages fund. He brought forth again Smith's tired maxims, and he reported indignantly: "Our Californian economist, in the most off-hand manner, bluntly contradicts such men as Adam Smith, Mill, and Buckle, and reproduces exploded theories as coolly as I here re-state the A B C of the science."[132]

Three highly respected and effective critics of the single tax had substantial influence in reducing Henry George's impact in the colonies, at least among intellectuals: they were Alexander Sutherland, Robert Mackenzie Johnston, and Andrew Garran. Sutherland, educator, amateur psychologist of international reputation, and student of Hearn, kept a sharp and skeptical eye on extravagant claims of land reformers.[133] In 1880, Sutherland examined critically estimates made by David Syme of allegedly excessive profits made by land-owners in Victoria. He discovered that when comparing relative rates of return on capital and land Syme had overstated the profit rate on real estate by calculating simple rather than compound interest on the sum paid originally for the land.[134] He suggested that Syme had given an appearance

131. J. Crozier, "Land Tenure," *Victorian Review*, V (1882), 414 and 416.
132. Samuel Rinder, "A Californian Political Economist—A Reply," *Victorian Review*, IV (1881), 416.
133. For Sutherland's other economic writings see below pp. 446 and 620.
134. Sutherland explained the correct mathematical solution of Syme's problem thus: "If r^1 be the rate per cent. per annum yielded by the rent of a piece of land, and r be the rate per cent. per annum of the increment in its value—If V^1

of false simplicity to estimates of real returns on land, whereas "The calculation of the exact rate at which the value of the land in Victoria has increased would involve the solution of an equation of the forty-second degree, and the labour so involved would not be compensated by the degree of accuracy obtained."[135] Sutherland concluded that a reasonable guess at the real annual increment in land values in the colony would be about six per cent, and he intimated that when added to annual rentals the total would not be very different from average returns on invested capital.

In 1885 Sutherland undertook another analysis of income from Victorian land, but on this occasion in greater detail and aimed directly at claims by followers of Henry George and Alfred Wallace. He set out specifically "to show from the case of Victoria that the returns given by land are not more than the average interest of capital." Sutherland estimated the total value of land by adding fifteen per cent to assessed tax ratings of real estate and subtracting costs of improvements. He then calculated the current value of the originial sum paid for land using a compound interest formula and assuming that this amount had been invested in government bonds. From the latter total he subtracted the capitalized value of actual rent payments on land so as to compare the net benefits accumulated by landowners (about forty-eight million pounds) against the value to government of the receipts from land sales. He estimated that land-owners had come out ahead by a mere one and one-half million pounds—"a not very serious amount." He concluded:

Hence we find that in a new country like this, land yields in rent and increase of value together only an interest equivalent to that obtained by capital. And that it should be otherwise would surprise us

---

be the price originally paid for land, V^2 the value after n years, then the value of r is obtained from the equation—

$$\log. (1 + r) = \frac{\log. V^2 - \log. V^1}{n}$$

If R be the value of r obtained from this equation, then $R + r^1$ is the annual rate per cent. received by the investor on his money." "On the Method of Calculating the Increment in the Value of Land," *Transactions and Proceedings of the Royal Society of Victoria*, XVI (1880), 152.
135. *Ibid.*, p. 150.

very much. If land yielded on the average a decidely better interest, no one would invest in anything else till every acre of land was bought up. If it yielded decidedly less, people would be slow in buying it, as their inducement would lie in motives much less strong and less speedy of action than the love of profit.[136]

At least one reformer, John Ross, became incensed at Sutherland's coldly dispassionate treatment of land as a productive factor. He rejoined: "it is a matter of some surprise to find Mr. Sutherland so deliberately reject the illustrations which old and thickly populated countries could supply, in favour of a *calculation*, in my opinion, entirely wide of the subject."[137] Sutherland replied with a further analysis of an "unearned increment" present in the value of almost all goods in a growing community. Even "A very dull clergyman might blossom into a bishop if he happened to be first in a district that afterwards became populous." "The theorist who is going to disentangle the unearned element from men's incomes," he observed, "has some little work before him."[138] Sutherland's polite demolition of the land-reformers' strongest economic argument was in sharp contrast to their own extreme statements and made a favorable impression on Victorian audiences.

In Tasmania Robert M. Johnston, the Government Statistician, waged a campaign of criticism against land reformers similar to that of Sutherland. In 1888 Johnston outlined to the Royal Society of Tasmania the rudiments of Malthusian population theory for the reason that "Mr. Henry George altogether failed to grasp the various elements of this problem . . . and has fallen into the most simple errors in his adverse comments upon Malthus."[139] Later Johnston argued that George mistakenly had drawn social reformers into a false cause. The real reason for economic difficulties, he insisted, was immobility of factors in the presence of changing tastes and technology in a free-

136. Alexander Sutherland, "Victorian Test of a Social Theory," *Melbourne Review*, X (1885), 182.
137. John Ross, "On Increment Value of Land," *Melbourne Review*, X (1885), 303.
138. Alexander Sutherland, "On Increment Value of Land," *Melbourne Review*, X (1885), 304–7.
139. R. M. Johnston, "The Problem of Malthus Stated," *Papers and Proceedings of the Royal Society of Tasmania*, 1888, p. 53, and see below pp. 413–15.

enterprise system.[140] Johnston pointed out several serious obstacles in the way of actually imposing a single tax. First, because much colonial land had been sold recently, unimproved land values would have to be returned to owners before a confiscatory rent tax could be introduced. Such compensation for Tasmania alone, he estimated, would cost eight million pounds. Second, practical difficulties of assessment would almost certainly result in taxation of marginal land and consequent reduction in total output. Finally, because the tax burden would depend solely upon ownership of land rather than upon total income, wealth, or services received, the incidence would be manifestly inequitable and unjust.[141] Johnston examined income and excise taxes with reference to Adam Smith's criteria and concluded that "all the advantages embodied in Dr. Smith's four maxims or principles cannot be directly or indirectly attained approximately by raising the *whole* of the necessary taxes by any *one method* whether direct or indirect."[142]

In Sydney, Andrew Garran maintained before the Australian Economic Association a temperate, balanced, and sustained opposition to extreme land reform proposals. He began by investigating carefully the history of settlement in the colonies, prices of land, and speed of alienation.[143] He went on to show that Henry George mixed value judgments with unsubstantiated policy proposals in a masquerade of scientific method.[144] Garran objected particularly to the assertion voiced repeatedly by land-reformers that increases in land values were attributable necessarily to community activity. In Australia, he maintained, a relatively few pastoralists had stimulated growth of the economy and were responsible almost single-handedly through their own

140. R. M. Johnston, "Root Matters in Social and Economic Problems," *Papers and Proceedings of the Royal Society of Tasmania*, 1889, pp. 143–204, and "Root Matters in Social and Economic Problems (2nd series)," *ibid.*, 1890, pp. 1–21.

141. Economist [R. M. Johnston], *Fallacies of the Single Tax Panacea* (Hobart, n. d.).

142. Economist [R. M. Johnston], *Taxation—Current Popular Fallacies* (Hobart, 1893), p. 8.

143. Andrew Garran, "On the Natural Demand for Land in New South Wales," *Australian Economist*, I (1888–90), 155–56.

144. Andrew Garran, "Henry George and the Scientific Method," *ibid.*, II (1890–93), 17–19.

efforts for increases in value of their holdings.[145] Garran supported a real estate tax as a valuable weapon in the government fiscal arsenal, but he argued that Georgian principles would be misleading if used as a guide for calculating rates.[146] Garran was supported in his critical attitude toward land reform by other members of the Australian Economic Association.[147] Arthur Duckworth reported that Garran's continued comment was partly responsible for imposition in New South Wales of a real estate tax as a conventional revenue device not designed specifically to capture an unearned increment.[148]

A variety of objections to land reform were voiced in the colonies during the 1880's and 1890's but were seldom as effective as the careful critiques of Sutherland, Johnston, and Garran. Many critics feared all interference with productive staple industries of the economy and denied that economic rent could be confiscated successfully without discouraging enterprise and destroying the colonies' attractiveness to labor and capital.[149] Charles Fairfield, a doctrinaire visitor from Britain, described Australian land-reformers as merely disgruntled and "unselected" combatants in the evolutionary struggle for survival trying collectively to compensate for individual failure. He called for a rally in defense of private property and "an evolution which shall reinstate primitive methods of getting and holding property." [150] Protectionists assailed land-taxers for their free trade views, while miscellaneous supporters of other panaceas condemned land reform in general as an inadequate single meas-

145. A. Garran, "Land Values: Their Origin and Increase," *ibid.*, II (1890–93), 196–200.
146. Andrew Garran, "Land Tax Exemptions," *ibid.*, IV (1894–97), 455–58.
147. See for example: A. Duckworth, "Wages and Capital: Mr. Henry George as a Political Economist," *ibid.*, I (1888–90), 220–21; and W. W. Carlile, "The Misuse of Paradox in Economic Science," *ibid.*, IV (1894–97), 533–34 and 535–36.
148. *Ibid.*, IV (1894–97), 517.
149. D. Brown, *Wealth and Wages in New South Wales* (Sydney, 1891), p. 33; Richard Teece, "A New Theory of the Relations of Wages and Profit," *Report of the Fourth Meeting of the Australasian Association for the Advancement of Science held at Hobart, 1892*, pp. 134–35; Prideaux Selby, "The Incidence of Taxation," *ibid.*, p. 584; Observer, *Journal of the Institute of Bankers of New South Wales*, VII (1898), *passim*.
150. Charles Fairfield, "Getting and Holding," *Melbourne Review*, IX (1884), 291–311. William Webster, an irate land nationalizer, replied to Fairfield with spirit. "Property in Land," *ibid.*, 393–404.

ure.[151] Considerable complicated and confused internecine rivalry took place between land-taxers and land-nationalizers; Alfred J. Taylor of Tasmania even criticized both "from the standpoint of a physicist."[152] A few opponents of reform resorted to crude ridicule and doggerel.[153] The Honourable L. F. Heydon blamed the strikes and depression of the 1890's on Henry George's visit and the malevolent effects of his ideas combined with those of Edward Bellamy. Heydon maintained: "All this disaster is directly and mainly due to the disturbance to labour and the discouragement of capital caused by Henry George's and Bellamy's socialistic doctrines, and to the depreciation of the selling value of land caused by Henry George's special doctrine as to the confiscation of land."[154]

After the turn of the century it was apparent that in all probability neither land nationalization nor the single tax would be imposed on a broad scale, and opposition accordingly diminished. Occasional criticism did continue for a few years, but without the former urgency and designed mainly to warn of the perils in economic heresy. For example, students at the University of Tasmania were asked in 1901 to reproduce on an examination Francis Walker's "refutation" of Henry George.[155] Alfred McLennan of Perth in 1908 began by ruling out such absurdities as the single tax in presenting "a simple arithmetic of political economy, to suit the adults who are, to the subject,

---

151. "Henry George on Protection," *Australian Magazine*, 1886, pp. 138–48; P. J. Gandon, *"Ecce Homo" in Political Economy: The Abolition of Poverty by the Single Tax. Letters Addressed to Henry George* (Sydney, 1890); David A. Andrade, *Our Social System, and How it Affects those who Work for their Living* (Melbourne, n. d.); Cynion, "The Land Question, its Development in Australia, and the Teaching of Henry George," *Australian Economist*, I (1888–90), 123–27.

152. Alfred J. Taylor, "Notes on the Value of Labor in Relation to the Production of Wealth: Regarded from the Standpoint of a Physicist," *Report of the Fourth Meeting of the Australasian Association for the Advancement of Science held at Hobart, 1892*, pp. 599–601; *Journal of the Adelaide Young Men's Society*, November 10, 1884; A. Forsyth, "Land Taxation and Nationalisation," *Australian Economist*, II (1890–93), 1–6.

153. E. G. Fitzgibbon, *Essence of "Progress and Poverty" Extracted from the American of Henry George and Gone into and Dealt with in Plain English* (Melbourne, 1884); and Percy Wakefield, *"Justice is Freedom," Fair Trade. Prologue for the Inauguration of a Fair Trade League for New South Wales* (Sydney, 1889).

154. L. F. Heydon, "Land Nationalisation," *Journal of the Institute of Bankers of New South Wales*, IV (1895), 425.

155. *Calendar of the University of Tasmania*, 1902.

as the infant class to the school."[156] E. W. H. Fowles of Brisbane, when searching for a cure for unemployment in 1911, explained at the outset that the single tax and other similar reforms had "been completely discredited."[157]

Conclusion

Professor Hancock has remarked: "The dominant theme in Australian political history is the lament of an unsatisfied land-hunger."[158] Another observer says: "One of the fascinating things about Australia is the sense of claustrophobia in the midst of such an infinity of space."[159] Throughout the period under study the Australian claustrophobic lament was accompanied by almost continuous economic enquiry into land policy.[160] Self-interest was the single most important consideration in the controversies, but the influence of foreign authorities was substantial. All major reform proposals—the Wakefield system, homestead settlement, nationalization, and taxation—were defended with dicta of British and American writers, and opponents of reform appealed in rebuttal to classical economic theory and to descriptions of the allocative benefits of laissez faire. Widespread familiarity with doctrine led to a willingness to undertake legislative innovation, but it also helped to stifle creative thought. In the area of land policy Australians faced challenging problems for economic analysis. But from the viewpoint of an economic theorist the results of sustained interest and almost continuous discussion were disappointing.

156. Alfred McLennan, *The Other Way Round* (Perth, 1908), p. 4.
157. E. W. H. Fowles, "On Unemployment," *Report of the Thirteenth Meeting of the Australasian Association for the Advancement of Science held at Sydney, 1911*, p. 457.
158. W. K. Hancock, *Australia* (New York, 1930), p. 72.
159. Alan Moorehead, *Cooper's Creek* (London, 1963), p. 9.
160. Outside observers made some of the most sensible comments about Australian land policy. For example: E. Fournier de Flaix, "Des Theories sur l'impot en Australie au XIXe siècle," *Revue d'économie politique*, I (1887), 52–63; Riccardo Dalla Volta, "Une Oeuvre posthume de M. Uge Rabbeno: la question foncière dans les colonies de l'Australie," *ibid.*, XIII (1899), 833–50; Louis Vigouroux, "L'Elevage en Australie," *ibid.*, XVI (1902), 168–78; Charles W. Dilke, *Problems of Greater Britain* (London, 1890), I, 193–95, and 281–82; A. F. Dodd, "Taxation of Land Values in Australasia," *Economic Journal*, XIV (1904), 401–12; and H. Heaton, "The Story of Australian Land Settlement," *Economic Record*, I (1925), 94–100.

· 5 ·

Banking and Currency: I. The Role
of the State

In chapters 5 and 6 controversy is described which surrounded
three aspects of banking and currency in the colonies: the role
of the state in monetary affairs, loans on the security of real
estate, and the desirability of bimetallic currency. These subjects
are not mutually exclusive nor were they at all times of the most
crucial importance in the development of the monetary system.
However, they bring forth frequent appeals to theory, reveal
clearly the impact of imported economic ideas, and submit to
independent treatment in separate sections. In this chapter concern is with discussion of the desirability of a "state," "national,"
or "public" bank, as a government monetary institution was
variously called. Writers who are examined often were unclear
and occasionally were uncertain as to the appropriate functions
for such an institution. But usually they regarded issue of a
uniform currency as a central feature and in varying degrees
favored some commercial activities and controls over private
banks. Proposals for a government bank ranged from appeals
for relatively conventional imitations of the Bank of England
to radical demands for agencies to issue irredeemable notes. As
with other controversial reforms, the intensity of agitation was
related inversely to the level of economic prosperity.

Early Demands for a Government Bank—Boom
and Depression in Wool and Gold

New South Wales. The earliest plan for a government bank
in the colonies was suggested in 1810 by Governor Macquarie;

it was based on recommendations made to him before his departure from Britain and on observations during his voyage of a bank at the Cape of Good Hope. The proposal, which was as much for provision of commercial bank services as for an institution of government control, was rejected by the Colonial Office.[1] Macquarie's demands were answered in part in 1817 by the issue of a charter to the Bank of New South Wales, and subsequently by the establishment of other corporate institutions.[2]

Occasional suggestions were made during the 1820's and 1830's that the several colonial banks amalgamate for greater strength.[3] However, the earliest detailed demands for a truly reformatory government note-issue bank were voiced in the 1840's during the first serious depression which followed a pastoral boom. Arguments were presented in the press, in the legislature, and in pamphlets to prove that the state by vigorous monetary action could revive the prosperity so inexplicably vanished. A representative writer in the *New South Wales Magazine* proclaimed that a government bank could stimulate economic activity both by issuing its own notes and by attracting British capital. "*A Government Loan Bank, and Bank of Issue,* based upon a *loan from England,* would confer upon the colony all the monetary advantage which it is capable of receiving, and in connection with the other measures we have recommended, restore it to prosperity, and again place it in a state of rapid advancement."[4]

In 1843 witnesses before a select committee of the Legislative Council on "the monetary confusion" gave evidence of widespread enthusiasm for some form of government intervention in monetary affairs. Their comments were inspired in part by general frustration with the depression and in part by dissatisfaction with activities of the commercial banks leading up to and fol-

1. S. J. Butlin, *Foundations of the Australian Monetary System 1788–1851* (Melbourne, 1953), pp. 76–79. I have leaned heavily on the exhaustive work of Professor Butlin for description of monetary history.
2. *Ibid.,* pp. 110 f.
3. *Ibid.,* p. 228.
4. "Credit—its Properties and Effects—Government Bank," *New South Wales Magazine,* 1843, pp. 575–83. Additional contemporary statements are reported by Professor Butlin, *Foundations,* pp. 541–44.

lowing the crisis. A typical critic complained of "the speculative mania fostered and encouraged by the Banks and by the Government." Most witnesses who favored experiments with government notes were undecided about the form these should take: an auctioneer suggested an issue of circulating government debentures, and a "landed proprietor" predicted that interest-bearing government bonds in small denominations would circulate slowly and would not depreciate.[5] W. C. Wentworth, an influential member of the committee, when examined as a witness made the only definite suggestion for creation of a "National Bank." He proposed that existing commercial banks be prohibited in future from issuing notes and that a government institution make available an amount of its own convertible currency equal to the present circulation. He argued that the public would be as willing to use state notes as private ones and that extra specie commercial banks would need to maintain a satisfactory reserve against deposits which would give added stability to the system.[6]

The committee, of which Richard Windeyer was chairman, concluded that monetary derangement was a cause of the recent crisis, noting "an undue contraction of the circulating medium, and the absence of all confidence and credit."[7] It regretted that currently land-owners found difficulty in obtaining loans, and it prescribed monetary expansion as a necessary antidote. The committee endorsed specifically a plan of government action presented by Thomas Holt, a Sydney merchant who had resided nine years in Prussia and "whose intelligence and opportunity of acquiring a thorough knowledge of the subject render his statements of the greatest value." Holt outlined two financial practices of the Prussian government: the first, purchase of land mortgages with negotiable guaranteed securities (called *pfand-*

---

5. "Report from the Select Committee on the Monetary Confusion, with Appendix and Minutes of Evidence," *Votes and Proceedings of the Legislative Council of New South Wales, 1843*, evidence, pp. 1, 28, 37, 42–49.
6. Evidence, pp. 62–65.
7. Richard Windeyer (1806–47) "was employed by *The Times*, and wrote extensively for the London *Sun*, in 1832–33 on politics and economics, expressing a strongly liberal point of view. He also took an active part in the early agitation against the Corn Laws." *Australian Encyclopaedia* (East Lansing, 1958), IX, 327.

briefes and discussed below pp. 211–13); the second, an issue of legal-tender notes convertible into gold by the Treasury and required for payments to the state.[8] The committee expressed concern over the "liability to abuse, by an over-issue of paper, and a refusal to pay coin in a time of pressure," and it suggested that "the good without the evil" might be preserved by combining the two practices, the state offering one portion of interest-bearing debentures and another portion of convertible notes for the purchase of "safe" mortgages on land. Windeyer pointed out that on the one hand property holders would be provided with emergency credit, and on the other the community would benefit from an increased but restricted circulation. He noted as precedent the British emergency monetary legislation of 1825–26, and he argued that his plan afforded "a means, by which the credit of the community may be safely interposed, as well to stay the further progress of the ruin which threatens so many, the richest, as well as the poorest—the most cautious and prudent, as well as the most rash, and speculative—as partially to place the currency of New South Wales, on a more stable foundation."[9] The committee suggested that the Treasury and a "Colonial Landboard" assume the issue, loan, and redemption functions of a central monetary authority, but it was reluctant to make such an extreme proposal as for creation of an actual "State Bank."

. . . your Committee, looking to the urgent wants of the Colony, have thought the more advisable course was, to confine their attention to some practical measure, which would not involve the necessity of erecting a State Bank; a step of vast importance, and only to be taken, after the most extended enquiry and mature deliberation.[10]

The committee's recommendations for issue of a government currency received support both from landowners and from spokesmen of the laboring class.[11] A bill to implement the plan

8. Evidence, p. 43.
9. Report, p. 3.
10. *Ibid.*
11. Michael Roe, *Society and Thought in Eastern Australia, 1835–1851,* Thesis Submitted for the degree of Doctor of Philosophy in the Australian National University, 1960, pp. 130–31, and 320–21.

was passed by the Legislative Council but was disallowed by Governor Gipps.[12] The question was not revived seriously after prosperity returned later in the decade.

Gold was discovered in large quantities both in New South Wales and in Victoria in 1851. During the 1850's, as thousands of miners poured into the colonies and tons of gold poured out, the question was raised again of government banks and note issue. Immediate reasons for the discussion were a critical shortage of currency which accompanied the booming prosperity, and allegedly high profits made by commercial institutions.[13] Banks purchased gold on the fields, or when it arrived in Sydney, Melbourne, or Adelaide from the interior, and they exchanged for the metal their own notes or coin, but at a substantial discount from specie value. Gold was shipped then to London to be coined at the full rate. Miners and their sympathizers argued that money should be augmented locally by colonial governments to prevent this deflation in value of a vital staple product and to retain profits of monetary expansion for local public purposes.

In New South Wales, the first method suggested for eliminating commercial bank arbitrage profit and for sustaining the domestic price level was a colonial mint to buy gold directly from miners and to give in return freshly coined legal tender. A select committee of the New South Wales Legislative Council concluded in 1851 that a local mint would be desirable, and after some discussion the Imperial authorities agreed.[14] In 1853 Captain E. W. Ward, R. E., was dispatched from Britain to head a new branch of the Royal Mint at Sydney with the rank of deputy master and with instructions to begin operations as quickly as possible. As one of his original assayers, Ward em-

12. S. J. Butlin, *Foundations*, pp. 329–32.
13. The gold-purchase activities of the colonial banks are described by Professor S. J. Butlin, *Australia and New Zealand Bank* (London, 1961), pp. 126–29.
14. "Report from the Select Committee on the Proposed Assay Office and Mint, with Minutes of Evidence," *Votes and Proceedings of the Legislative Council of New South Wales*, 1851. An account of the Sydney Mint's beginning is contained in A. S. Kenyon, "The Royal Mint and its Australian Branches," *Victorian Historical Magazine*, XV (1935), 61–82; see also Eric W. Dunlop, " 'The Golden Fifties' being the Story of the Influence of the Gold Discoveries in Australia in the 1850's; Part III," *Royal Australian Historical Society Journal and Proceedings*, XXXVII (1951), 168–214.

ployed the young William Stanley Jevons, and as part of his equipment he ordered "Books and Parliamentary papers, for reference on questions of currency and political economy." [15] The mint coined its first Sovereigns in 1854 and provided an immediate demand for raw gold. However, for several years, Sydney coins were legal tender only in New South Wales, and a thriving export trade in bullion persisted.[16] The mint was able to counteract locally the deflationary effects of a rapidly expanding staple trade, but it was limited by the legal-tender restriction from dispelling all criticism of monetary conditions.

The select committee which proposed formation of a mint in 1851 was divided on the propriety of suggesting also creation of a state bank. The influence was evident of controversy which had surrounded passage of the Peel Bank Act in 1844. One witness, at least, was firm in his convictions, and "in accordance with the more modern system," recommended "the establishment of a Government Bank of Issue, having no reference to banking matters," as approved "by all statesmen, and all the leading political economists." He testified that New South Wales faced a unique opportunity to create a note-issue authority strictly according to Currency School principles:

there is no country in the world—England not even excepted—that has the same facilities as this Colony for bringing the system of such a Bank of Issue into beneficial operation, inasmuch as the Bank would be enabled *strictly* to adhere to the great principle laid down—that not a single note should be issued beyond the amount of gold lying in its coffers. It should under no circumstances whatever enter into competition with any other banking establishment in matters connected with banking, strictly speaking.[17]

15. "Correspondence relative to Branch of the Royal Mint," *Votes and Proceedings of the Legislative Council of New South Wales*, 1854, pp. 6 and 9.
16. The Governor, Sir William Denison, complained in 1855 that "the establishment of a Mint was advocated by the Council here on wrong grounds altogether" and he suggested that the Mint thrived largely by accident. The Government of Victoria refused to recognize Sydney Sovereigns as legal tender, subjecting them to the same export duty as bullion. This action had exactly the opposite effect to that desired by causing the export only of duty-free British coinage and retaining Sydney coins for local circulation. Denison urged the Secretary of State unsuccessfully to make the colonial coinage a true "Coin of the Realm." Letter to Colonel Harness, R. E., dated Nov. 15, 1855, *Varieties of Vice-Regal Life* (London, 1870), I, 318–19.
17. Evidence of John Nicholas Beit, *loc. cit.*, p. 1.

Another witness explained in the same vein:

I consider that the circumstances in which this Colony is suddenly placed by the discovery of gold, present the most favorable opportunity which could be desired for carrying out the great principle which has been advocated by all the most able statesmen and financiers in Europe, viz., the establishment of a Government Bank of Issue, based wholly on the precious metals. Such a bank would command the confidence, not only of the Colonists, but of all the world, and tend to make this not only the chief entrepot for the goods, but also the settling place for all the money transactions of this hemisphere.[18]

John Darvall, the committee chairman, proposed insertion of a paragraph in the final report favoring a state bank of issue but he was overruled.[19]

In 1852 another select committee of the Legislative Council, with a distinguished membership which included W. C. Wentworth, John Darvall, James Martin, Charles Cowper, and Arthur Holroyd, set out specifically to examine the current monetary situation, the character of local institutions, and relevant statistics.[20] The chairman explained in his report that the committee began with unanimity of theoretical opinion, all members endorsing orthodox Currency School views.

Your Committee have not thought it necessary to examine any witnesses because the principles of currency and banking have been so repeatedly and so ably investigated by select committees of both Houses of Parliament, that an accumulation of speculative opinions here would be of little value, and because the bank returns have furnished them with the necessary statistical information. They have therefore availed themselves of the labors of those eminent statesmen and writers, who by general consent are looked up to as authorities on the subject.

The principles of currency and banking have been stated and proved in a few words, and without any extended variety of illustration.[21]

18. Evidence of J. H. Barlow, a Sydney merchant, *loc. cit.*, p. 28.
19. Darvall was educated at Eton and Trinity College, Cambridge; he practiced law in London and in Sydney after his arrival in 1839. He was a member of the first Senate of Sydney University. A. W. Martin and P. Wardle, *Members of the Legislative Assembly of New South Wales 1856–1901* (Canberra, 1959), p. 54.
20. In Darvall, Wentworth, and Holroyd the Committee included graduates of Cambridge, Oxford, and Edinburgh Universities.
21. "Report from the Select Committee on Currency and Banking," *Votes and*

The committee outlined the history of money and banking in Britain, noting the gradual assumption by the state of control over coinage, and it predicted that government authority over all paper currency was an inevitable development. "That reasons, equally cogent with those which have given the control of the metallic currency to the State, demand its interference with the paper currency also, your Committee feel fully persuaded." The committee defended the principle of state management of note-issue not alone on grounds of greater safety to note-holders, but also because of the need to limit business fluctuations which currently caused or at least were augmented by variation in commercial bank circulation.

. . . the increase or the diminution of a bank-note circulation has the same effect upon the value and convertibility of property, and influences trade in all its countless ramifications, in precisely the same way as an increase or diminution of the metallic currency would do were there no paper currency in existence. In the latter case, with the withdrawal of money from any country, the property of that country must fall in value, and become less convertible than before; and the converse is equally unquestionable.

So long, therefore, as this power of expanding or contracting the currency of a country is left to private speculators, so long will the prosperity of that country be constantly liable to the most violent and disastrous fluctuations. There must always be, in such a state of things, a probability of trade and speculation being unduly stimulated at one period and unduly depressed at another. An infinite number of unforseen causes may, at any moment, induce private banking institutions to expand their issues to an extent wholly disproportioned to the metallic capital of the country, and thus bring about a state of feverish excitement, the sure forerunner of a fatal collapse.[22]

The 1852 committee concluded that "To prevent a recurrence of these evils . . . a national bank is absolutely necessary." Government notes would be backed fully by specie and would be legal tender except at their source where they would be

---

Proceedings of the Legislative Council of New South Wales, 1852, p. 1. Geoffrey Eager stated in the Legislative Assembly in 1866 that "although this document bears the signature of Mr. [T. A.] Murray, it was, in fact, drawn up by my honorable friend Mr. Martin." James Thomson, ed., *The Financial Statements of the Colonial Treasurers of New South Wales* (Sydney, 1881), p. 190.

22. *Ibid.,* p. 2.

redeemable in gold. For existing commercial banks the committee recommended restriction and control: "That they should be confined to the only legitimate business of bankers—the dealing in and not the creating of money—appears to your Committee to be almost self-evident. If their functions can in any way be so limited without a direct prohibition, it would be desirable to adopt that course." Although the committee was influenced profoundly by the Bank Act of 1844, it did not condone the issue of any currency that was not fully gold-backed as were some Bank of England notes. Costs of a national bank would be paid "on the establishment of the mint in Sydney, either by a seigniorage sufficient to support both establishments, or by making the bank the means of collecting the revenue from the goldfields by compelling the whole produce of those fields to be sold to the bank at a fixed rate."[23] Like their counterparts in Britain during this period, would-be colonial bank reformers were concerned principally with strengthening the currency and not with the safety of depositors or the loan policies of private institutions.

Despite the prevalence of arguments for the introduction of government notes in New South Wales, no action was taken during the gold period. Later in the 1850's occasional demands for a "national bank" were voiced again, but were mixed with suggestions for abolition of the commercial banking system and were not accompanied by reasonable arguments as had been their predecessors.[24] E. W. Ward, reporting on the operation of the Sydney Mint in 1859, indicated one possible reason why discontent with monetary institutions diminished in the 1850's. The mint, he explained, had been able automatically to act in part as a central bank, and in particular almost to eliminate fluctuations in the exchange rate of Australian for British sterling, or more precisely, to maintain stability in Sydney of the price of bills of exchange drawn on London. Before the

23. *Ibid.*
24. See for example James Norton, *Government and Taxation of the Colony* (Sydney, 1856), p. 8.

discovery of gold in the colonies and establishment of the mint the bill rate varied seasonally and to the disadvantage of staple producers. During wool marketing periods, when the supply of bills on London from sales of wool was greatest in Sydney, the demands of colonial importers for bills exhibited little seasonality and remained at normal levels. The price of bills consequently fell, and wool-growers who needed cash were forced to sacrifice bills at a discount and with an effective loss on their product. Immediately after the discovery of gold and formation of the mint, gold-producers exported gold to London with little seasonality in flow, and provided thereby a supply of bills on London to match importers' increased demands for payments on miners' supplies. However, when wool sales began in Sydney and the price of bills on London fell as a result of the first wool exports, gold-producers found it more advantageous to bring gold to the Sydney mint for local coinage than to ship to London in return for depreciated bills. By trading with the mint when wool was brought to market, gold-producers relieved pressure on the bill market in Sydney just as wool-producers were increasing it, and as a result wool-growers received nearly full value in local currency for bills on London. Ward described this mint activity, which amounted to an automatic monetary adjustment of the exchange rate, with clarity, perception, and all the statistics he could muster. He wrote in part:

While the wool season lasted, the Mint continued to receive large quantities of gold from Victoria, as well as from New South Wales. At its close, about the end of January, the market and the Mint again came into competition, and the extraordinary demands on the Mint ceased. Since that period the Mint has operated in a similar manner in maintaining the value of gold, and of wool, as well as that of drafts against exports to the Mother Country. . . . Thus the influence of the Mint has been to reduce these fluctuations [of prices], year by year, until they have become insignificant. I have not sufficient data to estimate with accuracy the gain secured to the producing interests of the Colony, by the limit thus put to the fluctuation of the exchange. Assuming that the depression of the rate during the wool season has been reduced 4 per cent., and that but one-half of the exports are drawn against as soon as shipped, the saving to the producing class on the single article wool, of which about £1,200,000 is annually exported, amounts to £24,000 per annum.[25]

Ward suggested that his informal operations as a central banker might be extended and rendered even more valuable if the note-circulation of the colony, in addition to the coinage, were entrusted to his care roughly on the principles of the Peel Bank Act. He explained:

> That the Mint might act as I have stated, with the greatest effect, it should be connected with a note circulation, either of some existing bank, to which, for privileges conceded, the privilege of a legal circulation for their notes might be granted, or of a Government Bank of Issue, based on Bullion. . . . By this means a circulation of £500,000 could be maintained, the interest on which—£25,000 per annum—would be another source of Mint revenue. From these two sources the sum of £50,000 would be obtainable—or far more than sufficient to defray the expense of the bank, as well as of the Mint.[26]

Evidently Ward's proposal did not find favor.

Victoria. Although establishment of a mint in Sydney answered demands of many New South Wales banking critics, raw gold from Victoria had still to find a market either in Britain or in Sydney. Criticism of monetary conditions in Victoria was mobilized first by officers of the Bank of Victoria (which called itself "the sole banking institution in the Colony of a strictly local character") who hoped to obtain for their firm a position in the colony analogous to that of the Bank of England in Britain. In 1853, before a select committee formed to investigate a proposal that all government deposits be made with the Bank of Victoria in return for a loan to the government, John Matheson, Melbourne manager of the bank, argued that "the Government ought to exercise some control over the issue of notes when necessary," and that his institution might be used "as an engine to carry out their measures." Asked how he would have the government "interfere to check the improper issue of notes," he replied, "By compelling all banks of issue to keep a

25. "Sydney Branch of Royal Mint (Despatches and Reports Relative to Coinage at)," *Votes and Proceedings of the Legislative Assembly of New South Wales,* 1859–60, pp. 5 and 6.
26. *Ibid.,* p. 9.

proportionate amount of specie to their circulation; and I think the Government would be in a better position to control the currency by being connected with one bank only."[27] Hugh C. E. Childers, Victorian auditor general and later prominent British statesman, was one of the Bank of Victoria's strongest supporters. He hoped that, in light of extraordinary demands for public expenditures following the gold rushes, "the bank might act as the Bank of England has, and become the creditor of the public to a certain extent, or it might undertake the issue of debentures, and the management of a debt, arrangements which are exceedingly minute and complex, but which are peculiarly within the province of a bank." When questioned on the desirability of national banking in general, Childers replied: "As a principle, I am favorable to the policy of Sir Robert Peel's Currency Act, though I do not see that the regulation of the currency is involved in the present proposal; but, if the question is put to me generally, as to whether it would be advisable to establish the principles of that Act here, I should answer in the affirmative."[28] Childers had arrived at a conclusion reached by other legislators in new countries that a central monetary authority could become a valuable co-operating partner with the public treasury.[29] The select committee recommended finally that the Bank of Victoria be appointed "the sole depository of the Public Funds," in return for "a loan at interest from the Bank to the Treasury, to the extent of the average Public Deposits during the last twelve months. . . ."[30] The committee made no pronouncements about the desirability of state banking in any wider sense. A proposal for a central bank was discussed in the Victorian legislature during 1856, sponsored by Sir Charles Sladen, but came to nothing.

27. "Report from the Select Committee of the Legislative Council on Government Banking, together with the Proceedings of the Committee, and Minutes of Evidence," *Votes and Proceedings of the Legislative Council of Victoria*, 1853–54, questions numbered 175, 176, and 246.
28. *Ibid.*, questions numbered 552 and 559.
29. The Bank of Victoria's proposal, supported by Childers, was similar in spirit to a plan submitted to the Government of Canada in 1868 by the Bank of Montreal and endorsed by John Rose, then Minister of Finance. See my *Canadian Economic Thought*, p. 100.
30. "Report," unpaged.

Plans for establishment of the Sydney mint were viewed with some concern in Melbourne and stimulated discussion of plans for a local monetary authority. William Westgarth, a merchant, predicted correctly that because Sydney coins were not legal-tender in Britain, following Gresham's law, they would drive the more highly rated British coins from the colonies. The potential saving from having domestic currency coined locally, he added, was small. Westgarth acknowledged a debt to Captain Ward, Deputy Master of the Sydney mint, "for a variety of particulars regarding the probable cost of the mint Establishment, rates of seigniorage, powers of production, conditions as to legal tender, &c.," but Westgarth did not anticipate the important role the mint could play in stabilizing the exchange rate.[31]

Valentine Hellicar, another Melbourne resident, claimed in 1856 that Victoria had already an excess of coin and should not encourage, by making Sydney coins legal-tender, further retention of this "unproductive commodity." He wrote:

It is impossible to define with exactness what amount of circulating medium any country requires. It would appear to be governed generally by the population, and the amount of its internal trade; but what proportion it bears to these has never yet been satisfactorily shewn. Without attempting then to speculate upon the precise amount of gold currency wanted for this colony, I will venture, upon the data we have access to, to assert, that it is and has been not only abundantly but excessively supplied.[32]

Hellicar reported that during the previous four years, because of their active trade in bullion, Melbourne banks had maintained a startling average proportion of "specie on hand" to "notes in circulation" of 139.4 to 100.

By 1856 voices of new arrivals were heard in discussions of government banking in Victoria. J. Braché, a recently immigrated civil and mining engineer with experience in Europe and in America, explained to a legislative committee "on Gold" that Victoria needed badly a national bank patterned after either the

		31. William Westgarth, *Remarks upon the Proposed Branch of the Royal Mint about to be Commenced in Sydney* . . . (Melbourne, 1854), p. 3.
		32. *Coin and Currency: Being an Inquiry into the Probable Effect of Legalising as Currency the Coinage of the Sydney Mint* (Melbourne, 1856), p. 7.

Second Bank of the United States or the Bank of England. He claimed that "others" had convinced him of "the desirability of coming forward with the scheme." Braché contended that an additional colonial mint would not be worthwhile in itself, and he rejected objections to commercial bank profits on gold exports—"our gold occupies the same position as our wool. A profit must be realised by our merchants in buying wool here and having it shipped to and sold in England and other parts, to pay for the risk and trouble of shipping it. And similarly does this doctrine hold good with all other articles of trade. . . ."[33] He insisted that a government monetary institution should be designed principally to control private firms. Commercial banks, he claimed, had been responsible as note-issuing bodies for economic fluctuations of the early eighteen-fifties. "The whole population almost had, through the reckless credit system then prevalent through the example of the banks, been created into a body of gamblers and swindlers—a state of things that could not last, and of which the reaction must be at once sudden and severe." Braché proposed a government bank first of all as a currency reform measure:

to establish a banking system that would be really safe and beneficial to the community, it would be very desirable to confine the issue of paper to one source only. This, we believe, might be effected to a considerable extent by the establishment of a National Bank of Victoria. . . .[34]

But in addition he urged Victorians in the new situation of responsible colonial government and independence from New South Wales to issue irredeemable legal-tender notes as a financial measure. In an economy of rapid growth, he maintained, expansion of the money supply could finance public works and generate new employment without inflation. Braché illustrated the impatience and frustration of miners with what they considered was timid conservatism where bold imagination was required. He asked:

33. "Report from the Select Committee of the Legislative Council on Gold; together with the Proceedings of the Committee, Minutes of Evidence, and Appendix," *Votes and Proceedings of the Legislative Council of Victoria*, 1855–56, p. 54.
34. *Ibid.*

Why then should not our Government, under the New Constitution, follow the example of the British Parliament, and establish and support a bank which in this new country would have for its principal object the development of our vast natural resources? Railways are talked of and loans proposed for their execution; other reproductive public works are to be carried out; and why not use the vast capital which lies waste, and over which we shall have the control under the New Constitution, in the shape of the Crown Lands? Let the Government establish a Bank in connection with a National Mint and Assay Office, issue notes to be made a legal tender on the security of the Crown Lands, and the required capital will be created. Why pay interest on a loan when you have capital of your own lying idle and unemployed? Why incur a debt when you have boundless resources at hand? Why, I may ask, tax the people with interest to be paid to foreign bank shareholders and absentees, when there is an enormous capital lying useless for want of proper means being devised for its profitable investment?[35]

Braché's testimony in 1856 was evidence that in arguments for governmental banking, gold rushes had brought radicals, influenced by American and Continental ideas, to the side of the British Currency School. In particular to the case for a national bank, the explicit and powerful doctrine had been added that governmental manipulation of the money supply, in addition to altering income distribution and facilitating trade, could relieve unemployment and foster economic growth.

South Australia. Gold discoveries in Victoria and New South Wales caused monetary crises not in these colonies alone but in their smaller neighbors as well. As prospective miners streamed out of Adelaide to the gold fields, they withdrew coin from local banks to finance their adventures, and a multiple reduction in banknote circulation resulted. When, later, successful miners returned or directed remittances home, they bore nuggets and dust but little coin. As one South Australian explained some years afterward, the shortage of money by 1852 had become extremely serious:

35. *Ibid.* Braché acknowledged "the most valuable assistance" in preparing his statement "from Mr. Wm. Schultz, whose intimate acquaintance with the history of banking institutions I have found of great value."

crude gold, though easily saleable to the merchant was no legal tender at the banks, and bills, mortgage debts, &c. had to be paid. . . . It was a most extraordinary position, a Tantalus-like crisis, starvation in the midst of plenty, one that would have gladdened the heart of the political economist or Birmingham theoriser on the currency question. He would have rejoiced as the surgeon does over an interesting case.[36]

The solution was found in an emergency "bullion act" of 1852 authorizing assay operations to legitimize the new staple product as backing for bank currency. Gold was shaped into ingots of specified weight and quality which were made temporary legal-tender at an overvalued rate. Because the commodity employed thus as reserve happened to be gold, an aura of special respectability was given to the issue of what in fact were irredeemable notes.[37] A South Australian banker recounted thus a year after the event the deliberations which preceded the act:

The Chamber of Commerce met and considered the best remedy; a committee held a conference with the managers of the banks; and shortly there began to float on the public mind a scheme for a colonial mint, which was modified into a temporary measure for declaring assayed gold a legal tender. The Government, not estimating the difficulties of the colony so strongly as those who were urging this measure, delayed for a time acting upon this suggestion, and at first general and then legal difficulties were interposed, although at last [Governor] Sir Henry Young, urged by repeated solicitation and argument, took upon himself to recommend the Legislative Council to pass a law, which was accordingly done at one sitting, on 28th January, 1852, by which assayed gold was made a legal tender at 71s. per ounce.[38]

Opponents of the emergency bullion act were not slow in coming forward. Several merchants argued that the crisis should

36. Sir Arthur Blyth, "South Australia: Her Laws Relating to the Alienation of Agricultural Land, and Her Recent Industrial Progress," *Proceedings of the Royal Colonial Institute*, XI (1879–80), 182.
37. Governor Young explained in detail the conditions which made the Bullion Act of 1852 desirable in a letter to Lord Grey in 1851, reprinted in C. M. H. Clark, *Select Documents in Australian History 1851–1900* (Sydney, 1955), pp. 85–88.
38. *South Australia and the Gold Discoveries* (London, 1853), p. 10. Robert Torrens attributed "this able and useful tract" to the London Manager of the South Australian Bank. *Political Economy and Representative Government in Australia* (London, 1855), p. 5 n.

be left to run its course as a form of national purgative, and others insisted that newly assayed gold would simply leave the colony without increasing the note-circulation. Robert Torrens writing in London in 1855 remarked that the controversy generated in Adelaide was "somewhat analogous to that which had occurred in this country forty years before, when the restriction upon cash payments disturbed the equality between bank notes and coin. The question of depreciation, however, was neither so simple nor so easy of solution in Australia as it had been in England."[39] Torrens' son, R. R. Torrens, was South Australian Treasurer during passage of the act and was a leading exponent of the action taken.[40] Another observer writing in Britain described the controversy and concomitant developments as follows:

Thus in the early stages of the measure were parties divided as to its utility and worth. They argued upon old theories of political economy and abstract opinions of the depreciation and appreciation of the currency. The actual and substantial effects, however, rapidly brought the question to an issue. Gold was immediately deposited, when the Assay-office was once opened, and it was shortly perceived that a change had commenced, that those who anticipated only a disorganisation of the currency would find the best practical results following the measure. Instead of losing, the colony received large and ample resources, and trade again assumed an active and a healthy condition. What, in fact, was the working of the Act but an exact counterpart of the system adopted in this country?[41]

Even enthusiastic exponents viewed the South Australian bullion act as an emergency measure, and although the legislation was credited with having averted severe deflation and unemployment they were unwilling to sanction a permanent arrange-

39. *Political Economy and Representative Government in Australia*, p. 42. Torrens realized that a colonial mint would stabilize the price paid for bills of exchange on London in Sydney, and predicted the development that Ward described in detail several years later. See above p. 143. Professor Lionel Robbins has summarized the contents of Torrens' pamphlet in *Robert Torrens and the Evolution of Classical Economics* (London, 1958), pp. 344–45.
40. Extracts from R. R. Torrens' pamphlet *On the Present Effects and Future Tendencies of the Bullion Act* are appended to his father's tract, *op. cit.*, pp. 55–70. The criticisms of B. Herschel Babbage, another colonial representative of a prominent English family, are also appended pp. 70–75, with the younger Torrens' reply, pp. 75–82.
41. *South Australia and the Gold Discoveries*, p. 14.

ment which, it was believed, would permit an unrestrained issue of notes. In a desperate situation, South Australians had contrived a primitive central bank; with the return of normal conditions they were unwilling to continue this departure from orthodoxy.

Consolidation and Growth in the Colonies

New South Wales. Proposals for a government bank of issue, patterned either after the Bank of England or the Bank of the United States, continued to come from colonists at intervals throughout the nineteenth century. Financial crises were usually the excuse for renewed discussion. During the depression in the 1860's, the idea received particularly influential support. A select committee of the Legislative Assembly in 1865–66 on the "Present State of the Colony," under the chairmanship of Henry Parkes, heard extensive testimony from distinguished legislators in favor of a "National Bank." Edward Deas Thomson, last colonial secretary before responsible government, began with an apology: "I have on many occasions thought the subject over, but my ideas upon it have never assumed any very definite shape." Yet he was vehement in defense of Ricardo's writings on banking, and he read at length to the committee a sixteen point plan for a "National Bank" from "a posthumous paper by Ricardo, worked out by him with great care and thought. . . ."[42] Deas Thomson concluded regretfully: "The difficulty of establishing a Government Bank of Issue has always been the vested interests you would have to interfere with." Terrence A. Murray, currently president of the Legislative Council and in the 1850's chairman of an earlier select committee which favored central banking, again urged establishment of "a National Bank of Issue, in connection with the Mint." He was, he said, "contemplating a movement in that direction in the Legislative Council." Murray

42. "Progress Report from the Select Committee on the Present State of the Colony," *Votes and Proceedings of the Legislative Assembly of New South Wales,* 1865–66, p. 20. Deas Thomson read from "Plan for the Establishment of a National Bank," in J. R. McCulloch, ed., *The Works of David Ricardo, Esq., M. P.* (London, 1846), pp. 507–9.

did not always grasp the implications of his proposals and was easily confused by questioning. When asked to elaborate and defend principles of state banking, he preferred to fall back on references to authorities. He said: "There is of course a diversity of opinion upon the subject, but I think the views of Sir Robert Peel, Mr. M'Culloch, Mr. Norman, Lord Overstone, and Colonel Torrens, in 1844, were correct, and that the Bank Act of that year is sound in principle, and that principle should be acted on in this Colony, and in part in all the British Colonies."[43] Members of the select committee showed considerable interest in a proposal of Lord Sydenham, presented as Governor General of Canada in 1841, for a "Provincial Bank" in the North American colonies.[44] They quizzed several witnesses about the plan, but none was familiar with it.

Geoffrey Eager, Colonial Treasurer of New South Wales, made a lengthy appeal for a "Government Bank of Issue" when delivering his financial statement in 1866. He explained that "many individual members of the House have pressed it on the notice of the Government," and he felt compelled, therefore, to express his own views. Eager examined the course of state bank agitation from the beginning of the 1850's, and he argued that throughout the period commercial banks had been guilty repeatedly of causing financial crises. Government was more than justified, he insisted, in demanding controls:

what was desirable in 1852 is pre-eminently desirable at the present moment. If the Committee asks my reasons, they are these—because a crisis is impending, nay—has begun—and will, if not checked in time, go on to an alarming extent in this colony. And why? Because the banks have suddenly contracted their paper accomodation. For a long time past the banks in this colony have paid enormous dividends to proprietors by unduly stimulating the public credit; and after pushing it with great vigour for several years, there is now a sudden collapse, because the operations based on credit are now required to be realised by cash payments.[45]

43. "Progress Report from the Select Committee on the Present State of the Colony," *loc. cit.*, pp. 39–42.
44. *Ibid.*, pp. 21 and 55. For a discussion of Sydenham's plan, see my *Canadian Economic Thought*, pp. 77–79.
45. Geoffrey Eager, "Financial Statement made 27th September, 1866," in James Thomson, ed., *The Financial Statements of the Colonial Treasurers of New South Wales* (Sydney, 1881), pp. 189–91.

A depressed economy, Eager asserted, "imposes upon the Government of to-day or to-morrow the necessity of doing in this country, on a small scale, that which is done by the Bank of England on a large scale. It is high time for the Government to interfere, and to take into its own hands that right of creating and regulating the currency, with which it has improperly parted."[46] The gold mines of the colonies, Eager concluded as had his predecessors, could make possible a unique margin of safety for central bank operations.

The idea of reproducing in miniature the Bank of England in New South Wales, although never adopted, did not die. During the depression of the 1890's, defenders came forward in strength yet again. For example, E. Vethick observed in 1891 that government balances deposited by the Treasury with commercial banks were a source of dangerous instability, and he called for a "National Bank" to act as government financial agent, to issue all currency, and without usurping private business to assist commercial banks in emergencies. He suggested that a central bank in Australia should follow Currency School principles more closely even than the Bank of England itself:

> Although the working lines of such an institution as an Australian National Bank might very well be modelled to a great extent upon those of the Bank of England, yet, bearing in mind our democratic tendency out here, it would be almost necessary to insist on straiter lines. Dealing with private customers, as is done in exceptional cases by the Bank of England, should be stringently forbidden, as unduly interfering with the rights of other banks, and as, moreover, introducing the thin edge of a wedge which might in time attain the upper hand.[47]

Advocates of state banking had an opportunity to present their case in detail to a select committee of the Legislative Assembly which reported in 1893. Robert Osbiston, editor of the *Journal of the Institute of Bankers of New South Wales,* claimed that if the Bank of England were copied in the colony Sydney could become the London of the Pacific. An immigrant of only four years' residence, Osbiston justified thus his defense of British precedent:

46. *Ibid.*, p. 192.
47. E. Vethick, "A National Bank," *Sydney Quarterly Magazine,* 1891, p. 14.

I may say that I have been compelled to take the Bank of England as a type, not from any English prejudices, but from a careful comparison of that Bank with other institutions—such as the Bank of France, the Bank of Italy, and the State Bank of Russia. They are all impure as compared with the Bank of England. America, as you know, has a system of National Banks. I have taken the Bank of England as a type, because it is the purest type.[48]

Francis Kirkpatrick, Under Secretary for Finance and Trade, also favored a national bank, but only in the event of federation among the colonies. The committee examined and considered a variety of specific schemes. Eager's proposal in 1866 was reprinted in its entirety, and William Kapos, United States Consul in Sydney, described and recommended the American National Banking System. Several witnesses were remarkably misinformed in their evidence, as for example one who recommended as models of central banking the "National Bank of the United States" and the "Dominion Bank of Canada," neither of which, of course, existed.[49] The committee reported finally that private commercial banks had been guilty of undesirable malpractice, and that the state should assume control of the currency. It recommended formation of a comprehensive "Government Bank of Issue" operated by semi-autonomous commissioners to provide currency, to transact government financial business, and, by accepting deposits and making loans, to act as a competitor of the commercial banks. The most remarkable feature of this committee's very competent report was the close attention paid to banking theory and to reputable authorities. An appended "list of books and other publications bearing on the question of banking" included works by Macleod, Mill, Overstone, Poor, Sumner, McCulloch, Gilbart, and others. The thirty-eight page Final Report was thoroughly documented, and on specific points contained excellent summaries of "literature of the subject."

48. "Progress Report from the Select Committee on Post Office Savings Bank—National Bank; together with the Proceedings of the Committee, Minutes of Evidence, and Appendix," *Votes and Proceedings of the Legislative Assembly of New South Wales*, 1892–93, p. 31.
49. "Second Progress Report from the Select Committee on Post Office Savings Bank—National Bank; together with the Proceedings of the Committee, Minutes of Evidence, and Appendix," *Votes and Proceedings of the Legislative Assembly of New South Wales*, 1892–93, pp. 20–26.

Quotations from Mill, Macleod, Daniel Webster, and Alexander Hamilton were used to particularly good effect.[50]

W. H. Gocher, writing in support of the select committee's recommendations indicated the considerable emotional heat that was generated by the controversy. He declared that government had a positive obligation to guard the public from actions of irresponsible commercial banks—those "gambling pawnshops." "The State," he wrote, "has a just and perfect right to look after the monies of the people, and to protect them from these closing-up machines, which of late have sent so many to the lunatic asylums, and caused many more to commit suicide."[51] A "National Bank" plan was adopted by the Labour Party in 1891, and in 1894 became a plank in the party's important "fighting platform."[52]

Mounting sympathy for both the monetary and financial advantages of state banking was indicated in the 1890's by discussion before the Australian Economic Association at Sydney. A member in 1892 recommended increased public works to combat depression, and he added: "So long as the works are reproductive, it is only necessary to issue State-stamped paper money, backed by the credit of the State. . . ."[53] As the crisis worsened even several banker members of the Association conceded that government should control the note issue, at least so that "the Socialistic 'fad' of a National Bank may safely, therefore, be relegated to the dim and very distant future."[54]

By 1895 the Australian Economic Association was prepared to consider seriously such wildly radical schemes as a plan for irredeemable "greenback" notes.[55] R. L. Nash, financial editor of the Sydney *Daily Telegraph*, was able with impunity to advise the Institute of Bankers of New South Wales that note-issue

50. "Final Report from the Select Committee on Post Office Savings Bank—National Bank," *Votes and Proceedings of the Legislative Assembly of New South Wales*, 1892–93.
51. W. H. Gocher, *Australia, the Light of the World* (Sydney, n. d.), p. 2.
52. W. G. Spence, *Australia's Awakening* (Sydney, 1909), pp. 235, and 597–630.
53. J. P. Morice, "Surplus Labour," *Australian Economist*, II (1890–93), 273.
54. Comments by J. T. Walker, *ibid.*, III (1893–94), 331; and Reginald J. Black, "The Banking Crisis and its Lessons," *ibid.*, pp. 319–26.
55. Colonel Bell, "Some Unrecognised Economic Truths," *ibid.*, IV (1894–97), 585–89.

privileges should be reserved for government, a declaration which might have entailed personal peril only a few years earlier.[56] Also in 1895 Robert Osbiston reported to the Institute that both bankers and the public were becoming converted to, at least, some form of a "general reserve."[57] Nevertheless, the approach of Federation and a gradual return to prosperity during the late 1890's submerged state banking proposals once more.

Victoria. In Melbourne during 1860, a member of the Legislative Assembly, Archibald Michie, resurrected the Childers plan of six years before for a central bank. He explained: "the idea is not dead. Look into Mr. Ricardo's Works, and you will find ably and distinctly sketched his idea of a national bank, in which the state should have the profit of the banking operations. . . . I have revived the idea; let others work it out to practical issues."[58] Beginning in the 1870's James Mirams, another legislator, recalled the agitation of the 1850's and repeated Michie's proposal. In 1878 he asked for state bank notes, backed by government securities, to replenish commercial bank circulation depleted during a recent panic. A system of private banks, he complained, guarded most carefully the banks' own welfare, rather than the public good; in the important matter of note-issue, government control was essential. "Seeing, then, that the business of these institutions must, and will, be carried on, for and in the interests of the shareholders, it is idle to expect, where those interests clash with the benefit of the community at large, that the latter should receive the first consideration, even if it should obtain any at all."[59] Mirams discussed intelligently the relative merits of convertible and irredeemable notes, citing works by Overstone, Ricardo, Francis Walker, Mill, and Adam Smith. He concluded: "the question as to whether the notes issued should be partly of one kind and partly of another, is subordinate to the main ques-

56. R. L. Nash, "Combination in Coin Reserves," *Journal of the Institute of Bankers of New South Wales,* IV (1895), 319–38.
57. "The Theory of a General Reserve," *ibid.,* pp. 55–56.
58. Archibald Michie, *Victoria Suffering a Recovery: A Lecture* (Melbourne, 1860), p. 19.
59. James Mirams, "A National Bank of Issue for Victoria," *Melbourne Review,* III (1878), 292.

tion, of establishing the bank. The form or character of the notes is a matter of detail, involving the question of profit, more or less, which may be left for future consideration."[60] Mirams argued that a government bank with exclusive note-issuing authority could direct loans particularly to depressed areas and currently to small farmers and municipal governments. "Beyond this, every branch of business now engaged in by the banks would be left to them as they are at present."[61] Mirams continued to press the case for a state bank as late as the 1890's, taking pride in his reputation as "an acknowledged authority upon the question."[62]

Mirams' closest ally in demands for a national bank on the Bank of England model was R. Manuel, another radical Victorian politician. Manuel claimed in 1878 that he had espoused state banking as early as the 1850's and had even harangued miners on this theme at the gold fields of Ballarat in 1862.[63] Manuel leaned heavily on Ricardo for authority, on one occasion quoting an uninterrupted ten pages, but he did not hesitate to modify Currency School pronouncements. Specifically he proposed formation of "The National State Bank of Issue of Victoria," to have as "capital" all the unsold crown lands, annual government revenues from all sources, and the assets of the government savings bank.[64] Much more than Mirams, Manuel must have alienated potential supporters by extravagant claims. Apparently, he did not appreciate the relation between volume of money in circulation and the price level, and he called for unrestrained issue of government notes.[65]

60. *Ibid.*, p. 300.

61. *Ibid.*, p. 303.

62. James Mirams, *The Present Depression Its Cause and Cure* (Melbourne, 1892). Mirams described the controversy surrounding his advocacy of a state bank, and reprinted some of his utterances on the subject in *A Generation of Victorian Politics: Personal Records* (n. p., n. d).

63. R. Manuel, *The Present and Pending Crisis: A Lecture "On the Necessity and Advantages of Establishing a State Bank of Issue"* (Melbourne, 1878), pp. 3 and 8.

64. *Ibid.*, p. 14.

65. A difference between the views of Mirams and Manuel was indicated at a Conference of the National Reform League in Melbourne during 1879. Mirams proposed as a plank in the League's platform "a national bank of issue." Unsatisfied, Manuel insisted in a suggested amendment "That it was desirable to establish a national bank of issue embracing all branches of banking business." See "A National Bank of Issue," *Australasian Insurance and Banking Record*, III (1879), 204.

In 1871 an author under the pseudonym "Sigma" proposed creation of a National Bank solely on the ground that such an institution could restore and sustain full employment. He was bitterly critical of the commercial banks, which he believed were largely responsible for distress among the working class. He recounted: "after repeatedly musing on this momentous theme, during periods of enforced idleness, I registered a vow that, when the proper time came, a crusade should be commenced against *fontes que origines mali*, these pregnant sources of evil to the working many, for the benefit of the favored few. That time is now."[66] He accused banks of aiding land speculators, of exporting domestic capital, of encouraging rapacious middlemen, and finally of creating "a rapidly spreading feeling of insecurity and distrust, calculated, if not checked in time, to extinguish the last spark of that enterprise for which we were once becoming famous."[67] Commercial bankers, he insisted, had been responsible for rejection of Childers' scheme in Victoria and of Eager's plan in New South Wales. Sigma proposed only that a National Bank accept savings accounts, the proceeds of which would be used for public works, and assume responsibility for the note issue. Current account banking would be left with private firms. He insisted: "Let private enterprise have full scope, but let not the public be compelled to use money of doubtful value, and let the individuals constituting the public have a place of absolute security in which to accumulate their savings—neither advantage being obtainable at present."[68]

Colonel E. W. Ward, long a proponent of central banking when deputy master of the Sydney Mint, continued his campaign from a new position as head of the Melbourne Mint. He advised the Governor of Victoria in 1874: "the Mint and Treasury in the Colony should jointly discharge the duties, in respect to the circulation of a Government note, which in England are those of the Mint and the issue department of the Bank of England in

66. Sigma, *Money: How the Banks Make it Scarce and Dear! The Remedy! The Banks and their Stability!* (Melbourne, 1871), p. i.
    67. *Ibid.*, p. 12.
    68. *Ibid.*, p. 13.

respect to the Bank of England note."[69] Again Ward's ambitions came to naught.

Like most other reforms, plans for a central bank received greatest support during periods of crisis and depression. Yet proposals for a colonial imitation of the Bank of England did not generate wild enthusiasm even at the worst of times. Arguments in defense of the proposed new institution were generally cautious and well documented by citation of authorities and by reference to the experience of the "old country." From the tone of the writings it appears that Anglophilia, and in some cases homesickness, were elements in controversy. For example, in 1879 William Smith published a detailed plan of a "National Bank for Victoria" which was based word for word on the Bank of England charter. He used the works of Bonamy Price as guide, and he concluded "the National Bank would at once be like its great prototype, the safest institution in the country, and be only a bank of reserve, aid, and supply, controlling nothing, itself controlled by circumstances."[70]

Urquhart MacPherson in 1881 bolstered a scheme for a central bank by tracing banking through history to its triumphant culminations in Peel's Act of 1844 and to a lesser extent in foundation of the Bank of France. He conceded that European practice should be amended in minor respects for Australian conditions, in particular to permit loans for long-term development projects.[71] In a similar vein J. H. Brooke, in 1885, submitted to the Victorian Government a detailed plan for a direct colonial adaptation of the Bank of England.[72] In 1886 Charles H. Pearson, former Oxford don and currently Minister of Education, bearded that lions' den, the Bankers' Institute of Australasia, to propose with

69. "Royal Mint," *Votes and Proceedings of the Legislative Assembly of Victoria*, 1874, p. 5.
70. William Smith, *Paper for the Time: How to Found a National Bank in Victoria, Based on a Sound and Convertible Currency, like the Bank of England* (Melbourne, 1879), p. 17.
71. Urquhart MacPherson, "Commerce and Banking," *Melbourne Review*, VI (1881), 82–96.
72. Brooke's proposal was included as Appendix K of "Report of Royal Commission Appointed to Consider the Desirability of Establishing a State Bank and Royal Mint; together with Minutes of Proceedings, Evidence, Synopses, and Appendices," *Proceedings of the Parliament of South Australia*, 1889.

singular bravery formation of a central bank. He concluded that: "a National Bank carrying on a sound business—that is, with a large metallic reserve, and with little or none of its money locked up in securities not easily negotiable, may contribute powerfully to carry a State over a crisis of exceptional danger."[73] Despite these eloquent appeals the editor of the *Imperial Review* at Melbourne was able to report in 1886 that after the failures of Childers and Sladen the state bank "scheme was taken up by people who have always been looked upon as visionaries. It is never heard of at all nowadays."[74]

The serious depression which struck the colonies early in the 1890's afforded stimulus for revival of the state bank idea in Victoria as well as in New South Wales. In Melbourne as in Sydney, a few commercial bankers even gave qualified approval to the scheme. When the worst of the crisis approached in 1892, a member of the Melbourne Bankers' Institute noted wistfully that a "bankers' bank" would be a comforting source of emergency cash, and the Institute itself listened respectfully when Carl Pinschof, Consul for Austria-Hungary, recommended creation of a central reserve pool.[75] At the height of the panic in 1893, the *Australasian Insurance and Banking Record*, previously opposed unalterably to a central bank, conceded that such an institution would be useful at present. A leader in the *Record* said: "The question of a Central bank, to transact the official business of the colony and issue notes on an authorised basis, has, since the banking crisis, been discussed. No doubt such a measure would, if conducted on the basis on which the Bank of England, as regards Government and other transactions, is managed, be of advantage to banking concerns particularly. . . ."[76]

The vision of government currency as a cure for unemploy-

73. Charles H. Pearson, "National Credit as a Factor in Politics," *Australasian Insurance and Banking Record*, X (1886), 593.
74. "The Country Bankers," *Imperial Review*, October, 1886, pp. 73–75.
75. G. H. M., "Correspondence: A Bankers' Bank," *Bankers' Magazine and Journal of the Bankers' Institute of Australasia*, VI (1892–93), 929–30; Carl Pinschof, "Our Financial Organisation and the Present Crisis," *ibid.*, 1004–5, 1101–2, and 1125–29.
76. XVII (1893), 668.

ment had widespread appeal, as indicated by the fact that in 1893 "certain electors of Bairnsdale" petitioned the Legislative Assembly "that a State Bank of Issue for the Colony of Victoria may be established without delay, under such regulations as in the wisdom of the Assembly may be decided upon."[77] In the depths of the slump in 1894, the Commercial Travellers' Association heard Benjamin Hoare, a journalist and noted protectionist, cite Macleod, Smith, Ricardo, Peel, and Mill, making a case for "A State Bank of Issue" as the solution for the prevailing "stagnation."[78] Only government could "restore the wage fund," Hoare insisted, by placing money in circulation with expenditures on public works financed through a state bank. "There is a magic power in money," he said, "so long as it does not stagnate. Let it but live and move, and it is a miracle worker. Bury it, and it is a corpse." In 1895 a similar exponent, James Gray, quoted Leland Stanford, Herbert Spencer, and Macleod in another confused attempt to prove that a "state bank" could "give the unemployed constant work" and "relieve ratepayers, and the community generally, from the grasp of the 8 to 10 per cent usurers."[79]

A result of the general discussion of central banking during the depression was a Royal Commission appointed "to inquire into and report as to the question of the establishment of a State Bank. . . ." The commissioners consulted relevant literature and took evidence from "gentlemen possessing financial experience, and others having special knowledge," including Hoare, Pinschof, and Moreton Frewen, who claimed particular familiarity with central banking in other countries.[80] The commissioners added, as an appendix to their report, an article from the Melbourne *Age* by John Ross summarizing classical monetary thought. Although not unanimous in their conclusions, a major-

77. *Votes and Proceedings of the Legislative Assembly of Victoria*, 1893, p. 4.
78. Benjamin Hoare, "A State Bank of Issue and Its Uses," *Bankers' Magazine and Journal of the Bankers' Institute of Australasia*, VII (1893–94), 779.
79. James Gray, *The Labour Problem, or Social Salvation for Victoria* (Brighton, 1859), p. 15.
80. The Commissioners considered Henry Dunning Macleod "the leading authority on that branch of economic science which deals with banking and credit in all its forms," and they reprinted sizeable selections from his works. "Report of the Royal Commission on State Banking," *Papers Presented to the Parliament of Victoria*, 1895–96, pp. v–xiii.

ity of the commissioners recommended "that it would be desirable in the interests of the country that a State Bank should be established in Victoria." The institution they proposed would be formed by an amalgamation of two existing government savings banks, and would have "Banking" and "Issue" departments. It would possess exclusive note-issue powers, but would depart from Bank of England precedent by permitting unlimited circulation backed to the extent of twenty-five per cent in gold. Convertibility into legal-tender specie, the commissioners explained, would guarantee satisfactory operation of the international gold flow mechanism:

> The provision that it is compulsory on the part of the Issue Department, at its office, to pay all notes in gold supplies the means required to keep the notes at par, it being self-evident that if there is a discount on the notes holders will hasten to convert them into gold. This operation will continue until equilibrium is restored, provided that meanwhile further issues are stopped.[81]

The commission reprinted with approval the report of a meeting in Sydney of bankers from several colonies at which delegates expressed willingness to part with the note-issue privilege in return for assurance from government of emergency assistance. The commissioners hastened to add that such a bargain "would be in accordance with the views of economists and financial authorities, and also with the practice of the Bank of England."[82] The evident possibility of proximate colonial federation together with diminishing enthusiasm for reform after the crisis passed discouraged the Victorian government from taking action on the commission's report. Later in the 1890's discussion of a state bank became more and more in terms of an issuing authority for the new nation.[83]

South Australia. "The Desirability of Establishing a State Bank and Royal Mint" in South Australia was investigated by a Royal

81. *Ibid.,* p. ix.
82. *Ibid.*
83. See for example J. T. Walker, "The Federation of British Australasia: A Sketch from a Political and An Economic Point of View," *Report of the Seventh Meeting of the Australasian Association for the Advancement of Science held at Sydney, 1898,* pp. 905–6. See also Waldemar Bannow, *The Colony of Victoria Socially and Materially* (Melbourne, 1896), pp. 174–77.

Commission in 1889 by questioning with thoroughness South Australians, citizens of the other colonies, and "gentlemen representing the Governments of Germany, America, and New Zealand, present in Victoria in connection with the Centennial Exhibition." "Statements, reports and books" also were consulted. Lavington Glyde, a former colonial treasurer, told the commission that he had pioneered a state bank movement in South Australia and had even drafted but not submitted a national bank bill in 1874.[84] Ebenezer Cooke, Commissioner of Audit, and Henry Grainger, a "Financial Agent," testified that by increasing "confidence" and lowering costs of state debt a national bank would benefit both government and the public. James Mirams told of his unceasing campaign in Victoria, and he maintained even that "If Ricardo's maxims were followed there would be no fear of political corruption."[85] Detailed evidence was presented to illustrate the progress of government banking in New Zealand, Ceylon, British India, Germany, the Argentine Republic, France, and the United States. Significant documents related to state banking, including the New South Wales Select Committee Report of 1852 and Eager's plan of 1866, were reprinted. In their own report the commissioners hinted that the plethora of material which faced them was, in part, the reason why they did not propose establishment of a state bank. They concluded:

The question of establishing a Government bank has so wide a scope, and involves such exceedingly grave issues—upon which very few financial experts or students of political economy are as yet agreed—that we are unable to recommend the adoption of the proposition "That a Government bank should at once be established." We have no example or experience such as might be supposed to be afforded by the existence of a State bank in full development under conditions precisely similar to those that pertain to this province.[86]

As "preliminary steps in the direction of financial reform," the commissioners recommended that increased responsibilities be

84. "Report of Royal Commission Appointed to Consider the Desirability of Establishing a State Bank and Royal Mint; together with Minutes of Proceedings, Evidence, Synopses, and Appendices," *Proceedings of the Parliament of South Australia*, 1889. "The Incorporating Clauses of the Hon. Lavington Glyde's Bill Relating to the Public Debt Loans, and Establishment of a Government Bank, as Drafted in 1874" is Appendix B.
85. *Ibid.*, p. xxxix.
86. *Ibid.*, p. v.

placed upon the Treasury, and in particular that an experiment be undertaken with an issue of convertible Treasury notes. No immediate action was taken in this direction, but the idea of central banking was kept alive through the 1890's.[87]

Tasmania and Queensland. In the smaller colonies, the evident practicality of central banking was considerably less than in New South Wales, Victoria, or South Australia. During the nineteenth century, moreover, the economies of the less populous colonies were not as suceptible to the intellectual stimuli of boom and bust, and they attracted a smaller stream of immigrants with reformist ideas. Nevertheless, a carefully reasoned appeal for a "National Bank" was presented in Tasmania as early as 1874 by an anonymous Hobart author who offered three reasons for the institution:

1st. Because of the profit to the community arising out of it.
2nd. Because of its absolute safety.
3rd. Because of the opportunity it affords of averting or mitigating a financial crisis.[88]

The author argued that, rather than risk experiment, the colony should follow the monetary example of the Mother Country. The Bank of England, he emphasized, had been particularly successful in mitigating hard times.

So slight are the causes influencing the laws of wealth, that when through over speculation exchange becomes unfavorable, and gold is exported in quantities from the country, it is considered a sufficient corrective for the Bank of England to raise her rate of interest upon advances, and contract her issue. It is the lever this establishment affords the English Government of acting upon the currency that has probably saved the British nation from the financial calamities that

87. W. G. Spence states that a "state bank" was on the South Australian Labour Party's platform in 1892. *Australia's Awakening* (Sydney, 1909), pp. 597–630. Another select committee in 1894 heard testimony that a "state bank" would cure unemployment. "Final Report of the Select Committee of the Legislative Council on the Unemployed Problem; together with Minutes of Proceedings and Appendices," *Parliamentary Papers of South Australia*, 1894, p. 5. A confused appeal for monetary reform at the end of the century, probably by a woman writing under a pseudonym, was John Law, *Imperial Credit* (Adelaide, 1899).
88. "A National Bank," *Quadrilateral*, 1874, p. 7.

have overtaken the United States of America. . . . The colonies afford a favorable field for the further elaboration of a system similar to the British.[89]

Like other colonists this author expected a long succession of benefits from a central bank. He wrote:

A bank formed upon such a system as that advocated above would afford the public a convenient and secure place of deposit, and a ready means of investing surplus capital at a moderate interest, besides being a source of profit to the community, and affording a great relief from taxation. It would give the regulation of the currency into the hands of the Government, instead of leaving it with private and irresponsible individuals; and it would also avert an insidious and growing evil, the accumulation of certain capital in the hands of a few, that rightly belongs, and should revert to the community.[90]

Following the lead of New South Wales and South Australia the Tasmanian Labour Party placed a state bank on its platform in 1896.[91] But as in the larger colonies, no action was taken in Tasmania to implement the plan.

In Queensland, government notes were issued as an emergency revenue measure in 1866 when the Treasury circulated convertible bills, holding a reserve of one-third in gold.[92] Desire for long-run currency reform had a small part in this action, and the issue had few supporters as a permanent arrangement.[93] The last Queensland notes were retired in 1869. During the 1890's a state bank became a labor cry as in the other colonies,[94] J. J. Kingsbury, a member of Parliament for North Brisbane, maintained in 1894 that unless an institution similar to the Bank of England were created quickly "the conflagration . . . may come soon." Changing metaphors, he warned: "Unless we drop our attitude of

89. *Ibid.*, p. 6.
90. *Ibid.*, p. 9.
91. W. G. Spence, *op. cit.*, pp. 597–630.
92. T. A. Coghlan, *Labour and Industry in Australia*, pp. 1183–84.
93. The matter was examined by a Queensland Select Committee in 1867. See "Report of the Select Committee on the Issue of Treasury Notes; together with the Proceedings of the Committee and Minutes of Evidence," *Votes and Proceedings of the Legislative Assembly of Queensland*, 1867.
94. See reprinted selection from *The Worker* [Brisbane], 20 March 1893, p. 3, in C. M. H. Clark, *Select Documents in Australian History 1851–1900* (Sydney, 1955), pp. 306–7.

laissez faire, the storm must break. I firmly believe this, and I go further and state that it will involve us all."[95]

An Irredeemable Paper Currency

Whereas during the nineteenth century an issue of redeemable notes by a government bank was proposed often by eminently cautious and otherwise conservative statesmen, support for inconvertible notes came almost exclusively from radicals, at first from the "lunatic fringe," and later from the far political left. At no time did government plans for redeemable notes become widely popular, but projects for irredeemable money were seldom even a respectable subject for dispute. Economic depressions were the occasion for both types of currency proposal, but while proponents of a central bank on the Bank of England model sought reform seriously and with reasonable hope of success, advocates of irredeemable notes acted more in protest and rebellion against the economic system than in expectation of actual change. Arguments for redeemable notes, examined above, generally were more closely reasoned and made better use of theory than did those discussed in this section.

Victoria. In Victoria proposals for irredeemable notes were made as early as the 1850's and then regularly during the late 1860's and 1870's when problems of adjustment following decline in gold-mining led to an exhaustive search for economic panaceas. For example, Joseph Macardy, a disgruntled immigrant banker, expounded repeatedly in the 1850's a confused plan for a "General Deposit Bank" to issue irredeemable deposit slips as cash.[96] Macardy railed against both the operations of private banks and schemes such as Michie's proposed state bank. In similar fashion, Richard Capper told a Melbourne audience in 1868 that Victoria

95. J. J. Kingsbury, *The Financial Position of the Colonies in Relation to Banking* (Brisbane, 1894), p. 12.
96. Joseph Macardy, *A Brief Glance at State and Commercial Banks, &c.* (Melbourne, 1856); *Money: Where Shall I Deposit it for Security and Income?* (Melbourne, 1858), *A Glance at State Banks, &c., &c.* (Melbourne, 1860).

could experience the prosperity of Britain during the post-Napoleonic period if only it would duplicate the Bank of England with suspended specie payments. Capper based his arguments for a national bank mainly on the expected ability of such an institution to maintain full employment. He explained:

Abundance of money creates employment for labour, and labour should add value to money expended, by increasing the sources of national wealth. Where you have banks that can only issue under certain restrictions, they are obliged to be careful, chiefly on account of the enormous foreign demand made upon them, through imports so far exceeding exports. This compels them at times to contract their issues, and withhold assistance from their customers; this makes money scarce, checks the career of labour and the productiveness of invested capital. So it is at present, my friends; and all should join to check this foreign growth of demand upon our productive industry. This can only be done by establishing a source of money supply that may give it without limit in time of need, for in this lies the secret of success.

In every country where commerce, manufacturing industries, agriculture, mining, etc., are carried on, a plentiful supply of money in circulation is required to keep the wheels of prosperity safe in motion on their onward course.[97]

During the 1870's and 1880's proposals for irredeemable notes were revived again in Victoria. John Ebenezer Goodwin in 1878 recommended "an inconvertible paper currency" as part of an extensive program of social reform.[98] In the same year an issue of "greenbacks" was rumored to be contemplated as an emergency measure by the government of the day.[99] Edward Pratt in 1879 presented one of the few relatively cautious cases for irredeemable notes. He argued that society generally could effect a substantial financial saving if inscribed paper replaced gold as the monetary medium. He claimed:

it is an ascertained fact that the bank note circulation in Victoria has not for many years fallen below £1,200,000. It may, therefore, be

97. Richard Capper, *A Question for Electors! Why Should We Go to England to Borrow Money? A Lecture* (Melbourne, 1868), pp. 8–9.
98. J. E. Goodwin, *Scientific Legislation; or the Theory of Calculated Labour Equivalents* (Melbourne, 1878), p. 37.
99. See Alfred Deakin, *The Crisis in Victorian Politics, 1879–1881: A Personal Retrospect*, edited by J. A. La Nauze and R. M. Crawford (Melbourne, 1957), p. 18 n.

safely asserted that this sum (the amount being fixed by Act of
Parliament) might be issued by the Government in inconvertible
notes without causing any inconvenience to the public, except that
the banks would find many of their notes returned to them.[100]

In the same spirit R. Murray Smith published in 1882 a defense
of John Law, the great Scots master of inconvertible notes, "one
of that wonderful race, alike among the most cautious and most
speculative of mankind, with whom financial studies have long
been a favourite pursuit; who, possibly from that paucity of
money in their own country which Law lamented and sought to
cure, are unwearied in the pursuit of it elsewhere—who are ready,
in that quest, to start to Patagonia or Pekin, Toronto or Timbuck-
too, at an hour's notice. . . ."[101]

By the late 1880's demands for either complete abolition of all
banking or a government issue of inconvertible notes had become
commonplace in extreme reform proposals of Victorian radicals.
For example, David Andrade, a prominent anarchist, suggested
that "cooperative factories" be empowered to issue legal tender
notes. He wrote: "A labor currency bearing no interest, resting
on no fixed basis, redeemable by either labor or product, and
issued on the joint security of the cooperation, must be inaugurated at an early stage of the factory's career."[102] James Edwards
about 1890 expressed thus the ill feeling he felt towards commercial bankers:

They think bushranging is too dangerous, burglary is not respectable
enough, to beg they are ashamed. Therefore they say, "Go to, let us
amalgamate and open a bank, and gull the people into the belief
that we are assisting them, while we at the same time will be enabled
to live in luxury and idleness, while they go out into all weathers

100. Edward Pratt, "Money in its Relation to the State," *Melbourne Review,*
IV (1879), 85.
101. R. Murray Smith, "A Financial Genius: John Law," *Melbourne Review,*
VII (1882), 56. Murray Smith's article was praised and reprinted in part in
the *Australasian Insurance and Banking Record,* VI (1882), 8.
102. David A. Andrade, *An Anarchist Plan of Campaign* (Melbourne, 1888),
unpaged. Andrade added: "On the back of each note, should be a clear, concise
exposition of the nature of equity and usury, profitmaking and the cost principle,
and the general economic objects of the cooperation. . . ." See also David A.
Andrade, *Our Social System, and How it Affects Those Who Work for their Living* (Melbourne, n. d.).

and toil from morning to night to provide for us first, and themselves afterwards, if there should be anything left."[103]

Edwards insisted: "sweep away banks, and you can afford to give the worker an advance of 30 per cent. . . ."[104] Statements such as these did not increase the respectability of irredeemable notes.

New South Wales. A detailed plan for inconvertible notes was presented in New South Wales as early as 1865. The anonymous author deplored effects on society of price fluctuations, and he cited Adam Smith, Mill, and Fawcett to show that government could gain both control of the price level and extra revenue by issuing legal tender paper to the amount of present bank circulation. He added: "The [Sydney] *Herald* may perhaps object that Mr. Mill and Professor Fawcett are strenous advocates of universal suffrage, and that therefore their opinions are not worth much. But it is not a matter of opinion at all. It is one of as strict logical demonstration as a proposition of Euclid, and two sides of a triangle are greater than the third, even when a radical says so." [105] However, inconvertible notes did not achieve any substantial popularity until adopted by some spokesmen for the labor movement during the 1880's and 1890's.

Radical and labor enthusiasm for government legal tender began as in Victoria with a general feeling of enmity towards banks, which were regarded as tools of oppressive employers. The basis of protest was largely circumstantial and emotional, but was influenced in part by socialist and Marxist theory.[106] After the great strikes and financial collapse of the early 1890's, labor

103. Jas. Edwards, *Topics for the Development of Freedom. The Evils of our Banking System. (Aristocratic Pawnshops)* (Melbourne, n. d.), pp. 5–6.
104. *Ibid.*, p. 7.
105. *A Proposal to Meet the Financial Difficulties of the Country by the Partial Adoption of An Inconvertible Paper Currency* (Sydney, 1865), p. 8.
106. See, for example, the condemnation of money and "money power" in Henry W. S. Edmunds, "Land, Labour and Capital: Salus Populi Suprema Lex," *Sydney Quarterly Magazine*, 1885, pp. 37–49; Cinderella, *A Manual of Political Economy for Free Men* (Sydney, 1890); and Cinderella, *Money versus Wealth: or the Origin of Interest Clearly Explained by a Pupil of Henry George and John Ruskin* (Sydney, 1890), p. 14.

organizations became committed officially to monetary reform. Arthur Griffith, a labor spokesman, listed in 1893 land taxation and government currency as the two most vital objectives of working men. He asked: "On what ground, then, of either principle or expediency, can it be right to allow private money-grubbing syndicates to control the nation's finances?" And he added: "I have, I think, during the last year or two, heard every available argument against the establishment of a National Bank, but not one of them is based on reason, or verified by experience."[107] The Sydney *Bulletin,* after condoning gold-backed government currency but rejecting inconvertibility in 1891, reversed its stand in 1894 when the editor, commenting on discussion in Victoria, wrote:

The question to be decided is—could Victoria carry, for a limited period, £5,000,000 of inconvertible paper money, without depreciation? In all probability it could. Similar experiments have succeeded elsewhere, and their success depends solely on honest management. The circulation of such an amount in State-guaranteed notes would mean the extinction of the note issues of private banks, but that is a matter of exceedingly small importance, and would do more good than harm. . . . Anyhow, Victoria is just now a favourable field in which to try an experiment of the kind, for all the ancient methods of finance are played out.[108]

Several writers in Sydney echoed the *Bulletin's* change of heart toward government currency. J. R. Palmer illustrated the degree of confusion an enthusiastic amateur could achieve when wrestling with this complex subject. He wrote:

The public works of the colony would be carried out under a well regulated system of National Credit, each Credit Note being virtually a debenture issued upon the security of the public works themselves, and, if need arose, entitling the owner of each particular note to consideration as a shareholder to the extent of his or her note-possession, leaving the Government the advantageous possessors of assets, the number of claimants against which, would be in constantly

107. Arthur Griffith, *The Labor Platform: An Exposition* (Sydney, 1893), p. 9.
108. "Plain English: An Inconvertible Paper Currency," *Bulletin,* XIV (1894), No. 755, p. 7; also "An Australian Paper Currency," *ibid.,* XI (1891), No. 592, p. 6.

decreasing ratio to the increasing value created, thus rendering the position absolutely safe and well-nigh impregnable.[109]

South Australia. An early plan for irredeemable notes in South Australia in 1845 took a peculiar form. The author, under the pseudonym "Aristides," began with a "post-scriptum" because "this is at, or near the other end of the world." He provided a graphic and lurid account of financial panics caused by collapse of gold-based currencies (e.g. "Mrs. L.—covered with gore . . .") and then he proposed an issue of interest-bearing promissory notes to be redeemable in gold only at infrequent dates, and the rest of the time to be "a real representative of property" termed appropriately "moral credit." [110] The scheme was inspired by depression and had not been considered carefully.

A hesitant suggestion for interest-bearing government "Treasury Notes" was made in Adelaide in 1871 by an author who called himself coyly "B. Silent."[111] However, advocacy of inconvertible paper thereafter was almost entirely by one man, George W. Cotton, first labor candidate elected to the South Australian Legislative Council in 1888.[112] Cotton told a South Australian Banking Commission in 1889 that for more than two years he had "been collecting evidence on the subject from all sources— mercantile men, merchants, bankers, and others, and from all authorities on financial questions. . . ."[113] In evidence Cotton cited Gilbart, Paterson, and Peel with advantage, and he argued

109. John R. Palmer, *National Credit: How to Use It. A System of Finance Which Offers a Solution of the Unemployed Problem* (Sydney, 1895), p. 7. An equally confused indictment of the commercial banking system was Zouabi, *Australia's Incubus: The Banking System an Immediate Remedy* (Sydney, 1894). A tract on monetary reform entitled *The Vagabonds or the Bonded Vags*, by Sam Smith, an American and "Secretary of the Seamen's Union" was published in Sydney in 1894.
110. Aristides, *Commerce: its Laws; their Anti-Christian Spirit; their Anti-Constitutional Character; their Pernicious Consequences; and their Demoralizing Tendency; with a Plan for their Reformation* (Adelaide, 1845), pp. 3, 10, and 103–12.
111. B. Silent, *The Public Debt; and the Policy of Entrusting the Management to a Local Bank, Head Office in Adelaide . . .* (Adelaide, 1871).
112. For comments on Cotton's career see W. G. Spence, *Australia's Awakening* (Sydney, 1909), p. 338.
113. "Report of Royal Commission Appointed to Consider the Desirability of Establishing a State Bank and Royal Mint; together with Minutes of Proceedings, Evidence, Synopses, and Appendices," *Proceedings of the Parliament of South Australia*, 1889, p. 59.

convincingly that government should not be hindered by dependence on gold from manipulating the currency to promote economic stability and full employment. He testified: "when confidence is shaken, and there is a danger of things becoming depressed, instead of money being withdrawn it should be liberally distributed. . . . If we had a state bank of issue, it is manifest that this hostile policy of contracting the currency when it was most wanted, would not be followed as it has been in the past." [114] From reports of the Commission's proceedings it can be seen that Cotton was regarded as an eccentric heretic and was treated by questioners with considerable discourtesy.

In an address in 1891 to the Economic and Social Science Section of the Australasian Association for the Advancement of Science, of which he was president, Cotton elaborated his views on currency matters. He subscribed, he explained, to "a quantity or numerary theory of the currency" and regarded gold-backing as pure superstition:

The worth of gold, silver, copper, paper, as money depends solely on its total volume, and on the rapidity with which it circulates. This great dynamic fact has been purposely kept in the background till those who ought to know better have come to overlook its existence, in order that the public might, through not understanding the true doctrine of the currency, more easily become the victims of the money-changers.[115]

Cotton wished the colonies to "relegate gold and silver to the position of commodities, to be bought and sold for what they are worth, as men, women, and horses still continue to be." Government authorities, he suggested, should "cautiously ascertain what volume of currency will meet the expanding requirements of the country by carefully recording the issues and checking the results upon the business and productive energy of the country."[116] Cotton reasoned clearly and cogently, but his tone toward critics was somewhat impatient. He said:

The profound theorists who prosper under the present condition

114. *Ibid.*, p. 219.
115. G. W. Cotton, "A State Bank of Issue the Only Solution of the Domestic-Currency Question," *Report of the Third Meeting of the Australasian Association for the Advancement of Science, held at Christchurch, New Zealand, 1891*, pp. 333–34.
116. *Ibid.*, pp. 336–37.

of finance may ask, How is the State to discover what is an adequate emission of State paper? These querists will desire elaborate calculations and bewildering columns of figures. These are often the receptables of dust that they ever have at hand to blind the eyes of the public.[117]

Cotton characterized correctly many of his opponents in South Australia when he agreed with Del Mar that monetary reform "is never referred to by land reformers, because the subject is one usually beyond the scope of popular agitators, and who, besides, may fear to risk the popularity of their own remedy by acknowledging the existence of another."[118]

Queensland. The issue of convertible government notes in 1866 prompted a discussion also of irredeemable currency in Queensland. Before a select committee to examine the question, W. L. G. Drew, Under-Secretary of the Treasury, recommended inconvertible treasury notes to replace the commercial bank circulation, and he cited with approval Alexander Galt's issue of Dominion Notes in Canada in 1865. If limited in volume to "the requirements of the country," Drew insisted, government notes would remain at a par value with gold. He did not receive substantial support for this position.[119]

Central Banking in the Commonwealth

The Commonwealth of Australia Act in 1900 placed matters relating to banking and currency under Commonwealth jurisdiction, and controversy shifted thereafter to the federal arena. Advocacy of government banking immediately after federation came mainly from radicals whose real objective was indictment of the existing commercial banks, and in some instances, nationalization of the system. Cautious proponents of a central bank of issue and reserve, who patiently had pleaded their case through-

117. *Ibid.*, p. 336.
118. *Ibid.*, p. 331.
119. See "Report of the Select Committee on the Issue of Treasury Notes; together with the Proceedings of the Committee and Minutes of Evidence," *Votes and Proceedings of the Legislative Assembly of Queensland*, 1867, pp. 3–9. Objections of the Governor, Sir George Bowen, to the measure are contained in a series of his letters in Stanley Lane-Poole, ed., *Thirty Years of Colonial Government: A Selection from the Despatches and Letters of the Right Hon. Sir George Ferguson Bowen, G.C.M.G.* (2 vols.; London, 1889), I, 250–69.

out much of the nineteenth century, now increasingly remained silent. Several developments explain the disappearance by 1900 of this more conservative stream of reformist monetary agitation. First, intellectual heirs of early banking reformers were men concerned now singlemindedly with more pressing problems of the new nation. Second, after sixty years of defeat, many even of the most enthusiastic defenders of the central bank idea had become sufficiently discouraged to discontinue further demands. Thirdly, commercial bankers themselves had given some indications that under suitable arrangements they would not oppose government assumption of the note issue.[120] Finally, radical protests against the banking system, which confused central banking with measures of financial relief, had increased substantially during the 1890's and served to discredit more moderate proposals. Monetary reformers gained a reputation for extravagant claims and hair-brained schemes which restrained more reasonable critics from entering what seemed increasingly to be an arena of undisciplined radical protest and propaganda.

Tracts on state banking in the early years of the Commonwealth were emotional in tone and without well-reasoned argument. One of the more widely distributed works, published in 1903, was entitled *The Circulating Sovereign*.[121] The author, J. M. Scott, promised a panacea for all national ills in "nationalisation of the banking business." He explained:

It will increase the wealth of the Nation—the People individually and collectively. By this Policy we shall have absolute control of the Circulation of the Currency, and this is the Bridle that controls us. IT IS FINANCE PERFECTED. This Policy will give full play to working of the Law of Supply and Demand, and by the working of the Natural Law evils which at present exist will find their level, that is go out of existence.[122]

Scott's economic arguments are unworthy of detailed attention. In 1916, after a period during which he "stopped his crusade to try

120. S. J. Butlin, *Australia and New Zealand Bank*, pp. 340–45.
121. J. M. Scott, *The Circulating Sovereign* (Sydney, n. d. [1903]). Scott reported in a later edition in 1916 that 10,000 copies of the first edition were sold, and he reprinted laudatory passages from the New South Wales press, indicating, at least, widespread notice. J. M. Scott, *Response to Empire Call, The Circulating Sovereign, Book with a Purpose* (Sydney, n. d. [1916]), p. 4.
122. *The Circulating Sovereign*, p. 33.

and pay off his debts," he issued a second edition purporting to prove that war finance in addition to peace-time benefits could be achieved through expropriation of commercial banks.[123] Correctly or not, Scott claimed a major share of credit for strong Labour Party endorsement of state banking.

A variety of publications provided sermons on the urgent need for monetary reform. William Maloney described successful experiments with government notes in several different countries,[124] and Bertha McNamara traced all the evils of modern society to metallic currency. The latter wrote: "trafficking in gold as money is the greatest iniquity on earth, and has kept poor humanity in the devil's chains of usury. Without it, of course, modern capitalism and wage slavery become impossible."[125] Evident in most of these critiques, despite their naïveté, were a valid appreciation of the importance for society of sustained effective demand and a sympathy for and desire to end human suffering. For example, McNamara concluded:

> At present education proper, medical service, good dwellings, not to mention all our other numerous wants, are curtailed and crushed for the want of dead coin, notwithstanding that plenty of willing hands are waiting to do the work, and that Nature is teeming with good things, sufficient and to spare, for everyone. Words are scarcely strong enough, then, to condemn a cruel money system which, under all these advantages, permits men and women and innocent little children to starve and live in squalor.[126]

One radical publicist rested his case for reform on the assertion that "all the great classical authorities" of political economy "from Moses to . . . Henry George" had favored state banking.[127] But even when their arguments were valid, most radical proponents of government banking offended as many persons as they converted.

---

123. *Response to Empire Call, The Circulating Sovereign, Book with a Purpose,* p. 11.

124. Dr. William Maloney, *How to Issue Secured Federal Notes as a Legal Tender, Supplementary to Gold, for the Execution of Revenue Producing Public Works* (n. p., n. d., ca. 1905).

125. Bertha McNamara, *Paper Money* (Sydney, 1910), p. 3.

126. *Ibid.,* p. 6.

127. See for example Alexander W. Johnston, *Law and Liberty: A Manual of the Elements of Political Economy for the Use of Statesmen, Teachers and Students* (Sydney, 1910), p. vii; and Phillip J. Mulholland, *Facts of Finance* (Sydney, n. d.), p. 3.

King O'Malley, a colorful figure during the early years of the Commonwealth, was an enthusiastic advocate of a national bank. He was Tasmanian member of the Commonwealth House of Representatives from 1901 to 1917, and the Commonwealth Bank was established while he was cabinet member in the first Labour Government. O'Malley came from the United States where, by his own testimony, he had "established himself in banking in Georgia" after a career of evangelical opportunism in the tradition of Elmer Gantry.[128] Before emigrating to Australia, near death from consumption, he traveled widely in Europe and observed different financial systems in operation; he concluded that "the English system is the soundest in the world."[129] In a sense, the conservative and radical approaches to state banking were fused in O'Malley. He was pre-eminently an unrestrained social reformer, and much of the appeal to him of monetary reform was humanitarian. A state bank, he believed, was an institution which would bring closer the human millenium. And yet, at the same time, O'Malley read widely and was influenced by the reasonableness of the writings of such monetary pioneers as Alexander Hamilton and Sir Robert Peel. He was able to cite a variety of theoretical authorities and historical precedents. In his old age O'Malley and his admirers liked to consider his work for the Commonwealth Bank as path-breaking; [130] in fact, he was only one of the more vocal members in a long line of protagonists.

Immediately after entering the Commonwealth Parliament O'Malley began a campaign for a "People's Bank."[131] During 1907–8 he presented a scheme for a "National Postal Bank" of "Deposit, Issue, Exchange, and Reserve," which, excluding a provision for inconvertible notes, did not differ widely in essentials from the nineteenth century proposals of Childers, Michie, Mirams, Ward, Eager, and others. O'Malley recommended formation of a semi-public corporation to issue all currency which would be redeemable either in gold or in interest-bearing government securities "at the option of the Comptroller-General of the

128. See Dorothy Catts, *King O'Malley: Man and Statesman* (Sydney, 1957), p. 23 and *passim*.
129. *Ibid.*, p. 57.
130. See King O'Malley, *The Commonwealth Bank; the Facts of its Creation* (Melbourne, n. d.), p. 1.
131. Dorothy Catts, *op. cit.*, p. 87.

bank." This institution would conduct the financial business of all levels of government, and also would compete for private business with trading banks, whose reserves against deposits it would hold.[132] Apparently, O'Malley hoped to combine income redistribution with currency reform, and he did not consider that a conflict of functions would arise necessarily within a government agency acting both as a competitive commercial bank and as a central reserve and regulatory body. His recommendation for a possible issue of inconvertible notes was cause for particular concern among bankers.

While O'Malley was Minister for Home Affairs, the Commonwealth Bank Act was passed in 1911. However, the new institution which began operations in 1912 was similar in structure to a commercial bank, was not a central bank in any real sense, and provided thereby only one of the two functions desired originally by O'Malley.[133] Professor Butlin suggests that by his extravagant demands O'Malley actually delayed achievement of the central banking goals he sought—"the bank was . . . ironically a product of the rantings of O'Malley in support of a bank which would include note issue among its multifarious activities."[134] In 1910 the Treasury had quietly acquired an effective monopoly of the note-issue with small protest even from the banks.

After foundation of the Commonwealth Bank as a trading corporation, agitation for its further development as an organization to control both the commercial banks and the aggregate money supply came from two directions. First, a variety of critics expressed concern about the uncertain and haphazard issue policy of the Treasury, particularly during the periods of price fluctuation associated with World War I. Frank Anstey, a Labour member of parliament from Victoria, raised a "lonely voice" during the war in criticism of alleged commercial bank profiteering and excessive use of inconvertible notes.[135] After the war Anstey demanded that the Commonwealth Bank, that "emascu-

132. "Financial Relations of the Commonwealth and the States: Scheme for Adjusting, by the Hon. King O'Malley, M.P.," *Papers Presented to Parliament of the Commonwealth of Australia*, 1907–8.
133. See L. F. Giblin, *The Growth of a Central Bank* (Melbourne, 1951), p. 2.
134. *Australia and New Zealand Bank*, p. 350.
135. H. V. Evatt, *Australian Labour Leader: The Story of W. A. Holman and the Labour Movement* (Sydney, 1945), p. 374.

lated institution" formed by a Labour government which "softened by nose-rubbing with gentry of social and financial distinction had become Liberals in action," be transformed into a true "Bank of the Nation" with exclusive issue and reserve powers.[136] Anstey was intemperate in language and often obscure in argument, but he recognized the need for a central monetary authority as a tool of government policy. Other similar but less well-reasoned appeals for radical government monetary action were voiced after the war by L. G. De Garis and Frank Lock of Sydney.[137]

A second source of criticism of the early form of the Commonwealth Bank was a growing group of academic economists interested in monetary problems. During World War I, R. F. Irvine of Sydney University examined the usefulness and dangers of various techniques of war finance. He argued that a rigid gold standard had outlived its value, and he called for careful government planning and control of inconvertible currency and credit.[138] After the war, two of Irvine's disciples, L. T. and I. Watson, expanded this doctrine to cover problems of peacetime unemployment. They considered postwar depression an ironical paradox after wartime suffering and blamed the situation on prevailing monetary policy. They wrote:

The effect of our fallacious conceptions of the meaning of money is to put society in the absurd position of being unable to finance its own production. Each nation considers that it has not enough "money" to produce what is wanted by human beings; or, if it has produced, it believes itself unable to finance its production.[139]

The Watsons argued convincingly that government regulation of currency and credit could help to maintain effective demand and thereby restore prosperity.

Demand is incapable of estimate; it is perhaps limitless. But effective demand is dependent on credit, which is in turn dependent

136. Frank Anstey, *Money Power* (Melbourne, 1921), pp. 71, 74–75, and 102.
137. L. G. De Garis, *Labour or Gold* (Sydney, 1919); and Frank Lock, *The Nationalisation of Credit: The Only Cure for Industrial Unrest* (Sydney, 1919).
138. R. F. Irvine, *The Veil of Money* (Sydney, 1916), and *War Finance: Loans, Paper Money, and Taxation* (The Joseph Fisher Lecture in Commerce, 1917, Adelaide, 1917).
139. L. T. and I. Watson, *The New Frankenstein: An Examination of the Principles of Modern Finance in Relation to Present-Day Problems of Production and Distribution*, with a preface by R. F. Irvine (n. p., 1922), p. 53.

on productive power. Consumptive power is limited by purchasing power. If a nation has insufficient purchasing power to consume what it wants, that nation's home markets are limited, and the problem of the surplus becomes more acute. . . . The "money" required for this purpose is obtained from the credit (supposedly) inherent in the capital goods of the community, which is to be released by the State for the above purpose.[140]

They referred to recommendations of the Brussels and Genoa Conferences in favor of central banking, and they argued that the Commonwealth Bank should be reconstituted as a regulatory rather than a trading corporation. "The role, in fact, of the State should be neither that of borrower nor yet of lender, but of stabilizer."[141]

In the postwar period, monetary discussion among academics was dominated by Professor D. B. Copland, first of the University of Tasmania and later of Melbourne University. Beginning in 1920, Copland prepared and published a succession of careful analyses of Australian monetary conditions, and he spoke often publicly on the subject. He drew heavily on the theoretical work of Irving Fisher, and after examining statistically the components of the quantity equation for Australia attributed the wartime and immediate postwar inflation to a substantial increase in the money supply. He considered that recent changes in the velocity of money had been negligible, and he concluded: "The general level of prices may be regarded as the relationship between trade movements on the one hand and currency movements on the other."[142] Copland warned particularly of the perils for Australia in price fluctuations through their impact on foreign trade. As a solution for Australia's foreign exchange problems, he advocated in 1921 final abandonment of the gold standard and adoption of Irving Fisher's "multiple standard" which would be designed to stabilize both prices and the foreign exchange rate. Copland said: "Monetary theory has gone beyond the gold standard, as we knew it before the war, and a simple return to it will be no real

140. *Ibid.*, pp. 41–42.
141. *Ibid.*, p. 43.
142. D. B. Copland, *Currency and Prices in Australia* (The Joseph Fisher Lecture in Commerce, 1921, Adelaide, 1921), p. 19; also "Currency Inflation and Price Movements in Australia," *Economic Journal*, XXX (1920), 484–509.

advance. On the other hand, the successful adoption of a multiple standard is the next step forward."[143] In 1923 and 1924, Copland recounted for both British and Australian readers the course of postwar prosperity which had culminated in a substantial "trade depression." He placed monetary and financial factors high on his lists of causes of the "boom" and crisis, and he called for improved study and planning.[144]

Other university economists supported Copland in his enthusiasm for research, although some did not agree with his policy proposals. Edward Shann at Western Australia approved "effective control of credit supplies through the central banks" but feared in particular abandonment of the gold standard in favor of Fisher's multiple standard.[145] The example of active central banking experiments in other countries added strength to the demonstration by Copland of the need for monetary control. L. F. Giblin wrote that by 1924: "Ideas on central banking were in active circulation and stimulus had come from the recommendations of International Conferences at Brussels in 1920 and Genoa in 1922 and from the Imperial Economic Conference at London in 1923. . . . Central banking was in the air." [146]

In 1924 monetary stringency and deflation were met by reluctance on the part of the Treasury Notes Board to issue more currency and relieve pressure. Professor Giblin has suggested that careless interpretation of Fisher's quantity theory, Cassel's purchasing power parity theory, and "the theory of the banking creation of credit" had considerable influence in determination of this policy. "It was on somewhat facile applications of these theories that the Board built its haunting fears of serious inflation and justified its opposition to any addition to the currency."[147]

143. *Ibid.*, p. 43.
144. D. B. Copland, "The Trade Depression in Australia in Relation to Economic Thought," *Report of the Sixteenth Meeting of the Australasian Association for the Advancement of Science held at Wellington, 1923*, pp. 555–79; and "The Economic Situation in Australia, 1918–23," *Economic Journal*, XXXIV (1924), 32–51; "Monetary Policy and Its Reactions upon Australia," *Report of the Seventeenth Meeting of the Australasian Association for the Advancement of Science held at Adelaide, 1924*, pp. 495–534.
145. E. O. G. Shann, "The Present Position of Foreign Exchange (in abstract)," *Journal and Proceedings of the Royal Society of Western Australia*, IX (1923), 71.
146. L. F. Giblin, *The Growth of a Central Bank* (Melbourne, 1951), pp. 5–6.
147. *Ibid.*, p. 12.

A new Commonwealth Bank Act of 1924, by transferring the note-issue monopoly from the Treasury to the Bank, brought Australia one step closer to full central banking. The vicissitudes of this later evolution have been examined by Giblin in his *The Growth of a Central Bank*. When the period under examination closed in the late 1920's, Copland at Melbourne University continued his attacks on monetary mismanagement,[148] and a few radicals still looked to a state bank as an all-encompassing panacea.[149] Increasingly, however, significant discussion of central banking took place behind the closed doors of the Commonwealth Bank itself.

Opposition to Government Activity

Resistance to government control of the money supply came from two general categories of critics: commercial bankers who believed honestly that their own interest and that of the country lay with preservation of monetary private enterprise, and doctrinaire liberals who mistrusted and felt obliged to resist all government economic activity. Advocates of regulated money and banking met with little tangible success before formation of the Commonwealth Bank, but critics of reform schemes remained on the defensive throughout the colonial period. Apologies for free and unrestricted commercial banking, like critiques of government, were concentrated during times of economic crisis.

New South Wales. The first state bank plan in New South Wales, the unsuccessful scheme for government notes of Windeyer and Wentworth in 1843, brought forth vigorous protests

148. D. B. Copland, "The Commonwealth Bank of Australia," *Economic Journal*, XXXV (1925), 145–48; and "Report by Professor D. B. Copland, M. A., B.Sc., Dean of the Faculty of Commerce, Melbourne University. The Control of the Business Cycle with Special Reference to Australia," Appendix 1 to "Development and Migration Commission: Report of Unemployment and Business Stability in Australia," *Papers Presented to the Parliament of the Commonwealth of Australia*, 1926–27–28.

149. See for example: Fred. Saidy, *Workers' College Teaching: the Law of Cause and Effect, Economics and Political Science?* (Wollongong, 1929); and "Second Progress Report of the Royal Commission on National Insurance. Unemployment," *Papers Presented to the Parliament of the Commonwealth of Australia*, 1926–27, p. 10.

from immigrant liberals. Robert Lowe proclaimed passionately in the Legislative Council that this proposal conflicted with sound principles of political economy.[150] A writer in the *Weekly Register* noted a dangerous similarity between Windeyer's proposed *pfandbriefs* and notes issued by the dreaded John Law.

It will be seen at once, that the principle of Mr. Windeyer's scheme, and that of Law, is precisely the same, namely, to base the circulating medium upon the real property of the country, each land proprietor being, as it were, a shareholder in the National Bank. The error of both projectors consists in this, that they confound currency with credit and security. Bank paper is only valuable in so far as it represents those metals that have become the universal media of exchange between individuals and nations.[151]

The *New South Wales Magazine* said of Windeyer's Report: "We took it up with high expectations—we lay it down with the bitterest disappointment. The mountain has been long in labour, and the birth is that of a miserable starveling mouse."[152]

The report of a select committee in 1852 favorable to a state bank induced a dual argument in rebuttal from the Sydney *Empire*, that on the one hand banking had no relation to economic stability and should not be treated as a panacea, and on the other that present statistics were too meagre to permit enlightened government currency control. The *Empire* repeated the fallacious Banking School argument that commercial banks were prevented by circumstances from over-issue:

The notion that a bank can enlarge its issue of notes indefinitely, is simply absurd. A bank cannot extend its issue beyond the ordinary requirements of the district in which its notes circulate, and

150. See S. Elliott Napier, "Robert Lowe and his Associations with Australia," *Royal Australian Historical Society Journal and Proceedings,* XVIII (1932), pp. 1–31.
151. "The 'Monetary Confusion' Scheme," *Weekly Register of Politics, Facts, and General Literature,* September 2, 1843, pp. 73–74; and November 11, 1843, pp. 233–34. *The Sydney Herald* was equally critical of state banking. See Michael Roe, *Society and Thought in Eastern Australia, 1835–1851,* pp. 129–32.
152. "Monetary Confusion—Report of the Committee of Legislative Council—Proposed Remedy," *New South Wales Magazine,* 1843, p. 594. Even before the Committee's Report was published the *New South Wales Magazine* reviewed unfavorably a pamphlet by Mr. Patrick Grant, reportedly an immigrant from Europe who advocated state banking, entitled *An Inquiry into the Causes of the Present Monetary Depression of the Colony of New South Wales, with the Suggestion of a Remedy.* See *ibid.,* pp. 395–99.

it cannot issue its notes in excess of those requirements, without the certainty of having them immediately returned upon its hands. . . . The question is purely an abstract one, and we are certainly not yet in possession of sufficient data to legislate upon it to advantage.[153]

About the Report itself the *Empire* concluded: "One more vapid and puerile has, we imagine, rarely emanated from any body calling itself deliberative."[154]

A thorough defense of competitive banking was presented to a Sydney audience in 1859 by Edward Drury, a banker himself, who had recently arrived from Belgium.[155] Drury argued that banks were simply suppliers of a good called "money," and society was best served when the money market like all other markets was left unencumbered by "legislative interference." He insisted: "Free trade or unrestricted competition is the practical recognition of the great fundamental law of supply and demand, and there can be no philosophical ground for withholding its application from Banking rather than from any other branch of trade."[156] He claimed that competition wherein many banks issued notes was a ruthless destroyer of weak firms, and that the Peel Act of 1844 by preserving inefficiency would prove costly to Britain. Drury used a convincing Banking School argument to combat the Currency School contention that all notes beyond a fixed amount should be backed fully by gold. He pointed out that if the Currency School position (he cited Overstone) were accepted there was little apparent reason why fractional reserve deposit banking should be tolerated any more than fractional reserve notes, for "in principle there is no difference between cheques and bank notes." He elaborated:

this principle when carried out to its legitimate consequences, must inevitably lead to the suppression of banking, since the figures in a Ledger which indicate the amount of the Bank's debt to a depositor, are neither more nor less than certificates or tokens representing

153. "Currency and Banking," *Empire*, October, 5, 1852, No. 540, p. 1478.
154. *Ibid.*
155. Drury was born and educated in Belgium where his father, formerly a master at Harrow School, was tutor to sons of the King. Philip Mennel, *Dictionary of Australasian Biography* (London, 1892), p. 140.
156. Edward R. Drury, "Essay on Currency and Banking in New South Wales," *Sydney Magazine of Science and Art*, II (1859), 97.

sovereigns. They constitute, in fact, the Bank's promises to pay at the customer's order, to bearer on demand, a certain quantity of gold coin.[157]

On ground of equity: "the State has no more right to the profits arising from the issue of bank notes, than to those derived from the use of cheques, which means the profit resulting from the use of sums deposited in the Banks, the *promises to pay* which are inscribed in the Bank Books."[158] Like other bankers Drury was convinced that commercial banks, if left in a situation of free competition, could never issue more notes than were in the public interest: "The Banks can only issue as much paper as the country requires, because under a system of free competition and competing issues, with the admirable method of exchanging between themselves, all notes issued in excess, being paid into other Banks, are at once returned to the issuers who must redeem them with gold."[159] Drury recalled from history occasions when needy governments which possessed note-issue powers had inflated national currencies to relieve treasuries. All that was required to achieve a banking utopia, Drury maintained, was for government to supervise charter procedures, preferably on the Scottish model, and to publish periodically complete banking statistics.

Mistrust of commercial bankers in the reliability of colonial governments was their most valid ground for denying the desirability of government currency. In fact, bankers did have good reason for suspecting that penurious legislatures would come to regard the money supply as a financial as well as a monetary tool. Yet they could not demonstrate conclusively that this development would be undesirable from the public viewpoint. R. L. Nash, financial editor of the Sydney *Daily Telegraph*, assured the Bankers' Institute at Sydney in 1894 that "the natural limits of state interference" excluded a government bank from consideration.[160] To illustrate the potential weakness even of a public

157. *Ibid.*, p. 100.
158. *Ibid.*, p. 102.
159. *Ibid.*
160. R. L. Nash, "Banking Legislation, and the Natural Limits of State Interference," *Journal of the Institute of Bankers of New South Wales*, III (1894),

agency, Robert Osbiston, editor of the Institute's *Journal*, listed all occasions on which the Bank of England had been forced to suspend specie payments.[161] William McMillan, Colonial Treasurer from 1889 until 1891 and a founder of the Free Trade Association, identified "causes of the terrible collapse" without even mentioning banking instability. He thought a central bank reserve would be "rigid" and unnecessary.[162] In 1895, J. Henderson reviewed the course of central bank agitation in New South Wales from the 1840's and noted with pride the consistently successful opposition of bankers. He explained:

> It says a great deal for the continuity of our traditions and their influence in Parliament, that notwithstanding the strong recommendations of Select Committees and the pressure of circumstances from time to time during the last 50 years, the establishment of a National Bank is, apparently, no nearer fruition than ever, and I think we may well rest assured that the common sense of Parliament will not readily sanction any interference with our currency until such measures are proved to be necessary, and if any such measures ultimately become law, they will be properly safeguarded and conceived in a broad spirit, not inimical to the banks but for the benefit of the public generally.[163]

In 1899 the Institute *Journal* reported that Henderson's rejection of reform proposals, five years before, had influence, even despite a few bankers' panic-stricken admission of possible good in central banking.

> At the time of our last crisis, we saw the inevitable banking commission, with its long and tedious inquiry, resulting in a report now safely stowed away somewhere among the archives of the nation . . . a contribution in two parts appeared in this journal from the pen of Mr. James Henderson, which dealt very exhaustively with the history of our note issues. The result of his inquiry tended to establish the continuance of the present system of note issue. He showed that the financial troubles of 1893 were in no way traceable to any defect in the previously existing currency arrangements, and deprecated any

---

163–77; Robert Lucas Nash, *The Banking Institutions of Australasia* (London, n.d.), and "A State Bank," *Australian Economist,* II (1890–93), 146–48.
  161. Robert Osbiston, "The Bank of England Reserves and Australian Finance," *Journal of the Institute of Bankers of New South Wales,* III (1894), 287–304.
  162. Hon. W. McMillan, "Banks and Banking Legislation," *ibid.,* III (1894), 494–521.
  163. J. Henderson, "Our Paper Currency—Part 1," *ibid.,* IV (1895), 416–17.

change. Experience and authority seem to have confirmed this view, and there seems now to be no prospect of alteration. . . .[164]

With the prospect of federation only barely over the horizon, bankers were able effectively to forestall proposals for reform. As Reginald Black assured the Australian Economic Association in 1893: "When federation is an accomplished fact it will be time enough to think of a national or State bank, a dream which seems to perpetually haunt the minds of some of our legislators."[165]

Victoria. Several witnesses before the Victorian Select Committee on Government Banking in 1853 were enthusiastic in defense of unrestricted private banking and in opposition to transformation of the Bank of Victoria to a state bank. Representatives of other Melbourne banks did not look favorably on the Bank of Victoria's ambitions, and they stressed to the committee the virtues of competition. The manager of the Bank of Australasia said: "the Government ought to go upon the principle of free trade in this matter; that principle being now considered generally a sound one." The Union Bank manager added that a government bank would be "at variance with the principles of free trade, which, I think, are pretty generally acknowledged to be sound principles, and ought to be extended to banking as well as every other pursuit." The London Chartered Bank's representative repeated this answer almost word for word indicating that bankers may have prepared replies in advance; he said: "I think it objectionable, because it shows a departure from and is opposed to those liberal free trade principles which are now so generally held to be sound." John Badcock, the Bank of New South Wales' manager, criticized Bank of England regulation of note issue in accordance with gold flows; he alleged: "the Bank of England puts on the screw as soon as the exchanges are against that country. This principle of regulating the currency has been op-

164. "Our Note Currency," *ibid.*, VIII (1899), 4. For a similar denunciation of reform see Urbanus, "On the Proposal to Establish a State Bank," *ibid.*, 326–31.
165. Reginald J. Black, "The Banking Crisis and its Lessons," *Australian Economist*, III (1893–94), 324.

posed by economists, but the system has not been altered, because the Bank of England is a time-honored institution, and it would be difficult to remodel the system."[166] In response to a question framed in Currency School terms, he replied with Banking School argument. The exchange between Badcock and a Committee member was as follows:

[Committee member] Suppose, for the sake of argument, that there is nothing to prevent the issue of notes here to excess, may not the same thing happen here, as happened in England, when almost the whole of the banks stopped payment. That was in 1843 and 1844, when Sir Robert Peel introduced his measure restricting the issue of paper by the banks?—[Badcock] I think it almost impossible to have an over issue of paper; for if the note circulation is in excess of the wants of the community, the paper comes back upon the bank almost immediately, and, moreover, no advantage is gained by the bank's issuing in excess.[167]

During the late 1870's, when a state bank became again a live issue, criticism of reform proposals was revived. R. Murray Smith, an assiduous champion of laissez faire in all areas, led the attack on James Mirams' plan for government currency. Smith claimed that hard times had been caused by "national waste and extravagance" and that government monetary interference would lead only to disaster "more fatal to national prosperity than a costly war or a widespread conflagration." He insisted: "The only way in which a government can properly attempt to relieve financial pressure is by increased economy in dealing with the public funds, and by inculcating and aiding, as far as they can, the judicious husbanding and investing of the national resources."[168] The *Australasian Insurance and Banking Record* also greeted Mirams' proposal with cries of heresy. It said:

166. "Report from the Select Committee of the Legislative Council on Government Banking . . . ," *Votes and Proceedings of the Legislative Council of Victoria*, 1853–54, questions numbered 72, 253, 393, 529.
167. *Ibid.*, question numbered 402.
168. R. Murray Smith, "Paper Money," *Melbourne Review*, III (1878), 421. Mirams wrote that, in reply to Murray Smith, "I sent a rejoinder for publication in the succeeding issue [of the *Melbourne Review*]. It was refused insertion. I thereupon printed and circulated it in pamphlet form at my own expense." Mirams reprinted the rejoinder as part of *A Generation of Victorian Politics: Personal Records* (n. p., n. d.).

It is difficult to say which is the more surprising fact, the publication by one of our legislators of an elaborate essay on a subject to which he has devoted the best of his abilities, and seeks to force upon the attention of Parliament, but which bristles with the wildest fallacies, and is at variance with the A B C of political economy, or the acceptance of so crude a paper by the conductors of the *Melbourne Review*. . . .[169]

The *Record* noted a suggestion by Mirams that government notes might be irredeemable, and it described dreadful horrors which would befall a government lured into such perilous measures. The journal concluded:

But it is surely needless to multiply objections, which can be taken by scores, against a proposal antagonistic to British feelings, and at present unknown to any British community. It has never been resorted to except in desperate straits, when further taxation has become too grievous to be borne; with rare exceptions its outcome has been disastrous; the temptations to excessive use are so seductively facile that no human Ministry could hope to defend it from the log-rolling crusade that would bear down upon it.[170]

The *Record* repeated the assertion again and again that, even though government currency might begin as an honest attempt to bring about monetary improvement, it would end with irresponsible over-issue, inflation, and financial disaster.

Henry Gyles Turner, a prominent banker, historian, and a founder of the *Melbourne Review*, defended the Victorian banking system from reform protests in an address to the Melbourne Social Science Congress in 1880. He argued that banks, by advancing money on real estate, had been a crucial factor in Victorian development. Ironically, as the bank of which Turner was a senior executive fell early in the panic of 1893, he insisted that colonial institutions were eminently safe and sound. He declared: "we are, to a great extent, removed from the influence of that unreasoning panic which is a marked characteristic of Englishmen in times of doubt and difficulty, and, by long familiarity with the Scottish system of banking, have acquired that confidence in

169. "Mr. Mirams, M. P., on a National Bank for Victoria," *Australasian Insurance and Banking Record*, II (1878), 189.
170. *Ibid.*, p. 192. Mirams replied to the *Record's* attack in a letter, II (1878), 232.

the depositories of our surplus cash that is the marked distinction of the North Briton."[171] With the active support of Turner a Bankers' Institute was founded in 1884, in part as a forum for discussion.[172] Throughout the 1880's bankers expressed considerable interest in economic science and maintained that a "theoretical training" had become necessary to defend their institutions.[173]

George Griffiths in 1881 echoed the argument used by Turner and fellow bankers, that banking was no different from other business and that government was ill-advised to interfere with any aspect of commerce. He wrote:

Trading is not a function of State, and lending money is a trade. A Government which trades in money will disorganise its own money market, to the detriment of every interest under its care; but not only will it do harm in this way, but it will do injury to its own credit by losing on its loans; for as a Government is badly qualified for trading, it will certainly make losses.[174]

Griffiths used reasoning which Australians were quick to appreciate when he warned that mere contemplation of radical monetary reforms might discourage foreign lenders. "To establish a State Bank, or even to talk seriously of so doing, would slacken this competition, and frighten this money away."[175]

Mirams and Manuel encountered stiff opposition when they proposed a state bank to almost any group; before the National Reform League at Melbourne one critic complained that "the

171. H. G. Turner, "Victorian Banking Considered in Relation to National Development," *Australasian Insurance and Banking Record*, IV (1880), 403. See also Henry G. Turner, "Banking and Finance," in *Victoria and its Metropolis Past and Present* (Melbourne, 1888), I, 786–803.

172. A brief description of the founding of the Bankers' Institute of Australasia at Melbourne, in which Turner was very active, is given in *Imperial Review*, October, 1886, p. 73.

173. A. G. Eager, Accountant of the Bank of New South Wales, Melbourne, won a prize for an essay on the subject "On the Advantage of a Theoretical as Well as Practical Training for Bankers" awarded by the Bankers' Institute. Eager observed: "A correct knowledge of economic theories in persons who deal largely in money entrusted to them by others is, however, not only desirable, it is in point of fact necessary to the well-being of the community at large. What, for example, could be more disastrous than the adoption by the heads of banking institutions generally of any of the false notions in regard to the currency and kindred matters which have from time to time been promulgated in the political world?" *Australasian Insurance and Banking Record*, XI (1887), 767.

174. George Griffiths, "Some Objections to a State Bank," *Victorian Review*, V (1881), 232.

175. *Ibid.*, p. 242.

Government was doing too much for the people, which they were able to do for themselves, but were losing their self-reliance."[176] Supporters of other panaceas such as land reform feared that agitation for a central bank would weaken their own particular cause.[177] Opponents of a national bank took heart from the confident comments of Sir Charles Dilke, who remarked after a tour of "Greater Britain": "it is to the credit of the Victorian population that they should have rejected it as they did."[178]

During the depression which began in the late 1880's, Victorian bankers had frequent occasion to defend the principles behind their private banks and competitive system. The *Insurance and Banking Record* contended that state bank schemes were like childhood diseases to be endured quietly by commercial bankers but to be cured as quickly as possible before they could spread. The journal commented thus on the South Australian State Bank Commission of 1889:

> The State Bank disorder is a feverish eruption which is best left to "come out" of the patient in a natural manner. It is hardly surprising that in self-made communities, wherein force of character, apart from the equipments of education and experience, plays so conspicuous, and, on the whole, so worthy a part, a strong desire is constantly being manifested to search into the rudiments of a question in a manner which is occasionally calculated to tax the forbearance of those who have advanced further. But the agitations connected with the idea of a State Bank which have been carried on in various colonies, have hitherto practically ended by common sense vindicating itself as the untenability of the views held by the advocates of the system has been gradually demonstrated.[179]

During the crisis years 1892–93, bankers insisted that periodic financial difficulties, such as those being experienced currently, were inevitable; "quack remedies" would only worsen the situation. G. D. Meudell asked:

176. "A National Bank of Issue," *Australasian Insurance and Banking Record,* III (1879), 204.
177. e.g. Charles H. Pearson, "The Liberal Programme," *Victorian Review,* I (1880), 534.
178. Charles Wentworth Dilke, *Problems of Greater Britain* (London, 1890), I, 245.
179. "Report of the State Bank Commission of South Australia," XIII (1889), 554.

When will the public understand that industry is periodic, and that commercial bubbles and manias, with their attendant commercial crises or collapses, are merely tides of industry as certain as the procession of the equinoxes? Men are speaking and writing to-day as Mirams and his kind did in 1878, and as though what is happening had never happened before, and as though the decay of industry and the decline and fall of Victoria had commenced![180]

Bankers resurrected the spectre of "Lawism" and French monetary excesses once again. The *Bankers' Magazine* cautioned urgently against such schemes:

It is in times like these that "cranks" bring out their proposals for State banks and forced issues of notes, and the fear is that in the temporary distrust in the hour of trial of old, tried systems, such as our adaptation of the Scotch system of banking, we may do as others have done to their peril, and take up with some such schemes as those of the French revolutionary republic with their issue of *Livres* that depreciated a thousand-fold, the fallacies of John Law, or the Cedula banks of Argentina.[181]

Apart from bankers themselves who were almost unanimously opposed to any form of government banking, the division of opinion over the monetary role of the state followed lines somewhat similar to those drawn over commercial policy. During the 1870's, the doctrinaire protectionist James Mirams was met by the dogmatic free-trader R. Murray Smith, and in the 1890's free-trader Max Hirsch condemned bitterly the state bank scheme of protectionist Benjamin Hoare.[182] A reason why protection was introduced in Victoria and government banking was not may have been the extra weight of argument and vituperation added by bankers. Informally and through their institute bankers maintained a barrage of criticism. In 1894, unsatisfied with the strength of current statements, the *Bankers' Magazine* issued the following characteristic appeal:

180. G. D. Meudell, "A New Way to Pay New Debts," *Bankers' Magazine and Journal of the Bankers' Institute of Australasia*, VI (1892–93), 1050.
181. "The Financial Panic and its End," *ibid.*, VI (1892–93), 1417.
182. See *ibid.*, VII (1893–94), 779–82. Reporting on Hoare's lecture to the Commercial Travellers' Club the *Bankers' Magazine* said: "This is the first time this convivial resort has been perverted to such purposes as the study of abstruse points in economics." *Ibid.*, p. 662.

Wanted, someone to knock the State-bank fad on the head. Why do not some of the lecturers at the Bankers' Institute tackle the subject? It is not sufficient to reply that banking men are already assured of the danger of a State bank and its inexpediency; at any rate in the form it is generally presented by the gentlemen of socialistic tendencies and profound financial imbecility who offer it to impecunious but hopeful crowds at open-air meetings as the one thing needful. The teaching would go beyond the Institute, and might help to educate aright the whole public mind of Australasia, which now is somewhat inclined to it for want of better knowledge.[183]

The magazine's request for "better knowledge" was answered throughout the 1890's by continued propaganda aimed directly at public persuasion in its own pages and in those of other publications.[184]

The Smaller Colonies. In the smaller colonies, proposals for government banking were relatively few and poorly supported; opposition was correspondingly weak. The South Australian State Bank Commission in 1889 did arouse some concern among defenders of private banks but only temporarily. One particularly vehement witness before the Commission feared that with a government bank "All growth would be stopped, and we should arrive at a petrified civilisation of the Chinese type."[185] P. Glynn, a Commission member, was led to publish separately his own "Case Against a State Bank" in which he emphasized dangers of inflation and cited classical economists on the virtues of free trade.[186] During the depression of the 1890's, bimetallism was a more widely discussed method of currency reform than government notes. As comment on George W. Cotton's scheme for irredeemable money, one bimetallist remarked contemptuously in

183. "Editor's Notes," *ibid.*, VIII (1894–95), 146.
184. See for example: Edward Davies, *Capital: The Friend and Ally of Wage-Earners and the Mainspring of Commerce* (Melbourne, 1896); and William Bateman, *Australian Produce: The Best Means of Realising Thereon* (Melbourne, 1897).
185. "Report of Royal Commission Appointed to Consider the Desirability of Establishing a State Bank and Royal Mint; together with Minutes of Proceedings, Evidence, Synopses, and Appendices," *Proceedings of the Parliament of South Australia*, 1889, p. liv.
186. P. Glynn, *The Case Against a State Bank* (Adelaide, 1889).

1893: "An inconvertible currency is the last resort in national financing, and the communities on which it is inflicted are either in the throes of some national commotion, or have not yet fully emerged from the domain of barbarism."[187]

The Commonwealth. After Federation in 1900, a few commercial bankers continued their attacks on the idea of a state bank. A. P. Stewart in 1906 cited Francis Walker, Bonamy Price, and Leroy-Beaulieu in support of unrestricted private banking.[188] J. Russell Butchart was a particularly articulate critic of plans for centralization, and both during and after World War I he pleaded for retention of the gold standard and of the principle that bank loans should be extended exclusively on commercial paper. He was alarmingly condemnatory of R. F. Irvine's suggestion during World War I that government introduce a managed irredeemable currency. He said: "Of the 13th century we are told that the man who introduced paper money into Persia when the King was hard up was first cursed and then hanged; so far we have not arrived at the cursing stage."[189] However, other bankers gradually became convinced of the need for a central reserve capable of giving emergency assistance to trading banks, and in 1928 A. C. Davidson of the Bank of New South Wales actually deplored the barrier to such a development posed by the Commonwealth Bank acting as a competitor.[190] Davidson was concerned principally about increasing the safety of the banking system, and he was skeptical about use of a central bank as a macroeconomic tool. He insisted: "The position is that the banker has a very limited capacity to create credit. There is no action of his which in a period of depression or stagnation can start the

187. David Murray, "Bimetallism," *Report of the Fifth Meeting of the Australasian Association for the Advancement of Science held at Adelaide, 1893,* p. 563.
188. A. P. Stewart, "On Currency," *Journal of the Institute of Bankers of New South Wales,* XV (1906), 202–24.
189. J. R. Butchart, *Money and its Purchasing Power* (Melbourne, 1918), p. 5. See also *idem, Money, Credit, and Exchange* (The Joseph Fisher Lecture in Commerce, 1923, Adelaide, 1923). Similar arguments were voiced in Western Australia by F. E. Allum, "Modern Currency Problems," *Journal and Proceedings of the Royal Society of Western Australia,* VIII (1921–22), 1–16.
190. A. C. Davidson, *Central Reserve Banking* (Sydney, 1929).

wheels of industry and commerce again by the creation of credit."[191]

Academic opinion after formation of the Commonwealth was divided on the question of government banking. All university economists did not, like Copland and Giblin, have faith in the virtues of monetary control. W. Neill at the University of Adelaide opposed creation of the Commonwealth Bank in 1911 and feared an issue of irredeemable currency.[192] Sir Henry Braddon, who had lectured at Sydney University, compared Australian departure from the gold standard and use of government notes with the catastrophic French issue of *assignats*.[193] In 1929, Edward Shann, at Western Australia, supported formation of "a true central reserve, managed with the single aim of maintaining through the ordinary banks the free play of individual initiative;" but he disliked the present form of the Commonwealth Bank, mistrusted "the cult of centralizing everything in government hands," and rejected categorically an issue of inconvertible notes. He said: "Some are foolish enough to think that a printing-press in a government bank of issue can do, at less cost, the work that the mines used to do. Their faith in fiat money is still unshaken after the miseries of war and post-war finance in Europe. They are but few —the 'lunatic fringe.' "[194]

191. A. C. Davidson, *Banking, Credit and Industry* (Melbourne, n. d.), p. 3.
192. W. Neill, *The Commonwealth Note Issue* (A Lecture delivered before the University Society of Commerce, Adelaide, 1911).
193. Sir Henry Braddon, "Paper Money," in *Commonwealth Accountants' Students' Society Lectures* (Melbourne, n. d.), and "The French 'Assignat' Issues 1790–1797," in *Essays and Addresses* (Sydney, 1930), pp. 16–42.
194. Edward Shann, Preface to A. C. Davidson, *Central Reserve Banking* (Sydney, 1929), pp. 10–11, and *Bond or Free?* (Sydney, 1930).

6

Banking and Currency: II. Price Levels and Property Loans

A discussion of two questions in monetary policy which reflected above all the special conditions of a fast-growing staple-producing economy is examined in this chapter. The first was the relationship between price levels and prosperity, and particularly the desirability of a bimetallic currency as a price-support device. The second concerned modification of the commercial bank injunction against loans on the security of real property.

Price Levels and Bimetallism

Preoccupation with price levels. During the early years of colonial banks, their critics expressed continuing concern at the prospect of unrestrained note-issue. For example, when the Derwent Bank was proposed in Van Diemen's Land in 1828, one commentator insisted that the "extra money" this institution would create could only "find circulation" by "raising the prices."[1] Another, with memories of the old country, predicted national disaster from inflation:

That a depreciated currency is injurious in the highest degree, it requires no more than the example of England to prove, for the vast increase of paper in that country, having created an immense sum of unemployed capital, formed as it were, a financial water spout, which bursting over the people in consequence of a spirit of false speculation, ultimately carried ruin wheresoever it went.[2]

1. "Finance," *Murray's Austral-Asiatic Review,* I (Hobart Town, 1828), 27.
2. "The Banking System," *Colonial Advocate, and Tasmanian Monthly Review and Register* (Hobart Town), April 1, 1828, p. 55.

However, colonists learned quickly that their banking system was destined to be predominantly mercantile in character and relatively conservative in issue policy. Bankers seldom proposed abandoning convertibility with gold, and serious fears of inflation disappeared quickly.

Deflation rather than inflation became the question of most bitter dispute. During the 1840's staple-producers discovered for the first time that falling prices for products could threaten their very survival; costs of mortgaged property and borrowed capital were fixed contractually while incomes, dependent upon export sales, declined. A variety of remedies for deflation were discussed: a national bank, special government loans, land reform, and tariff protection. One proposal, supported energetically by Wentworth and other land-owners, was for a usury law which would reduce interest costs of staple production by legislative enactment. This measure was opposed successfully by creditors with eloquent appeals to "every principle of political economy" and with reminders of the sanctity of free trade.[3] Rising prices and technological innovations late in the 1840's, together with hectic prosperity following gold discoveries, arrested temporarily concern with deflation.

Prices of Australian exports fell steadily from 1864 until 1894, with a sudden drop after 1884.[4] The *Australasian Insurance and Banking Record* noted the sudden deflation in 1884 and expressed hope that an increased real value of gold exports would compensate for reduced wool and grain receipts:

> That England will be the gainer, and that those countries which, like Australasia, have borrowed largely from outside sources will be the losers by this appreciated value of gold, there can be little doubt. If our wool and wheat are to sell at permanently lower prices, it is clear that we shall have to sell more wool and wheat than formerly to pay the same interest on our national and private debts. But we shall

3. The controversy over usury legislation has been discussed in detail in David S. Macmillan, *The Debtors War* (Melbourne, 1960). A proposal in Tasmania for a voluntary "equitable adjustment" of interest charges was contained in "Past, Present, and Future Position of Tasmania," *South Briton; or, Tasmanian Literary Journal*, I (Hobart Town, 1843), 25–32.

4. T. A. Coghlan's "Price-level of Exports" index (1900 prices = 1000) stood at 1931 in 1864, at 1345 in 1884, and was down to 780 by 1894. *A Statistical Account of the Seven Colonies of Australasia, 1901–1902* (Sydney, 1902), p. 376.

feel the loss less acutely than other large borrowing countries, because one of our great products is this very gold which is becoming appreciated in value.[5]

Increasingly Australians grew concerned about the price decline, and some came to believe that the fundamental cause of endemic deflation was a worldwide money shortage resulting from strict adherence to the gold standard. Gold-mining, it was pointed out, had not kept pace with production of other goods and services. One writer suggested that after an initial price decline gloomy expectations had worsened and sustained deflationary effects. He said:

The largely increased production of commodities during the last twelve years, accompanied by a stationary supply of gold, was probably the cause of the original downward movement. This downward movement, whatever its cause, having once begun, dealers and consumers of commodities in the face of falling prices have, as a rule, bought only from hand to mouth and speculation has been almost dormant. In this way the slight original natural fall, whatever its cause, has been intensified and greatly magnified by the contracted use of credit, for the supply of money offered for commodities has been reduced to the narrowest possible limits, and, therefore, prices have fallen lower and lower.[6]

Bimetallism. A substantial group of colonists concluded by the 1880's that to restore price stability the money supply would have to be supplemented by monetization of silver. Undoubtedly, discovery of rich silver deposits at Broken Hill in New South Wales, near the South Australian border, gained support for this plan, but the main impetus came from staple-producers caught in the squeeze of falling prices and constant costs.

As early as 1883 William Westgarth, living in London, out-

5. "Increase in the Purchasing Power of Gold," VIII (1884), 95.
6. "Are the Low Prices of Commodities Due to a General Over-production?," *Australasian Insurance and Banking Record,* IX (1885), 145. The *Record's* editor added in a footnote: "Under the title of this paper appears the word 'communicated'—an unusual precaution in the *Record.* We are not prepared to go so far as the writer in his explanation of the causes which have led to the undesirable fall in the prices of commodities, nor do we altogether agree with him. But we esteem the paper as a thoughtful and intelligent exposition on a subject of the deepest interest, and as entitled to the prominence which we accord it."

lined the Australian case for bimetallism.[7] By 1887 the scheme
had attracted widespread attention in the colonies.[8] Edmund Jowett, a prominent pastoralist and wool merchant, explained to
the Bankers' Institute in Melbourne the bimetallists' most appealing argument, that the worldwide decline of prices lowered
unfairly Australia's export receipts while increasing steadily her
debt burden.[9] He was supported with varying amounts of enthusiasm in proposing monetization of silver by Institute members.[10] In Sydney, discussion had become sufficiently intense by
1889 to mobilize monometalists in defense of the gold standard.[11]
In South Australia during 1889, a particularly emphatic plea for
bimetallism came from Jens Bolvig, a Danish immigrant nursery-
man, who saw in colonial adherence to the gold standard a
British plot to increase the debt of dependencies and to impoverish colonists by exploiting their raw material production. He
advocated minting an Australian coin which would contain only
one part of gold to fifteen parts of silver.[12] In 1889 the *Australasian
Insurance and Banking Record* suggested as a less radical alternative to bimetallism a "third element in the rate of interest,"
reminiscent of Wentworth's usury bill, which would adjust debts
automatically according to changes in the "purchasing power of
the medium of exchange."[13]

During the depression years after 1893, bimetallism enjoyed a

7. William Westgarth, "Correspondence: The Bi-metallic Argument," *Chamber
of Commerce Journal*, II (London, 1883), 272–74.
8. Students at Sydney University were asked on their political economy examination in 1887: "What is meant by the Bi-metallic system? What advantages are
claimed for it, and under what conditions might those advantages be secured?"
Sydney University, *Calendar*, 1888, p. clxii.
9. E. Jowett, "Low Prices and the Appreciation of Gold: How are they Caused,
and Are They Likely to Last?," *Journal of the Bankers' Institute of Australasia*,
(1887–88), 14–21. See also Edmund Jowett, *The Ruinous Fall in the Prices
of Produce and the Prevailing Scarcity of Money: or, Why Australia Needs International Bimetallism* (Melbourne, 1893). A biographical description of Jowett
is contained in Edwin J. Brady, *Australia Unlimited* (Melbourne, n. d.), p. 990.
10. *Journal of the Bankers' Institute of Australasia*, II (1887–88), 240–50, and
288–97.
11. Monetas Ganesha, "The Gold and Silver Question," *Sydney Quarterly
Magazine*, 1887, pp. 90–94; and Henry Siebel, "Money," *Bulletin*, X (1889),
No. 510, p. 4.
12. "Letter by Jens Gerdt Bolvig on Bi-metallism," *Proceedings of the Parliament of South Australia*, 1889.
13. "A Third Element in the Rate of Interest," *Australasian Insurance and
Banking Record*, XIII (1889), 388.

surge of popularity. Falling prices were an evident symptom of recession and were diagnosed also as a cause. The bimetallists' complaint of an inadequate metallic base for the money supply appeared eminently reasonable, and their reform proposal followed directly from their argument. Bimetallism was espoused with special enthusiasm by articulate middle-class liberals who could not countenance other reforms. Bitter strikes of the early 1890's dimmed hope for a general program of "co-operation," while the alleged virtues of collectivism had yet to be demonstrated. Adoption by radicals in the labor movement of land reform, tariffs, and a government bank as panaceas for depression encouraged more cautious reformers to accept bimetallism as an alternative answer to economic problems. Liberals turned to bimetallism as a solution to recession which could be defended on a lofty theoretical plane with plausible arguments and with assistance from respectable allies in other countries. Bimetallists were comforted particularly by realization that, if adopted, their plan would bring dual benefits to Australia by restoring prosperity and at the same time providing a buoyant market for the new domestic staple, silver.

Discussion of bimetallism occurred in all the colonies during the depressed 1890's, but debate was particularly vigorous in South Australia which anticipated increased trade with silver-producing Broken Hill. David Murray, an enthusiastic advocate, outlined arguments to the Adelaide Chamber of Commerce, of which he was president, in a lengthy address that nearly anesthetized the worthy merchants. Murray set forth (with diagrams) the quantity theory of money under "guidance of those who have given our monetary system a life long study" (including the bimetallists Soetbeer, Seyd, and Laveleye, as well as J. S. Mill) to illustrate that currency had been in short supply throughout the world since demonetization of silver in the 1870's. For twenty years, he explained, entrepreneurs had suffered falling prices; workers increasingly were unemployed; and government faced mounting relief costs.

At present the farmer, the woolgrower, the mineowner, has to give twice the quantity of his produce for the labour he employs that he required to give twenty years ago. One might suppose that the labourer is thereby enriched, but such is not the case. Although the necessaries of life have fallen somewhat in price the reduction is small, when purchases are made in retail quantities, compared with that to which the producers have to submit, while, on the other hand, as a consequence, we find in some industries efforts are made to reduce wages, in others labour is curtailed and labourers are discharged, who swell the ranks of the unemployed that resort to Government in their extremity.[14]

Murray restated his case to the Economic Science and Agriculture section of the Australasian Association for the Advancement of Science in 1893. On this occasion he sought to prove that monometallism was the main cause of depressions by disputing other explanations. He said: "all of them are more the result than the cause, and individually they have existed in good times without producing any injurious result."[15] Murray urged colonial legislatures to blackmail the British government into bimetallism by threats of debt repudiation:

These Governments have a voice in the counsels of the mother-country—let them exert their influence. Let them say to creditor England—We must by some means be released from this strain; we demand your attention to the currency question; its increase by means of the remonetisation of silver gives promise of relief, and your present apathy and inaction is irritating to us, and may eventually bring us into the condition of inability and unwillingness any longer to bear the intolerable burden.[16]

Murray received some public support for his proposal. A petition with 448 signatures was presented to the South Australian Parliament in 1893 with a request that, in view of "the depression from which nearly all branches of industry are suffering, not only in this province, but throughout Her Majesty's dominions," the British government be urged to call an international conference "for the regulation of the laws relating to metallic currency."[17]

14. David Murray, *Appreciation of Gold* (An Address read before the Adelaide Chamber of Commerce, Adelaide, 1893), p. 17.
15. David Murray, "Bimetallism," *Report of the Fifth Meeting of the Australasian Association for the Advancement of Science held at Adelaide, 1893*, pp. 561–62.
16. *Ibid.*, p. 572.
17. "Petition in Favor of International Monetary Conference," *Proceedings of the Parliament of South Australia*, 1893.

However, Murray also met formidable opposition. Robert Barr Smith, a prominent Adelaide financier, suggested that Murray and other bimetallists were simply advocates of debt repudiation in new guise making use of pseudo-scientific jargon.[18]

William Alison, president of the Bi-metallic League of New South Wales, was the principal spokesman for Sydney bimetallists. Like Murray in South Australia, Alison subscribed to a strict quantity theory of money drawn from Mill and Hume; he interpreted history in terms of changing price levels caused by a fluctuating relationship between gold production and the volume of overall economic activity. With regard to current difficulties he asked:

> Can it be doubted that the cause of the decline in prices is from the appreciation of gold, caused by its increased use, its decreased production, and an increasing population? To say that the cause is overproduction is to argue too much of everything in the world beyond the needs of its population. This is deductively absurd.[19]

The *Australian Pastoralists' Review* published some of Alison's writings, and in these contributions he did not fail to emphasize the dangers of secular deflation for wool-producers. He said in phrases that could be understood clearly: "When most of the money was borrowed the bale of wool sufficed to pay its proportion. Now two bales are required."[20] Alison and other Sydney bimetallists called for international agreement on currency reform as the only alternative to repudiation of debts.[21]

Alison's most effective critic in Sydney was R. L. Nash, leader of the Gold Standard Defence Association, who pointed out such technical problems of bimetallism as the difficulty in maintaining a fixed rate between two metals under a dual monetary standard.

18. R. Barr Smith, *Bimetallism and What Bimetallism May Do for South Australia* (Adelaide, 1893), and *The Bimetallic Question* (Adelaide, 1893).
19. William Alison, *Bimetallism: Wool and Gold, Prices and Wages. The Historical Aspect of the Currency* (Sydney, n. d.), p. 5.
20. *Ibid.*, p. 7.
21. Other presentations of bimetallist views were: Julius Salenger, "Silver," *Journal of the Institute of Bankers of New South Wales*, II (1893), 447–53; J. Currie-Elles, "Financial Review," *ibid.*, III (1894), 4–6; President Aldenham, *The Indian Currency Question: An Appeal to Australasian Producers and Traders* (Sydney, n. d.); W. H. Gocher, *Australia, the Light of the World. The National Bank. The Coining of Our Own Silver. The Backing-Up of Our Silver. The Modification of Bryanism. The Solidification of Federation* (Sydney, n. d.).

Nash argued that bimetallism was based mainly on propaganda of would-be profiteering silver-producers. In direct refutation of Alison he wrote:

That there are some professors in England tainted with the bi-metallic doctrine I admit. But they are outnumbered by twenty to one. Now, as regards the United States. As a matter of fact, the populous Eastern States are overpoweringly monometallic in their views. But it is in the Western and silver-producing States, which, whatever their population, have an equal representation in the Senate, that we find the great strong-hold of the silver party.[22]

After a spirited "rejoinder," in which Alison cited a list of authorities and additional statistical proof of deflation, Nash replied with an autobiographical defense. He said:

Mr. Alison considers that Dr. Giffen is "more scientific than Mr. Nash," and modesty, if nothing else, ought to stand in the way of my disputing the point. Yet it is a strange coincidence that in support of that very assertion Mr. Alison quotes a comparison of prices from Giffen's essays, which Giffen in turn quoted from the *Economist*. Now, for years the preparation of those comparisons of prices happened to be the work of Mr. Nash. Mr. Alison also makes reference to the Silver Commission, which unhappily resulted in a lamentable division of opinion. I was at the time much impressed with the fact that those "index numbers" which Mr. Alison quotes were seriously misleading, and I assisted Mr. Inglis Palgrave, who was a member of the Silver Commission, in the preparation of a series of revised tables, which were printed as an appendix to the Reports of the Commission. I wish I had them by me.[23]

Nash and other critics of bimetallism feared that if Australia remonetized silver unilaterally, or without the complete unanimity of all other countries, Gresham's law would have effect and gold would disappear from circulation.[24]

Several prominent members of the Australian Economic Asso-

22. R. L. Nash, "The Impossibility of an Unfettered Bi-Metallic Currency," *Cosmos Magazine*, I (1895), 503–7. Nash wrote in reply to William Alison, "The Importance of a Bi-Metallic Currency to Australia," *ibid*., pp. 457–60.

23. R. L. Nash, "Bi-metallism: Mr. Alison's 'Rejoinder'," *Cosmos Magazine*, I (1895), 592.

24. See for example J. Medway Day, "Is Bimetallism a Remedy?," *Bulletin*, XIV (1894), No. 761, p. 6.

ciation gave qualified support to bimetallism. Arthur Duckworth began the discussion in 1893 by drawing attention to the prevailing deflation and by noting that gold seemed no longer to be fulfilling its appointed functions as a stable "store of value and standard of deferred payment." He said: "Any cause . . . which may affect the selling price of our product is of great importance to the colony, and the continued depreciation naturally makes us anxious as to the future position of this metal." [25] At first members treated plans for bimetallism merely as the special pleading of an ailing silver industry,[26] but as the depression continued the schemes received a more thorough hearing.[27] Finally, in 1897, Professor Walter Scott of Sydney University set forth an elaborate defense of a bimetallic arrangement to be adopted universally by all important trading nations. He summarized his argument by use of a popular mechanical analogy:

At present, the values of gold and silver may be represented by the height of the water in two unconnected tanks, each having an irregular and intermittent inflow and outflow. Open a connection between the two tanks, and any increased inflow into one of them will slightly raise the level in both, instead of more largely raising the level in one. The bimetallic law would serve the purpose of a connecting pipe.[28]

Scott was joined in support of bimetallism by Duckworth, William Pearse, and the head of the Sydney Chamber of Commerce,[29] but he was opposed vigorously by Alfred De Lissa and W. H. Chard.[30] The Association disbanded before there was time to act on an appeal from the Bimetallic League of Great Britain "to Australia to make her voice heard before it is too late, and to assist, by public protests from her citizens and legislatures. . . ."[31]

25. A. Duckworth, "Is Bi-metallism a Remedy?," *Australian Economist*, III (1893–94), 300.
26. *Australian Economist*, III (1893–94), 340, and IV (1894–97), 513.
27. The following works by well-known bimetallists were reprinted in the *Australian Economist:* W. H. Grenfell, "Bimetallism," IV (1894–97), 565–66; Bimetallic League of London, "What is Bimetallism?," *ibid.*, 580–81; and Francis Walker, "Bimetallism," *ibid.*, V (1897), 14–16.
28. Walter Scott, "Inaugural Address," *ibid.*, V (1897), 13.
29. *Ibid.*, V (1897), 30–31, 40, and 64.
30. *Ibid.*, V (1897), 18 and 20.
31. *Ibid.*, VI (1898), 48.

By 1895 discussion of bimetallism dominated meetings of the Institute of Bankers of New South Wales. Both sides of the question were examined *ad nauseam* with "reading lists" and reprints of foreign authorities both pro and con.[32] However, enthusiasm for bimetallism was correlated closely with the downward movement of prices, and, when towards the end of the 1890's prices began to rise, supporters of the panacea melted away. Alison assured a disconsolate annual meeting of the Bimetallic League in 1899 that prices would soon resume their slide and make their program again "a live question."[33] But his hopes were in vain.

Discussion of bimetallism in Victoria followed the pattern of the other colonies. F. A. Keating, president of the local Bimetallic League, explained repeatedly the doctrinaire bimetallist position whenever he could find an audience.[34] G. A. Russell, a moderate bimetallist, presented a balanced case for currency reform to the Bankers' Institute in 1893. Like other more reasonable bimetallists, Russell attacked principally the evils of deflation without making excessively extravagant claims for the remedy. His study of history, he said, had indicated that a modern economy could not adjust easily to falling prices.

> Times of falling prices are of necessity times of slackening enterprise. New works are not so readily undertaken, and old works once stopped from any cause, are often not re-started. Employment is restricted in all directions, and must so continue until stability of prices, on a lower plane of value, having been once more attained, the work of production can proceed without apprehension of continued reductions in the gold price.[35]

32. "The Currency Question," *Journal of the Institute of Bankers of New South Wales*, IV (1895), 97–103; W. C. Corlette, "Bimetallism (From a Commonplace Point of View)," *ibid.*, 143–48; Moreton Frewen, "Bimetallism," *ibid.*, 201–10; W. Alison, "Monometallism: A Rejoinder," *ibid.*, 219–23; C. McKay Smith, "Bimetallism: A Faith or a Superstition?," *ibid.*, 235–60; W. Alison, "Bimetallism: A Faith or a Superstition? A Rejoinder," *ibid.*, 354–57. There were numerous other minor contributions on the topic throughout 1895.

33. *Ibid.*, VIII (1899), 158.

34. F. A. Keating, "Bimetallism, and the Present Crisis in Currency," *Bankers' Magazine and Journal of the Bankers' Institute of Australasia*, VI (1892–93), 1110–15, and 1189–99; see also the report of a lecture at the Melbourne Town Hall by Keating entitled "The Latest Aspects of the Currency Question," *Australasian Insurance and Banking Record*, XVIII (1894), 22.

35. G. A. Russell, "Appreciation of Gold," *Bankers' Magazine and Journal of the Bankers' Institute of Australasia*, VII (1893–94), 79.

Russell conceded that structural weaknesses in the Australian economy had caused the current depression, but he insisted that collapse had been accentuated by worldwide deflation. "It is not pretended for a moment that there would be no financial crises if there were no gold appreciation; but it is urged that given gold appreciation, and financial crises are likely to be more frequent, more intense, and more general."[36]

In Melbourne, as in Adelaide and Sydney, reprints were issued of both American and British monometallists and bimetallists.[37] The currency controversy, with its insistent repetition on both sides, was described appropriately by the *Bankers' Magazine* as "a kind of intellectual sword play."[38] A visit to Melbourne in 1895 by Moreton Frewen, a prominent international bimetallist called by the *Bankers' Magazine* "the present high priest in these latitudes of bimetallism," gave a temporary fillip to discussion, but as in the other colonies an end came with rising prices.[39]

Tasmania was the only colony, in addition to New South Wales, to produce sizeable quantities of silver, and as might have been expected it yielded also its share of bimetallists. Led by a Dr. Benjafield, Tasmanian bimetallists exhibited a characteristic unanimity of doctrine. Benjafield set forth a rigid economic interpretation of history and traced the world's problems to demonetization of silver.

In 1873, the link between silver and gold was broken by law, and from that date the disasters in the great trading centres commenced . . . demonetization of silver has wrought such mischief in so short a time. We say it has lowered prices, increased the burden of debt

36. *Ibid.*, p. 80.
37. See for example, A. J. Utley, *Bimetallism* (Melbourne, 1896), an American bimetallist tract; and H. S. Foxwell, "Comments on Some Points of the Currency Controversy," *Bankers' Magazine and Journal of the Bankers' Institute of Australasia,* VI (1892–93), 1392–95, a memorandum from a professor of economics, University College, London.
38. Later specimens of the literature are: J. E. Mackey, "Some Fallacies of Bimetallism," *Bankers' Magazine and Journal of the Bankers' Institute of Australasia,* VI (1892–93), 1455–57; William Turner, "Some Strictures on Bimetallism," *ibid.*, VII (1893–94), 686; An Old Banker, "The Currency Question Stated in Homely Terms," *ibid.*, VIII (1894–95), 14–18.
39. "Is Bimetallism a Fad? Its Upholders Entitled to a Respectful Attention," *Bankers' Magazine and Journal of the Bankers' Institute of Australasia,* VIII (1894–95), 477–80; Moreton Frewen, "Currency and Tariff Developments in the United States," *ibid.*, 482–85; opposition came from Waldemar Bannow, *The Colony of Victoria Socially and Materially* (Melbourne, 1896), pp. 175–77.

on all debtors, spoilt investments, and caused stagnation in enterprise; all resulting in bank failures, private bankruptcies, and national troubles.[40]

Benjafield aroused spirited opposition when he called monometallists "drones in the world's hive who neither toil nor spin but luxuriate on others earnings not satisfied with a fair margin of interest for their amassed gold, but they would fain grab everything."[41] Like Murray in South Australia, Benjafield urged Australians to blackmail Britain into adoption of a bimetallic standard through threats of non-payment of debts.

All we have to do is to tell Lombard Street they, by their laws, have so altered the amount of our liabilities that we must demand alteration. If they saw the interest on £400,000,000 trembling in the balance, to say nothing of the principal, they would quickly swallow bimetallism. United Australia now holds a lever which would remove the Lombard Street opposition more quickly than anything.[42]

Several Tasmanian defenders of the gold standard voiced strong opposition to bimetallism. R. M. Johnston argued that because the exchange rate between silver and gold could not be both fixed and in strict accordance with real costs, therefore, bimetallism would be impossible. He said:

if it be . . . admitted that cost of production is the true primary law of economic value or price, then it may be confidently affirmed that any attempt made by governments to fix arbitrary laws for determining the relative exchange values of any two commodities—such as gold and silver as in the scheme of bimetallism—would be as futile as to pass arbitrary laws for determining their absolute specific gravities.[43]

Johnston's objection would have been valid in the case of unilateral bimetallism, but if international agreement had pegged gold and silver at the same relative values in all countries, relative

40. Dr. Benjafield, *Bimetallism: The Remedy for our Depression* (Hobart, 1895), pp. 1 and 5.
41. *Ibid.*, p. 12.
42. *Ibid.*, p. 13.
43. R. M. Johnston, "The Primary Law of Value or Price . . . ," *Papers and Proceedings of the Royal Society of Tasmania*, 1894–95, p. 95. See also "Cost of Living," *ibid.*, 1893, pp. xxiii–xxiv, probably prepared for use in the bimetallism controversy.

production costs would have been significant only for determining levels of profit to producers of monetized silver.

R. J. Lucas, in opposition to currency reform, voiced the type of improbable argument which bimetallists loved to cite. He said:

the true cause of the fall in prices is attributable, not to the scarcity of money, even if that were a fact, but to the cheapness of production, caused by the phenomenal development of mechanical appliances, steam and electricity, facilitating rapidity and cheapness of production; cheapness of water and land carriage, increased facilities of exchange, and the grinding taxation of the great nations for the maintenance of the bloated armaments which have converted Europe into one vast military camp.[44]

Lucas maintained in contradiction to bimetallists that falling prices were in some respects desirable, and were in other respects of no concern because "the law of supply and demand will in due course bring about an adjustment."[45] If legal-tender silver coins were introduced, he added, "bad" money would soon drive out "good." "Sir Thomas Gresham's treatise contains the essential and fundamental principles of a sound currency and is generally so accepted by leading economists, and it is on these principles that monometallism has been developed."[46] A. J. Ogilvy formulated one of the most reasonable cases against bimetallism when he suggested that shortage of effective demand rather than of coin was the cause of deflation and depression. He called for changes in income distribution instead of in the currency.[47]

Sir Samuel Griffith in Queensland discussed bimetallism in 1895 from the viewpoint of a gold-producing colony. He found it necessary to begin by assuring his audience at the Brisbane Technical College that "I am not going to weary you with a discourse on bimetallism, which is thought by some people to be the most dismal branch of the 'dismal science.' I believe that a whole literature on the subject exists, which I have heard described as sufficient to fill a fair-sized private library."[48] Grif-

44. R. J. Lucas, *Bimetallism* (Hobart, 1895), p. 2.
45. *Ibid.*, p. 3.
46. *Ibid.*, p. 11.
47. A. J. O., *The Appreciation of Gold* (Hobart, 1897); and above p. 114.
48. Sir S. W. Griffith, *University Extension, Presidential Address, the Appreciation of Gold, Local Council of Education* (Brisbane, 1895), p. 7.

fith suggested that the currency question should be analyzed in terms of the relation between the costs of producing gold and other goods. "If it should turn out," he said, "that the cost of production of gold has seriously increased, its appreciation or rise in value as compared with everything else would be pro tanto accounted for. The consequences of such a discovery would be far reaching."[49] Griffith predicted that if examination showed the relative production cost of gold to have risen steadily, then the world would be forced before long to recognize that the metal had "become unfit to discharge the function of a standard for measuring debts." With gold production costs permanently advanced, an increased gold supply could not be expected in the future to reverse the price trend. The problem of finding a new monetary standard would be complex, Griffith insisted, and would not be eased by preoccupation with silver. The answer to the currency question, he concluded, was still not known, but he doubted that it lay with the proposals of bimetallists.

The bimetallism controversy was a natural outcome of conditions in the Australian colonies during the 1880's and 1890's. Falling prices were a major cause for concern, and during the prolonged depression many amateur economists became disillusioned with other panaceas. Bimetallist statements contained a kernel of reasoned argument based on a recognition of price inflexibility and the significance for full employment of sustained effective demand. However, the bimetallists' fatal weakness was doctrinaire insistence on a remedy which seemed to be special pleading for a particular industry and promised creation of as many new monetary difficulties as it proposed to solve. The theoretical position of many bimetallists in the 1890's was not unlike that of some pioneer macroeconomists in the 1920's who called for managed currency as a tool of government policy.[50] But colonial bimetallists did not confine themselves to such sensible demands, and the essential weakness of the bimetallic remedy consigned it to oblivion at the end of depression. After fed-

49. *Ibid.,* p. 9.
50. See for example D. B. Copland, *Currency and Prices in Australia* (The Joseph Fisher Lecture in Commerce, 1921, Adelaide, 1921).

eration, bimetallism was seldom revived in discussions of price movements.[51]

Loans on Real Property: Early Agitation

Banking in nineteenth century Britain was developed, and in some instances was controlled, by merchants who established a principle that legitimate security for lending should be, in the main, "self-liquidating commercial paper," meaning claims upon goods destined for proximate resale. Real estate and other forms of fixed property were viewed as illiquid and, even though income-producing, excessively risky backing for loans. In part this principle rested on pure self-interest in that merchants, by restricting the number of eligible recipients for bank funds, obtained relatively low interest rates on their own borrowing and were, in some cases, able also to undertake profitable relending. Furthermore, however, bankers recognized correctly that the market for real property in Britain was remote from the frontiers of economic progress, was particularly prone to wide price fluctuations, and was a favorite resort of speculators.

When carried to new countries where economic development took place principally through exploitation of natural resources, this so-called "real bills doctrine" came under sharp attack. Initially, fledgling colonial banks attempted to follow closely British practice; they were encouraged for a time to confine their lending to commercial security also by the unreliability of local property markets. As early as the 1840's, special mortgage companies, large merchant-lenders, and savings banks helped to relieve pressure on trading banks for funds.[52] But the lure of high profits proved too strong. As in other parts of the Empire, the banks arranged an extension of the "commercial" principle to include loans on the security of goods still in the process of production under a

51. F. E. Allum presented a rather Quixotic defense of monometallism during World War I in "Principles of Currency," *Journal and Proceedings of the Royal Society of Western Australia*, II (1915–16), 35–44.
52. S. J. Butlin, *Foundations*, pp. 308, 312, 449, 454–65; and *A. N. Z. Bank*, 25–26, 212, 213, and 236.

system of wool liens and stock mortgages.[53] Banks were led at different times also to accept mortgages on the simple pragmatic ground that sufficient commercial paper could not be obtained.[54] Charles Swanston informed his clients from Hobart in 1838: "In this colony there are only two modes of investing money, one is by mortgage on landed security and the other by investments in bank shares."[55] Although mortgage lending was blamed often for economic crises and was discouraged explicitly by the British Treasury, it became a significant feature of Australian banking in the nineteenth century. The most serious attempts to offer theoretical justification for property loans, by appeals to European precedent, are described in this section.

Schemes for low-cost lending on mortgage security attracted both banking and land-reformers. The former sought liberalization of the commercial loan principle while the latter wished encouragement to settlement on the land. In the early years, opposition to the "real bills doctrine" from both types of advocate took the form merely of appeals for a break with banking tradition without presentation of rival theory in self-justification. For example, in 1830 the President of the Agricultural and Horticultural Society of New South Wales asserted that "the Proprietors of shares of both our Banks ought to step forward and lend their notes upon mortgage, at moderate interest; such notes not to be payable in less than three years."[56] During the crisis year, 1843, schemes for institutions to be called land banks were prepared both in Tasmania and in New South Wales.[57] On the strength of evidence from a witness who had spent some time in Prussia, a select committee on "the monetary confusion" in New South Wales suggested that the colonial authorities act as intermediary in the flotation of loans on the security of real estate. Under this

53. S. J. Butlin, *Foundations*, pp. 340–45.
54. *Ibid.*, pp. 402, and 501–9; and *A. N. Z. Bank*, pp. 96 and 249–50.
55. Cited in S. J. Butlin, *Foundations*, p. 231; and see *ibid.*, pp. 355–60.
56. John Jamison, *Report of the Agricultural and Horticultural Society of New South Wales for 1830* (Sydney, n. d.), p. 72.
57. It was reported in Hobart that a group was attempting to "organize a species of Land Bank" to seal "the doom of usury." "Past, Present, and Future Position of Tasmania," *South Briton; or Tasmanian Literary Journal*, I (1843), 30–31; and S. J. Butlin, *Foundations*, p. 338.

proposal, government would have advanced to colonists, on mortgage up to one-third of the market value of land, interest-bearing public securities similar to *pfandbriefes* issued by Prussian land boards or *landschaften*.[58] These guaranteed debentures could be sold in the open market for par value.[59] *Pfandbriefes*, it was argued, would return to pioneer settlers the essential capital of which they had been deprived by land sales. Charles Griffith suggested a physiological analogy to indicate how mortgage lending could relieve depressed conditions in the Port Phillip District:

if the blood all goes to the head, a man dies just as much as if he was bled to death—the only difference being between apoplexy and inanition. If indeed government had in the first instance retained the money in its hands, and then lent it back to the purchasers of land under the system of *pfandebriefe* [sic], this might have acted like cataplasms to the natural body, and the circulating medium have been thus re-distributed through the body politic—in short, things would have been much where they started.[60]

Despite its temporary popularity, the *pfandbriefe* scheme was judged by the Colonial Office too great a departure from orthodoxy for a fledgling colony with a banking system barely thirty years old.

Proposals for agricultural banks or some other type of formalized mortgage lending were made at irregular intervals after the 1840's, generally during recessions and usually with continued inspiration from Continental experience. Robert R. Torrens in 1858 recommended that an institution of *crédit foncier* be established in South Australia to make loans on land registered under his new Real Property Act. Under Torrens' scheme, mortgages would have been accepted as security against both notes

58. Pfandbriefe operations are described in: M. Tcherkinsky, *The Landschaften and their Mortgage Credit Operations in Germany (1770–1920)* (Rome, 1922); and H. Belshaw, *The Provision of Credit with Special Reference to Agriculture* (Cambridge, 1931).
59. "Report from the Select Committee on the Monetary Confusion, with Appendix and Minutes of Evidence," *Votes and Proceedings of the Legislative Council of New South Wales*, 1843.
60. Charles Griffith, *The Present State and Prospects of the Port Phillip District of New South Wales* (Dublin, 1845), p. 110.

and deposits, with a one-third reserve ratio of specie against deposits and note-issue restricted to two-thirds the amount of paid-up bank capital. Torrens believed that a land bank, in addition to accelerating growth of the colony, would be found "greatly to promote habits of frugality, encouraging the practice of daily savings from incomes for the redemption of debt."[61] Despite insistence by Torrens and others on the need for modification of the commercial banking practice, British tradition remained strong, and mortgage loans continued to be approved often in practice but seldom in principle. A prominent banker, Henry Gyles Turner, contended as late as 1880 that the prosperity of the past twenty-five years had justified departure from orthodoxy in the granting of loans on mortgage; yet he too attempted only to offer empirical proof of this assertion. He said:

The special circumstances of the colony, and the experience of a quarter of a century, justified the belief that such advances, within judicious limits, might be safely and profitably made by banks of issue. The practice, though discountenanced by English authorities, had been of immense value in promoting the settlement of the colony, and the development of those resources which must ultimately become the mainstay of its prosperity.[62]

In the 1880's and 1890's, schemes for what were given during this period the title *crédit foncier* (landed credit) joined homestead settlement, the single tax, land nationalization, protective tariffs, and government banking as a popular panacea for depression. Details of plans differed, but real estate loans were a common feature and the French term was used as a general designation. Charles H. Pearson listed as one important element of his "Liberal Programme" for Victoria in 1880 "something like the Banks of Agriculture that have been established for many years in Prussia and other European countries. Deriving their

61. Robert R. Torrens, *Project for the Establishment of a South Australian Land Bank, on Principles Similar to those of the "Institution des Credits Fonciers," on the Continent of Europe, Earnestly Recommended to the Attention of Capitalists, Landowners, and the Public of South Australia* (Adelaide, 1858), p. 9.
62. H. G. Turner, "Victorian Banking," *Argus* (Melbourne), November 23, 1880, p. 6.

funds partly from a State loan, partly from trust money on deposit, and partly from shares, these banks are administered by local men under Government inspection, and advance money on land, on timber, and on stock."[63] W. E. Adcock, in the same tradition, presented in 1881 a detailed plan for a "State Agricultural Loan Bureau."[64]

The report of a South Australian Royal Commission on state banking in 1889 revealed the prevalence of land bank ideas and their continued Continental inspiration. George W. Cotton, a radical member of the Legislative Council, recommended strongly as a witness that a government bank be formed to undertake mortgage lending on the *pfandbriefe* pattern. The Commission, which was more conservative in sentiment than was Cotton, appended to its report translations of writings on the subject by Otto Swoboda and E. Merkel, but concluded that except for possible operations by a government savings bank the system "seems at present impracticable."[65]

During the 1890's, bank failures and curtailment of credit caused the question of mortgage lending to be discussed urgently, and in several colonies special agricultural relief measures were introduced.[66] Outstanding spokesmen for Continental principles of land-banking were two European immigrants, H. L. E. Ruthning and Carl Pinschof. Ruthning, a solicitor and president of the Queensland Farmers and Graziers Alliance, began in the 1880's to portray mortgage banking as a vital element in a broad system of social co-operation wherein capital and labor could work together in harmony and prosperity. He wished strict application of the Prussian model of *landschaften* as described by "German and Continental writers," including in particular provisions for

63. Charles H. Pearson, "The Liberal Programme," *Victorian Review*, I (1880), 533.
64. W. E. Adcock, "Is a State Agricultural Loan Bureau Desirable?," *Victorian Review*, IV (1881), 735–39.
65. "Report of Royal Commission Appointed to Consider the Desirability of Establishing a State Bank and Royal Mint; together with Minutes of Proceedings, Evidence, Synopses, and Appendices," *Proceedings of the Parliament of South Australia*, 1889, p. vi.
66. S. J. Butlin, *A. N. Z. Bank*, p. 322; and W. Pember Reeves, "Colonial Governments as Money-Lenders," *Report of the Seventieth Meeting of the British Association for the Advancement of Science*, 1900, transactions, pp. 848–49.

close community supervision of mortgaged property, long-term advances, gradual repayment conditions, and negotiability of debentures on an open market.[67] Ruthning was a doctrinaire purist and he condemned all suggestions for Australian deviations from imported theory.[68] He was dismissed by the *Journal of the Bankers' Institute of Australasia* as one who "treats the present subject in an abstruse and academic fashion, which, together with his foreign mode of expression, would render him unintelligible to Australians accustomed to a plainer, if less cultured, method of expression."[69]

In Victoria during the 1890's, a special agency was established within the government savings bank, ostensibly on principles of *crédit foncier* but in reality simply to assist farmers and pastoralists whose sources of credit had been contracted by bank failures. Carl Pinschof, consul for Austria-Hungary in Melbourne, was the foremost advocate of the scheme, and he was responsible at least in part for acquainting local bankers with methods of operation of French and other land banks. He was less doctrinaire in prescription than was Ruthning, and he wished merely for agricultural loans on easy repayment terms without insistence on exact conformity to any particular principle.[70] The Melbourne Chamber of Commerce endorsed Pinschof's proposals and reported in 1893 that a lecture by him had stimulated a wave of public enthusiasm:

The importance of the question is now universally admitted, and although, for the reasons above stated, no immediate result followed Mr. Pinschof's lecture to this Chamber, the seed then sown has been germinating, and the committee believe that good fruit will follow in the near future. Amid the conflict of party questions, the "soul of goodness" in the essential principles of the Credit Foncier has been

67. H. L. E. Ruthning, "Co-operation and its Possibilities," *Australian Economist*, I (1888–90), 25–26; "A Crédit Foncier," *ibid.*, IV (1894–97), 502; "The Crédit Foncier," *Journal of the Institute of Bankers of New South Wales*, VI (1897), 373–76; and "How Should the Principles of Crédit Foncier be Applied?," *ibid.*, VII (1898), 23–28.

68. H. L. E. Ruthning, "The Victorian Crédit Foncier," *Australian Economist*, V (1897), 41–43.

69. "The Victorian Crédit Foncier," XI (1897–98), 5.

70. Carl Pinschof, "Our Financial Organisation and the Present Crisis," *Bankers' Magazine and Journal of the Bankers' Institute of Australasia*, VI (1892–93), 1004–5, 1101–2, and 1125–39.

recognised by all sections of the press, and the public mind has lately been made thoroughly familiar with its objects and methods.[71]

The editors of the *Bankers' Magazine* affirmed in 1894 that "we consider that Mr. Pinschof was really and entirely the means, by his lecture at the Bankers' Institute, Melbourne, of introducing the Foncier plan."[72] Only a year later, however, they gave evidence of general fatigue with Pinschof's continuous propaganda:

> Regarding Carl Pinschof . . . he is undoubtedly clever, and if he had not such an awful name, might have been Treasurer of Victoria ere this. . . . The intelligent Victorian thinks the scheme foreign directly P. opens his mouth, and will not hearken to the voice of the charmer. Herr P. is a man with a mission, and he is like the ancient mariner telling his story to the wedding guest:
> "He held him with his glittering eye."
> And if Pinschof's eye fails, he hooks you with a massive forefinger and murmurs into your ear soft nothings about "irredeemable bonds," or "unification of loans." It is useless to try to stave him off with feeble protestations such as "Excuse me, the wife says I must be home to dinner at five o'clock." He has a financial mission. It may be the voice of one crying in the wilderness; but nothing short of an earthquake, or an attack of influenza, will stop the genial and gallant Hungarian stuffing financial truth into the weary wayfarer while the latter can stand on his legs.[73]

Although the views of Ruthning, Pinschof, and other exponents of European land banking were reported widely, and a variety of experiments were undertaken throughout the colonies with government loans to farmers, it is unlikely that Continental experience was decisive in any one instance.[74] Authorities from

71. "The Credit Foncier. The Chamber of Commerce (Melbourne) Report," *Bankers' Magazine and Journal of the Bankers' Institute of Australasia*, VII (1893–94), 665–66; Pinschof's address to the Chamber was published as "The Credit Foncier System," *ibid.*, VI (1892–93), 1183–87 and 1397–1405.
72. "The Credit Foncier Bill (Victoria)," *ibid.*, VII (1893–94), 808.
73. "Editors' Notes," *ibid.*, VIII (1894–95), 800–801.
74. Writings by Pinschof on land banking were recommended by a New South Wales Committee on a Post Office Savings Bank—National Bank in 1892–93. See "Progress Report; together with the Proceedings of the Committee, Minutes of Evidence, and Appendix," *Votes and Proceedings of the Legislative Assembly of New South Wales*, 1892–93. The experience of South Australia with government loans on mortgage is described in "Report of the Select Committee of the Legislative Council on the State Bank; together with Minutes of Proceedings, Evidence, and Appendices," *Proceedings of the Parliament of South Australia*, 1909. A "short history" of legislation relating to agricultural banks in Western Australia is contained in "Report of the Agricultural Bank Royal Commission," *Minutes and Votes*

other countries also were passed in review, in particular the
American Senator Leland Stanford,[75] and Australians themselves
seemed little concerned with consistency to one model. Agricultural credit drew support from a variety of different adherents.
In addition to financial doctrinaires, others during the depression
grasped at a proposal for institutional change which seemed
likely to encourage community co-operation.[76] In dire straits as
many of them were, farmers and pastoralists were willing to
accept any principles which promised relief. Henry Gyles Turner was probably close to the truth when he contended that
crédit foncier was accepted in Australia not from conviction but
in response to irresistible demands from beleagured borrowers
for "cheap money."[77] After federation, demands for mortgage
lending were submerged beneath proposals for a Commonwealth bank.

The two matters examined in this chapter, price-level fluctuations and property loans, were of urgent concern in a dependent staple-producing economy. Inspiration for proposed
reforms came from abroad, and local discussion consisted largely
of imported arguments. Examination of these controversies reveals ways in which foreign idea systems were able to penetrate
the colonies at appropriate times; it reveals also the formidable
conservative influence of orthodox British tradition.

---

and Proceedings of the Parliament of Western Australia, 1934, pp. 4–6. An incomplete and partly inaccurate account of "state banks and land mortgage credit institutions in Australia" can be found in Anwar Iqbal Qureshi, *State Banks for India*
(London, 1939), pp. 23–130.

75. Leland Stanford, *Great Money Question* . . . (Melbourne, 1893).

76. John Plummer, "The Possibilities of Co-operative Agricultural Production
in Australia," *Australian Economist*, V (1897), 54–55; B. R. Wise, "The People's
Banks of Italy and Germany," *Journal of the Institute of Bankers of New South
Wales*, III (1894), 357–73. For views expressed in this article Wise was labeled
by the Sydney *Bulletin* "essentially a man of book-knowledge and slow to learn
by personal observation." XIV (1894), No. 759, p. 7.

77. "Views of Mr. Henry Gyles Turner," *Bankers' Magazine and Journal of the
Bankers' Institute of Australasia*, XI (1897–98), 11–13. Similar caustic comments
by bankers were contained in *Australasian Insurance and Banking Record*, e.g.,
XVIII (1894), 69–70.

7

Economic Fluctuations

Australian colonies experienced their first recognizable trade cycle in the 1820's, and subsequently booms and recessions occurred at intervals with particularly deep depressions dominating the 1840's and 1890's.[1] Economists today are far from agreed on the causes of and cures for economic fluctuations, and Australians in the nineteenth century understandably were either puzzled or sharply divided on these questions. Analysts usually rejected as ludicrous or preposterous explanations of trade cycles which differed from their own, and in this chapter contributions to the debate are treated without close regard to the enthusiasm with which they were received by contemporaries or to their current respectability. Reasons which were offered for economic fluctuations fell into three broad categories and are examined here in separate sections; these were: temporary but unavoidable irregularities in the system of a free economy, misguided policies of government, and deficiency of total effective demand.

Irregularities in the Economic System

Paradoxically, writers during the early years of the nineteenth century who were most familiar with sophisticated economic theory often were least able to account for economic fluctuations. Classical and neo-classical economists confined their analysis in most cases to problems of an hypothetical smooth-running sys-

1. An economic fluctuation in the 1820's is described by R. M. Hartwell in "Australia's First Trade Cycle. Boom, Crisis, Depression and Recovery in New South Wales, 1820–1832," *Royal Australian Historical Society Journal and Proceedings*, XLII (1956), 51–67.

tem wherein consumers, according to their buying power, received at minimum cost the goods they desired, and fully employed producers were rewarded in proportion to their productivity. Economists took some notice of possible monopolistic distortions and warned against evil effects of restrictive legislation, but with a few exceptions such as Malthus and Lauderdale they were unable to offer reasonable explanations for the serious crises and periods of stagnation which took place around them. Disciples of British political economists living in the colonies seldom had more insight than did their masters, and usually they too listed frictions in the economic mechanism as causes of difficulties.

Psychological factors. A favorite reason put forth for the existence of fluctuations was the development of collective psychological aberrations amounting to a form of mass neurosis. For example, a writer in the *New South Wales Magazine* asked rhetorically in 1843 "To what causes, then, is it owing, that with all these commercial and territorial wealth, the colony is now so much embarassed and depressed?," and he replied wonderingly, "It is plainly not from *natural* causes, such as earthquakes, plague, pestilence, and famine; the evils must, therefore, have arisen from *mis-management*, on the part either of the Government, of the colonists, or of both."[2] After investigation, the writer concluded that the "mismanagement" seemed to be caused by a condition resembling national manic depression. At the beginning of a cycle, rapid immigration and new discoveries led to exaggerated excitement until, when reality failed to match hopes, excessive reaction began a downturn to depression. In terms of this theory of fluctuating expectations, the first great boom and collapse of pastoralists during the 1820's was described thus:

The demands of this affluent body, superadded to those of the capitalists regularly arriving on our shores, strengthened the general confidence in colonial resources, created a growing spirit of adventure in rural pursuits, and caused a rapid enhancement of the nominal

2. "The Affairs of New South Wales," *New South Wales Magazine*, 1843, p. 243.

value of property. Here was about the first example of "OVER-ACTION" in New South Wales. Expectations of profit were unduly raised; capital was invested with incautious precipitancy; liabilities were incurred without prudent regard to the ways and means whereby they were to be met; credit was too easily obtained; paper money commanded too ready a currency; and when about three-fourths of the ten years of which we are speaking had passed away, the re-action —and a fearful re-action it was—began to make itself felt.[3]

Several colonial writers came to believe that, as a rule of human nature, economic elation and optimism were followed inevitably by deep dejection and black pessimism. In Tasmania during the 1840's, T. J. Ewing contended that boom and collapse were initiated by new discoveries and price fluctuations but were sustained by this fundamental human emotional instability. He wrote that in 1839–40:

the gambling propensities of human nature were called into action; and there were few, possessing the means, who did not venture to embark some portion of their property in schemes which would now startle many from their wildness. At length the tide turned, and a sudden transition took place from unbounded confidence to general distrust.[4]

William Mackintosh in Melbourne suggested that an occasional recession acted as a necessary purgative for the human psyche. He reported gratefully in the 1840's that as "bitter fruits of over speculation, and careless extravagance, which caused the revulsion of 1841–2–3 . . . careful distrust of speculation, prudent attention to business and frugality in expenditure, are now the pleasing results that everywhere meet the eye."[5] The Sydney *Empire* during the gold rush of the 1850's reprinted long passages from "the celebrated McCulloch" setting forth the need for calm and reason to compensate the speculative boom.[6]

3. *Ibid.*, pp. 244–45.
4. Rev. T. J. Ewing, "Statistics of Tasmania, 1838–1841: Extracts from the Introductory Letter to his Excellency Sir John Franklin," *Tasmanian Journal of Natural Science, Agriculture, Statistics, &c.,* II (1846), 143.
5. William Mackintosh, *General Statistical and Commercial Report of the Province of Australia Felix, for the Year Ending 31st July, 1847* (Melbourne, c. 1848), p. 3.
6. "Commercial Record: Speculation and Monopoly," *Empire*, August 23, 1851, pp. 78–79.

J. D. Lang in 1852 described a recent cycle exclusively in biological terms. He wrote: "In short, the body politic of the colony
has passed through a crisis of violent and unnatural excitement,
which, according to the well-known maxim of Hippocrates, the
father of medicine, must necessarily be followed by a corresponding crisis of unnatural depression."[7] Christopher Rolleston,
Registrar General of New South Wales, indicated that by 1867 the
manic-depressive theory had obtained wide currency, and that as
a result the inevitability of depressions had become universally
accepted. He explained:

I am satisfied to fall in with the general opinion that we *are* suffering
from the effect of previous overtrading and extravagance. This is no
new thing. Young and vigorous communities like ours are peculiarly
liable to fluctuations of this kind. Depression follows excitement as
naturally in the body social as in the body physical, and I know of
nothing in the climate or constitution of New South Wales which
should exempt us from this law.[8]

During the 1880's and 1890's the psychological theory of fluctuations was used first to urge restraint during the boom and then
during depression to combat other explanations which implied
the need for radical social or economic reform. Catherine Spence
in South Australia in 1881 claimed that a human propensity to
gamble and to speculate was the only possible reason for crises.
"No doubt the production and the consumption have been somewhat badly adjusted; but the real main reason of these industrial
crises has been over-speculation, and especially over-speculation
in land."[9] The *Australasian Insurance and Banking Record* in
1884 "preached caution" in regard to the wave of excitement it
saw developing, and it remarked: ". . . we certainly incline to
the opinion that both Australian Governments and Australian
merchants have been going too fast. A time of retrenchment
always follows such a period of inflation, and business must be
very sound indeed to survive the reaction without some sort of

7. J. D. Lang, *An Historical and Statistical Account of New South Wales* (London, 1852), I, 216.
8. Christopher Rolleston, *The Condition and Resources of New South Wales*
(London, 1867), p. 4.
9. C. H. Spence, "A Californian Political Economist," *Victorian Review*, IV
(1881), 143.

shock."[10] A contributor to the *Record* in 1885 warned that sudden reversals in price expectations would soon generate fluctuations in the money supply and effective demand. Because instruments of credit formed a major portion of the money supply, small price changes up or down might react on the volume of bank loans and thereby strengthen the price movement in the same direction. He wrote:

. . . without any change whatever in the quantity of gold coin in the world, the demand for commodities, and therefore the prices paid for them, may undergo the most violent fluctuations in very short spaces of time. If they have reason to expect a rise in the prices of some commodities, men naturally buy freely, making an extensive use of their money and their credit, and a rise far greater than the one they anticipated is often produced. On the other hand, if there be reason to apprehend a fall in the price of commodities, dealers and consumers naturally buy as little as possible, that is, they do not use their money and credit freely, and prices naturally fall.[11]

W. H. Irvine, lecturer in political economy at the University of Melbourne, subscribed to a trade cycle theory based entirely on changes in expectations. He wrote:

We see in all things a perpetual oscillation between too much and too little, the middle position being seldom long retained. Some of the phenomena of supply and demand afford good instances of this. The demand, let us suppose, for a certain article is raised by the too sanguine expectations of traders to a point not warranted by actual demand of the consumers. Prices are high and too much of the article is produced. Soon there succeeds a period of depression. Dealers hardly buy at all, their sanguine timerity [*sic*] having given place to a want of confidence and timidity as excessive on the other side. Prices fall abnormally low, and production almost ceases. But the same causes which brought about the depression, being as it were in an inverted position, give rise to a new increase in the demand. In this way the whole process repeats itself.[12]

Although some writers late in the century were able still to explain fluctuations entirely in terms of psychological change,

10. "Have the Australian Banks Been Over-Advancing?," *Australasian Insurance and Banking Record*, VIII (1884), 140.
11. "Are the Low Prices of Commodities Due to a General Over-Production?," *Australasian Insurance and Banking Record*, IX (1885), 145.
12. W. H. Irvine, "Prof. Bonamy Price on the Doctrine of Rent," *Victorian Review*, X (1884), 223.

others included this factor in a larger eclectic theory. In London during 1883, William Westgarth set forth a detailed trade cycle hypothesis based on assumed changes in expectations but embodying also descriptions of overproduction and inventory oscillations. He claimed that during an upswing overoptimism encouraged excessive expenditure on investment goods which, when in operation, never yielded satisfactory returns. As soon as investors realized their folly the crash began. Westgarth elaborated:

> Crisis, then, comes chiefly of disproportion; it comes of great expenditure disproportionately restored. During the excited times which as the rule precede great crises, there is rarely any want of producing energy to keep even a full pace with the spending energy. Indeed the lavish expenditure in question is mostly for reproduction of some kind; but the reproduction is not proportionate in its various items, so as to restore duly the capital expended, and thus to maintain the stocks of trade in their suitable proportions for business wants. And thus the society is impoverished by reduced capital, while the market is, in some apparent contradiction, dull and stagnant, alike through the overstocks and understocks of its disproportioned contents.[13]

Westgarth concluded that revival occurred when inventories declined, memories of the collapse dimmed, and "the natural tendencies to a reproduction proportionate to expenditure has restored the normal equipoise." During the 1890's, when a variety of explanations for prevailing depression came under review, psychological theories such as those described here were considered often again.[14]

Inflexibility of resources. In addition to the psychological factor, immobility of labor was a favorite reason for unemployment suggested particularly by defenders of a free economy. Immobility was blamed usually on "lazy" city workers unwilling to adapt to changing conditions. If only part of the urban population would move to the country and become truly "productive," the argument ran, greater employment would be provided for persons

13. William Westgarth, "Practical Commerce versus Theoretical Political Economy: Crises," *Chamber of Commerce Journal*, II (1883), 328.
14. See for example: *Journal of the Institute of Bankers of New South Wales,* II (1893), 62–65; and J. Currie-Elles, "Financial Review," *ibid.,* III (1894), 4–6.

who remained in cities, and national output would increase. For example, a writer in New South Wales proclaimed during a recession in the late 1850's that "it is vain to expect any considerable amelioration in our circumstances, until some of the now productive hands which hang uselessly behind the counters of our shops, and are half employed in our mercantile offices, are employed in raising wealth from the soil."[15]

H. L. Lindsay in Victoria observed that although "in establishing a new country, the more the population can be scattered, the better for the ultimate benefit, both of the country and themselves," the lure of gold-mining had attracted labor to a few congested centers.[16] When the temporary profits of surface mining diminished, Lindsay predicted, only a recession and general price decline would stimulate the dispersion necessary for long-run prosperity. Some critics extended condemnation of congregation in cities to wasteful high living which resulted from urbanization, and they called for return to the rural virtues of thrift and abstinence. In 1878 R. Murray Smith warned:

We have spent too much, and made too little; we have eaten and drank, and clothed ourselves too extravagantly; our harvest has been deficient, our wool clip has fallen short of our calculations, our capital has, partly through financial, partly through political causes, been diverted to other colonies. We have spent most of the money which we borrowed from England; and while we are feeling the pressure of payment of interest, we are pursuing an unprofitable and wasteful system of finance.[17]

R. M. Johnston, the Tasmanian government statistician, believed that unemployment through immobility could be overcome by scientific discovery of appropriate proportions of the labor force which should be directed to various economic sectors. If labor were allocated proportionately, he claimed, all could be employed. He calculated that for equilibirum in his own colony the pastoral, mining, and agricultural sectors should contain together about 50 per cent of the labor force, unskilled city

15. "Future Prospects," *Sydney Magazine of Science and Art,* II (1859), 149.
16. H. Lill Lindsay, *The Industrial Resources of Victoria, with Practical Suggestions on Agriculture, Employment of Labor, Water Supply, &c.* (Melbourne, 1856), p. 4.
17. R. Murray Smith, "Paper Money," *Melbourne Review,* III (1878), 420.

artisans and laborers should constitute about 30 per cent, and skilled professions should number not more than approximately 20 per cent of the total. Misallocation of labor in proportions other than the ones he prescribed, Johnston asserted, entailed unemployment and widespread distress. In particular, he warned, too many colonists should not be encouraged to gain skills in the production of secondary goods and services for which there could be no demand. He said:

It is largely due to the flooding of particular kinds of employment beyond the strict proportions which local wants demand that inconvenience or distress is felt in young as well as old countries. The numbers which can find entry into the higher industrial, the commercial, and professional divisions cannot, without unhealthy competition, be increased beyond the relative proportions which these divisions must bear to the producing industries of the particular country; and these dominating industries in Australasia are agricultural, pastoral, and mining.[18]

Johnston acknowledged that optimum factor proportions were changing constantly because of alterations in taste, technology, and stage of development. But he maintained that economists overestimated the ease of factor mobility necessary to permit smooth adjustments in employment, and he argued that frictions in the movement of economic resources should be gauged and taken into account in the same way as costs of transporting physical goods. "Because the Political Economist does not think, or does not choose to think, that the transfer of a labourer or capitalist to a new place or to a new kind of occupation involves a process analogous to the movement of inanimate bodies, it is not the less true."[19]

Johnston insisted that socialists and land-reformers misunderstood the real causes of unemployment and therefore advocated false cures. He said:

Noble as are the ideals of the better class of socialistic writers, I am, nevertheless, convinced that the selfishness of landlordism or

18. Robert M. Johnston, "Observations on Current Social and Economic Problems," *Report of the Second Meeting of the Australasian Association for the Advancement of Science held at Melbourne, 1890,* p. 130.
19. *Ibid.,* p. 145.

capitalist is not the cause of our miseries, and that placing more people on the land than the economic conditions of the particular country requires would, instead of removing the present evils, increase them tenfold. . . . The congestion of labour, so called, in crowded centres is not due to such a cause at all. It is entirely due to the lack of knowledge how to allocate the breadwinner each day added to the population in accordance with the exact division of labour in which fresh services are required.[20]

Perhaps because of his position as a civil servant, Johnston seldom put forward specific and detailed proposals for economic reform, but he did observe that, short of full state management of the economy, higher levels of employment might be achieved by close study and government planning to assist private decision-makers. He concluded:

What is needed . . . is something like omniscience, to continually devise and regulate the training of breadwinners in the proportions in which their services will be in demand. We must not, therefore, despise the defective machinery—capitalists and organisers of industry—which hitherto have performed roughly this grand service for us. At least we owe them so much that we cannot desire to see them removed until it can be clearly shown that a better provision can take their place.[21]

Johnston reasoned that even if the colonies did not wish to interfere with the voluntary location of their existing labor force they could at least control the flow of immigrants in correct proportions, and he emphasized that in a staples-producing economy the number of workers employed in secondary industry would be determined rigidly by the volume of primary production.[22] Johnston believed that apart from misallocation other causes of Australian depressions lay beyond the country's control, and in particular inexplicable worldwide disturbances of product and capital markets.[23] For a brief period Johnston experimented, like

20. R. M. Johnston, "Consumable Wealth," *Report of the Seventh Meeting of the Australasian Association for the Advancement of Science held at Sydney, 1898*, p. 883.
21. *Ibid.*, p. 884.
22. R. M. Johnston, "Conditions upon Which the Healthy Growth of the Population of Young Colonies Depend," *Papers and Proceedings of the Royal Society of Tasmania*, 1903–5, pp. 27–33.
23. R. M. Johnston, *Handbook of Tasmania for the year 1893* (Hobart, 1894), p. 94.

William Stanley Jevons, with correlations of economic and "super-terrestrial" phenomena.[24]

Other Australians shared Johnston's belief in the significance of correct employment proportions for preservation of economic stability, and Alfred De Lissa, whose writings are discussed in Chapter 14, recommended formation of a labor bureau to assign jobs to the unemployed.[25] When Professor Walter Scott of Sydney University investigated causes of unemployment in 1890 he too concluded: "The answer must be for want of proper *organisation*" and he also advocated "labour bureaux." Scott had boundless faith in the ability of economic science to provide answers for macro-economic problems, and for this reason he said: "We want knowledge of economic truth, because knowledge is power; and all who care whether they or their neighbours are richer or poorer, over-worked or unemployed, are by that very fact interested in the study and progress of Political Economy. . . ."[26] In 1900 the possibility of planned labor allocation was discussed by members of a Victorian Board of Inquiry on Unemployment who named "insufficiency of organization" and "concentration in the metropolis" as two principal causes of hard times.[27] Like Johnston, De Lissa, and Scott, the Board recommended creation of a "Public Department of Labour" and a "Labour Bureau" as co-ordinating bodies.

Economic ignorance. In addition to psychological instability and factor immobility, some colonists also blamed want of ac-

24. R. M. Johnston, "Remarks on the Observed Periodicity of the Death-Rate, with Suggestions as to its Possible Relation with the Periodicity of Solar and Other Super-Terrestrial Phenomena," *Papers and Proceedings of the Royal Society of Tasmania*, 1884, pp. 236–39. Johnston was criticized effectively by A. B. Biggs in "Observations on Mr. R. M. Johnston's Vital Statistics," *ibid.*, pp. 276–80; and he replied in "A Rejoinder to Mr. A. B. Biggs' Criticism on Observations Made in Respect of the 'Observed Periodicity of the Death Rate' Etc.," *ibid.*, pp. 280–82. Johnston may have been inspired by a contribution to the proceedings of the London Statistical Society: B. G. Jenkins, "On a Probable Connection Between the Yearly Death-Rate and the Position of the Planet Jupiter in his Orbit," *Journal of the Statistical Society*, XLII (1879), 330–33.
25. See below p. 516.
26. Walter Scott, "Inaugural Address of the Eighth Session of the Australian Economic Association," *Australian Economist*, II (1890–93), 95 and 97.
27. The Board, which included such prominent free traders as R. Murray Smith and Max Hirsch, took evidence only from W. H. Renwick, Secretary of the Free Trade Democratic Association. "Report of the Board of Inquiry on Unemployment," *Papers Presented to the Parliament of Victoria*, 1900.

curate information for the existence of economic fluctuations. If knowledge of the economy was incorrect, it was argued, miscalculations were inevitable. A Victorian legislative committee in 1856 decided that improved statistics would both stabilize domestic prices and limit development of unproductive sectors of the economy. The committee reported with regard to agricultural data that,

These Returns, if made immediately after harvest, would afford the information necessary to enable the mercantile community to decide upon the necessity or otherwise for foreign supplies, and thus protect the home producer in some measure against unnecessary importations. They would also enable the farmers of the Province to decide with certainty as to the most profitable articles of cultivation for the future, and at the same time furnish information to those who might be desirous of settling, as to the particular district in which their peculiar knowledge would be most profitably turned to account.[28]

Christopher Rolleston, Registrar General of New South Wales, explained also in 1856 that the derangement of markets resulting from gold discoveries after 1851 might have been minimized if statistics of demand, supply, and prices of all goods had been available to merchants and producers. He explained that currently farmers faced particularly great uncertainty:

The absence of accurate information on the subject of agriculture is found to be productive of inconvenience to all classes, owing to the uncertainty which prevails as to the quantity of land under the different descriptions of cultivation in each year; as to the supplies of food which exist in the country at any given time, and consequently as to the quantities that may be required from abroad to make up the deficiency in home-grown produce, thus giving rise to extreme fluctuations in bread, and encouraging hazardous speculations in corn.[29]

During the decline of the late 1880's and 1890's, "want of knowledge" both of principles and of data was mentioned repeatedly as the root of economic troubles. One New South Wales banker argued that because so many past crises had been brought

28. "Report from the Select Committee of the Legislative Council on Agricultural and Horticultural Statistics; together with the Proceedings of the Committee, Minutes of Evidence, and Appendices," *Votes and Proceedings of the Legislative Council of Victoria*, 1856, p. iii.
29. Christopher Rolleston, "The Science of Statistics," *Sydney Magazine of Science and Art*, I (1858), 256.

228   *Theory and Policy*

on by irresponsible statements of unprincipled demagogues the best antidote for current difficulties was concentrated teaching of enlightening political economy. He emphasized: "Indeed to political action arising from ignorance of the correct theories in regard to credit and the currency we may ascribe the monetary panics which (in this colony) we have occasionally witnessed, rather than to any real failure in our sources of wealth."[30] Throughout the deep depression of the 1890's, observers both in the colonies and in Britain repeated the claim that disaster had followed overexpansion caused by excessively optimistic misinformation.[31]

Colonial peculiarities. A few writers conceded that peculiar characteristics of colonial economies complicated the functioning of their free enterprise systems and could account for periodic distress. In particular, during the 1850's and 1860's, variations in the flow of immigrants were blamed for fluctuations in economic activity. The Sydney *Empire* asserted in 1852 that sustained growth required continuous and regular immigration because new workers in a new country both provided a demand for goods and furnished the labor needed for increased production.

Labourers are themselves consumers, and therefore contribute to employment in proportion to their numbers. No department of industry can be productive without labour, and without adequate labour it will barely sustain itself, to say nothing of the expansion of the principle of social activity abroad. The influx of labour should always be higher than the previous demand, in order to ensure the requisite supply, exhausted by contingencies and advancements, and to give an ever-increasing momentum to enterprise.[32]

Subsequently, this argument was expanded to state that a colonial economy became adjusted to and dependent upon a rapidly

30. A. G. Eager, "On the Advantage of a Theoretical as Well as Practical Training for Bankers," *Australasian Insurance and Banking Record*, XI (1887), 767. See also pleas for informative statistics of "the provident habits" of the colonists in H. D'E. Taylor, "The Direction of Thrift. A Savings Bank Comparison," *Victorian Review*, IV (1881), 703–11.
31. See for example, "Final Report of the Commission on Agriculture," *Minutes and Votes and Proceedings of the Parliament of Western Australia*, 1891–92; and "Gold-Bewitched Victoria," *Investors' Review*, II (1893), 145–74.
32. "The Causes of Depressed Wages," *Empire*, June 25, 1852, p. 1130.

growing population. Any decline in immigration led inevitably to domestic crisis and depression.[33]

As early as the 1840's, some colonists speculated that alternating overenthusiasm and excessive skepticism of foreign investors rather than of domestic entrepreneurs were the root cause of business fluctuations.[34] John Dunmore Lang, in a widely accepted account of the boom and depression of the 1820's, claimed that the newly formed and British-capitalized Australian Agricultural Company had misled colonists with false hopes. Lang wrote:

no sooner had the existence of the Agricultural Company been duly announced, and its operations been commenced in right earnest, than the *sheep and cattle mania*—a species of madness undescribed by Cullen, and formerly unknown even in the colony—instantly seized on all ranks and classes of its inhabitants.[35]

During the depression of the 1890's, Australians replied to attacks on the soundness of the colonial economies by insisting that irregular capital imports were the reason for all difficulties.[36] Even in the 1880's, when only the first signs of recession had appeared, astute observers such as B. R. Wise in New South Wales and H. G. Turner in Victoria maintained that inconsistency in capital imports was contributing substantially to current "irregularity of

33. See particularly: Archibald Michie, *Victoria Suffering a Recovery* (Melbourne, 1860), p. 13; Francis H. Nixon, *Population; or, A Plea for Victoria* (Melbourne, 1862), p. 11; "Report from the Select Committee on Immigration," *Journals of the House of Assembly of Tasmania*, 1865, p. 4; "Progress Report from the Select Committee on the Present State of the Colony; together with the Proceedings of the Committee, and Minutes of Evidence," *Votes and Proceedings of the Legislative Assembly of New South Wales*, 1865–66, p. 1. See also chapter 12 *passim*.

34. "Report from the Select Committee on the Monetary Confusion, with Appendix and Minutes of Evidence," *Votes and Proceedings of the Legislative Council of New South Wales*, 1843, evidence, pp. 1, 16, 19, 29, 62; A. G. L. Shaw, *The Economic Development of Australia* (London, 1955), p. 58.

35. J. D. Lang, *An Historical and Statistical Account of New South Wales* (London, 1852), I, 213; and R. M. Hartwell, "Australia's First Trade Cycle . . . ," *loc. cit.*

36. Two of the most devastating critiques of colonial "extravagance" were: A. G. V. Peel, *The Australian Crisis of 1893* (London, 1893); and J. W. Fortescue, "The Seamy Side of Australia," *Nineteenth Century*, XXIX (1891), 523–37, and "The New South Sea Bubble," *ibid.*, XXXIV (1893), 22–33. The course of the 1890's recession is described in H. L. Harris, "The Financial Crisis of 1893 in New South Wales," *Royal Australian Historical Society Journal and Proceedings*, XIII (1928), pp. 305–43.

unemployment and uncertainty in the rate of wages."[37] In the depths of the crisis, Australian bankers and others complained that British direct investors and depositors in colonial banks had been singularly ill-informed about the circumstances of their investment. In some cases, Australians admitted, foreigners had been duped by unscrupulous promoters, but in most instances external capitalists had built their own unreasonable and unjustified expectations. The effect for Australia had been a rapid investment boom during which prices had risen, imports had jumped, and with mounting production costs export industries had languished. Finally, panic had brought on a sudden cessation of investment funds and stagnation.[38] Catherine Spence accused a single lowering of the return on public securities in Britain of causing a serious boom and collapse in the colonies. "For the recent terrible financial crisis British capitalists are much to blame. Mr. Goschen's conversion of the Three per Cents. was the signal for sending millions of money out to banks and finance companies, to inflate the monstrous land boom of Melbourne and its suburbs."[39] Explanation of the 1890's crisis as a reaction to a fluctuation in British foreign lending was accepted widely in Australia, and was repeated in 1927 by Edward Shann as a warning of the possibility that a similar disaster might occur again in the 1920's for the same reasons as thirty years before.[40]

Some colonists reflected that income fluctuations might be caused as much by heavy dependence on production and sale

37. B. R. Wise, "Industrial Grievances in Australia," *Sydney Quarterly Magazine*, 1886, p. 379; and "Mr. H. G. Turner's Address to the Melbourne Chamber of Commerce," *Australasian Insurance and Banking Record*, XIII (1889), 314–15.
38. Variants of this explanation are contained in: Reginald J. Black, "The Banking Crisis and Its Lessons," *Australian Economist*, III (1893–94), 319–26; Nathaniel Cork, *The Australian Banking Crisis of 1893* (London, 1894); "Mr. Cork on the Late Australian Banking Crisis," *Australasian Insurance and Banking Record*, XVIII (1894), 283–85; Theodore Fink, "Foreign Loans and A Young Democracy," *Bankers' Magazine and Journal of the Bankers' Institute of Australasia*, VI (1892–93), 1245–55 and 1301–10; C. M. H. Clark, *Select Documents in Australian History 1851–1900* (Sydney, 1955), pp. 295–300; H. G. Turner, "Booms," *Bankers' Magazine and Journal of the Bankers' Institute of Australasia*, X (1896–97), 299–305.
39. C. H. Spence, "Social and Intellectual Aspects of Australian Life," *Proceedings of the Royal Colonial Institute*, XXVI (1894–95), 30.
40. E. O. G. Shann, *The Boom of 1890- and Now* (Sydney, 1927); and see A. St. Ledger, *Australian Socialism: An Historical Sketch of its Origin and Developments* (London, 1909).

abroad of a few raw materials as upon variations in flows of
labor and capital, and they turned to the study of market behavior. In a few cases this train of thought led to crude explanations of a primitive "cobweb cycle" wherein assumptions were
made that primary producers planned future output on the
basis of present prices, were unable to store their products, and
made little attempt to second-guess the market. One writer described an early cobweb fluctuation in Western Australia, in
which prices and output oscillated around an equilibrium. In the
boom period he wrote:

> The rapid increase of stock might have warned the settler that
> the number must soon exceed the local demand, and the profits conse-
> quently fall; but this increase viewed only in connection with existing
> prices, encouraged speculation and large purchases of imported stock
> very inferior in quality to our own. . . .
> This, occurring when the supply and demand were fast approaching
> to a level, caused a reaction in general opinion, and a disproportionate
> depression of prices; which embarrassing and alarming the farmer,
> and, by his retrenchment of expenditure, reducing the means of the
> citizen, produced a sudden cessation of speculation, a stagnation of
> enterprise, retirement of capital, and consequent reduction of the
> market-price of all property.[41]

A pessimistic writer in Sydney during 1838 warned New South
Wales wool-producers of the probable onset of a market cycle,
and he advised against the temptations to overproduction. He
said:

> although, in the natural course of events, a corresponding depression
> must always be expected to follow a considerable elevation, and that
> decline again be succeeded by an advance; yet we would caution our
> wool-growing friends against too sanguine expectations of a very
> rapid or extensive re-action in the wool markets of Great Britain.[42]

When William Westgarth described the new settlement at Victoria in 1848 he maintained that income fluctuations would continue there so long as the new country depended upon production

41. *Journal of the Agricultural and Horticultural Society of Western Australia,*
I (1843), 4.
42. "Present Financial Situation of the Colony and Future Prospects," *Australian
Magazine,* I (1838), 59.

of staple goods for sale abroad and did not develop a substantial home market. He suggested that under existing conditions periodic recessions were an effective method of curtailing production to foreign demand and helped to prevent catastrophic excess supply.

These commercial crises, as they are termed, appear to be the appointed mode of relief from a plethoric state of the general market, which would probably, but for some such check, produce, in general, results still more detrimental to society at large; and although it is not desirable, nor indeed usual, to see such sudden and violent changes in the social relations as those just described, yet such must be the occasional lot of a young and still limited colony, situated at a remote distance from its sources of supply, and therefore exposed to irregularities in its commercial transactions.[43]

Policy implications. A general conclusion reached by most adherents to classical political economy was that whether economic fluctuations were caused by emotional instability, factor immobility, lack of knowledge, or colonial dependence, periodic bad times were probably inevitable.[44] Moreover, they believed that extravagant attempts to bring about uninterrupted prosperity might injure fatally the delicate economic system and might perhaps even extend depressions. Man, they decided, was the victim of "the irresistible operation of economic laws."[45] Some colonists suggested that crises, like fever in the human body, helped to purge the system of its ills and to stimulate improvements. With regard to the effects of depressions on advancement in techniques of economic analysis, John Plummer said: "Experience has shown that the occurrence of a period of commercial or industrial depression generally has the effect of stimulating inquiry into the principles which govern the production and accumulation of wealth, and its distribution and consumption."[46] As Carl Pinschof told the bankers of Victoria in 1892: "those who

43. William Westgarth, *Australia Felix: or, a Historical and Descriptive Account of the Settlement of Port Phillip, New South Wales* (Edinburgh, 1848), p. 191.

44. A good statement of the inevitability thesis was: Senex, "Financial Sickness and Recovery," *Bankers' Magazine and Journal of the Bankers' Institute of Australasia*, VI (1892–93), 1173–75.

45. *Australasian Insurance and Banking Record*, XVII (1893), 292.

46. John Plummer, *Sir Matthew Decker and Adam Smith* (Publication of the Australian Economic Association, n. p., n. d.), p. 1.

have at all studied the 'Periodicity of Crises' will be inclined to think that so long as man is mortal these catastrophes will recur, and we can only do our best to avoid them, asking Providence to protect us from these as from all other evils."[47]

Legislatures, and particularly those dominated by free-traders, were usually in a quandry during periods of depression as to the wisdom of all compensatory actions. They welcomed statements such as the following by Waldemar Bannow that "As a canon in political economy, it must be clearly understood that the Government has no obligation to find employment for men out of work, least of all, in their special trades or callings; it is only when the necessities become extreme then it becomes the duty of the Government to prevent actual starvation."[48] Significantly, the only positive actions sanctioned by a Victorian Board of Inquiry which, in 1900, collected indubitable evidence as to the seriousness of unemployment, were small relief payments to destitute paupers and sponsorship of expeditions by the unemployed "fossicking" for gold, "rabbit trapping," and "track cutting."[49] Even into the twentieth century, as more and more evidence was collected illustrating the ability of government to control economic activity, vigorous protests against efforts toward greater stability continued to come from convinced economic liberals on grounds of danger to the system.[50]

Defective Social Policies and Institutions

So long as no single explanation of economic fluctuations was accepted widely, participants in a variety of colonial controver-

47. Carl Pinschof, "Our Financial Organisation and the Present Crisis," *Bankers' Magazine and Journal of the Bankers' Institute of Australasia,* VI (1892-93), 1005. Similar expressed beliefs in the inevitability of business cycles are contained in: William Coote, *Railway and Loan Policy of Queensland* (Brisbane, 1879), p. 27; and B. R. Wise, "What Parliament Can Do for Labour," *Sydney Quarterly Magazine,* 1891, pp. 220–37.
48. Waldemar Bannow, *The Colony of Victoria Socially and Materially* (Melbourne, 1896), p. 189.
49. "Report of the Board of Inquiry on Unemployment," *Papers Presented to the Parliament of Victoria,* 1900. See also "Report of Select Committee on the Unemployed," *Journals and Printed Papers of the Parliament of Tasmania,* 1894.
50. E.g., F. W. Eggleston, *State Socialism in Victoria* (London, 1932), p. 308.

sies were able to blame hard times on particular policies or institutions ranging from tariffs to road tolls. The argument behind specific indictments was usually that any iniquitous element in society disturbed the proper functioning of all parts. Types of accusations were as numerous as the controversies themselves, but the debates seldom contributed to a genuine understanding of the reasons for depression.

Tariffs and free trade. Conflict over commercial policy gave rise to charges that both free trade and protection rendered a colonial economy particularly susceptible to crises. Free-traders insisted that protection produced a "sterilising effect upon the development of natural resources."[51] When isolated from the healthy pressure of international competition, they argued, firms became sickly and liable to failure. Moreover, government tended to degenerate morally from exposure to the temptations of high tariff revenues, and its dissolute condition and corrupt principles were transmitted to private industry. One representative free-trader explained that protectionist governments sowed the seeds of disaster through their policies both of collecting revenue and of expenditure. Extravagant projects undertaken initially with tariff proceeds, he wrote, later required funds from other sources and never yielded satisfactory returns. Protection was simply a prelude to depression.[52]

On the other side of the tariff debate, protectionists used the powerful argument that high tariffs alone could support full employment. While Australia remained exclusively staples-producing under free trade, they maintained, neither city artisans nor small farmers could expect rising or even stable demands for products.[53] This claim was attended most sympathetically when serious unemployment actually threatened and protectionists could promise, as did Henry Dwyer in Sydney during 1887, that

51. "Some Proximate Causes of the Australian Crisis," *Australasian Insurance and Banking Record,* XVII (1893), 849.
52. C. M. Smith, *Trade Depression and Wasted Resources; with Some Remarks on Popular Government in New South Wales* (Sydney, 1887), p. 6. See also chapter 2 above.
53. See for example, C. O. Waldow, *The Present Depression in Trade: Its Cause and Remedy* (Sydney, 1887), p. 21.

"Protection is the enchanting wand which will raise from the ashes of adversity the Phoenix of our national prosperity."[54]

Land policy. The policy of land sales, from the earliest years of its introduction in New South Wales, was credited often with causing depressions. Critics at an early date reasoned that funds taken from colonists in payment for land and then used for subsidized immigrant passages were removed from circulation and reduced domestic demand. Thomas Bannister, in Van Diemen's Land in 1833, approved land sales so long as proceeds were spent internally, for otherwise, he insisted, the colony would surely stagnate "losing its very life blood in a great portion of its capital being constantly withdrawn from circulation, by being sent away, and receiving in exchange but a pauper population. . . ."[55] Repeating a favorite analogy of the economy to the human body, a New South Wales legislative committee on land sales reported during the depression of 1843 that, as a result of the past outflow of land funds, "The circulating medium which, like the blood in the animal system, diffused life and activity through every part, has been withdrawn from use, and the Colony is now in a state of inanition."[56]

When ideas of Edward Gibbon Wakefield came to influence colonial policy, critics of land sales complained that the restrictive device of a "sufficient price" merely added to the deleterious effects of reduced circulation. Excessive land charges circumscribed domestic industry, gave rise to needless unemployment, and thereby discouraged immigration and growth. A writer in the *New South Wales Magazine* during 1843 summarized contemporary criticism thus:

The causes of the present "depression" of the colony seem deducible by our analysis in the following order:

54. Henry Dwyer, *Pauperism in New South Wales: Its Cause and Cure* (Sydney, 1887), p. 6.
55. Thomas Bannister, *A Letter on Colonial Labour, and on the Sale of Lands in Austral-asia Addressed to the Right Honourable the Secretary of State for the Colonies* (Hobart Town, 1833), p. 15.
56. "Report from the Select Committee on the Crown Land Sales Act, with Minutes of Evidence and Appendix," *Votes and Proceedings of the Legislative Council of New South Wales,* 1843, p. 3.

Causes

Primary.	1st.	The raising the price of land to a higher rate than the usual operation of capital, labour, and population would bear.
Secondary.	2nd.	The effect of that high price of land on emigration from England.
	3rd.	Interruption from other causes of the current of immigration; changes in its quality.
	4th.	The discontinuance of that immigration to the colony which made capital in it worth 10 per cent.[57]

Opponents of a high land price were often would-be land-owners motivated mainly by self-interest; nevertheless their analyses of potential depressing effects were usually convincing and presented in a cogent manner.[58] Many colonists continued to believe fervently throughout the century that if only labor could gain free access to land hard times would disappear forever.[59]

Class warfare. Both sides in the struggles between capital and labor in the colonies attributed economic instability to actions of the other. As early as the 1840's, employers complained that ruinous demands by workers threatened general prosperity,[60] and when during the 1890's the beginning of a major depression coincided with a period of extreme union unrest this coincidence again did not pass unannounced by opponents of organized labor. John Hurst outlined to the Australian Economic Association no less than eight alleged economic ill effects of union activity, including: inflation, distortion of resource allocation, and dis-

57. Q. E. D., "An Enquiry into the Causes of the Former Prosperity and Present State of the Colony of New South Wales," *New South Wales Magazine*, I (1843), 408.
58. See for example: "What is to Become of the Colony?," *New South Wales Magazine*, I (1843), 615–25; Gideon Scott Lang, *Land and Labour in Australia* . . . (Melbourne, 1845), pp. 14–15; Charles Griffith, *The Present State and Prospects of the Port Phillip District of New South Wales* (Dublin, 1845), p. 109; and William Bland, *Letter to His Excellency Sir Charles Augustus Fitzroy, Governor-in-Chief of New South Wales* (Sydney, 1850), p. 8.
59. "The 'Prevailing Depression,'" *Bulletin*, XII (1892), No. 634, p. 6; and J. Medway Day, *Idlers in the Market Place: Practical Suggestions Towards the Solution of the Unemployed Problem* (Sydney, 1896).
60. C. M. H. Clark, *Select Documents in Australian History 1788–1850* (Sydney, 1950), p. 412.

couragement of recuperative enterprise.[61] The Honourable W. Forrest assured the Brisbane Chamber of Commerce in 1893 that "The undue forcing up of wages was a prime factor in our Labour troubles,"[62] and J. Currie-Elles told the bankers of New South Wales that labor demands for experiments in socialism had discouraged industry, brought on depression, and threatened the very survival of a free economy. "The cry for the State to support and foster fungoid growths by the aid of borrowed capital— taxing, for its maintenance, a community which cannot stand taxation, should be discouraged, as it has nearly run its course."[63] In 1905, C. E. S. Turner accused communist labor leaders of helping to render a free economy inoperative by knowingly bringing on crises in key industries. He charged that "attacks are being made upon every factory and factory owner to hinder him in his business so that relinquishment becomes preferable to the persecution he is suffering . . . it is hoped to close every factory, or place them in a restraining harness of which Trades Unions hold the reins."[64]

Spokesmen for labor replied to complaints of employers by claiming that monopoly, usury, and capitalist exploitation were the true causes of crises. David Andrade, an anarchist leader, observed that "money power" was at the root of all evil:

It is the legal monopolized currency which holds men in slavery. It is that which makes industrial depressions. Everything is subservient to money. The owners of money swallow up the proceeds of labor, rob the moneyless of the lands which they have been compelled to mortgage to them, control the public morals, the press, the judiciary, make the laws, and control all the destinies of the nation.[65]

The radical Queensland Social-Democratic Federation, which with remarkable eclecticism embraced the teachings both of Marx and of Pope Leo XIII, insisted that depressions were an inescap-

---

61. John Hurst, "Trade Unions," *Australian Economist*, II (1890–93), 127–33.
62. Hon. W. Forrest, *The Present Depression: Its Cause and Cure* . . . (Brisbane, 1893), p. 3.
63. J. Currie-Elles, "Financial Review," *Journal of the Institute of Bankers of New South Wales*, III (1894), 5.
64. C. E. S. Turner, *Unemployment—The Remedy* (Sydney, 1905), p. 1.
65. David A. Andrade, *An Anarchist Plan of Campaign* (Melbourne, 1888), unpaged.

able feature of a capitalist economy. "This irregularity of production is one of the most lamentable phases in our present system of industry. The employer does not like it, neither does the workman."[66] The Sydney *Bulletin* endorsed radical explanations of economic fluctuations, and particularly the growth of monopoly, partly on the ground that other explanations were not convincing. The magazine during the 1890's ridiculed accounts of alleged overproduction because everywhere could be seen unemployment, misery, and want. "A presumably sane and intelligent population accepts this as a perfectly reasonable theory, owing chiefly to that dismal ignorance that makes every population believe whatever it is told to believe, if the statement is only loud enough and made with sufficient energy."[67]

Some observers of labor-management relations who did not enter the controversy strenuously on either side suggested that the real cause of unemployment was neither capitalist avarice nor socialist extremism, but was rather the continued manufacture of an increasing quantity of labor-saving machinery. Henry Copeland in Sydney detected a paradox in the contemporaneous existence of idle workers and accelerated production of more machines. His lament has a modern ring.

The ominous cry of "over-production" is sounded from all the centres of manufacturing industry, yet the most active and intelligent brains of the age are busily at work day and night to discover other inventions which will enable them to produce a still greater amount with a lesser expenditure of manual labour than at present. Each labour-saving invention of importance, when brought into general use, must be the means of dispensing with the labour of hundreds and it may be thousands of able-bodied men.[68]

B. R. Wise agreed that depression in the late 1880's was a result of rapid accumulation of efficient machinery, but he recommended in the tradition of J. S. Mill that only symptoms and not the cause of the depression be checked.

The introduction of machinery has caused appalling suffering, and probably a large portion of the present trade depression is owing to the

66. *What is Socialism?* (Leaflets for the People, No. 1, Brisbane, n. d.), p. 5.
67. "Commercial Depression," *Bulletin*, XI (1891), No. 577, p. 6.
68. Henry Copeland, *Adam's Curse and Labour-Saving Inventions: An Enquiry into the Labour Question of the Future* (Sydney, 1885), p. 18.

increasing number of labour-saving machines. . . . But the policy which allows wealth to increase the fastest, allows the greatest saving to be made, and is thus the safest guarantee that the distress in any single branch of trade will soonest pass away. The true benevolence is to offer the sufferers every means of finding relief in other fields, and not to prolong their agony by tempting them to continue in an occupation which is doomed.[69]

William Maston, a moderate representative of the Trades and Labour Council of New South Wales, conceded that labor-saving devices were a critical cause of unemployment, and he added: "This problem of surplus labour is a vital one, it is the gangrene which is slowly yet surely gnawing the very vitals of society. . . ."[70]

Interruption of Effective Demand

As early as the 1820's it became apparent to some colonists that during recessions the amount of purchasing power expended on goods and services diminished in proportion to the general decline. They explained this phenomenon in one of two ways: either, they concluded, the money supply itself was poorly constituted and inefficient, or certain structural features of the economy generated fluctuations in money flows. The first explanation focused attention directly on the banking and currency system.

Monetary interruptions. Banks received blame for causing depressions throughout the period under review. In 1828 Andrew Bent's *Colonial Advocate* in Hobart Town described how banks in other countries issued excessive notes and thereby depreciated all domestic currency. As a result of banking, costs rose to domestic producers, and because products were sold on world markets selling prices were unaffected and profits fell. Employers were compelled ultimately to cut wages, labor strife abounded, and a

69. B. R. Wise, *The Mutual Relations of Imports and Exports* (Australian Economic Association Papers, No. 1, Sydney, 1887), pp. 40–41.

70. William Maston, "The Surplus Labour Problem," *Australian Economist*, II (1890–93), 168.

widespread crisis usually concluded the inflation. The journal described thus post-Napoleonic experience with banking in England and warned of the danger of similar developments in the colonies.

The prices of commodities were raised to the manufacturer, thereby encreasing his expences [sic]. Foreign competitors started up: he was therefore compelled to lower the market prices of his manufactured goods, and consequently his profits were decreased. Machinery was introduced to lessen the expence of manual labour—low wages followed—discontent among the operatives subsequently appeared—and the ultimate result has been the present wretchedly low state of trade in the Mother Country. How long it will be before such an effect is produced in Van Diemen's Land, by a superabundance of paper, it is not for us to determine.[71]

During the depression of the 1840's, banks again were accused of generating instability. Bank critics acknowledged the tendency of humans to gamble and to formulate unreasonable expectations, but they argued that banks fostered this propensity through extravagant lending in a boom and contraction during a crisis.[72] The sudden destruction of credit by banks in a panic, they contended, resulted in immediate interruption of the production of real wealth. One writer in Sydney summarized the importance of sustained bank credit to a new country:

It gives equal impulse to both buyer and seller—nay, the very knowledge that it exists, renders it unnecessary to call it into action. Its hypothetical wealth is gradually transmuted into real wealth, and acts like real wealth during the process . . . if we look at it merely as the foundation of all the contrivances to economize the use of money, and by doing so, to prevent that extreme depression of prices which would destroy production of commodity, except under the most favourable circumstances, we shall see that whilst it is of vast importance to the oldest, the strongest, and the wealthiest nations, it is essential to the very existence of a young country in which vast sources of wealth are known to exist, but are imperfectly developed.[73]

71. "The Banking System," *Colonial Advocate, and Tasmanian Monthly Review and Register*, April 1828, p. 55.
72. "Report from the Select Committee on the Monetary Confusion, with Appendix and Minutes of Evidence," *Votes and Proceedings of the Legislative Council of New South Wales*, 1843, Minutes of Evidence, pp. 1, 8, 19, 37, 39, and 59.
73. "Credit—Its Properties and Effects—Government Bank," *New South Wales Magazine*, 1843, p. 576.

This writer proposed formation of a government bank to assure a constant supply of credit even in hard times. After two more years of crisis without reform, a South Australian in 1845 exclaimed in anger that because the colony's money supply consisted mainly of bank credit "The trading world is, in fact, owing to the laws by which it is governed, a sea of bubbles, which are ready to burst on the slightest touch." He asked: "Should not the laws of commerce be framed, not to *induce*, but to *prevent* periodical convulsions?" And he recommended that some form of long term promissory notes replace bank paper payable on demand.[74]

By mid-century the basic necessity of retaining a system of commercial banks was accepted by most people, and critics accused banks less of actually causing crises than of intensifying and extending them. The recession which followed the 1850's gold rush brought forth vigorous critiques of banking and demands for legislative restraint. For example, J. Braché told a Victorian legislative committee:

this crisis, which swept over the land, was increased in density by the banks. When they suddenly found their coffers filled with the produce of the mines, and when enormous amounts of gold weekly flowed in upon them, they extended their credit most unwarrantably, and encouraged and fostered the mad projects and speculations of the day among individuals as well as societies. This they went on doing long after the exchange had set in considerably against the Colony. And when, after this fever heat of speculation, which ought to have been checked by the banks and not encouraged, there came that violent reaction from which the Colony is now slowly recovering, the banks again became most unmercifully severe, and their conduct on that occasion will be remembered by many a merchant whose credit was suddenly stopped, and who, although he might have pulled through the crisis, was thereby driven into the Insolvent Court.[75]

Some opponents of unrestricted commercial banking advocated an issue of inconvertible government notes. They empha-

---

74. Aristides, *Commerce: Its Laws* . . . (Adelaide, 1845), pp. vii and 103.
75. "Report from the Select Committee of the Legislative Council on Gold; together with the Proceedings of the Committee, Minutes of Evidence, and Appendix," *Votes and Proceedings of the Legislative Council of Victoria,* 1855–56, Appendix I, p. 54.

sized that, unlike notes dependent for their value on the credit-worthiness of a private institution, legal-tender currency would remain in circulation even during an actual or threatened financial crisis.[76] A state bank or issuing authority could circulate notes at times of low confidence and might thereby reverse the downward movement in income by restoring purchasing power. So long as government notes were not overissued they could not cause inflation or other ill effects. An enthusiast in Melbourne wrote: "Private institutions may become insolvent and fail to meet their promises to pay, or, in other words, their bank notes may become no better than waste paper; but the public can never become distrustful of their own ability, as a corporate body, to pay, nor, when once its properties and peculiarities are understood, can there ever be a run on a National Bank."[77] James Mirams, an extremely vocal proponent of national banking, exclaimed in 1892: "What we want is more currency. The banks, through whom the supply of currency alone reaches us, cannot, under existing circumstances, supply what is required; or what amounts to the same thing they do not."[78] Mirams insisted that shortage of money was the true cause of financial crises and that only blind prejudice stood in the way of a managed currency and elimination of instability forever. He remarked sadly that: "There is something comical, or rather there would be, were it not so terribly tragical in its results, in the fact of a country which has close upon 600 millions of accumulated capital [Hayter's estimate], quietly submitting to such a condition as that we are now suffering from, for the want of some two millions or less of currency, through fear of departing by one hair's breadth from the old financial track. . . ."[79] In the trough of the depression of the 1890's, several observers were compelled

76. See for example: *A Proposal to Meet the Financial Difficulties of the Country by the Partial Adoption of an Inconvertible Paper Currency* (Sydney, 1865); and Richard Capper, *A Question for Electors! Why Should We Go to England to Borrow Money?* (Melbourne, 1868).

77. Sigma, *Money: How the Banks Make it Scarce and Dear! The Remedy! The Banks and their Stability!* (Melbourne, 1871), pp. 13 and 17. See also "A National Bank," *Quadrilateral*, 1874, pp. 6–9.

78. James Mirams, *The Present Depression: Its Cause and Cure* (Melbourne, 1892), p. 24; and see also James Mirams, "A National Bank of Issue for Victoria," *Melbourne Review*, III (1878), 288–303.

79. *The Present Depression: Its Cause and Cure*, p. 25.

to accept the reasonableness of Mirams' analysis even though they were reluctant to endorse his radical remedy.[80]

A severe bank crisis shook the colonies in 1893 and for a short time caused the bankers to pay serious attention to the causes of their own difficulties. Melbourne bankers were advised by the local bankers' association to read carefully Juglar's *History of Panics,* and they were directed to a variety of additional appropriate works on political economy.[81] The banking community tolerated a remarkable amount of introspection and self-condemnation, and they listened patiently while radical speakers laid responsibility for the country's ills at their doorstep, even lending a sympathetic ear to discussion of radical banking reform.[82] Before long, however, bankers returned to their position held before the crash that factors other than monetary derangement were responsible primarily for economic instability.[83]

Part of the case bimetallists put forward during the 1880's and 1890's for a currency based on silver as well as on gold presupposed the need for a stable volume of money in circulation to sustain total purchases of goods and services. Bimetallists were concerned mainly with the depressing effects of secular deflation on expectations and incentives, but they were conscious also of the need for short-term maintenance of money flows.[84] Although bimetallists concentrated on the impact of long-run trends, they exhibited an awareness in common with advocates of national banking and government currency of the importance for economic stability of adequate effective demand.

D. B. Copland was the first professional economist to explain

80. For example: J. J. Kingsbury, *The Financial Position of the Colonies in Relation to Banking. "Rocks Ahead!"* (Brisbane, 1894); and W. McMillan, "Banks and Banking Legislation," *Journal of the Institute of Bankers of New South Wales,* III (1894), 499–500.
81. *Bankers' Magazine and Journal of the Bankers' Institute of Australasia,* VII (1893–94), 86–87 and 394.
82. See for example: F. T. Hickford, "The Depression and Federation," *ibid.,* pp. 355–57; and James Smith, "Financial Crises, Their Cause and Cure," *ibid.,* pp. 4–7.
83. J. Currie-Elles, "Supply and Demand," *Journal of the Institute of Bankers of New South Wales,* III (1894), 415–25, and 439–51.
84. D. Murray, "Bimetallism," *Report of the Fifth Meeting of the Australasian Association for the Advancement of Science held at Adelaide,* 1893, pp. 557–72; William Alison, *Bimetallism* (Sydney, n. d.); Dr. Benjafield, *Bimetallism: The Remedy for Depression* (Hobart, 1895).

business fluctuations mainly in terms of monetary factors. He admitted that "commercial crises" were "due partly to psychological factors and partly also to variations in the general productivity of the world," but he declared that "it is through the defective standard of value that these psychological factors operate."[85] Using the work of Hawtrey, Mitchell, Fisher, Lavington, and Keynes, Copland set out to show that price movements were the motive force of swings in economic activity. He accepted a quantity theory of money and observed that prices were determined largely by the volume of purchasing power issued in Australia by the banking system. During a period of monetary expansion, he observed, the business community became excessively optimistic in response to rising prices. Banks continued to supply bountiful requests for new loans until finally reserve limitations necessitated restraint. Recession resulted from the cumulative process operating in reverse. Tight money brought on a price decline which, in turn, discouraged borrowers and led to even more deflation. A lagged and extended monetary cycle was generated in Australia, Copland said, by the practice of governmental wage regulation:

In years of rapidly rising prices wages lagged behind when the productivity of industry might have justified higher rates, but in the period of depression wages are relatively higher than before, and the readjustment is slow. This shows the rigidity of the arbitration system and the difficulties that arise through the regulation of industrial costs on so artificial a standard.[86]

Appropriate counter-cyclical policy, Copland proposed, would include governmental regulation of the banking system, careful study of macro-economic variables, and provision of public information to dispel mistaken expectations.[87]

85. D. B. Copland, *Currency and Prices in Australia* (The Joseph Fisher Lecture in Commerce 1921, Adelaide, 1921), p. 24. See also "Currency Inflation and Price Movements in Australia," *Economic Journal*, XXX (1920), 484–509.
86. D. B. Copland, "The Trade Depression in Australia in Relation to Economic Thought," *Report of the Sixteenth Meeting of the Australasian Association for the Advancement of Science held at Wellington, 1923*, p. 575.
87. D. B. Copland, "Monetary Policy and Its Reactions upon Australia," *Report of the Seventeenth Meeting of the Australasian Association for the Advancement of Science held at Adelaide, 1924*, pp. 495–534. See also D. B. Copland, "The Economic Situation in Australia, 1918–23," *Economic Journal*, XXXIV (1924), 32–51.

Breaks in the circular flow. English classical economists confined their attention mainly to specific market analysis and ignored relationships between aggregates of the national economy. Writing as they were in a complex economic system where a large number of diverse industries contributed to national product, where distribution patterns remained comparatively stable, and where growth took place through a slow process of income saving and an excess of births over deaths, they concluded that the economic woods could be understood best by focusing attention on a single economic tree. In the colonies, however, conditions were different from Britain, and macro-economic problems assumed special importance and meaning. The small number of industries were dependent on sale abroad of raw materials and determined thereby the level of national income. Additions to capital and labor were gained not in appreciable amount through a process of gradual accumulation but in uneven waves from other countries, attracted by the lure of high returns. Australians were well aware of the dramatic impact on their well-being of a sudden infusion of new resources, a technological innovation, or an alteration in the price of some output component. It was only natural that they should attempt to understand and to explain theoretically these phenomena, and through their findings to improve their knowledge of business fluctuations.

Several early settlers were conscious of the circulation of money in their economy and particularly of its relation to external trade. W. C. Wentworth in 1819 observed that a continued outflow of funds for imports, even if balanced by an inflow of British government expenditure, prevented an uninterrupted internal circular flow and therefore prohibited the existence of a stable colonial currency supply. He wrote:

Of the whole colonial income about £100,000 annually may be considered as arising from the labours of the agricultural body. This is undoubtably that portion of the colonial wealth which gets into most general circulation; but even *it* is far from undergoing that minute subdivision and universal diffusion which are requisite for the maintenance of a constant internal circulating medium. Created in the first instance by the government in payment of the grain, meat, &c. furnished by the settlers, it is immediately handed over by them to the traders to whom they may be indebted, and from these again passes to the importing merchants, on whom they may be dependent for their supplies of merchandize, who in their turn eventually transmit it to their foreign correspondents.[88]

It was recognized that payments to absentee landlords, by causing a reduction in colonial circulation, could entail more loss to the colonies than equivalent payments to domestic land-owners who would consume or invest goods to the amount of their rent and would thereby bestow employment on their neighbors. There is implied in the following critique of absentee *rentiers* by Thomas Bartlett an intuitive awareness of the existence of an international trade multiplier.

A particular school of political economists, may consider it immaterial in what place the interest of money is spent, but it would not be difficult to prove, that when the interest of a large capital invested in a colony is spent in Europe, it is so much money lost to the small community in which it is raised. . . . It is clear that it would be for the advantage of a colony to pay a larger interest for the use of his money to a resident capitalist than to the absentee proprietor in Europe.[89]

Colonists discerned at an early date differing levels of relative national importance between economic sectors, and in particular the crucial role of primary production as the supplier of foreign currency. They realized that so long as a steady proportion of all expenditures went for imported goods colonial growth was limited strictly by the ability to obtain foreign exchange. Australian writers stressed dependence on land not from a belief in physiocracy but from realization of their export dependence. One commentator explained:

This colony is pre-eminently based upon land-owning and land-occupying. These created a demand for articles not produced upon the

88. W. C. Wentworth, *A Statistical, Historical, and Political Description of the Colony of New South Wales, and its Dependent Settlements in Van Diemen's Land* (London, 1819), pp. 206–7.
89. Thomas Bartlett, *New Holland: Its Colonization, Productions and Resources, with Observations on the Relations Subsisting with Great Britain* (London, 1843), pp. 107–8.

land—the merchants and traders came to supply that demand, at first, like hawkers, bringing their wares, and inviting, or calling upon their customers, then, as do hawkers, taking shops in the centre of their connection, and becoming resident—and then, having opened and furnished their shops, they seek new connections of whom to buy, and to whom they may sell, and thus comes foreign trade—but all is based upon the land.[90]

The dangers in external leakages from the circular flow were emphasized in several acrimonious policy controversies during the nineteenth century. Immigration subsidies with revenues from land sales were condemned for the resulting contraction of local effective demand and consequent depressing effects on domestic industry.[91] An effective argument used in support of protective tariffs was that leakage from monetary circulation was minimized, and therefore the prosperity of the entire community was most stable and the economy balanced. For example, a Victorian civil engineer advocated protection of farm products after the gold rush by pointing out:

All these articles we could raise ourselves, and we ought to raise them; if we did, then the one and a half millions of money which we pay for them would go into the pockets of our Victorian farmers, instead of into the pockets of the farmers of other countries. And therefore so much more money would be in circulation among us, for the encouragement of colonial enterprise and industry.[92]

Professor W. E. Hearn at the University of Melbourne was an ardent free-trader and exponent of laissez faire. Nevertheless, he stressed the interdependence of sectors in an economy and in his *Plutology* provided inadvertently a rationale for government action to restrain those activities of individuals which threatened the maintenance of effective demand. He wrote:

the effects of a benefit or of an injury done to one class are rapidly felt throughout the whole community. The insolvency of the capitalist throws the labourer out of employment. The prosperity of the labourer brings with it an increased demand for the use of capital and increased

90. "Legislative Council—Prospects of the Colony," *New South Wales Magazine*, 1843, pp. 510–11.
91. See above pp. 64–82.
92. William E. Bryson, "On the Resources of Victoria, and their Development," *Transactions of the Philosophical Institute of Victoria*, I (1859), 144.

profits. When times are good, rent is well paid. When rents are well paid, there is a fresh stimulus given to profits and to wages. The bankruptcy of even one great firm sometimes, as we know, involves in its fall numerous distant, and in appearance even unconnected, establishments.[93]

John Winthrop Hackett, a colleague of Hearn at Melbourne University, re-examined for the colonies in 1877 the vexatious question of how to treat absentee property owners, and he performed a competent analysis of the macro-economic issues involved. He set about his task strictly as an economist, "The simple matter at issue being—is the sum available for enjoyment in the country greater or less as the property-holder may happen to live at home or abroad?"[94] Hackett enlarged on Senior's critique of McCulloch's claim that absentees, in the same way as residents, received income in the form effectively of commodities produced on their own property.[95] Senior remarked that absentee income was extracted actually in money and not necessarily in goods, and Hackett suggested that the crucial matter for investigation was the comparative proportions of income spent internally by absentees as opposed to residents.[96] When any income receiver made purchases within the colony "out of his payments much, by the action of ordinary economic laws, may find its way to the fund for the productive employment of industrial labour; much more may be saved for beneficial accumulation by the recipients; and further . . . the very retaining this income for use in any place will confer no insignificant advantage."[97] Hackett noted that local income receivers as well as absentees spent part of their income on foreign goods and services, but he admitted that even allowing for substantial imports by residents it was difficult to deny that "residence may actually increase the funds applicable to the payment of domestic or industrial services in the country." [98] So long as income receipts were retained and were ex-

93. W. E. Hearn, *Plutology* (London, 1864), p. 385, and see also p. 402.
94. John Winthrop Hackett, "Should Absentees be Taxed?," *Melbourne Review*, II (1877), 80.
95. Nassau William Senior, *An Outline of the Science of Political Economy* (London, 1938), p. 156.
96. *Ibid.*, p. 160.
97. Hackett, *op. cit.*, p. 76.
98. *Ibid.*, p. 77.

pended internally to employ local labor they would stimulate domestic capital accumulation "as this expenditure passes from class to class, and from seller to buyer, the margin of profit, constantly demanded and constantly accruing, (all taken in the last resort out of the pocket of the consumer), forms the natural basis of the new fund for investment."[99]Naturally, the longer money remained active and circulated in the colony before departing in payment for imports the better: "the longer and more winding the channel of its descent, the more are the opportunities of saving, and the greater may be the possible gain of the nation."[100] Hackett concluded that the leakage from circulation as a result of income received by absentees was probably substantially greater than was the import leakage from the expenditures of residents. But he asserted that national gains from having extra capital provided by absentees exceeded by far the problems created thereby, and he opposed all plans to penalize or tax nonresidents. "If we establish the tax there might be fewer absentees, —there would be fewer investors."[101]

Beginning in the 1870's, crude expositions of the need to sustain a circular flow of purchasing power for the maintenance of economic stability were voiced by a variety of economic reformers. Statements were similar to early writings on underconsumption, usually unsophisticated in form and neglecting in particular the role of investment as a source of effective demand. However, at least during periods of deep depression, proposals to stimulate consumer spending were eminently reasonable, farsighted, and a refreshing contrast to the fatalism of laissez faire.

During the last troubled years of the 1870's, John Ebenezer Goodwin published in Victoria an eccentric program for economic reconstruction which, although ludicrous in detail, illustrated fundamental recognition of the principle that measures to regulate aggregate spending could promote constant full employment and might increase prosperity. Goodwin proposed a large number of specific reforms, including wage and price regulation, a national bank, and a system of welfare payments.

99. *Ibid.*, p. 79.
100. *Ibid.*, p. 77.
101. *Ibid.*, p. 85.

He hoped to stimulate effective demand so that sales could be guaranteed for all goods produced. He explained: "The increasing poverty through want of employment is due to low wages and the multiplied production-power of machinery, whilst the consumption in most things remains the same."[102] Goodwin recounted in graphic detail the pure joys of income equality and full employment which would be possible in a managed economy and welfare state. He mused:

> Fair wages would give the majority the means of luxury. Luxury would be the same or greater perhaps, but much better diffused. The swagman, instead of buying fusel-oil alcoholics to poison and excite his overworked system, would buy a piano and learn to play it; and instead of walking himself footsore, and coiling himself up in a blanket like a snake and sleeping under a gum-tree, will be able to travel on free rail, eat and sleep in a hotel, and indulge in sherry cobblers for his own pleasure and the benefit of trade and the revenue.[103]

Goodwin cited Smith, Ricardo, Mill, and Whately; and he was influenced or confused by Louis Blanc, Proudhon, Chevalier, and Owen.[104]

Land-reformers of the colonies laid great stress on the importance for economic stability of transferring income through a tax or by nationalization from wealthy *rentiers* with a low propensity to consume to persons who would consume a large proportion. During 1883, Henry Edmunds in Sydney blamed monopoly of natural resources for difficulties encountered in recovering from trade recession, and he asserted that prosperity could be rendered permanent through social reform aimed at functional income redistribution. He reasoned:

> Trade depressions, the result of over-speculation and over-production, frequently arise, causing glutted markets; yet by some of the sapient teachers of the people we are informed that the only way to cure this state of things is by paying less wages, working longer hours, and by producing more rapidly. This would but increase the glut, and add to the existing difficulty.

102. John Ebenezer Goodwin, *Scientific Legislation; or the Theory of Calculated Labour Equivalents* (Melbourne, 1878), p. 29.
103. *Ibid.*, p. 36.
104. *Ibid.*, pp. 17–18, and 50.

To remedy this state of affairs, there must be created a new order of things more suited to the public requirements and the present times. It is evident that the error of our present system lies in its defective and false organization, and that the required reform is more social than political.[105]

In South Australia, reformers contended that world-wide land nationalization, by redistributing income and increasing consumer demand, would raise prices and extend markets for the colony's staple products. They announced confidently: "Wheat is cheap now, not because its quantity is in excess of what consumption, with the present population of the world, can reach; but because the number of actual consumers is artificially diminished by bad social adjustments, and desire and means exist in inverse proportions in the same people."[106]

During the depressed 1890's, several colonial land reformers prepared detailed and incisive statements of underconsumption theory. In Tasmania, A. J. Ogilvy pointed out the necessity for uninterrupted circulation and the sharp distinction which should be made between real capital accumulation and mere abstinence from consumption.

What the abstainers will save is money. If they saved it in the shape of coin, hoarding it, there would again be no accumulation. The money would be lying uselessly idle instead of circulating usefully, and that is all. A little wear and tear would be saved no doubt, but that is hardly worth mentioning. The money was coined for the sole purpose of being circulated, and the withdrawal of so much of it from circulation would disturb prices, cause a tightness in the money market, and derange trade generally.[107]

Ogilvy appreciated that some investment expenditure did take place. He explained: "we know that the saving will not be effected by hoarding coin any more than by hoarding goods. It will be

105. Henry W. Sanderson Edmunds, "Social Science," *Sydney Quarterly Magazine*, 1883, p. 259.
106. *Manifesto of the South Australian Land Nationalization Society* (Adelaide, 1884), p. 15.
107. A. J. Ogilvy, "Is Capital the Result of Abstinence?," *Report of the Fourth Meeting of the Australasian Association for the Advancement of Science held at Hobart*, 1892, p. 532. Ogilvy published this paper separately under the title *Saving and Spending* (Hobart, 1896), and together with a number of his other writings in the volume *The Third Factor of Production and Other Essays* (London, 1898).

effected by contracting expenditure. . . ."[108] But he did not investigate investment determinants. He was concerned mainly
with the principle that saving without compensating investment
expenditure led to unemployment, and with the fact that hoarding might stand in the way of capital formation. Ogilvy's description of a cumulative economic decline initiated by saving
without investment would, if written today, be considered perfectly orthodox and distinctly Keynesian in tone. He said:

> Those who have been supplying the abstainers with bread, boots, and
> tobacco will suddenly find a quarter of their goods left on their
> hands. There will be stagnation in those trades, with all its inconven-
> ience and distress. After a while, finding their customers are resolved
> to buy only the reduced quantity, the sellers will have to clear out
> their goods at whatever price they can get, even at a loss, and will
> have to reduce their production for the future in view of the dimin-
> ished demand, thereby throwing so many people out of employment,
> who, under the existing conditions of society, will either crowd into
> other employment, bringing down wages, or will have to be main-
> tained by charity.
> Thus there will be a dead loss all round. The abstainers will have
> lost their accustomed comforts, the producers their market, and the
> labourers their employment. There will next year be no more old ac-
> cumulations standing over, while there will be fewer newer accumu-
> lations brought into existence.
> Saving, then, which consists not in preserving goods but in ceasing
> to buy them, is illusory.[109]

Ogilvy attacked with clever ridicule policies of frugality and
parsimony proposed by others as cures for depression. He pictured a businessman, named "T", faced by able-bodied but unemployed workers and implored by his soft-hearted wife to offer
them charity.

> But T, who has studied political economy, shakes his head and says,
> "No, that would never do. Gratuitous alms only pauperise, relieving
> the evil for the moment only to intensify it by and by; degrading the
> men and impairing their usefulness."
> "Well," says the wife, "suppose you clear that waste piece of
> ground at the back of the house and make a lovely pleasure ground
> of it. That will give the men employment."

108. "Is Capital the Result of Abstinence?," p. 532.
109. *Ibid.*

But T says sadly, "No, that would be worse still. It would dissipate my savings, and so do away with the very fund that maintains labour. It would be downright sin in these times to waste good money in frivolous unproductive expenditure. There is a crisis, my dear, and we must all save so that capital may again become abundant and trade revive."[110]

The depression worsens, Ogilvy recounts, until unknown to T, the beneficent wife "who doesn't half understand, but does wholly detest the doctrines of Political Economy, can stand the sight of those poor men no longer," and she devises her own make-work project on which she pays workmen ten shillings to "grub up the roses and root out the bulbs, and dig up the paths, and the fountain, and the summer houses, and turn the whole place upside down, and leave it a desolation." Wonder of wonders, the result of the wife's kind act and its attendant destruction is that ten shillings pass through countless hands, and in each case bring forth new production and employment.

But for T's wife, none of these goods—boots, table, lock, etc., worth ten shillings each, would have been produced; so that society is the richer by the whole series of them through her act. . . . Directly she turned the tap the stream flowed forth, trade revived, and production began afresh.[111]

Like other underconsumptionists, Ogilvy failed to give adequate attention to investment spending, and he blamed a long-run decline in consumer expenditure for deficient effective demand. He affirmed without evidence, that the rich were becoming richer and were buying less, and he expressed concern particularly about exploitative features of land monopoly (he termed land rent "tribute"). Ogilvy deplored concentrated industrial organization, and he regretted technological innovations which were unfavorable to an increasing demand for labor. He summarized thus his understanding of the cause of depression:

the true explanation of the fall of prices is what is called overproduction, but is really under-consumption, due to the contraction of "effective demand," which again is caused by the present unequal

110. A. J. O., *The Cause of a Crisis* (Hobart, 1894), pp. 11–12.
111. *Ibid.*, p. 13.

and apparently inequitable apportionment of the annual product. . . . Hence the many poor cannot buy all they want, and the few rich are increasingly disinclined to buy all they could. Discoveries and inventions have so increased the productiveness of labour that the supply of this "effective demand," limited as it is by poverty at one end, and "saving" at the other, is effected without employing all the workers, whence ensues intense competition amongst the workers for employment, bringing down the price of work and of the products of work.[112]

Ogilvy exhibited admirable analytical insight, and on urgent contemporary policy questions he offered sound advice. But his close identification with doctrinaire principles and specific reform organizations labeled his writings as propaganda in the minds of many readers. Apart from his fellow land-reformers, he does not appear to have made a substantial impact on his audience.[113]

The basic policy position held by Ogilvy, that an increase in national income could be achieved by appropriation of land rent, soon became a land reform cliché. For example, Max Hirsch in Melbourne told a printers' union in 1894: "Increase wages and there will be greater consumption, increase them more, and consumption will still follow. Increase wages to their natural limit—the full value of the labourer's produce—and the consumption of the labourers will also come close to that value, making a general over-production of goods absolutely impossible." Hirsch then qualified this statement and warned that higher wages must be sought through land reform and not by union organization or other means. "Open the earth and the riches which it contains to the labour of men; make it necessary for the men who now hold natural opportunities out of use, or full use, to get them used to the fullest possible extent, and wages must rise— not only the wages of the men who work on land, but all wages —printers' wages included."[114]

Several heretical members of the otherwise conservative Aus-

---

112. A. J. O., *The Appreciation of Gold* (Hobart, 1897), pp. 5 and 6.
113. An equivocal review by J. Bonar of Ogilvy's *The Third Factor of Production* was contained in *Economic Journal*, IX (1899), 74–75.
114. Max Hirsch, *The Solidarity of Labour* (Melbourne, 1894), pp. 5 and 9.

tralian Economic Association advocated strong measures of social reform during the 1890's to sustain effective demand. W. H. Chard explained to a skeptical audience in 1894:

the supply of commodities is even now after five years of depressed trade larger than the purchasing power in almost all industries. Yet according to the teachings of political economy, production cannot properly exceed demand, because demand is practically unlimited.[115]

Chard deplored what he considered a mistaken but widely held belief that parsimony and retrenchment were real cures for depression. He continued:

I regret to think that in the present state of public knowledge, but few persons would agree that it is desirable to distribute more in wages of all kinds and less in interest and rent. On the contrary there seems to be a hazy notion that good times will be brought about by a rise in value of land, and further loan money being invested—i.e. by more rent and interest. It is not generally understood that the common idea of saving labor, discharging workers, cutting down salaries and wages, and general retrenchment will never make good times or cure commercial depression.[116]

Colonel Bell, the United States consul in Sydney, may have been influenced in discussions of underconsumption before the Australian Economic Association by the writings of A. J. Ogilvy. From his American experience, Bell explained how wide ownership of land—what he and Ogilvy both called "the third factor in production"—could bring about equitable income distribution through large and uninterrupted consumer spending. In language similar to that used by Ogilvy, Bell asserted:

Production can be carried on without money, man can subsist without money, but commerce cannot exist without money, and commerce is the basis of civilisation. Money moves all, inspires all, directs all. It is the magic wand that has led humanity from barbarism. It is mighty. It should be a ministering angel—it may be a relentless despot.[117]

115. W. H. Chard, "Commercial Depression and the Appreciation of Gold," *Australian Economist*, IV (1894–97), 512. Similar expositions were contained in: Martin Simmat, "Unproductive Consumption," *ibid.*, I (1888–90), 66–69; and J. P. Morice, "Surplus Labour," *ibid.*, II (1890–93), 271–74.
116. "Commercial Depression and the Appreciation of Gold," p. 513.
117. Colonel Bell, "Some Unrecognised Economic Truths," *Australian Economist*, IV (1894–97), 588.

To restore money circulation, Bell recommended the American expedients of subsidized homestead settlement and an issue of greenbacks.

Like Ogilvy, Chard, and Bell, other underconsumptionists set forth their macro-economic analysis usually in conjunction with an appeal for radical social reform, and as a result they met spirited opposition and little dispassionate consideration. Richard Teece, before the Australian Economic Association, dismissed "quack remedies" which "betrayed an ignorance of the first principles of economics," and he insisted "The obvious cause of the unemployed class was that a large number of these people would not work."[118] Professor Walter Scott criticized underconsumptionists for failing to appreciate that savings do return to the expenditure stream as investment, and he insisted—a little hollowly during the disaster year 1893—that the true cause of the crisis had been a few business miscalculations.[119] Attacks on Chard's restrained and cogent presentation in 1894 became so vicious and unreasonable that he refused to reply to critics.[120]

Throughout the depressed 1890's, the arguments of persons who recognized a deficiency in total effective demand influenced discussion. Suggestions for greater private and government spending were voiced often during the period, and a few legislators even considered public policy measures to supply the need. D. M. Charleston, a legislative councillor in South Australia, told a parliamentary committee that widespread social reconstruction would be the most satisfactory method of restoring monetary circulation and of curing depression. He maintained that "land monopoly and control of capital" permitted "the few" to obtain a growing proportion of total income and prevented the creation of sufficient demand to match increased production of goods. Charleston feared long-run stagnation more than he did occasional fluctuations. He said:

Under the exploiting system the consuming powers of society are cramped by limitations quite independent of the possible amount of

118. *Australian Economist*, II (1890–93), 280 and 281.
119. W. Scott, "Surplus Labour: A Criticism," *Australian Economist*, III (1893–94), 291–94.
120. *Australian Economist*, IV (1894–97), 536–40.

production, consumption being limited not by the capabilities of society to produce, nor its capacity to consume, but by the amount the controllers of production and industries decide upon or consent that society should consume. It therefore follows that with every increase in production greater contributions of wealth must fall to the share of the capitalists if they fail to utilise that share by limiting their personal wants, or refuse to employ it in the production of some other form of wealth, and the demand for what is produced must of necessity be diminished. As the value of things is fixed according to demand, if there be no demand the things are valueless, and further production will necessarily cease. This will lessen the demand for labor, and its value will fall; partial employment at best will only be found for large numbers, and many of the workers will be compulsorily idle.[121]

Charleston concluded that instability would disappear and employment would remain full if society were reconstituted to permit universal participation in the benefits of progress, on foundations of "justice and equity" and "sound basic economic principles." Accordingly, the committee to which he addressed his remarks recommended accelerated construction of public works and new measures for redistribution of income and wealth.[122]

At the onset of depression in Queensland, Premier Samuel Griffith considered measures to restore prosperity, and in 1892 he risked political suicide by reversing his traditional policy regarding colored immigration and supporting temporary admittance of Polynesian labor. In a "Manifesto" in defense of this action, Griffith reasoned that the condition of the sugar industry was fundamental to the welfare of the total community, and that the need for relief to this primary sector transcended momentarily social or moral scruples. He said:

It cannot be too often impressed upon our minds that we all directly or indirectly depend for our livelihood on the products of the land of the colony. Any serious falling off in its productiveness, from whatever cause is therefore a matter of national concern. It has been urged that a revival of the sugar industry, which is at present in a condition

121. "Final Report of the Select Committee of the Legislative Council on the Unemployed Problem; together with Minutes of Proceedings and Appendices," *Parliamentary Papers of South Australia*, 1894, p. 23.
122. *Ibid.*, p. 5.

of depression and uncertainty, would result in a restoration of prosperity throughout the colony.[123]

In 1896, having in the interim become Chief Justice of Queensland, Griffith set forth the economic theory which may have inspired his earlier bold action. In an address to the Australasian Association for the Advancement of Science, he explained that he regarded a national economy as similar in form to an animal body, each part dependent on the activities of all the other parts, the system both producing and consuming at all times.

Whether it be an actual objective fact, or only a pretty conceit, that a nation or community is a real and distinct entity, with physical and mental attributes of its own—the individual member bearing to the whole a material relation analogous to that of a cell to an animal—there is no doubt that there are many striking points of resemblance between an individual and a body politic.[124]

Griffith believed that the secret of depressions was revealed from a study of the circulatory process within an economy.

It is necessary, then, in order to gain a proper knowledge of the material condition of a body politic, to investigate its sources of income (or food), both as to quantity and quality, the manner in which this income or a sufficient part of it is digested—that is, brought into the form in which it can be made available for consumption as food, clothing, and shelter—and the manner in which it is circulated through the community to perform the functions of repairing waste and providing for growth.[125]

A basic prerequisite of prosperity, Griffith asserted, was that the natural resources be adequate. However, he added, it was just as necessary for flows within the economy to be smooth-running, so as to distribute national income.

If this fund is sufficient for its purpose, and if the process of circulation or distribution is effective, every member of the community should be supplied with a sufficiency of food, clothing, and shelter, and there

---

123. Reprinted in C. M. H. Clark, *Select Documents in Australian History 1851–1900* (Sydney, 1955), p. 216. Griffith's policy was supported by "J. E. D.," in *The Way to Revive The Prosperity of Queensland* (Mackay, 1893).
124. Samuel Griffith, "A Plea for the Study of the Unconscious Vital Processes in the Life of Communities," *Report of the Sixth Meeting of the Australasian Association for the Advancement of Science held at Brisbane, 1895*, p. 659.
125. *Ibid.*, pp. 660–61.

should be something to spare for growth and accumulation. If, however, although the fund is sufficient, the process of circulation is ineffective, we may expect to find some parts of the body politic in a state of congestion or atrophy.[126]

Griffith was uncertain about appropriate methods of examining an economy, and he posed many questions without answering them. Like Alfred De Lissa, he hoped for illumination from the *Tableau Économique*. He continued:

It may, I think, be asserted with some confidence that this flow of circulation is governed by definite laws. Probably it takes place along the lines of least resistance. Probably there is in every healthy community a normal flow. The actual flow is certainly capable of being observed and investigated, and the laws governing it are probably open to discovery. I am not aware of any investigation of the subject from this point of view since the once celebrated *Tableau Economique* of Quesnay, the chief of the Physiocrats, which obtained such unbounded praise from the elder Mirabeau. The *Tableau* appears, however, to be lost, and I have not been able to meet with either of the books in which it was described in some detail.[127]

Although not clear in his own mind about the actual operation of an economy, Griffith did recognize that interruption at any point in the circular flow could initiate a cumulative contraction and recession. He said:

If there is a law regulating the flow of the material life-blood of a community, it is quite certain that any failure to obey that law will result in disturbance of the health of the body politic. When the body is healthy the supply of nutriment to every part of it is adequate. If, then, we find at any time that some members of the community suffer want or privation while others have enough, and perhaps to spare, the natural inference is that some law of health has been violated, and either that the total supply of nutriment is insufficient or that the proper flow of circulation is obstructed.[128]

Griffith's expressed appreciation of interdependence within an economy helps to explain his great anxiety in 1892 to relieve by any means the depression of a major industry caused by falling prices.

126. *Ibid.*, p. 665.
127. *Ibid.*, and see below p.514.
128. Samuel Griffith, "A Plea . . ." p. 667.

The significance of sustained effective demand for maintenance of economic stability was discussed seldom after the 1890's. Apparently, however, concern lurked in the minds of a few academic economists. William Mitchell observed quizzically in 1911: "not all professional economists appear to have reconciled the truth in the two opposite statements that 'demand for commodities is not demand for labour,' and that 'want of work is due to underconsumption.' "[129] R. F. Irvine at Sydney speculated in 1914 that new measures for income redistribution, by strengthening total demand, would have the unexpected result of increasing national production. He told a meeting of the British Association: "The new force of demand, coming as it does from the millions, will be persistent and reliable, and will set in motion forces which tend to progressive improvements in machinery, in processes, in organization, and finally in reduced costs."[130] Irvine's interest in the relation of production and consumption grew in the 1930's into whole-hearted acceptance of underconsumption theory and sympathy for the doctrines of social credit.[131]

Conclusion—The Twentieth Century

Discussion of economic fluctuations, by its nature, experienced oscillations correlated inversely with the level of economic activity. After the 1890's, Australia did not experience another deep depression until the 1930's, a decade which is beyond the scope of this study. Accordingly, most of the writings examined here were from the nineteenth century. In the first thirty years of the twentieth century, minor recessions occurred but were obscured for intellectuals by other exciting events, notably federation, World War I, and postwar reconstruction. Interest in business cycles did not disappear entirely during this period, but few investigations were carried out or additions to knowledge made.

129. *Encyclopaedia of Religion and Ethics* (Edinburgh, 1911), IV, 81–83.
130. R. F. Irvine, "The Influence of Distribution on Production," *Report of the Eighty-Fourth Meeting of the British Association for the Advancement of Science: Australasia, 1914* (London, 1915), p. 481.
131. R. F. Irvine, *The Midas Delusion* (Adelaide, 1933), pp. 57–67 and 99–117. Studies by Irvine of the relationship between the money supply and economic fluctuations have been examined in Chapter 5 above.

E. W. H. Fowles, president of the Social and Statistical Science Section of the Australasian Association for the Advancement of Science, reported in 1910 that awareness abroad of unemployment as a social problem had mounted steadily during the previous decade, and he appealed for renewed enquiry in Australia:

Ten years ago unemployment was regarded as a good subject for kind-hearted benevolent societies and pious millionaire philanthropists, but not worth the serious attention of statesmen. The unemployed were an annual winter spectacle in England—harrowing, it is true, but temporary, and their troubles were usually mitigated by soup-kitchens and a respectable subscription list headed by the Queen. In year-books or statistical returns the subject of unemployment, if noticed at all, was relegated to an appendix or foot-note where uncertain figures were bolstered up by vague references to what was done in Germany, Switzerland, and other places on the Continent.[132]

Fowles condemned advocates of "one cure-all" for unemployment, and he emphasized that "Sentimental treatment of the unemployed is futile; the time has come for a scientific handling of the problem." He proposed formation of public and private agencies to provide work during depressions and to insure against unemployment. But Fowles himself remained puzzled as to the causes of cyclical variations in economic activity, and he was able only to ask embarrassing rhetorical questions.[133] Despite his urgency and enthusiasm others did not hasten to provide the answers.

On several occasions the Commonwealth government sponsored attempts to analyze a recession. In 1910 G. H. Knibbs, the first Commonwealth statistician, related developments in social insurance programs in other countries, and he was led naturally to examine "causes of unemployment." Rather uncertainly Knibbs attributed a decline in the demand for labor to "seasonal conditions," "changes in conditions of the money market," and labor disputes. He cited for authority works by Sismondi in particular. Knibbs urged study of unemployment with "the undi-

132. E. W. H. Fowles, "On Unemployment," *Report of the Thirteenth Meeting of the Australasian Association for the Advancement of Science held at Sydney, 1911,* p. 456.
133. *Ibid.,* pp. 457–71.

vided attention of a well-informed mind" rather than "either a dilettante or a merely academic consideration."[134] In 1912 Knibbs proposed formation of an association in Australia to channel the study of unemployment; but he reported in disgust that he met only "lack of interest."[135]

A postwar recession in the 1920's revived government awareness of unemployment. A Royal Commission on National Insurance reported in 1926, evidently without conviction, that seasonal factors, drought, and "the action of those who control the supply of currency and credit" seemed to be "causes of unemployment." The Commission recommended establishment of an "unemployment council," "labour bureaux," and improvement in the flow of economic information. It doubted that insurance could be devised to cope with such widespread catastrophes as the unemployment generated by lengthy depressions.[136] The Development and Migration Commission also reported on unemployment in 1928, leaning heavily on Douglas Copland's interpretation of the business cycle. It proposed measures to improve mobility and knowledge, monetary reform, and scheduling of public works during recessions.[137]

On the brink of the great depression of the 1930's, Australian economists had not advanced substantially beyond the point their predecessors had reached in the 1890's in the study of economic fluctuations. Little empirical investigation had yet been carried out, and contemporary theories of cycle behavior had been anticipated forty years earlier, at least in unsophisticated form. Certainly by 1930, the postwar revival of economics had not produced such precocious insights or brilliant technical inno-

134. "Social Insurance: Report by the Commonwealth Statistician, G. H. Knibbs," *Papers Presented to the Parliament of the Commonwealth of Australia*, 1910, pp. 70 and 93.
135. "Unemployment: Report on the Conference of the International Association on, Held at Ghent, September, 1913—By Mr. Donald Campbell, Commonwealth Representative; together with Note by the Commonwealth Statistician," *Papers Presented to the Parliament of the Commonwealth of Australia*, 1913.
136. "Second Progress Report of the Royal Commission on National Insurance. Unemployment," *Papers Presented to the Parliament of the Commonwealth of Australia*, 1926–27, pp. 10 and 14.
137. "Development and Migration Commission. Report on Unemployment and Business Stability in Australia," *Papers Presented to the Parliament of the Commonwealth of Australia*, 1926–27–28.

vations as were contained in the nineteenth century works of Musgrave and De Lissa, treated in Chapter 14.

By the end of the period examined here, little concensus had been reached as to the reasons for economic fluctuations in Australia. Reluctance by governments to introduce reforms designed to improve stability may be explained in part by widespread acceptance of the general conclusion that crises were inevitable and incurable features of a free capitalist system. In discussions of the effects of specific government actions such as tariffs and land disposal upon economic stability, as many proponents and as many convincing arguments were marshalled on one side of the debates as upon the other. Colonists who traced economic fluctuations to periodic deficiencies in effective demand came closest to what is accepted today as a reasonable description of the contraction process. However, these persons employed incomplete arguments and usually combined and confused analysis with proposals for radical social reform. It can be said in summary that before the professionalization of economics, enlightened understanding of economic fluctuations was rare, and ironically, the less orthodox were cycle explanations and schemes for amelioration the more they approached the truth.

· 8 ·

Transport Development

Australian colonists from the early years of settlement were keenly aware of the significance for economic development of improvements in transport facilities.[1] However, before the middle of the nineteenth century they were prevented from improving water transport by the inadequacy of Australian rivers and from making important changes on land by the high costs of roads and railways relative to sparse population. Moreover, capital was scarce and the Colonial Office cautioned against excessive public borrowing and expenditures.[2] Then, at midcentury, significant changes took place. In 1846 Colonial Office conservatism was modified when Secretary of State Gladstone, as part of a general liberalization of British economic policy, notified colonial governors that railways, recently perfected in Britain, could be undertaken by the colonies at their own discretion; he suggested from British experience certain principles of construction and operation that might with wisdom be adopted.[3] Gladstone's announcement touched off a decade and a half of vigorous discussion and inquiry into railway economics, which was sustained by local legislative enthusiasm, by actual commencement of railway construction, by grants to the colonies of responsible government, and by gold discoveries which attracted both capital and immi-

1. For example, W. C. Wentworth argued in 1819 that the progress of humanity had been determined largely by advances in navigation. *A Statistical, Historical, and Political Description of the Colony of New South Wales* (London, 1819), pp. 79–84. Governor Macquarie endorsed wholeheartedly public development of transport facilities. A. G. L. Shaw, *The Economic Development of Australia* (London, 1955), p. 27.
2. See Paul Knaplund, *James Stephen and the British Colonial System 1813–1847* (Madison, Wisconsin, 1953), p. 27.
3. T. A. Coghlan, *Labour and Industry in Australia* (London, 1918), p. 830. A discussion of Gladstone's policy reversal is contained in S. J. McLean, "An Early Chapter in Canadian Railroad Policy," *Journal of Political Economy*, VI (1897–98), 323–52.

grants with new ideas.[4] Debate was concerned both with the wisdom of completing specific projects and with the relative desirability of private and public enterprise. In this chapter some of the writings on railways are examined which were produced during the years of greatest controversy: first a selection of optimistic railway *apologia,* and then a group of critical analyses in reaction to optimism. The studies themselves were not important contributions to the literature of economics, but viewed as a whole reveal the climate of informed contemporary opinion. For this reason they help to explain the pattern of colonial growth and indicate the part played by imported ideas.

Initial Enthusiasm for Railways

The possibility of railway contruction was discussed in Australia as early as 1833, but the first serious debate followed Gladstone's dispatch in 1846.[5] An enthusiastic public meeting was held at Sydney to collect information, and a committee headed by Ralph Mansfield, a local entrepreneur, cleric, and amateur statistician, issued a favorable report. Heady optimism was the dominant feature of railway discussion in the late 1840's, and a pamphlet by John Curr in 1847 was only the first of many engineers' tracts to deal hopefully with the technicalities of railways in New South Wales.[6] Curr and his successors did not neglect to mention any of the manifold blessings which they were convinced would follow construction.

No official action on railways was taken in 1847, but in 1848 a select committee of the Legislative Council, with Charles Cooper chairman, reported strongly in favor of railways in general, and

4. Attitudes of the Colonial Office toward Australian railways, and particularly their significance for federation, are described in John M. Ward, *Earl Grey and the Australian Colonies, 1846–1857* (Melbourne, 1958), pp. 101–2, 153, 175, 178, 328, 330, and 361. Adoption by the colonies of conflicting railway gauges is discussed, *ibid.,* pp. 271–77.

5. See Alan Birch, "The Sydney Railway Company, 1848–1855," *Royal Australian Historical Society Journal and Proceedings,* XLIII (1957), 49–92; and George A. Gilder, "The Early History of the Railways of New South Wales," *ibid.,* XVII (1931), 215–38.

6. John Curr, *Railway Locomotion, and Steam Navigation: Their Principles and Practice* (London, 1847).

in particular of government assistance to private companies, on grounds of "expediency." The committee gathered together a little information on physical aspects of routes, and on probable costs and revenues of lines; but it based its recommendations principally on the successful experiences of other countries, and on faith. The committee concluded that profitability of railways could not be measured by calculating existing road traffic, but only by estimating potential community development. It reported:

That the introduction of Railways into Europe, and other civilized portions of the world, has been attended by a rapid and almost incredible development and increase of all the sources and appliances of national industry, is a fact so universally admitted as to require no argument for its proof.[7]

As a result of the committee's deliberations, a Sydney Railroad and Tramway Company was incorporated in 1849, and construction began in 1850. Public support for the enterprise was aroused by such propaganda pieces as *The Sydney Railway Pamphlet* which used currently fashionable catechistic literary technique.[8] In 1849 another select committee urged the British Government to make available a guaranteed loan.[9] Construction proceeded slowly, and costs quickly exceeded estimates as labor became scarce with the discovery of gold. Nevertheless, enthusiasm for the new method of transport steadily increased rather than diminished both in New South Wales and in the other colonies.

Railway polemics reached a peak in the 1850's.[10] Advocates of construction were either military engineers, civil servants, or

7. "Report from the Select Committee on Railways, with Minutes of Evidence," *Votes and Proceedings of the Legislative Council of New South Wales*, 1848, p. 457. An account of the public meeting held at Sydney in 1846 forms Appendix B of this document, and Mansfield's report is Appendix D.

8. Publicus, *The Sydney Railway Pamphlet; or, the Subject Generally, Succinctly Considered, in a Series of Questions and Answers; with Extracts from Mr. Shields' Evidence, before the Select Committee of the Legislative Council, of the Cost per Mile, Etc. Etc. and an Outline of the Act of Incorporation* (Goulburn, 1849).

9. "Report from the Select Committee on the Sydney Railway Bill, with Minutes of Evidence and Appendix," *Votes and Proceedings of the Legislative Council of New South Wales*, 1849.

10. An extravagantly optimistic railway prospectus of 1853 is reprinted by T. A. Coghlan, *Labour and Industry in Australia*, pp. 832–34.

actual and would-be promoters who hoped to interest private investors and colonial legislatures in financing projects. Despite initial setbacks and hardships encountered by the Sydney Railway Company during its first years, a New South Wales select committee in 1854 received extensive and sanguine testimony from engineers and others on the desirability of more lines. The committee reported that past difficulties were in themselves sufficient reason for government to come to the aid of railroads, and that "the time has arrived when the construction of Railways ought to be taken up on a large and comprehensive system. Whatever may be the cost . . . their general introduction into the Colony ought not any longer to be deferred."[11] Prompted by the imminent collapse of private enterprise, the New South Wales legislature took the committee's advice and inaugurated the first government railways in Australia in 1854. In 1857, despite repeated financial discouragements on existing projects and recommendations of caution in further expansion by such authorities as Captain Ward of the Sydney Mint, Jacob L. Montefiore, chairman of a new select committee to investigate "the Most Advisable Plan for Securing the Formation of the Great Trunk Lines of Railway in New South Wales," proved that legislative enthusiasm was not easily dampened. He proposed government subsidies in land to any new private companies which might wish to establish themselves.[12]

In Victoria excitement over railways became intense by the mid-1850's.[13] Some schemes included plans for development of reservoirs, water power, and harbors. Frederick Acheson, C.E., contended in 1856 that railways in Victoria should be inaugu-

11. "Final Report from the Select Committee on Roads and Railways, with Minutes of Evidence," *Votes and Proceedings of the Legislative Council of New South Wales*, 1854, p. 2.
12. "Report from the Select Committee of the Legislative Council, Appointed to Consider and Report on the Most Advisable Plan for Securing the Formation of the Great Trunk Lines of Railway in New South Wales," *Journal of the Legislative Council of New South Wales*, 1857.
13. Representative tracts of the period were: Lieut. Amsinck and "An Old Backwoodsman", *Two Competing Essays on Internal Communication* (Melbourne, 1856); and N. W. Pollard, *Prize Essay on Internal Communication* (Melbourne, 1856). These essays were entered in a competition "for the premium of fifty guineas" awarded by the Melbourne Chamber of Commerce.

rated by a line to the Yan Yean reservoir and establishment of a
water-driven quartz crusher. He wrote: "To carry out . . . the
scheme of internal communication by railways successfully, it is
quite as necessary to provide for the reproductiveness of the
capital invested, by making arrangements for the creation of
traffic, as it is to construct the lines of railway in the first instance."[14] Railway enthusiasts often took their proposals to legislative committees which were not unreceptive. Henry N. Smith,
C.E., among others, explained to a Victorian committee, which
reported in 1854-55, that bountiful returns had followed railways
in other countries. He concluded:

> They [railroads], therefore, should be constructed, it being a maxim
> *"That the civilization, progress, and prosperity of a country may be
> judged of by the state of its roads."*
> The Railway being the best form of road, it follows, that the coun-
> try which relatively possesses most mileage of Railway, is the most
> civilized, most progressive, most prosperous.
> By no other known means can the resources of a country be so
> rapidly developed, its internal commerce increased, or comfort and
> cheapness of living become general.[15]

The committee recommended strongly that government sponsor
trunk lines, on the ground that: "The evidence which has been
taken before your Committee distinctly shews the advantage of
one comprehensive scheme of railway communication."[16] Accordingly, in 1855 the Victorian government assumed responsibility

14. "On Motive Power in Victoria, Economically Considered," *Transactions of
the Philosophical Institute of Victoria*, I (1855–56), 110. A similar plan was contained in Thomas Oldham and Thomas E. Rawlinson ("engineers"), *Treatise on
Railway & Harbour Accomodation for Victoria: with Remarks on the Formation of
Storage Reservoirs for the Pastoral, Agricultural, and Gold-Mining Population*
(Melbourne, 1855).
15. "Progress Report from the Select Committee of the Legislative Council on
Railways; together with the Proceedings of the Committee, Minutes of Evidence,
and Appendices," *Votes and Proceedings of the Legislative Council of Victoria*,
1854–55, p. 24.
16. *Ibid.*, p. iii. George Ward Cole, a prominent Melbourne merchant, warned
the Committee—"as I have contended over and over again, the power of borrowing
[for railways] should be invested in the government *alone*, fully to protect the
future interests of the country." p. 32. See also "Report from the Select Committee
of the Legislative Council on Railways; together with the Proceedings of the Committee, and Minutes of Evidence," *Votes and Proceedings of the Legislative Council
of Victoria*, 1855–56.

for all but suburban rail lines. Another select committee rebutted critics who suggested that more careful study of profitability should precede construction, and it reported: "The effects of railway communication should not be measured exclusively by the commercial value of the undertaking. The same beneficial results which have followed in other countries the establishment of improved internal communication, may with safety be anticipated here."[17] A government line to connect Melbourne with the gold fields was commenced in 1858.[18]

Railway mania in the 1850's was not confined to the two colonies with gold rushes and the largest populations. Hon. S. Davenport, South Australian Commissioner of Public Works, outlined eleven "general propositions" of railway operation to a select committee in Adelaide and advised accelerated construction with state support.[19] When the separate colony of Queensland was formed in 1859, it too inherited from the parent New South Wales a characteristic faith in the wonders of railways. A select committee "on Internal Communication," without making any estimates of either probable costs or returns, reported:

[The Committee] beg to direct the serious and earnest consideration of the Legislature to the necessity in the early period of the history of this colony of adopting the best and most economical means of developing the vast resources of the interior, by establishing a permanent, effectual, and certain means of communication between the outlying districts and ports of shipment.

This object once attained the wealth and importance of our towns and thickly populated portions of the colony will be daily increasing and the illimitable tracts of pasture lands on our Western frontier which, with our present means of conveyance, can never be reached, will then be rendered available.[20]

17. "Report of the Select Committee of the Legislative Assembly upon Railways; together with the Proceedings of the Committee, Minutes of Evidence, and Appendices," *Votes and Proceedings of the Legislative Assembly of Victoria, 1856–57*, p. v.
18. T. A. Coghlan, *Labour and Industry in Australia*, p. 755.
19. "Report of the Select Committee of the Legislative Council, Appointed to Report on Railways and Tramways; together with Minutes of Evidence and Appendix," *Proceedings of the Parliament of South Australia, 1857–58*, pp. 1–9.
20. "Report from the Select Committee on Internal Communication; together with the Proceedings of the Committee and Minutes of Evidence," *Votes and Proceedings of the Legislative Assembly of Queensland, 1860*, p. 6.

Skepticism and Railway Economics

Against this background of official lightheadedness based on high optimism and poorly substantiated claims, a succession of Australian colonists in the 1850's reviewed the economic functions of railways and produced a body of critical comment which would have done credit to a society more advanced in the conventional evidences of culture. Authors of railway critiques were inspired in part by concern with what they considered grossly extravagant policies pursued or proposed by immature governments. In addition, these writers, like other educated men of the period, were acquainted at least in a general way with "principles of political economy," either through Adam Smith, Malthus, Ricardo, or a popular text, and they were accustomed to judging policy measures according to these principles. They observed that aggressive government action in a major area of the economy was clearly a departure from laissez faire and could be justified only after careful examination of effects on production and distribution and clear demonstration of benefit to society.

All students of railway economics after 1850 had the benefit of Dionysius Lardner's monumental work, *Railway Economy,* and this book had substantial influence in the Australian colonies.[21] Beyond giving extensive data on "the progress of transport" and technicalities of railway operation, Lardner applied classical economics to railway rate policy and arrived at an analytical system similar to present-day theory of the firm.[22] He indicated the need for some government interference with private railway compa-

21. *Railway Economy: A Treatise on the New Art of Transport, its Management, Prospects, and Relations, Commercial, Financial, and Social* (London, 1850) was one of the first dozen or so books on economics in the Library of Melbourne University in 1856. *Catalogue of the Library of the University of Melbourne, Victoria* (London, 1856), p. 28. It was also listed among the 107 books on "Politics and Political Economy" in the Parliamentary Library of Tasmania in 1869. "Report of Commissioners on the Parliamentary Library," *Journals of the House of Assembly of Tasmania,* 1869.

22. Lardner constructed a total cost curve (consisting of fixed and variable portions) and a total revenue curve, and he observed correctly that a profit-maximizing monopolist would produce at an output and sell at a price where the latter lay farthest above the former. See *Railway Economy,* p. 288, and corrected diagram following p. xxiii.

nies, because of the monopolistic character of their operations, and he recommended a semi-autonomous state "board of control" —similar to the railway commissions instituted in all the Australian colonies during the nineteenth century.[23] Above all Lardner called for careful and sustained study and analysis of proposals for construction of railways, and their subsequent operations.

Beginning in November, 1852, Henry Parkes published in his newspaper the *Empire* the first reasonably objective study of colonial railroad economics, an anonymous treatise in eleven instalments entitled "The Economy of Railways in Australia," and constituting "an inquiry into the mechanical principles of Railways, and their influence in developing the resources of a country—into the cost of constructing, maintaining, and working them —and into the means by which the expense may be confined to the lowest scale, consistent with the full attainment of the objects of such works in Australia."[24] United States railroads (built by "that prudent and far-seeing people") were described in some detail and judged "so much better than the costly system followed in the United Kingdom."[25] The author laid great emphasis on inexpensive construction and operation, and suggested use of horses instead of steam engines for motive power. He reminded his readers that "the cost at which goods and passengers can be carried on a railway will be as the interest on the capital expended, added to the cost of working the line, and inversely, as the number of passengers or quantity of goods carried."[26] Realistic estimates were compiled of construction costs in New South Wales, and eight "collective benefits of railway communication," "taken from a recent publication" (probably Lardner), were listed.[27] The author concluded: "Such national enterprises should be protected from all unnecessary expense—from all extravagant demands and vexatious opposition—and have a strong claim on

23. *Ibid.*, pp. 502–24.
24. The study was serialized in the following issues of the *Empire* during 1852: Nov. 11, p. 1610; Nov. 13, p. 1618; Nov. 19, p. 1638; Nov. 24, p. 1654; Nov. 30, p. 1674; Dec. 4, unpaged; Dec. 10, p. 1710; Dec. 15, p. 1726; Dec. 20, p. 1742; Dec. 25, p. 1766; Dec. 31, p. 1786.
25. *Empire*, Nov. 13, 1852, p. 1618.
26. *Empire*, Nov. 11, 1852, p. 1610.
27. *Empire*, Dec. 31, 1852, p. 1786.

the protection of the Government."[28] In this series Parkes did not
introduce a novel approach to the analysis of railways, but he did
provide a stimulating example of straight thinking on the subject,
and perhaps a healthy antidote to the boundless optimism of the
times.[29]

When it became clear in 1854 that both the Victorian and New
South Wales governments might assist railways on a large scale,
independent discussion and enquiry increased. Reasoned arguments were advanced both for and against the proposed state
support. An unidentified writer in the first issue of the *Sydney
University Magazine* in 1855 launched a scathing attack on methods which had been used in New South Wales for investigating
the subject. Comparing Australian construction costs, inflated by
the gold rushes, with prices in Europe and in the United States,
as reported by Lardner, the author claimed railways in the colonies could never be economical.

> The true state of the case is simply this. The population is too small
> to support a Railway in any part of the colony. It would require a very
> large traffic, and very high charges, to cover the working expenses. The
> first requirement is impossible without a dense population; and with
> any amount of population is incompatible with the second.[30]

The author denied that alleged traffic-creating powers of railroads should be given serious consideration in calculating
probable profitability, and he claimed that an analogy often
drawn between the United States and Australia during the gold
rush period was basically invalid. The character of the Australian
frontier and the pattern of development were different in important respects from their American counterparts. He explained:

> The Atlantic States of America are densely peopled; the natural
> increase of the population is large; the annual immigration from

28. *Empire*, Nov. 13, 1852, p. 1618.
  29. The *Empire's* railway policy was expounded again at later dates: for example, "Hints for the Railway Committee," Feb. 3, 1854; and "The Philosophy of
Railways," Feb. 8, 1854.
  30. "Railways," *Sydney University Magazine*, January, 1855, p. 35. The author
was careful to concede that: "Of all the known modes of overland transport, the
cheapest, the safest, the quickest, in every respect the best, is by Railway, *where
the traffic is sufficiently great* to justify such an undertaking." But he added: "We
cannot sufficiently emphasize this condition; where it does not hold, a Railway is
an absolute loss." *Ibid.*, p. 24.

Europe is enormous, equal to, if not greater than, the whole population of New South Wales. From these causes there is a restless and needy surplus population constantly seeking for an outlet in the west. A railway through an unsettled, rich, alluvial district presents such an outlet. A rush is made; the effect so often described is produced; the wilderness is changed into a garden. But no such wonders can be expected here. We have not the wilderness, the rich alluvial wilderness; nor have we the overflowing population at one end of the line eager to rush in and fill up the void.[31]

For the New South Wales Select Committee on Roads and Railways of 1854 the Sydney University critic had only harsh criticism.

No evidence, except of the most vague and unsatisfactory kind, was obtained respecting the probable traffic and working expenses. The Council is persuaded to rush with inconsiderate haste into an expense of £700,000 upon the bare statements of the engineer who is to superintend the works, and of the contractor who is to carry them out.[32]

The *Sydney University Magazine* aroused the anger of railway supporters, and James Norton, a member of the Legislative Council, replied to the article with more spirit than careful argument. Norton deplored excessive emphasis on commercial profitability in considerations of public utilities in a new country, and he insisted that the incalculable social economies of railways, including savings in ordinary road repairs and the accelerated pace of overall colonial development, justified a government subsidy. He wrote: "we might expect that the author of a work addressed to us from the fountain of literature and science, would, in a paper on railways, aim at higher things than the pecuniary profit likely to result from the capital employed in their construction."[33] Speculating that his opponent was a faculty member at Sydney University, Norton aimed close to home by suggesting that transport was analogous to higher education in value to society:

The writer appears to think that no expenditure of money can be proper that is not capable of a full and perfect return. This is the

31. *Ibid.*, pp. 33 and 37.
32. *Ibid.*, p. 40.
33. "Rail Communication in Australia," in James Norton, *Australian Essays on Subjects Political, Moral, and Religious* (London, 1857), p. 35.

argument, not of the political economist, but of the shopkeeper. Is the Sydney University an institution that will yield to the colony any interest for the money expended in upholding it?[34]

Norton was able only to speculate about possible gains from railways, and he was at a disadvantage with his adversary in the *Sydney University Magazine* who was able to illustrate clearly through accepted principles how railways could disturb resource allocation and cause the community loss. Norton's one reservation about the desirability of railways was particularly candid and in a sense far-sighted. He mused: "it is painful to contemplate the accidents which, amongst an ignorant and drunken population, must result from steam propulsion."[35]

In Victoria in 1855, Richard Woolley expressed views very similar to those of Norton in New South Wales. He defended government control of railways by citing McCulloch on the wastes of competition which could exist where conditions of "natural" monopoly prevailed. He claimed considerable personal acquaintance with both the theory and practice of railways:

as I have for years past made this subject my study, and have enjoyed ample opportunities in Europe of becoming thoroughly conversant with it in all its bearings, including the comparative benefits and disadvantages of the various systems in operation there for constructing and managing Railways, I trust I shall not be charged with presumption if I venture to speak with some confidence upon it.[36]

Woolley argued that a government railway commission could raise capital more easily and at lower interest rates than could a private company, would be willing to accept a smaller rate of profit, would charge the most socially desirable fares and freight rates, could minimize costs by using convicts and other public facilities, and would obviate the unhealthy speculation connected with a joint stock corporation. However, like Norton, Woolley was able only to express undocumented personal conviction of the social values in railways.

Thousands of immigrants from the United States poured into

34. *Ibid.*, p. 38.
35. *Ibid.*, p. 37.
36. Richard Woolley, *Railways: By Whom Shall They be Made and Managed?* (Melbourne, 1855), p. 5.

Australia in the 1850's, drawn both by the lure of gold and by profits in industries and occupations ancillary to gold. Their views on railways, reflecting home experience, were expressed often in the literature of the period. Many of the more enterprising transport promoters were American, notably George F. Train and Freeman Cobb who helped revive the Melbourne Chamber of Commerce as a powerful transport lobby.[37] But critics as well as enthusiasts came from and were inspired by the United States. One opponent of "premature" railway construction, using the pseudonym "American" and writing in Hobart, declared that a Tasmanian scheme to construct a main trunk line was grandiose, extravagant, and liable to detract from legitimate efforts to develop staple production. He pleaded with Tasmanians to give railroads a dispassionate examination, first to collect data revealing costs and revenue and then to judge proposed lines strictly on their economic merits. He insisted:

the question is not the mere possibility of discovering a line, as many seem to think, but the benefits it will confer on the community, and the consequences it may entail on us for good or evil, now and hereafter.

The prospect of the success of this project depends on the solution of one simple question—will the inland traffic of Tasmania support 120 miles of rail with a reasonable hope of profit to all concerned?[38]

"American" presented blue-book statistics of external trade as the best available "thermometer of commerce," and he concluded that the proposed railroad could not possibly be remunerative. He described thus a local engineer who cited Lardner in lyrical terms on the value of railways in other countries:

"The book-full blockhead, ignorantly read,
"With loads of learned lumber in his head."[39]

37. L. G. Churchward has estimated that 16,000 Americans arrived at Sydney and Melbourne between 1852 and 1856. "The American Contribution to the Victorian Gold Rush," *Victorian Historical Magazine*, XIX (1941–42), 85–95; and, "Australian-American Relations during the Gold Rush," *Historical Studies Australia and New Zealand*, II (1942–43), 11–24.
38. *The Letters of "American," on the Projected Railroads, and the Public Lands of Tasmania* (Hobart, 1856), p. 12.
39. *Ibid.*, p. 16. Construction of the proposed Tasmanian line was not undertaken until the 1870's.

In a similar vein a South Australian parliamentary committee reported that it had "not been inattentive to Lardner and other authors on the railway system in the United States," but it regretted that:

Those whose knowledge is altogether theoretical, and whose opinions have been formed from works published with reference to the advantage and benefits of railways in older and more populous countries, appear to your Committtee to have arrived at the conclusion, that certain effects have been produced in other countries under certain circumstances, therefore the same results will follow here under circumstances altogether dissimilar.[40]

The most valuable contribution to railway discussion in Melbourne during the 1850's was a moderate and balanced study entitled *Railway Economy in Victoria* by Francis A. Corbett, chief clerk of the 1854 Victorian census.[41] Corbett claimed he had no personal or political objectives for his writings, but wished only to "determine the broad principles in accordance with which our works should be formed."[42] Apparently, he was versed in classical economics, and like Smith and Ricardo he stressed the importance of improvements in transport for economic development. "High carriage," he wrote, "has all the injurious consequences of a barren soil or unpropitious climate, in retarding the progress of wealth and population; it has an almost incalculable effect in rendering labour less productive, because it confines men to the cultivation of the poorer and more barren soils near large cities."[43] He agreed with less cautious advocates of railways that external economies as well as commercial profit should be assessed when contemplating construction, but he insisted on a careful weighing of aggregate benefits against costs, and he deplored the absence of serious analysis prior to recent railway legislation. He hoped to provide in his little book useful information for the colonial government when planning rail-

40. "Report of the Select Committee of the Legislative Council, Appointed to Report on Railways and Tramways," *Proceedings of the Parliament of South Australia, 1857–58,* p. 1.
41. Major Campbell, Registrar-General and director of the census, praised Corbett's statistical labors in "Statistics in Victoria," *Melbourne Monthly Magazine of Original Colonial Literature,* I (1855), 249.
42. Francis A. Corbett, *Railway Economy in Victoria* (Melbourne, 1857), p. 8.
43. *Ibid.*, pp. 25–26.

roads. He objected: "The fact is, we have been legislating without reflection, and not upon principle, and the legislation of caprice can never be other than a series of blunders and inconsistencies, always discreditable, and often injurious."[44]

Corbett cast most of his enquiry in general terms dealing with transport as only one industry affecting colonial development; his arguments could have applied as well to other areas of the economy. He asserted that in matters affecting national growth private ownership of capital was subservient to the public responsibility of government, and if individuals did not of their own accord select the most socially desirable directions for investment the state was obliged to interfere. Apparently, Corbett was deeply impressed by the high productivity and rate of return on capital goods he saw around him. In Victoria, he argued, where no satisfactory transportation facilities existed at his time of writing, government should not tolerate unrestricted private railway construction which might result on the one hand in wastes of competitive operation and generation of excess capacity, or on the other hand in exploitative monopoly. In his view, the legislature was compelled by the need to make optimum use of capital either to manage or to control closely all new transport enterprise. He urged—"be it remembered that it is as much the charge and duty of Government, provided it can do so without infringing private rights or liberty, to guard against that portion of the capital which is in private hands, being squandered or wasted, as it is to preserve that which is more immediately under the charge of the Executive."[45]

Corbett decided that, on balance, fewer problems would be presented by public ownership of railroads than by state control of private firms. He justified his approval of a single public railway corporation rather than many smaller private companies thus: "If the people are taxed for a general system of railways, every man in the community, even the poorest, gets a recompense for what he pays in the reduction of all the commodities he consumes, or in the increase of employment occasioned by the prog-

44. *Ibid.*, p. 15.
45. *Ibid.*, p. 13.

ress and extension of industry; but the benefit derived from private lines is only local, and they, in too many cases, become public nuisances."[46]

Corbett was extremely perceptive when dealing with the extent and form which railways should take in undeveloped countries; his reasoning involved implicit use of a marginal productivity theory of capital. He listed purposes for which funds beyond a bare minimum could be expended in railway construction (increases in durability, speed, or length of track), and he stated as a principle that every pound spent must yield a net return equal to the rate of profit prevailing throughout the colony. To insure the observance of this principle, he insisted that detailed calculations of both revenue and cost be made prior to commencement of railway building, including forecasts for all segments of the market for transport services and expense of future reconstruction and repairs—questions of real concern in a territory passing through a gold rush and attendant inflation. He explained:

> The additional expenditure . . . is dependent, amongst other things, on the value of money, which varies in all countries; on the probability of such a fall in the wages of labour and in materials, as may admit of the renewal of works at a cheaper rate than that at which construction of a durable character is at present attainable; on the possibility of the discovery in this new country, of cheaper and better materials than are now known, and on the probability of alterations in the lines being found advisable, in consequence of their having been made through an unsurveyed country, or owing to the shifting of the population.[47]

Corbett outlined how and why in a new and booming economy returns on invested capital exceed greatly returns in an older country. He described a condition all colonists knew existed, but whose explanation and implications they were inclined to forget. He wrote:

> In new countries of great natural resources, where the population is rapidly increasing as every day rolls on, new opportunities for the investment of capital are opened. . . . If you take £100 by

46. *Ibid.*, p. 17.
47. *Ibid.*, p. 54.

taxation from a capitalist in England, you deprive him of only from
£3 to £4, and a man in business of £5 or £6 per annum. Here
if you take the same sum from a capitalist, he loses £12 per annum,
and a tradesman suffers at least £20 yearly.[48]

The vital significance for railways of differing rates of return on
capital between old and new countries, Corbett found, was that
construction and employment of capital goods profitable in an
old economy could result in loss in a new one. He estimated the
pure interest rate in Britain at four percent and in Victoria at
twelve and one-half percent, and he argued that because of this
disparity it was sensible to build works of less durability, size,
and complexity in the colony than in the mother country. No matter whether costs were paid from borrowings or from taxation of
inhabitants, the more profitable alternative uses for capital in the
colony required economically defensible expenditures on public
utilities to result in far higher increases in yield (marginal productivity) than in Britain. For example, he explained, it would be
folly to deprive Australian residents of the use of capital through
taxes or loans to the same extent as Englishmen to give a railway
work added length of life. The capitalized value of returns from
increased durability, because of a higher prevailing market interest rate, was lower and therefore a worse national investment in a
new country than in an old one. He wrote: "it would not be
justifiable to save the people of England a portion of a tax, if by
so doing, works were made to last less than eighteen years; whereas, in this colony, it may be sound policy to make them of little
more than six years durations, and renew the tax so often for the
purpose of putting them up again and again."[49] Corbett combatted
a fallacy of economic thinking which is prevalent even in our
own time, that one country can dogmatically prescribe its own
institutions, tools, and methods for use in another land. This mode
of thought was particularly strong in Victoria in the 1850's after

48. *Ibid.*, p. 55.
49. *Ibid.*, p. 56. With regard to capital borrowed abroad, Corbett explained:
"No matter at what rate we may be able to procure loans, money is worth to us our
current rate of interest, and should be husbanded with equal care as if the higher
rate were paid for it." p. 58.

an influx of immigrants accustomed to techniques and capital uses of an old country and unconvinced as yet of the need for adjustment to new conditions of factor scarcity. He noted some of the basic errors that could be made in Australia by British railway entrepreneurs or planners:

> It is a very general impression that there is a gain in making costly works, if the durability be augmented in a higher proportion than the increase of outlay . . . but no doubling of outlay for any amount of permanency, beyond the period of capital doubling, is justifiable on the grounds of economy alone, whatever it may be for other reasons. . . . stone bridges being several times more expensive, are by no means economical in a country where capital is exceedingly precious. Now, economy is the chief thing to be considered in railways as well as in machinery.[50]

Corbett emphasized the need for public utilities to yield immediate aggregate benefits equal to the return on private capital throughout the economy, but he also predicted that construction costs would fall in the colonies as population increased. He believed that the sum of all his arguments was conclusively in favor of temporary and inexpensive railway construction, carefully planned to maximize revenue and minimize costs.[51]

As corollaries to his general conclusions, Corbett recommended first that Australian railways be designed principally for the transport of freight and not of passengers as in Europe, and second that lines be planned to pass through fertile areas ending eventually in markets, but without specific regard to shortest or fastest routes. When determining length of line, Corbett advised engineers to remember always the prevailing interest rate on capital; he showed by an example how a relatively long and elaborate line could be undertaken if funds were available at three percent interest and how a shorter more simple system would be indicated if capital cost five percent. He warned repeatedly that English engineers would not accept easily either the developmental role of railways in the colony or the changed relationship of factor

50. *Ibid.*, pp. 57 and 58.
51. *Ibid.*, pp. 59–60.

costs, and that they would require close direction and supervision. In England, he wrote, railways:

are principally constructed with a view to the traffic between the
termini, and with very little reference to the intermediate districts.
It is necessary, therefore, to have the different circumstances of the
two countries well impressed upon the minds of those who have the
laying out of our railways, as there is a strong tendency amongst us
to imitate the systems of the mother country, without sufficiently investigating the reasons for their adoption.[52]

The impact of Corbett's perceptive discussion of colonial railways cannot be assessed with precision. He wrote at a time when
the decision to proceed with government lines in Victoria had
already been made, and his influence would have been greatest
on the extent and form of new construction. Corbett claimed that
a member of the Victorian Legislative Assembly quoted with
approval from his manuscript before publication, and certainly
government officials who were concerned about railways had few
other local authorities to consult.[53] The period was characterized
by social ferment and considerable sympathy for intellectual
enquiry, and reflective legislators and planners may well have
been led by Corbett's work to examine skeptically theoretical
preconceptions and their own particular schemes.[54]

Sir William Denison, Lieutenant Governor of Van Diemen's
Land (Tasmania) from 1846 to 1854 and Governor of New South
Wales from 1854 to 1861, expressed great personal interest in
transport development. He reported to Lord Grey from Hobart
in 1851: "The prosperity of the agricultural interests of the colony must depend very much upon the facilities which are afforded for the conveyance of produce to market."[55] He wrote
from Newcastle, New South Wales, in 1855: "I hope . . . to digest
a scheme of railroads, applicable to a country like this, which

52. *Ibid.*, p. 33.
53. *Ibid.*, pp. 3–4.
54. Other aspects of intellectual activity in the Australian colonies during the
1850's are discussed in George Nadel, *Australia's Colonial Culture* (Melbourne,
1957).
55. Cited in C. M. H. Clark, *Select Documents in Australian History 1851–
1900* (Sydney, 1955), p. 85.

will throw the interior open to settlers, who have been kept from it hitherto by the impossibility of getting stores up or produce down. I am sanguine of being able to do this, and shall spend the next five or six months in experiments."[56] He related to an officer of the Royal Engineers, also in 1855:

> I look forward to a great extension of our public works, especially of all those which tend to improve the means of communication. . . . Roads there are none worthy of the name; for canals you have no water. What is to be done, then, to rescue this country from the sterility to which it is condemned? What means have we of opening it out, and giving to the land a value which will ensure its becoming saleable? Roads, say some;—railroads, say I.[57]

In 1856 Denison was instrumental in founding at Sydney a "Philosophical Society," an ancestor of the present Royal Society of New South Wales, and he selected the topic "railways" for both his inaugural address and his first serious paper to the Society.[58]

Denison began by urging skepticism of railways, and he suggested that careful studies be made of their value: "a clear and definite idea should be formed of the nature of the benefit which the country is supposed to derive from improved means of communication, more especially from railroads; and it would be desirable, if possible, to make some approximation to the amount of this benefit, as measured according to some pecuniary standard."[59] But he conceded that all calculations of the worth of public utilities were particularly complex in new countries. "In this case, the *direct benefits*, which are measured by the profits of the railway as a speculative investment of capital, and the *indirect benefits*, which are those resulting to society at large from the use of the railway, are merged together, the community being

56. Letter to Mrs. Denison, dated March 18, 1855, in Sir William Denison, *Varieties of Vice-Regal Life* (London, 1870), I, 308.

57. Letter to Colonel Harness, R. E., dated November 15, 1855, *ibid.*, p. 319.

58. Denison wrote to Sir Roderick Murchison: "I determined that I would not be President of an effete body, so I called the members together, read a paper on railroads, got them to agree to meet regularly once a month for eight months in the year, and shall now, by the help of occasional papers from myself, and of suggestions to others, manage, I dare say, to generate, first, an appetite for writing, and then a taste for observation, in order to have something to write about." Letter dated June 25, 1856, *ibid.*, p. 354.

59. Sir William Denison, "A Brief Outline of the Development of the Railway System of England, with Suggestions as to its Application to the Colony of New South Wales," *Sydney Magazine of Science and Art*, I (1858), 10–11.

both proprietor and employer of the railway. . . ."[60] Denison prepared a table "showing the present cost of Transport throughout the Colony" listing freight charges between fifty-eight successive points and Sydney, and he estimated part of the potential "indirect benefits" which might result from a single proposed railway line to Campbelltown by multiplying the difference between actual road and expected railroad carriage rates by the present volume of traffic. The sum at which he arrived, £21,533 per annum, was, he explained:

but a portion of the indirect benefit conferred upon this district by the substitution of a railway for a turnpike road—I say but a portion; for, in the first place, I have made no allowance for the saving of money and time to the passengers on the road; I have not calculated on the increased amount of traffic, which will most assuredly be the result of the introduction of railway communication; neither have I taken the increased value given to property into consideration.[61]

Denison agreed with other Australian writers that rigid economy should be practiced on colonial railways, possibly with horses used instead of steam engines; and he observed wisely that Australian staple products, with the exception of Newcastle coal, were low in bulk and although able to justify construction of simple lines would not warrant investment in expensive rolling stock. Neither wool nor gold, because of their relatively small volume, could be expected to afford rapid growth in demands for haulage, and "as the agricultural products can only command a limited market, their increase cannot be depended upon to an extent sufficient to create a traffic for any great length of railway."[62] Because of Australian dependence on mining and pastoral industries compared with American exploitation of agriculture, Denison argued that "the analogy between Canada and New South Wales is not close enough to justify the inference that railways will succeed here because they have done so there."[63]

The method of estimating social benefits of railways pioneered

60. *Ibid.*, p. 11.
61. *Ibid.*, p. 12.
62. Sir William Denison, "Railroads," *Sydney Magazine of Science and Art*, I (1858), 68.
63. *Ibid.*

by Denison, who computed the difference in costs of carriage before and after opening of lines, had some value when employed carefully. However, wildly extravagant and speciously accurate calculations were made by other analysts. For example, Captain Martindale, the New South Wales Railway Commissioner, in 1857 placed the annual net "gain to community, by the construction of railways" in New South Wales at precisely £303,236 18s. 1d.[64] Henry Samuel Chapman, a member of the Victorian Legislative Council from 1856, Attorney General off and on between 1857 and 1859, lecturer in law at Melbourne University, and close friend of John Stuart Mill,[65] gave only a slightly more reasonable assessment of Victorian railway benefits. He explained to the Statistical Society of London during 1863 that although the railways of Victoria maintained an annual operating deficit of £200,000, this loss was more than compensated by "the great economical gain to the country from the cheapness of transport generated by these railways." Chapman subtracted current railroad freight rates from horse and bullock charges before railways existed, and multiplied the difference by the current volume of freight. He concluded:

This makes an average saving of 2l. 6s. 6d. per ton, or a total of 311,550l. gain, against the revenue deficiency of 200,000l. In this calculation nothing is allowed for the superior condition of the goods when delivered; nothing for time; nothing for the absence of depredation, which used to be considerable; nothing for passengers and their convenience; and nothing for the revenue of the Echuca line when completed, for the 200,000l. is charged on the whole. Taking all these into account, I do not doubt that the economical advantage distributed over the whole country is a least *half a million*, secured at a guarantee of insurance charge of 200,000l.; and as the charge is not subject to increase, but may be reduced as the traffic extends, the advantage must be deemed progressive. . . .[66]

Chapman assured his British audience that they could not visualize the enormous improvement railways brought to a new coun-

64. Martindale's report brought unfavorable comment from the *Sydney Magazine of Science and Art* (December, 1857, p. 40), and is discussed by Professor J. A. La Nauze, *Political Economy in Australia: Historical Studies*, p. 32.
65. Letters from Mill to Chapman are contained in: Hugh S. R. Elliot, ed., *The Letters of John Stuart Mill* (London, 1910), I, 208–11, and II, 53–56.
66. H. S. Chapman, "The Industrial Progress of Victoria, as Connected with its Gold Mining," *Journal of the Statistical Society*, XXVI (1863), 439–40.

try. "Englishmen, who only know, the change from our four-horse coaches, splendidly appointed and worked, to the railway, can form no conception of the revolution which we have experienced. It is a change from misery to comfort—a sudden jump from the eighteenth to the middle of the nineteenth century."[67]

Denison, Martindale, Chapman, and others who sought to estimate the social benefits of railways were grasping really to express in money terms a quantity amounting to the increase of Marshallian consumer's surplus which accrued to users of transport services as a result of railway subsidies. They hoped to show that the value of this increase exceeded the amount of subsidy, not considering whether receivers of the surplus would be the same persons who would be taxed to pay the subsidy. In addition to questioning this risky use of *ceteris paribus* in rapidly changing colonial conditions over a substantial time period, it is possible to show that these analysts made their calculations with a theoretical misconception. Either, as Denison, they selected the volume of traffic before the existence of railways, or, as Chapman, they used the volume of freight after establishment of lines to multiply by the rate change and obtain the increase of surplus. In the first instance the growth of consumer surplus was understated, and in the second it was exaggerated. Logically, they should have projected the elasticity of demand over the range between prices before and after railways and calculated the surplus accordingly.[68] This technical correction is in no way a condemnation of the commendable analytical insight of these pioneers. They were conscientious planners who felt compelled to assess the value of

---

67. *Ibid.*, p. 440–41. When a supreme court judge in New Zealand in 1870 Chapman reflected on his experience with railways in Victoria in the 1850's and said: "As I had some share in carrying into operation an extensive railway system . . . I have necessarily turned my thoughts a great deal to that which I have ventured to call 'the political economy of railways'. . . ." At this date Chapman estimated the cumulative gain to Victoria from railways at a relatively conservative £792,278. "On the Political Economy of Railways," *Transactions and Proceedings of the New Zealand Institute*, III (1870), 337–51.

 68. In terms of a simple diagram illustrating the market for transport services, and showing supply before (S) and after (S¹) railways subsidies, it can be seen that Denison estimated the increase in consumer surplus resulting from market equilibrium shifting from E to E¹ as the figure PP¹QE. Chapman suggested PP¹E¹Q¹, and the correct amount is PP¹E¹E.

railway subsidies, and they used the best theoretical tools available.

Persuasion from Denison probably was responsible for several other papers on railway economics which were delivered to the Philosophical Society of New South Wales. W. G. Pennington provided "a careful analysis of the railway systems of America and Canada," and recommended that government encourage rail construction by land grants to private firms. He warned particularly against accumulation of public debts, the evils of which "our American brethren have found to their cost."[69]

Morris Birkbeck Pell, Fellow and Senior Wrangler of St. John's College, Cambridge, and foundation professor of mathematics and natural philosophy at Sydney University from 1852, discoursed to the Philosophical Society in 1856 on "some general principles from which to ascertain under what circumstances railways are really conducive to the material prosperity of a community."[70] Pell put forward the best case voiced during the 1850's for opposition to government railway subsidies. He argued that transport, like any other industry, was not deserving either of special favors or of discouragement. He conceded that, because of natural monopoly conditions, government might build and operate lines, but he insisted on a principle of complete self-support. Pell observed that in primitive communities transport facilities were of use mainly to a few individuals and were maintained through payments to entrepreneurs by users. In a more advanced economy, when a network of well-travelled roads was required, tolls became impractical and the state was forced to provide roads supported through taxation. But, he warned, even in the case of ordinary roads, "if the traffic is so small that the saving to the community is not equivalent to the interest upon the money expended, and the cost of maintenance—then the road, so far from being an advantage, is a constant drain upon the resources of the community."[71] Pell insisted that this lesson of road operation

---

69. W. G. Pennington, "The Means of Constructing Railways Financially Considered," *Sydney Magazine of Science and Art*, I (1858), 75–76 (in abstract).
70. M. B. Pell, "On the Application of Certain Principles of Political Economy to the Question of Railways," *Sydney Magazine of Science and Art*, I (1858), 124.
71. *Ibid.*, p. 125.

applied as well to railroads, and accordingly: "The natural course of an enquiry into the expediency of constructing railways seems to be, first, to determine, if possible, some general principle fixing the point in the progress of a community at which such undertakings become advisable; and next to ascertain whether the particular community under consideration had arrived at that point."

Where railways differed in one important respect from ordinary roads, Pell declared, was in the ease with which all travellers and shippers could be charged for the use of rails; and for this reason, he denied categorically that it was ever desirable to support railways from the public purse. Citizens spread throughout an economy could, indeed, benefit from railways without actually making direct use of them. But if benefit equaled indirect cost, all gainers would voluntarily pay their share of ultimate charges through a chain of interacting markets. If a railroad were constructed by government and could not be made to survive on returns from freight charges and passenger fares alone, Pell insisted: "In this case I say, the railway is a loss and a burden, and would be so even if every person in the whole community were included in the list of those availing themselves of the railway, and if a tax could be devised, which should fall upon every one of them in a perfectly equitable proportion. . . . The fares and charges are a perfectly equitable tax."[72] Some governmental functions, Pell admitted, notably the administration of police and justice, could not be operated on a self-supporting basis. But, he added, "This problem, which does not appear in general to admit of an exact solution, presents no difficulty, as I have endeavoured to show, in the case of a railway."

Pell was not sanguine about the probability of railways being self-supporting, and therefore desirable, in the colonies. In the belief that immediate and extensive construction was contemplated at a time when it was wisest to wait several years, he set out to attack and destroy the arguments repeated most frequently by railroad promoters. In addition to denying that railways generated truly external economies, Pell disputed the suggestion that

72. *Ibid.*, p. 126.

rail construction and operation, by increasing expenditure in domestic industries and reducing imports, could add to local employment. He explained: "The whole difficulty arises from viewing
the case through what is called by Mill the 'hazy medium of a
money transaction'. . . . The loss is . . . occasioned . . . by
the withdrawal of labour and capital from full productive employment."[73] He rejected allegations that subsidised railways
could be a valuable tool for opening Australia's empty spaces. "It
might happen indeed that the inhabitants of a particular district
would derive great advantage from a railway maintained by the
country at large; they might fatten upon the resources of the rest
of the community and grow wealthy at the expense of their
neighbours, but the whole community would scarcely benefit by
the process. There would be an apparent increase but in reality
only a concentration of wealth."[74] Nor could railroads be counted
upon to promote colonial growth in any wider sense and thereby
pay for themselves in the long run. Pell explained:

The great bulk of the traffic consists of wool, and of ordinary articles
of consumption. The population is fully employed. Production and
consumption must have reached very nearly their maximum point, so
that nothing can materially increase the traffic except an increase
of population. To suppose that a railway will exercise any great
influence in attracting population from other countries is contrary to
reason and to experience.[75]

Finally, Pell contradicted assertions that government should build
railways in order to render public lands saleable. Returns from
land sales above what they would have been without a railroad,
he pointed out, would exceed construction costs only if the line
would, in any case, have been self-supporting. He illustrated this
argument with an example:

Suppose, for instance, that in consequence of £1,000,000 having been
spent upon railways, 1,000,000 acres of land become worth and are
sold at the rate of 25s. per acre (which were not previously saleable
for more than 5s. per acre). A person who purchases an acre of land
under these circumstances, in reality pays 5s. for the land and £1 for

73. *Ibid.*, p. 127.
74. *Ibid.*, p. 127.
75. *Ibid.*, p. 128.

the use of the railway, which is, therefore, worth to him annually the interest upon £1. He would be exactly in the same position if he paid only 5s. for the land, and the interest upon £1 in the form of an increase upon the railway charges; and this increase, when extended to all the purchasers of the 1,000,000 acres, would be just sufficient to pay the interest upon the outlay. The railway would, therefore, in this case be actually self-supporting, and consequently, according to my view of the subject, a real advantage to the community.[76]

Pell formulated a clear statement of static classical theory applied to a single industry in an economy. He showed that optimum resource allocation and maximum total satisfaction could be achieved only by leaving each producer and each consumer unhindered but without special encouragement and free to pursue his own self-interest. He implied that growth should take place in this system automatically and with government in the background. Evidently four years in a colonial environment which, from its very beginning, had depended on a paternal state for progress and even for existence had not caused Pell to waver in his conviction that "all artificial restrictions upon trade are detrimental to the prosperity of a community, and artificial stimulants would be found equally so."[77] Other educated immigrants generally concurred with Pell's views. Young William Stanley Jevons, a recently arrived assayer at the Sydney Mint, endorsed and repeated Pell's "irresistible conclusions" derived from "the most indisputable truths of Political Economy."[78] W. E. Hearn did not examine specifically the question of railway development in his book *Plutology* (1863). However, citing Lord Durham's *Report* on Canada, he conceded that: "In every new country . . . the construction of the means of communication and the disposal and management of the waste lands form part of the duties of the state."[79] *Plutology* was essentially a defense of laissez faire, and while Hearn admitted "In such cases the interference of govern-

76. *Ibid.*, pp. 127–28.
77. *Ibid.*, p. 128.
78. "Railway Economy," *Empire*, December 29, 1857. Jevons' remarks on railways, which were contained in a series of letters to the *Empire*, are similar to those of Pell and are discussed fully by Professor La Nauze, *op. cit.*, pp. 32–33, and 40–41.
79. I have discussed the economic policy of the Durham *Report* in my *Canadian Economic Thought* (Durham, 1961), pp. 25–30.

ment, if judiciously applied, may accelerate and assist the ordinary processes of natural development," he felt compelled to add, "Unfortunately the judgment shown in this interference is seldom very sound."[80]

Serious discussion of railway economics continued until the end of the 1850's, but with less enthusiasm as more and more miles of track were laid, as colonial governments became closely involved with construction, and as gold discoveries and rapid population growth made cautious analysts seem out of style.[81] In 1859 a Melbourne critic exclaimed wearily that colonials had listened at great cost to self-interested railway engineers, and he declared that any observer examining railway legislation "would be struck by a meagre paucity of idea, and, we say it with all respect, an absolute ignorance of those sound principles upon which all railways not only ought to be, but must be, founded, in order to succeed."[82] In all except technical matters, he insisted, testimony of engineers should be rejected and "the capitalist, the money-dealer, the economist must be appealed to."[83] By 1860 railway critics had established a tradition of skepticism among intellectuals in the colonies, but increasingly questions as to the desirability of already existing lines became academic. Moreover, on matters of detail, governments found it possible either to follow precedent or to accept advice from a growing number of experienced public servants. During the 1860's tariff and land reforms caught the imagination of thinkers on economic subjects, and interest in transport declined.

80. W. E. Hearn, *Plutology* (Melbourne, 1863), pp. 415 and 380; and see Professor La Nauze, *op. cit.*, p. 79.
81. The failure of private railway enterprise in the colonies has been attributed by Professor Noel G. Butlin to competitive attractions in the pastoral industry, difficulties of obtaining capital, and "the absence of entrepreneurial ability and organization by private individuals." "Colonial Socialism in Australia, 1860–1900," in Hugh G. J. Aitken, ed., *The State and Economic Growth* (New York, 1959), pp. 39 and 41. In contrast, earlier observers in the United States and in Germany attributed this failure principally to colonial reluctance to inaugurate a generous land-grant policy. Victor S. Clark, "Australian Economic Problems. I. The Railways," *Quarterly Journal of Economics*, XXII (1907–8), 399–451; and Moritz Kandt, *Ueber die Entwickelung der australischen Eisenbahnpolitik, nebst einer Einleitung über das Problem der Eisenbahnpolitik in Theorie und Praxis* (Berlin, 1894), and reviewed at length by Carl C. Plehn in *Annals of the American Academy of Political and Social Science*, V (1894–95), 112–15.
82. L., "The Railway Policy of the Colony," *Victorian Monthly Magazine*, June, 1859, p. 3.
83. *Ibid.*, p. 4.

A period of colonial rail expansion occurred in the 1870's, inspired in New South Wales by the Governor, Sir Hercules Robinson, but this did not stimulate serious study apart from some desultory discussion of how to arrange government control and how best to set freight rates.[84] During the 1880's advocates of private enterprise occasionally castigated government ownership of railways and pointed (without looking too closely) to the success of private land-grant companies in the United States.[85] At the other extreme, labor spokesmen in the 1890's demanded abolition of railway tolls, and after Federation proposed nationalization of all state lines.[86] Although writings on railways late in the century contained much speculation and many outrageous claims, they included little serious economic analysis.[87]

The only nineteenth century Australian writer after the 1850's to examine railways in the manner of Denison, Corbett, and Pell— reasonably, objectively, and with knowledge of economic theory —was the enormously energetic Tasmanian Government Statistician, Robert Mackenzie Johnston. Bank failures and financial crisis early in the 1890's led several British periodicals to publish

84. See for example H. M. Franklyn, "The Victorian Railways and their Management," *Victorian Review*, 1879, pp. 311–20; and George S. Griffiths, "Cheap Freights and Colonial Industries," *ibid.*, 1881, pp. 336–55. For comment on railways of the period see T. A. Coghlan, *Labour and Industry in Australia*, p. 1420; and A. St. Ledger, *Australian Socialism: An Historical Sketch of its Origin and Developments* (London, 1909), p. 144.

85. See for example, John Wisker, "The American Railway System and Ours," *Victorian Review*, 1883, pp. 88–106; and J. Reid, "State Railways," *Sydney Quarterly Magazine*, 1887, pp. 138–44. A Western Australian Select Committee reported in 1883 in favor of constructing a transcontinental railway on the American land grant model. "Report of the Select Committee of the Legislative Council Appointed to Consider and Report upon the Question of the Construction of Railways in Western Australia," *Votes and Proceedings of the Legislative Council of Western Australia*, 1883. A land grant contract was negotiated with Anthony Hordern in 1884 for construction of a line from Perth to Adelaide; and in Queensland Premier McIlwraith proposed a land grant transcontinental in 1880, but was defeated on this issue in the election of 1883. See Coghlan, *Labour and Industry in Australia*, p. 1756.

86. See Alexander W. Johnston, *Strikes, Labour Questions, and Other Economic Difficulties: A Short Treatise on Political Economy* (London, 1895); and *Report of the Commonwealth Labour Conference, held at Trades Hall, Sydney, 1902* (Brisbane, 1902), p. 3.

87. A detailed compilation and analysis of Australian railway statistics was prepared by a member of the London Statistical Society at the end of the century: Price Howell, "Comparative Statistics of Australasian Railways," *Journal of the Statistical Society*, LXII (1899), 83–114. Certain aspects of Australian railway growth during the twentieth century are discussed in "The Economics of Australian Transport," *Economic Record*, VI (1930), supplement, and T. Hytten, "Some Problems of Australian Transport Development," *ibid.*, XXIII (1947), 5–19.

bitter and often unfair attacks on the colonial economies, and particularly on the active role of government. In 1892 Johnston replied on behalf of the colonies to these charges of mismanagement, and particularly to accusations of a "grossly extravagant" railway policy.[88] He denied that Australian public expenditure had been in any sense unwise, and he explained to his British audience a fact which had been recognized in the colonies for half a century, that legitimate government functions were of necessity much greater in new than in old economies. "In the self-governing colonies of Australasia," he wrote, "the scope of general government—owing to the peculiar condition of lands thinly populated with vast undeveloped areas—embraces many functions which it would be impossible to resign to local bodies or to private enterprise as in older countries."[89] To complaints that public debt in the colonies had risen more quickly than population, Johnston retorted that where government performed functions fulfilled elsewhere by private corporations an increasing national debt represented mounting capital accumulation and was both a cause and a sign of economic growth. Colonial borrowing, he emphasised, should not be confused with public indebtedness incurred by older countries during wartime. He explained:

Now, as the Governments of Australasia hold the position of capitalist and *entrepreneur*, in respect of the great industries connected with transport and communication, it follows that they constitute in themselves the most important employers of labour in the community; and if they fail to make the necessary provision for bringing improved means of transport to settlers in the freshly invaded areas of land, they arrest the production of wealth and the further development of

88. Several of the British critiques of Australian policy were: Matthew Macfie, "Aids to Australian Development," *Proceedings of the Royal Colonial Institute,* XXI (1889–90), 53–82; W. M. Acworth, "Government Railways in a Democratic State," *Economic Journal,* II (1892), 629–36; "Gold-bewitched Victoria," *Investors' Review,* II (1893), 145–74; Nathaniel Cork, "The Australian Banking Crisis of 1893," *Journal of the Institute of Bankers,* April, 1894; J. W. Fortescue, "The Seamy Side of Australia," *Nineteenth Century,* XXIX (1891), 523–37, and "Guileless Australia: A Rejoinder," *ibid.,* XXX (1891), 430–43. A contemporary American critique in a similar vein was: William Hill, "State Railways in Australia," *Journal of Political Economy,* III (1894–95), 1–23. Writings by two allies of Johnston were: Howard Willoughby, " 'The Seamy Side of Australia': A Reply from the Colonies," *Nineteenth Century,* XXX (1891), 292–302; and R. G. C. Hamilton, "Lending Money to Australia," *ibid.,* XXXII (1892), 194–202.
89. R. M. Johnston, "The Attack on the Credit of Australasia," *Nineteenth Century,* XXXI (1892), 607.

the country. If such provision be made only according to the ratio of increase of population or public revenue, no positive advance could occur. As a matter of fact no country, in the earlier stages of its history, can ever prosper whose capital investments in the machinery of transport and production do not in ratio of increase greatly exceed the ratio of increase of either people or public revenue.[90]

Johnston believed that railways were of great importance to the colonies and that freight revenues represented "the merest flea-bite as regards the actual value added to the country's wealth." He summarized the "principal additions to the wealth of the country due to railways" as "(1) . . . saving of time and cost of transit. (2) . . . giving commercial value to vast natural products hitherto lacking value, owing to lack of cheap means of transit. (3) . . . impetus given to the creation of fresh wealth in areas formerly unproductive."[91] He reasoned that items numbered (2) and (3) could "only vaguely be guessed at," but for (1) he performed a comparative cost analysis similar to those of Denison and Chapman thirty-five years before, and he concluded:

in the year 1890 alone, the actual benefit to the colonies, arising from the introduction of railways, represents a sum of 17,000,628*l.* equal to 15.78 per cent. of the total capital invested in railways open for traffic in the same year, after discharging all expenses connected with working the railways, and the yearly charge for interest on borrowed capital.[92]

Edwin C. Nowell, Johnston's predecessor as Tasmanian Government Statistician, spoke from retirement in general support of Johnston's position regarding railways. Nowell said to the Royal Statistical Society in London in 1895:

It is an opinion very generally held, that Government railways should not be constructed unless they are expected to return the whole or a major part of the interest on construction in addition to their working expenses. But no such condition is required in the case of ordinary roads, and there does not appear to be any reason whatever why any such distinction should be made. . . . The real question then to be asked when a railroad is projected would seem to be, not: Will it pay

91. *Ibid.*, p. 616.
90. *Ibid.*, p. 614.
92. *Ibid.*, p. 617.

working expenses and interest? but: Are the advantages, direct and indirect, likely to result from it sufficiently great to justify the expenditure?[93]

In 1908 Johnston repeated his assessment of railway benefits and reaffirmed his thesis that colonial public debt was more analogous to the equity of private corporations than to the national debt of older countries. He criticized plans for establishing sinking funds to eliminate Australian state debts on the ground that public works were still amply productive, and because by parallel reasoning it could be contended that profitable joint-stock companies should struggle to reduce their original capitalization.[94]

Railway Theory and Policy

The writings examined in this chapter were not lasting contributions to economic science. Taken together, however, they constitute an impressive collection of attempts to study seriously an urgent contemporary problem. In addition to mere panegyrics, they include rigid interpretations of classical theory by the *Sydney University Magazine*, Pell, and Jevons; speculations about possible gains to the community by Parkes, Norton, and Woolley; estimates of costs, revenues, and external economies by Denison, Chapman, and Johnston; and perceptive observations on uses of railway capital by Corbett. The authors were not professional economists, but rather were enthusiastic amateurs in politics, the civil service, journalism, and universities. Generally, it appears that willingness to treat railways as a special industry worthy of government attention strengthened with the length of a writer's residence in the colonies.

These railway enquiries have had parallels at other times in the history of Australian economic thought. In particular, tariff discussions of the 1920's (examined below) culminating in 1929

93. Edwin C. Nowell, "Comparative Statistics of the Principal British Possessions and Foreign Countries," *Journal of the Royal Statistical Society*, LVIII (1895), 489.
94. R. M. Johnston, "State Borrowing, and Sinking Funds for the Redemption of State Debts, Regarded from an Economical Point of View," *Papers and Proceedings of the Royal Society of Tasmania*, 1908, pp. 10–30.

in the monumental report *The Australian Tariff: An Economic Enquiry*, bear resemblances in scope and purpose to the earlier railway debates. In both periods a group of economists with a genuine sense of social responsibility set out not so much to defend or to destroy particular policies as to clarify issues according to principles which they understood, and to make government and the public aware of real costs and benefits. In both cases the most competent authors condemned extreme measures and recommended government moderation.

One dominant feature of the railway discussions was that conservative critics of state-subsidized railways had the benefit of more closely reasoned arguments than did advocates. Proponents of state sponsorship were many, but they must never have been as convincing to sophisticated audiences as were opponents. This distinction was a reflection not of the more radical economists' ability or sincerity of intention, but rather of the state of economic science at the time they wrote. Immigrants to Australia in the nineteenth century were schooled in a body of economic theory which was essentially static and dealt with determination of the optimum use of available resources and productive power for the satisfaction of human wants. Economists who had been educated in this tradition were poorly trained, or were even mistrained, to analyze colonial conditions where ample undeveloped resources promised bountiful growth and potential production but where immediate returns were slight. Technological change was rapid in the Australian environment, and as settlers improvised to overcome new difficulties they discovered that startlingly high rewards followed imaginative ventures which, in a static sense, had appeared impractical at the outset. For example, any cautious economic analyst would certainly have shown that a large-scale wool industry could not succeed in the colonies before Macarthur and his followers, while building this industry, had conquered numberless technical problems of pastoral operations; and no static theorist would have approved plans for substantial wheat production before Ridley, under pressure of colonial circumstances, had developed his revolutionary "stripper," and Farrer had bred a rust-proof wheat. However, sheep thrived, wheat was harvested, and the colonies prospered while economists had little dynamic theory to account for or guide this growth process. When these examples of the successful use of intuition by Australian pioneers are remembered today, as they certainly were kept in mind by railway advocates in the nineteenth century, it can be understood that colonists were not anti-theoretical on principle when they fell back on arguments which amounted only to belief that railroads would be an important stimulant to economic growth. They were aware from personal experience that preliminary cost and revenue projections, prescribed by static theorists, had not been sound guides to action in the past, and they felt justified, where science had been proved inadequate, in resorting to a conditioned sixth sense. However, despite the reasonableness of their position as seen today after substantial advances in economic theory, defenders of subsidized railways in the colonies did not, as did the more successful contemporary tariff advocates, have statements from List, Carey, Mill, or other authorities to justify their break with laissez faire; and, unable to match argument for logical argument, they usually left critics easily holding the field. The ideal railway economist during the 1850's would have gauged the dynamic as well as the static elements in his surroundings, and on this dual basis he would have passed judgment on railroad projects. Such an analytical procedure might have brought approval either for more or for less construction than actually took place.[95] But, as economists today are still far from confident when performing judicial functions in dynamic situations, the Australian economists can only be pardoned for adopting the expedient of acting from static considerations alone.

The influence of discussion on colonial railway development cannot be assessed with any certainty. It is worthwhile, however, to outline briefly the sequence of events which may link thought with action. During the 1850's, the New South Wales, Victorian, and South Australian governments set out with a will first to assist private railway companies and then to undertake construc-

95. Professor Noel Butlin has discussed ways in which railway construction may have both advanced and retarded capital accumulation in Australia. *Op. cit.*, pp. 72–75.

tion on their own. Coghlan commented on the activity of the 1850's thus:

The Governments of Australia, in undertaking the carrying out of a comprehensive system of railway extension, knew that the development of their territory was a consideration that stood above all others, and it was in this spirit that the railways were undertaken.[96]

By 1861, 243 miles of track had been opened, a not inconsiderable feat for the difficult gold rush period during which it was achieved. In the later years of this decade, most of the critical discussion described above took place.

In the 1860's the pattern of colonial railway development changed radically. Although groundwork had been laid in the previous decade for rapid extension of track, mileage increased only to 1030 by 1871, and colonial governments exhibited substantial loss of enthusiasm for railway operations. Coghlan wrote in a very different tone of this period which followed the railway critiques:

The main object of railway construction, the opening up of the country by affording cheap conveyance of products to market, was almost neglected, and everywhere made subordinate to the necessity of making lines pay. The railways were in fact worked as a private company might have been expected to work them, the possible future gain to the whole community not being thought sufficient compensation for the adoption of a policy or principle of action entailing large immediate sacrifices.[97]

The pace of railway construction increased markedly in the colonies after 1870, by which time the memory of economists' skepticism had faded.

It seems possible that formulation in the nineteenth century of the views described in this chapter was a significant determining factor in the development of government attitudes toward railways. Other reasons, not discussed here, can be offered to explain why Australia in the 1850's, unlike Canada and the United States, did not experience a period of wild abandon in railroad expansion. However it is reasonable to conclude that

96. T. A. Coghlan, *Labour and Industry in Australia*, p. 836.
97. *Ibid.*, p. 1219.

trained economists were one restraining force. Undoubtedly these colonial railway economists of the nineteenth century performed valuable service in exposing wildly impractical schemes and in forcing legislators, promoters, and the public to face realities of transport projects. It may be argued also, however, that their sermons were far too cautious and that Australian development might well have been saved from these friends.

9

The State and Economic Growth

To a large extent, Chapters 1 through 8 have been concerned with analyses of economic growth. It has been shown that discussions of tariffs, land disposal, banking, and transport were conducted largely in terms of effects on national development. Australia's preoccupation with progress has been epitomized in the country's motto "Advance Australia." In this chapter debate on the wider question of the overall place of government in the growth process is examined. In general, writers held one of two conflicting policy positions: either that growth proceeded most quickly in a competitive free market system where government had minimal functions, or that an active state was equipped best to plan and to mobilize for change. A profound influence on all analysts of growth was discoveries in the theory of biological evolution; this influence is examined in the following chapter.

Defense of Laissez faire

During the first half of the nineteenth century when colonists discussed the role of government in the economy they considered almost exclusively the activities of the Colonial Office and its representatives. The complication of a locally elected legislature had barely appeared. In this period in Britain and in Australia, mercantilism began as the reigning economic philosophy and was replaced only gradually by commercial liberalism buttressed with classical political economy. Principles of laissez faire were brought to the colonies by immigrants and in imported literature.

The change in outlook of the mother country from restrictionism to liberalism was mirrored by the child.

W. C. Wentworth, one of the first Australian-born students at Oxford, became an early convert to the teachings of Adam Smith, Ricardo, and other classical economists. In 1819 Wentworth published a pioneering book *A Statistical, Historical, and Political Description of the Colony of New South Wales, and its Dependent Settlements in Van Diemen's Land,* in which he admitted at the outset that he "developed no new principle of political economy, and . . . only travelled in the broad beaten path in which hundreds have journeyed before him."[1] In this work he provided the first careful analysis of Australian growth in terms mainly of classical theory. Wentworth selected for investigation certain factors in Australian development, in particular, changes in transport technology. Improvements in ocean travel, he observed, had made possible exploration, while a shortage of north-south rivers had prevented rapid creation of a diversified and self-sufficient economy.[2] Wentworth laid special stress on social determinants of growth, and he stated positively: "Not only the records of the years that are no more, but the experience also of the present day, concur in proving that the prosperity of nations is not so much the result of the fertility of their soil, and the benignity of their climate, as of the wisdom and policy of their institutions."[3] He maintained that colonies would prosper best where free enterprise and political liberty were guaranteed:

> Prosperity is a plant that can only flourish in an atmosphere fanned by the wholesome breath of freedom. The highest fertility of soil, the greatest benignity of climate, the most commanding superiority of position, will otherwise be unavailing. Freedom may in the end convert the most barren and inhospitable waste into a paradise; but the inevitable result of tyranny is desolation.[4]

Wentworth's fascination with the process of economic growth led him to construct pathbreaking national income estimates.[5]

1. W. C. Wentworth, *A Statistical, Historical, and Political Description of the Colony of New South Wales, and its Dependent Settlements in Van Diemen's Land* (London, 1819), p. xi.
2. *Ibid.,* pp. 79–84.
3. *Ibid.,* p. 159.
4. *Ibid.,* pp. 87–88, and 164.
5. See below p. 466.

Wentworth was influenced profoundly by classical growth theory and particularly by Adam Smith's description of "the natural progress of opulence" in which Smith observed that: "According to the natural course of things . . . the greater part of the capital of every growing society is, first, directed to agriculture, afterwards to manufactures, and last of all to foreign commerce."[6] Wentworth concluded that for fundamental economic reasons commerce with other parts of the Empire was vital for Australia from the outset, but he insisted, in agreement with Smith, that for many years pastoral and agricultural industries alone should receive encouragement. Not until all arable land had come under cultivation should manufactures be contemplated.[7] If let alone, he argued, primary agricultural industries ultimately would thrive and prove thereby their merit, but judicious assistance could accelerate this process and bring greater prosperity at an earlier date.

There is but one remedy for the disease of the colony: it is to give due encouragement to agriculture, and to promote the growth of exportable commodities, which its inhabitants may offer in exchange for the productions of other countries. The manufacturing system which has begun to take root, will then wither away of its own accord; since it will then be the least productive manner in which capital and labour can be employed.[8]

Wentworth advocated toleration of colonial distilleries to permit, through greater use of grain, agricultural economies of scale and to provide a steady market for farmers.[9] He recommended assistance to incipient wool-producers and, to promote the introduction of new agricultural products, "a colonial plantation, in which a certain number of the most enterprizing youths might be instructed in their culture and preparation."[10] He hoped that Australian fisheries could become a "nursery for seamen," valuable both to the colonies and to the mother country.[11]

Wentworth was opposed rigidly to establishment in New South

6. Adam Smith, *An Inquiry into the Nature and Causes of the Wealth of Nations* (Modern Library edition, New York, 1937), p. 360.
7. *A Statistical, Historical and Political Description*, pp. 189–90.
8. *Ibid.*, pp. 192–93.
9. *Ibid.*, pp. 253–55, and 340.
10. *Ibid.*, pp. 279–81.
11. *Ibid.*, p. 311.

Wales of manufacturing industry which, he believed, could survive only as an artificial creation of government. Both colonists and the Colonial Office should avoid grandiose schemes for urban expansion and confine their energies to production of staple commodities. He wrote:

The manufacturing system, now so rapidly gaining ground, has been one of the retributive consequences of the shortsighted and illiberal policy of which this unfortunate colony has been so long the victim, and will cease of itself, whenever the existing impediments to the extension of agriculture shall be removed, for the best of all reasons, because no person will select a less profitable undertaking when a more profitable one, and one requiring less skill, capital, and assiduity, lies open to him. Agriculture, therefore, as soon as it shall be freed from its present restraints, will afford the readiest and most accessible channel for carrying off the large accumulation of stagnant labour which at present infests this colony.[12]

Like Adam Smith, Wentworth was no doctrinaire advocate of laissez faire, and he listed several functions he considered legitimate for government. A "wise and considerate government," he said, would take appropriate steps to achieve "public objects."[13] In particular, government in the colonies might arouse private entrepreneurs from the deep lethargy of mercantilism. He explained:

Industry, though one of the most active principles of human nature, settles when long restrained into a habit of inertion, which cannot be instantly overcome. When the bounds within which this principle has been long confined, are suddenly removed, it will not of itself rush at once into every new channel in its way, and stop only when it has found its own level. It is not like fluids possessed of inherent elasticity and tendency to motion, but requires a directing impulse to set and continue it in activity, and its activity will then only be in proportion to the power and energy applied. . . . There is a timidity in man, which though not sufficient to curb the adventurous spirit of his nature, tends materially to check and repress it.[14]

Wentworth did believe in acceptance without fundamental alteration of the most efficient structure of production and of a

12. *Ibid.*, pp. 382–83 and 277–78.
13. *Ibid.*, pp. 269–70.
14. *Ibid.*, pp. 380–81.

free-price economy. The state in his view should be a source of occasional vital assistance but not a dominant force.

Colonial staple-producers became accepted standard-bearers for classical growth theory and particularly for the stage hypothesis elaborated by Wentworth. They argued that progress should take place "naturally" with expansion first of the most efficient pastoral sector. Manufacturing industry, they explained, could not be viable before agricultural and pastoral activities had been established firmly. One early resident of Victoria cautioned:

> the wisest course to pursue is, not to attempt to hurry on the current of events, or anticipate an order of things which time will itself bring round, but, recognising facts as they exist, to derive from them the greatest amount of good of which they are capable. As population increases and the arts take root, manufactures are established, and agriculture and husbandry assume the important position which is their recognised place in all long established communities.[15]

Spokesmen for pastoralists conceded the importance of technological change, but they intimated that improvements would occur spontaneously, and they focused attention on methods of adding to the two variable resources, capital and labor. They accepted the free market as the best mechanism for allocating materials to worthy entrepreneurs, and they denied categorically the desirability of artificially balanced growth.

Initially the Colonial Office ruled the colonies with little concern for local consent, and so long as the franchise even of the legislative councils was limited, discussion of economic growth could be conducted in the colonies in relatively callous terms. Development was considered a process of increase in total output through resource use in which the lower the price of factors the better.[16] Labor was treated as an input supplied in the form of convicts or free immigrants and little different from other elements of total cost. As one pastoralist explained in 1845: "the object kept constantly in view throughout, is to discover how and in what proportions *Capital, Capitalists, Labour, and Live Stock* must be

15. "Our Social Tendencies," *Australia Felix Monthly Magazine*, June, 1849, p. 16.
16. For example, "The Progress of South Australia in the Elements of Wealth," *South Australian Magazine*, July, 1841, p. 73.

combined so as to cause the Colony to yield the highest possible amount of benefit to the Mother Country."[17]

During the 1830's and 1840's, a succession of legislative committees in New South Wales, containing among others the Lord Bishop of Australia, examined the course of immigration as the process of importing the scarce and essential commodity labor; they ignored considerations of human welfare and confined their attention to means of improving immigrant quality and of minimizing costs (i.e. wages) without market derangement.[18] Continued convict transportation was favored widely as a source of cheap labor, and was defended on grounds of economic benefits to the colonies and to the mother country. In an open letter to Charles Buller during 1839, the Australian Patriotic Association led by Wentworth, Bland, Ralph Mansfield, and others, presented a convincing case for transportation by listing specific "economical, political, and maritime advantages," including savings of prison maintenance, increased colonial production, and expanded British markets.[19] T. Potter MacQueen set forth the same arguments in 1840. He wrote:

> Although transported convicts do not, *in the first instance*, personally enjoy the fruits of their labour, still by means of it, their employers greatly add to their consumption of British manufacture [sic], and a large subsequent increase takes place, as on the expiration of their sentences, the convicts become labourers on their own account, increase their earnings, and expend on themselves the proceeds of their labour; they generally behave well, perhaps because they find it more advantageous to do so, even if not from change of principle, whilst a continued supply of fresh convicts enable their late employers not only to continue their consumption, but to increase it with increased income.[20]

17. Gideon Scott Lang, *Land and Labour in Australia* (Melbourne, 1845), p. 3.
18. "Report from the Committee on Immigration," *Votes and Proceedings of the Legislative Council of New South Wales*, 1838, 1839, 1840, 1841, 1842, 1845, and 1847. See also C. M. H. Clark, *Select Documents in Australian History 1788–1850* (Sydney, 1950), pp. 174 and 391.
19. "Report from the Select Committee on the Renewal of Transportation, with Appendix, and Minutes of Evidence," *Votes and Proceedings of the Legislative Council of New South Wales*, 1846, Appendix B.
20. T. Potter MacQueen, *Australia as She is & as She May Be* (London, 1840), p. 18. Similar views are expressed in "Past, Present, and Future Position of Tasmania," *South Briton; or, Tasmanian Literary Journal*, I (1843), 25–32.

For a few years after the grant of responsible government, colonial writers continued to treat optimum economic growth as the process simply of combining factors at least cost. In 1862, Francis H. Nixon observed that as "an agreed principle in Colonial economy" capitalists ought to receive a "substantial guarantee" of continuing availability of workers at low wages; "such steps should be taken as would secure a regular and sufficient supply of labour at a reasonable rate."[21] Only a year earlier, however, William Westgarth predicted wisely that policies such as that proposed by Nixon, and even the basic virtue of rapid economic growth, would become the subject of controversy. Newly enfranchised workers, he pointed out, now opposed the depressing effects of subsidized immigration on wages, even if such a device could be expected to bring a larger national income.

The democratic institutions latterly adopted in the principal Australian colonies, including manhood suffrage, have called up instinctive opposition to this policy. It is naturally associated with the employing interest, who seek to supply their labour-market, and who, under the old regime, were all-powerful to that end. On the other hand, the employed classes, who may now be considered predominant, look rather to local expenditure and the enhanced wages for the time being.[22]

Economists as well as politicians were compelled to recognize that democracy raised to prominence considerations of distribution as well as of growth.

Some observers of colonial development, influenced by classical political economy, laid heavy emphasis on the necessity for continuous private capital accumulation either from individual abstinence or from foreign borrowing. Robert Lowe, an acknowledged disciple of English classical economists, explained in his newspaper the *Atlas*: "capital increases fast in the hands of an industrious people; but slowly, or not at all, in those of a Govern-

21. Francis H. Nixon, *Population; or, a Plea for Victoria* (Melbourne, 1862), pp. 17–18.
22. William Westgarth, *Australia: Its Rise, Progress, and Present Condition* (Edinburgh, 1861), p. 248. A similar observation was made to the Royal Colonial Institute in 1889 by Matthew Macfie, "Aids to Australian Development," *Proceedings of the Royal Colonial Institute*, XXI (1889–90), 59.

ment."[23] Lowe insisted that one major disadvantage of colonial
subservience to a distant metropolis was the substantial danger
of government waste of national capital—"if money be raised in
large sums from the colonists, it will be recklessly spent by the
Home Government."[24] Lowe was by no means alone in his admiration for private capital accumulation. One exasperated critic
of government activity remarked concerning the leaders of an
early protection movement:

It serves nothing to demonstrate to such gentlemen that the industry
of society can augment only in proportion as its capital augments; that
its capital can augment only in proportion to what can be gradually
saved out of its revenue; but that the immediate effect of protective
duties is *to diminish* its revenue, and therefore that which diminishes
its revenue is certainly not very likely to augment its capital.[25]

A number of writers argued that, because of the need for uninterrupted capital accumulation, land should be made available
freely to settlers and government should spend all revenues internally. One Victorian remarked: "We say without hesitation
that our wisest course is to draw the capital required for bringing
in population, from the place from which the population comes."[26]
Every effort was made to show that Australia was an appropriate
outlet for "surplus" British capital, and English investors were
assured that the colonial economy was little different from those
of other associated territories such as Ireland. Another Victorian
asked: "why should colonies, formed wholly of a British population, be looked upon as *dependencies* at all? and not as parts of
the British empire—without reference to whether it is St. George's
channel, or sixteen thousand miles of ocean, which separate them
from the head quarters of the nation?"[27]

23. *Atlas* (Sydney), December 7, 1844, p. 15.
24. *Ibid.*
25. "Corn Laws," *Weekly Register of Politics, Facts, and General Literature,*
March 30, 1844, p. 504.
26. "How is Immigration to be Paid for in Future?," *Australia Felix Monthly
Magazine*, October, 1849, pp. 159–60; and also *Expenditure of the Land-Fund
of New South Wales in the Colony, and Principally on Public Works; as a Means
of Promoting and Supporting Immigration* (Sydney, 1842).
27. "The Spirit of our Future Policy," *Australia Felix Monthly Magazine*, June,
1849, p. 43; and also "National Emigration and Colonization," *New South Wales
Magazine*, 1843, pp. 583–88; and Aristides, *The Approaching Crisis of Britain and
Australia: with a Way to Escape the Ruin it Threatens* (Melbourne, 1853).

Occasionally representatives of the merchant community and other urban interests joined staple-producers in defense of a growth policy of laissez faire. After the grant of responsible government, revulsion against all forms of government control was widespread.[28] A writer in the Sydney *Empire* explained that merchants were indispensable middlemen in the free enterprise system, bringing capital from old countries to new ones and allocating resources to most efficient uses. He outlined the merchant's role in the growth process thus:

> In every country where arbitrary restrictions do not exist, where *free trade* is the rule, and prohibitory duties is [*sic*] the exception, the mercantile and trading interests become the true bulwarks of the country. They are in possession of its whole floating and surplus capital [estimated for N. S. W. at £5,000,000 and £800,000 respectively]. They do not lead it into a wrong channel, because profit with them is the *primum mobile*.[29]

In discussions of growth, free competition was described as an essential selection procedure. One Tasmanian reported: "While it is the interest of the producer to narrow competition, it is the interest of the consumer to enlarge it; and the advantage of consumers is clearly the advantage of the country at large; for every man is a consumer, even the producers themselves, who, though they may be desirous of preventing competition in their several walks, must yet wish for it in all other species of commerce."[30] Another contributor to the Sydney *Empire* concluded that laissez faire should be the guiding principle for all enlightened colonial policy: "Self-interest is the best guide in the matter, and by allowing industry to take its own course, unimpeded by fanciful theories and arbitrary rules of government, will successful colonization alone be attained."[31]

During the 1850's, the first decade of responsible government, the colonies underwent revolutionary economic change following the discovery of gold. A wave of immigration, blossoming new

28. T. A. Coghlan, *Labour and Industry in Australia*, p. 844.
29. Publicola, "Social and Political Conditions of Australia—No. 2. The Mercantile Interest," *Empire*, 1851, No. 90, p. 374.
30. James Barnard, "Statistics of Van Diemen's Land for 1844–1846 . . . ," *Tasmanian Journal of Natural Science, Agriculture, Statistics, &c.*, III (1849), 447.
31. "Model Colonies," *Empire*, January 14, 1852, p. 570.

communities, and shortages in many critical areas created formidable tasks for the state, even in the provision of essential services. Although colonial governments in fact had little choice in acceptance of magnified responsibilities, this fact did not leave defenders of laissez faire less concerned. A Melbourne writer in 1855 reacted bitterly to an overpowering state he saw developing. After citing appropriate selections from works by Adam Smith and John Stuart Mill, he summarized his views thus:

In a word, if Government would allow men to form their contracts at their own discretion, and would not disturb the ordinary operations of the market by its interference as a dealer; but if it would direct its attention to the best and quickest and most certain means of enforcing these contracts, and of preventing any individual from doing injury to public rights, it would save itself a great deal of unnecessary and disagreeable labour, and the interests of society would be much more efficiently served.[32]

J. Aikenhead, proprietor of the Launceston *Examiner* and a prominent free-trader, illustrated in lectures to a mechanics' institute how, until mid-century, colonial progress, with minimal state interference, had followed the course prescribed by Smith of pastoral and agricultural development. He deplored the new and expanded functions he believed were being usurped currently by government. "It is a grievance," he said, "whether in Turkey, England, or Tasmania, if officials seize on as much spoil as they can. The sooner such a system is overthrown the better for humanity."[33]

Pastoralists experienced worsening labor shortages and market fluctuations at the same time that they observed increases in government activity, and they did not fail to relate these developments. Land-holders deplored particularly proposals for government encouragement of small homestead settlement; Colin Campbell, a prominent Victorian land-owner, maintained:

If every country should engage in those branches of labour which it can carry on with the greatest advantage, then every one in the country should be left in a natural way to do that which he can do,

32. "State Interference," *Melbourne Monthly Magazine of Original Colonial Literature*, I (1855), 76–83.
33. J. Aikenhead, *Principles of Political Economy* (Tasmania, 1856), p. 33.

so as best to promote his own personal interest. It is the part of the State to hold true the scales of justice, and to afford full protection both of person and of property to all its subjects through its executive and legislative functions.[34]

In the 1850's and 1860's, as has been shown above, prophets of laissez faire were particularly influential in opposing subsidized railway development, reflecting always the classical economists' skepticism both of monopoly and of government intervention in industry.

Critics of a developing gold-based economy were disturbed especially by apparent distortion of the national growth process described by Smith. Premature distraction of settlers from pastoral and agricultural enterprises, they feared, could retard development permanently. H. Lill Lindsay, an immigrant Irish land surveyor, announced formally that he took "A. Smith" for his "guide," and then he condemned what he considered a misguided attempt by Australians to by-pass the agricultural stage of development and to move via mining directly from pastoral activity to manufacturing. He explained:

labor is the gold of this or any other country; it is by labor that the gold is found, and though individual profits might not be so rapidly made at more legitimate pursuits, yet labor legitimately directed and economically carried out, would be of a lasting, while the other affords but a transient benefit; by the one, all individual enterprise would reap an advantage; while by the other, the benefits occur by chance, and for one that may be enriched, one hundred may be left penniless.[35]

Lindsay faced a dilemma in endorsing wholeheartedly classical growth theory. He accepted the wisdom of laissez faire only to find that in the colonies non-intervention by the state led paradoxically to deviation from the prescribed "natural progress of opulence." As a way out of the dilemma, he chose to tolerate temporary state sponsorship of such measures as irrigation and

34. Colin Campbell, *The Squatting Question Considered with a View to its Settlement* (Melbourne, 1861), pp. 12–13.
35. H. Lill Lindsay, *The Industrial Resources of Victoria with Practical Suggestions on Agriculture, Employment of Labor, Water Supply, &c.* (Melbourne, 1856), p. 4. Similar views were expressed by N. L. Kentish in *Question of Questions: Just Shewing How to "Speed the Plough" in Victoria . . .* (Melbourne, 1855).

homestead farming to restore a healthy growth sequence. He
wrote:

How far the promotion of agriculture may tend to bring about manufacturing pursuits, it would be difficult at present to predict; but one
thing is certain, that as men become settled, as a steady yeomanry,
they will soon find means of satisfying their wants, in establishing
local manufactories, to suit the circumstances of the country; it may
therefore be safely asserted, that the employment of labor, in the
promotion of agriculture is only the first step towards developing the
great industrial resources of the country, and that capital to a very
large amount will be created by the reproductive labour attendant
on manufacturing pursuits, and also that a considerable number of the
population, will be gradually attracted to undertakings of that character, for the present the subject can only be noticed as a *sequitur* to
the cultivation of the soil. Thus agriculture appears to be the great
project to begin with,—the industry—the employment of labour,—the
providing of food, for the inhabitants, and the creation of capital,—all
depend upon its due and rapid promotion.[36]

Samuel Davenport in South Australia, using the same arguments as Lindsay in Victoria, urged settlers to accept "prominent
truths" appropriate for their changed environment and to seek
the most economic industrial enterprise. He insisted that staple
production should remain the first concern of any new country:
"In the progress to wealth of the early occupants of newly inhabited countries, agricultural precede manufacturing industries; or, as a rule, the production of raw material attaches more
especially to new and thinly peopled communities. Therefore,
the industries to which we owe attention are chiefly agricultural,
or closely allied to those."[37] Although in principle a free-trader,
Davenport was willing to tolerate government interference to the
extent of temporary encouragement for such new products as
silk and tobacco. After gold mining had complicated seriously
the problems of the Australian economy in the 1850's, it became
difficult even for the most sincere devotee of laissez faire seriously
to recommend unconditional non-intervention.

The stage theory of economic development became an impor-

36. H. Lill Lindsay, *op. cit.*, p. 28.
37. Samuel Davenport, *Some New Industries for South Australia, Silkworms,
Mulberry, Olives, Tobacco, Etc., Etc.* (Adelaide, 1864), p. vi.

tant element in the thinking of several early professional economists. J. S. Elkington, Professor of History and Political Economy at the University of Melbourne, maintained that colonies could be expected to exhibit sequential growth characteristics identical to those of parent European nations:

a new country, in the sense of a country colonized from an old one, will be harassed by no exceptional conditions. Such communities take with them fully developed capacities for economic and jural organization; their institutions bear a general resemblance to those of the parent state, but adjust themselves by natural and spontaneously developed agencies to the novel conditions in which their exercise is called for.[38]

Elkington subscribed to the classical explanation of British economic development, and he suggested that in the colonies as in the old country urban manufacturing naturally and in due course would supercede agriculture.

The manufacturing industry of the nation gradually passed from the domestic stage of hand-weaving, hand-knitting, &c., which for a long time were ordinary occupations of rural families, to the organized or factory stage, which entails an ever-increasing division of employment, and leads to the concentration of many persons on a small area. This development of national resources led to the voluntary abandonment by artisans of the less remunerative occupations incidental to tillage in the country, and their seeking instead the more remunerative occupations which the growth of manufactures and of national commerce offered them in the towns.[39]

Elkington concluded that the success of Britain in obtaining relatively high living standards by moving without interference through successive growth stages warranted colonial simulation and adoption of the principle that "The action of the State cannot be just when it meddles with freedom of exchange between individuals."[40]

Henry Gyles Turner suggested in 1880 that the contemporary primitive development stage of the Australian economy pointed

38. J. S. Elkington, "An Historical Glance at the Land Question," *Melbourne Review*, II (1877), 256–57.
39. *Ibid.*, p. 241.
40. *Ibid.*, p. 264.

to the desirability of continued pursuit of pastoral and agricultural production. Dependence on staple industries, he added, justified departures from banking practices appropriate for older countries, in particular loans on real estate.[41] Robert M. Johnston, employed a stage theory early in the twentieth century to defend immigration restriction and to project—successfully—the growth of Australian population.[42] Johnston viewed economic growth as a process of satisfying wants by overcoming "obstacles," and he believed this could be mobilized best by private entrepreneurs with, at most, guidance from the state. Government might be justified in altering the pattern of income distribution but it should avoid carefully misallocation of available resources.[43] In discussions of population problems during the 1920's, a stage theory, implying that the Commonwealth would move progressively from raw material production to manufacturing, remained influential.[44]

Pastoralists recognized that contemporary growth theory afforded reasonable justification for their continued unrestricted operations,[45] and they joined disciples of classical economics to repeat arguments for "natural" growth through stages.[46] In reply to assertions that an energetic state was essential to prosperity, they countered that the crucial element in national development was "the character of the people, its physical, mental and moral fibre." These virtues, they implied, were present in unusually large doses on a sheep station. One spokesman, identifying clas-

41. Henry G. Turner, "Victorian Banking Considered in Relation to National Development," *Australasian Insurance and Banking Record*, IV (1880), 401–4, and above p. 212.
42. R. M. Johnston, "Conditions upon which the Healthy Growth of the Population of Young Colonies Depend," *Papers and Proceedings of the Royal Society of Tasmania*, 1903–5, pp. 27–33.
43. R. M. Johnston, "Observations on Current Social and Economic Problems," *Report of the Second Meeting of the Australasian Association for the Advancement of Science held at Melbourne, 1890*, pp. 120–59; "Observations Regarding some Economic Aspects of the Eisenach Social Equality Programme," *Papers and Proceedings of the Royal Society of Tasmania*, 1903–5, pp. 125–35.
44. E. T. McPhee, "Drift of Population to the Cities," *Report of the Seventeenth Meeting of the Australasian Association for the Advancement of Science held at Adelaide, 1924*, pp. 535–50; and P. D. Phillips and G. L. Wood, eds., *The Peopling of Australia* (Melbourne, 1928), pp. 63 and 221.
45. T. A. Coghlan, *Labour and Industry in Australia*, pp. 844 and 1221.
46. See for example, Samuel Cook, *The "Wagga Wagga Advertiser" Prize Essay on the Future Land Policy of New South Wales* (Sydney, 1870).

sical theory with grazing interests, recalled that Spain's decline under mercantilism could "be directly traced to ignorance, ignorance of the most rudimental principles of political economy on the part of its successive rulers, and ignorance the most dense and shameless of the first elements of education on the part of the people."[47] Even pastoralists, however, were willing to accept government assistance for their own purposes, and by the end of the century, after drought and depression, they too made few appeals for unconditional governmental impotence.

After the effectiveness of state activity in the economy had been demonstrated in the 1850's and the memory of Colonial Office domination had begun to fade, criticism of the role of government in economic growth took the form mainly of opposition to specific public policies: tariff protection, national banking, homestead settlement, or subsidized railways. Criticism of particular policies was usually pragmatic in tone. For example, J. Reid insisted that with regard to public management of railways: "the Government is the very worst servant the public can possibly have, and for this reason, that the state (as it is the fashion to call it) is exempt from all those influences which make private capitalists, whether singly or as joint stock companies, exert themselves to enlarge the businesses in which they are engaged."[48] Opponents of land reform appealed occasionally to general principles, but usually only as a tool of argument; J. Crozier wrote in condemnation of land nationalization: "The prosperity of the community depends on the prosperity of the individual, and captious interference is the surest way of marring the happiness of the individual, and consequently of society."[49] Sophisticated free-traders took pains to distinguish between low tariffs and a general policy of laissez faire. B. R. Wise explained regretfully in 1892: "Popular impressions die hard; and it will probably be as difficult to persuade Protectionists and Socialists that Laissez faire is not a necessary part of economic teaching as it is to persuade Individualists that Socialism does not mean either re-

47. T. F. Bird, "The Basis of National Prosperity," *Melbourne Review*, I (1876), 99 and 101.
48. "State Railways," *Sydney Quarterly Magazine*, 1887, p. 142.
49. "Land Tenure," *Victorian Review*, V (1882), 416.

distribution of private property or the abolition of capital. Nevertheless, the attempt must be made." Wise outlined carefully the criteria governments should consider before interfering in the growth process:

the principles by which any act of State interference should be tested may be summarised as follows:—
1. The State ought in no case to weaken the motives for morality.
2. The State should not do that which might be done as well by private persons.
3. The state should never act in such a way as to weaken individual self-reliance.
But where the object to be gained is one of national importance, which the efforts of individuals cannot accomplish, and when it can be gained without discouraging any from making efforts on their own behalf, or from entering into union for a common purpose, then all the conditions are present which are required to justify State action.[50]

Apart from works of evolutionists examined in the next chapter, the few expositions of doctrinaire laissez faire voiced in the colonies, late in the century, were negative in tone and constituted indirect attacks on contemporary socialist theory.[51] In the twentieth century, academic economists added condemnation of government interference in the growth process to more generalized attacks on redistributive social policies.[52]

Development through Collective Action

Australian settlement began during a period when British colonial policy rested on principles of eighteenth century mercan-

50. *Industrial Freedom: A Study in Politics* (Melbourne, 1892), pp. 145 and 164.

51. Bruce Smith, *Liberty and Liberalism* (Melbourne, 1887); Charles Fairfield, "State Socialism in the Antipodes," in Thomas McKay, ed., *A Plea for Liberty* (London, 1892), pp. 124–72; Henry Wrixon, *Socialism: Notes on a Political Tour* (London, 1896), and reviewed unfavorably by F. M. Butlin, *Economic Journal*, VII (1897), 413–15; Max Hirsch, *Democracy versus Socialism* (London, 1924).

52. Edward Shann, *Bond or Free?* (Sydney, 1930); O. de R. Foenander, "The Shipping Enterprise of the Australian Commonwealth Government," *American Economic Review*, XIX (1929), 605–18.

tilism under which colonies were regarded as suppliers of raw materials, markets for finished goods, sources of tribute, nurseries for seamen, and, in the case of Australia, receptacles for convicts. James Stephen, who dominated the Colonial Office from the 1830's until the 1850's, was in close sympathy with proposals for liberalization of colonial economic policy and with attempts to forge imperial links of friendly association rather than of close domination.[53] Under Stephen, the Colonial Office continued to exercise tight control of Australian affairs, but with demonstrated faith in the ability of private enterprise to accomplish growth unhampered by close state supervision.

The first and only extensive official exercise in application of mercantilist principles to Australia was carried out by Thomas Bigge, a special commissioner of investigation sent to examine conditions in New South Wales. Bigge treated the Australian continent as one giant enterprise to be operated, like any firm, in the most efficient manner. He was impressed profoundly by experiments in adaptation of the wool industry to the colonies, and he recommended government assistance to remove all "obstacles" to this development. Bigge insisted:

> Upon the expediency of promoting in the colony of New South Wales the growth of fine wool, and creating a valuable export from thence to Great Britain, no doubt can be entertained, as it appears to be the principal, if not the only source of productive industry within the colony, from which the settlers can derive the means of repaying the advances made to them from the mother country, or supplying their own demands for articles of foreign manufacture.[54]

Bigge proposed that favorable treatment, including tariff protection, be afforded attempts to manufacture tobacco and flax in the colonies. His reports engendered considerable controversy, in part because of condemnation of actions taken by Governor Mac-

---

53. See Paul Knaplund, *James Stephen and the British Colonial System, 1813–1847* (Madison, Wisconsin, 1953), p. 64; J. C. Beaglehole, "The Colonial Office, 1782–1854," *Historical Studies Australia and New Zealand*, I (1940–41), 170–89; and E. Trevor Williams, "The Colonial Office in the Thirties," *ibid.*, III (1944–49), 141–60.

54. *Report of the Commissioner of Inquiry, on the State of Agriculture and Trade in the Colony of New South Wales* (London, 1823), p. 18.

quarie, but their impact was not great.[55] Sheep-raising during
the 1820's and 1830's became sufficiently profitable without government assistance for Bigge's mercantilist proposals not to warrant serious consideration.

Some early settlers believed that continuance of aggressive
mercantilism, changes in British policy notwithstanding, was in
the interest both of the mother country and of the colonies.
During the first half of the nineteenth century, pleas were voiced
as strenuously for reversal to rigorous imperial control as for
movement toward economic independence. For example, the
Colonial Advocate at Hobart argued in 1828, using information
from Postlethwayt's *Universal Dictionary of Trade*, that closely
managed colonial public enterprise had alone made possible
imperial prosperity. The journal predicted that Australia could
replace the United States as Britain's most profitable overseas
possession and therefore deserved close attention; it concluded:
"We consume a great portion of the manufactures of Great
Britain, and we also consume an immense quantity of her articles
of trade. We prove a market for an extraordinary number of gal-
lons of West India rum, and much East India produce. How
then can it be otherwise than that we are increasing the wealth of
the Mother Country?"[56] Colonists doubted that private initiative
in a new environment could equal the efficiency of British government. Robert Dawson maintained in 1831 that rapid colonial
growth was possible only through subsidized transfer of capital
and labor organized under methodical state planning.[57] The
"Wakefield System" discussed above, dominated government
thinking during the 1830's and 1840's, but the good or ill of state
control were neither confirmed nor disproved by experience. As
William Westgarth was forced to conclude in 1848:

55. A complimentary review of Bigge's reports was published in the *Edinburgh Review*, February, 1823, pp. 85–104. A discussion of Bigge's activities in Australia is: J. Dennis, "Bigge versus Macquarie," *Royal Australian Historical Society Journal and Proceedings*, XXIII (1938), 411–72.
56. "Colonial Policy," *Colonial Advocate, and Tasmanian Monthly Review and Register*, May 1, 1828, p. 116. For similar statements see John Lhotsky, *Illustrations of the Present State and Future Prospects of the Colony of New South Wales* (Sydney, 1835).
57. Robert Dawson, *The Present State of Australia* (London, 1831).

No definite system has yet appeared. The question at present is clouded with difficulty, and perhaps nothing has yet been proposed that is worthy of consideration, or even possible in practice, as a great scheme of national emigration. But an important preliminary is attained; the continuous attention of the public mind cannot fail to result in some practical measure, adapted to the circumstances of our age and country.[58]

John Dunmore Lang was an energetic and articulate advocate of aggressive government policies for accelerating economic growth.[59] He emphasized particularly the complementary character of old and new economies, and he illustrated how wise imperial action might permit the excess capital and labor in one to remedy the shortage in the others. Lang favored encouragement of individual initiative wherever possible, but directed if necessary by the community.[60] He conceived distinctive developmental functions for the state, including particularly in new countries the attraction of prosperous settlers.[61] Unlike many of his contemporaries Lang believed that in the colonies government retained unambiguous obligations to any workers who became unemployed involuntarily; a legislative committee of which he was chairman reported thus during the depression year 1843: "Your Committee . . . have no hesitation in expressing their belief and conviction, that the Government have other duties to discharge, in regard to the unemployed, besides that of merely sympathising with them in their present condition; it is the

58. William Westgarth, *Australia Felix; or, a Historical and Descriptive Account of the Settlement of Port Phillip, New South Wales* (Edinburgh, 1848), p. 303.
59. Lang's writings are described in A. C. Child, "Studies in the Life and Work of John Dunmore Lang," *Royal Australian Historical Society Journal and Proceedings*, XXII (1936), 69–90, 208–28, and 298–311.
60. Lang proposed in 1833 that British poor-rates be discontinued and that paupers be given a choice between starvation and free passage to the colonies. John Dunmore Lang, *Emigration; Considered Chiefly in Reference to the Practicability and Expediency of Importing and of Settling Throughout the Territory of New South Wales, a Numerous, Industrious and Virtuous Agricultural Population* (Sydney, 1833), p. 4.
61. "Minutes of Evidence Taken Before the Committee on Immigration," *Minutes and Proceedings of the Legislative Council of New South Wales*, 1834, pp. 295–99; John Dunmore Lang, *Immigration; the Grand Desideratum for New South Wales: and How to Promote it Effectually* (Sydney, 1870); and *An Historical and Statistical Account of New South Wales, from the Founding of the Colony in 1788 to the Present Day* (London, 1875), particularly I, 289.

bounden duty of the Government, to afford relief, and the means of subsistence, to the utmost extent practicable in the actual circumstances of the Colony."[62] Lang was preeminently a man of action, and in the emergency situation which he believed characterized colonial growth he was willing to sanction with few limitations the strong hand of the state.

Tasks imposed on colonial governments by the gold rushes demonstrated conclusively that the state could play a vital role in economic development. Exploration and surveys were undertaken, emergency transport and police services were provided, and special relief was afforded both to distressed miners and to other groups which suffered sudden dislocations. It became clear, as one witness informed a Victorian legislative committee in the 1850's, that: "The timely provision for opening up our natural resources and making room for an increase in our population, by encouraging a well directed national enterprise, is one of the wisest laws or principles of political and social economy."[63] In 1862–63 a Victorian Royal Commission cited John Stuart Mill to defend government construction of public utilities, improvement of public knowledge, and special bonuses and favors for activities of benefit to the community. The Commission concluded confidently:

> It affords much satisfaction to your Commissioners to add that there exists the most abundant evidence that our mineral deposits are practically inexhaustible, and that all that is required is the clearing away of unnecessary legal and official obstructions, the passing of efficient mining laws, liberal departmental regulations, the equitable combination of capital and labor, together with the employment of the best mechanical and chemical appliances, to insure to the miners of Victoria a long and prosperous future.[64]

62. "Report from the Select Committee on the Petition from Distressed Mechanics and Labourers, with Minutes of Evidence," *Votes and Proceedings of the Legislative Council of New South Wales*, 1843, p. 3.
63. "Report from the Select Committee of the Legislative Council on Gold; together with the proceedings of the Committee, Minutes of Evidence, and Appendix," *Votes and Proceedings of the Legislative Council of Victoria*, 1855–56, Appendix 1, p. 46.
64. "Report of the Royal Mining Commission Appointed to Enquire into the Condition and Prospects of the Gold Fields of Victoria," *Papers Presented to Both Houses of the Parliament of Victoria*, 1862–63, p. 51. See also Charles Mayes, *Essay on the Manufactures more Immediately Required for the Economic Develop-*

By the end of the turbulent 1850's, many colonists remained critical of particular developmental policies of government, but as most critics received public assistance in some form or other they came to accept, tacitly at least, the need for an active state.

Sanguine hopes of Australians, during the 1850's, for continued growth and prosperity based mainly on mineral exploitation were not justified. Problems posed by the failure of alluvial gold-mining and memories of satisfactory government performance during years of success made the question of continued state participation in the growth process somewhat academic. By the 1860's, continuance of a strong state was assumed, and critics as well as defenders of laissez faire turned to detailed questions of particular policies. More than any other single problem the place of land in the growth process preoccupied colonists.[65] The Wake-field system, which prescribed use of proceeds from land sales to attract immigrant labor, was one suggestion; sub-division of pastoral holdings to make small farms was another. Even though colonists could seldom agree on a single course of action, they believed almost without exception that correct use of the land was the key to prosperity and social tranquility.[66] Mining and manufacturing had their share of advocates, but with the presence of a nearly empty continent these could not often vie successfully with land for attention.

The conventional classical explanation of economic growth as a process of saving and accumulation puzzled some Australians. A. J. Ogilvy in Tasmania rejected the motive of abstinence as a reasonable description of capital increase in a new country, and he suggested instead:

speaking broadly, accumulations are due, not to abstinence, but to a variety of causes, the three chief of which are—

ment of the Resources of the Colony, with Special References to those Manufactures the Raw Materials of which are the Produce of Victoria (Melbourne, 1861).
65. Controversy over land policy is described in Chapters 3 and 4 above.
66. See particularly: *Direct Remission Advocated* (Sydney, 1848), p. 3; James J. Casey, "The Land Systems of South Australia and Victoria Compared," *Melbourne Review*, II (1877), 1–22; William Coote, *Railway and Land Policy of Queensland* (Brisbane, 1879); "Final Report of the Commission on Agriculture," *Minutes and Votes and Proceedings of the Parliament of Western Australia*, 1891–92; and Alexander C. Wylie, "The Relations between Capital and Labour," *Victorian Review*, XII (1885), 369–78.

1. To extra exertion: that is, a man having satisfied his immediate wants, proceeds to produce something else which he does not want now, but expects to want hereafter.

2. To the natural durability of most of the articles we produce, in consequence of which they are produced faster than they are worn out, and so accumulate.

3. To the exercise of ingenuity and advance of knowledge, whereby with the same labour that we formerly produced a mere sufficiency we can now produce a surplus.[67]

Perhaps because of his environment, Ogilvy did not distinguish clearly between consumption and investment spending, but he did appreciate the importance for full employment and growth of sustained monetary circulation.

A number of colonial observers concluded that the peculiar feature of economic growth in a new country was the vital role played by public capital accumulation. Private saving, they suggested, was limited fundamentally in scope by the nature of a young economy and could increase only in proportion to public capital. R. M. Johnston claimed in 1892: "In the colonies . . . the major part of the so-called *public debt* is as much a commercial asset as the capital invested in railways and tramways in England, and with the exception of about one or two per cent. the remainder is represented by public works of a permanent character, whose value, as wealth-producing auxiliaries, enormously exceeds the nominal debt standing against them."[68] Critics of state activity condemned the rapid growth of a national debt, but they objected less and less often to the vital public works which resulted.[69]

From an early date, Australians were concerned about their apparent inability to understand and thereby to guide the course of economic growth. Sir Charles Nicholson complained to the Royal Colonial Institute in London that British economists had been of little assistance with this enigma. He said: "It is a re-

67. "Is Capital the Result of Abstinence?," *Report of the Fourth Meeting of the Australasian Association for the Advancement of Science held at Hobart*, 1892, pp. 525–26.
68. "The Attack on the Credit of Australasia," *Nineteenth Century*, XXXI (1892), 611.
69. James E. Fitzgerald, "Public Debts and Sinking Funds," *Victorian Review*, XII (1885), 257–68; Crito, *The Present Crisis: Are Tasmanians Oppressively Taxed?* (Launceston, n. d. [c. 1872]), pp. 7–8.

markable and significant fact that at a period when political economy had in England been erected into a science, and professors appointed for inculcating its principles in our Universities, a subject so germane to its inquiries, if not of its very essence, viz., 'colonisation,' should have been virtually ignored."[70] One result of the prevailing inability to comprehend the growth process was that political leaders of all complexions seldom employed doctrine in defense of state action.[71] Alfred Deakin, converted to the importance of a strong state by the polemical writings of Carlyle and Ruskin, considered a policy of "let be" a mere "fad," and yet he did not embrace socialist theory or other strong doctrinal justification for the powerful state which developed while he was prime minister.[72] William Morris Hughes and G. H. Knibbs subscribed to a biological theory of the state, examined in the next chapter, and they justified government encouragement of growth mainly as legitimate nourishment of an organism.[73] Interest of Prime Minister Bruce in unexplained processes of development led to enquiries by the Development and Migration Commission in the 1920's.[74] The Commission explained in its first annual report: "We have never had a stocktaking of our resources with a view to determining the industries that, having regard to our natural advantages, should be promoted. The Commission will consider all schemes submitted by State Governments, or that come before it from other sources, and, generally, it will advise the Government in relation to all questions of developmental policy, in order to ensure the best utilization of our resources and the most effective and rapid method of dealing with them."[75]

70. "The Principles which Ought to Regulate the Determination of the Political and Municipal Boundaries and Divisions of the Colonies," *Proceedings of the Royal Colonial Institute,* XII (1880–81), 318.
71. J. B. Brigden, "State Enterprises in Australia," *Report of the Eighteenth Meeting of the Australasian Association for the Advancement of Science held at Perth, 1926,* pp. 597–98; and S. M. Ingham, "Political Parties in the Victorian Legislative Assembly, 1880–1900," *Historical Studies Australia and New Zealand,* IV (1949–51), 241–56.
72. "A Fair Field and No Favour," *Australasian Critic,* July, 1891, *passim;* and *The Crisis in Victorian Politics, 1879–1881: A Personal Retrospect,* edited by J. A. La Nauze and R. M. Crawford (Melbourne, 1957), pp. 3–5.
73. See below pp. 347–49.
74. Gordon Greenwood, ed., *Australia: A Social and Political History* (Sydney, 1955), pp. 305–6.
75. "First Annual Report of the Development and Migration Commission," *Papers Presented to the Parliament of the Commonwealth of Australia,* 1926–27, pp. 5–6.

F. W. Eggleston offered a convincing apology for public economic activity in the Australian economy before the British Association in 1914; but his arguments were largely pragmatic, and he admitted readily: "It is characteristic of Australian democracy . . . that no systematic attempt has been made to weigh these advantages and disadvantages to utilise the strength and eliminate the specific weaknesses of the system."[76]

Conclusion

By the end of the period under study, Australians had little more understanding of the process of economic growth and the correct functions of the state than they had at the beginning. In this respect, they were like citizens of other countries. It is noteworthy, however, that even the rapid, exciting, and in many ways unique development of their continent did not stimulate important study of the subject. The absence of operationally meaningful theories of economic growth, domestic or foreign, prevented doctrine from exerting a decisive influence on many aspects of economic policy in Australia.

Imported ideas were dominant in discussions of the place of government. Disciples in the colonies of British classical economics included such powerful figures as W. C. Wentworth, Robert Lowe, Henry Gyles Turner, and other representatives of the pastoral, mercantile, and financial communities. In the universities and public services, early professional economists seldom questioned the dictates of Smith or Mill. Most opponents of a positive state in the economy were willing on occasion to sanction government action in their own self-interest, but they defended none the less vehemently the principle of laissez faire in general. Advocates of vigorous government activity in most instances supported their favorite programs piecemeal. They endorsed land reform, tariffs, or a national bank but seldom the basic rationale of strong government. Apart from occasional claims that national

76. "The Australian Democracy and its Economic Problems," *Economic Journal*, XXV (1915), 350.

destiny transcended individual commercial freedom, or that special problems of a new country dictated state interference, they did not provide a defense of their basic theoretical position. The greater respectability among intellectuals of laissez faire discouraged investigation into the relationship between the state and economic growth, and innovation was confined to discussions of analogies from biological evolution examined in the next chapter.

10

Evolution Theory and Social Thought

Knowledge of developments in the theory of evolution, high-lighted in biology by the work of Darwin and in the social sci-ences by Spencer and Comte, came to Australia in the minds of educated immigrants and in literature imported from Britain and America.[1] That Darwin's own impressions of Australia were not favorable did not dampen enthusiasm for his ideas; he had re-marked regarding the colonies: "My opinion is such that nothing but rather sharp necessity should compel me to emigrate."[2] Dur-ing the second half of the nineteenth century, evolutionary thinking became a powerful element combined with and sup-plementary to classical economic theory in Australian discussions of colonial growth.

Professor Hofstadter has suggested that in the United States interpretations for social growth of evolutionary theory had sig-nificant influence in at least two directions. First, beginning in the 1860's and 1870's, explanations of social development in biological terms were employed in defense of doctrinaire laissez faire. "In so far as it defended the status quo and gave strength to attacks on reformers and on almost all efforts at the conscious and directed change of society, social Darwinism was certainly

---

1. The impact of evolution theory on American social thought has been de-scribed in Stow Persons, ed., *Evolutionary Thought in America* (New Haven, 1950), and in Richard Hofstadter, *Social Darwinism in American Thought* (re-vised edition, Boston, 1955). A bibliography to 1955 is contained in Hofstadter, pp. 205–16.

2. Another oft-quoted comment by Darwin on leaving the colonies brought him the special enmity of future generations. He said: "Farewell, Australia! You are too great and ambitious for affection, yet not great enough for respect. I leave your shores without sorrow or regret." Charles Daley, "Charles Darwin and Australia," *Victorian Historical Magazine*, XVII (1938–39), 68–69.

one of the leading strains in American conservative thought for more than a generation."[3] Second, evolutionary theory was used to defend racial conflict at the national level. "Although Darwinism was not the primary source of the belligerent ideology and dogmatic racism of the late nineteenth century, it did become a new instrument in the hands of the theorists of race and struggle."[4] In part, the development of evolutionary thinking in Australia followed a pattern which was very similar to that of the United States; the doctrine of beneficial struggle was adopted first by conservative thinkers for application to the domestic economy and was expanded later to justify international racial competition. However, evolution theory had perhaps its greatest impact in Australia in a third direction. A concept of integral national growth as a process of biological evolution found great favor and influence in Australia at a time when governments were undertaking a variety of bold social experiments. Whereas in America support for an organic theory of social development, as distinct from a theory of struggle among individuals, was manifested by defenders of a prevailing advocacy of laissez faire, in Australia an organic interpretation of society was used to justify a comprehensive program of aggressive state activity.

In this chapter, the extent to which social evolutionary ideas penetrated Australia is described first; the influence of these ideas on conservative individualist thought is outlined next, followed by their place in radical collectivist thought. Finally, their lasting impact on Australian thinking is discussed.

Evolution Theory in Australia

From their beginnings after mid-century, Australian universities gave evolutionary theory an important place in their curricula. William Edward Hearn, foundation professor of history and political economy at the University of Melbourne, was an

3. *Op. cit.*, p. 7.
4. *Op. cit.*, p. 172.

acknowledged disciple of Darwin, Spencer, and Comte, as well as of classical political economists.[5] In his book, *Plutology* (1863), Hearn discussed at length the biological development of organisms, and devoted an entire chapter to "the industrial evolution of society," in which he noted analogies between biological change and the process of economic growth. "In every organism," he observed, "there have been found to exist certain well-defined and fundamental laws of growth." In general, simplicity gives way to complexity and also mutual interdependence.

The homogeneous structure gradually becomes heterogenous; and the uniformity of function gives way to variety. The division of employments is established between the several parts of the organism. Their separate existence is merged in the larger collective life; and they become the component parts of an organized whole.[6]

Society like other organisms, Hearn continued, moved from uniformity to multiplicity of dissimilar parts and a process of mutual interaction: "Society therefore, like the individual organism, tends to become more complex, and its parts consequently become more closely interdependent. The more complex is the individual organism, the greater is its activity; and the keener is its sense of enjoyment."[7] Healthy growth of society, Hearn explained, occurred in the same way as in other organisms. Under favorable conditions, excess nutriments caused sectors to expand both in size and in shape in proportion to resources received. "In societies as in organisms, growth and development, increased bulk and increased complexity of structure, ought always to proceed with equal pace."[8] A limiting factor peculiar to the growth of social organisms, Hearn pointed out, was the human ability to recognize consequences and to practice restraint. "Man seldom *will* do all that he *can* do." Hearn claimed optimistically that, given satisfactory institutions, economic evolution led naturally

    5. Hearn's intellectual debts as well as praise from his contemporaries and successors are described in detail by Professor John La Nauze, *Political Economy in Australia: Historical Studies*, pp. 49–53 and 59–65. See also Douglas B. Copland, *W. E. Hearn: First Australian Economist* (Melbourne, 1935), pp. 78–79.
    6. William Edward Hearn, *Plutology: or the Theory of the Efforts to Satisfy Human Wants* (Melbourne, 1863), p. 383.
    7. *Ibid.*, p. 384.
    8. *Ibid.*, p. 393.

both to a solution of the problem of potential excess multiplication of population and to a process of continuous capital accumulation. "Wealth implies capital; and capital implies foresight, intelligence, and frugality. The development of these qualities thus tends at once to increase wealth and to restrict population."[9] Hearn tested his hypothesis of social development with copious examples from history, and he concluded confidently that as he had speculated, the "inter-dependence of the parts of any organism is a portion of its evolution."[10]

Although unique policy implications of Hearn's economic evolution theory were not self-evident, he offered only one interpretation. He pictured the world economy as an evolving organism of progressive complexity and with vital interrelationships between parts dependent upon free exchange of goods. "The rents of the peer are well paid, the wages of the artizan are large," he wrote, "when there is an abundant wool-clip on the Murrumbidgee, or when the miners at Ballarat have luck. Abundance is indeed the parent, not less than the offspring, of exchange."[11] Hearn maintained that free trade and outward-looking national policies were obvious dictates of his theory and that provincialism and tariff protection led implicitly to evolutionary retrogression. Often these conclusions did not appear as obvious to others as they did to Hearn, and his insistence on doctrinaire free trade seemed to critics a rather shallow rationalization of old and familiar precepts of classical economics. In the judgment of Professor La Nauze, "Hearn's grafting of biology on to economics was an original experiment but one which in his own case bore little fruit."[12]

Despite Hearn's failure to pursue this experimental line of reasoning, he established firmly the social evolutionary principles expressed in *Plutology* in the teaching of history and economics at Melbourne University. Works by Spencer held a prominent place on reading lists,[13] and students testified to the profound im-

9. *Ibid.*, p. 394.
10. *Ibid.*, p. 402.
11. *Ibid.*, p. 403.
12. *Political Economy in Australia: Historical Studies*, p. 64.
13. University of Melbourne, *Calendar*, 1868–69, p. 120.

pact of evolutionary thought. John Simeon Elkington, one of Hearn's first-class honours students and his successor in the chair of history and political economy, told a Victorian Royal Commission as late as 1902: "I base my teaching necessarily upon historical lines. Evolutionary lines is a modern phrase that about fits the situation."[14] Alfred Deakin, second prime minister of the Commonwealth, related that in the 1870's, after studying under Hearn, he was "saturated with the doctrines of Spencer, Mill, Buckle, superimposed upon an earlier and more durable foundation from Carlyle, Ruskin, and Emerson."[15] Henry Bournes Higgins, cabinet minister and pioneer labor arbitrator, also studied under Hearn in Melbourne, and like Deakin he accepted evolutionary theory although subsequently rejecting a policy of laissez faire, and becoming a convinced advocate of a strong state.[16]

Literary and intellectual activity outside the University in Melbourne reflected also the influence of Darwin, Spencer, Hearn, and other evolutionary writers. Prophets of evolution were cited with reverence, as for example when one Melbourne author declared in 1886: "Darwin and Buckle enormously strengthen and buttress moral foundations by their physical demonstration of the universality of order, method and law." He concluded that *The Origin of Species* was "one of the four most important books published in London since Macaulay."[17] Evolutionist works were available readily in bookstores throughout the colonies,[18] and on one occasion in 1870 the Land Reform League of Victoria even reprinted and distributed a substantial portion of Spencer's *Social Statics*.[19] Controversy over evolutionary theory abroad was

14. "Royal Commission on the University of Melbourne: Minutes of Evidence on Administration, Teaching Work, and Government of the University of Melbourne," *Papers Presented to the Parliament of Victoria*, 1903, p. 88.
15. Alfred Deakin, *The Crisis in Victorian Politics, 1879–1881: A Personal Retrospect*, edited by J. A. La Nauze and R. M. Crawford (Melbourne, 1957), p. 3.
16. Nettie Palmer, *Henry Bournes Higgins: A Memoir* (London, 1931), p. 65.
17. *Imperial Review* (Melbourne), July 1886, pp. 32–34.
18. Petherick bookstores in Melbourne, Adelaide, and Sydney in 1890 stocked fourteen different titles by Darwin and eleven by Spencer. *Australasian Critic: A Monthly Review of Literature, Science and Art*, October 1, 1890, p. ix.
19. Herbert Spencer, *The Right to the Use of the Earth*, Land Reform League Tracts, Number 1 (Melbourne, 1870). The impact on social thought in Melbourne of spiritualism and harmonialism, which were linked in some respects with views on land tenure and evolution theory, are described in Henry Mayer, *Marx, Engels and Australia* (Melbourne, 1964), pp. 54–63.

watched carefully, as for instance when Edward Langton, a prominent free-trader, read to a group of Melbourne bankers a translation of an address, strongly evolutionary in tone, by Jules Roche to the French Chamber of Deputies.[20]

Interest in evolutionary thought was not confined to Melbourne. A literary group in Tasmania which published the distinguished periodical *Quadrilateral* included several enthusiastic adherents. In 1874 Alfred J. Taylor, a prominent biologist, explained that evolution was a process common to all organisms: "Dame nature is very parsimonious. Niggardly and economising she wastes nothing and utilises every thing. . . . In her work she is progressive, but her progression consists rather in evolution, than arbitrary creation; that which appears to be new being simply a new combination and arrangement of the elements out of which the old was wrought."[21] During the intense labor strife of the 1890's Taylor commented: " ' . . . there *has* been, and *is proceeding*, an Economic Evolution, practically independent of our individual desires or prejudices;' and holding this as an article of my political faith, I do not contemplate the future of Unionism with fear or misgiving."[22] In 1883 Moncure Conway, the American rationalist theologian, visited the colonies and lectured on Darwin to interested groups in Melbourne, Sydney, and Hobart. Conway reported that in Tasmania where he was received warmly by friends he also "had the honour of being attacked in the papers by orthodox writers."[23] At Sydney University, evolutionary doctrines had no publicist equal to Hearn at Melbourne, but Spencer in particular was praised highly by the omniverous Professor Francis Anderson.[24] R. F. Irvine, first professor of economics at Sydney, called in 1914 for greater study of economic change, but he deplored use of evolution theory to justify perpetuating economic individualism and laissez faire. He

20. "State Socialism and Protection," *Bankers' Magazine and Journal of the Bankers' Institute of Australasia*, VIII (1894–95), 154–55.
21. A. J. T., "Nature's Circle," *Quadrilateral*, 1874, p. 94.
22. Alfred J. Taylor, "Trade Unionism as a Factor in Social Evolution," *Papers and Proceedings of the Royal Society of Tasmania*, 1892, p. 41.
23. Moncure Conway, *My Pilgrimage to the Wise Men of the East* (London, 1906), pp. 87 and 104.
24. Francis Anderson, *Sociology in Australia: A Plea for its Teaching* (Sydney, 1912), p. 9.

complained: "economists have most clearly shewn their practical denial of evolution in their hesitation to accept public or collective effort as a true cause of social evolution."[25]

Evolution as a Bulwark of Conservatism

To the beleaguered defenders of laissez faire in the colonies, and particularly in Victoria where the impact of gold discoveries was greatest, explanation of social development as a process analogous to biological evolution came as a welcome supplement to arguments against government activity derived from classical political economy. The theory that "natural selection" was as important a principle to humans living together as it was to other species implied that interference by government with economic aspects of the selection process could result in social stagnation, or even deterioration. Destruction of the weak was the only way to assure success for the strong. In addition to the familiar unseen hand, the state was pictured as facing a "natural" order of growth which it could alter only at its peril. The doctrine of social evolution in this crude form was particularly attractive to successful members of the business and pastoral community and to all advocates of rugged individualism. In the colonies, where laissez faire implied continuation of unrestricted staple production, economic liberalism was essentially a conservative policy; and conservatives became vocal evolutionists.

Henry Keylock Rusden and Henry Gyles Turner were outstanding exponents in Victoria of doctrinaire applications of social evolution theory. Rusden, a pastoralist for a time, then a public servant, secretary of the Royal Society of Victoria, and "the foremost rationalist and atheist in Melbourne,"[26] rejected absolutely on evolutionary grounds all attempts "to interfere with private economy further than as, by laws, the protection of one individual

25. R. F. Irvine, *The Place of the Social Sciences in a Modern University* (Sydney, 1914), p. 15.
26. A. G. Austin, *George William Rusden and National Education in Australia 1849–1862* (Melbourne, 1958), pp. 7 and 126.

against another is provided for."[27] He argued that "laws" of economic evolution were immutable and should never be disobeyed: "the data of political economy—the laws of the pressure of population, of demand and supply, of natural selection and the survival of the fittest—are simply impregnable inductions from the phenomena of nature and of human society." He insisted "it would be as reasonable to quarrel with the inherent properties of numbers, as with them."[28] Rusden cautioned against evil effects for all social classes of wage and price determination by other than free-market forces, and he warned particularly of discouragements to saving: "Any restriction upon or impediment to the accumulation by natural capitalists of the results of labour, accumulate nothing,—of so much accumulatable wealth. The loss is of course greater to those who cannot accumulate for themselves than for those who can."[29] A typical capitalist, Rusden explained, was "a social trustee of the results of the labour of others" and ought to be assisted by society in this trusteeship. Attempts by less successful citizens to wrest wealth from prosperous capitalists through injudicious legislation impeded the evolutionary process and threatened the welfare of future generations.

Rusden called attention to the potential danger of rapid population growth, and he insisted that if moral restraint did not prove adequate to restrain human multiplication, "positive checks" of famine and disease ought not to be impeded in their operation. "The positive checks to population are the only other means which are not fatally invidious of determining who should give place to the others in the struggle for existence. Some must be pressed out or down; and who should they be, if not the criminal, the lunatic, the stupid, the weak, the diseased and the incompetent? The survival of the fittest is best."[30] Rusden applied an evolutionary test to all proposed public welfare programs, and he approved specific measures only if they did not interfere with

27. H. K. Rusden, "Labour and Capital," *Melbourne Review*, I (1876), 68.
28. *Ibid.*, p. 69.
29. *Ibid.*, pp. 72 and 76.
30. *Ibid.*, p. 79.

healthy struggle. He was led even to a remarkably brutal justification for extermination of primitive races. He wrote:

The survival of the fittest means that might—wisely used—is right. And
thus we invoke and remorselessly fulfil the inexorable law of natural
selection (or of demand and supply), when exterminating the inferior
Australian and Maori races, and we appropriate their patrimony as
cooly as Ahab did the vineyard of Naboth, though in diametrical opposition to all our favourite theories of right and justice—thus proved to
be unnatural and false. The world is better for it; and would be in-
calculably better still, were we loyally to accept the lesson thus taught
by nature, and consistently to apply the same principle to our conventional practice; by preserving the varieties most perfect in every
way, instead of actually promoting the non-survival of the fittest by
protecting the propagation of the imprudent, the diseased, the
defective, and the criminal. Thus we surely lower the average of, and
tend to destroy, the human race, almost as effectually as if we were
openly to resort to communism.[31]

Rusden may have been strengthened in his evolutionary conviction and in his support for laissez faire by a letter from J. S. Mill
in 1870 affirming Rusden's "proposition that human freedom
should not be interfered with, except by such precautions as are
necessary to prevent injury to society."[32]

Henry Gyles Turner, banker and historian, was no less uncompromising than was Rusden in opposition to public assistance for
private persons on grounds of interference with the evolutionary
process. In 1898 he restated an objection to medical care for the
indigent which he claimed to have been expressing publicly and
consistently for thirty years.[33] Society, he argued, could not afford
to nurture or to encourage unfit persons who had been defeated
in the struggle for existence.

It would of course be unreasonable and foolish to look for any measure
that could stimulate a sense of independence in a debilitated frame

31. *Ibid.*, p. 82.
32. Hugh S. R. Elliot, *The Letters of John Stuart Mill* (London, 1910), II, 266.
33. Turner reported that between 1870 and 1898 evolutionary doctrine achieved
some measure of respectability. He said: "I was denounced vehemently for the
views I ventured to put forth in the 'Argus,' but public opinion is so far modified
that recently Dr. Bevan [Llewelyn David Bevan, a prominent cleric] dealt with
the subject on almost equally drastic lines, and his views met with wide approval."
"The Treatment of Paupers," *Bankers' Magazine and Journal of the Bankers' Institute of Australasia,* XII (1898–99), 618.

racked by disease or deformity. Under the rule of nature, the survival of the fittest, this class would be ruthlessly eliminated, but we do our utmost to check this process of elimination—we build asylums for them, we institute poor laws, our medical brethren exert themselves to keep them alive to the last moment, and we shrink from the obliquity which would be incurred by any general attempt to prevent them propagating their species, though we know that the consequences must be a marked degeneration of the race.[34]

Workers unemployed because of incompetence or any other reason, Turner maintained, deserved no sympathy. They should be "let alone to reform or starve," and in the latter eventuality society could murmur "good riddance." He said:

> Why are our cities congested with pale-faced, dispirited, listless mendicants who curse the Chinaman and other foreign competitors— who clamor for suburban relief works and other State aid nostrums, and rail at the capitalist as their bitterest foe? Because these prefer the squalid companionship of the slums—the garish attractions of Bourke Street on Saturday night,—even the dismal horrors of a Sunday in Melbourne, to the hard graft, the rough fare, and the rougher surroundings of the bushman's sphere of toil. . . .
> The conclusion I have come to is that the only way to bring to him a proper recognition of his rights and wrongs, is to let him severely alone . . . if he is worth saving, he will resolutely apply himself to the task of becoming useful in some form or other; if he cannot or will not do this, the assumption must be that he is not worth saving,— though society will probably order us to take every care of him.[35]

Turner put forth a proposal, reminiscent of Australia's origins, that in order to relieve the state of an intolerable burden "confirmed criminals" be cast upon a desert island, there either to live by their own labors or else to starve and to destroy themselves.

Charles Fairfield, an immigrant English journalist, was impressed deeply by pronouncements of Moncure Conway and other lecturers in the colonies on evolution, and in 1884 he elaborated conclusions he himself had drawn from social Darwinism. Economic progress, Fairfield argued, was limited strictly by a natural force driving social evolution onward. Legislation could impede and hinder this force but could not alter its char-

34. *Ibid.*, p. 613.
35. *Ibid.*, pp. 614–15.

acter. Welfare measures designed to protect the weak and preserve the unselected were not only injudicious but were doomed
to failure. He explained:

If the usages which Darwin proclaimed constant in the lower world
be potent among men also, we find ourselves confronted by impulses,
pushing humanity, surely though slowly, like some huge jack screw
and perhaps these may be altogether too strong for us. We may find
that when men discuss *laissez faire*, the *laissez* is an impertinence,
so to speak, since a supreme force, abler than our legislation, *fera
faire* whether we "let" it or not. We may find also why nothing can
be permanently altered by Acts of Parliament which propose to run
counter to or fail to recognize the scientific obligation of natural
selection and the struggle for life, two prime movers, which are ever
at work underneath the varnish and coatings of civilization.[36]

Fairfield was less enthusiastic about the laissez faire policy dictates of evolutionary theory than were some of his contemporaries
such as Rusden and Turner. Nevertheless, he agreed that an
unimpeded struggle for existence was legitimate and necessary.
Protection of incompetent humans could result only in disaster
for the race. "Infinite charity towards feeble types would, in a
few generations, cause the enslavement or destruction of the race
which has indulged in it. It again seems a cruel rule which con-
demns all weak, unselected folk to constant failure and ultimate
annihilation. Yet, how invent a better?"[37] Fairfield was pessimistic
about the future of humanity because he believed that economic
development accompanied by universal suffrage would lead to
misguided social welfare measures and consequent degeneration
—"the very improvements in sanitation and medicine, and the
exertions of philanthropists, increase the stringency of competition, by keeping thousands of deformed and sickly people alive
who under former dispensations would have been allowed to
die."[38] He was certain that misguided workers with unrestrained
political power in their hands would destroy eventually both

36. "Getting and Holding," *Melbourne Review*, IX (1884), 293. Conway is
mentioned on p. 291.
37. *Ibid.*, p. 295.
38. *Ibid.*, p. 305.

themselves and all of society by contradicting evolution—"in proportion as we moderns perfect the competitive machine, we hasten the time when it must grind itself to pieces."

During the last years of the nineteenth century, Australian conservatives found three main reasons for worry about the path of human evolution. First, widening of the suffrage appeared to be leading steadily to creation of a monolithic, state-controlled economy with attention devoted to redistribution rather than to production. In the colonies governments already were building railways, protecting industry, controlling immigration, operating schools, and regulating settlement. In addition, experiments were contemplated or under way in wage arbitration, government banking, and a variety of nationalized industries. Of greatest seriousness, an increasingly restive labor movement called for creation of a welfare state in which all semblance of selection of the fittest through economic struggle would be removed. A second cause for concern was the awakening in Asia illustrated by growing Japanese commerical and military strength and magnified in significance by the contrast between Australia's empty north and the population expansion in China and India. Most Australians had few doubts of their own evolutionary superiority, and gains by colored races either in numbers or in economic status seemed to them certain retrogression of the human species.

Finally, conservatives were deeply distressed at the economic difficulties which overtook the colonies and the rest of the world in the late 1880's and 1890's. It became progressively more difficult to predict confidently man's great destiny while thousands of his kind remained unemployed and starving for little apparent reason. Indications of mounting pessimism among Australian evolutionists were evident in statements by Fairfield, but they were epitomized in 1893 by a book of Charles H. Pearson, a former Victorian minister of education, entitled *National Life and Character: A Forecast.*

Pearson outlined a detailed prophecy of global development based in part on an observation of population growth in the temperate zone which he concluded from Australian experience was

the only area where the white "higher races" could live.[39] He
accepted Malthusian doctrine that population was destined to
increase steadily the pressure on resources, and he reasoned that
if "emigration, which is the rough substitute for the organization
of labour, becomes impossible, the tendency to State Socialism,
which is already strongly marked in certain British colonies, will
become more and more powerful."[40] The progress of humanity,
Pearson maintained, would be arrested soon through overcrowding and the need for rigid political control—"the gradual decay
of faith, the diminished importance of family life, and the loss of
original power, as genius is deprived of its noblest fields, will be
serious offsets to the material development of life . . . even physical conditions will be worse, as cities grow upon the world, and
as the field of adventure in unsettled regions is closed."[41] Pearson's forecast was in essence an elaboration of the classical thesis
of ultimate progress to a stationary condition, and he even used
familiar language in his projection. He said:

Unless we can assume, what is most unlikely, that the struggle for
existence will become less and less severe as numbers multiply and
the earth fills up, we must suppose that countries in the Temperate
Zone at least will gradually approximate more and more to the
stationary state.[42]

But Pearson expected as an additional disaster that highly developed whites would suffer domination by "inferior" colored races
and mankind would slip backward to a lower evolutionary stage
—"since it has become impossible to deny inferior races the protection of the law in civilised communities, they are bound to increase faster than the privileged part of the nation. The case of
the Jews in Russia is peculiarly instructive, because they were a
mere fraction of the population when Lithuania and Poland
were first incorporated, and are now numerous enough to appear

    39. Colored races outside the temperate zone "though they may in parts accept
the white man as a conqueror and organiser, will gradually become too strong
and unwieldy for him to control, or if they retain him, will do it only with the
condition that he assimilates himself to the inferior race." *National Life and
Character: A Forecast* (2nd ed.; London, 1894), p. 68.
    40. *Ibid.*, p. 1.
    41. *Ibid.*, p. 28.
    42. *Ibid.*, p. 342.

a danger to the Empire."[43] Western humanitarians, Pearson observed, were "the blind instruments of fate for multiplying the races that are now our subjects, and will one day be our rivals. We carry the sanitary science and the engineering skill of Europe into the East."[44]

Pearson claimed that even if social decay did not come about through racial deterioration, humanity was doomed nevertheless because of a propensity to misguided interference with the internal selection process. From experience in Victorian state government, he described how the tendency of contemporary society was to preserve its unfit members. Altruism of the strong and selfish use of political power by the weak combined to check the process of selective race improvement. He elaborated:

To some it has seemed that the struggle for existence, which the English theory of unlimited competition involves, is unutterably brutal, and that the survival of the fittest in industrial war means the extinction of all who are weak, of all who have other interests than gain, of all who are scrupulous. It is not the purpose of this argument to consider whether there is any truth in this point of view. All that is contended is, that if anything like the democratic programme of the day comes to be realised; if every man, weak or strong, skilled or unskilled, is assured work on fairly equal terms; if the hours of labour are limited; if the State takes the employment of labour more and more into its own hands, buying up lands and factories and mines, the change will practically be as great as that which has transformed serfs or slaves all over the world into free labourers.

It will also be a change that will reproduce many conditions of primitive society and conditions that we associate with inferior races.[45]

Pearson's pessimistic forecast of social evolution was accepted readily in Britain and America during the depressed 1890's, and his book constituted the first instance after Hearn of influence outside the colonies by an Australian evolutionist.[46] Pearson's merit

43. *Ibid.*, p. 85.
44. *Ibid.*, p. 88.
45. *Ibid.*, p. 112.
46. Richard Hofstadter, *op. cit.*, pp. 185–86; review by A. C. Lyall, *Nineteenth Century*, XXXIII (1893), 892–96; and J. M. Tregenza, *The Life and Work of C. H. Pearson 1830–1894*, Thesis Submitted for the degree of Doctor of Philosophy in the Australian National University, 1959, p. 503.

was viewed by critics as in large part a healthy and realistic antidote to a succession of overoptimistic predecessors. As one American reviewer remarked: "There is a homely proverb to the effect that a long succession of dainties makes brown bread taste good."[47]

Reports of discussions at meetings of the Australian Economic Association in Sydney indicate that evolutionary ideas found adherents among conservatives in New South Wales as well as in Victoria. Andrew Garran, journalist and politician, asserted that in human development the struggle for survival occurred at the economic level and that substantial capital accumulation was prima facie evidence of fitness. He examined the history of primitive man and concluded: "When the test of the survival of the fittest comes, the tribe that has most saved and that has best invested its surplus will show to the most advantage."[48] H. A. Ellis agreed with the crude social evolution thesis, but he suggested that knowledge of the struggle for survival might permit its amelioration.[49] R. A. Woodthorpe, discouraged by developments both in deductive and historical approaches to economics, called for renewed attempts to employ the lessons of natural science in analysis of economic evolution. "The growth of the Biological sciences and the change in historic methods have impressed upon our minds two facts: that human nature is not a fixed product, and that institutions are in a state of incessant change. Economics, as the science which deals with the economic activities of man, must study carefully phenomena which are not merely a complex but are vitally interconnected."[50] William McMillan, an influential member of the New South Wales Legislative Council, "held firmly" the principle that "all channels of industry" should be "left free in the struggle of capital, brains, labour, thrift," and that "the State" should be "confined as much as possible to the duties of the policeman and the sanitary inspector."[51]

47. C. H. Lincoln in *Annals of the American Academy of Political and Social Science*, V (1894–95), 140.
48. Andrew Garran, "The Genesis of Capital," *Australian Economist*, II (1890–93), 46.
49. H. A. Ellis, "The Theory of Malthus," *ibid.*, pp. 38–41.
50. R. A. Woodthorpe, "The Philosophical Basis of Economics," *ibid.*, p. 155.
51. W. McMillan, "The Services of the State," *ibid.*, IV (1894–97), 575.

W. H. Chard reported confidently just before the demise of the Association that "the law of evolution forces some kind of progress upon us."[52]

Adaptation to Radicalism

A new and radically different interpretation of evolution theory became evident in the colonies during the late 1880's and 1890's, and was illustrated clearly in the proceedings of the Australian Economic Association. Appeals to biological analogy no longer concluded necessarily with exhortations to doctrinaire acceptance of governmental impotence. For example, in 1890 Professor Walter Scott of Sydney University and J. Percy Creed both objected vigorously to Garran's evolutionary justification of laissez faire. Scott argued that no conclusive argument for economic non-intervention could be derived from evolution theory, and that in fact optimum community growth seemed to require collective action for the "public good."[53] Creed maintained that although capital might have passed naturally to the most able members of primitive tribes, inheritance and not physical or mental fitness had become the critical factor in determining contemporary economic performance.[54] Some Association members attempted to combine elements of Marxian dialectic with evolutionary theories taken from Darwin and Spencer. For example, J. P. Morice assured a somewhat hostile audience that "the course of evolution" would ultimately "bring about thorough national collectivism by the spontaneous working of economic forces."[55] Thomas Roseby, a Christian-socialist clergyman, rejected unmodified Spencerian theory as morally unsatisfactory and based on an erroneous premise that human behavior was identical with that of other animals. He said that Spencer's "philosophy leaves us still under the old brutal laws of force and guile. The race is to the swift and the

52. W. H. Chard, "Future Economic Progress," *ibid.*, V (1898), 58.
53. W. Scott, "Notes on Dr. Garran's Paper, 'The Genesis of Capital,'" *ibid.*, II (1890–93), 60–61.
54. J. Percy Creed, "A Criticism of 'The Genesis of Capital,'" *ibid.*, pp. 67–68.
55. J. P. Morice, "Surplus Labour," *ibid.*, p. 272.

battle to the strong. . . . There are those of us who are profoundly dissatisfied alike with this philosophy and with its economic results."[56] Roseby suggested that Australians could
discover more appropriate policy principles from Plato than from
Spencer. "To read the ideal of the state as contained, e.g., in the
Crito of Plato, and then to read Herbert Spencer's idea of the
state is like passing from a palace into an aboriginal gunyah."[57]
Despite spirited opposition from old-line evolutionists, Roseby
reiterated on several occasions his conviction that "the *dicta* of
Herbert Spencer" had not "settled our social questions for us
for ever."[58]

The reaction of opponents of doctrinaire laissez faire to social
applications of biological theory was at first rejection to be followed later by a gradual and brilliant assimilation with their own
arguments.[59] Radical critics of social Darwinism became for a
time almost as vocal as conservative advocates. An article by
Charles Fairfield in the *Melbourne Review* brought forth a scathing reply from William Webster, who argued that even if evolution led to or was affected by a strong state, progress under
socialism still could bring increases in democracy and in material
well-being. Webster's attack was more on moral than on economic
grounds. He wrote:

Mr. Fairfield's doctrine, in short is that might is right; always has
been right; and that there never has been, and never will be, any other
than might. This, he further contends, is the "scientific" doctrine; the
sole sacred and scientific right to property is might; and evolution, he
prophesies, "shall reinstate primitive methods of getting and holding
property." Few getters or holders of property, we venture to say, are
prepared to accept and avow this doctrine, no matter how skillfully

56. Thomas Roseby, "Is There any Social Question?," *ibid.*, IV (1894–97), 466.
57. *Ibid.*, p. 467.
58. Thomas Roseby, "Remarks on W. McMillan's 'The Services of the State,'"
ibid., p. 595; and for comments by opponents, *ibid.*, pp. 484 and 522–25.
59. Critiques of social evolutionary theory were anticipated in part as early as
the 1850's by Henry Parkes' newspaper, the Sydney *Empire*, which proclaimed in
1851 that wealthy colonists should never be excessively confident of their own
particular fitness in the struggle for survival. " 'The race is not always to the swift,
nor the battle to the strong,' truly; and the virtuous and hard-striving have gone
down with sorrow and grey hairs to the grave, in New South Wales as well as in
old countries. . . . " "The Suicidal Measures of our Wealthier Classes," *Empire*,
I (1851), No. 59, p. 230.

it may be couched in and entrenched behind pseudo-scientific terminology. . . .[60]

J. H. Barrows replied to an evolutionist statement of Edward Langton by saying that divine law superseded biological theory and dictated obligations of the state to individuals. He insisted: "No government has the least claim to the respect or loyalty of the people which does not seek to promote in every way the happiness and welfare of all classes of the people."[61] A. J. Ogilvy in Hobart complained that economic liberals offered neither convincing explanations of contemporary worker distress nor adequate solutions. He said:

The Economist and the Statesman alike admit that the labourer's toil is long and his pay poor, but declare that the Government cannot help him. Some say that the remedy is in his own hand, as wages are a matter of free contract, and it is his own business to insist on better terms . . . others, again, say that it is the result of an iron law of nature for which there is no remedy, poverty being the necessary lot of the unfit and the superfluous in the struggle for existence. . . .[62]

Henry Gyles Turner's paper on social evolution to the Bankers' Institute of Australasia raised a storm of protest. A Bendigo banker considered Turner's recommendations barbaric, and the radical Melbourne *Age* complained that Turner "bases his conclusions on the logic of pagen philosophy—of the survival of the fittest, the fittest being always those who are most capable of suppressing the others."[63]

George Lacy, a British journalist who spent much of his life in Australia and New Zealand including three years of "active participation in public affairs in Sydney," published in 1888 a monumental indictment of "political economy" in general, and of Herbert Spencer in particular. His book, entitled *Liberty and Law*, was dedicated to a former minister for lands in New South Wales. Lacy set out first to prove that laissez faire was an im-

60. "Property in Land," *Melbourne Review*, IX (1884), 404.
61. J. H. Barrows, "The Obligations of Modern Society to its Members," *Bankers' Magazine and Journal of the Bankers' Institute of Australasia*, VIII (1894–95), 168–69.
62. A. J. O., *Labour v. Capital* (Hobart, 1895), p. 3.
63. "The Treatment of Paupers and Criminals," *Bankers' Magazine and Journal of the Bankers' Institute of Australasia*, XII (1898–99), 684–703.

proper policy interpretation of evolutionary theory. He argued that a complex system of restraining laws and positive economic functions of government were themselves products of evolution and were, therefore, more "natural" than a return to economic anarchy.

If the customary laws of the primitive man are natural and commendable, why are the "positive" laws of the civilised man opposed to natural processes, and therefore to be denounced? There is absolutely no answer to this question, except on the assumption that evolution ceases when civilisation begins.

But how can such a proposition as this be for an instant maintained? If evolution be a fact, then the genesis and development of man's faculties must as surely be a part of it as the development of his physical form . . . if man's faculties are developed in the same way as all other phenomena, then surely, in the nature of things, all the results from the exercise of those faculties must be a manifestation of evolution, as much as the development of the faculties themselves.[64]

Lacy insisted that a fair and beneficent evolutionary struggle was not possible unless a strong state controlled the avaricious propensities of human beings. "The question of the survival of the fittest cannot arise so long as wealth is inherited; or so long as capital absorbs all profit."[65] He pointed to Australasia for examples of the satisfactory results which could follow enlightened co-operative action. "Most men, if they once get the opportunity, are capable of far greater things than they can effect when bound down by the chains that free competition lays upon them. Large numbers attain to eminence in the colonies who would in the old country have remained in the positions of mere wage-earners. . . ."[66]

During the late years of the century, radical collectivists joined conservative defenders of economic individualism in a remarkable use of evolutionary theory to support their own conflicting economic policies. In part this development reflected adherence by colonial labor intellectuals to socialist writers who

64. George Lacy, *Liberty and Law* (London, 1888), pp. 86–87.
65. *Ibid.*, p. 176.
66. *Ibid.*, p. 175.

had come to accept evolution as a process, particularly Marx. But also it followed naturally from recognition that analysis of social development and economic change did not lead inevitably to a single set of policy conclusions.[67] For example, D. M. Charleston, a member of the Legislative Council of South Australia, pointed out that study of "the laws of evolution" revealed clearly the need for an active state in the economy. He accepted part of the Marxian dialectic and agreed that contemporary capitalism contained within itself the seeds of its own destruction, but he denied the inevitable demise of the capitalist system. Charleston claimed that the free-price economy could be preserved indefinitely if basic inequalities and contradictions were removed through timely reforms. He said: "The power given at present to a few through land monopoly and control of capital is opposed to such sound basic economic principles. But justice and equity are the only sure foundations upon which to build society; all others bear in themselves the germs of decay which sooner or later must develop."[68]

Adaptation of evolutionary theory to the defense of radicalism was illustrated well from the middle of the 1880's in contributions to the Sydney *Bulletin,* one of the most influential journals of the period. Writers in this periodical accepted principles of biological evolution as valid, but interpreted the struggle for survival as supplying adequate reason for benevolent state intervention in an economy and for opposition to laissez faire.[69] *Bulletin* authors rejected the beautiful simplicity of selection by fitness and described instead the brutality, waste, and imperfec-

67. The ideas of pioneer Australian labor leaders are discussed in Bruce E. Mansfield, "The Socialism of William E. Morris: England and Australia," *Historical Studies Australia and New Zealand,* VII (1955–57), 271–90; and P. J. O'Farrell, "The Australian Socialist League and the Labour Movement. 1887–1891," *ibid.,* VIII (1957–59), 152–65. For Marx's views on evolution see Henry K. Grossman, "The Evolutionist Revolt Against Classical Economics," *Journal of Political Economy,* LI (1943), 381–96, and 506–22, and reprinted in part in Joseph J. Spengler and William R. Allen, *Essays in Economic Thought* (Chicago, 1960), pp. 500–524.
68. "Final Report of the Select Committee of the Legislative Council on the Unemployed Problem; together with Minutes of Proceedings and Appendices," *Parliamentary Papers of South Australia,* 1894, p. 25.
69. For example, "The Coming Revolution," *Bulletin,* IX (1888), No. 445, p. 4.

344 Theory and Policy

tions of economic anarchy. One contributor in 1888 compared the writings of Darwin and Spencer with those of Marx, Carlyle, and Gronlund, and he concluded regretfully:

It is almost universally assumed by the sort of political economy which is taught in universities and believed in by the powers that be, that the chief and distinguishing glory of the present era of industrialism is the lovely theory of competition, by which it is unctiously announced the best man always fills the best place. The terrible waste and loss to humanity of splendid energy and cultivated talent, which is worn away in the hideous attrition of competition, is never mentioned, or only with a sort of impatience, as one of those trivial concomitants of progress hardly worth considering in our magnificent and highly-developed civilisation.[70]

The *Bulletin* greeted enthusiastically a suggestion made by Thomas Huxley that the struggle for existence had progressed from jungle warfare among individuals to a series of contests between nations and races.[71] The journal announced that Huxley's position justified once and for all aggressive tariff protection and immigration restrictions, particularly against the Chinese—referred to as "Chows." Australians, it insisted, should not shirk the challenge of an inferior race by adopting laissez faire. "Let us take up the gage thrown down by Istar, and instead of figuring at the cannibal repast, trussed and roasted on a dish, larded and ready for filling the maws of our rivals, let us sit down amongst the guests—but in the place of honour, with an appetite sharpened by the struggle for existence. . . ."[72] The *Bulletin* adopted Huxley's favorite biological analogies between the human body and the body politic to justify public welfare measures. The labor movement was pictured as a healing force in society working always against the virulent "infections" of selfish capitalists and inferior races. One writer explained:

the white blood-corpuscle, the minute cell of protoplasm which floats in the vital fluid of man, has as great or greater, a battle for existence,

70. "The Brutality of Competition," *Bulletin*, VIII (1888), No. 415, p. 4; and similar statements in "Organisations of the Discontented," *ibid.*, XI (1890), No. 599, p. 6 and No. 565, pp. 4–5.
71. T. H. Huxley, "The Struggle for Existence: a Program," *Nineteenth Century*, XXIII (1888), 161–80.
72. "Protection—a National Necessity," *Bulletin*, IX (1888), No. 433, p. 4.

as the lordly creature through whose veins it pulses life. The deadly bacteria are ever at hand, and protection and free trade, land nationalisation and universal suffrage, cruel battle and hideous strife, are going on incessantly. All the fierce problems that rack the social organism are working out their evolution in a single drop of blood.[73]

The *Bulletin* did not lose interest in the social significance of evolution theory as it did in a variety of panaceas such as the single tax, and as late as 1894, readers were still being advised to examine carefully biological literature. The editor remarked:

The development of the theory of evolution, that grand conception which unites all phenomena in one splendid synthesis under uniform law, remains the most attractive feature of contemporary science. From year to year the hypothesis is altered in its details, but its general truth becomes always clearer, and those who now reject it do so only by impugning the quality of their intellect. It is not as if there were rival theories of defensible validity. All the facts point one way. For creation or emanation there are assumptions and presumptions innumerable, but not a vestige of ponderable proof. For evolution there is all the proof that is. Its chain of evidence may not be complete; the links that are wanting have probably been lost for ever; but sufficient remain to amply justify the general judgment of scientists.[74]

The *Bulletin* recommended careful perusal of works by Spencer and in particular of C. H. Pearson's *National Life and Character* ("a remarkably able book"). To one reader who wished immediate revolutionary reform the editor replied: "Everything is a matter of evolution: we must go step by step, add line upon line."[75]

The Lasting Impact of Evolution Theory

By the 1890's and during the early years of the twentieth century, Australians on the right and on the left advocated sharply conflicting social policies using arguments which made serious appeals to different interpretations of the same evolutionary theory. Doctrinaire defenders of laissez faire continued to in-

73. "The Verdict of the Microscopes," *Bulletin*, IX (1888), No. 436, p. 4.
74. "Contemporary Science," *Bulletin*, XIV (1894), No. 764, inside cover.
75. "Things as they are," *Bulletin*, XVI (1895), No. 798, p. 6.

sist that economic struggle and the selection process should never be inhibited by government action. At the same time proponents of a strong and beneficent state maintained that national development was an organic process which required direction and control. In this century open debate subsided, partly from boredom and partly from disillusionment with all forms of doctrine. There is considerable evidence, however, that evolution theory had lasting impact.

After the internal strife and depression of the 1890's only the most rigid advocate of laissez faire could continue to glorify unmitigated evolutionary struggle. A few such advocates remained, however, particularly among pastoralists and unbending opponents of all government restrictions. For example, during the labor struggles of the 1890's, Edmund Mitchell, a spokesman for squatter opposition to a shearers' union, condemned worker organization on the ground that economic progress could come only with freedom of contract and with competition in the labor market. He concluded: "We live in a world of evolution" not revolution.[76] Max Hirsch, an indefatigable free-trader, assured the Australasian Association for the Advancement of Science in 1909 that social justice and human improvement could be achieved only through an uninhibited free market mechanism. He said:

> The admitted object of every action of the State being general happiness, it follows that the State must abstain from any action which disturbs the relation between efficiency and reward. It must neither increase the reward of the more capable at the expense of the less capable, nor must it increase the reward of the latter at the expense of the former, i. e., it must not confer special privileges on any individual.[77]

Interest increased after the 1890's in use of evolution theory for justification of a strong state in Australia. Supporters of land reform, government banking, tariffs, and wage arbitration denied that humans should be left unrestricted to pursue their personal

76. Edmund Mitchell, *The Labour Question in Australia* (Melbourne, 1892), *passim.*
77. "The Limit of State Action," *Report of the Twelfth Meeting of the Australasian Association for the Advancement of Science held at Brisbane, 1910*, p. 530.

self-interest. Mankind, they argued, could alter and improve development. Collectivist evolutionists often were eclectic in their endorsement of theory. For example, one Queensland socialist in the 1890's professed admiration for both Darwin and Spencer but explained in Marxian terms that socialism was the natural sequence to capitalism in the evolutionary process. Wise government, he added, would assist this development.

> Socialism is not a paper constitution; it is not proposed to establish it forthwith; it is an evolutionary movement, going on whether we will or no. We may, indeed, by discovering its tendencies, put ourselves in harmony with it, and so accelerate its progress; or by ignorance, negligence, indifference, and willful opposition we may retard it; but stop it we cannot.[78]

Australians of less radical beliefs also accepted evolution theory while rejecting social Darwinism. Alfred Deakin, an early convert to Spencer, did not continue long an advocate of laissez faire on evolutionary or any other grounds. He explained: "My scruples as to state interference easily vanished and gradually I became satisfied that fiscal interference in the interest of the working classes and their industries was justifiable and necessary."[79] Deakin condemned scathingly a denunciation by Charles Fairfield of "State Socialism in the Antipodes" published in a collection of essays introduced by Spencer.[80] Deakin's early enthusiasm for and subsequent conversion to collectivism were repeated by the labor leader W. A. Holman.[81]

William Morris Hughes, prime minister during World War I, denied explicitly laissez faire conclusions of social Darwinism, but he employed evolutionist theory to justify state activity.[82]

78. *Religion, Science, and Socialism* (Leaflets for the People No. II, Brisbane, 1892), p. 12.
79. Alfred Deakin, *The Crisis in Victorian Politics, 1879–1881: A Personal Retrospect*, edited by J. A. La Nauze and R. M. Crawford (Melbourne, 1957), pp. 5–6.
80. Charles Fairfield, "State Socialism in the Antipodes," in Thomas Mackay, ed., *A Plea for Liberty* (London, 1891); and Alfred Deakin, "A Fair Field and No Favour," *Australasian Critic*, 1891.
81. H. V. Evatt, *op. cit.,* p. 9.
82. As early as the 1890's Hughes was active in the intellectual ferment which preceded formation of a New South Wales labor party. See L. F. Fitzhardinge, "W. M. Hughes in New South Wales Politics, 1890–1900," *Royal Australian Historical Society Journal and Proceedings*, XXXVII (1951), 145–68.

Hughes believed that society was a developing organism which required extensive government interference in its more advancd stages. He explained:

The sphere of state activity is not definite and immutable. On the contrary, it is ever changing, and in modern society ever extending. Acts permitted in primitive communities without restraint are in a more advanced state of civilisation subject to the most rigid regulations, or not allowed at all. . . .

The modern State, considered as an organism, exhibits those marks which invariably accompany higher development. It responds more readily to stimuli, it specialises functions, and it has evolved new organs, or, what is the same thing, rudimentary organs have developed until they perform functions entirely new, or formerly very imperfectly performed by the individual.[83]

Hughes regarded an active government, protecting and assisting individuals, as a legitimate luxury of mature society. Laissez faire and the struggle for survival were necessary and appropriate only for primitive and economically undeveloped peoples whose resources were in desperately short supply. Selection and reward in modern economies, he argued, should be based on more humane criteria than mere brute strength or business shrewdness.

Competition, perhaps, is the primary law of life, but co-operation is certainly that of society. Amongst primitive communities the State generally protects the individual but slightly. With civilisation the restraint of the individual for the benefit of the community becomes more marked. Life and property are protected from the operations of the strong and unscrupulous. The weaker individuals by co-operation prevent the stronger from exercising their strength against the rest of the community. . . .

As for the law of the "survival of the fittest," in one sense civilisation itself is an interfgrence with the operation of this principle. Every law is such an interference, as is every custom and every act which restrains the exercise of mere brute strength or cunning. Society is a protest against it. No form of government known to men tolerates it, unless it be that negation of government—anarchy.[84]

In 1911 Hughes used his organic theory of the state in an appeal for a constitutional amendment which would legalize extended

83. W. M. Hughes, "The Limits of State Interference," *Report of the Eleventh Meeting of the Australasian Association for the Advancement of Science held at Adelaide, 1907*, pp. 623–24.
84. *Ibid.*, pp. 627 and 631.

economic functions of the federal government.[85] This interpretation of evolutionary principles by Hughes was very different from the statements of thirty years earlier by Rusden and Turner. During the twentieth century, although excitement diminished over specific application of biological theory to social development, the influence of evolutionary thought remained evident in discussions of public policy. For example, in 1910, George Knibbs, the Commonwealth Statistician, mindful perhaps of criticism on evolutionary grounds which had greeted plans for welfare measures in the past, took pains to elaborate an organic theory of the state before proposing a scheme for social insurance. In the tradition of Huxley and the *Bulletin* he cited Lassalle and Fichte to prove that the health and preservation of every individual were necessary in the struggle for greatness between nations. In his proposal he minimized appeals to such Benthamite ends as the lessening of human suffering and stressed rather the relevance of public health to national security.

This notion of solidarity, viz. that the strong must carry the weak, is regarded as essential to a favorable development of the nation, and it is recognised that the national welfare requires sacrifices to be made by those able to make them, for the well-being of its weaker elements. In other words, it is required that, in order to advance the prosperity of a nation as a whole, and to conserve its vital forces, it is better that a misfortune falling on an individual should be distributed and borne lightly by the whole community, rather than that the individual should be crushed by the weight of his own misfortune. And although the results of an efficient system of social insurance must necessarily be philanthropic in their effect in individual cases, yet the basic principles of such a system are neither philanthropic nor individualistic in their nature, but aim at the general betterment of the community and at the proper guidance of national destiny.[86]

Knibbs was not alone among statisticians in his view of society as an evolving organism. Also, in 1910, E. M. Moors, assistant professor at the University of Sydney, prescribed a pension program as necessary medicine for the social malady of unemployment. He concluded: "It is becoming more and more widely

85. H. V. Evatt, *op. cit.*, p. 265.
86. "Social Insurance, Report by the Commonwealth Statistician, G. H. Knibbs," *Parliamentary Papers of the Commonwealth of Australia*, 1910, pp. 11–12, reviewed favorably in *American Economic Review*, II (1912), 939.

recognized that a community or a nation is an organism—a unit in itself—that the nation as a unit suffers from diseases of the body politic, even as every individual suffers from his particular individual ills."[87]

C. H. Wickens, Knibbs' successor as Commonwealth Statistician, subscribed also to a biological theory of social growth. He claimed that "the community may be said to be a living organism continuously growing and adapting itself to its environment, the human units corresponding to the cells of which the microscopists tell us that living bodies are composed."[88] Wickens used his organic theory to justify a restrained immigration policy. "As an organism we can satisfactorily grow only by absorption, not by mere accretion, and in any measure taken to stimulate growth much more attention needs to be devoted to the nature of this wonderful organism than is usually paid by those whose main advice is to 'get large quick.' "[89]

After the novelty of social evolution theory diminished and its ambiguous implications became clear, the topic was seldom discussed at length on its own. However, the underlying principles had become sufficiently familiar for their influence on social policy discussions to remain powerful. Three final examples may illustrate the continuing impact on both collectivist and individualist thinking. R. F. Irvine, Professor of Economics at Sydney University, regarded evolutionary evidence as conclusive proof of the need for an aggressive and strong government which would foster "the interaction of individuals and groups of individuals." He claimed that "the collective will expressed in legislation is just as natural as these other social forces and may be among the most powerful factors in progress. It may, of course, in certain forms be destructive of progress, but so may any other social force or influence."[90] W. Jethro Brown, an arbitration court judge, employed

87. E. M. Moors, "Pension Funds," *Report of the Fourteenth Meeting of the Australasian Association for the Advancement of Science held at Melbourne, 1913*, p. 506.

88. C. H. Wickens, "Australian Population: its Nature and Growth," in P. D. Phillips and G. L. Wood, eds., *The Peopling of Australia* (Melbourne, 1928), p. 66.

89. *Ibid.*, p. 67.

90. R. F. Irvine, *The Place of the Social Sciences in a Modern University* (Sydney, 1914), p. 15.

evolution theory during the 1920's in defense of government-controlled eugenic breeding. He said: "I do not suggest that a scientist should go around with an axe and a bath, smashing half the men and drowning half the women. Such loose measures might attain good results. But, no, that sort of thing is not done in polite society."[91] Brown appealed for "public authority of the right to marry" and "segregation or sterilization of obviously defective types." During the depths of depression in 1932, F. W. Eggleston, diplomat, politician, and a graduate of the University of Melbourne, came to an opposite conclusion from that reached by Irvine and Brown. He wrote: "Our study of the structure of society shows the obstacle to planning as a form of progress, and gives no hospitality to the idea that the method of evolution can be changed to a saltatory progression. Indeed, the changes in pattern of the social structure all point in the opposite direction."[92] Despite the continuing conflict of opinions illustrated here, it is evident that the influence of evolution theory remained strong.

Conclusion

The theory of biological evolution was viewed as one of the most startling discoveries of the Victorian age in Australia as in the rest of the world. Supposed implications of evolution theory for social policy became clear first to colonial conservatives. They argued that human improvement had occurred in the past through beneficial struggle wherein the fittest alone had survived. Intervention by the state with the natural growth process of an economy, they concluded, could lead only to stagnation and race deterioration. Radical collectivists replied with counter claims that societies and not individuals were the crucial developing organisms. They insisted that primary responsibility of government, as custodian of the community wisdom and power, was to regulate relations between citizens and to seek with every available means

91. W. Jethro Brown, "Economic Welfare and Racial Vitality," *Economic Record*, III (1927), 27.
92. F. W. Eggleston, *State Socialism in Victoria* (London, 1932), p. 340.

the highest possible national destiny. Evolution theory was used effectively by collectivists to defend the broad program of social experimentation undertaken in the colonies and continued after federation.

To sophisticated observers in all countries it became apparent quickly that simple analogies between biological and social phenomena were basically invalid and could be manipulated for support of almost any policy position. Nevertheless the plausibility of the arguments remained and their impact cannot be denied.

· 11 ·

Labor and the Economy

Classical economists had little practical advice to offer colonists on the subject of functional income distribution. The tautological wages-fund doctrine, taken from Smith and perfected by Ricardo and John Stuart Mill, shed little light on the determination of wages' share. It did, however, highlight the dependence of labor upon the size of capital stock and led to frequent formulation in the colonies of a "doctrine of co-operation" which enjoined workers always to assist rather than impede their employers. A second, and very different, interpretation of classical distribution theory was that national product could be attributed exclusively, both directly and indirectly through capital as embodied labor, to the efforts of workers. Radical thinkers in Australia accepted this latter doctrine happily as justification for measures of extensive social reform, either through the Marxian revolutionary process or through legislative action. Failure of most Australians to appreciate or to accept the marginal productivity theories of functional income distribution developed in Europe and America before 1900 may explain in part their considerable enthusiasm for and faith in schemes for government regulation of wages. Arbitration courts and wages boards were justified usually by assertions similar to those of Mill and his disciples that although laws of production were "natural," distribution of the national output could be regulated with impunity by the collective will of the people. Not until after World War I did university economists proclaim loudly in Australia the Marshallian and Clarkian objections to wage-price control and point out that distortion of the competitive markets for productive factors might cause resource misallocation and a diminution of total national income.

In this chapter these questions of the place of labor in the economic process are examined in separate sections.

The Doctrine of Co-operation

Writers on economic matters in the Australian colonies during the first half of the nineteenth century, whether authoritarian or liberal in outlook, viewed labor as similar in character to other productive factors. Income of workers, they argued, was and ought to be determined by market forces, and could be altered only by changes in the demand for and supply of labor services. For example, W. C. Wentworth wrote in 1819—"labour, like merchandize, will rise and fall with the demand which may exist for it in the market where it is disposable . . . the moment it becomes the interest of the employer to give higher wages, he will do so. . . ."[1] Generally, writers in this early period were not wage-earners themselves, and they considered increasing "labor" income inimical to economic growth and sufficient justification for such measures as accelerated convict transportation and sub-sidized immigration.[2] They condemned public welfare measures in particular as invitations to idleness and dissipation.[3]

A severe depression in the 1840's aroused the first articulate opposition to callous treatment of colonial workers. Labor organizations were formed, such as the Mutual Protection Association at Sydney in 1843,[4] and one representative critic castigated thus legislators who favored wage reduction as a remedy for the emergency:

1. W. C. Wentworth, *A Statistical, Historical, and Political Description of the Colony of New South Wales, and its Dependent Settlements in Van Diemen's Land* (London, 1819), p. 107.
2. "Past, Present, and Future Position of Tasmania," *South Briton; or, Tasmanian Literary Journal*, I (1843), 25–32; "Report from the Select Committee on Immigration, with Appendix and Minutes of Evidence," *Votes and Proceedings of the Legislative Council of New South Wales*, 1843, p. 1; William Bland, *Letter to His Excellency Sir Charles Fitzroy, Governor-in-Chief of New South Wales* (Sydney, 1850), p. 9; Francis H. Nixon, *Population; or, a Plea for Victoria* (Melbourne, 1862), p. 11. See also C. M. H. Clark, *Select Documents in Australian History 1788–1850* (Sydney, 1950), pp. 174 and 412.
3. "A Short Sketch of the Origin and Progress of Poverty," *Australian Magazine* (Sydney), February, 1838, pp. 113–15.
4. Gordon Greenwood, ed., *Australia: A Social and Political History*, p. 58.

They appear to think that cheap labour is essential to public prosperity; and that because, in their individual experience, they have found cheap compulsory labour to pay well, therefore high wages are a great disadvantage to society. They forget that society is principally composed of labourers—they forget that they themselves are now the representatives, not of the few individuals who own the sheep and the lands, but of the community at large, including all who earn their livelihood with their own hands.[5]

Early attempts to form labor combinations for mutual welfare and collective bargaining brought forth horrified resistance from many colonists. A Tasmanian reviewer in 1854 deplored a work by J. R. McCulloch which implied that unions legitimately might affect the wage rate; he explained:

Combinations are unnecessary; the price of labor regulates itself and is regulated in precisely the same way that prices of other commodities are regulated; a good steady workman will always obtain a fair and sufficient return for his work, and a bad workman—no matter what the rate of wages may be—will never receive so much, while he who is by nature discontented or given to irregular habits, and society and evils generated at the beer shop will never be paid enough. Of these three classes of workmen all combinations are invariably set on foot by one or other of the last two. . . .[6]

Even Henry Parkes, a leading labor spokesman and reformer who expressed repeatedly during the 1850's and 1860's serious concern for worker well-being, at the same time abhorred any tendency toward collectivism.[7] Parkes' newspaper, the Sydney *Empire*, voiced consistently the anxiety shared by most economic liberals that worker organizations would increase monopoly in the labor market, and it warned in 1854: "There is a philosophy—a law of economy in such matters as well as in everything else,

5. "Immigration," *Weekly Register of Politics, Facts, and General Literature,* I (1843), 57.
6. *Tasmanian Athenaeum; or Journal of Science, Literature, and Art,* I (1853–54), 179.
7. See for example the reports of two legislative committees of which Parkes was chairman: "Report from the Select Committee on the Condition of the Working Classes of the Metropolis; together with the Proceedings of the Committee, Minutes of Evidence, and Appendix," *Votes and Proceedings of the Legislative Assembly of New South Wales,* 1859–60; and "Progress Report from the Select Committee on the Present State of the Colony; together with the Proceedings of the Committee, and Minutes of Evidence," *ibid.,* 1865–66.

and of this strikes are totally unobservant."[8] The newspaper continued at greater length:

The sacred law—"If any man will not work, neither should he eat"—is at the very foundation of political economy. . . .

Labour, like everything else, must have its price, which will be regulated on free-trade principles by the demand, and this in turn will be regulated by the market for productions. Much may be done in smaller matters by a friendly spirit of adjustment between the employees and the employed, and it is an extreme folly for either side to be rigid. But it is not in the power of either side to force wages up or down, without inflicting a damage on both parties, and on society, proportionate to the extent of the violence.[9]

The *Empire* cautioned against possible inflationary effects of artificial wage increases: "It is a thing which infallibly drags all other costs in its train, and the recipient of the augmented wages ceases to derive advantage."[10] The paper called for restrained immigration policy as the only legitimate safeguard against wage decline.[11] The *Empire* made clear its sympathy with the plight of the working class and its approval in principle of high wages; however, it insisted upon the inviolability of the free-market mechanism and rejected all proposals for imposed or administered prices. It concluded: "it would be easy to show that high wages in this new country stimulate rather than retard prosperity by attracting population, and then returning into the channels of commerce and trade. But, for the present, in this controversy in hand, it would be superfluous to cast political economy to the dogs."[12] In Melbourne the *Argus* newspaper, arguing in unison with the Sydney *Empire*, warned that trade unions, by interrupting the full operation of "demand and supply of labour," would lead certainly to unemployment and would injure the very workers they sought to protect.[13]

Colonial economists during the nineteenth century interpreted for their own environment the wages-fund doctrine developed in

8. "The Economy of Strikes," *Empire*, February 21, 1854, p. 4.
9. *Ibid.*
10. "Wages and their Effects," *Empire*, July 6, 1854, p. 4.
11. "The Causes of Depressed Wages," *Empire*, June 25, 1852, p. 1130.
12. "A Socialist in Sydney," *Empire*, June 1, 1853, p. 2334.
13. Selections from the *Argus* (Melbourne), November, 1860, reprinted in *Journal of the Royal Statistical Society*, XXIV (1861), 129–30.

Britain by Adam Smith and refined by John Stuart Mill and other classicists.[14] This doctrine stated that a fixed quantity of resources was destined at any time for payments to the factor "labor," and implied clearly that a single group of wage-earners could alter its own particular share only at the expense of others. The responsibility of the state was to protect all workers from the selfishness of a few, and to encourage labor to bring about an increase in income by the only practicable device, economic progress through capital accumulation. Wages-fund theorists maintained that collective bargaining distorted the wage structure without enlarging labor's share, and thereby disturbed resource allocation and reduced the necessary savings needed for growth. As one writer warned Melbourne workers in 1878: "The true interest of the labourer requires that capital should increase faster than population, for thus only can want and misery be kept in check . . . the unfortunate antagonism between the labourer and the capitalist is not only mistaken, but suicidal."[15] It was argued that all public welfare measures constituted a reduction of the wages-fund; in 1868 a typical speaker assured the Royal Society of New South Wales with citations from Mill that "actual destitution presents the only claim to relief."[16]

The views of colonial observers toward the chances of amicable relations between all productive factors remained generally optimistic until late in the nineteenth century. The environment of an empty new continent promised ample and increasing returns for all residents without the need for pressure to change distributive shares. Workers were assured that conflict over immediate income distribution would jeopardize improvement in future production and might prevent achievement of national greatness. The need for continuous "co-operation" among capitalists, land-

14. *The Wealth of Nations* (Modern Library Edition, New York, 1937), pp. 64–86; and J. S. Mill, *Principles of Political Economy* (4th ed.; London, 1857), I, 409–30.
15. Prideaux Selby, "Thoughts on Taxation," *Melbourne Review*, III (1878), 217.
16. Alfred Roberts, "On Pauperism in New South Wales," *Transactions of the Royal Society of New South Wales*, II (1868), 108. Similar statements were contained in a paper presented to the Melbourne Social Science Congress by J. A. Reid entitled "Poverty Among the Working Classes," and reported in the *Argus*, November 26, 1880.

owners, and laborers was the theme of numerous presentations to groups of working men. For example, W. G. Pennington told the Sydney School of Arts in 1854 that current social problems could undoubtedly be solved without struggle between classes.[17] Similarly, G. K. Holden advised members of the Sydney Mechanics' Institute in 1867 to avoid both "the false principles of Trades Unions" and "Socialism, Communism, St. Simonianism, Fourierism, Owenism, and other schemes for reaping the advantages of co-operation without recognizing those rights of property which are essential to maintain the natural stimulus of industry in each individual."[18] He explained hopefully:

First came the era of master and slave, then that of capitalist and hired servant, and now we are approaching that of partnership or co-operation,—or rather we are consummating it, for it has long since embraced the whole of the capitalist class without reference to their relative wealth as individuals,—and all that remains is for it to comprehend also the labourer in a more perfect brotherhood of industry.[19]

A premise of much economic discussion in the 1860's and 1870's was that a uniquely "just" and "equitable" division of income could be discovered by competing productive factors if only they would give the problem their sincere, unselfish, and undivided attention. David Syme expressed a widely held belief when he asserted in 1876 that: "The moral element is, indeed, absolutely essential to industry. It is the foundation on which the whole industrial system rests."[20]

Writings by renowned authorities in economics often were thrust at workers to bolster pleas for industrial "co-operation." E. C. Nowell suggested to the Royal Society of Tasmania in 1872 that widespread familiarity with political economy might bring

17. "School of Arts. Literature of Working Men. Substance of a Lecture Delivered to the Members by W. G. Pennington, Esq.," *Operative: a Journal of Progress in the Interest of the Working Classes,* October 14, 1854, pp. 12–13.
18. G. K. Holden, *An Enquiry into the New Relations between Labour and Capital Induced by Co-operative Societies, Labour Partnerships, and other Forms of Productive Industry in Which Labour is Employed on a Footing more Independent than Common Hire, with some Reference to Special Features of Colonial Industry* (Sydney, 1867), pp. 6 and 10.
19. *Ibid.,* p. 33.
20. David Syme, *Outlines of an Industrial Science* (London, 1876), p. 174.

about an era of complete social tranquility. He claimed that "A thorough, intelligent study of the principles of political economy will demonstrate that the commercial intercourse of individuals and nations is quite as much promoted by the practice of the great Law of Love as is their moral welfare."[21] Writings of John Stuart Mill and Frédéric Bastiat were considered the most effective texts for presentation to workers and were employed both negatively to show the folly of such measures as pauper relief, and positively in support of co-operative societies.[22] Writers in the Hobart *Quadrilateral*, for whom Mill was virtually the patron saint, maintained: "The co-operative system would go far to remove class differences and jealousies, and we trust to see it universally adopted before the present century closes."[23] In South Australia, William Roby Fletcher from the University of Adelaide lectured working men on the application of political economy to social problems, and lest his audience misunderstand the principle of competition, he emphasized that: "Self in relation to self is a vice, self in relation to others a virtue."[24]

In most instances, advocates of industrial co-operation viewed the working classes with ill-concealed condescension. Well-intentioned as their motives may have been, they gained little support through pronouncements such as the following by James Smith of Victoria:

If, in the goodness of Providence, and by favour of natural capacity or of special circumstances, some of us have been placed in a position in which we can say that life is sweet and pleasant to us, and that we find it abounds in intellectual enjoyments and innocuous pleasures —we wish, in all these respects, to bring the toiling masses up to our

21. E. C. Nowell, "Political Economy," *Monthly Notices of Papers and Proceedings of the Royal Society of Tasmania*, 1872, p. 13.
22. Alfred Roberts, "On Pauperism in New South Wales," *Transactions of the Royal Society of New South Wales*, II (1868), 107–20; G. K. Holden, *op. cit.*, pp. 14 and 23; and Argyle McCallum, *The Social Unrest of the Present Day and What Causes it* (Yass, n. d.), p. 2.
23. "England at the Close of 1873," *Quadrilateral*, 1874, pp. 18–19; and also "John Stuart Mill," *ibid.*, pp. 45–46.
24. W. Roby Fletcher, "An Evening's Instruction and Amusement in the Study of Political Economy," *Journal of the Adelaide Young Men's Society*, July 15, 1878, p. 5; and in the same vein, C. Proud, "Capital and Labour," *ibid.*, January 19, 1879, p. 5.

own level, and to make them participators in the *agrémens* familiar to ourselves.[25]

Proposals for industrial co-operation were rooted in the same tenets of optimistic economic liberalism as were the homestead settlement and land reform schemes of the period. Liberals believed that with appropriate legal and institutional structures in both the agricultural and industrial sectors workers would acquire a fair share of productive factors and abandon distributional conflict.[26]

Appeals for worker "co-operation," meaning both rejection of collective bargaining and organization of constructive community activity, assumed a more aggressive tone as the century progressed and as more radical reform proposals began to capture the imagination of labor. Advocates of co-operation insisted that preservation of the free-price system required collaboration rather than conflict among component units. Specific programs for co-operation were seldom presented, however, and argument was usually in terms of ethical generalities. For example, a resident of New South Wales proclaimed in 1878:

A red demon is abroad—the maniac Communism, bred out of the craze for equality of Parisian workmen, and the cravings of German mechanics ground down by the Bismarck policy. It has already infected the usually sober workmen of the United States; and its ravings have found a kindred echo among our neighbours in Victoria. . . . Capital, whether public or private, is too sensitive to live in contact with communism. Funds are abstracted and go elsewhere—work ceases—then production—finally the necessaries of life become scarce, and the buying power scarcer yet. . . .

Co-operation, not communism, will provide the true key to the workman's paradise.[27]

25. James Smith, "The Abolition of Labour," *Victorian Review*, I (1880), 361. For biographical information concerning Smith and a discussion of the complex doctrinal background of appeals for co-operation in Melbourne during the 1870's, see Henry Mayer, *Marx, Engels and Australia* (Melbourne, 1964), p. 47 and *passim*.
26. Charles H. Pearson, "On Property in Land," *Melbourne Review*, II (1877), 129–48; W. B. Worsfold, "The Rights of Labour," *Australian Economist*, I (1888–90), 200–203; W. H. Chard, "Labour and Capital," *ibid.*, II (1890–93), 104–8. See also Chapters 3 and 4 above.
27. Capricornus, "Labour and Immigration," *Australian*, I (Sydney, 1878–79), 198–99.

For some Australians the notion of co-operation had almost a religious attraction, and writings on the subject retained over the years a missionary tone. Free enterprise was regarded as a moral "good" to be obtained and state control an "evil" to be avoided. Arguments that co-operation could achieve desired ends were based more on faith than on analytical thought. Appeals to authority were customary; George Lacy, writing in Sydney, advised workers to consult publications of the English author George Holyoake "the greatest living authority on the subject," and he maintained that study of political economy, almost as of revealed truth, would provide necessary guidance for co-operative action. Lacy concluded:

Among all splendid contrivances for the more equitable distribution of material wealth, which have emanated from the human intellect, there can be no question that the discovery of the principle of Co-operation holds the first place; and yet, strange to say, it is the one above all others concerning which the greatest amount of ignorance is displayed. . . . The one thing deemed to be needful appears to be a knowledge of political economy, and as political economy has, as yet, to a very limited extent, taken cognisance of these questions, they are, in consequence, entirely neglected. And thus Communism, Socialism, Rationalism, Co-operation and Internationalism are confused together and mixed up in the most bewildering and amusing manner.[28]

Workers were assured throughout the turbulent 1880's and 1890's that co-operation was the only desirable antidote for falling wages and for technological unemployment. Trade unions, they were told, should attempt to improve the productive process and not to disrupt activity with industrial warfare. The message aimed repeatedly at labor by the middle class was that social betterment could be achieved only as a result of increase in the total economic product and not from destructive wrangling over the size of particular shares.[29] The biologist Alfred J. Taylor in

28. George Lacy, *Co-operation: the Social Equalizer, the Pacificator of all Antagonism between Capital and Labour, the Goal of all Industrial Enterprise* (Sydney, 1880), pp. 5–6; and see also George Lacy, "State Socialism, A Warning," *Australian*, V (Sydney, 1881), 92–101; and *Liberty and Law* (London, 1888).

29. See for example: F. J. Carter, "On Wages: a Reply," *Victorian Review*, II (1880), 860–63; John Ross, "Co-operation amongst the Working Classes," *Melbourne Review*, VI (1881), 39–52; Henry Copeland, *Adam's Curse and Labour-Saving Inventions* (Sydney, 1885); B. R. Wise, "Industrial Grievances in Australia," *Sydney Quarterly Magazine*, 1886, 377–84; Waldemar Bannow, *Australasia's*

Tasmania called for "wider recognition of equality and brotherhood than has yet been realised in the world's history."[30] Professor Walter Scott of the University of Sydney, joined by colleagues in the Australian Economic Association, deplored the
development of an exclusive "cash-nexus" between employers
and the employed. Influenced by Carlyle and Ruskin, these middle-class liberals yearned for restoration of dignity and creativity
in industry.[31] Even such a radical periodical as the Sydney *Bulletin* cited Carlyle and Ruskin during the 1880's in the hope that
workers, through co-operative enterprise, might experience a real
sense of participation and accomplishment.[32] Percy Wakefield, a
nephew of Edward Gibbon Wakefield, epitomized in doggerel
the aspirations of co-operationists. He wrote:

> But what is the use? There's only one plan
> To brighten for ever the lot of man—
> Co-operation—the plan I propose,
> As plain as a wart on the tip of your nose.
> "Freetrade," "Protection!" Oh, the jades!
> Let them be given to the burying trades.[33]

Advocates of co-operation speculated that the severe labor conflict which began during the late 1880's was a result of inappro-

Future: How to Shape it (Melbourne, 1890). For description of the important
part played by John Ross as a proponent of co-operation in Victoria see Henry
Mayer, *op. cit.*, pp. 51–53.
  30. Alfred J. Taylor, "Trade Unionism as a Factor in Social Evolution," *Papers
and Proceedings of the Royal Society of Tasmania*, 1892, p. 43.
  31. Walter Scott, "The Cash Nexus," *Australian Economist*, I (1888), 2–6, and
discussion by B. R. Wise, J. T. Walker, and John Plummer, *ibid.*, pp. 7–12. Writings by Carlyle and Ruskin were reprinted and cited liberally for the benefit and
guidance of workers, for example: W. H. Gresham, *Land (Tenure) Reform League
Tract No. 5* (Melbourne, 1872); E. S. Armstrong, "John Ruskin, Considered as a
Political Economist," *Sydney Quarterly Magazine*, 1889, pp. 317–31; P. J. Gandon,
"*Ecce Homo*" In *Political Economy* (Sydney, 1890), p. 2; Cinderella, *Money
versus Wealth, or the Origin of Interest Clearly Explained by a Pupil of Henry
George and John Ruskin* (Sydney, 1890); and Cinderella, *A Manual of Political
Economy for Free Men* (Sydney, 1890). Cinderella observed: "Competition *ripens*
into Co-operation as naturally as corn ripens and yet the Market remains." *Ibid.*,
p. 46.
  32. "What is Socialism?," *Bulletin*, III (1885–86), No. 146, p. 5, and No. 147, p.
9; and "The Brutality of Competition," *ibid.*, VIII (1887–88), No. 415, p. 4.
  33. Percy Wakefield, "*Justice is Freedom.*" *Fair Trade. Prologue for the Inauguration of a Fair Trade League for New South Wales* (Sydney, 1889), p. 7.
The buoyant tone maintained throughout the monumental Australian edition of
the *History of Capital and Labour in All Lands and Ages* (John Norton, ed.,
Sydney, 1888) reflects the initial optimism of the developing labor movement.

priate application of competitive economic ideas imported from and designed for the old world. H. H. Champion, an itinerant British journalist, suggested that Chartist influence, grounded in the hardships of overpopulated England at mid-century, was responsible for misguided agitation to shorten working hours in labor-short Australia.[34] Richard Teece, in his presidential address in 1892 to the Economic and Social Science and Statistics Section of the Australasian Association for the Advancement of Science, argued that recent maritime and shearer strikes were caused by erroneous expectations of unionists that they stood to gain from prolonged conflict with employers. In a new country, in contrast to an older one where already much liquid wealth had been accumulated, wage increases could come only from growth of total income and not from reductions in returns to other factors. Teece explained sadly:

the greatest difficulty in the way of harmonising the relations of labour and capital lies in the fact that labourers and capitalists have both been taught to believe that their respective interests are opposed to one another. Generation after generation has been nurtured in this fallacy, and until it is exposed there can be no hope of a reconciliation; there may be a temporary truce, but never a lasting peace.[35]

Nothing but widespread awareness among all social classes of the common interest in economic growth, Teece concluded, could make possible uninterrupted national development.

In the first place, it will tend to make labour more efficient, because the labourer will realise that he is a partner in the enterprise, and that his remuneration will tend to increase in proportion to the zeal and skill with which he applies himself to the performance of his task. In the next place, it will tend to induce the employer to provide the most efficient means to aid the labourer, to husband his strength, to make his circumstances as comfortable as possible, in order that

34. H. H. Champion, "The Origin of the Eight Hours System at the Antipodes," *Economic Journal*, II (1892), 100–108; see also John Rae, "The Eight-Hours Day in Victoria," *ibid.*, I (1891), 15–42.

35. R. Teece, "A New Theory of the Relations of Wages and Profit," *Report of the Fourth Meeting of the Australasian Association for the Advancement of Science held at Hobart*, 1892, p. 140. Similar statements of dismay over conflict between labor and capital were contained in Arthur Duckworth, "The Australian Strike, 1890," *Economic Journal*, II (1892), 425–41; and "The Broken Hill Strike," *ibid.*, III (1893), 148–54.

he may be able to utilise his efforts to the best advantage. In the third place, by persuading both capitalist and labourer that their interests are mutually dependent, and not antagonistic, it will tend to make capital more productive and labour more efficient by the union of the two forces acting in the same direction instead of in opposite directions.[36]

Industrial strife and prolonged depression during the 1890's together with rapid growth of a powerful labor movement destroyed even the most sanguine expectations of achieving quickly in the colonies a genuine spirit of co-operation and understanding between capitalists and workers. However, some hopes were sustained and "co-operation" remained as the favored alternative offered by liberals to continued conflict or drastic reform.[37] For example, praise of the medieval guild system by Sir Henry Braddon, president of the Sydney Chamber of Commerce, reflected a longing for return to an era when all productive agents had combined effectively and in harmony against consumers.[38] Middle-class support for the Workers' Educational Association after 1913 came partly in hope that laborers could be taught a more "reasonable" attitude toward employers.[39] After World War I, experiments with co-operative manufacturing and distributing enterprise and with profit-sharing mirrored earlier attempts to frustrate radical socialism by providing "practical" training in co-operation.[40] Even a few radicals continued to speak wistfully in the twentieth century of progress that might be achieved with the willing collaboration of all productive factors. Professor R. F.

36. R. Teece, *op. cit.*, p. 141.
37. B. R. Wise, "The People's Banks of Italy and Germany," *Journal of the Institute of Bankers of New South Wales*, III (1894), 357–73; William Bateman, *Australian Produce: the Best Means of Realising Thereon* (Melbourne, 1897).
38. Sir Henry Braddon, *The Guilds, A Survey of the Old Guild System, and a Comparison of some of its Features with our Conditions To-day under our Industrial Laws* (the Joseph Fisher Lecture in Commerce, Adelaide, 1925). Other post-depression appeals for co-operation were: Waldemar Bannow, *The Colony of Victoria Socially and Materially* (Melbourne, 1896); Frank C. Pulsford, *Co-operation and Co-partnership: the Way of Social Salvation* (Sydney, 1913); and H. M. Murphy, *Wages and Prices in Australia: Our Labour Laws and their Effects, also a Report on How to Prevent Strikes* (Melbourne, 1917).
39. E. M. Higgins, *David Stewart and the W. E. A.* (Sydney, 1957), *passim*.
40. B. R. Marshall, "Co-operation and Political Education," *Historical Studies Australia and New Zealand*, IV (1949–51), 257–68.

Irvine of the University of Sydney remarked in 1916: "I am not saying that the workers should not continue to be watchful of their interests. On the contrary, I believe that they cannot afford to disregard their interests for a moment; but I say emphatically that these interests require an efficient production, and this depends to a very large extent upon their own co-operation."[41]

The doctrine of co-operation gained prominence because of the apparent conflict between accepted principles of ethics and of classical political economy. Liberals who had been taught to believe on the one hand in the virtues of love and charity and on the other in the need for competitive higgling in the market place, saw a resolution of this contradiction in the ill-defined process of "co-operation." Contemporary faith in the power of reason and the characteristic optimism of a new country gave strength to the view. The doctrine survived as a powerful force until the end of the century when bitter class conflict inspired a search for concepts which would be more useful operationally and promised more immediate returns.

The Spirit of Radicalism

A tradition of rebellion against wealth and authority developed in the colonies as a result, in part, of origins and environment. Convicts and their descendants nourished bitterness toward a social system which had resorted to exile, while political extremists such as Chartists from Britain and Canadian rebels helped to articulate resentment. Many free settlers, and especially goldminers, like convicts, felt antipathy toward the old world which in their cases had been unable to provide employment and a satisfactory living standard. The large body of Irish colonists nourished a particular national and religious grudge. Both bond and free immigrants viewed with alarm any indications of development in Australia of the stratified society they had left behind,

41. R. F. Irvine, "Trade Unionism and Efficiency," in Meredith Atkinson, ed., *Trade Unionism in Australia* (Sydney, 1916), p. 34.

and when they found their local government a potent force for economic improvement, they turned naturally in this direction for amelioration and control of social change.[42]

From the first years of legislative autonomy in the 1850's, some colonial radicals suggested the desirability of fundamental social reconstruction, and they voiced complaints at an early date against monopolistic exploitation.[43] However, until the 1890's, most reformers devoted their energies to campaigns for specific alterations of the existing economic system through piecemeal changes in commercial, industrial, fiscal, immigration, monetary, and land policy. A typical colonial radical in the 1870's and 1880's appealed less for the overthrow of capitalism than for free homesteads, land taxation, immigration restriction, industrial regulation, an inheritance tax, the eight hour day, a national bank, and in some instances tariff protection.[44] Deities held sacred by early radicals were Henry George, John Stuart Mill, Herbert Spencer, Thomas Carlyle, John Ruskin, and finally Edward Bellamy who was termed by some "the prophet of the era."[45]

Bellamy's *Looking Backward* was read widely and gave strength to hopes for long-run improvement from social reform.[46] A utopian dream rather than an exhortation to revolution, Bellamy's work was received enthusiastically by pioneers of the labor movement, and was both circulated intact to union members and serialized

42. J. W. Hackett, "Social and Economic Conditions in Australia," *Journal of the Society of Arts*, LV (1907), 67–84; W. K. Hancock, *Australia* (New York, 1930), pp. 41, 63, and 71–73; and Russel Ward, "Collectivist Notions of a Nomad Tribe," *Historical Studies Australia and New Zealand*, VI (1953–55), 459–73.

43. For example, Frederick Vines, *The Cue to Prosperity: or, Our Lands, and How to Get Them* (Melbourne, 1856).

44. Sigma, *Money: How the Banks Make it Scarce and Dear!* (Melbourne, 1871); H. W. Edmunds, "Social Science," *Sydney Quarterly Magazine*, 1883, pp. 252–68; H. W. Edmunds, "Land, Labour and Capital. Salus Populi Suprema Lex," *ibid.*, 1885, pp. 37–49; A. C. Wylie, "The Relations Between Capital and Labour," *Victorian Review*, XII (1885), 369–78; David A. Andrade, *An Anarchist Plan of Campaign* (Melbourne, 1888); James Edwards, *Topics for the Development of Freedom* (Melbourne, n. d.); *The Labour Question* [Extracts from writings of G. P. Macdonnell, Henry George, and Richard T. Ely] (Melbourne, 1890); and see above chapters 1–6, and 8. Professor Henry Mayer has shown that Marxist ideas, mixed with those of Mill and others, were influential to a limited extent in Melbourne at least as early as 1872. *Marx, Engels and Australia* (Melbourne, 1964), pp. 13–23, and 147–48.

45. "Looking Backward," *Pacific Quarterly*, I (1890), 30; and Alexander W. Johnston, *The New Utopia, or Progress and Prosperity* (Sydney, 1890).

46. "Looking Backward," *Bulletin*, XI (1890), No. 521, p. 5; "Some Economic Sophisms," *ibid.*, No. 552, p. 6.

in the *Worker* newspaper.[47] The radical labor leader, William Lane in Queensland, was a tireless propagandist for Bellamy: summarizing, reprinting, and organizing study groups among workers.[48] George Reid remarked in 1905 that "during the past fifteen or twenty years some people's notions of socialism have been very much coloured by Bellamy's one little solitary 'idea' about 'equality of wages.' "[49] Bellamy's vision was as appealing to rich as to poor, and particularly so because it contained no prescription for immediate confiscation of wealth.[50]

During the late 1880's and early 1890's, significant new economic conditions affected discussion of labor's place in the economy. Whereas throughout the previous quarter century relatively steady economic growth had brought uninterrupted gains in worker income, characteristic features of this period were industrial stagnation, financial crises, and violent industrial disputes. Throughout these years of social turbulence only the most sanguine observer could view the economic future with confidence and attach great hope to piecemeal proposals for reform. In an atmosphere of depression and despondency, old radical authorities lost adherents and schemes for revolutionary social reconstruction found favor.[51] In the Sydney *Bulletin*, for example, the change in attitude was evident.[52] During 1888 writers in this

47. William G. Spence, *Australia's Awakening* (Sydney, 1909), p. 549; and Vance Palmer, *The Legend of the Nineties* (Melbourne, 1954), pp. 68–77.

48. A. St. Ledger, *Australian Socialism: an Historical Sketch of its Origin and Developments* (London, 1909), pp. 10–11, 14, 35–39.

49. *Journal of the Institute of Bankers of New South Wales*, XIV (1905), 341.

50. "A Banker," "Socialism," *Bankers' Magazine and Journal of the Bankers' Institute of Australasia*, VI (1892–93), 857–63.

51. Radical intellectual ferment during this period has been discussed in the following works: June Philipp, "Historical Revision: No. 1. 1890—The Turning Point in Labour History," *Historical Studies Australia and New Zealand*, IV (1949–51), 145–54; L. G. Churchward, "The American Influence on the Australian Labour Movement," *ibid.*, V (1951–53), 258–77; Bruce E. Mansfield, "The Socialism of William E. Morris: England and Australia," *ibid.*, VII (1955–57), 271–90; P. J. O'Farrell, "The Australian Socialist League and the Labour Movement, 1887–1891," *ibid.*, VIII (1957–59), 152–65; Gordon Greenwood, ed., *Australia: A Social and Political History* (Sydney, 1955), pp. 148–61; Vance Palmer, *op. cit.*, pp. 81–93; and H. V. Evatt, *Australian Labour Leader* (Sydney, 1945), pp. 1, 21, and 39.

52. The influence of the *Bulletin* in Australia has been discussed in Ailsa G. Thompson, "The Early History of the Bulletin," *Historical Studies Australia and New Zealand*, VI (1953–55), 121–34; and Gordon Greenwood, ed., *Australia: A Social and Political History*, p. 148.

journal predicted that "the ranks of the social army," led by such generals as Henry George, soon would triumph over their adversaries: "Every day the enemy is getting weaker and fewer."[53] By 1889, the year of George's Australian tour, the *Bulletin* had cooled considerably towards single-minded advocates of land reform, and in 1890 it designated Karl Marx's *Das Kapital* "the greatest work on social and political economy that it [the world] has yet seen."[54] Whereas in 1890 readers of the *Bulletin* were advised to consult carefully Bellamy's *Looking Backward*, in 1892 they were informed that this book was of little practical use because Bellamy "altogether failed to explain how the new order of things was to be brought about."[55] As prophets of radicalism, Bellamy and Henry George were supplanted increasingly during the 1890's by European and American socialists of a more aggressive character, and particularly by Marx, Engels, Nordau, Bax, and Gronlund.[56] The departure of William Lane for Paraguay removed the most effective exponent of Bellamy's work, and implied the failure of Bellamy's ideas. In fact, during the disastrous strike-ridden early 1890's, Bellamy's utopian dream seemed bitter irony. One disillusioned critic remarked in 1891: " 'Looking Backwards' requires that we should go to sleep till the year 2000, and sleep even for a shorter period than that is apt to be haunted with dreams."[57]

During the early years of the 1890's, when a mounting body of unemployed came to believe that they had little to gain under the existing economic system, extreme radicalism found its strongest appeal. In the absence of more plausible explanations, Marxian theories of unemployment were accepted enthusiastically. An army of idle labor was pictured as a structural feature of capitalist colonial economic development. For example, D. M. Charleston, a member of the Legislative Council of South Australia, advised

53. "The Coming Revolution," *Bulletin*, IX (1888), No. 445, p. 4.
54. A. G. Yewen, "The Single-Tax and Socialism," *Bulletin*, XI (1890), No. 522, p. 5.
55. "Looking Backward," *Bulletin*, XI (1890), No. 521, p. 5; and "Bursting the Big Estates," *ibid.*, XII (1892), No. 636, p. 6.
56. "Weighed and Found Worthy," *ibid.*, XIV (1894), No. 771, inside cover.
57. A. Gosman, *Socialism in the Light of Right Conduct and Religion* (Melbourne, 1891), p. 31; and also, Edmund Mitchell, *The Labour Question in Australia* (Melbourne, 1892).

a select committee in Marxian terms during 1894 that capitalism was engaged upon a headlong decline into overproduction and underconsumption. He said:

The demands of animal nature being more inexorable than those of the higher nature, men are compelled to bid against each other for bare subsistence. Consumption falls to the lowest point, increasing the distance between possible production and actual demand. The evil of holding unused surpluses and the locking up of the means of production grows in intensity until depression and privation reign supreme, and society, with accelerated speed, deteriorates in physique, nobility of character, ability and energy, and rapidly descends to the barbarism from which it had slowly and painfully evolved.[58]

After surveying the probable ineffectiveness of such contemporary reform proposals as land taxation and a national bank, one disconsolate rebel concluded: "The existing evils of society are too gigantic to toy with. . . . These 'remedies' are no remedies at all."[59] Attempts were made to reconcile revolutionary radicalism with opposing philosophies and institutions. The Queensland Social Democratic Federation declared unequivocally that its object was simply "State Socialism . . . whereby the whole of the natural resources, as well as the means of production and exchange of any country, shall belong to the people of that country."[60] Yet the Federation made every effort to illustrate that this objective was entirely consistent with Christianity, land reform, and restricted immigration.[61] One publication of the Federation bore a quotation from Marx on the cover and contained copious discussion of scripture within.[62]

In all probability most Australian socialists absorbed their theory secondhand from local interpreters who themselves had only vague comprehension of detailed doctrine. One contempo-

58. "Final Report of the Select Committee of the Legislative Council on the Unemployed Problem; together with Minutes of Proceedings and Appendices," *Parliamentary Papers of South Australia,* 1894, p. 23.
59. David A. Andrade, *Our Social System, and How it Affects Those Who Work for Their Living* (Melbourne, n. d.), unpaged.
60. *What is Socialism?* (Leaflets for the People, No. 1, Brisbane, n. d.), p. 3.
61. *Religion, Science, and Socialism,* and *The Catholicity of Socialism* (Leaflets for the People, No. 2 and No. 3, Brisbane, n. d.). See also H. V. Evatt, *op. cit.,* p. 37.
62. *For God and Home, Humanity and Fatherland* (Brisbane, n. d.).

rary writer recounted facetiously in the following terms a doctrinal dispute conducted with a friend.

We were discussing "Capital," not that either of us knew much about that famous work of Karl Marx, and were consequently discussing it in the abstract, not in the concrete. He had investigated the cover, I had probed further, just turned it over. "To study Marx," said he, "one requires a hard seat, a bare table, and a head swathed in wet, ice-cold towels." I don't know whether he meant the towels to keep the head from swelling, or keep down the temperature. Then I agreed with him—but I don't now. Warmth causes the blood to flow, and the brain to quicken. My experience is that nice, warm, comfortable surroundings, not elaborate, but with a degree of comfort, are most conducive to the studying of Marx's stupendous effort.[63]

A lighthearted approach to theoretical authority was not uncharacteristic of the period. Marxian influence, however, was no less significant.

By the late 1890's, after the worst years of depression had passed, the influence of revolutionary writers became blended with the more permanently appealing and moderate social critiques of Mill, Carlyle, and Ruskin.[64] Visits by prominent British labor leaders such as Sidney and Beatrice Webb and H. H. Champion, together with campaigns by less radical local spokesmen such as W. M. Hughes, W. A. Trenwith, and Henry Bournes Higgins, assisted the process of integration.[65] W. A. Holman was able to argue convincingly by 1905 that Mill was the chief inspiration for Australian radicalism and that it was "a mistake to imagine that English or Australian socialism owes much to Karl Marx or the Continental writers."[66] Socialist doctrine came to be

63. The Vag, *Random Ramblings* (Sydney, n. d.), p. 36.
64. G. V. Portus, *Happy Highways* (Melbourne, 1953), pp. 50 and 154.
65. H. H. Champion, "The Crushing Defeat of Trade Unionism in Australia," *Nineteenth Century*, XXIX (1891), 225–37; South Australian Fabian Society, *Second Annual Report of the Executive Committee*, 1893–94; L. F. Fitzhardinge, "W. M. Hughes in New South Wales Politics, 1890–1900," *Royal Australian Historical Society Journal and Proceedings*, XXXVII (1951), 145–68; Nettie Palmer, *Henry Bournes Higgins: a Memoir* (London, 1931), pp. 129–30.
66. W. A. Holman, "Is Socialism Possible? A Reply to Mr. Nash's Recent Paper," *Journal of the Institute of Bankers of New South Wales*, XIV (1905), 328–29. In a much publicized debate Holman and G. H. Reid competed to pay respect and homage to Mill. *Socialism as Defined in the Australian Labor Party's Objective and Platform: Official Report of a Public Debate in the Centenary Hall, Sydney* (Sydney, 1906), p. 41.

employed less and less to justify complete social reconstruction and more and more to support familiar and long-standing demands for land, banking, and currency reform, control of monopolies, and public welfare measures.[67] In the years that followed depression, influential labor leaders advocated moderate experimental social legislation, and particularly schemes for wages arbitration, in attempts to improve conditions of workers without introduction of overall public ownership and rigid economic control.[68] Complete public ownership of economic resources came even to be questioned as a cure for unemployment. E. W. H. Fowles informed the Australasian Association for the Advancement of Science in 1911: "State remedies may go far to reduce the undesirable classes, and indeed . . . there are many indirect means by which the class of the unemployed can be brought within comparatively easy handling, but neither in communism, nor in collectivism, or in any plan, however skillfully devised of socialism, will unemployment automatically cease."[69] Marx was revered as a prophet of the working man, but was placed side by side in some discomfort with Henry George, Alfred Russel Wallace, and even Sir Robert Peel.

Revolutionary socialist literature retained popularity in Australia long after the 1890's. In Sydney, Bertha McNamara's book-

67. For example: H. S. Taylor, *Tucker Prize Essay on the Single Tax* (Adelaide, 1892); Arthur Griffith, *The Labour Platform: an Exposition* (Sydney, 1893); Alexander W. Johnston, *Strikes, Labour Questions, and Other Economic Difficulties: a Short Treatise of Political Economy* (London, 1895); Ebenezer, *A Plea for Democracy: or the Land for the People, a Treatise on the Political and Economic Conditions of New South Wales* (Sydney, 1896); Sam. Smith, *The Vagabonds or the Bonded Vags. A Tale about Money* ("Workman" Social Reform Series, Sydney, 1894); A. J. Ogilvy, *Labour v. Capital* (Hobart, 1895); A. J. Ogilvy, *The Appreciation of Gold* (Hobart, 1897); John Law, *Imperial Credit* (Adelaide, 1899); Vida Goldstein, "Socialism of To-day—an Australian View," *Nineteenth Century*, LXII (1907), 406–16; M. D. McRae, "Some Aspects of the Origins of the Tasmanian Labour Party," *Tasmanian Historical Research Association: Papers and Proceedings*, III (1954), 21–27.
68. Discussion in the 1890's by J. C. Neild, a New South Wales legislator, of the responsibilities of a paternalistic state attracted attention. See *Report on Old Age Pensions and Charitable Relief and State Insurance in England* (Sydney, 1898); and H. V. Evatt, *op. cit.*, pp. 119, 168, and 183. A compilation of social and economic legislation from 1890 to 1909 in New South Wales is contained in: John B. Trivett, "Comparative Legislation Relating to the Industrial Classes," *Report of the Twelfth Meeting of the Australasian Association for the Advancement of Science held at Brisbane*, 1909, pp. 532–52.
69. E. W. H. Fowles, "On Unemployment," *Report of the Thirteenth Meeting of the Australasian Association for the Advancement of Science held at Sydney*, 1911, p. 469.

shop and, in Melbourne, Andrade's continued to find a steady clientele for current and classic socialist literature. Local popularizers sustained an output of theoretical regurgitations and applications of principle to domestic conditions.[70] Even after the emigration of William Lane, Queensland remained a stronghold of radicalism; as evidence of sincerity of purpose Brisbane socialists in 1919 issued a manual "to help the beginner over the first steps—that most difficult period—and lead him by easy stages to the real scientific works . . . study of which alone can fit him to take an active part in the Socialist movement in the fight to overthrow Capitalism and usher in Socialism."[71] The socialist novice in Queensland was referred particularly to works by Marx, Engels, Daniel De Leon, and the Irish nationalist James Connolly.[72] Socialist writings were imported in large quantities from Britain and from the United States, and at least one Melbourne publisher made available works by Marx and other prominent communists at special low rates.[73] Between 1905 and 1909, doctrinaire socialists in Australia were particularly well organized under the leadership of the English labor leader Tom Mann.[74] However, Mann

70. For example, W. S. McClure presented a modified Marxian economic interpretation of history to prove the inevitability of socialist revolution. *Socialism* (a paper read before the Albany Press Club "Socialist Night," Sydney, 1907). Similar accounts are Phillip J. Mulholland, *Facts of Finance: A History of the Great Error of Civilization, and the Bridge between Present-day Wage Slavery and the Perfect Civilization of the Future, as Outlined in the Labor Party's Objective* (Sydney, n. d.), and "Dogmatist," *The Materialist Conception of History, an Introduction to its Study* (Melbourne, n. d.). The labor theory of value was expounded (with diagrams) in Chas. Eyre, *The Economics of the Eight-Hours' Day* (Originally written for the International Socialist Club by the late Chas. Eyre. Now revised and brought up to date by the General Executive of the Socialist Federation of Australasia, Sydney, 1907).
71. Norman R. Freeberg, *Socialism: What is It?* (Brisbane, 1919), p. 3.
72. *Ibid.*, p. 141.
73. The following works by Marx were published in Melbourne: *Wage-Labor and Capital* (Melbourne, n. d.), *Value and Surplus Value* (Melbourne, n. d.). Importation of American socialist literature is described in L. G. Chruchward, "The American Influence on the Australian Labour Movement," *Historical Studies Australia and New Zealand*, V (1951–53), 266.
74. Tom Mann described thus in 1906 the activities of the Australian Socialist Party in Melbourne. "In June, 1905, we commenced Sunday afternoon lectures on Socialism in the Gaiety Theatre; these proved a decided success. Then, when the Queen's Hall was available for us on Sunday evenings, we commenced there too. As the summer weather came on we gave up the Gaiety and commenced out-door agitation on the Yarra Bank. . . . We commenced an Economics Class and a Speakers' Training Class, and fully 60 comrades have been engaged in the voluntary work of the Socialist advocacy indoors and out during the year. We have averaged fully ten propagandist meetings a week, or 500 meetings during

left the country after only five years; he was disillusioned finally with the limited enthusiasm that could be generated in the Antipodes for truly revolutionary goals. Socialists remained vocal during and after World War I, but met increasing opposition from critics who viewed with mounting horror the spectacle of communism in operation in the Soviet Union.[75]

Certain features of revolutionary socialist doctrine had greater permanent impact on Australian thought than did others. The suggestion that capitalism tended to generate a body of unemployed workers was noted carefully during depressions, as were the predicted progressions toward monopoly, concentration of wealth, and immiserization of the laboring class. However, most Australian socialists like co-operationists were affected to some extent by the optimism of a new country, and they could not accept wholeheartedly the inevitability of capitalist, and free market decay. They designated the social strife and depression of the 1890's as satisfactory proof of important contradictions within their economy; but they indicated by political action that they believed the structure could be reclaimed and might be reconstituted in satisfactory form by imaginative change. When R. F. Irvine of Sydney University discussed in 1914 the variety of social reforms during the previous quarter century, he emphasized the continuing influence of diverse imported doctrine. He concluded: "Our experimentation seems to me, in moments of self-criticism, less due to energy of creative thought than to a certain sporting courage in adopting ideas that other countries have hesitated to act upon, and to the general weakening—perhaps a fortunate weakening—in Australia of some of the traditional forces of social control."[76] A French observer in 1901 categorized the Australian social structure as "socialisme sans

the last twelve months." Article reprinted in *Tom Mann's Memoirs* (London, 1923), p. 205. See also, Tom Mann, "The Political and Industrial Situation in Australia," *Nineteenth Century*, LVI (1904), 475–91.

75. Concern with developments in Russia was evidenced by publication of "A Collection of Reports on Bolshevism in Russia. (Paper presented to British Parliament)," *Papers Presented to the Parliament of the Commonwealth of Australia*, 1917–18–19. A postwar restatement of Marxist principles was W. H. Emmet, *Marx's Economics and Professor Meredith Atkinson* (Sydney, 1920).

76. R. F. Irvine, *The Place of the Social Sciences in a Modern University* (Sydney, 1914), p. 8.

doctrines."[77] A more accurate description might have been "beaucoup de doctrines."

Reaction to Radicalism

Economic liberals greeted with horror the growing popularity of collectivist doctrine during the 1890's. They repeated with increasing frequency their fundamental contention that the solution to economic distress was increased private production and not redistribution or government ownership. B. R. Wise stated emphatically, although somewhat hollowly, in 1891 that the only defensible economic reforms open to government at that time were a reduction in public expenditure and legislation designed to reduce distribution costs of consumer goods. In the best liberal tradition, Wise cited for authority "John Stuart Mill—the wisest and most even-minded writer upon public affairs that the English language possesses."[78] Others viewed socialist theory as a contagion rooted in ignorance and susceptible of cure through education. As one speaker informed the Australasian Association for the Advancement of Science in 1892:

> Whatever of hopefulness there is in the outlook for the future will lie in the fuller education of the people to a perception of their real wants, and a realisation that neither from their own side nor from their opponents, will they obtain redress for evils that are entirely of their own causing, and that can only be removed by a change in their own dispositions.[79]

Liberals were willing to tolerate worker organizations—either unions or labor parties—only so long as the "natural" pattern of income distribution was not disturbed; attempts to obtain a larger wages share, they insisted, resulted inevitably in unemployment, inflation, social inequalities, and ultimate stagnation.

77. Albert Métin, *Le Socialisme Sans Doctrines* (Paris, 1901).
78. B. R. Wise, "What Parliament Can Do for Labour," *Sydney Quarterly Magazine*, 1891, p. 222.
79. Mrs. A. Morton, "The Evolution of Hostility between Capital and Labour," *Report of the Fourth Meeting of the Australasian Association for the Advancement of Science held at Hobart, 1892*, p. 553.

Traditional wages-fund doctrine was emphasized repeatedly, as for example when D. Brown observed: "no trade, or body of men, can have their share of the produce increased, either by a strike or by the award of a Board of Conciliation, without reducing the share of some other wage receiver."[80]

When collectivists became rapidly more influential during and after the crisis year 1893, their liberal opponents also became more vigorous and in some cases more extreme. Andrew Garran told the Australasian Association for the Advancement of Science in 1895 that all "systems of political economy" had been "moulded unconsciously by contemporary conditions," and he argued that Marx was merely an inevitable but transitory product of the times who had "done the most to give form to the complaint of the worker and to argue that he is exploited and robbed by his employer."[81] Garran suggested that when a truly objective system of economic analysis unrelated to any class interest was developed, interest in Marxism would wane. Others, however, were not so confident, and pictured Schäffle, Marx, and Lassalle as the established prophets of collective compulsion, sloth, and the "government stroke."[82] A member of the Australian Economic Association offered the following definition:

> What is a Socialist! One who is willing
> To fork out his penny and pocket your shilling.[83]

As depression deepened, workers were informed that their political and economic extremism was in fact a cause and not an effect of the catastrophe. Proponents of wages-fund theory reminded the public that all along they had warned that agitation

---

80. D. Brown, *Wealth and Wages in New South Wales: an Examination of the Income of the Community, its Source and its Application* (Sydney, 1891), p. 37; similar statements are contained in: John Hurst, "Trade Unions," *Australian Economist*, II (1890–93), 127–33; Andrew Garran, "Trade Unions: a Criticism," *ibid.*, 144–46; and J. F. N., "Strikes," *Sydney Quarterly Magazine*, 1887, pp. 23–30.

81. Andrew Garran, "Three Systems of Political Economy," *Report of the Sixth Meeting of the Australasian Association for the Advancement of Science held at Brisbane, 1895*, pp. 695 and 697.

82. Colin McKay Smith, "On State Socialism," *Australian Economist*, III (1893–94), 295–99; W. M'Millan, "Public Finance and the Duty of Citizens," *Journal of the Institute of Bankers of New South Wales*, II (1893), 314–25.

83. *Australian Economist*, III (1893–94), 313.

for high wages would bring unemployment.[84] Advocates of specific panaceas such as the single tax insisted that less drastic reforms than those demanded by socialists would not have destroyed confidence and jeopardized worker welfare.[85] To counteract the outpouring of socialist literature in the 1890's, selections from the writings of orthodox economists were made available in inexpensive editions.[86]

Robert Mackenzie Johnston was a notably active and articulate opponent of radical economic writing. He argued that poverty, unemployment, and depression resulted only from disproportions and immobilities in the free market economy, and he insisted that worker welfare could be improved most effectively by government planning of private activity and not through public ownership or radical distributional reform.[87] Labor organizations, Johnston asserted, were likely to discourage private capital formation upon which growth depended, and at best could only redirect a larger proportion of the total wage share to their own particular members while decreasing the amount flowing to other workers. During the attendant struggle, moreover, a cumulative rise in the general price level would probably occur; he explained:

it is possible to regulate and alter the distribution of the aggregate wealth of consumable necessaries of life, but so long as this aggregate

84. For example, C. E. S. Turner, *Completing the Ruin, Trades Unions and Communism*, Series 1. *Unemployment—How Caused*, and Series 2. *Unemployment —the Remedy* (Sydney, 1905).

85. J. Currie-Elles, "Financial Review," *Journal of the Institute of Bankers of New South Wales*, III (1894), p. 5; L. F. Heydon, "Land Nationalisation," *ibid.*, IV (1895), 423–38; Max Hirsch, *The Solidarity of Labour* (Melbourne, 1894); A. W. Johnston, *Law and Liberty* (Sydney, 1910).

86. For example, Edward Davies, *Capital: the Friend and Ally of Wage-Earners and the Mainspring of Commerce: Extracts and Notes by a Wage-Earner for More than Half a Century* (Melbourne, 1896). A critic of writings by Tom Mann wrote: "Mann's programme is that of the German Social Democrats, and it may be taken as certain that Australia is entered for the race with New Zealand, in flouting what Carlyle termed the Dismal Science of Political Economy." "Tom Mann," *Imperial Review* (c. 1903), No. 39, p. 58.

87. R. M. Johnston, "Root Matters in Social and Economic Problems . . . ," *Papers and Proceedings of the Royal Society of Tasmania*, 1889, pp. 143–204; "Root Matters in Social and Economic Problems (2nd Series)," *ibid.*, 1890, pp. 1–21; and "Observations Regarding the Production and Distribution of 'Consumable Wealth' and 'Economic Capital,' with an Inquiry into the Probable Effect of Arbitrary Regulation of 'Minimum Wage' Standards upon the 'Cost of Living,'" *Report of the Fourteenth Meeting of the Australasian Association for the Advancement of Science held at Melbourne, 1913*, pp. 454–55.

wealth fails to be increased per capita per year, Strikes cannot increase the *real wages* or the purchasing power of a day's labour of *all* wage-earners. In a word they cannot divide more than what has actually been created or produced, although the *nominal rates of wages* and *nominal prices of commodities* may both be raised to any extent without real benefit to anyone.[88]

Johnston was convinced that much radical writing and labor agitation was based on theoretical misconceptions perpetrated by economists. In particular he maintained that wealth inventories which excluded the capitalized value of labor services exaggerated the apparent economic power of land and capital. "Socialistic writers and others . . . invariably measure the distribution of the wealth created purposely for human consumption and personal satisfaction among the wage-earning classes by the proportions which the ownership of fixed or monopolised capital-producing instruments, &c., show among the people generally."[89] With this false picture of income distribution, labor leaders were led to demand a land tax and a capital levy.[90] Johnston was sympathetic with the plight of the poor and of the unemployed, and he wrote enthusiastically in support of such programs as government old-age pensions.[91] However, he opposed consistently all measures which he believed would interrupt economic development, and he was a powerful foe of the collectivist

88. R. M. Johnston, "Observations on the Influence of Strikes upon Real Wages," *Papers and Proceedings of the Royal Society of Tasmania*, 1890, p. 198. Johnston refuted effectively a critic who maintained that unions might extract a share of rent payments and profit from employers and might facilitate wage increases by improvements in productivity. A. J. Ogilvy, "Can Strikes Really Improve the Condition of the Masses?," *ibid.*, pp. 202–7; and R. M. Johnston, "General Increase of Wages Falls upon Consumers of Products, and in No Way Encroaches upon Rent or Profits of Capitalists," *ibid.*, pp. 208–31.

89. R. M. Johnston, "Consumable Wealth," *Report of the Seventh Meeting of the Australasian Association for the Advancement of Science held at Sydney, 1898*, pp. 875–76.

90. R. M. Johnston, "Observations on Current Social and Economic Problems," *Report of the Second Meeting of the Australasian Association for the Advancement of Science held at Melbourne, 1890*, pp. 120–59; "Notes on the Natural Limits to Occupation on the Land," *Papers and Proceedings of the Royal Society of Tasmania, 1892*, pp. 1–8; "Observations Regarding some Economic Aspects of the Eisenach Social Equality Programme," *ibid.*, 1903–5, pp. 125–35; "Observations Regarding Accumulated Capital Wealth," *ibid.*, 1918, pp. 1–8.

91. R. M. Johnston, "The Ethical and Economic Aspects of Old Age Pensions," *Papers and Proceedings of the Royal Society of Tasmania*, 1903–5, pp. 95–112.

spokesmen of the time. His influence was evident in both public documents and private writings in Tasmania.[92]

After the turbulent discussions of the 1890's, only a small body of academic social scientists remained as vociferous and vocal opposition to collectivist economic doctrine. Francis Anderson at Sydney University retained faith in the ability of objective analysis to reveal appropriate policies, and he saw danger for society in rigid adherence to socialist or any other doctrine. He described thus the development of socialist thought: "the scientific problem was soon lost sight of, by both Marx and his followers, in the heat of revolutionary zeal. The scientific thesis was transformed into a political dogma. The creed of collectivism was preached with the fervour, and its almost invariable accompaniment, the intolerance of the religious devotee."[93] G. V. Portus and other followers of Anderson took similar positions in opposition to doctrine, and they preached the gospel of objective social sciences in the University and in the Workers' Educational Association.[94] Professor William Mitchell at Adelaide University took pains to lecture publicly on such matters as "the rate of interest" in refutation of Marx and Henry George.[95] J. A. Gunn at Melbourne instructed his tutorial classes on finding an economic solution to the "workers' problem," and he assured his audience that the answer rested in the study of economic growth: "the question whether or not in fact too much is paid as remuneration for saving, and hence too little for working."[96] Considerable early economic and

92. "The Unemployed: Report of Select Committee, with Minutes of Proceedings, Evidence, and Appendices," *Journals and Printed Papers of the Parliament of Tasmania*, 1894; Alfred J. Taylor, "Trade Unionism as a Factor in Social Evolution," *Papers and Proceedings of the Royal Society of Tasmania*, 1892, pp. 32–44; and "Notes on the Value of Labor in Relation to the Production of Wealth: Regarded from the Standpoint of a Physicist," *Report of the Fourth Meeting of the Australasian Association for the Advancement of Science held at Hobart*, 1892, pp. 599–601.

93. Francis Anderson, *Sociology in Australia: A Plea for its Teaching* (Sydney, 1912), p. 9; and see also "Liberalism and Socialism," *Report of the Eleventh Meeting of the Australasian Association for the Advancement of Science held at Adelaide*, 1907, pp. 217–26.

94. See for example, G. V. Portus, *An Introduction to the Study of Industrial Reconstruction* (Sydney, 1919).

95. Professor Mitchell, *Lecture on the Rate of Interest* (Adelaide, 1909).

96. J. Alexander Gunn, *Distribution of the National Dividend* (Melbourne, 1925), p. 53.

statistical research was designed to throw light on the true relations between factors.[97]

Government Regulation of Wages

The principle of administered wages gained support in the Australian colonies for several reasons: general concern over the effects of steadily increasing urbanization and industrialization; disillusionment with timeworn panaceas such as land, banking, and tariff reform; and anxious desire to alleviate through institutional change the depression and labor warfare which developed near the end of the nineteenth century. Wage regulation was a concept which appealed particularly to men of moderation, order, and strong moral sense. Wise judges and legislators, they reasoned, should be as capable of discovering "just" levels of factor payments as of rendering decisions under civil and criminal law. Arbitration and conciliation were viewed as means of introducing order into economic chaos, and a powerful analogy was drawn often between warfare in an unregulated labor market and social anarchy before introduction of the rule of law.

Until the crisis years of the 1890's, suggestions for government wage control were in most cases made to an unreceptive audience. Drastic departures from labor market laissez faire were considered seriously only in occasional extreme situations. For example, in 1878 John Ebenezer Goodwin of Melbourne presented virtually unnoticed an elaborate plan whereby government would fix wages according to the level of average labor productivity. Scientific justice incorporating the labor theory of value in statutes would, he argued, guarantee industrial peace. He explained:

We require to establish a Labour Department for organising labour in all industries, and for calculating units of labour, units of labour-wages, and the prices of goods.

The time values of every different tradesman's and labourer's pro-

97. Particularly the works of James T. Sutcliffe: *The National Dividend* (Melbourne, 1926), and *History of Trade Unionism in Australia* (Melbourne, 1925).

ductions can be equated and expressed in terms of the unit of value, viz.—*an hour's work of an average worker.* . . . science, aided by Government, may be applied to organise labour, and find out how much wealth a working man creates by his hour's or day's work, and how much of consumable articles he must have distributed to him in equitable exchange for that work. There is no reason to believe that scientific legislation applied to the regulation of labour and capital would do anything but abolish the present universal antagonism now subsisting between these two conflicting elements of social life.[98]

Goodwin rejected the classical wages fund and subsistence theory of wages: "This reduces the working man to a working and limited-stock-perpetuating animal for the convenience of the capitalist, who is to keep all the production the working man creates in excess of his family's feed &c."[99] However, Goodwin's own recommendation for payment according to "calculated labour equivalents" was neither closely reasoned nor operationally useful and is interesting mainly as a precocious curiosity. At the time Goodwin wrote, his combination of boundless faith in the omnipotence of "science" with sympathy for the working class had little widespread appeal. Moreover, Goodwin and others with pioneer suggestions for wage control were no match in open debate for defenders of "supply and demand."[100]

In the 1880's and 1890's, business recession and labor unrest gave rise to the first real enthusiasm among politicians, businessmen, and labor leaders for some form of labor-market regulation. Faced with the apparent collapse of the free enterprise system even some doctrinaire liberals turned in desperation to the promise of emergency government intervention. Through reform in the system of distribution, it was hoped, both the volume of production and social tranquility could be restored.[101] Reasoned expectations for the results of experiments with arbitration were of two broad types, and the distinction was important. One group

98. John Ebenezer Goodwin, *Scientific Legislation; or the Theory of Calculated Labour Equivalents, Containing Constitutional, Banking, Railway, Medical, Law, Departmental, Labour, and Prices Reform* (Melbourne, 1878), pp. 17 and 50.
99. *Ibid.*, p. 18.
100. Another early proposal for government interference in the labor market which induced an immediate refutation was: John Woods, "Wages," *Victorian Review*, II (1880), 640–51; and F. J. Carter, "On Wages: a Reply," *ibid.*, pp. 860–63.
101. See for example, S. W. Griffith, *Wealth and Want* (Brisbane, n. d.).

looked to courts of law to discover and to impose the prices for labor which would have been established naturally in a truly competitive market. Strikes and depression were accepted by these persons as evidence of the absence of competition in the Australian economy but not as an indictment of the *theory* of a competitive economy. They reasoned that because the classical economic model did not imply the existence of unemployed resources some government authority could merely discover and enforce an approximation to competitive prices and guarantee thereby full employment and smooth functioning of the system. The second type of expectation for arbitration was that judges, by fixing factor payments, could mold the pattern of income distribution according to standards of social justice and do so without affecting adversely the efficiency of the system. In defense of this latter position, two Sydney lawyers explained in 1911, "It is the business of law in every department of life to see that reasonable expectation is fulfilled."[102]

In the early years of experiments with wage control, the exact purposes of particular schemes were seldom articulated clearly, and active support came largely on pragmatic grounds. Employers looked to labor market regulation for restoration of industrial peace, and workers hoped for higher wages. First in the despair of depression, and later in the exhilaration of federation, the concept of wage control captivated and brought together persons whose views on other matters were mutually antagonistic: co-operationists, liberal economists, radical labor leaders, and conservative businessmen. Only after the first flush of enthusiasm passed did the contradictory character of some hopes for wage control become abundantly clear.

Machinery for wages regulation, conciliation, and arbitration was introduced in the colonies during the 1880's and 1890's with particular advances in Victoria under Peacock, in South Australia under Kingston, and in New South Wales led by B. R. Wise. The purposes of the earliest schemes were to prevent "exploitation"

102. Philip S. Eldershaw and Percy P. Olden, "Industrial Arbitration in Australia," *Annals of the American Academy of Political and Social Science*, XXVII (1911), 221.

or "sweating" of unprotected groups in the labor force through
establishment of a minimum wage, and to deal with emergency
strike situations in vital industries. Gradually, and particularly
after formation of the Commonwealth, enthusiasm grew for development of a wider code of industrial jurisprudence which would
give legitimacy and permanence to the industrial wage structure.[103] Legislative innovation took place in an intellectual climate
favorable to change. By the late 1880's, vocal advocates of conciliation and arbitration had appeared among radicals, moderates,
and conservatives. For example, several members of the Australian Economic Association in Sydney campaigned openly for ex-

103. Government regulation of the labor market, more than any other single
topic, attracted the attention both of foreign observers of the Australian
economy, and of domestic economists. In the extensive literature on the subject
the following are works particularly useful for description of the early period:
June Philipp, "Historical Revision: No. 1. 1890—the Turning Point in Labour
History?," *Historical Studies Australia and New Zealand,* IV (1949–51), 145–
54; R. J. Cameron, "The Role of the Arbitration Court," *ibid.,* VI (1953–55),
204–14; Victor S. Clark, "Recent Changes in Australasian Laws Against Strikes,"
Quarterly Journal of Economics, XXIV (1909–10), 561–63; "Present State of
Labor Legislation in Australia and New Zealand," *Annals of the American
Academy of Political and Social Science,* XXXIII (1909), 440–47; and *The
Labour Movement in Australasia* (New York, 1906); Matthew B. Hammond,
"The Minimum Wage in Great Britain and Australia," *Annals of the American
Academy of Political and Social Science,* XLVIII (1913), 22–36; "Wages Boards
in Australia," *Quarterly Journal of Economics,* XXIX (1914–15), 98–148, 326–
61, 563–630; and "Judicial Interpretation of the Minimum Wage in Australia,"
American Economic Review, III (1913), 259–86; Paul H. Douglas, "Wages Regu-
lation and Children's Maintenance in Australia," *Quarterly Journal of Economics,*
XXXVII (1922–23), 643–86; Philip S. Eldershaw and Percy P. Olden, "Industrial Arbitration in Australia," *Annals of the American Academy of Political and
Social Science,* XXVII (1911), 203–21; G. V. Portus, "The Development of
Wage Fixation in Australia," *American Economic Review,* XIX (1929), 59–75;
William Pember Reeves, *State Experiments in Australia and New Zealand* (London, 1902); "The Minimum Wage Law in Victoria and South Australia," *Eco-
nomic Journal,* XI (1901), 334–44 (with critique by Clara E. Collet, *ibid.,* pp.
557–65); "Mr. Wise's Industrial Arbitration Act," *ibid.,* XII (1902), 320–26;
George W. Gough, "The Wages Boards of Victoria," *ibid.,* XV (1905), 361–73;
George S. Beeby, "The Artificial Regulation of Wages in Australia," *ibid.,* XXV
(1915), 321–28; F. A. A. Russell, "Industrial Arbitration in New South Wales,"
ibid., XXV (1915), 329–46; F. W. Eggleston, "The Australian Democracy and its
Economic Problems," *ibid.,* XXV (1915), 347–59; H. Heaton, "The Basic Wage
Principle in Australian Wages Regulation," *ibid.,* XXXI (1921), 309–19; Mary
T. Rankin, *Arbitration and Conciliation in Australasia: the Legal Wage In Victoria and New Zealand* (London, 1916); A. St. Ledger, *Australian Socialism*
(London, 1909), p. 50 f.; William G. Spence, *Australia's Awakening* (Sydney,
1909), pp. 108–9; Vance Palmer, *The Legend of the Nineties* (Melbourne, 1954),
pp. 143 and 162; Anton Bertram, "Le Mouvement ouvrier en Australasie," *Revue D'Economie Politique,* XI (1897), 35–53; Antoine Bertram (traduit par M.
Moncharville), "Quelques experiences de conciliation par L'état en Australasie,"
ibid., XI (1897), 539–65; Charles Schindler, "L'Australie et le régime travail-
liste," *ibid.,* XXVII (1913), 339–60.

perimentation with government intervention in the labor market. In 1888 Archibald Forsyth, a protectionist manufacturer, appealed for a conciliation board to supplement "the law of supply and demand."[104] Andrew Garran, chairman of a Royal Commission in 1891 on "Strikes and their Causes," recommended inauguration of both conciliation and arbitration.[105] Several legislators viewed wage control as the primrose path to social harmony: Bruce Smith in Victoria called for creation of an arbitration court whose awards would be absolute and binding, while G. R. Dibbs in New South Wales proposed the nomination of special "wisemen" with dispute-settling powers patterned after the "prudhommes" at medieval fairs.[106] Faced with extreme labor conflict and recession in Queensland, Sir Samuel Griffith proposed radical legislation to govern industrial working conditions and minimum wages.[107] In 1891 the radical Sydney *Bulletin* gave qualified endorsement to suggestions for government intervention; it denied the validity of the wages-fund theory but conceded that when confined to the process of collective bargaining labor was limited strictly in the extent to which it might alter income distribution.[108] Writers in this journal suggested that if through legal action workers could reduce the "earnings of capital" to a "just" level they might "live like lords." Compulsory arbitration, they claimed, could be expected to determine wages according to right principles:

The present system of "trial by combat," which decides against the party that starves first, and in favour of the one whose resources hold out longest, is utterly opposed to all the principles of justice, as justice is now understood. In all disputes save only those between Capital and Labour, the law arrogates to itself the right to decide between the conflicting parties.[109]

104. Archibald Forsyth, "Relations between Capital and Labour Examined," *Australian Economist,* I (1888–90), 99–103.
105. Arthur Duckworth, "The Australian Strike, 1890," *Economic Journal,* II (1892), 425–41.
106. *Australian Economist,* I (1888–90), 127; and George R. Dibbs, *Address to the Trades and Labour Council* (Sydney, 1890), p. 5.
107. The Honourable Mr. Justice Matthews, "A History of Industrial Law in Queensland with a Summary of the Provisions of the Various Statutes," *Historical Society of Queensland Journal,* IV (1948–52), 150–80.
108. "Wages," *Bulletin,* XI (1891), No. 596, p. 6.
109. "Compulsory Arbitration," *Bulletin,* XII (1892), No. 648, p. 6.

Critics of wage regulation replied vigorously to advocates and insisted that at most government should attempt only to assist the market in finding a natural level. Professor Walter Scott of Sydney University in 1895 set forth a catalog of economic ills which would follow indiscriminate interference with the free-market mechanism, including: inflation, distortion of income distribution, unemployment of subnormally efficient workers, and loss of export markets. Scott concluded that "the fixing of a minimum *above certain limits* would be unmixed harm to all concerned."[110] The Reverend Reginald Stephen, as did Scott, emphasized that the clear eventuality of fixing wages above the free-market level would be unemployment. He insisted that Australians recognize clearly this threat:

It is assumed that Society is bound to provide for the unemployed. Those who can get work are to be paid fair wages. But those who are excluded from the artificially restricted circle of employment are to be maintained at the expense of their more fortunate neighbours. Of the reasonableness of this plea I have nothing to say at present. But it must be taken for granted if a living wage is to be given.[111]

A few skeptical labor organizers joined in criticism of proposed wage regulation suspecting at the very least a trick by employers to weaken unions. Tom Mann explained that by 1908 his long-standing fears had been justified: "As a result of the working of these Acts, the unions grew in membership, but lost fighting efficiency. The whole of industrial negotiation was in the hands of the legal fraternity."[112] Although both doctrinaire defenders of labor-market competition and advocates of unrestricted collective bargaining presented reasonable theoretical arguments why wages might increase more rapidly without than with government intervention, the unanswerable flaw in their case was the evidence, clear to all, that during the 1890's wages did not increase. After this apparent failure of conventional economic analysis,

110. Walter Scott, "On Fixing a Minimum Wage," *Report of the Sixth Meeting of the Australasian Association for the Advancement of Science held at Brisbane, 1895*, p. 162.
111. Reginald Stephen, "A Living Wage," *Report of the Sixth Meeting of the Australasian Association for the Advancement of Science held at Brisbane, 1895*, p. 685.
112. Tom Mann, *Tom Mann's Memoirs* (London, 1923), pp. 224 and 235.

Australians turned readily to considerations of justice and morality as criteria for income distribution.

Well-informed, literate, and articulate persons were among those who designed and operated the first agencies for wage regulation. B. R. Wise, Attorney General of New South Wales, a student of Arnold Toynbee at Oxford, and champion of free trade, explained in 1901 that his Industrial Arbitration Act of that year was drafted only after careful study of experience in other colonies and with suggestions from Sidney and Beatrice Webb.[113] George S. Beeby, who introduced legislation in 1912 to strengthen Wise's machinery, was acquainted fully with criticisms of government interference by economists, and he based his defense on the probability of aggregate social benefits, including industrial tranquility, exceeding possible economic loss.[114] However, early legislators were compelled often by the imprecise nature of their subject matter and the obscure economic significance of their proposals to make such assertions as those of a Tasmanian Royal Commission in 1907 that certain workers received "inadequate payments" and that all "toilers" should by rights be paid wages sufficient "to provide the ordinary home comforts and necessaries of life for themselves and those dependent upon them."[115] A New South Wales Royal Commissioner, charged to "inquire into the working of compulsory conciliation and arbitration laws," acknowledged the limitations of his findings and reported regretfully "I have quoted figures occasionally, but I do not rely on them so much as on my own observation." He concluded: "I have no wish to embody in my report a treatise on political economy, a task which would be as unpleasant as it would be difficult."[116]

Henry Bournes Higgins, President of the Commonwealth Court

113. B. R. Wise, "What I Expect from the Industrial Arbitration Act," *Review of Reviews for Australasia*, XIX (1901), 551–53.
114. George S. Beeby, "The Artificial Regulation of Wages in Australia," *Economic Journal*, XXV (1915), 321–28. A similar report is: F. A. A. Russell, "Industrial Arbitration in New South Wales," *ibid.*, pp. 329–46.
115. "Royal Commission on Wages and Wage-Earners in Tasmania. Report of the Commissioners," *Journals and Printed Papers of the Parliament of Tasmania*, 1907, p. 15.
116. "Report of Royal Commission of Inquiry into the Working of Compulsory Conciliation and Arbitration Laws," *Votes and Proceedings of the Legislative Assembly of New South Wales*, 1901, pp. 19 and 34.

of Conciliation and Arbitration from 1907 until 1921, was chief architect of wage regulation at the federal level, and by example, indirectly in the states.[117] Prime Minister Alfred Deakin determined in 1907 that full powers of the Commonwealth government, including even a system of conditional tariffs known as "new protection," should be employed to guarantee for all workers economic justice and a fair minimum wage. Higgins was selected to implement this policy, and he became the first official to grapple seriously with the substantial problems of translating Deakin's principles into hard and defensible practice. Although a student of Hearn in political economy at Melbourne University and a consistent advocate of commercial education,[118] Higgins based his wage decisions less on the economic facts of the Australian environment than on what he considered universal principles of social equity. In his first years on the bench, he explained, he had "to learn the business, with no book of instructions, no teacher other than experience, no kindly light except from the pole star of justice."[119]

In a volume entitled *A New Province for Law and Order*, composed of essays prepared for the *Harvard Law Review*, Higgins set forth in detail the principles which underlay his judicial decisions and which became established precedents for his successors. At the outset he eschewed all theory which prescribed wage payments strictly according to labor productivity or value received by employers; he adopted instead "a standard based on 'the normal needs of the average employee, regarded as a human being living in a civilized community.' "[120] He calculated a minimum standard by estimating "average necessary expenditures" of a typical workman derived from an arbitrary inventory of essential goods which he believed should be purchased with an appropriate "living wage." This amount constituted a level of payment below which employers under the court's jurisdiction could not offer employment. Higgins added to the basic wage

117. Higgins observed in 1915 that the state "wages boards frequently look for guidance in their action to the reasoning of the Federal Court." H. B. Higgins, *A New Province for Law and Order* (London, 1922), p. 32.
118. See below pp. 579–80.
119. *A New Province for Law and Order*, p. v.
120. *Ibid.*, p. 3.

a "secondary wage" computed from an index of traditional income differentials among skilled occupations. Despite the long-standing Australian concern with population growth, Higgins refused to adjust the basic wage between married and unmarried workers; he stated: "It rests on Walt Whitman's 'divine average,' and the employer need not concern himself with his employee's domestic affairs."[121] Higgins was vague and equivocal about the significance for the basic wage of corporate profits; he explained: "The wages cannot be allowed to depend on the profits made by the individual employer, but the profits of which the *industry* is capable may be taken into account." He insisted that employers should be permitted only in very exceptional circumstances to set a wage below the basic level, but in the event of a firm experiencing radically reduced capacity to pay the courts might adjust downward the secondary wage.[122] Higgins was torn between an awareness of restraints imposed by economic expediency and a desire to mold society according to tenets of pure justice.

Institutional problems of wage adjustment multiplied for Higgins during his years on the bench, and he was compelled reluctantly to face and accept numerous inconsistencies of principle. On the one hand he was led to declare that firms of subnormal profitability should not be permitted to share losses with workers, and yet he felt unable to raise objections to union insistence upon wage payments above the conventional standard in the event of excess business profits. A basic assumption held by Higgins was that in a free market the bargaining power of workers acting independently was less than that of their employers, and wage rates therefore would be lower under competition than in markets either regulated by government or organized by trade unions. He stated categorically: "freedom of contract is a misnomer as applied to the contract between an employer and an ordinary individual employee. The strategic position of the employer in a contest as to wages is much stronger than that of the individual employee."[123] Yet Higgins held mixed views about unions. He sympathized with wishes of workers to bargain col-

121. *Ibid.*, p. 6.
122. *Ibid.*, pp. 7 and 143.
123. *Ibid.*, p. 19.

388 Theory and Policy

lectively, but he recognized that unrestrained struggle was irreconcilable with the principle of public regulation: "Arbitration by the Court is meant to be a substitute for the method of strike, and 'you cannot have award and strike too.' "[124] When forced to make a choice between objectives, Higgins held that preservation of "industrial peace" should be the principal aim of arbitration courts, and that discovery of absolute distributive justice was important but of secondary significance.[125]

The ideas and practices of Higgins and his fellow pioneers in wage regulation attracted considerable attention abroad, and before World War I influential observers from Britain, the United States, and Germany studied and described the experiments favorably.[126] Victor S. Clark visited Australia and New Zealand in 1903-4 under commission from the United States government and produced an influential report.[127] Minimum wage legislation introduced to the United Kingdom in 1909 followed close study of Australian experience.[128]

By World War I two major difficulties had appeared to plague authorities responsible for wage regulation. The first was a weakening of all segments of public support resulting from reaction to exaggerated expectations. Visionaries who had hoped for the coming of an industrial millenium under a system of arbitration grew disappointed quickly with the reality of continued antagonism between management and labor. Workers whose support from the beginning had been pragmatic expressed increasing doubt that their income share would in fact be less under unrestricted collective bargaining than it was under arbitration. Industrialists deplored the continued government toleration of work stoppages. The problem of public support was accentu-

124. Ibid., p. 23.
125. Ibid., pp. 35-37.
126. M. B. Hammond, "Judicial Interpretation of the Minimum Wage in Australia," American Economic Review, III (1913), 259-86; and M. B. Hammond, "Wages Boards in Australia: IV. Social and Economic Results of Wages Boards," Quarterly Journal of Economics, XXIX (1914-15), 563-630.
127. The Labour Movement in Australasia (New York, 1906).
128. M. B. Hammond, "The Minimum Wage in Great Britain and Australia," Annals of the American Academy of Political and Social Science, XLVIII (1913), 22-36; and J. Ramsay MacDonald, "The Labour Legislation of the Australasian States," Report of the Seventy-Seventh Meeting of the British Association for The Advancement of Science, 1907, transactions, p. 596.

ated after 1914 by the strain of a major war effort under which prices rose rapidly and the proportion of national income available for personal consumption diminished. Workers who had come to believe confidently that, regardless of hardships, courts could guarantee a steadily rising standard of living expressed their disillusionment through a wave of strikes. Employers complained with justification that even in a national emergency the arbitration system could not preserve industrial peace.

The second major difficulty which faced arbitration authorities by World War I was a basic weakness in the process of operation. After twenty years, no definitive standard had yet been devised for establishment of "equitable" wage levels. Arbitrators found universally that the "just" wage was easier to discuss in general terms than to identify in fact. At the outset of his term on the federal arbitration court, Higgins was presented unequivocally with the dilemma of obtaining appropriate data and of cataloging criteria for determination of a minimum wage. Parliament expressed confidence that his judicial wisdom would reveal true standards of equity. A memorandum in 1907–8 expressed the prevailing optimism of legislators about the omniscience of the judiciary; it explained:

> It has been objected that the term "fair and reasonable," as applied to wages, is too vague to be put into an Act of Parliament, and that some definition is required from the Legislature of the meaning to be attached to the words. As they stand, they express the intention of Parliament clearly though generally, and it is not imperative to attempt a complete definition of them in the Statute. The difficulty lies not in their interpretation, but in their application. Hence it has been deemed best to leave these words to be interpreted, whenever necessary, by a well-informed and impartial tribunal, possessing the fullest opportunity for investigation and consideration before it arrives at a decision, and also of varying that decision should occasion require.[129]

Using the investigative powers of his court Higgins set out valiantly to discover a just minimum wage through budget and price surveys, and he enforced his findings in the celebrated

129. "New Protection—Explanatory Memorandum in Regard to," *Papers Presented to the Parliament of the Commonwealth of Australia*, 1907–8, p. 1.

Harvester decision of 1907. The incomplete and arbitrary character of his results, however, was disturbing to him as well as to others, and a Labour and Industrial Branch was added to the Commonwealth Statistical Bureau to render professional assistance.[130] Subsequently the suspicion grew that the process of determining a minimum wage was not, after all, susceptible to scientific treatment.

During World War I, rapid inflation and mounting criticism from all quarters with operation of the arbitration system led to demands for a new and exhaustive enquiry into the meaning of the minimum wage. At the war's end the Prime Minister, W. M. Hughes, in a speech at Bendigo in 1919 reaffirmed the philosophy underlying the system; he repeated the familiar cry that "Labour is entitled to a fair share of the wealth it produces," and he called for full implementation of economic "justice." However, Hughes accepted the need for an investigation.[131] Higgins recommended that the task of redetermining the basic wage "be committed to the Statistician, with all his experience and facilities and his cool, scientific, impartial attitude."[132] Instead, a Royal Commission with A. B. Piddington as chairman was formed and charged to ascertain the just basic wage by discovering the current "cost of living" for an "average" family of man, wife, and three children. Although critical of techniques employed by predecessors, the commissioners did not question the fundamental validity of their quest, and they arrived at a minimum which, like that computed by Higgins in 1907, included "reasonable standards of comfort, not by reference to any one type or group of employees, but by reference to the needs which are common to all employees, following the accepted principle that there is a standard of living below which no employee should be asked to live."[133] A par-

130. Gerald Lightfoot, "Labour Statistics," *Report of the Fourteenth Meeting of the Australasian Association for the Advancement of Science held at Melbourne, 1913,* pp. 537–38. Gerald Lightfoot, chief of the branch, set forth his own views on "the judicial determination of the minimum wage" in a series of lectures sponsored by the Melbourne University Extension Board. *Extension Work: Aim, Methods, and Syllabus of Lectures* (Melbourne, 1915), p. 13.
131. "Report of the Royal Commission on the Basic Wage," *Papers Presented to the Parliament of the Commonwealth of Australia,* 1920–21, p. 8.
132. *A New Province for Law and Order,* p. 135.
133. "Report of the Royal Commission on the Basic Wage," 1920–21, p. 17.

ticularly disturbing feature of the Piddington report was that, after sixty-six sittings and perusal of numerous tables and items of evidence, the Commission arrived at a minimum wage which if paid to all Australian workers would, in the opinion of the Commonwealth Statistician, have more than exhausted the entire national product.[134] This anomalous finding together with disturbing statements that the Commissioners had "consistently excluded political and economic views as being no part of their function," gave a peculiar air of irrelevance and unreality to the report.[135] A later suggestion by Piddington that the "impossible" basic wage could be rendered practicable by discriminating among single and married workers through a system of child endowments did little to redeem the report.[136]

The Piddington report stimulated a new wave of attacks on the principle of wage regulation. Criticism had been uninterrupted from the beginnings in the 1890's, but skeptics at first were restrained by the boldness and imagination of the new experiments and by the weakness of their own critical equipment. The awards set down by Higgins had been impressive both for awareness of economic realities and for desire to implement principles of fairness and charity; it was left for the Piddington Commission to show clearly the potential inconsistency of these considerations.

The machinery of wage regulation was contrived during lean years in the history of wage theory. John Stuart Mill offered his famous recantation of the wages-fund doctrine in 1869, and no alternative authoritative body of theory was presented immediately to fill the gap. Economists remained divided and uncertain as to whether wages were an original or residual share in the national income and as to whether institutional regulation could alter the pattern of distribution without disastrous results. Marginal productivity theory was perfected late in the century by

134. *A New Province for Law and Order*, p. 136.
135. G. V. Portus, "The Development of Wage Fixation in Australia," *American Economic Review*, XIX (1929), 59–75.
136. D. T. Sawkins, "The Australian Standard of Living," in Persia Campbell, R. C. Mills, and G. V. Portus, eds., *Studies in Australian Affairs* (Melbourne, 1928), pp. 27–48.

J. B. Clark, Alfred Marshall, and the Austrians, but this new approach did not become accepted doctrine in Australia until the twentieth century. The first well-documented objections to the basic principle of wage arbitration were the consequence of belated application by Australian economists after World War I of the new marginal theory to their domestic conditions. Professor Hancock observed in 1930 that "The Australian conception of 'fair and reasonable' is ethical, like the medieval idea of the just price."[137] It was clear recognition of this fact for the first time in the 1920's which touched off a reaction analogous to the classical critique of scholasticism.

Even the most unsympathetic critics of wage control seldom questioned the high moral purpose of the reform. Rather, they denied the possibility of achieving the desired goals of justice and peace through this device. In 1911 H. Y. Braddon observed that while arbitration might on balance have reduced unrest, the courts appeared to operate far more effectively during periods of prosperity, when firms could absorb increasing labor costs, than in depression. He wondered wistfully whether a method could be devised of reconciling morality with the "economic wage," and he concluded: "Society awaits the genius who can suggest a feasible method for bringing about industrial peace."[138]

The complex problems during the 1920's of adjustment from wartime economic conditions afforded a sombre background for extended criticism of wage regulation. The doubts expressed by Braddon were elaborated in particular by a new breed of university economist. The principal objection raised to administered wages rested on the contention that if a minimum level were established above the value to employers of a marginal worker's service this worker would not find employment. Advocates of regulation replied to this objection by asserting that wages above the free market level, in addition to tapping monopoly profits, stimulated worker productivity and justified thereby their own payment. W. Jethro Brown stated in 1920: "In order to make

137. W. K. Hancock, *Australia* (New York, 1930), p. 85.
138. H. Y. Braddon, "The Compulsory Principle in the Settlement of Industrial Disputes," *Report of the Thirteenth Meeting of the Australasian Association for the Advancement of Science held at Sydney, 1911,* p. 504.

possible a high state of industrial efficiency on the part of the employees, it is necessary that the wages should be such as to ensure the workman sufficient to maintain him in a high state of industrial efficiency and to provide his family with the necessaries for physical health and physical well-being."[139] An underconsumptionist argument, that high wages were necessary to sustain purchasing power and employment, was used as well to justify arbitration; Brown continued: "as economists have frequently pointed out, high wages mean an increase in the demand for those commodities which involve a maximum of employment."[140] However, it was not difficult to illustrate that the validity of both these defensive arguments was uncertain, and that, at best, their application was limited. It could not be demonstrated effectively that maintenance of a minimum wage above the free market level would not cause unemployment, except to the extent that employer monopsonistic advantage was counteracted.

Critics of wage arbitration during the 1920's objected to the practice rather than to the principle of the system. Herbert Heaton in 1921 outlined anomalies which had developed, culminating in the Piddington Report, and he called for more extensive study of the subject.[141] In 1925, three influential economists, R. C. Mills, J. B. Brigden, and J. T. Sutcliffe, combined as Queensland Economic Commissioners to launch a frontal attack on establishment of wage minimums according to workers' needs rather than employers' capacity to pay.[142] In this report and elsewhere these men rejected categorically the desirability of calculating the basic wage on any other standard than worker productivity. Under stable economic conditions, Sutcliffe suggested, the conventional cost of living might come coincidentally to approximate the value of labor to employers, but during periods of rapid change any official definition of the living standard might lag behind productivity to a disastrous extent. He explained:

139. W. Jethro Brown, "The Judicial Regulation of Industrial Conditions," in Meredith Atkinson, ed., *Australia: Economic and Political Studies* (Melbourne, 1920), p. 220.
140. *Ibid.*, p. 22.
141. H. Heaton, "The Basic Wage Principle in Australian Wages Regulation," *Economic Journal*, XXXI (1921), 309–19.
142. *Report of the Economic Commission on the Queensland Basic Wage* (Brisbane, 1925).

The cost of living basis may give satisfactory results in times when production is not changing materially or rapidly. Where such changes occur the cost of living basis ceases to be equitable. If production is increasing, the cost of living basis will fail to give to the workers any share of that increasing production. If production is decreasing, then the fixing of wages on a basis which takes no account of that decrease may lead to unemployment, and to an even greater decrease by making the production costs exceed what can possibly be paid.[143]

In the Pitt Cobbett lecture for 1925, Brigden endorsed the fundamental principle of wage arbitration but he appealed for awards on the basis of the potential income levels of firms.[144] The sentiments of these Australian economists generally were greeted enthusiastically by their professional colleagues at home and abroad.[145]

Professor Douglas Copland emphasized, more than did most other contemporary critics, macro-economic dangers in wage regulation. He too deplored the misallocative results of determining factor returns by criteria other than productivity, but in addition he expressed particular concern with the destabilizing effects of an increase in overall price rigidity introduced by cumbersome judicial machinery. Any single country which tolerated a high degree of price inflexibility, he explained, might find its products unsaleable during worldwide deflation. Copland listed specifically as one of the "causes of economic crisis" in postwar Australia "the difficulties of regulating industrial costs to the changing price-level."[146] He implied even that arbitration designed to increase living standards of workers had instead lowered returns to labor through lagged response to general price increases in boom and creation of unemployment during reces-

143. J. T. Sutcliffe, "Wages and Production," *Economic Record*, I (1925), 64–65.
144. J. B. Brigden *et al.*, *Employment Relations and the Basic Wage: Lectures and Papers Published in Connection with the Pitt Cobbett Foundation* (Hobart, 1925).
145. See for example, A. Duckworth, "Notes on Australian Affairs," *Economic Journal*, XXXV (1925), 321–24; and G. F. Shove, "Review of *Report of the Economic Commission on the Queensland Basis Wage*," *ibid.*, pp. 499–500. At the beginning of the depression in 1929 Senator Colebatch prescribed a cut in real wages as "the one known remedy" for unemployment. *The Economic Outlook* (Melbourne, 1929), pp. 9–10.
146. D. B. Copland, "The Trade Depression in Australia in Relation to Economic Thought," *Report of the Sixteenth Meeting of the Australasian Association for the Advancement of Science held at Wellington, 1924*, p. 567.

sion: "in years of rapidly rising prices wages lagged behind when the productivity of industry might have justified higher rates, but in the period of depression wages are relatively higher than before, and the readjustment is slow."[147] Like the majority of critics Copland attacked the standard used for wage arbitration, and not the process itself. In fact he regretted the unfavorable impact on public opinion of what he considered misguided operation of the arbitration machinery. He wrote: "failure to apply a principle soundly should not, as many suppose, warrant the condemnation of that principle. The productivity of industry is the final source of wages, and arbitration cannot be successful if it ignores this factor. . . . The position thus revealed has created a very difficult situation in Australia, and is to a large extent responsible for the reaction that has set in against arbitration . . . in general it is the most disturbing factor in the economic situation at the present moment."[148]

Schemes for wage regulation were undertaken in response to the urgent economic and social problems of the 1890's. After decades of experimentation with land and immigration policy, Australians were perfectly willing to risk this new piece of doctrinal heresy to preserve the viability of their new nation. The early programs of arbitration were multi-purposed, designed to eliminate conflict between workers and employers and at the same time to prevent exploitation of vulnerable worker groups. Pioneer wage decisions, and particularly those of H. B. Higgins, were made in recognition of productivity limitations on court action, but with a basic belief in the applicability of transcendent standards of justice. The restraint of early arbitrators in accepting economic limitations in fact if not always in theory and the anemic condition of economic science prior to the 1920's delayed attack on the system. The possibility of inconsistency between ethical and economic criteria was made particularly clear by the Report of the Piddington Commission in 1920 and drew critical attention from a growing body of professional economists. A noteworthy feature of economists' comments was the direction of

147. D. B. Copland, "The Economic Situation in Australia, 1918–23," *Economic Journal*, XXXIV (1924), 47.
148. *Ibid.*, p. 45.

critiques not against the system itself, but against operations thusfar. They called for change in the method of making awards, by productivity rather than cost of living, but accepted the permanence of the arbitration structure. After thirty years of mixed experience Australians generally remained willing to stand by their experiment in government control. The traumatic 1890's left a lasting scar on Australian memories, and except for a few devoted adherents the concept of a free labor market had few friends left.

12

Population Studies

For two reasons, population studies held a special fascination for Australians. First, Australians hoped through analysis of population growth to understand and to control the development of their new and empty continent. Second, they saw in the population increase of their Asian neighbors a threat to national survival. In the first section of this chapter the impact of population theory on Australian thought is discussed. The second section deals with the place of population analysis in controversies surrounding major public policies. The third section traces the collection of vital statistics, and the last considers some pioneer studies of special population problems.

Population Theory and Australian Thought

An important assumption of nineteenth century British colonial theory was the classical population doctrine that humans tend to multiply more rapidly than do food supplies, a balance being maintained by the operation of certain "checks" on the increase of people. Acceptance of Benthamite utilitarian principles prevented Molesworth, Torrens, Wakefield, and other colonial theorists, from subscribing to a mercantilist position that labor, regardless of its rate of remuneration, was valuable to a nation and should not be encouraged to leave. Therefore, they suggested that when population grew too quickly the surplus should be assisted in emigrating. So long as excess population moved from old countries to colonies the need for positive population checks of "misery and vice" would be minimized and the sum of human happiness could be increased. Through the teachings of Malthus, British intellectuals came thus to regard the colonies as more than mere suppliers of raw materials and an extension of the home market. The unsettled parts of the Empire were to become the means of allaying temporarily the Malthusian spectres of poverty and overcrowding. The place of the Australian colonies in the scheme of classical economics was represented dramatically by Harriet Martineau in one of her *Illustrations of Political Economy*. She portrayed an honest but unemployed English workman encouraged by his enlightened parson to proceed with his sister to Van Diemen's Land. In the colonies, the parson advised, the worker would find prosperity while in Britain his fellows would experience relief from competition.[1]

Australians followed closely discussion of population problems in the mother country and particularly suggestions that Britain should assist the movement of free labor to the colonies. T. Potter MacQueen, an early settler in New South Wales, stressed the complementarity of old and new economies and noted that after the Napoleonic Wars positive checks to British population growth had diminished. An outlet for surplus capital and labor was needed immediately. MacQueen hoped to convince Britain that, in her own self interest, she should foster and maintain colonies. He explained:

The surplus population now so rapidly increasing, and from a long state of peace relieved from those checks which in former days reduced it, must demand the anxious care of our legislation . . . but place them in these Colonies, where from high wages and cheap provisions they can earn *four times the amount necessary for their subsistence*, and they will become the best consumers of the staple exports of England, and at the same time encourage our mercantile navy.[2]

John Lhotsky, a particularly astute observer of colonial conditions, expressed the same thoughts as MacQueen in more picturesque language. He wrote:

1. *Illustrations of Political Economy: No. X. Homes Abroad, A Tale* (London, 1832).
2. *Australia As She Is & As She May Be* (London, 1840), pp. 17–18. For a similar statement by MacQueen, see "Minutes of Evidence taken before the Committee on Immigration," *Minutes and Proceedings of the Legislative Council of New South Wales, 1834* (printed at Sydney, 1847), pp. 283–322. The same conclusions were also reached by the author of "National Emigration and Colonization," *New South Wales Magazine*, 1843, pp. 583–88.

When a nation has arrived at such a pitch of refinement, and departure from the law of God and nature, that one portion of the (superabundant) population are enjoying incommensurate and godless luxuries, the majority are leading a wretched and degraded life; it is obvious, and it becomes a necessity for, and a duty of Government, to ejaculate and discharge as quickly as possible such feculous and infected matter from its bloated political body. In this respect these Colonies and the Canadas might become the salvation of Great Britain, and thus perhaps prevent or delay the eruption of one of those civic tornados, which (as in the natural world) are sometimes destined to purify a pestiferous and overcharged political atmosphere.[3]

British fear of overpopulation was greatest and Australian offers of a home for surplus workers were received most enthusiastically during the first half century following the Napoleonic Wars. By 1858 attitudes had changed and Sir James Stephen was able to assure an English audience that Britain, through social reform and technological innovation, would be able after all to employ her growing labor force. He said: "Wise and enlightened as he was, Mr. Malthus did not perceive that the political abuses which he justly deplored as the cause of so much social evil, were even then undermined and tottering to their fall. He did not see that he was standing on the very threshold of the great English revolution of the nineteenth century."[4]

Many colonial intellectuals in the nineteenth century came to accept Malthusian theory as an article of faith. Copies of Malthus' *Essay on Population* were contained in most well-stocked private and public libraries,[5] and Malthusian principles permeated discussions of settlement policy. W. C. Wentworth suggested in 1819 that the Australian colonies were unusual instances of land where plentiful natural resources could for a time permit unlimited

3. [John Lhotsky], *Illustrations of the Present State and Future Prospects of the Colony of New South Wales* (Sydney, 1835), p. 27.
4. "Colonization as a Branch of Social Economy, by the Right Hon. Sir James Stephen, K. C. B.," reprinted in Paul Knaplund, *James Stephen and the British Colonial System 1813–1847* (Madison, Wisconsin, 1953), p. 288.
5. From auctioneers' catalogs preserved in the Mitchell Library, Sydney, it is known that in the 1840's the *Essay* was possessed by such distinguished colonists as Roger Therry, Alexander McLeay, and John Dunmore Lang. The Australian Subscription Library in 1834 and the New South Wales Legislative Council Library fifteen years later both contained several works by Malthus. See *Catalogue of the Australian Subscription Library* (Sydney, 1834); and *Index to the Legislative Council Library* (Sydney, 1849).

increase of human numbers without the operation of checks imposed in older countries by a niggardly nature. In the colonies, population growth from internal fertility alone might be expected to occur at a geometric rate, as Malthus explained was theoretically possible. Wentworth even alleged that any lesser rate of increase indicated a situation of artificial scarcity and was evidence of misgovernment and failure by the colonists to exploit economic opportunities. With this reasoning Wentworth attacked the colonial administration thus:

> Mr. Malthus, who has immortalized himself by his essay on this branch of political economy, has so satisfactorily shewn that the increase of population is proportioned to the facility of procuring subsistence, and administering to the various wants of a family, that it is quite unnecessary for me to repeat arguments with which every one ought to be familiar, to prove that this colony has not been exempt from the destructive influence of causes whose operation has been steady and invariable in all ages and in all countries. The inference that this difficulty has been a preventive to marriage, and to the consequent progress of population is self-evident: to be understood it only requires to be stated. But the numerical increase of the colony has been checked in a still greater degree, perhaps by the constant returns from its shores which are daily occasioned by the same causes.[6]

John Dunmore Lang suggested that population pressure in some old countries could have distinctly happy results through migration to colonies. Without citing Mandeville, from whose writings he obviously drew inspiration, Lang compared communities of humans to hives of bees, continually growing and producing new swarms so long as they were well governed. Men, like bees, had to export surplus population before it became an inconvenience. Lang believed man could learn from bees that when establishing new colonial communities all elements of society—a hive in miniature—should be transferred to the new environment. Haphazard settlement, Lang explained, was doomed to failure. Lang even saw an analogy between convict transporta-

6. *A Statistical, Historical, and Political Description of the Colony of New South Wales* . . . (London, 1819), pp. 214–15.

tion and expulsion by bees from the hive of unproductive drones. Drones, like many early colonial convicts, met a quick end in unfamiliar and inhospitable surroundings. A part of Lang's remarks is worth repeating here because his casual speculations are probably the earliest attempt in the colonies to formulate a model of colonial population growth. Lang wrote:

Without pretending . . . to anything like superior discernment in the science of political economy, I hold that the most important and fundamental axioms of that science are to be found in the outset of the book of Genesis—in that passage where this injunction is divinely given to our first parents. *"Multiply, and replenish the earth, and subdue it."* This injunction, when translated into the language of political economy, reads as follows, "Let there be no artificial check to the increase of population. Let marriage be encouraged by all means; and when the population in any country becomes excessive, let a portion of the inhabitants of that country emigrate to the waste and uninhabited lands in other parts of the world."

These divinely derived axioms of political economy are embodied in the practice and procedure of a divinely constituted community, from which I conceive the more important communities of men might learn a salutary lesson. The community I allude to is that of bees. There are no checks to population thought of in the beehive; but whenever the hive becomes overpopulous, as it regularly does at least once every year, what do its little inhabitants do? Do they divide the cells as an Irish farm is divided among all the families of several successive generations of the lineal descendants of the first tenant, till it affords to each at last nothing more than a miserable potato-garden? No, the matter is managed much more wisely and much more comfortably to all concerned—the redundant population of the hive swarms off at the proper season in one great body and forms a flourishing colony somewhere else, which perhaps in a very short period rivals the parent hive. The bees, it is true, have a sort of transportation-law like ourselves, in virtue of which a kind of forced emigration, of a very limited extent however, takes place from their little community; they banish the drones from the hive, and they even sometimes, as is gravely told us by their historians put these pests of society to death. But these desultory and solitary instances of forced emigration or banishment are never found to supersede the grand, annual, national, voluntary emigration. The drones or convicts are banished in dozens, but the great swarm of free emigrants leaves the hive in tens of thousands. As Solomon therefore says to the indolent, *"Go to the ant, thou*

sluggard," I would say to all those persons in Great Britain who ignorantly declaim against emigration—that divinely appointed remedy
for the evils of a superabundant population—"Go to the bee, ye would-
be political economists!"[7]

Throughout his life Lang supported a policy of attracting
population to the colonies by all practicable means: immigration
companies, subsidized passages, or free homesteads.[8] In his old
age, however, Lang suspected that overpopulation might become
a problem even in New South Wales itself. He proposed in 1871
that Australia begin a hiving-off process of its own so that with
their "large floating population" the colonies might become
imperial powers in their own right. He asked:

May we hope . . . that such principles will be recognized and established, with the concurrence of the Imperial Government, as will
make this city of Sydney, like the ancient city of Miletus in the
flourishing period of Grecian colonization, the mother city of a whole
series of flourishing colonies in New Guinea and in the numerous and
beautiful islands of the Western Pacific.[9]

When some measure of political autonomy was granted the
colonies in the 1840's and 1850's, colonists became concerned
seriously for the first time about future economic relations with
Britain. Clearly, it seemed, the mother country could not be
expected to regard colonies both as politically independent and
at the same time as economic responsibilities. Yet the colonies
were still largely dependent on British trade and on imports of
British capital and labor. In place of the traditional concept of
possession, settlers felt constrained to establish compelling reasons why fostering care should continue, and to this end colonial
writers outlined to a British audience with renewed vigor the
problem of overpopulation that faced old countries, and the
solution that was presented by emigration. An Australian pro-

7. *Emigration; Considered Chiefly in Reference to the Practicability and Expediency of Importing and Settling Throughout the Territory of New South Wales,
A Numerous, Industrious and Virtuous Agricultural Population . . .* (Sydney,
1833), p. 3.
8. *Immigration; the Grand Desideratum for New South Wales: and How to
Promote it Effectually* (Sydney, 1870), p. 42 and *passim.*
9. "New Guinea—a highly Promising Field for Settlement and Colonization,
and How Such an Object Might be Most Easily and Successfully Effected,"
Transactions of the Royal Society of New South Wales, 1871, p. 47.

ponent of immigration to be assisted by the country of origin wrote in 1848:

it is applicable alike to every country and to every colony, as an arrangement under which the whole of the waste lands of the earth may be made to receive the unfed and destitute population of the older countries, which must continue to increase to an enormous extent so long as the present peaceful disposition prevails amongst the nations; and whilst all the improvements in the arts of life are making such wonderful progress, but whilst cultivatable land is not available to a sufficient extent, or attainable at a sufficiently remunerative rate.[10]

After the introduction of responsible government in the 1850's colonial writers emphasized with special enthusiasm the interests held in common by new and old countries. The horrors of a crowded island, short of food and racked by misery and vice, were described to the home government with vivid illustration. One Melbourne writer who signed himself "Aristides" explained in an open letter to the Secretary of State for the Colonies in 1853:

So certain as the roaring waves of the Atlantic forbid the extension of Britain's territory, so certain is it that a redundant population, increasing its millions, as every decade indicates, with an accelerated impetus, will ultimately make her almost entirely dependent on the world for bread, and subject her, in cases of contingency, to all the horrors of famine, death, or cannibalism, unless timely prevented.

Have I announced a startling fact, my Lord? Apply the test of anthropometrical progression to the multiplying millions of a redundant population in a limited territory, and you will find in every census demonstrative tokens of a coming event, the neglect of which may issue in an awful crisis.

Britain's great danger lies, not in any peculiarity of her government, nor in this or that administration, nor even in her liability to foreign invasion, great as that may be at all times, but in over population, annually multiplying her wants of subsistence, and her consequent temptations to crime.[11]

Giving the other side of the coin, Archibald Michie, a member of the Victorian Legislative Assembly and a prominent economic

---

10. *Direct Remission Advocated: Being a Consideration of the Connexion between Waste Lands of the Colonies and Emigration* (Sydney, 1848), p. 18.

11. *The Approaching Crisis of Britain and Australia: With a Way to Escape the Ruin It Threatens* (Melbourne, 1853), pp. 9–10.

reformer, cited Malthus effectively to show that rapid colonial development could not be achieved without immigration:

"Find us fresh customers!" cry all, from the shopkeeper, listless, and almost helpless, over his wares, to the artificer, whose tools are idle in his basket. Fresh customers! Most willingly, but where are they to come from? From natural increase of our present population? Hardly so. Read the Rev. Mr. Malthus's book on the principle of population— the book of a very wise, a very amiable, a very much abused, and certainly not a too well understood man. He will show you that, under the most favourable circumstances, you may double your population, from within in some fifteen or twenty years. Will you wait so long for your new customers? Where will they come from then, but from across the seas? What! Immigration? Ay, Immigration![12]

W. E. Hearn, in his *Plutology*, formulated an optimistic interpretation of Malthusian theory. Humans, like all living things, Hearn explained, had a propensity to increase "in geometrical proportion." However, he continued, humans were restrained by their innate good sense from breeding to the point of overpopulation. He wrote:

Population is year by year increasing; and such an increase, slow though it be, must at some remote period, if it continue, fill the world. But we need not dread the approach of such a period, and we cannot foresee the means by which this tendency will be controlled. The preventive check is sufficient to retard almost indefinitely the question of over-population; and when that question does present itself, the people to whom it will come will doubtless be enabled to deal with it.[13]

Hearn believed that national economies of scale occurred as population grew and as natural resources were exploited by increasingly labor-intensive techniques.

If wealth bring with it population, population in its turn brings with it wealth. The most favourable circumstances for the exercise of all the industrial aids, but especially of co-operation and exchange, are found amidst a large population. . . . A large population therefore, if

12. *Victoria Suffering a Recovery: A Lecture* (Melbourne, 1860), p. 13. See also "Speech by Mr. Michie on the Immigration Vote in the Legislative Assembly of Victoria, 2 June, 1870," reprinted in C. M. H. Clark, *Select Documents in Australian History 1851–1900* (Sydney, 1955), pp. 246–47.

13. William Edward Hearn, *Plutology: or the Theory of the Efforts to Satisfy Human Wants* (London, 1864), p. 394.

it be duly organized, ought to be more wealthy, and consequently to have a greater capacity for increase, than a small one.[14]

Hearn asserted that Australia contained abundant resources for population growth and that relatively remote areas such as Queensland and the Northern Territories stood in relation to the settled regions as the colonies stood to the mother country.[15]

Not all colonial interpretations of Malthusian theory pointed to continued good fortune from the old world's overcrowding. H. K. Rusden, the first secretary of the Royal Society of Victoria, drew pessimistic conclusions from Malthus even for the Australian environment with its apparently bountiful natural resources. He argued that the cloud of population pressure threatened not only the mother country but also the colonies.

Yet there are persons to be found who deny these effects of the pressure of population upon the means of subsistence, and assert that over-population is an impossibility in a country or a world where there are many unoccupied square miles of land. Is it not certain from experience that there must be pressure of population wherever it is concentrated? Is it not the nature of civilization to concentrate population? And must there not be over-population wherever the concentration exceeds that of the means of subsistence?[16]

A Queensland writer suggested that an uncontrolled population was quickening the approach of a stationary state in Europe and that this development in itself would restrict colonial growth. A staples-producing economy, he contended, could expand only with the markets for its products, and should the old world become stagnant both the demand for wool and Australian economic progress would reach their limit.

That "stationary state" which Malthus predicted, and Mill saw no reason to "deprecate" may be nearer, as to the mother country, as to wealth and profits, than superficial observers imagine. And it does not follow that if we could produce one hundred million pounds of wool instead of twenty-two millions, that profitable sale would be found for the larger quantity.[17]

14. *Ibid.*, pp. 391–92.
15. *Ibid.*, p. 96.
16. "Labour and Capital," *Melbourne Review*, I (1876), 78.
17. William Coote, *Railway and Loan Policy in Queensland, in Connection with its Bearing upon the Position of the Colony, as Illustrated by its Financial and Commercial History* (Brisbane, 1879), p. 27.

Critics of Malthus as well as admirers made themselves heard in the colonies. The enormous and empty Australian continent suggested to several settlers that the pressure of population on resources was exaggerated as a world problem and was yet far off. In 1845, Robert Lowe's newspaper, *The Atlas*, praised a Legislative Council report which had said "it may be justly alleged that whilst in old countries one of the greatest of social evils arises from the population pressing upon the sources of subsistence, the converse of that proposition may be held, to a certain degree, as justly applicable to this colony." *The Atlas* later printed a facetious report of a "GREAT MEETING OF CATS" with the following account:

> Mrs. Creamlap next addressed the meeting—but in so low a voice that she was sometimes almost inaudible. However, we understood her to say, that the wrongs of cats were past belief. No creature suffered more from the tyranny of political economists. Even house-maids were bitten with the notion of superabundant population, and drowned kittens by fives and sixes. She herself had only a fortnight since lost four little ones—all of 'em soused in a pail (*Sensation.*)[18]

Colonial radicals and social reformers voiced criticism of Malthus at an early date. Pioneer labor leaders discovered quickly that export of Britain's excess population threatened disruption of their working conditions and weakness to their organization; they argued that colonial development should take place not with continued immigration but through domestic population increase. Malthus, they insisted, had exaggerated the population problem of the old world.[19] A critic of subsidized or "bounty"

18. *The Atlas* (Sydney), October 11, 1845, p. 541, and November 22, 1845, p. 619. For a similar skeptical statement of the relevance of Malthusian theory in the colonies, see Thomas Bartlett, *New Holland: Its Colonization, Productions and Resources, with Observations on the Relations Subsisting with Great Britain* (London, 1843), p. 26.

19. A writer in Sydney argued in 1843: "These legislators of ours have studied their political economy among scourges and fetters. They appear to think that cheap labour is essential to public prosperity . . . are we to be told in the middle of the nineteenth century that high wages *are* a disadvantage to society? The fact is the very reverse, as all know who are in the least acquainted with the science of political economy. 'What improves the circumstances of the greater part of society,' says Adam Smith, 'can never be regarded as an inconvenience to the whole. . . .'" "Immigration," *Weekly Register of Politics, Facts, and General Literature*, August 26, 1843, pp. 57–58. T. A. Coghlan noted in 1918: "The great body of the wage-earners have been, if not hostile, entirely indifferent to taking steps to introduce new population." *Labour and Industry in Australia* (London, 1918), p. 874. A. St. Ledger has drawn attention to the contradictory position held by labor spokesmen late in the century when they were forced to defend

immigration wrote in 1855: "What we should desire to bring about, is an increase of wealth in proportion to numbers, and not of numbers in proportion to wealth. If we adopt this as a maxim, jealousy of high wages will cease, and the pretensions of those who live by labour will not appear so irksome and offensive."[20]

Colonial radicals objected to the pessimism they saw—or thought they saw—in Malthus' writings. The picture of an uncontrollable population running away from resources was completely inconsistent with their belief that Australia could become a promised land. Jorgen Jorgenson, a colorful and eccentric immigrant to Van Diemen's Land, pointed out that in the scriptures "It was expressly commanded man to 'go forth and multiply.'" Jorgenson castigated

the accursed theory of Malthus, and those like him, affecting the highest interests of posterity, if I may be allowed the expression—for should theories such as that of Malthus be acted upon, many would never be born who would otherwise enjoy life. If eternal happiness is the true end of the creation, the more that are the partakers of the feast, the better.[21]

In the second half of the nineteenth century, Malthus came under sustained fire specially from land-reformers who argued that if land or its benefits were made freely available the population problem would disappear. Before the end of the 1850's, easily accessible gold supplies began to diminish in the colonies, and miners were forced to turn elsewhere for employment. Agitation for homestead provisions resulted in an important series of

at the same time both a Marxian labor theory of value and restricted immigration. *Australian Socialism: An Historical Sketch of its Origin and Developments* (London, 1909), p. 150.

20. *Bounty Immigration, a Letter to the Members of the Legislative Council, from One Who Has Handled the Spade* (Melbourne, 1855), p. 8. Similar critiques of immigration to the colonies are reprinted in C. M. H. Clark, *Select Documents in Australian History 1851–1900* (Sydney, 1955), pp. 248 and 249.

21. *Observations on the Funded System; Containing a Summary View of the Present Political State of Great Britain, and the Relative Situation in Which the Colony of Van Diemen's Land Stands Towards the Mother Country* (Hobart Town, 1831), pp. viii and ix. See also Michael Roe, *Society and Thought in Eastern Australia, 1835–1851*, Thesis Submitted for the degree of Doctor of Philosophy in the Australian National University, 1960, p. 327, where it is noted of a New South Wales labor leader in the 1840's "To him both 'the devilish doctrines of Malthus' and laissez faire appeared as cloaks for pulling down the standards of the poor."

land legislation reforms, and the presence of unemployed labor was the strongest argument for change. Reformers were quick to reject all explanations of the unemployment which did not condemn the ill effects of land monopoly, and they attacked vigorously the fatalistic Malthusian hypothesis which they interpreted to mean that labor was doomed always to increase faster than employment and to press on natural resources. Henry Edmunds, an active New South Wales advocate of land nationalization, explained:

> For ages to come the population question, which has given so much trouble to political economists, will be only a question of subjugating and cultivating man's heritage for the common good. Land is now taken by public law for railways, schools and various other public purposes, from individuals, whether they consent or not—whether or not they be satisfied with the compensation they receive for their private interest therein. In this the supremacy of the State is duly recognised. We have but to extend the principle and we shall speedily arrive at a satisfactory solution of that all-important and most difficult problem, the Land Question.[22]

Henry George's supposed refutation of Malthus was copied and praised highly. Percy R. Meggy summarized George's arguments thus:

> Malthus . . . maintained that the tendency of population is to increase faster than the means of subsistence, and consequently the more mouths there are to feed, the less there would be to put in each. It was reserved for Henry George to show the complete fallacy of both these assumptions, and to prove (1) that, wages, instead of being drawn from capital, are in reality drawn from the product of the labour for which they are paid, and (2) that population does not tend to increase faster than the means of subsistence at all. . . . Political economy, as guided by its reverend professor, does not say, like Punch, to those about to marry—don't; but to those about to have children—don't. The mere statement of such a hideous, grossly immoral, and, I need not say, thoroughly irreligious doctrine, is enough to damn it in the eyes of every decent person.[23]

22. "Social Science," *Sydney Quarterly Magazine*, 1883, p. 267. See also H. W. S. Edmunds, "Land, Labour and Capital. Salus Populi Suprema Lex," *ibid.*, 1885, pp. 37–49.
23. "Land Nationalisation—What is it?," *Sydney Quarterly Magazine*, 1889, pp. 313–14. For a similar statement see F. Cornell, "Progress and Poverty: A Defence," *Victorian Review*, VIII (1883), 608.

After George's visit to Australia in 1890, his critique became a land reform cliché. A *Bulletin* correspondent in 1891 conceded that population limitation might slow progress toward poverty, but it would also, he argued, delay fundamental reforms. "The sooner the evil comes, the sooner will the remedy be found, for the human race is a slow-moving concern, which travels only under the pressure of necessity, and never looks for a cure until the disease is upon it."[24] E. W. Foxall, honorary secretary of the New South Wales Land Nationalization League, accused Malthus of religious heresy, and he remarked sarcastically: "it is cause for some surprise that the revised version of the scriptures did not leave out the text—Happy is the man that hath his quiver full of them."[25] The winner of an essay competition in 1892 concluded: "the theories of the check-population professors are gradually shrivelling into matter dry-as-dust."[26]

A. J. Ogilvy, a reasonable and influential land-reformer, examined population theory in detail. He denied that population expansion was a social problem on the ground that death before marriage, celibacy, and barrenness all tended to reduce the potential rate of increase. In fact, he said:

we find that in countries like Australia, where there is work for all who choose to work and at what is recognised as "high wages," where subsistence is cheap, land fit for cultivation but uncultivated in abundance, and where there are no catastrophic checks, the actual rate of increase is only about 2 per cent. per annum, thus doubling about every 35 years. We may call this, then, the normal rate of increase of population. It is far from being a "geometrical" rate.[27]

Social progress, Ogilvy said, could be expected to cause a decline in fertility among humans analogous to the deterioration which took place in wild animals when domesticated.

. . . as brain power is cultivated and as life becomes more artificial reproductive power diminishes, so that, with a rising standard of comfort, a more regulated life and higher intellectual tastes, a sort of Law

24. "How Rents Keep Up," *Bulletin*, XI (1890–91), No. 578, p. 6.
25. E. W. Foxall, "Henry George," *Australian Economist*, VI (1898), 14.
26. Harry S. Taylor, *Tucker Prize Essay on the Single Tax* (Adelaide, 1892), p. 25.
27. "The Malthusian Doctrine," in a collection of essays by Ogilvy entitled *The Third Factor of Production and Other Essays* (London, 1898), p. 159.

of Diminishing Return comes in, and the increase of population slackens from causes having little or nothing to do with "prudential restraint."[28]

Ogilvy supported his assertions about population change with a stage theory of economic development. In the first two stages, through which much of the world had already passed, men lived as hunters and herdsmen, and subsistence increased slowly. Then—

there comes a time, when man begins to invent and to improve; when he begins systematically to observe and to reflect, to conceive new ideas and carry them out, investigating the laws of nature, and perfecting his instruments and his social and industrial organisation. From the moment that he once fairly enters this progressive stage his power of producing subsistence increases rapidly; indeed, so long as there is land enough, the rate of increase of production (whether of subsistence or other things) may much more fairly be described as "geometrical" than his rate of increase in population.[29]

Ogilvy argued, on the basis of his experience in Australia, that increasing returns from "Scientific discoveries, mechanical inventions, improved communications, diffused education, co-operation and organisation" could be expected to counteract diminishing returns from limited natural resources.[30] He believed that classical growth theory, formulated in a European environment, had misled economists in Australia into taking for granted diminishing productivity of natural resources over time. Diminishing returns, he maintained, required a limited and fully employed cultivatable area, and did not apply in the colonial situation. Ogilvy marveled at the paradox in new countries of pessimistic economic doctrines retained in the face of rapid increase in per capita income.

The curious thing is that the Malthusian economist sees perfectly well that the production of *wealth* is becoming daily more easy; but,

28. *Ibid.,* p. 160.
29. *Ibid.,* p. 161.
30. Ogilvy said, "My point is that the facilities in all these numerous departments increase much faster than the increase of return from *the land* diminishes; and, as a consequence, it becomes *easier* every year to procure subsistence, notwithstanding the increase of population; indeed, in great measure *because* of it." *Ibid.,* p. 165.

misled by the Law of Diminishing Return, he thinks that it is that kind of wealth only that consists of superfluities, and does not include subsistence—subsistence being dependent on cultivation, and the increase from cultivation tending to fall off.[31]

Ogilvy denied that colonial territorial expansion occurred merely as a response to population pressure with marginal land employed in the Ricardian pattern only as food supplies grown on more productive property became inadequate. Australian settlement, he contended, was stimulated not by increasing scarcity but by successive autonomous technological innovations.

The true explanation, we submit, is that as knowledge and skill improve and appliances multiply, lands that formerly could not be cultivated with profit now become worth cultivating; and so *invite* resort to them, no matter whether subsistence be short or not; subsistence becoming *easier* to procure in consequence of the diminishing labour required to secure a given product, and the increasing area rendered available.[32]

Ogilvy concluded from the evidence of rapid colonial development that the twin bogeys of classical economics—land shortage and redundant population—were not legitimate matters for concern in the foreseeable future. Above all, he insisted, economists should not let their attention be distracted from true social evils, particularly the growth of monopolies and inequitable income distribution.

In addition to land-reformers, other writers were critical of Malthus' work. W. H. Irvine, a lecturer in political economy at Ormond College of Melbourne University, rejected the scientific method of Malthus in a general indictment of the use of induction in economics. Irvine declared:

It is always a matter for regret that writers on these subjects should like Malthus, with his arithmetical and geometrical ratios—pretend to invest with an appearance of precision principles which *ex natura rei* are incapable of anything like exactitude. In Political Economy a quantitative analysis is usually impossible; all that is required is that its theories should be correct qualitatively. To attempt more merely

31. *Ibid.*, p. 166.
32. *Ibid.*, p. 167.

discredits the truth which does exist in them, by making them appear to claim recognition under false colours.[33]

Andrew Garran, in 1890, questioned the value of Malthus' arithmetic and geometric progressions and deplored excessive attention to overpopulation as a social problem. "Let us," he said, "always beware of single cause philosophers."[34]

Socialists objected to Malthusian theory for the same general reasons as land-reformers. They believed that advocacy of social change was inconsistent with pessimistic population expectations. Socialist misrepresentation of Malthus was occasionally quite shameless, as in the following comment.

Malthus would get rid of the pauper in this way. He says, "To marry without a competency to start with, is clearly an immoral act; such a man must be taught that God and nature rightly doom him and his family to starvation, and that it has no claim on society for the smallest portion of food. A child born under such circumstances has no business where he is. At nature's feast there is no vacant seat for him; she tells him to be gone." Malthus's remedy for the pauper is, "Starve him to death," and this, mind you, was the gospel preached in the present century by the fortunate class, whose circumstances only called for a profession, and not the practice, of the laws laid down by Malthus.[35]

One critic of evolutionary theory regarded Malthus as a grim prophet of "survival of the fittest," and said "the canon of Darwin and the theory of Malthus, culminates in force."[36]

A Queensland socialist in the 1890's maintained that concern with population pressure and "the parsimony of Nature" had withdrawn critical attention from the fundamental role of government in society and the need for overall social reform.

It is scarcely too much to say that a mighty movement towards political and industrial freedom was decisively checked, confused, and broken

    33. "Prof. Bonamy Price on the Doctrine of Rent," *Victorian Review*, X (1884), 228. A less cogent critique of Malthus is "Bonar's Malthus," *Imperial Review*, January, 1886, pp. 42–43.
    34. A. Garran, "A Criticism of Malthus' Doctrine," *Australian Economist*, II (1890–93), 61. Garran objected to Malthus rather than to population study generally, and at a meeting in 1892 "Dr. Garran said that whenever we dug down to bedrock on any great social question, we always found the population question there to meet us." *Australian Economist*, II (1890–93), 281.
    35. "Socialism," *Bankers' Magazine and Journal of the Bankers' Institute of Australasia*, VI (1892–93), 861.
    36. William Webster, "Property in Land," *Melbourne Review*, IX (1884), 403.

up by a book. That book was the famous "Essay on Population," and its author was the reverend T. R. Malthus. . . . Capitalism was exonerated, political incompetency and corruption were shown to be of little moment; the chief cause of the terrible impoverishment of the masses, and of all the evils which poverty brings in its train, was over-population.[37]

Australia, stated this writer, was existing proof that social ills did not disappear where population was small and resources were plentiful. The economic system rather than the economic environment required alteration. The new world could show the old that the classical statement of dangers facing mankind was faulty, and that the wrong evils had been named. Capitalism, not scarcity, was the real cause of human suffering.

It is admitted, of course, that the Malthusian ideal community has never yet been realised, but there have been, and are now, close approximations to it. Take, for instance, our own fair Australia today. Here, surely, population is sufficiently sparse, while there is practically no limit to the wealth which the soil will afford them. . . . Yet even here, enjoying all these advantages, we have poverty in all its horrid aspects, and with all its accompanying evils. It drives men here to sin and crime, and women to degradation, as it does in older lands. It fills our prisons, our pauper houses, and our lunatic asylums.[38]

A writer in the Sydney *Bulletin* in 1885 summarized succinctly the sentiment behind much of the opposition to Malthusian theory. He said: "if *Mr. Malthus* be correct in his ideas, the Word of God is all wrong, and as Plenty is unattainable, Peace also is impossible, and consequently the Millenium is an absurd fancy."[39]

Frequent attacks of land-reformers, socialists, and other critics inspired defenders of Malthus. R. M. Johnston presented in 1888 a summary of Malthus' population theory to the Royal Society of Tasmania suggesting that Henry George had "altogether failed to grasp the various elements of this problem." Using symbols, Johnston assumed various possible growth rates and alternative

37. *The Catholicity of Socialism* (Leaflets for the People, No. 3, Brisbane, n. d., circa 1892), p. 5.
38. *Ibid.*, pp. 6–7.
39. "The Millenium," *Bulletin*, II (1885), No. 100, p. 3. Similar statements were made in "Malthus and Vanderbilt," *ibid.*, III (1885–86), No. 149, p. 4; and "Quack Remedies for Social Ailments," *ibid.*, XI (1890–91), No. 556, p. 6.

checks to construct a simple model of population change. In this way he hoped to prove that the significant contribution of Malthus was an analytical system and not a specific prophecy.[40] Johnston argued that mechanical inventions and geographical discoveries had delayed but had not eliminated the potential problems revealed by Malthusian analysis.

> Had it not been for the fortunate discovery of the steam engine, the perfecting of means of transport, and the discovery of new fertile continents (Australia and America) thinly populated, opening out vast additional sources of production and affording relief to the pressure of crowded European centres, it is certain the state of Europe would be very different at the present hour. . . .[41]

Johnston considered that calculation of a total population which would make possible the greatest general welfare was crucial even for a country as thinly peopled as Australia. If the optimum population level were once passed it might never be regained. He said:

> While there are different stages of civilisation in existence, over-population is a relative term applicable to the particular country, and not an absolute quantity to be determined by an absolute number of persons to a given area as most erroneously indicated by Mr. George. This is clear to any one who studies the civilisation and the sanitary state of different countries.[42]

Johnston condemned persons who wished for Australia a mere increase in total national product at the expense of what he

---

40. Johnston isolated as factors of the problem: "P.—Actual population. I.— Natural tendency to increase. . . T.—Natural limit of life; death at extreme old age. C.—Checks, cutting off life before the healthy limit of life has been reached [he mentions six separate groups]. . . M.—Moral Restraint operating upon I. E.—Means of subsistence, varying with season, but increased absolutely by numbers and increasing knowledge of natural resource; the ratio per individual, however, gradually lessening as the poorer lands and waters are invaded by swelling numbers. F.—The absolute limit when a greater density for each square mile of the earth's surface is reached by removal or the minimising of all checks. G. The final stage, the world peopled to its full limit, and the struggle for existence only permitting a perpetuation of the maximum population at F by the effects of T, and the failure of either in any degree, again re-introducing of necessity checks C, . . . and so producing a decline in population, although the natural tendency I to multiply may still be conceived to be as vigorous and prolific as at the first." "The Problem of Malthus Stated," *Papers and Proceedings of the Royal Society of Tasmania,* 1888, pp. 53–54.
41. *Ibid.,* p. 58.
42. *Ibid.,* p. 57.

believed was the correct goal of public policy, the improvement of welfare per capita. He concluded:

Few recognise the truth that individual welfare depends less upon the greatness of the aggregate wealth of a country than upon the proportion which freedom from excessive competition gives each individual over the local natural sources of utility, including primary wants; and that the country possessing the greatest aggregate of material wealth may, owing to the competition of excessive numbers, present the spectacle of a small privileged minority absorbing an unparalleled share of luxurious wealth, while the masses are struggling for the barest subsistence.[43]

Beside Johnston other spokesmen came to the defense of Malthus in Australia. A Melbourne reviewer in 1890 condemned Edward Bellamy for ignoring the "unanswerable" population problem, and he rejected Henry George's denial of Malthusian theory thus: "a perusal of his [George's] arguments reveals the fact that he has missed the very kernel of the law, and devotes his energies to pounding the husks."[44] H. A. Ellis reminded the Australian Economic Association that Malthus alone had discovered a way of avoiding the Darwinian struggle through voluntary limitation of numbers by moral restraint.[45] S. Clemes suggested to the Australasian Association for the Advancement of Science at Hobart in 1892 that: "The Population question is the root matter in all economic reasoning" and "Malthus deserves all honor as being the first to attempt a scientific statement of the question." He added: "we must not ignore the many sides of it which Malthus overlooked," and particularly the possibility of unrestricted increase in Australia.[46] A stoical writer in the *Bulletin* observed: "The world cannot by any process at present available, avert the increase of population, but none the less its tendency to whoop and let off rockets because of the spread of

43. "Observations on Current Social and Economic Problems, Presidential Address in Section F," *Report of the Second Meeting of the Australasian Association for the Advancement of Science held at Melbourne, 1890*, p. 158.
44. "Looking Backward," *Pacific Quarterly*, I (1890), 31.
45. H. A. Ellis, "The Theory of Malthus," *Australian Economist*, II (1890–93), 38–41.
46. "A Layman's Criticism of Current Theories of Population, an abstract," *Report of the Fourth Meeting of the Australasian Association for the Advancement of Science held at Hobart, 1892*, p. 590.

that incurable complaint called Man is a sight to make angels weep."[47] Annie Besant's Malthusian popularization of *The Law of Population* was published at Sydney in 1889, and Mrs. Besant herself toured the colonies in 1894 lecturing on theosophy and other matters.[48]

As late as the 1920's, university professors still were defending Malthus from misrepresentation. In 1925, R. C. Mills of Sydney University presented a summary of Malthusian theory, like Johnston calling for determination of an optimum population—"the number which will produce the greatest average material welfare."[49] A few years later, J. B. Brigden at the University of Tasmania asked the question "What right have our workers to enjoy a higher standard of comfort than would-be workers from other countries?" He answered with the words of Edwin Cannan: "It is better that (a people) should learn that over-population is an evil, and how to avoid it, in one country or continent, than after extending it all over the world."[50]

Toward the end of the nineteenth century, Malthusian theory came to be discussed in the colonies not as in earlier years with reference only to Australia and to Britain, but now applied to Asia, Africa, and the need for selective immigration. The Australian policy of excluding colored immigrants originated in workers' fears of excessive competition; in the 1850's and 1860's conflicts on the gold fields between whites and Chinese and on the Queensland sugar plantations between whites and Pacific Islanders led to widespread clamor for restricted Asiatic admission.[51] Ulti-

47. "The Increase of Population," *Bulletin*, XI (1890–91), No. 590, p. 6.
48. Annie Besant, *The Prosecuted work. The Law of Population: Its Consequences and Its Bearing upon Human Conduct and Morals* (Sydney, 1889). The editor of the *Bankers' Magazine* in Melbourne reported regretfully: "Half the public in the southern capitals have been rushing to hear Mrs. Besant talking about heaven, according to the tenets of her very last creed. The other half have been enjoying themselves in their peculiar fashion by looking at a dance, usually called the 'can-can,' which used to be prohibited, and should be put a stop to now." "Editors Notes," *Bankers' Magazine and Journal of the Bankers' Institute of Australasia*, VIII (1894–95), 299.
49. "Economic Aspects of Population," *Australasian Journal of Psychology and Philosophy*, III (1925), 248–53. Another statement of Malthusian principles was contained in J. Alexander Gunn, *Livelihood* (Melbourne, 1927).
50. "Population: The World and Australia," in *Pitt Cobbett Essays and Addresses*. (*Second Series*) (Hobart, n.d., c. 1927), unpaged.
51. See A. H. Charteris, "Australian Immigration Policy," in P. D. Phillips and G. L. Wood, eds., *The Peopling of Australia* (Melbourne, 1928), pp. 77–78. See also C.M.H. Clark, *Select Documents in Australian History 1851–*

mately, non-whites were prevented in a variety of ways from immigrating in large numbers, and the urgency of the problem declined for some years.[52] Would-be Asiatic immigrants were regarded as enterprising individuals attracted by Australia's opportunities but without the support of their own governments and not constituting a menace as potential invaders and dangerous only when landed on Australian shores.

In the 1880's and 1890's, a few farsighted writers suggested that the problem of Asian exclusion might become more sinister and serious through time. Their fear rested on expectations of a future population expansion in the non-white countries of the world. R. M. Johnston warned the Royal Society of Tasmania that even if the colonies were successful in discovering and maintaining an optimum population level their Asian neighbors, driven to desperation by the pressure of unemployed and redundant labor, might insist on gaining entrance and thereby destroy the Australian success. A white Australia, although unanimously desired at home, could still be in peril from the Malthusian problem abroad. Johnston asked:

if a higher culture could be enabled by provident moral or self-control to successfully grapple and overcome the present enigmas of social science, now is it possible that such a culture could be effectually preserved if it were open to be disturbed by the cheap labour or the starvation price products of other nations, who, by improvidence and lack of moral control, were still sunk in the abyss of that wretchedness which is due to over-population?[53]

Johnston was one of the first to express the Australian fear of Asian overpopulation which grew with worldwide recognition of

---

1900 (Sydney, 1955), pp. 68, 216–17, and 240; and Colin Clark, *Australian Hopes and Fears* (London, 1958), p. 47.

52. Discussions of the "White Australia Policy" by contemporary observers are contained in: Joseph Lee, "Anti-Chinese Legislation in Australasia," *Quarterly Journal of Economics*, III (1888–89), 218–24; John Douglas, "Asia and Australasia," *Nineteenth Century*, LII (1902), 43–54; Frank Parsons, "Australasian Methods of Dealing with Immigration," *Annals of the American Academy of Political and Social Science*, XXIV (1904), 209–20; and Philip S. Eldershaw and P. P. Olden, "The Exclusion of Asiatic Immigrants in Australia," *ibid.*, XXXIV (1909), 410–23.

53. "Root Matters in Social and Economic Problems. (Is the Poverty of the Masses a Necessary Concomitant of Increased Accumulation of Wealth in the Aggregate?)," *Papers and Proceedings of the Royal Society of Tasmania*, 1889, p. 204.

a social and economic awakening in Asia. Australians came forcibly to realize that the problem of discouraging would-be migrants pulled by the country's resources might soon be complicated by the actions of more aggressive invaders pushed from their homelands by sheer necessity.

The most detailed and carefully reasoned statement of the new Australian concern with Asian overpopulation came from Charles H. Pearson. In his widely acclaimed book, *National Life and Character: A Forecast,* Pearson assumed as a self-evident fact that the white race was at a higher evolutionary stage than the colored races, and he proceeded to show that a larger proportional white increase was a desirable but, with present rates of population growth, a highly unlikely development. He wrote:

> It is a very small matter to the world at large whether titled and landed aristocracies show a tendency to gradual extinction, but it cannot be accounted a matter of indifference if the higher races increase very much more slowly than the lower. Even if we assume higher and lower to be merely relative terms, and that the negro is capable of becoming as fine a specimen of humanity as the Englishman or the Frenchman, it has to be recognised that very favourable conditions and a long period of time are required for the transmutation, which, after all, is more than a little doubtful.[54]

Pearson used classical economic growth theory to prophesy world development, and accordingly he predicted that developed nations in the near future would face the conditions of a stationary state: a crowded population living at subsistence levels with an absence of innovation and accumulation. For Pearson, however, the force impelling change was not internal population growth as in the simple classical model, but rather population pressure from Africa and Asia. He presented statistical proof that in certain European countries, notably France, population increase had almost ceased, while in most tropical Eastern countries it had been very large. When the tropics became intolerably crowded, Pearson argued, colored races would inevitably swarm into temperate zones that were traditionally the exclusive

54. *National Life and Character: A Forecast* (London, 1894), p. 78; and see above pp. 335–38.

habitat of whites. Because of a desire to preserve their higher civilization, whites had restricted members voluntarily, but their restraint would be of no use so long as the colored population of the world increased unabated. Pearson predicted that gradually as whites were threatened and restricted they would take final refuge in socialism and other inferior political forms. Before they were overwhelmed, whites would experience slow racial deterioration; "while the lower races are raising themselves to the material level of the higher, the higher may be assimilating to the moral and mental depression of the lower."[55]

Pearson regarded Australia as one of the last strongholds of the white race, but already threatened by the Chinese and on the brink of final destruction. On this ground he justified the colonies' policy of racial discrimination as an emergency measure, and he complained of British criticism and misunderstanding.

The fear of Chinese immigration which the Australian democracy cherishes, and which Englishmen at home find it hard to understand, is, in fact, the instinct of self-preservation, quickened by experience. We know that coloured and white labour cannot exist side by side; we are well aware that China can swamp us with a single year's surplus of population; and we know that if national existence is sacrificed to the working of a few mines and sugar plantations, it is not the Englishman in Australia alone, but the whole civilised world, that will be the losers. . . . We are guarding the last part of the world, in which the higher races can live and increase freely, for the higher civilisation. We are denying the yellow race nothing but what it can find in the home of its birth, or in countries like the Indian Archipelago, where the white man can never live except as an exotic.[56]

Pearson's prophecy was born of despair. He could see no escape from an uncontrollable colored population, advancement of humanity to a low stationary state, and inevitable social decay. Nevertheless, his forecast formulated almost seventy years ago and regarded at the time as fantastic, reveals when examined today startling instances of predictive accuracy. For example, he wrote concerning Asia and Africa:

55. *Ibid.*, p 101.
56. *Ibid.*, p. 17.

The day will come, and perhaps is not far distant, when the European observer will look round to see the globe girdled with a continuous zone of the black and yellow races, no longer too weak for aggression or under tutelage, but independent, or practically so, in government, monopolising the trade of their own regions, and circumscribing the industry of the European; when Chinamen and the nations of Hindostan, the States of Central and South America, by that time predominantly Indian, and it may be African nations of the Congo and Zambesi, under a dominant caste of foreign rulers, are represented by fleets in the European seas, invited to international conferences, and welcomed as allies in the quarrels of the civilised world. The citizens of these countries will then be taken up into the social relations of the white races, will throng the English turf, or the salons of Paris, and will be admitted to intermarriage.[57]

Pearson's warning did not go unheeded by Australians. Two spokesmen from Ballarat called him "One of the most intellectual statesmen who ever resided in Australia" and praised his efforts to prevent growth of "the Asiatic canker-spot." They concluded:

There is no selfishness in endeavouring to preserve Australia as a heritage for the white races—not exclusively, be it remembered, for the Anglo-Saxon race— unless it be the selfishness of patriotism, since it aims at nothing which has not a place in the creeds of the greatest Englishmen. It is a policy dictated by common-sense and prudence, and based on the best interests of humanity.[58]

George Handley Knibbs, the first Commonwealth Statistician, succeeded Pearson as the most outspoken prophet of the danger to Australia in world population growth. In an appendix to his 1911 Census, Knibbs warned that humanity faced an imminent population crisis and that soon either numbers or living standards would have to be restricted.[59] In 1921 Knibbs explained to the Australasian Association for the Advancement of Science that in the face of dire peril Australia should fill her empty spaces and reduce her attractiveness to the world's impatient victims of overcrowding.

57. *Ibid.*, pp. 89–90.
58. Oswald P. Law and W. T. Gill, "A White Australia: What it Means," *Nineteenth Century*, LV (1904), 150.
59. *Commonwealth of Australia, Report of Census*, 1911, I, Appendix A, p. 453.

. . . a study of the statistics of the last century discloses the fact that population cannot increase for long at the rate which has characterized the century just closed . . . to rapidly people countries with sparse populations can alone give them a measure of safety . . . a rapid rate of growth involves the support as dependents of a very large fraction of the population, and can be reached only by hard work, thrift, abstemious living, and more than ordinarily efficient production.[60]

By 1926 Knibbs had become a staunch advocate of what he termed "The New Malthusianism."[61] In *The Shadow of the World's Future* (1928), Knibbs examined historical and contemporary rates of population increase and concluded that if present growth continued the world would reach its maximum human density in less than two hundred and fifty years. He emphasized again the need for rapid protective Australian increase. Racial discrimination among prospective immigrants posed a problem of conscience for Knibbs, but he did not treat the matter as a moral issue. He argued that migration conditions should be satisfactory both for migrants and for receiving countries, and that above all migration should not be viewed principally as a means of relieving overcrowding in older countries. He explained: "migrations of human beings are only a palliative of the kind of difficulties that are arising, and are merely a very partial and temporary solution of the troubles occurring through large increases of population."[62] In overpopulated countries, birth-control was the only long-run solution, and migration should never be pictured as an alternative. In the receiving country, migration presented crucial problems, and necessary conditions for successful absorption were complex. Without mentioning the desirability of Asian exclusion from Australia, Knibbs listed several convincing reasons why some types of immigration could cause undesirable friction and how on certain grounds discrimination among immigrants was justified.

60. "Statistics in Regard to World and Empire Development," *Report of the Fifteenth Meeting of the Australasian Association for the Advancement of Science held at Melbourne, 1921, (Hobart Meeting)*, p. 197.
61. See G. H. Knibbs, "The New Malthusianism in the Light of Actual World Problems of Population," *Scientia*, 1926, pp. 379–88.
62. G. H. Knibbs, *The Shadow of the World's Future* (London, 1928), p. 107.

Among different peoples the ordinary standards-of-living vary greatly. Because of this, and also because of racial and national vanities, not always well-based, migrants are not always welcome. And even if they were very welcome, there are economic difficulties in the way of reaching relatively equal degrees of population-saturation. Usually great hardships have to be faced in opening up new country, and also in developing new conditions. Satisfactory migration often requires that the migrants should possess some capital, and it is to be noted that the capacity of any people to receive migrants with small amounts of capital or none at all, is usually very limited indeed, as things are at present, or as they are likely to be.[63]

Knibbs concluded with an eugenic argument for selective migration. A new country receiving immigrants would benefit humanity as well as itself by choosing only the best stock from which to breed its citizenry.

One of the most important questions, even at the present time, is a proper selection among the various possibilities of migration, etc. It is self-evident that the world's empty spaces would be better filled by the progeny of the superior human stocks, rather than by that of the more degenerate. Peoples who are robust physically, temperamentally stable, just, equitable, friendly and forceful in life, mentally well-endowed, have pre-eminent rights not merely in their own interests but in the interests of the world's future. The gap between human derelicts and degenerates and the finer specimens of humanity is enormous. . . . the time has arrived when defectives and degenerates should not be allowed to reproduce their kind . . . .[64]

The implications for Australian public policy of Malthusian theory applied to population growth in Europe and at home differed widely from the implications when this theory was used to interpret population increase in Africa and in Asia. During most of the nineteenth century, Australians regarded population pressure as a future domestic threat and a current European problem understandable most easily by a comparison of arithmetic and geometric progressions. They cautioned themselves to exercise restraint and to profit from errors of the old world by limiting numbers and selecting only the most desirable immigrants. Then, in the 1890s, non-white population expansion elsewhere in the

63. *Ibid.*
64. *Ibid.*, p. 112.

world was identified as a real and pressing danger, and domestic population growth, instead of posing a long-run threat, came to be regarded as a major defense against hordes from the north. Subsequently, Australia's emptiness in the face of Asia's multitudes dominated most discussion of population policies and problems.

In this section it has been shown that population theory was a controversial discussion topic from the early days of Australian history. Classical doctrines were supported by colonists who approved subsidized migration from old countries, and they were attacked by labor spokesmen, optimistic social reformers, and others. Malthus' theories were defended by students of political economy and were revived by worried observers of rapid population growth in neighboring lands.

Population Analysis and Public Policy

Throughout the nineteenth century most discussion of public policy in the colonies made reference to size of population. Before responsible government was introduced at mid-century, however, workers tended to be regarded more as units of a commodity "labor" than as autonomous citizens, and "labor" was treated as a valuable factor of production whose price should be kept low through continual increases in supply. A New South Wales legislative committee in 1845 argued thus in favor of steady immigration:

The resources of a new country can only be developed by constant additions to its population. However great such resources may be, their value and importance bear a direct relation to the means employed in rendering them available. The gradual and natural increase of population, arising from excess in the number of births over that of deaths, would present a scale of augmentation far too slow to meet the demands of the Colony.[65]

65. "Report from the Select Committee on Immigration," *Votes and Proceedings of the Legislative Council of New South Wales*, 1845, p. 1. Similar statements are contained in Reports of Select Committees on Immigration, 1838, 1839, 1840, 1841, 1842, and 1847.

This committee expressed sentiments which in a few years would
have horrified legislators elected by democratic process. For
example, the report explained, "It is with much anxiety, that
your Committee have learnt that there is a considerable augmentation in the rate of wages, of pastoral and agricultural labour,
over what has prevailed for the past two years."[66]

Early advocates of subsidized immigration argued that increase in colonial population would generate economies of scale
and raise average per capita income. John Dunmore Lang, an
active exponent of this position, reasoned that the colonies were
far below optimum population density and would be justified in
borrowing funds with which to sponsor and attract immigrants.
He wrote: "In short, it would only be an investment of capital on
the part of the colony, on which a high interest is to be expected,
and on which a high interest would infallibly be realized."[67]

Colonial governments agreed in general that population increase was of great value, and a typical Tasmanian select committee reported in 1865:

Without a dissentient voice they [the Committee] have come to the
conclusion that it is absolutely necessary for the best interests of the
Colony that the Government and the Legislature should devise some
means of attracting additional population to our shores. In no other
way, they feel assured, will the natural resources of Tasmania be properly developed; in no other way will her lands be settled by an industrious and thriving population; in no other way will the elasticity
of the Public Revenue be secured, and the burden of taxation be
rendered light and easy to be borne; in no other way will a sound and
substantial foundation be laid for the certain and permanent prosperity
of all classes in the community.[68]

It was admitted widely that population density was an important
determinant of land values. T. C. Aldrich explained in 1883: "It
is perfectly true that the value of land is almost wholly deter-

66. "Report from the Select Committee on Immigration," 1845, p. 2.
67. *Emigration; Considered Chiefly in Reference to the Practicability and
Expediency of Importing and of Settling Throughout the Territory of New
South Wales, A Numerous, Industrious and Virtuous Agricultural Population*
(Sydney, 1833), p. 7.
68. "Report from the Select Committee on Immigration," *Journals of the
House of Assembly of Tasmania,* 1865, p. 4.

mined by the amount of population upon or adjoining it. Only the presence of man makes land a marketable commodity."[69]

By the turn of the century, the crucial significance of population growth had become a stock assertion of statesmen, and in 1925 W. M. Hughes listed yet again economies of scale that could be achieved with a large population.[70] S. M. Bruce, when discussing advantages of establishing the Development and Migration Commission in 1926, pointed to the inseparability in Australia of population increase and economic development. He said: "We cannot develop unless we have more population, and we cannot absorb more migrants unless we develop. . . . We have never, in this country, really faced the problem of development."[71]

In addition to recognizing the long-term value of increased population, colonists believed also that their economy had become accustomed to steady immigration and would have to undergo painful adjustments if migration ceased. A writer in the Sydney *Empire* contended in 1852 that a reduction in the rate of immigration would not increase wage rates, as claimed by some workers, but by deranging "demand and supply" would cause depression and would actually lower wages.

Labourers are themselves consumers, and therefore contribute to employment in proportion to their numbers. No department of industry can be productive without labour, and without adequate labour it will barely sustain itself, to say nothing of the expansion of the principle of social activity abroad. The influx of labour should always be higher than the previous demand, in order to ensure the requisite supply, exhausted by contingencies and advancements, and to give an ever-increasing momentum to enterprise.[72]

A Melbourne writer in 1862 suggested that depression which followed a decline in gold-mining in the 1850's was caused in

69. "The Land Laws of New South Wales," *Victorian Review*, VIII (1883), 490.
70. *Australian Industries: The Interdependence of "Primary & Secondary"* (an address delivered before the Chamber of Manufactures of New South Wales, Sydney, 1925).
71. "Speech by the Prime Minister on the second reading of the Development and Migration Bill," reprinted in "Development and Migration Commission. First Annual Report for period ending 30th June, 1927," *Commonwealth of Australia, Parliamentary Papers*, 1926–27, p. 5.
72. "The Causes of Depressed Wages," *Empire*, June 25, 1852, p. 1130.

part by a lessening in the rate of increase in effective demand for domestic products associated with a reduced inflow of new miners. He recommended assisted immigration to revive prosperity through restoration of population increase, and he explained: "Abundant consumption of natural products and of excisable articles, of course, operates favourably upon the revenue and commerce of the country; and, by a parallel of reasoning, anything which tends to check the growth of the population must act prejudicially in the same directions."[73] After the financial collapse of 1893, subsidized immigration was again suggested as an anti-depression measure. J. Currie-Elles told the bankers of New South Wales: "The certain outlet for Australian products will be promoted by the increase of population, and all energies should be directed to aid immigration of the most desirable class, and give the immigrants some *locus standi*."[74]

The New South Wales Treasurer in 1878 stated his general approval of all public expenditures which resulted in increased population.

It is the population of a country that makes it great, prosperous, and wealthy, for without population there would be no produce obtained from the land—the origin of all wealth; there would be no local consumers, and no enterprise to give value to that produce, even when yielded, by introducing it into foreign countries and creating and stimulating an external demand for it; in effect, the land would be comparatively if not absolutely valueless.[75]

A writer defending assisted immigration in 1881 declared that population was an important part of real capital in a new country, and he calculated that in Victoria "Every fresh immigrant that lands upon our shore is worth £160 to us, and if as many came out as between 1851 to 1879, they would be wroth £80,000,000 to us. If the economic value of immigration has no weight in

73. Francis H. Nixon, *Population; or, A Plea for Victoria* (Melbourne, 1862), p. 11.
74. "Financial Review," *Journal of the Institute of Bankers of New South Wales*, III (1894), 5.
75. "Financial Statement of Hon. Henry Emanuel Cohen, 31st January, 1878," contained in James Thomson, ed., *The Financial Statements of the Colonial Treasurers of New South Wales* (Sydney, 1881), p. 397.

such a case, what stronger argument can be employed in its favour?"[76]

Major political controversies were argued occasionally in terms of the effects of particular policies upon population growth. Discussion of railway construction in the 1850's centered on the ability of the colonial population to support public works. Advocates of government-sponsored lines argued that settlement would follow transport improvements, and others claimed that population should precede railroads. A critic of subsidized railways in New South Wales wrote:

> The true state of the case is simply this. The population is too small to support a Railway in any part of the colony. It would require a very large traffic, and very high charges, to cover the working expenses. The first requirement is impossible without a dense population; and with any amount of population is incompatible with the second.[77]

One Tasmanian author called for free land grants to attract settlers, and construction of roads rather than railroads. He exclaimed: "I aim at higher objects than those comprized in any mere mercenary considerations; such as the general advancement of the country; the full exposition of her productive capacity; and above all, the accumulation of a stationary population; without which everything we do is useless."[78]

Commercial policy was debated frequently with reference to the effects of protection or free trade upon the size of population. In defense of free trade, Henry Parkes traced the British population from the beginning of the eighteenth century to the middle of the nineteenth century to show a sudden increase in the growth rate after repeal of the Corn Laws in the 1840's.[79] Protectionists replied that population would increase only where society was "balanced," and that for this reason secondary manu-

76. James Allen, "Immigration: Australia's Great Want," *Victorian Review*, III (1881), 746.
77. "Railways," *Sydney University Magazine*, January, 1855, p. 35.
78. *The Letters of "American," on the Projected Railroads, and the Public Lands of Tasmania* (Tasmania, 1856), p. 33.
79. "Speech in the Legislative Assembly of New South Wales, 1873," in Henry Parkes, *Speeches on Various Occasions Connected with the Public Affairs of New South Wales 1848–1874* (Melbourne, 1876), pp. 389–90.

facturing should be encouraged in a staples-producing country. Francis Gould Smith explained in 1877 that without protective tariffs Victoria could never have more than a few centers of population and would remain governed by a merchant class. He argued:

> With a generally diffused system of judicious and discriminating protection, concentrating the industry of EACH COUNTRY on ITS OWN soil and indigenous materials, industries flourish, wealth increases, commerce follows, population multiplies throughout the entire globe. But without such artificial legislation, population, industry and wealth have a tendency to concentrate and to confine themselves to favoured spots.[80]

Other protectionists pointed to rapid population growth in the protected United States, and they predicted a flood of immigration to Australia following the imposition of high colonial tariffs. One South Australian explained:

> In order that a country may progress and become wealthy, a large population is absolutely necessary. The paucity of population in this colony has always been recognised as one of the great drawbacks, and in order to supply the deficiency no other system appears to have occurred to our legislators but to import immigrants. This is no doubt a very primitive way of settling a difficulty, but it does not speak much in favour of the perspicacity of the governing classes. If more attention had been paid to making the colony attractive, and every possible assistance rendered to the establishment of manufacturing industries and the development of natural resources, people would have been flocking here now and for many years past at their own expense, because they would be sure of plenty of profitable employment.[81]

The *Australasian Insurance and Banking Record* commented on controversy surrounding a lessening of the Victorian population growth rate in the 1870's and took a neutral position on the influence of commercial policy. The journal reported:

> While one section of the press laments this halting in the race, and ascribes it to the protectionist policy of the Government, another section denies the allegation, or, while admitting it to a certain extent,

80. *The Australian Protectionist* (Melbourne, 1877), p. 22.
81. *Protection or Free Trade* (Adelaide, 1880), p. 15. For a similar statement on the importance of protection to population growth see J. W. Cheek, *Protection: as it Affects the Farming Industry of Tasmania* (Launceston, c. 1888), p. 7.

applies the salve to its conscience, that though the colony may be poorer in population than was expected, it is richer per head. From both of these extreme deductions we dissent, and think the truth lies between the two.[82]

The Prime Minister's committee of economists which reported on the effects of the Australian tariff in 1929 argued that one of the principal benefits of protection had been increased ability of the Australian economy to support population. The authors said:

We have to recognise in the tariff as a whole, in spite of its un-doubted extravagances, a potent instrument in maintaining at a given standard of living a larger population than would have been otherwise possible. It seems certain that without the tariff we could not have offered the same field for immigration, and would not have been able to maintain our growth of population.[83]

As Professor Jacob Viner has pointed out, the committee's claim of increased carrying capacity attributable to protection varied throughout the report, and "the authors have not given adequate weight to the possibility of securing these ends by means more economical of the national income."[84] Nevertheless, it is significant that the committee considered a larger population an end for which the Australian people were willing to make substantial sacrifices.

If discussion of population theory outlined in the first section of this chapter, and the attention to population policy described in this section are kept in mind, the enthusiastic collection of statistics and analysis of problems examined in the following sections may be seen in perspective. A writer in 1894 expressed succinctly the characteristic confidence of Australians in the importance of population study. He said:

the study of population returns rises to supreme importance, and furnishes a large amount of valuable information, from which it is possible

---

82. "The Census of Victoria: Its Results and Its Lessons," V (1881), 244.
83. J. B. Brigden, D. B. Copland, E. C. Dyason, L. F. Giblin, and C. H. Wickens, *The Australian Tariff: An Economic Enquiry* (Melbourne, 1929), p. 84. And see above pp. 34–39.
84. *Economic Record*, V (1929), 308–9. Mr. Colin Clark has written of the committee's estimate of Australia's increased population as a result of protection: "These contentions were ingenious but just not correct." *Australian Hopes and Fears* (London, 1958), p. 146.

to arrive at a closer approximation to the actual state of a community, than is to be found in any other statistics . . . there is little room for doubting that vital statistics afford as reliable a test of progress as can well be found.[85]

Pioneer Vital Statistics

In the early years of settlement, knowledge of human numbers was vital for government. Supplies were imported, and the size of shipments from home depended on accurate calculations of need. So long as the colonies remained predominantly penal settlements, "musters"—with all heads counted physically—were vital also to prison discipline.[86] When Australia developed as an important source of wool, the mercantilist vision of colonies as economic units for the benefit of the mother country, receptacles for unwanted citizens, and producers of raw materials, implied that a close tally be kept of colonial resources. Owners of firms requested periodic statements of accounts, and in the same way the mother country required a list of its colonial possessions. In response to need, statistics of population were provided by colonial governors in annual "Blue Books."

In the 1840's and 1850's, convict transportation to the eastern Australian colonies ceased. In the same period, a British domestic policy of economic liberalization resulted in gradual repeal of the Corn Laws and Navigation Acts. Britain became less certain of the value of colonies as close appendages, and self-government grad-

85. A Correspondent, "Population," *Journal of the Institute of Bankers of New South Wales,* III (1894), 105.
86. A remarkably detailed and thorough analysis of an economic census of the prison colony of Norfolk Island was presented to the London Statistical Society in 1843 by Captain Maconochie, R.N., late Superintendent of Convicts. He discussed the geography, geology, and agricultural history of the island together with characteristics of the present and former residents, including their place of origin, religion, sentence, cause of death, age of conviction, and education. Maconochie made good use of his confined statistical universe and the information available from convict indentures to make recommendations for changes in government policy. Captain Maconochie, "Criminal Statistics and Movement of the Bond Population of Norfolk Island, to December, 1843," *Journal of The Statistical Society,* VII (1845), 1–49, and summarized as "On the Statistics of the Criminal Population of Norfolk Island," *Report of the Fourteenth Meeting of the British Association for the Advancement of Science,* 1844, transactions, pp. 93–95.

ually was introduced. With growing independence, the colonies inherited a host of new burdens, including responsibility for finding solutions to many social and economic problems. This section covers the work and thought of a few individuals who faced the challenge of autonomy and undertook collection and presentation of essential population data.

New South Wales. The first Australian census was taken in New South Wales in 1828 and was followed by others in 1833, 1836, and every subsequent five years until 1861, when the decennial sequence was introduced.[87] A nominated Legislative Council was created in New South Wales in 1823, and the concession of partial elective representation in 1842 coincided with improvement in census procedures. However, census reports continued to be published, like results of earlier musters, in colonial Blue Books, without analysis and in a form not readily available or comprehensible to the public. A member of the Royal Statistical Society in London complained that the 1846 census of New South Wales was "very defective" in form and "involves the necessity of many calculations to render it intelligible."[88]

Interpretation of early census statistics was provided by private persons in non-official publications, in the first instance by Ralph Mansfield, a cleric and amateur statistician who like other notable contemporary divines combined religion with business and public affairs.[89] Mansfield advised a committee of the Legislative Council in 1845 to accept recommendations for census reform made by a committee of the London Statistical Society in 1840.[90] He noted with approval in 1847 that his suggestions had been accepted:

87. G. H. Knibbs, *The First Commonwealth Census, 3rd April, 1911, Notes* (Melbourne, 1911), pp. 5–6; and Reginald H. Hooker, "Modes of Census-Taking in the British Dominions," *Journal of the Royal Statistical Society,* LVII (1894), 289–358.
88. F.G.P. Neison, "Analysis of the Census of New South Wales," *Journal of the Statistical Society,* XI (1848), 38.
89. In addition to Mansfield's writings the following works contained digests of census results: "Colonial Statistics," *Arden's Sydney Magazine,* October, 1843, p. 90; "Australian Statistics," *New South Wales Magazine,* 1843, pp. 4–8.
90. "Report from the Select Committee on the Census Bill, with Minutes of Evidence," *Votes and Proceedings of the Legislative Council of New South Wales,* 1845.

Previously to the Census of 1841, the returns were meagre and unsatisfactory; but in that year, under the able guidance of the present Colonial Secretary, the Honorable Edward Deas Thomson, Esq., they exhibited a fulness of information and a perspicuity of arrangement which seemed to meet almost every wish that the statistical enquirer could have formed. In each of these qualities, however, the tables of 1841 are immeasurably surpassed by those of 1846.[91]

Mansfield was an enthusiastic advocate of special census studies, and he helped to convince a select committee of the Legislative Council in 1846 that the desirability of railway construction could be assessed only from adequate statistics of population density and probable freight requirements. He became chairman of a citizens' subcommittee which gathered information and submitted a report on the subject.[92]

After introduction of responsible government in New South Wales, annual "Statistical Registers" replaced the more limited Blue Books; these were compiled first under the direction of Christopher Rolleston, an emigrant from Nottinghamshire. Rolleston had a genuine interest in social enquiry, and he found much in common with the scholarly Governor Sir William Denison, whose private secretary he became in 1855. In 1856 Rolleston was appointed Registrar General, and he soon reformed the hitherto inaccurate and unsatisfactory methods of registering births and deaths. In 1858 he took charge of the Statistical Branch of the Colonial Secretary's office, and thereby he accepted responsibility for the census. Rolleston had a deep sense of purpose and wide knowledge of statistical undertakings elsewhere in the world. He was concerned with many types of statistics, but he considered the census to be one of the most significant. He explained to the Philosophical Society of New South Wales in 1856:

Of all statistical inquiries, the census of the people is among the most important which a government can undertake, as its results must form

91. *Analytical View of the Census of New South Wales for the Year 1846* (Sydney, 1847), p. 1. cf. Ralph Mansfield, *Analytical View of the Census of New South Wales for the Year 1841* (Sydney, 1841).

92. See "Report from the Select Committee on Railways, with Minutes of Evidence," *Votes and Proceedings of the Legislative Council of New South Wales*, 1848, esp. Appendix B and Appendix D.

the basis for administrative and economical measures of the highest consequence, and supply the elements of almost every statistical investigation.[93]

Rolleston outlined progress made in the census of other countries, and he urged uniformity in the statistics of the colonies. He observed that a precedent for inter-colonial co-operation could be found in proposals of a recent conference held at Brussels:

Taking instruction from the recommendation thus adopted by the statistical congress at Brussels, the advantages of a similar uniformity in the time and method of ascertaining the state of the population in the Australian colonies, cannot be too strongly impressed upon their respective governments; we should thus have a basis of comparison which would illustrate severally and unitedly their social condition and progress, and facilitate the means by which they may be beneficial to one another.[94]

Rolleston regarded collection of population statistics through the census and under the recently reformed Registration Acts as an important function leading to progress in the social sciences.

There can be no doubt that a series of statistical returns prepared under these Acts, relating to a large population, and to a period of years, and embracing every variety of physical and social condition, will afford materials from which several important laws (general as to this country) may be satisfactorily deduced, whilst the laws special to particular localities, will be brought out in the working of the problem. . . .[95]

Timothy A. Coghlan was the first New South Wales Government Statistician independent of the Registrar-General's office. He took responsibility for the census as well as for collection of general statistics. Coghlan's interests and contributions were many, but his most significant work in vital statistics concerned analysis of the birth-rate, examined in the next section.

Tasmania. In Tasmania, as in New South Wales, vital statistics in the early years were interpreted to the public by private or

93. "The Science of Statistics," read to the Philosophical Society, December 10, 1856, *Sydney Magazine of Science and Art*, I (1858), 255.
94. *Ibid.*
95. *Ibid.*

semi-official persons. In 1846, T. J. Ewing, a cleric, at the request
of Lieutenant Governor Sir John Franklin, published a statistical
summary of data collected by government. Beginning in 1849,
Lieutenant Governor Sir William Denison commissioned James
Barnard to prepare "by order" a series of statistical digests and
analyses "compiled from Official Records in the Colonial Secretary's Office."[96] Barnard paid special attention to population
statistics and was particularly fond of comparing growth rates
in Australia with those of other countries, notably the United
States. In a paper to the Royal Society of Van Diemen's Land,
Barnard discussed American actuarial life-tables, and he urged
that similar tables be prepared for Australia.

. . . they would form a basis for the equitable distribution of life-in-
terests in estates, pensions, and legacies; they would assign the true
valuation of life annuities, assurances, and reversions of heritable
property, and tend to protect the public from many ill-adjusted financial schemes, founded in ignorance of the true probabilities of life;
they would correct a multitude of prejudices and misconceptions respecting the healthiness of different localities; and, besides this, form
a common standard of reference in all those moral, sanitary, and mercantile statistics which have brought to light most valuable truths and
generalizations, and which give promise of still greater benefits in the
advancement of civilization.[97]

In 1867, E. C. Nowell was appointed Tasmanian Government
Statistician with James Barnard as his assistant. Nowell hoped to
accomplish two purposes from the collection and study of population statistics: attraction of immigrants by publicizing the
healthy Tasmanian environment and probability of long life,

96. See Rev. T. J. Ewing, "Statistics of Tasmania, 1838–1841. . . ," *Tasmanian Journal of Natural Science, Agriculture, Statistics, &c.*, II (1846), 141–
50; James Barnard, "Statistics of Van Diemen's Land for 1844–1846. . . ,"
ibid., III (1849), 444–55; "Observations on the Statistics of Van Diemen's
Land for 1848 . . . ," *Papers and Proceedings of the Royal Society of Van Diemen's Land*, I (1849–50), 102–34; "Observations on the Statistics of Van
Diemen's Land for 1849 . . . ," *ibid.*, II (1851–54), 1–33; "Observations on
Tasmanian Statistics for the Decennial Period 1844 to 1853 . . . ," *ibid.*, III
(1855–62), 9–36.
97. "Observations upon the Census of the United States, taken 1st June,
1850. From the Official Report of the Superintendent of Census," *Papers and
Proceedings of the Royal Society of Van Diemen's Land*, II (1851–54), 382;
see also "Observations upon the Census Taken Throughout Van Diemen's Land,
1st March, 1851," *ibid.*, pp. 33–40.

and direction of social reform by isolating areas of poor health and high mortality. After one investigation, Nowell discovered that the death rate was higher in Tasmanian towns than in the countryside, and he suggested that this discrepancy was proof of the need for municipal sanitary improvement.[98] Robert M. Johnston succeeded Nowell as Tasmanian Government Statistician, and with wide interests in population questions he continued and extended the collection of data.

Victoria. Prior to gold and independence from New South Wales in 1853, residents of Victoria had to turn for colonial statistics mainly to the writings of William Westgarth, a Port Phillip merchant.[99] After separation, W. H. Archer was appointed Assistant Registrar General and conducted the first census in 1854.[100] With Henry H. Hayter as chief clerk, Archer began an outstanding statistical department: he published periodic "essays" of high quality and encouraged inter-colonial statistical co-operation.[101] In 1861, at Archer's invitation, colonial representatives met at Melbourne to discuss united statistical action, and in 1871 the census was taken simultaneously in New South Wales, South Australia, and Victoria.[102]

After Archer's retirement, Henry Hayter became Government Statistician of Victoria. He was less imaginative than either of his outstanding contemporaries, Coghlan or Johnston, but his

98. E. C. Nowell, "On the Vital Statistics of Tasmania, with Especial Reference to the Mortality of Children," *Papers and Proceedings of the Royal Society of Tasmania*, 1875, pp. 108–26. A "Statistical Account of Tasmania from 1804 to 1823," *Journals of the House of Assembly of Tasmania*, 1856, may have been prepared by Nowell.
99. See for example, *Australia Felix* (Edinburgh, 1848); and a series of "Reports" on "the District of Port Phillip" in the 1840's. William Mackintosh continued Westgarth's Reports in *General Statistical and Commercial Report of the Province of Australia Felix* (Melbourne, c. 1848).
100. Major Campbell, the Registrar General, reported: "There were 45,880 schedules to abstract, many of which were almost as difficult to decipher as an Egyptian inscription, without any mention of the Chinese returns." "Statistics of Victoria," *Melbourne Monthly Magazine of Original Colonial Literature*, I (1855), 249.
101. A discussion of the work of Archer, Campbell, and Hayter during the 1850's is contained in D.R.G. Packer, "Victorian Population Data, 1851-61: A Preliminary Analysis," *Historical Studies Australia and New Zealand*, V (1951–53), 307–21.
102. W. H. Archer, *The Progress of Victoria: A Statistical Essay* (Melbourne, 1873), p. 3.

tenure of office from 1874 to 1891 spanned the formative period
of Australian vital statistics. He was an effective critic and was
always influential offering advice and urging co-operation.[103] On
several occasions as he neared retirement, Hayter emphasized
the transcendant importance he attached to population studies.
He argued that in the colonies the census should be taken more
often than every ten years because, among other reasons, enumerators forgot their techniques.[104] He wished more detail in questionnaires and all possible care in planning and performance.[105]
In 1893 he claimed that defective registration procedures were
destroying the value of population estimates between censuses.
Officials employed greater energy listing entries to than exits
from a colony, and a person who traveled between Australian
ports was often counted as a new immigrant. The solutions Hayter
put forward for difficulties of vital statistics were those he recommended for most Australian statistical problems: closer inter-
colonial co-operation, a more frequent census, and more careful
statistical techniques.[106]

Other colonies. Apart from New South Wales, Tasmania, and
Victoria, other Australian colonies did not produce notable
pioneers in the collection or presentation of population data.
Josiah Boothby was a competent Under-Secretary and Government Statistician of South Australia in the 1870's, but his statistical labors were not distinguished.[107] In 1878, Henry Hayter

103. See below pp. 477–79..
104. "On Official Statistics," *Report of the First Meeting of the Australasian
Association for the Advancement of Science held at Sydney, 1888*, pp. 417–33.
105. Hayter said: "Having been connected officially with four censuses of
this colony, the last two of which have been entirely under my own management, I can confidently say that upon the intelligence and forethought exercised
in devising and planning the preliminary arrangements, the success of a census
mainly depends." "The Coming Census," *Report of the Second Meeting of the
Australasian Association for the Advancement of Science held at Melbourne,
1890*, p. 579.
106. "Disturbance of the Population Estimates by Defective Records," *Report of the Fourth Meeting of the Australasian Association for the Advancement of Science held at Hobart, 1893*, pp. 537–41; and reprinted in *Journal
of the Royal Statistical Society*, LVI (1893), 327–30.
107. Boothby provided a "Statistical Sketch" for William Harcus, ed., *South
Australia: Its History, Resources, and Productions* (London, 1876). This
included, among the statistics, a photographic view of "Park Side Lunatic
Asylum."

read a paper to the Philosophical Society of Adelaide in which he used South Australian statistics to illustrate remarkably high infant mortality. The sensational discovery some months later that Hayter's disturbing conclusions rested on faulty data may have inspired subsequent improvement in South Australian statistical technique.

The Commonwealth. The Australian Commonwealth Constitution gave to the Federal Parliament authority "to make laws . . . with respect to Census and Statistics," and accordingly the Commonwealth Bureau of Census and Statistics was created in 1906.[108] George Knibbs, first Commonwealth Statistician, saw as his primary task "unification and co-ordination" of statistical effort, and he helped to achieve these goals by a conference of state statisticians in 1906.[109] In subsequent years, with the co-operation of the states, vital statistics of the Commonwealth were steadily improved. Knibbs' reputation as a vital statistician was worldwide, and in 1920 he acted as chairman of the Census Committee of the Imperial Statistical Conference.[110] C. H. Wickens succeeded Knibbs as Commonwealth Statistician and maintained a steady interest in population study.[111]

Analysis of Special Population Problems

It has been shown in the previous sections of this chapter that colonists demonstrated consistent interest in the size and growth rate of their population. Until late in the nineteenth century most special population studies by Australians were concerned prin-

108. F. R. E. Mauldon, *The Use and Abuse of Statistics with Special Reference to Australian Economic Statistics* (Melbourne, 1933), pp. 18–19.
109. "Unification of Australasian Statistical Methods and Co-ordination of the Work of the Commonwealth and State Bureaux. Conference of Statisticians of the Commonwealth and States of Australia and Colony of New Zealand. Melbourne—November and December, 1906," *Commonwealth of Australia, Papers Presented to Parliament*, 1907–8.
110. "Statistical Conference (British Empire). Report and Resolutions Accompanied by Explanatory Memorandum and Observations by the Commonwealth Statistician," *Commonwealth of Australia, Papers Presented to Parliament*, 1920–21.
111. For Wickens' views on the census see his *Professional Paper on Census Taking* (Sydney, 1910).

cipally with the volume of immigration. Occasional surveys were made of domestic birth and death rates, but most of these were designed either to indicate the need for sanitary reform or to convince prospective settlers of an environment's comparative "healthfulness" and freedom from positive population checks.[112] In this section, attention is directed to several population studies which illustrated notable competence or imagination. These studies included: pioneer actuarial analysis by Morris Pell, models of population growth by R. M. Johnston, explanations of urban population concentration by Henry Hayter, birth rate enquiries by Timothy Coghlan, and improvements in demographic theory and statistics by G. H. Knibbs.

Morris Birkbeck Pell, Senior Wrangler at Cambridge in 1849 and foundation professor of mathematics at Sydney University, was the first to apply sophisticated analytical techniques to the population statistics of New South Wales.[113] In 1867, having taken part-time work as actuary with a local life insurance firm in addition to his university duties, Pell constructed a pioneer Australian life-table. He explained his methods and purpose to the Royal Society of New South Wales in that year:

> I have undertaken the task of examining the reports of the Registrar-General, from the year 1856 to the present time, and the Census returns for the years 1856 to 1861, for the purpose of ascertaining and exhibiting, as exactly as the data will permit, the rates of mortality at various ages; so that a comparison may be made between this colony and England, so far as regards the effect of the climate and condition of the people upon the duration of life. Another object which I had in view in undertaking this investigation was the formation of a complete mortality table, to serve as the basis of exact calculations respecting Life Assurances, and Life Annuities.[114]

112. See for example: Dr. Hall, "Climate and Vital Statistics of Tasmania for Fifteen Years, 1857–1871," *Monthly Notices of Papers and Proceedings of the Royal Society of Tasmania*, March, 1872, pp. 1–4; Thomas Borthwick, *A Contribution to the Demography of South Australia* (London, 1891); James Jamieson, "An Attempt to Estimate the Population of Melbourne at the Present Time," *Proceedings of the Royal Society of Victoria*, VII (1895), 173–79; R. M. Johnston, "The Health of Hobart," *Papers and Proceedings of the Royal Society of Tasmania*, 1896, pp. 1–21.

113. See Cecil W. Salier, "Professor Morris Birkbeck Pell: A Biographical Note," *Royal Australian Historical Society Journal and Proceedings*, XVIII (1932), 246–51.

114. "On the Rates of Mortality and Expectation of Life in New South Wales as Compared with England and Other Countries," *Transactions of the Royal Society of New South Wales*, I (1867), 66.

Pell discovered some of the problems which face all students of colonial population statistics: for example, that variable yearly immigration of persons of mature age prevents confident projection of population growth and estimates of proportions at different ages. He explained:

In a country such as England, where the existing population is the result chiefly of natural increase, not much affected by emigration or immigration, the increase from year to year proceeds according to laws which remain almost constant during a considerable period; and of the population living at any particular time, the numbers at the several ages are connected by relations which may be considered almost invariable. It was possible therefore in England, from the results of two censuses taken at an interval of ten years, together with the records of deaths during the intervening years, to estimate with considerable accuracy, by the method of Finite Differences, the numbers of the population and their ages, at intermediate and subsequent years. In this colony, however, where so large a proportion of the increase of the population is due to immigration, which is variable and uncertain, the methods alluded to can scarcely be applied. The natural proportion also amongst the numbers living at different ages is entirely destroyed here by the large influx of persons of mature age. These causes, as well as the comparatively small total numbers, have rendered the subject more than usually difficult to deal with, and at the same time the results more uncertain than those obtained from a larger experience in more populous and more settled countries.[115]

Pell found that rates of infant and child mortality were lower in New South Wales than in England, and he attributed this disparity to greater economic well-being of colonial parents and to the later age at which children were sent into fields and factories. Pell wished for calculations in more detail, but he noted that data which would permit such distinctions as Australian natives from foreign born were "buried" in the Registry Office and could be unearthed only at "considerable expense."[116] Pell retained his interest in population analysis, and in 1877 he

115. *Ibid.*, p. 67.
116. Pell said plaintively: "I wish that I could undertake to furnish some answer to the interesting question, whether the rate of mortality amongst the native born population is greater or less than amongst those born elsewhere—to foretell, in fact, whether the rates of mortality generally will increase or diminish as the proportion of the population born in the colony increases, and to ascertain whether a native of England increases or diminishes his expectation of life by coming to reside in New South Wales." *Ibid.*, pp. 69 and 73.

revised his life-table.[117] He remained convinced of the social significance of his findings, apart from their use to insurance companies, and he claimed "nothing . . . affords so clear a proof of
the real and general well-being of the people as the figures which
I now report."

The North American experience of economic development accompanied by extensive homestead settlement influenced profoundly Australian social thought throughout the nineteenth
century. As a result, Australians were relatively slow to examine
logically their own distinctive development pattern of rapid urban growth and large, thinly settled, pastoral land holdings. Both
new immigrants and old colonists were reluctant to concede that
climate, internal geography, and distance from markets gave
Australasia a heavy comparative advantage in wool production,
a process which was overwhelmingly labor-extensive and land-
intensive. Critics of the wool economy, who yearned for creation
of a sturdy landed yeomanry, argued that the large proportion
of arable land devoted to pasture and the relatively low returns
from food production were results mainly of monopoly and unjust legislation. Many land reforms proposed and enacted in the
nineteenth century were designed, as one writer said in 1879, to
overcome what was regarded as "the huge pernicious growth of
centralization, which is now gnawing away our resources and
corrupting our people."[118] Pastoralists and their defenders replied
that urban concentration reflected the aversion of immigrants to
"real" labor and fondness for the "fast" city life. J. W. Fortescue, a
British critic of Australian social policy, complained of "the met-
ropolitan populations, fully a third of the whole, disinclined for
hard work, bent upon the enjoyment of an easy and comfortable
life, and seeking to crush competition by restraint both upon
immigration and natural increase."[119] Cautious observers suggested that urbanization might be the most efficient disposition
of Australian labor, but they faced criticism from both sides,

117. "Rates of Mortality and Increase of the Population of New South Wales,"
Australian Practitioner, No. 3, April, 1878, pp. 145–75.
118. Capricornus, "Labour and Immigration," *Australian*, I (1878–79), 198.
119. J. W. Fortescue, "The Influence of Climate on Race," *Nineteenth Century*, XXXIII (1893), 871.

either of conservatism and inhumanity or of softness towards luxury and debauchery.

Only a few persons ventured to elaborate the unpopular economic explanation of urban growth, but statisticians were among the most valiant. In 1892 Henry Hayter explained that heavy population "concentration," although not necessarily socially desirable, was a natural economic development in Australia, and he predicted a still greater increase during the twentieth century in response to improvements in transportation. He made the relatively heretical assertion that the colonies might even gain socially as well as economically from urban expansion, and he favored particularly the development of a few large centers rather than numerous smaller ones.

It would no doubt be desirable, especially in newly settled States, that more persons should live in the country, where they are generally producers of wealth, than in either small or large towns, where a much larger proportion of them are merely distributors or dependents; but, since this cannot be the case, the balance of advantage is . . . in favour of cities being large and few instead of small and numerous.[120]

In response to British allegations in the depression of the 1890's that Australian difficulties could be traced to artificial and luxurious urbanization, R. M. Johnston replied that "the science of demography" showed "ratios of urban population" were not variables which could be altered by governments at will. The growth of cities was a function of agricultural technology, efficiency of transport, and generally the "progress made in civilisation."[121]

Confusion over the causes of urbanization did not end in the nineteenth century. In 1918 a select committee of the Victorian Parliament listed no less than nine unconvincing reasons for the "Drift of Population from the Country Districts," including old arguments of governmental "neglect," "want of systematised rural organizations," and "general dullness of country life."[122] In 1924,

120. "The Concentration of Population in Australian Capital Cities," *Report of the Fourth Meeting of the Australasian Association for the Advancement of Science held at Hobart, 1892*, p. 545.
121. "The Attack on the Credit of Australasia," *Nineteenth Century*, XXXI (1892), 602–22.
122. "Report of the Select Committee upon the Causes of the Drift of Population from Country Districts to the City," *Votes and Proceedings of the Legislative Assembly of Victoria*, 1918.

E. T. McPhee of the Commonwealth Bureau of Census and Statistics presented a critique of this report and like Hayter and Johnston he explained the "primary cause" of urbanization: Australian farms and sheep stations required relatively little labor, and with technological improvement employed "a continuously diminishing *proportion* of the community."[123]

Some Australians suggested that because the colonies were capable of producing adequate food supplies and contained bountiful unsettled land, the population when unrestricted by disease should increase at a rate approaching Malthus' geometric progression. Evidence conflicting with this assumption was discovered occasionally, but until the late 1880's was explained usually as the exception to a general rule. For example, in 1880, Henry Hayter and J. J. Fenton both reported to the Melbourne Social Science Congress a decline in the Victorian marriage rate and in the numbers of population at certain ages. Hayter commented that these developments were caused merely by a "falling-off in the number of males at marriageable ages, simultaneously with a continuous increase in the total population" associated with recent fluctuations in immigration.[124] This unusual situation, Hayter said, would correct itself quickly. The propensity to eventual population increase was not challenged seriously.

R. M. Johnston reaffirmed in 1884 that, in the colonies, economic scarcity was seldom a limiting factor, and he concluded that the death rate attributable to disease was the crucial element affecting internal population growth. He suggested that certain astronomical phenomena might explain important fluctuations in mortality.[125] After presenting a few simple correlations between astronomical and social data he proposed to the Royal Society of Tasmania an hypothesis that sunspot activity and the orbit of

123. "Drift of Population to the Cities," *Report of the Seventeenth Meeting of the Australasian Association for the Advancement of Science held at Adelaide, 1924*, pp. 535–50; and reprinted as "The Urbanisation of Australian Population," in P. D. Phillips and G. L. Wood, eds., *The Peopling of Australia* (Melbourne, 1928), pp. 165–87.
124. *Argus* (Melbourne), November 26, 1880, p. 10.
125. "Remarks on the Observed Periodicity of the Death-Rate, with Suggestions as to its Possible Relation with the Periodicity of Solar and Other Super-Terrestrial Phenomena," *Papers and Proceedings of the Royal Society of Tasmania*, 1884, pp. 236–39.

Jupiter, through meteorological change, affected the virulence of disease. Johnston was criticized sharply by an astronomer who considered the evidence insufficient even for formulation of a hypothesis, and he did not pursue the investigation further.[126]

Johnston, in one of his last discussions of the subject, made a remarkably accurate prediction of Australian population based on a stage theory of economic growth. Johnston explained that in the first or "pastoral" stage of a new country's development immigrants poured in to settle unoccupied lands, and export trades in staple raw materials were established. The labor absorption potential of a new country remained high throughout the pastoral stage until most of the land passed into private hands. In a second or "agricultural" stage a new country remained dependent upon the sale abroad of staple products, but the products were diversified. During the second stage, and unlike the first, unless a diminution in per capita income occurred, the domestic economy was able to offer new employment only to the extent that the labor intensity of staple production increased. Employment on the land, Johnston maintained, would have to keep in a fixed proportion to employment throughout the economy, and he suggested that in Tasmania the ratio was about four persons employed in staple production to ten employed in total. Whenever Tasmanian employment increased by ten workers, four new jobs in export industries had to be created. Johnston believed that in 1900 Australia had already reached the second development stage; most of the arable land had been settled and growth would take place through intensified wool, meat, and mineral production. Additions to population could be absorbed successfully less rapidly than in the first stage. The present residents of Australia, he argued, could not be expected to permit a reduction in their own living standards to make room for more immigrants. Therefore, it might be a full century before raw material exports had expanded sufficiently to permit the Australian economy to reach the third development stage where wide internal markets finally made large-scale production possible and manufacturing profit-

126. A. B. Biggs, "Observations on Mr. R. M. Johnston's Vital Statistics," *Papers and Proceedings of the Royal Society of Tasmania*, 1884, pp. 276–80; and Johnston's "Rejoinder," pp. 280–82. See above p. 226.

444   *Theory and Policy*

able. Only in this last stage would the Australian nation become truly independent. Johnston summarized his theory thus:

Broadly speaking, therefore, the development of a new colony passes, naturally, through three great successive predominating stages, partly overlapping, viz.: (1) The predominance of the pastoral stage. (2) The predominance of the agricultural stage. (3) The predominance of the manufacturing stage, as in England, Scotland, and Belgium. The last of these stages is a long way off so far as the Australasian Colonies are concerned, because density of population—involving a greater struggle for existence among the laboring classes—is essential to the establishment of great manufacturing industries which can successfully and independently compete with other countries in the external or open markets of the world. But pastoral and agricultural interests alone cannot support many persons to the square mile of territory, and hence, in young colonies, the rate of development, so far as population is concerned, is usually less rapid when all the more available and accessible lands have been encroached upon, and when the third or manufacturing stage is approached.[127]

Because, Johnston maintained, Australia had entered the intensification or agricultural stage of staple production in the decade before Federation, and because in this stage "the numbers engaged in the primary industries determine very rigidly the number of persons that may be employed with advantage in any other form of occupation" a prediction of the growth of primary employment alone made possible a population forecast for the entire economy. On the basis of this hypothesis, which amounted to the application of an international trade multiplier to population, and from evidence of increase in employment in staple industries during the previous ten years, Johnston calculated 1.73 per cent as the probable annual growth rate of Australian population through the twentieth century. Using this rate, Johnston forecast a population of 10.5 million in 1960, giving an error of only 2 per cent from the actual total of 10.3 million.[128]

In the 1880's and 1890's, observant writers expressed uneasi-

127. "Conditions upon which the Healthy Growth of the Population of Young Colonies Depend," *Papers and Proceedings of the Royal Society of Tasmania,* 1903–5, p. 29.
128. L. F. Giblin, Johnston's successor as Tasmanian Statistician, also evidenced continued interest in population problems after Federation. He discussed some peculiarities of the 1911 Census in "The Demography of Tasmania," *Papers and Proceedings of the Royal Society of Tasmania,* 1913, pp. 173–76.

ness about mounting evidence of an unusually slow rate of Australian population increase.[129] Most commentators believed that the prevailing depression had imposed temporary population checks of "poverty and misery," but others saw long-run changes of a more serious kind. J. W. Fortescue, a particularly vocal British critic of Australian society, asserted in 1893 that the evidence proved white men could never reproduce effectively and thrive in the antipodes. He remarked: "the people of Sydney wear in summer a limp, parboiled appearance resembling that of the degenerate whites in Barbadoes. . . ." In tropical regions, he maintained, "Somebody must be found to do work in this territory; white men will not, cannot do it, so coloured men must." He concluded arrogantly: "England ought to take over tropical Australia, and govern it as a part of our Asiatic Empire, to which, indeed, it really belongs. . . ."[130] Although rejecting Fortescue's pessimism, R. M. Johnston modified his earlier position in 1894 and cautioned colonists from concentrating excessively upon the death-rate as the only significant determinant of population growth. He drew attention to other factors, including the birth-rate and the age distribution both of the local population and of immigrants.[131]

At the turn of the century, T. A. Coghlan, the New South Wales Statistician, made a startling disclosure. In a carefully prepared and well-documented study, he proved that although immigration had declined seriously for at least a decade the birth-rate in New South Wales had also fallen steadily. He concluded:

No people has ever become great under such conditions, or, having attained greatness, has remained great for any lengthened period. The problem of the fall of the birth-rate is, therefore, a national one of overwhelming importance to the Australian people, perhaps more than

129. See for example, "Low Birth Rate and Slow Increase of Population," *Australasian Insurance and Banking Record*, VII (1883), 413; and Arthur Duckworth, *A Comparison of Populations and Rates of Mortality in New South Wales and Victoria* (read before the Insurance Institute, July, 1894), and reviewed by F. Y. Edgeworth, *Economic Journal*, IV (1894), 691–92.
130. J. W. Fortescue, "The Influence of Climate on Race," *Nineteenth Century*, XXXIII (1893), 868–71.
131. "How Far Can the General Death-Rate for all Ages be Relied upon as a Comparative Index of the Health or Sanitary Condition of Any Community?," *Papers and Proceedings of the Royal Society of Tasmania*, 1887, pp. 13–35.

to any other people, and on its satisfactory solution will depend whether this country is ever to take a place amongst the great nations of the world.[132]

In 1901 J. W. Barrett and Alexander Sutherland showed that Coghlan's findings applied to Victoria as well as to New South Wales.[133] These revelations caused considerable consternation, particularly as they were voiced at the time of colonial federation and when the strength and aggressive power of an awakening Asia to the north were making Australians aware of a need to populate their empty continent.[134] As Richard Teece explained in 1904, the colonists had accepted for years as a "truism of political economists that an increasing marriage rate is the accompaniment of increasing prosperity and is a consequence of it." Consequently, news of a decline was indeed "a shock to the State of New South Wales."

An immediate result of Coghlan's discoveries was appointment of a special commission of investigation.[135] The commission concluded that if immediate action were not taken decline in the birth rate would continue and the Australian people must come soon to accept a philosophy of race suicide; "unless some effective change is quickly introduced in the mental attitude of the people towards the question of reproduction, the material provided by the present generation for the continuance of the race in New South Wales will be inadequate to maintain even its present rate of increase in the numbers of the native-born population."[136]

Viability of the new Australian nation was the Commission's foremost concern. It reasoned that if the pace of internal popula-

132. *Childbirth in New South Wales: A Study in Statistics* (Sydney, 1900). Coghlan had studied characteristics of birth-rates during the 1890's, and his examination of "Deaths in Child-Birth in New South Wales," was hailed by the Royal Statistical Society in 1898 as a pioneer work with no equivalent in Britain. T. A. Coghlan, "Deaths in Child-Birth in New South Wales," *Journal of the Royal Statistical Society*, LXI (1898), 518–28; and *ibid.*, LXII (1899), 157–59.
133. See J. W. Barrett, "Presidential Address to the Medical Society of Victoria, January 20, 1901," in J. W. Barrett, *The Twin Ideals* (London, 1918), I, 317–50.
134. See for example, Percy F. Rowland, "The Beginnings of an Australian National Character," *Nineteenth Century*, LII (1902), 400–411.
135. Royal Commission on the Decline of the Birth-Rate and on the Mortality of Infants in New South Wales, "Report; together with Copies of Commissions, Diagrams, Statistical Evidence, and Statistical Exhibits," *Joint Volumes of Papers Presented to the Legislative Council and Legislative Assembly of New South Wales*, 1904, p. 52.
136. *Ibid.*

tion growth was not maintained, hopes for a British, or even for a white Australia were dim. "With a decay of individual and social morality we must expect the loss of all those qualities which have made the British race predominant. . . . The future of the Commonwealth, and especially the possibility of maintaining a 'white Australia,' depend on the question whether we shall be able to people the vast areas of the continent which are capable of supporting a large population." The Commission stated explicitly a fear of Asian population pressure from the north:

while Russia and Japan, prospective rivals of Australia for supremacy in the Western Pacific, are already seeking outlets beyond their own borders for the energies of their ever-growing people, it will be forty-six and a half years before Australia, with her three and three-quarter millions of inhabitants, and dependent alone on her natural increase (if this even be maintained at its present rate), will have doubled her population; 113 years before she will have twenty millions of people; and 168 years before her numbers will have reached the present population of Japan.[137]

The Commission's reform proposals included prohibition of contraceptive devices and also sanitary improvements to increase the fertility of women. Considering the gravity with which the Commission viewed the declining birth rate these were not notably imaginative suggestions. However, the *Report* probably had greatest influence by focusing national attention in a dramatic way on a new and pressing problem. Such matters as Asiatic restriction and subsidized European immigration were shown clearly to be related closely to the chances of survival for the new Commonwealth.

In the years immediately following the New South Wales Birth-Rate Commission, population studies achieved a sudden increase of popularity. An indication of new enthusiasm was an emotional volume entitled *Racial Decay* by Octavius Beale, one of the Commissioners and President of the New South Wales Chamber of Manufactures.[138] Beale reprinted lengthy excerpts from the works of numerous writers on population problems,

137. *Ibid.*, p. 53.
138. *Racial Decay: A Compilation of Evidence from World Sources* (Sydney, 1910).

including Garnier, Malthus, and Annie Besant. He attempted then to refute all arguments for birth control. Beale predicted that if the birth rate continued to fall Australia would follow ancient Rome to depopulation and national decadence. Shortly before World War I, the birth-rate reversed its decline, and by 1912 Arthur Duckworth was able to report that Australian fears of depopulation had practically disappeared.[139]

At Federation in 1900, responsibility for the census and for collection of other population statistics passed to the Commonwealth Government. State statisticians retained mainly an informal and unofficial interest. G. H. Knibbs, first Commonwealth Statistician, expressed special interest in population problems. In addition to prescribing policy, Knibbs made substantial contributions to population theory.[140] He collected and analyzed data and suggested and tested possible relationships between variables. Knibbs' best known theoretical work was "The Mathematical Theory of Population," published first as an appendix to his 1911 Census and later separately. This exhaustive treatise on statistical analysis of population data "received almost universal praise from a number of statisticians the world over." Arne Fisher called it "one of the leading works on mathematical statistics of the twentieth century."[141] William Bailey remarked that "one would search long to find a better piece of analytical work than this."[142] Horace Secrist termed it "unique in studies of population" and "a monumental piece of statistical technique."[143] Knibbs' other writings on particular problems of population study were concerned with such questions as the characteristics of multiple births, the influences of climate on population, and the incidence of disease.[144] Arne Fisher wrote, in a general review of

139. Arthur Duckworth, "White Australia: A Study of Australian Vital Statistics," *Economic Journal*, XXII (1912), 421–35.
140. See C. H. Wickens, "Sir George Knibbs," *Economic Record*, V (1929), 334–35.
141. *Publications of the American Statistical Association*, XVI (1918–19), 156 and 157.
142. *Ibid.*, XV (1916–17), 802.
143. *American Economic Review*, IX (1919), 379–83.
144. See for example, G. H. Knibbs, *The Classification of Disease and Causes of Death, from the Standpoint of the Statistician* (Melbourne, 1907); *Proposals of the International Statistical Institute Regarding the Statistics of Tuberculosis* (Melbourne, n. d.); *Four Professional Papers* [on the statistics of disease]

Knibbs' work: "small pamphlets from the hands of Mr. Knibbs have always brought to the present reviewer a very refreshing breeze of stimulating thought and a stream of new and original ideas. They have always been admirable in their brevity and lucid expression and stand in a class by themselves as examples of a clear and lucid exposition of thought."[145] Knibbs believed that in "young countries where the flux of population, owing to migration differences, is essentially different from that of old populations" all relevant factors affecting population growth should be considered carefully.[146] He hoped that regular census reports could be enlarged to include discussions of statistical methodology, extended interpretation of data, and description of socio-economic background (technology, natural resources, and human customs): "an ordinary population census can be made to tell a far more interesting, instructive, and valuable story than it does at present."[147] C. H. Wickens, and others in the Commonwealth Bureau of Census and Statistics, continued the tradition begun by Knibbs of giving special attention to analytical problems of vital statistics.[148]

(Sydney, 1913); *Mathematical Analysis of Some Experiments in Climatological Physiology* (London, 1912); "On the Influence of Infant Mortality on Birthrate," *Journal and Proceedings of the Royal Society of New South Wales*, XLII (1908), 238–50; "Note on the Influence of Infant Mortality on Birth-Rate," *ibid.*, XLIV (1910), 22–24; "Suicide in Australia. A Statistical Analysis of the Facts," *ibid.*, XLV (1911), 646–90; "Multiple Births, their Characteristics and Laws Mathematically Considered," *ibid.*, LIX (1925), 128–45; "The Human Sex-Ratio and the Reduction of Masculinity Through Large Families," *ibid.*, pp. 212–22; "Protogenesis and Ex-Nuptial Natality in Australia," *ibid.*, LXI (1927), 73–114; "Rigorous Analysis of the Phenomena of Multiple Births," *ibid.*, pp. 190–217; "Proof of the Laws of Twin-Births," *ibid.*, pp. 347–53; "The Theory of Large Population-Aggregates," *Metron*, I (1920), No. 1, pp. 113–25; "The Growth of Human Populations, and the Laws of Their Increase," *ibid.*, V (1925), No. 3, pp. 147–62.

145. *Publications of the American Statistical Association*, XVI (1918–19), 156.

146. "The Problems of Statistics," *Report of the Twelfth Meeting of the Australasian Association for the Advancement of Science held at Brisbane, 1909*, p. 515.

147. G. H. Knibbs, "The Analysis of a Census," *Publications of the American Statistical Association*, XVII (1920–21), 185; and see also "The Laws of Growth of a Population," *Journal of the American Statistical Association*, XXI (1926), 381–98; and continued *ibid.*, XXII (1927), 49–59.

148. See for example, Charles H. Wickens, "Investigations Concerning a Law of Infantile Mortality," *Report of the Fourteenth Meeting of the Australasian Association for the Advancement of Science held at Melbourne, 1913*, pp. 526–36; and "Human Capital," *Report of the Sixteenth Meeting of the Australasian Association for the Advancement of Science held at Wellington, 1923*, pp. 536–54.

By the end of the 1920's, centralization of vital statistics in the Commonwealth Government, widespread appreciation of the national need for economic growth, and increasing prestige for the social sciences in universities combined to give impetus to population study in Australia.[149] The scope of the activity was evidenced in 1928 by publication of a collection of essays in which five social scientists, three natural scientists, and three statisticians examined problems related to "The Peopling of Australia." Although the generally high quality of contributions to the volume indicated that substantial work was being carried out already on population problems, the editors, P. D. Phillips and G. L. Wood, called for more study by a "Bureau of Economic Research"—to correct what they described as "Australia's self-centred attitude . . . a curious sensitiveness, almost nervousness, in discussion." They noted particularly a growing fear in Australia "that 'migration' might at some time cease to be a pure question of domestic jurisdiction and become a subject matter of international law."[150] They anticipated that, through misunderstanding of population questions, Australians might attempt to grow too quickly and too much. They called for "reasoned consideration" of the subject and rejection of the belief that "bigness is synonymous with greatness." They asked for a clear definition of national goals followed by "a courageous probing of many of the assumptions which underly existing policies."[151] Ideas which had been discussed in the colonies for almost a century were debated again in *The Peopling of Australia*. The need for discovering an optimum population which would yield the largest possible per capita welfare was mentioned in most essays, and was discussed exclusively by F. C. Benham in application to Australian conditions.[152]

149. M. H. Belz in 1929 built on the work of Knibbs in explaining population growth by fitting Australian population data to Pearl and Reed's logistic curve. "Theories of Population and their Application to Australia," *Economic Record*, V (1929), 253–62.
150. P. D. Phillips and G. L. Wood, "The Australian Population Problem," in P. D. Phillips and G. L. Wood, eds., *The Peopling of Australia* (Melbourne, 1928), pp. 7, 10, and 12.
151. *Ibid.*, p. 23.
152. "The Optimum Size of Population," *ibid.*, pp. 246–72.

Conclusion

Population studies had a significant place in the development of Australian policy and thought. Recognition of the particular relevance of demography to the colonial environment led numerous Australians, including several of the most able early economists, to investigate the subject in detail. Initial stimulus came from acquaintance with classical population theory formulated for conditions of the old world. Malthus' writings, it was discovered, provided justification for subsidized migration and at the same time demonstrated dangers inherent in unrestrained local population growth. The influence of Malthus was evident throughout early debates over restrictive immigration, public works development, encouragement of domestic reproduction, commercial policy, and land settlement.

Most colonists were content to make a simple application of imported doctrine to domestic conditions, but a few enterprising innovators such as John Dunmore Lang advanced on contemporary thinking. As in other countries, the pessimistic implications of Malthusian theory were anathema to reformers who believed explicitly in the perfectibility of human society. But as fear developed late in the nineteenth century of an Asian threat to Australia's empty spaces, the relevance for Australia of external population increase was accepted almost without question. The dark forecasts of Pearson and Knibbs attracted worldwide attention.

The challenge of Australian population problems attracted a number of remarkably able analysts, led by government statisticians. At least four pioneer demographers were worthy of international attention. Henry Hayter in Victoria arranged for perfection and standardization of early censuses. His statistical publications were models for contemporaries. R. M. Johnston suggested imaginative hypotheses to explain population change and tested his models with the meagre facilities available to

Tasmania. Timothy Coghlan prepared detailed studies of special demographic problems, stimulated intercolonial comparisons, and detonated a major furor in New South Wales at the turn of the century with an analysis of birth-rate trends. George Knibbs directed the Commonwealth Bureau of Census and Statistics in extensive studies of demographic matters.

With the exception of Morris Pell, whose interests in population were extra-curricular, Australian universities did not contribute materially to population discussion until after World War I. Such competent economists as Hearn and his successors were familiar with Malthusian theory, but they made no attempts to provide local interpretations or to advance the level of understanding.

Population studies in Australia were undoubtedly an example of intellectual endeavor taking place in response to a demonstrated need.

Part Two

The Science of Enquiry

13

Economic Statistics

Demand for Statistical Knowledge

Interest in economic statistics developed in Australia during the 1840's and 1850's, a period of rapid but uneven economic growth and achievement of self-government. As the colonial economies moved from a penitentiary function to become separate and distinct societies with complicated domestic problems, they discovered quickly a pressing need for local information. In the 1840's, Australians were given strong reason for the first time to experience intense concern over the condition of their economy. During the previous two decades, autocratic power of governors slowly had been restricted by formation of legislative councils, and at the same time active wool markets had brought unprecedented industrial and commercial progress. Then in the early 1840's, clouds appeared on the economic horizon as drought and falling prices caused widespread hardship. Pessimism replaced the heady optimism of a few years before, and colonists sought accurate data about the extent, causes, and probable duration of the decline.

As early as 1841, a South Australian writer expressed the view that formation of a local statistical service could be a vital step on the road to economic recovery. He said: "In all new colonies, the diffusion of sound statistical information is one of the best means of enabling the public to judge of their true condition, and one of the best methods of promoting and ensuring their prosperity and advancement."[1] The editor of *Arden's Sydney*

1. "The Progress of South Australia in the Elements of Wealth," *South Australian Magazine*, 1841, p. 73.

Magazine regretted also the paucity of published official statistics and the difficulties encountered by colonial observers in obtaining information. He explained: "Although the Newspaper Press of the Colony has been laudably engaged in recording, from time to time, statistical data for the use of the future Colonial Historian, yet the search amongst their scattered, and too frequently imperfect, columns must prove laborious and unsatisfactory to the reader desirous of such information."[2] Thomas Bartlett, a British critic, deplored the poor quality of the few statistics that were published in the colonies, and he accused settlers of making available only favorable data. He castigated colonial authors thus:

Misrepresentations,—to use no harsher word,—both direct and indirect, and of every conceivable variety, are indulged in: and, although each is loud in his denunciation of the fallacies sent forth by his opponents, he scruples not to endeavour to raise the colony which he has taken under his especial protection by precisely the same means.[3]

A contributor to the *New South Wales Magazine* in 1843 discussed the importance of statistics in some detail. He outlined the history, use, and present development of statistical technique, with mention of current work being carried out by the British Association and the Statistical Society of London. A strong recommendation was made for improvement in Australian statistics, both to assist formulation of domestic policy and to assure the mother country of the basic good health of the colonial economy. He commented:

From the rapid extension of the Australian colonies, and the unexampled advancement of some of them in wealth and population, it has become desirable that their statistics should be diligently collected, clearly arranged, and published in a connected form. The various facts relating to their physical, moral, and political elements may be supposed, from the peculiarities of these settlements, to possess more than common interest in the eyes of philosophers and statesmen. The attention of our public authorities has for some years

2. "Colonial Statistics," *Arden's Sydney Magazine*, October, 1843, p. 90.
3. Thomas Bartlett, *New Holland: Its Colonization, Productions and Resources, with Observations on the Relations Subsisting with Great Britain* (London, 1843), p. 5, and see also p. 25.

past been turned to statistical enquiries; and hence many of the papers published by order of the Legislative Council contain tables drawn out with great skill, and exhibiting much valuable information as to the resources and progress of the Colony. These publications, however, are not within the reach of readers in general. True, many of their contents are transcribed into our newspapers; but newspapers are so seldom bound into volumes, and when bound, are so ponderous and unwieldy, that for purposes of reference they are of all things the most inconvenient.[4]

This writer in New South Wales hoped that the deficiency in statistics of the colonies could be overcome by the periodical press.

The turmoil caused by gold discoveries in the 1850's brought new demands for improvements in economic statistics. The *Melbourne Monthly Magazine* in 1855 observed regretfully that scarcity of data, particularly regarding income and prices, prevented accurate identification of specific areas of gain and loss from rapid growth and made difficult the task of devising equitable taxation. It complained: "In a new colony it is next to an impossibility to acquire correct data as to the income of its inhabitants, and the taxation contributed by different classes to the state. This want of information leads to misconception, and misconception on such a vital point is sure to beget injustice and mislegislation."[5]

Henry Parkes in the New South Wales legislature and press combined concern for the welfare of the growing working class with wide knowledge of economic and statistical literature. In an address to the Legislative Council in 1855, Parkes "thought it would not be disputed that to be in such a state as we now were, without some correct public statistics as to the supply of food from the soil, was to be in a condition not at all in accordance with the public safety."[6] Parkes proceeded to read aloud a portion of a recent report to the Statistical Society of London on agricultural statistics, and he outlined how recommendations contained

4. "Australian Statistics," *New South Wales Magazine*, 1843, p. 5.
5. "Financial Prospects," *Melbourne Monthly Magazine of Original Colonial Literature*, I (1855), 185.
6. Henry Parkes, *Speeches on Various Occasions Connected with the Public Affairs of New South Wales 1848–1874* (Melbourne, 1876), p. 44.

therein could be implemented in the colony. From his newspaper, the Sydney *Empire*, Parkes directed scathing criticism at government statistical efforts; of the published documents he said "the statistical tables are a kind of Procrustean bedstead to which everything must square, even the very bars and joints of it being unalterable and unimprovable by science."[7] Parkes believed that government supervision of the colonial economy should be similar to private management of a business corporation, and in both cases "correct and complete statistics are a corner-stone in the foundation of equitable and perfect administration." He presented a very strong case for a special government statistical office:

The government of a country is altogether analogous to that of any more limited establishment, a commercial company, a benefit club, an hospital, or a household. In every one of these the knowledge of all details of expenditure and income, of debts and credits, of offices, officers, and servants, and of their various efficiency or deficiency; of the sufficiency of income to meet expenditure, of profit and loss; and of the mechanical operation of every part of the administration—everybody knows that without this knowledge, there is the greatest risk of dangerous inequalities which may ultimately ruin the concern. . . .[8]

In 1859, as chairman of a legislative committee on the "Condition of the Working Classes," Parkes proved his own practical enthusiasm for statistical compilation. From abundant testimony and evidence received by the committee, Parkes prepared and appended to his report valuable tables of social statistics.[9]

During the 1850's, colonists were influenced significantly by statistical developments in other countries. The active Statistical Society of London paid some attention to Australia in its early years,[10] and the interest was reciprocated; the University of Melbourne Library opened with a complete set of the Society's

7. "Defective and Erroneous Statistics," *Empire*, August 24, 1854, p. 4.
8. "The Importance of Complete Statistics," *Empire*, August 31, 1854, p. 4.
9. "Report from the Select Committee on the Condition of the Working Classes of the Metropolis; together with the Proceedings of the Committee, Minutes of Evidence, and Appendix," *Votes and Proceedings of the Legislative Assembly of New South Wales*, 1859–60.
10. See below pp. 467–68. The Statistical Society of London became the Royal Statistical Society in 1887.

Journal.[11] In Victoria, where American influence was pronounced during the gold-rush period, considerable enthusiasm was expressed for statistical labors of the United States government.[12]

In the less spectacular decades which followed the exciting gold-rush 1850's, accurate and respected statistics were recognized by colonists as a means of making known to the rest of the world, and particularly to Great Britain, Australia's recent development and great potential. Australians themselves were confident of their own great promise but were conscious as well of geographical isolation and of stiff competition in markets for capital and immigrants.[13] In Victoria and New South Wales the task of providing statistical information and publishing it in attractive form was particularly well performed by Henry Hayter and Timothy Coghlan, as will be explained below. Support for their statistical activities was strengthened by a vigorous and sometimes acrimonious rivalry which began soon after separation of the two colonies and reached a peak in the late 1880's. The competition revolved around alleged effects of divergent commercial policies of free trade in New South Wales and protection in Victoria. Protagonists of each policy endeavored to show conclusive superiority by repeated comparisons of statistical series ranging from "number of letters received and despatched" to "number of men at soldiers' age." Protectionists in Victoria, led by the Melbourne *Age*, used judicious selections from Hayter's *Yearbook* to "prove" the case for high tariffs, and, until the appointment of a New South Wales government statistician, they held a decided advantage over free-traders.

Edward Pulsford, a prominent free-trade champion, used material published in Michael Mulhall's *Dictionary of Statistics* in refutation of protectionists,[14] but he remarked regretfully shortly

11. *Catalogue of the Library of the University of Melbourne, Victoria* (London, 1856), p. 42.
12. "American Statistics," *Victorian Monthly Magazine*, I (1859), 59–70.
13. The value of responsible statistical reporting in the colonies, as opposed to unreliable propaganda, was stressed to the Royal Colonial Institute in 1876 by John Plummer, who in this respect was in substantial accord with the views of many Australian statesmen. John Plummer, "The Colonies and the English Labouring Classes," *Proceedings of the Royal Colonial Institute*, VIII (1876–77), 144–79.
14. Edward Pulsford, *Free Trade and Protection* (Sydney, 1885), p. 15. The

after Coghlan's appointment in 1886: "Had a Government Statistician been appointed in this colony ten years ago, the erroneous
ideas possessed by many people with regard to Victoria, would
never have been entertained."[15]

In 1887 the *Age* accelerated its campaign and suggested that
Coghlan's figures were "themselves not to be depended upon."[16]
New South Wales free-traders replied to the extravagant protectionist claims with streams of their own calculations, and they
reacted to slurs against Coghlan with shocked indignation. The
report of a meeting addressed by Pulsford indicates the high
level of excitement generated by the *Age*'s charges. Pulsford said:

I think you will all feel that public servants who fulfill their duties
faithfully and honorably are worthy of our esteem, and I cannot
think of anything more painful than that men, who are thus entitled
to the esteem of the public, should be represented as guilty of actions
to which no honorable man would stoop for love or money (Loud
cheers.) . . . I presume that Mr. Coghlan and his assistants—sup-
posing them to have honestly done their best, as I believe they have,
cannot but feel pained and indignant that a charge of public lying
should be brought against them, and the knowledge that such charges
would carry pain and annoyance, ought to have caused some hesitation in the minds of their authors. (Hear hear.) . . . The British
race in Australia has lost none of its love of fair play, one, I take it,
of its greatest characteristics, and though misrepresentation may
prosper for awhile the common sense and love of fair play of the
people will in the end justify where justification is due, and condemn
where condemnation has been earned. (Applause)[17]

As a result of the *Age* accusations, Coghlan's honor as a
responsible statistician became a favorite question for debate,
and another free-trader, James Martin, reported triumphantly
to the Free Trade and Liberal Association that "although it was

---

controversy was described by William Westgarth in "The Battle between Free
Trade and Protection in Australia," *Report of the Fifty-seventh Meeting of the
British Association for the Advancement of Science*, 1887, transactions, pp. 833–
34.

15. *Freedom in New South Wales versus Oppression in Victoria: A Reply to
the "Age" Articles* (Sydney, 1887), p. iii. And see above pp. 54–56.

16. *Protection in Victoria versus Free-Trade in New South Wales, Reprinted
from "The Age"* (Melbourne, 1887), p. 19; James Mirams, *The Progress of
Victoria* (London, 1883).

17. Edward Pulsford, *New South Wales' Statistics and Victorian Critics* (Sydney, 1889), pp. 29–31.

a favourite topic of the protectionist to throw stones at Mr. Coghlan's figures, he would tell them that Mr. Hayter, the Government Statistician in Victoria, accepted Mr. Coghlan's statistics. (Applause)"[18] W. H. Renwick, an outspoken free-trader, announced in 1901 that the *Age* had itself perpetrated some statistical falsification, and he warned legislators: "As it is possible that many members of the Federal Parliament may be unaware of the reputation of the 'Age' newspaper for unveracity on fiscal matters, and may therefore attach some value to the positive statements which it makes, we deem it important to place before you an exposure of the assertions made in this article."[19]

Keen public interest in the contest between Victoria and New South Wales explains in part the generous support received by government statisticians for publication of elaborate yearbooks and for continued searches after new indicators which, each colony hoped, would prove favorable to its own position. A South Australian federalist remarked optimistically from the sidelines in 1876: "A healthy rivalry between the colonies is not adverse to their federal connection and general prosperity. Such a rivalry these statistics are eminently calculated to promote."[20] On the other hand, sustained public scrutiny and high emotional fervor must have placed uncommon temptations before the government statisticians to collect and publish mainly those statistics which accorded with public preconceptions. In fact, from the tenor of many of their statistical publications, it is apparent that neither Hayter nor Coghlan did forget entirely the instant demise of the messenger who brought Emperor Alexander bad news.

Robert Giffen, visiting the colonies in 1892, set forth dangers inherent in overemphasis on statistical comparison, and he gave a polite but pointed warning to a gathering of the Australasian Association for the Advancement of Science. He said:

All the leading branches of statistics without exception, when examined, give numerous illustrations of the dangers of taking the figures

18. *Report of the Proceedings and Public Meetings of the First Annual Conference of the Free Trade and Liberal Association of New South Wales* (Sydney, 1889), p. 111.
19. W. H. Renwick, *An Exposure of "Age" Statistics* (Melbourne, 1901), p. 1.
20. *South Australian Advertiser*, November 2, 1876.

relating to them from dictionaries or works of reference at haphazard for international comparison, as if the figures called by the same names in different countries meant the same things, or the units had the same values . . . the figures as such may be right enough, though there are many difficulties as to the data themselves to be faced in statistics, but the exact meaning of the figures called by the same name, when place and circumstances are different, may require a great deal of elucidation. . . . When one knows, for instance, how intrinsically difficult it is to prove statistically the greater prosperity of one country than another when the differences between them are not very great, it is not difficult to estimate at its due weight any argument in which the difficulties are ignored and statistics are dealt with by short cuts when they seem to support the side on which the arguer has ranged himself. If we help by this discussion to strengthen the wholesome attitude of doubt, and to discredit the short cuts of the amateur partisan, the discussion, it may be hoped, will not have been wholly in vain.[21]

In addition to pressures for publicity abroad and from inter-colonial competition within, government statisticians faced other demands. Particular types of economic statistics had special significance for colonial problems. Widespread and continuous concern with population study and vital statistics has been discussed above. In the early years, statistics of crime were used to protest and prove the ill effects of continued transportation.[22] Labor statistics were analyzed by politicians and others concerned about worker welfare,[23] while some observers contended that improved information about economic growth, including calculations of the domestic propensity to save, could increase the development rate and permit state planning and control. T. F. Bird wrote in 1876: "the reliable and exhaustive statistics relating to every department of national activity in all civilized states which are now available to the political student, place him on a vantage-ground far above his predecessors, and render it possible

21. Robert Giffen, "International Statistical Comparisons," *Report of the Fourth Meeting of the Australasian Association for the Advancement of Science held at Hobart, 1892,* pp. 485–86.
22. For example, William Westgarth, "The Statistics of Crime in Australia," *Journal of the Statistical Society,* XXVII (1864), 505–19.
23. Two examples are, Henry Copeland, *Adam's Curse and Labour-Saving Inventions: An Enquiry into the Labour Question of the Future* (Sydney, 1885); and *The History of Capital and Labour in All Lands and Ages* . . . (Sydney, 1888), p. 908 f.

to determine the elements and conditions of national prosperity with almost mathematical accuracy."[24] The Australian Economic Association came into existence in 1887 with social improvements through collection of statistics as one of its goals.[25]

During the 1890's, Australian economists grew increasingly concerned about falling prices and mounting unemployment. Alfred De Lissa laid heavy emphasis on the value of detailed statistics for discovering explanations of economic fluctuations, and he made use of Coghlan's pioneer national income calculations to construct a macro-economic multiplier model.[26] Bimetallists, with particularly narrow interests, argued that statistical comparison of price declines with trends in gold production and world trade volume revealed the real cause of the crisis. Sir Samuel Griffith called for careful calculations of national income and expenditure statistics both to reveal reasons for unemployment and to provide a picture of the national economy as a guide to government policy. He asked:

What is the annual income of the body politic of Queensland or of any other Australian province, or, for that matter, of any other country, and how much of it is available for itself after discharging its foreign obligations? What is the total amount available annually for the supply of food, clothing, and shelter to the people, and what surplus is left for growth? An answer to these questions would show at once whether a country was progressing or retrogressing in material prosperity. And without an answer to them, and without the inquiries that are necessary to afford an answer, how can the true condition of a community be ascertained with any degree of accuracy? . . . Besides the knowledge of the actual condition of the community, which I conceive to be highly important, if not essential, to its welfare, and which might be acquired by the investigations I have suggested, some other interesting facts would be disclosed—for instance, the proportion of the annual produce that is disposed of in discharge of foreign obligations and for no present equivalent, the proportion of the whole income of the community that is taken

24. T. F. Bird, "The Basis of National Prosperity," *Melbourne Review*, I (1876), 95. See also, Henry D'Esterre Taylor, "The Direction of Thrift. A Savings Bank Comparison," *Victorian Review*, IV (1881), 703–11; and "International Statistical Uniformity," *Transactions and Proceedings of the Royal Society of Victoria*, XXII (1886), 35–48.
25. See below p. 629.
26. See below Chapter 14.

464   *The Science of Enquiry*

by the State to defray the cost of government, the actual burden of an income tax or a property tax, and—which I anticipate would be the most surprising of all—the average amount annually expended upon the food, clothing, and shelter of each individual.[27]

Complaint about inadequate macro-economic statistics was not confined to private individuals. A Victorian board of enquiry appointed to examine the extent and causes of current unemployment discovered in 1900 the deficiencies noted by De Lissa and Griffith, and in its official role called loudly for improvement.[28]

After 1906 pressure for improved statistical data was focused on the newly formed Commonwealth Bureau of Census and Statistics.[29] The most urgent demands were of two basic types. The first arose as a result of determination in the colonies to develop a system of industrial arbitration or distributive jurisprudence, based on "economic justice" and apart from the familiar higgling of the market place and labor warfare. A pressing need discovered quickly by arbitration court judges was for data on which to base their decisions. Mr. Justice Higgins and his colleagues developed a formula for administered wages based on estimated cost of living, but they were inhibited in the confident implementation of plans by an absence of trustworthy cost information.[30] Not only were statistics not collected but confusion was widespread about the mere meaning of the term price change.[31] Rapid inflation during World War I, the need for wartime administered prices as well as wages, and the evident inadequacy of amateurs called to investigate and to wrestle with

27. Sir Samuel Griffith, "A Plea for the Study of the Unconscious Vital Processes in the Life of Communities," *Report of the Sixth Meeting of the Australasian Association for the Advancement of Science held at Brisbane, 1895,* p. 664.
28. "Report of the Board of Inquiry on Unemployment," *Papers Presented to the Parliament of Victoria,* 1900.
29. F. R. E. Mauldon, *The Use and Abuse of Statistics with Special Reference to Australian Economic Statistics* (Melbourne, 1933), p. 19.
30. See above pp. 386–90.
31. See for example the following incoherent discussions of price movements: "Report of the Royal Commission on Wages and Wage-Earners in Tasmania," *Journals and Printed Papers of the Parliament of Tasmania,* 1907; and A. Duckworth, "Notes on the Increased Cost of Living," *Report of the Thirteenth Meeting of the Australasian Association for the Advancement of Science held at Sydney, 1911,* pp. 505–7.

price problems, made only more urgent the need for professional inquiry.[32]

A second type of demand for improved statistics was voiced during the recession after World War I; this amounted to a revival of appeals made in the 1890's for statistics of such macro-economic variables as production, income, and other financial aggregates. The case for statistical improvement of this kind was made most effectively by Douglas Copland, L. F. Giblin, and other members of the growing body of university economics teachers. Complaints from these and other professional economists were expressed more and more often before such influential bodies as Royal Commissions, and legislative committees.[33]

Discussion in the following two sections of advances in the collection, analysis, and presentation of statistics in Australia should be examined in the context of these demands for change.

Non-Official Statistics

As soon as it became evident in the 1820's and 1830's that Australia was suited for profitable production of wool and other staple products, prospective immigrants, capitalists, and traders in Britain were attracted by the resources and economic potential

32. See Herbert Heaton, "The Basic Wage Principle in Australian Wages Regulation," *Economic Journal*, XXXI (1921), 309–19; Colin Clark, *Australian Hopes and Fears* (London, 1958), p. 136; Gordon Greenwood, ed., *Australia: A Social and Political History* (Sydney, 1955), pp. 281–82; "Report of the Royal Commission on the Basic Wage," *Papers Presented to the Parliament of the Commonwealth of Australia*, 1920–21. Sir Charles G. Wade, a government official, reported confidently in 1919 that wartime inflation had been the result of "trusts and profiteers" and could be eliminated by "public investigation" through a system of "tribunals" designed to restore competition. Hon. Sir Charles G. Wade, "Price-fixing, with Special Reference to Australian Experience," *Report of the Eighty-seventh Meeting of the British Association for the Advancement of Science*, 1919, transactions, pp. 246–47.

33. D. B. Copland, "The Trade Depression in Australia in Relation to Economic Thought," *Report of the Sixteenth Meeting of the Australasian Association for the Advancement of Science held at Wellington, 1923*, pp. 555–79; "Second Progress Report of the Royal Commission on National Insurance. Unemployment," *Papers Presented to the Parliament of the Commonwealth of Australia*, 1926–27; "First Annual Report of the Development and Migration Commission," *ibid.*; and "Development and Migration Commission. Report on Unemployment and Business Stability in Australia," *ibid.*, 1926–27–28.

466   *The Science of Enquiry*

of the continent. The British public provided a market for statistics and description while, at the same time, colonists themselves
grew anxious that their story be told to bring tools and labor
needed for development. Before the grant of responsible government in the 1850's, colonial officials did not provide economic
information in satisfactory form or detail. The Colonial Office
required collection of certain statistics considered necessary for
efficient management of the territories: these consisted principally of the census, volume of foreign trade, bank returns, and
land sales. Data were collected, however, because of their usefulness in the formulation of essential fiscal policies, and not directly
for analytical or publicity purposes. Statistical returns were
printed in Colonial Office "Blue Books" in relatively undigested
condition and with little interpretation or explanation.

In the absence of useful government publications, demands for
economic statistics were met in part by private authors who were
either resident colonists, returned military personnel, or temporary visitors. They prepared "accounts" of the colonies usually
combining historical and geographical descriptive outline with
statistics garnered from Blue Books and other sources. Works by
these amateurs varied in quality from the valuable studies of
Wentworth and Lang, which included perceptive and influential
critical comment, to pedestrian "immigrants' handbooks."[34] Most
writings were excessively optimistic in tone, both to please
colonial readers and to encourage prospective immigrants. Only

34. W. C. Wentworth, *A Statistical, Historical, and Political Description of the
Colony of New South Wales, and its Dependent Settlements in Van Diemen's
Land* (London, 1819); second edition, 1820; and greatly enlarged in a third
edition published as *A Statistical Account of the British Settlements in Australasia; including the Colonies of New South Wales and Van Diemen's Land* (London, 1824); John Dunmore Lang, *An Historical and Statistical Account of New
South Wales, both as a Penal Settlement and as a British Colony* (London, 1834);
second edition, 1837; third edition, 1852; fourth edition, 1874. Other well prepared early descriptive works were: P. Cunningham, *Two Years in New South
Wales* (London, 1827); Henry Melville, *Van Diemen's Land; Comprehending a
Variety of Statistical and other Information, Likely to be Interesting to the Emi-
grant, as well as to the General Reader* (Hobart Town, 1833); Henry Melville,
*The History of the Island of Van Diemen's Land, from the Year 1824 to 1835 In-
clusive. To Which is Added, a Few Words on Prison Discipline* (London,
1835); J. Syme, *Nine Years in Van Diemen's Land* (Dundee, 1848); J. S., *The
Land of Promise: Being an Authentic and Impartial History of the Rise and
Progress of the New British Province of South Australia* (London, 1839); J. F.
Bennett, *Historical and Descriptive Account of South Australia: Founded on the
Experience of a Three Years' Residence in that Colony* (London, 1843).

a few disgruntled critics made themselves heard.[35] Several writers, such as the Reverend Ralph Mansfield in New South Wales and the Reverend T. J. Ewing in Tasmania, worked in close collaboration with government officials.[36] Occasionally authors were emboldened even to attempt precocious and imaginative estimates of such variables as national income, aggregate capital, domestic prices, and average sheep-station budgets.[37] During the depression of the 1840's, several periodicals published statistics in an effort to reassure flagging confidence.[38]

During their early years, the Royal Statistical Society, founded in 1834, and the British Association for the Advancement of Science, meeting for the first time in 1831, devoted some attention to colonial statistics and to the Australian territories in particular.[39] J. T. Danson in 1849 described and criticized Colonial Office statistics and called for their reform.[40] During the gold-rush years, interest of the two bodies increased, and extracts from Australian newspapers were inserted regularly in the Statistical Society's

35. For example, Robert Dawson, *The Present State of Australia* (London, 1831); and Thomas Bartlett, *New Holland: Its Colonization, Productions and Resources, with Observations on the Relations Subsisting with Great Britain* (London, 1843).

36. See Mansfield's testimony in "Report from the Select Committee on the Census Bill," *Votes and Proceedings of the Legislative Council of New South Wales*, 1845. Mansfield's analyses of the census are discussed above pp. 431–32. Ewing, at the request of Governor Sir John Franklin of Tasmania, compiled "certain Statistical Returns connected with this Colony for the three years ending with 1841," in "Statistics of Tasmania, 1838–1841; Extracts from the Introductory Letter to His Excellency Sir John Franklin," *Tasmanian Journal of Natural Science, Agriculture, Statistics, &c.*, II (1846), 141–50. A similar semi-official account of Western Australia was *Report on the Statistics of Western Australia in 1840; with Observations by the Colonial Committee of Correspondence* (Perth, 1841).

37. For example, W. C. Wentworth, *op. cit.*, 1819, p. 113; "State and Prospects of New South Wales. Jasoniana," *New South Wales Magazine*, 1843, pp. 299–322; "Disadvantages of a Sheep Station out of the Boundaries of the Colony of New South Wales, in a North-West Direction, in 1837," *Australian Magazine*, 1838, pp. 135–45; Marcus Collisson, *South Australia in 1844–45* (Adelaide, 1845), pp. 103–6.

38. "Colonial Statistics," *Arden's Sydney Magazine*, October, 1843, pp. 90–104; and "The Affairs of New South Wales," *New South Wales Magazine*, 1843, pp. 195–203.

39. For example: Captain Maconochie, "Criminal Statistics and Movements of the Bond Population of Norfolk Island, to December, 1843," *Journal of the Statistical Society*, VIII (1845), 1–49, and see above p. 430. F. G. P. Neison, "Analysis of the Census of New South Wales," *ibid.*, XI (1848), 38–54.

40. J. T. Danson, "Some Particulars of the Commercial Progress of the Colonial Dependencies of the United Kingdom, during the Twenty Years, 1827–46," *ibid.*, XII (1849), 349–439 and particularly 399–407.

journal.[41] After normal conditions had returned and improvement had taken place in statistical facilities within the colonies during the 1860's, formal interest decreased but did not disappear.[42]

In Victoria William Westgarth acted for several years as a private one-man statistical bureau. He had the energy and eye of a truly dedicated economic historian, and his work deserves special recognition. During the 1840's, he published a series of "Reports, Commercial, Statistical, and General," for the purpose of "disseminating facts and local information throughout the world," and which he maintained had "afforded some agreeable and improving exercise for leisure time." Westgarth was anxious not only to provide statistics for immediate use but to furnish a record of the colony's early history. He wrote:

The illustration of every British settlement by the regular issue of such a document, recording local facts and occurrences, which may in general be so easily seized upon, and so correctly delineated, at the time of their appearance, is a desideratum that can scarcely be too highly prized. There may thus be furnished, for some future occasion, an interesting retrospect of the early days of settlement whose career cannot but be regarded with the greatest interest, and whose progress hitherto stands unparalleled in the annals of colonial history.[43]

Westgarth was very sympathetic to the problems of Australian aboriginal natives, and he did much to publicize their plight.[44]

41. G. M. Bell, "Historical and Statistical View of the Colony of Victoria," *ibid.*, XVII (1854), 258–74; "Remarks on the Irregularity of the Statistical Phenomena Observable in the Australian Colonies since the Gold Discovery of 1851; and Statement of the Production of Gold in Australia to the Close of 1859," *ibid.*, XXIV (1861), 198–207; P. L. Simmonds, "On the Growth and Commercial Progress of the two Pacific States of California and Australia," *Report of the Twenty-fifth Meeting of the British Association for the Advancement of Science*, 1855, transactions, pp. 188–91; Henry John Porter, "On the Census of Sydney, New South Wales," *ibid.*, Twenty-seventh Meeting, 1857, p. 167; Hon. Thomas M'Combie, "On the Statistics of the Trade and Progress of the Colony of Victoria," *ibid.*, Twenty-ninth Meeting, 1859, pp. 218–23.

42. E. T. Blakely, "On the Commercial Progress of the Colonies and Dependencies of the United Kingdom," *Journal of the Statistical Society*, XXVIII (1865), 34–55; William E. Stark brought up to date G. M. Bell's article in "Statistics Relating to the Colony of Victoria, Australia," *ibid.*, XXXVIII (1875), 438–62; John Beddoe, "Notes on the Statistics of Victoria (Australia)," *Report of the Forty-seventh Meeting of the British Association for the Advancement of Science*, 1877, transactions, pp. 163–64.

43. William Westgarth, *A Report, Commercial, Statistical & General, on the District of Port Phillip, New South Wales, for the Half Year Ended 31st July, 1846* (Melbourne, 1846), preface. The series ran from 1841 until 1846, and was continued for one year by William Mackintosh as *General Statistical and Commercial Report of the Province of Australia Felix. Being a Continuation of Observations, &c., by "William Westgarth, Esq."* (Melbourne, 1848).

44. W. Westgarth, *A Report on the Condition, Capabilities, and Prospects of*

He opposed convict transportation and supported free emigration and self-government. During the gold rush he continued to publish balanced accounts of the colonies, and his writings were appreciated for their judicious tone by his fellow settlers.[45] In 1860, after Westgarth had moved to Britain as agent general, he represented Victoria at the International Statistical Congress in London.[46]

After the colonies gained self-rule, government officials gradually assumed from private writers the functions of providing economic information for immigrants, legislators, and other interested observers. The transition process was slow, however, and authors of descriptive and statistical works continued to find markets throughout the nineteenth century.[47] The lag of New South Wales behind Victoria in appointment of a government statistician independent of the Registrar General permitted sus-

---

the *Australian Aborigines* (Melbourne, 1846); and *Australia Felix; or, a Historical and Descriptive Account of the Settlement of Port Phillip, New South Wales: Including Full Particulars of the Manners and Condition of the Aboriginal Natives, with Observations on Emigration, on the System of Transportation, and on Colonial Policy* (Edinburgh, 1848).

45. *Southern Spectator,* I (1857–58), 133. See also William Westgarth, "Report," *Illustrated Australian Magazine,* I (1850–51); *Commerce and Statistics of Victoria, from the Commencement of the Colony* (Melbourne, 1856); *Victoria and the Australian Gold Mines in 1857; with Notes on the Overland Route from Australia, via Suez* (London, 1857); and "The Commerce and Manufactures of the Colony of Victoria," *Report of the Thirty-first Meeting of the British Association for the Advancement of Science,* 1861, p. 269.

46. William Westgarth, *Australia its Rise, Progress, and Present Condition* (Edinburgh, 1861), pp. 41–43.

47. Respectable economic accounts of the colonies during the transition to official statistics were: Charles St. Julian and Edward K. Silvester, *The Productions, Industry, and Resources of New South Wales* (Sydney, 1853); Anthony Forster, *South Australia: Its Progress and Prosperity* (London, 1866); J. E. Calder, *Tasmanian Industries: with some Notices of Those of the Australian Colonies and New Zealand* (Hobart Town, 1869); Salvador Morhange, *Étude sur L'Australie, 1862–1869* (Bruxelles, 1869); G. H. Reid, *An Essay on New South Wales, the Mother Colony of the Australias* (Sydney, 1876); Sir Archibald Michie, *Readings in Melbourne: with an Essay on the Resources and Prospects of Victoria, for the Emigrant and Uneasy Classes* (London, 1879); W. A. Brodribb, *Recollections of an Australian Squatter, or Leaves from my Journal Since 1835* (Sydney, 1883); J. P. Stow, *South Australia: Its History, Productions, and Natural Resources* (Adelaide, 1883); Theophilus P. Pugh, *A Brief Outline of the Geographical Position, Population, Climate, Resources, Capabilities, Form of Government, Land Laws, Trade, Revenue, etc. etc. of the Colony of Queensland* (Brisbane, 1861); William Harcus, ed., *South Australia: Its History, Resources, and Productions* (London, 1876); Waldemar Bannow, *The Colony of Victoria Socially and Materially* (Melbourne, 1896); and the works of James Bonwick, a bibliography of which is George Mackaness, "A Bibliography of James Bonwick (1817–1906), Australian Historian," *Royal Australian Historical Society Journal and Proceedings,* XXIII (1938), 355–60.

tained private statistical activity in that colony. Private publications in co-operation with government were not unusual, and a
useful set of consular reports by G. W. Griffen, United States
Consul at Sydney, was published by the New South Wales
government printer.[48] John Plummer, immigrant journalist, mu-
sician, artist, amateur economist, and friend of John Stuart Mill,
maintained a stream of statistical interpretation and description
in pamphlets, periodicals, and the *Year Book of Australia*.[49]
Edward Pulsford, leading the crusade for free trade in New South
Wales, prepared his own elaborate computations and diagrams
to wage war on Victorian protectionists who were armed with
material from their official statistician, Henry Hayter.[50] The Australian Economic Association formed a statistical committee at
its inception in 1887, and at least for the first year gathered some
data and published findings.[51] Appointment of the energetic
Timothy Coghlan as Government Statistician of New South
Wales in 1886 put an end to most non-official statistical endeavor
in that colony.

Official Statistics

Systematic collection and publication of colonial statistics was
introduced during the administration of Lord Bathurst as Secretary of State for War and the Colonies from 1812 to 1827. This
period coincided with the transformation of Australia from the
equivalent of an offshore prison hulk to the embryo of a viable

48. G. W. Griffen, *New South Wales: Her Commerce and Resources* (Sydney, 1888); see also Charles Robinson, *New South Wales: the Oldest and Richest of the Australian Colonies* (Sydney, 1873); Thomas Richards, ed., *New South Wales in 1881: Being a Brief Statistical and Descriptive Account of the Colony up to the End of the Year, Extracted Chiefly from Official Records* (Sydney, 1882). W. H. Knight, *Western Australia: Its History, Progress, Condition, and Prospects; and its Advantages as a Field for Emigration* (Perth, 1870).
49. John Plummer, "Some Personal Recollections of John Stuart Mill," *Victorian Review*, III (1881), 542–49; and *Sir Matthew Decker and Adam Smith* (Sydney, 1887). An album of newspaper articles contributed by Plummer to local newspapers in the 1890's entitled "Australian Bank Troubles" is contained in the Mitchell Library, Sydney. Plummer's personal copy of the *Year Book of Australia*, 1897, with Plummer's many anonymous contributions clearly marked, is in the author's possession.
50. See above pp. 54–56.
51. *Australian Economist*, I (1888–90), 71.

new nation. Bathurst began the preparation of the Blue Books which contained statistics necessary for colonial administration, and he stimulated accumulation of additional data by the appointment of special investigators such as J. T. Bigge, who visited and reported on New South Wales. Professor Beaglehole has written: "Lord Bathurst had no affection for political economy *by name*, but to the results of a wise combination of Colonial measures, which in their character might more or less belong to the science of political economy, no man was more alive. . . ."[52]

New South Wales. After the grant of partial self-government in the 1850's, responsibility for statistics passed in each colony from the colonial secretary to an official appointed by the legislature. In New South Wales, Christopher Rolleston, an immigrant from Britain in 1838, was named Registrar General in 1856 and took charge of the statistical branch of the Colonial Secretary's Department in 1858. Rolleston came to his new position with more than ten years' local civil service experience, and he had been associated closely with the governor, Sir William Denison, becoming his private secretary in 1855. Rolleston explained to the Philosophical Society of New South Wales in 1856 why he attached great value to economic statistics; he said: "The collection and comparison of facts which illustrate the condition of mankind and tend to develop the principles by which the progress of society is determined, form a science which has attained very great importance, both in society and legislation, not in England alone, but throughout Europe."[53] He outlined the development of statistics in other countries, and mindful of inflammable local controversies, he stressed the statistician's correct role as nonpartisan observer. He explained: "The science of statistics differs from political economy, because, although it has the same end in view, it does not discuss causes, nor reason upon probable effects; it seeks only to collect, arrange, and compare that class of facts which alone can form the basis of correct conclusions with respect

52. J. C. Beaglehole, "The Colonial Office, 1782–1854," *Historical Studies Australia and New Zealand*, I (1940–41), 177.
53. Christopher Rolleston, "The Science of Statistics," *Sydney Magazine of Science and Art*, I (1858), 254.

to social and political government."[54] He emphasized the need
for rigid observance of scientific method and avoidance of unsubstantiated speculation: "it is simply required that all conclusions shall be drawn from well attested data, and shall admit
of mathematical demonstration." Rolleston viewed the statistician
primarily as a servant of the statesman, able to give guidance on
practical matters and prepared to test "scientific and philosophical writings." He mistrusted particularly the deductive method
in economics:

it being impossible not to observe a growing distrust of mere hypothetical theory, and *a priori* assumption, and the appearance of a
general conviction that in the business of social science, principles
are valid for application only inasmuch as they are legitimate inductions from facts accurately observed and methodically classified,
that all conventional rules in order to be permanently beneficial
must have a strict conformity with the physical and moral laws of
nature, which are ascertainable only by observing, collecting, and
registering the positive facts of experience—that, in short, statistical
data must constitute the raw material of all true systems of economy
and legislation.[55]

Rolleston expressed special interest in improvement of the census and in collection and elaboration of agricultural statistics
to afford an approximate index of annual production. He claimed
that data on raw material output were "indispensable as the
basis on which a correct appreciation of the social and economical
progress of the population must be founded."[56] Rolleston called
for careful gathering also of information about education, crime,
industry, and trade, because these were matters about which
colonial governments had urgently to legislate. He warned that
extravagant or immediately observable results should not be anticipated, and he advised: "The only fair way of determining the
worth of statistical collections is to ask the question 'had similar
accounts been kept 50 or 100 years ago would they have been
of use at the present day?' "[57]

54. *Ibid.*
55. *Ibid.*, p. 255.
56. *Ibid.*, p. 256.
57. *Ibid.*, p. 257.

Rolleston managed to bring about substantial improvements in government registration methods, and he began publication of a statistical register in place of the old Blue Books.[58] He was not able to undertake the ambitious reforms he had hoped for, however, and despite his good intentions his tenure on the whole was not marked by outstanding innovations in economic statistics. He appears to have encountered marked disinterest in his superiors, and in 1867 he complained again of "the unsatisfactory mode of collection" of agricultural statistics.[59] In 1874 he found it necessary to defend on strictly practical grounds a proposed improvement in criminal statistics; he explained hopefully that "by examining the nature of the offences and the condition of the offenders, we may elicit the local causes which create an excess."[60]

E. G. Ward, Rolleston's successor as Registrar General, also did not make noteworthy statistical contributions. As long as the duties of government statistician were combined with those of public record-keeper, they remained relatively inconsequential.

Timothy A. Coghlan was appointed the first New South Wales Government Statistician in 1886, and he made up quickly for time lost in formation of a separate statistical department. He published several major series of periodical handbooks and numerous other works.[61] He collected much of the historical and descriptive material gathered for earlier official publications in his monumental and non-official *Labour and Industry in Australia*.[62] Coghlan had special interests in population study and in the census, but because there were few other trained economic consultants he was summoned for advice also on such matters

---

58. "Registration of Births, Deaths, and Marriages for the year 1858," *Votes and Proceedings of the Legislative Assembly of New South Wales*, 1859–60.
59. Christopher Rolleston, *The Condition and Resources of New South Wales* (London, 1867), p. 20.
60. Christopher Rolleston, "Criminal Statistics of New South Wales, from the Year 1860 to the Year 1873," *Transactions of the Royal Society of New South Wales*, 1874, p. 26.
61. Coghlan's serial publications included: *The Wealth and Progress of New South Wales*, superceded by *Official Year Book of New South Wales*; *A Statistical Account of the Seven Colonies of Australasia* (nine issues between 1891 and 1902); *Statistics of the Seven Colonies of Australasia* (issues from 1897 to 1903); *A Statistical Account of Australia and New Zealand* (two issues, 1902–3 and 1903–4). He was also responsible for such minor official publications as: Greville Tregarthen, *New South Wales 1860 to 1889, a Statistical Sketch* (Sydney, 1890).
62. London, 1918, four volumes.

as banking legislation.[63] One of Coghlan's most remarkable achievements was a series of estimates of Australian "income" and "wealth," compiled initially using methodology developed by Michael Mulhall in his *Dictionary of Statistics*.[64] Coghlan achieved an enviable international reputation, and his writings and opinions were viewed with respect abroad.[65] His appointment as Agent General in 1905 was a serious blow to Australian statistics.[66]

Victoria. Several outstanding political figures in Victoria during the 1850's had special awareness of the significance of statistics for economic development. Hugh Childers, Auditor General in 1852 and Commissioner of Trade and Customs in 1855, read political economy at Cambridge and "almost knew by heart" Smith's *Wealth of Nations.* Childers wrote to his mother from

63. "Progress Report from the Select Committee on Post Office Savings Bank—National Bank; together with the Proceedings of the Committee, Minutes of Evidence, and Appendix," *Votes and Proceedings of the Legislative Assembly of New South Wales* 1892–93, pp. 14–23.

64. Coghlan's national income statistics have been discussed fully in Heinz W. Arndt, "A Pioneer of National Income Estimates," *Economic Journal,* LIX (1949), pp. 616–25; and Noel G. Butlin, *Australian Domestic Product, Investment and Foreign Borrowing 1861–1938/39* (Cambridge, 1962), pp. 36–49. Professor Arndt has written that Coghlan's statistics "were the first official estimates of national income anywhere; and he also seems to have been the first (if Gregory King be left in a class by himself) to have attempted parallel estimates of national income, output and expenditure on lines at least approaching modern techniques." p. 616. Mulhall's statistics were used extensively by writers in New South Wales during the 1880's before the appointment of a government statistician. See for example, Thomas Richards, ed., *New South Wales in 1881* (Sydney, 1882), pp. 2–3; Henry Copeland, *Adam's Curse and Labour-Saving Inventions* (Sydney, 1885), p. 62 n; Edward Pulsford, *Free Trade and Protection: An Answer to Mr. Forsyth's Pamphlet* (Sydney, 1885), p. 15. Henry Parkes' own copy of Mulhall's *Dictionary* is in the author's possession.

65. R. P. F., "Review of *A Statistical Account of the Seven Colonies of Australasia,* 1895–96," *Publications of the American Statistical Association,* V (1896–97), 227–8; George H. Wood, "Changes in Average Wages in New South Wales, 1823–98." *Journal of the Royal Statistical Society,* LXIV (1901), 327–35; and "Changes in Average Prices in New South Wales, 1820–98," *ibid.,* pp. 661–76; B. M. [Sir Bernard Mallet], "Obituary: The Hon. Sir Timothy Coghlan, K. C. M. G., 1857–1926 (Hon. Fellow, 1893–1905)," *ibid.,* LXXXIX (1926), 785; A. St. Ledger, *Australian Socialism: An Historical Sketch of its Origin & Developments* (London, 1909), pp. 100–101; Robert Giffen, "Protection for Manufactures in New Countries," *Economic Journal,* VIII (1898), 3–16; "Statist Coghlan," *Imperial Review* (Melbourne, c. 1906), No. 41, pp. 60–62.

66. Even as Agent General Coghlan retained his interest in statistics and their presentation. See his "Memorandum by Agents General on the Question of Publishing Information and Removing Misconceptions as to the Commonwealth; and Advertising its Resources and Developments, Etc.," *Papers Presented to the Parliament of the Commonwealth of Australia,* 1905.

Melbourne in 1852: "You will, I dare say, see a good deal of my statistics in the House of Commons emigration papers. All the returns of wages, prices, arrivals, etc., go through me, and are certified by my signature, and I dare say many will be thought interesting enough to be copied. . . ." He added a few months later: "Some of the statements and projects which we read of in the newspapers are so amusing that I almost feel inclined to write a true account of the colony, for general information. But I suppose others have the same intention, and far more time to do it in."[67] H. S. Chapman, Attorney General between 1857 and 1859, related to the Statistical Society in London the progress made by Victoria during the gold rush, and he remarked: "this very gold of ours has enabled us to *buy* . . . appropriate talent in every department of our Government."[68] The first "purchases" of personnel authorized by the new colonial Parliament included a competent staff for a registrar-general's department.

A Major Campbell was appointed Registrar General in 1853, but his assistant, William Henry Archer, soon succeeded to the position. Archer explained to a select committee concerned with agricultural statistics in 1855 that the tasks facing the new statisticians were formidable. He reported: "I found that the returns obtained by the Colonial Secretary were anything but what could be desired, and that the collection was of a very doubtful nature as to results." Archer recommended exhaustive reform of all statistical services at the outset of self-government and co-ordination through one office. He testified:

I should have been glad to have seen a motion embracing an extensive view of statistics *generally*, that is to say, of all or most subjects relating to the social well-being of the community. Then, instead of having as now, partial, isolated, fitful attempts by different departments for various special purposes, a full and more economical organi-

67. Spencer Childers, *The Life and Correspondence of the Right Hon. Hugh C. E. Childers 1827–1896* (London, 1901), I, 17, 44, and 48.
68. H. S. Chapman, "The Industrial Progress of Victoria as Connected with its Gold Mining," *Journal of the Statistical Society*, XXVI (1863), 426. See also H. S. Chapman, "On the Statistics of New Zealand," *Report of the Twenty-first Meeting of the British Association for the Advancement of Science*, 1851, transactions, p. 98.

zation might be formed on a uniform system for the Census, the Elective Franchise, Education, Agriculture, Horticulture, Live Stock and every other division of statistics that the Legislature might regularly or from time to time require.[69]

Archer admired the statistical advances of Quételet in Belgium, and observed that "England is perhaps the worst off of any European country for statistical information concerning its agriculture." He found that in the colony "surgeons" were particularly well suited to act as statistical enumerators because "they know personally or by repute most other people in their district, and are found to be intelligent and efficient agents." He noted also, strange as it seems today, that physicians could be engaged (with horse) for a mere thirty shillings a day. One irate citizen testified in favor of medical enumerators and protested that a police constable who last had collected his returns "was very inefficient, in fact he was very drunk" and "in such a state he could not get away the night he came."[70]

Archer received considerable support for his endeavors, and he was able to engage a competent staff.[71] In 1860 a committee of the Royal Society of Victoria, organized by Professors F. Mueller and M. H. Irving of the University of Melbourne, prepared a report on the economic condition and potential of the colony using Archer's statistics and other data to show that prosperity need not be transitory and was not dependent wholly on gold.[72] For publicity purposes Archer issued "statistical essays" in 1861, 1867, and 1873, on the "Progress of Victoria," including data on prices, wage rates, public finance, banking, production, foreign trade, employment, land sales, and transport. He was able to report by the time of his retirement in 1873:

The statistical records of Australia are not excelled either in fulness or in accuracy by those of any other country; and as the statistical

69. "Report from the Select Committee of the Legislative Council on Agricultural and Horticultural Statistics; together with the Proceedings of the Committee, Minutes of Evidence, and Appendices," *Votes and Proceedings of the Legislative Council of Victoria*, 1856, p. 1.
70. *Ibid.*, pp. 2, 3, 5, and 9.
71. Archer's first chief clerk was Francis Corbett, whose work on transport questions is discussed above pp. 276–81. The Select Committee in 1856 recommended immediate improvement in agricultural and horticultural statistics. *Op. cit.*, p. 3.
72. *Report on the Resources of the Colony of Victoria* (Melbourne, 1860).

system initiated in Melbourne in 1853 is gradually being followed by statisticians in surrounding states, there is every reason to hope that, at no distant date, thorough unity will exist both of purpose and of action in relation to all the leading lines of statistical work throughout Australasia.[73]

Henry Heylen Hayter, Archer's assistant, became the first Victorian Government Statist in 1873. In the following year, in place of the cumbersome annual *Statistical Register* and Registrar General's *Report*, he began his famous series of *Year Books*. Hayter explained in the first issue:

It was . . . considered desirable by the Government that the information contained in the Report should be disseminated somewhat largely, both in this colony and in Europe; and it was thought that if the work were issued in a pamphlet or book form it would be more convenient for reference than if circulated on the large-sized and somewhat formidable looking pages upon which the Parliamentary Papers of this colony are printed.[74]

Hayter declared firmly that he would endeavor "to record facts with correctness and impartiality; to comment upon them only so far as may be necessary to elucidate them properly; to set up no theories except such as may be fairly deducible from the materials before me; and, in drawing inferences, to exercise perfect fairness to all sections of the community."[75] He followed conscientiously these self-imposed rules, and he enlarged steadily and improved his *Year Book* with useful discussion and comparative data. William Newmarch reviewed the volume for 1878 before a meeting of the Statistical Society in London, and he is reported to have said:

The handbook is almost a perfect model of what such a publication should be. The contents are most carefully classified according to subjects, and the tabular details are arranged scientifically and skilfully. There is also as much descriptive discussion as is required to bring out the true bearing of the figures. The speaker [Newmarch] said it had been his painful duty to examine handbooks, official and otherwise, and to be afflicted by the careless and unskilful manner in

73. William Archer, *The Progress of Victoria: A Statistical Essay* (Melbourne, 1873), p. 3.
74. Henry Heylen Hayter, *Victorian Year Book, Containing a Digest of the Statistics of the Colony for the Year 1873* (Melbourne, 1874), p. iii.
75. *Ibid.*, pp. iii–iv.

which they were framed. But Mr. Hayter's work, on the contrary, was not marked by any of these defects, and Mr. Newmarch would go so far as to say, that the statistical department of the Imperial Government might with advantage follow to a large extent in Mr. Hayter's steps, and profit by his example.[76]

Hayter gained a commanding position among Australian social scientists, and in 1888 he was elected first president of the Economic and Social Science and Statistics Section of the Australasian Association for the Advancement of Science. In his presidential address, he appealed directly to the other colonies to follow the long-standing example of Victoria and the more recent lead of New South Wales by appointing full-time government statisticians. He said:

Facts most important in statistical enquiries, can scarcely ever be got at by persons who have not access to State documents, and who do not possess the authority to collect information. But the State ought to supply machinery adequate to the purpose, and should not allow the preparation of statistics to be mixed up with other duties, such as for instance investigating the titles to, and regulating the dealings with real property. Where this is done, the chances are that the statistics will suffer. . . .[77]

Hayter insisted that reliable statistics were of vital importance in new countries where economic conditions were changing constantly. He himself devoted his energies to areas he considered particularly dynamic: he made substantial contributions to population study, and only a few years after Coghlan he produced an estimate of national income.[78] Hayter, joined by Coghlan and R. M. Johnston in later years, was mainly responsible for the excellent reputation enjoyed by Australian statistics throughout the world by the end of the nineteenth century.[79] Sir Charles Dilke

76. *Journal of the Statistical Society*, XLI (1878), 160.
77. H. H. Hayter, "On Official Statistics," *Report of the First Meeting of the Australasian Association for the Advancement of Science held at Sydney, 1888*, pp. 431–32.
78. See above pp. 474 and N. Butlin, *op. cit.*
79. A writer in the London *Investors' Review*, critical of almost all phases of Australian life, was forced to admit that Hayter was "the head of all men of his vocation in Australasia. Not only is he painstaking and accurate in the collection of statistics relating to his own colony; he also made not inconsiderable progress in the study of comparative statistics, and goes less astray therein than is the habit with some more pretentious men here at home." "Gold-bewitched Victoria," *Investors' Review*, II (1893), 145–74.

concluded in 1890: "Victoria has almost from her birth been at the head of all countries in statistics, and the Year-Book of the Government statist and the other productions of his office are as nearly perfect as such works can be."[80] Hayter was succeeded shortly before Federation by James J. Fenton.

Tasmania. Apart from Blue Books compiled by the Colonial Secretary, the earliest semi-official publication of statistics in Van Diemen's Land took place in the 1840's and 1850's by James Barnard, a clerk in the Colonial Secretary's Office. Barnard provided useful discussion and analysis of data drawn principally from the census, and he compared Tasmanian progress with that of other colonies and of the United States.[81] In addition to Barnard's publications, a precocious collection of historical economic statistics, running from 1804 to 1823, was issued officially in 1856.[82]

Edwin C. Nowell, Clerk of the Legislative Council, became the first Tasmanian Government Statistician with Barnard as his assistant. Nowell regarded statistics as a valuable complement to political economy and absolutely necessary if the scientific method was to be applied to economic problems. He explained:

In its simplest enunciations, political economy is nearly as much an exact science as mathematics; as for example, when it lays down the proposition that *the demand creates the supply,* or that *competition lowers prices,* for these are matters of pure reason, and are

80. Sir Charles Wentworth Dilke, *Problems of Greater Britain* (London, 1890), I, 187.

81. James Barnard, "Statistics of Van Diemen's Land for 1844–46, Compiled from Official Records in the Colonial Secretary's Office, and Published by Order of the Lieut.-Governor, 1847," *Tasmanian Journal of Natural Science, Agriculture, Statistics, &c.,* III (1849), 444–45; "Observations on the Statistics of Van Diemen's Land for 1848 . . . , *Papers and Proceedings of the Royal Society of Van Diemen's Land,* I (1849–50), 102–34; "Observations on the Statistics of Van Diemen's Land for 1849 . . . ," *ibid.,* II (1851–54), 1–33; "Observations upon the Census taken Throughout Van Diemen's Land, 1st March, 1851," *ibid.,* 33–40; "Observations on the Census of the United States, taken 1st June, 1850, from the Official Report of the Superintendent of Census," *ibid.,* 372–93; "Observations on Tasmanian Statistics for the Decennial Period 1844 to 1853 . . . ," *ibid.,* III (1855–62), 9–36.

82. "Statistical Account of Tasmania from 1804 to 1823," *Journals of the House of Assembly of Tasmania,* 1856.

universally true; but when facts have to be observed, and disturbing elements are introduced, its character becomes more mixed; but it is always a *science* still, and never an art.[83]

Nowell was encumbered by other duties in addition to those as statistician, and he was restricted from ambitious publications by the form and limited scope of his annual report. However, he was able to undertake an occasional special study, such as an analysis of census data, and he prepared useful "statistical essays" for publicity purposes.[84] Nowell retained his enthusiasm for statistics even into retirement, and he addressed the Royal Statistical Society in London as late as 1895 on comparative rates of colonial growth.[85]

In 1882 the Tasmanian government established a distinct statistical bureau and appointed Robert Mackenzie Johnston, one of the most remarkable intellectual figures in nineteenth century Australia, Registrar General and Government Statistician. Son of a Scottish crofter, orphaned soon after birth, and without formal education beyond the elementary level, Johnston arrived in the colonies in 1870 at the age of twenty-five and began work as an accountant with the Launceston and Western Railway.[86] He remained Government Statistician for thirty-seven years, until his death in 1918, and during his half century in Tasmania he was an indefatigable student of both natural and social sciences. He contributed a total of eighty-five papers to the Royal Society of Tasmania on geological and biological subjects alone, and two volumes he published on the geology of Tasmania were path-breaking classics.

Johnston began his statistical work by enlarging and improving the annual *Statistical Register*, changed in title to *Statistics of*

83. E. C. Nowell, "Political Economy," *Monthly Notices of Papers and Proceedings of the Royal Society of Tasmania*, 1872, p. 16.
84. E. C. Nowell, "On the Vital Statistics of Tasmania, with Especial Reference to the Mortality of Children," *Papers and Proceedings of the Royal Society of Tasmania*, 1875, pp. 108–26; [possibly by Nowell] *Tasmania: A Description of the Island of Tasmania and its Resources* (Launceston, 1876).
85. Edwin C. Nowell, "Comparative Statistics of the Principal British Possessions and Foreign Countries," *Journal of the Royal Statistical Society*, LVIII (1895), 480–505.
86. Brief "biographical notes" on Johnston are contained in *The R. M. Johnston Memorial Volume* (Hobart, 1921). This book contains reprints of some of Johnston's economic and statistical writings, but because some condensation was carried out reference is made here to the originals.

the Colony of Tasmania, and in 1890 he began publication of the *Tasmanian Official Record,* a handbook patterned after the series produced by Hayter and Coghlan. He announced in the preface to his first volume:

For some time past the want of a handy official book, especially relating to Tasmania and its affairs, has been greatly felt. Hitherto the only authoritative information furnished by the Statistical Office was contained in the Report prefixed to the bulky volume of yearly statistics, and was solely restricted to the analyses of tables relating to departmental, economic, and social matters. That work is still most necessary as a source of reference, but it is too costly and somewhat cumbersome; and it lacks information much sought after bearing upon Early History . . . the Author has endeavoured to meet all these wants in the present volume. . . .[87]

With his new handbook, which lasted only until the depression year of 1893, and occasional special essays, Johnston was able to increase his statistical output with reasonable certainty of publication.[88]

Johnston intended many of his papers and articles on economic statistics as antidotes for what he considered extreme and unjustified claims of contemporary reformers.[89] In particular he objected to arguments that while labor was the principal source of all production, the distribution of national income was determined by ownership of real capital. The major part of real capital, he insisted, consisted not of tools, equipment, and natural resources, but of the capitalized value of current services of workers. Johnston regarded statistical calculations of "national wealth," such as that made by Coghlan for Australasia, as misleading and a reason why radical thinkers were excessively preoccupied with the ownership pattern of physical capital. Summations of national wealth which included only the value of tangible real goods and neglected the overwhelming importance of potential labor distorted the appearance of forces able to direct income. He wrote:

87. R. M. Johnston, *Tasmanian Official Record,* 1890, p. iii.
88. During the depressed 1890's Johnston gave a spirited and convincing defense of the Australian economy from British critics in: R. M. Johnston, "The Attack on the Credit of Australasia," *Nineteenth Century,* XXXI (1892), 602–22.
89. Johnston's study of business cycles, his defense of Malthus, and his critiques of land reform and socialism are discussed above pp. 223–26, 413–15, 127–30, and 376–78.

The so-called "Statistician's wealth," to which attention of Social Reformers of existing individualistic democratical organisations is invariably restricted excludes the primary source of all wealth in exchange (consumable wealth) viz., the existing productive personal services of man (Karl Marx's labor unit), although the annual monetary effective value is fully three times as great.[90]

Examination of per capita distribution of physical "wealth" rather than of annual income, Johnston maintained, suggested a degree of economic inequality far in excess of that which existed. He called for careful analysis of national income and its distribution, and abandonment of all attempts to compile an inventory of existing real goods. He continued:

the true distribution of wealth in the community—wealth in consumption being the major factor—can alone be accurately determined by the average annual earnings or claims upon wealth. The proportion of fixed wealth owned by individuals affords no clue to current distribution of total wealth. It can merely show how the 30 per cent. devoted to fixed instruments is distributed.[91]

Johnston calculated that labor's share of "national income" in Tasmania during 1891 was 69.11 per cent, a proportion which would not have been suggested by a study merely of the concentration of capital ownership.[92] Johnston focused attention correctly on analysis of economic returns over time, and he performed a useful service in illustrating that humans, by their reluctance to assign the producer of labor a capitalized market price, render calculations of aggregate wealth of limited value.[93]

Shortly before and after the turn of the twentieth century, Johnston prepared statistical analyses of the financial implications for Tasmania of federation among the colonies. In 1897 and 1899 he helped Sir Philip Fysh to illustrate that states with relatively low per capita incomes stood on balance to lose eco-

90. R. M. Johnston, "Observations Regarding Some Economic Aspects of the Eisenach Social Equality Programme," *Papers and Proceedings of the Royal Society of Tasmania*, 1903–5, p. 125.
91. R. M. Johnston, "Consumable Wealth," *Report of the Seventh Meeting of the Australasian Association for the Advancement of Science held at Sydney, 1898*, p. 876; and reprinted *Australian Economist*, VI (1898), 2–6.
92. *Ibid.*, p. 881.
93. A later article on this theme was: R. M. Johnston, "Observations Regarding Accumulated Capital Wealth," *Papers and Proceedings of the Royal Society of Tasmania*, 1918, pp. 1–8.

nomically under terms of current federal proposals.[94] In the year
of Federation itself, Johnston joined Judge Inglis Clark in arguing
that neither the "Opimeter, or revenue-yielding method" nor
"the Populimeter, or population basis" but rather "the just and
natural Inopimeter, or compensation for actual loss method"
should determine proposed federal payments to the states.[95] In
subsequent years, Johnston reiterated the view that small and
predominantly rural states, because of the peculiar character of
their economies, deserved special treatment in a federal system.
He concluded in 1910:

As a general rule history shows that the larger the population of
several federating States of the same stage of civilisation the *larger
is the absolute cost of the Government,* concomitant *with a smaller
cost per head of population.*
It logically follows that, in any true federation of States for the
sake of common interests, the smaller States must, even on the basis
of per head of population, *entail a greater sacrifice* for the common-
weal than, that entailed by, the greater or more advanced States.
This view is also clearly borne out by the experience of the six
Australian States in the years prior and subsequent to Federation.[96]

94. "Federal Finance: Memoranda Prepared and Statistics Collected for the
Basis of an Address Delivered to Members of Hobart Chamber of Commerce,
May 27, 1897, with Subsequent Amendments, Additions, and Explanatory Text,
by Sir Philip Fysh, K. C. M. G.," *Journals and Printed Papers of the Parliament
of Tasmania,* 1897; "Tables Showing Probable Effect of a Uniform Tariff Upon
Finances of Tasmanian State Treasury, as Estimated by R. M. Johnston, Government Statistician," *ibid.,* 1899.
95. "The Federal Finance Problem: Further Observations by R. M. Johnston,
F. S. S., Government Statistician, Tasmania, with an Introductory Note by his
Honour Mr. Justice Clark," *Journals and Printed Papers of the Parliament of Tasmania,* 1900.
96. "Considerations Regarding the Federation of States which Differ Materially,
at the Initial Stage in the Magnitude of Population or Development, by Robert
M. Johnston, I.S.O., F.S.S., Government Statistician," *Journals and Printed
Papers of the Parliament of Tasmania,* 1910, p. 1; see also "Federal Finance
Problem and the Way Out," by R. M. Johnston, I.S.O., Government Statistician,"
ibid., 1907. Johnston hoped for introduction of a decimal currency in the Commonwealth. See comments upon a paper by the Bishop of Tasmania entitled
"The Decimal System, as Applied to Weights, Measures, and Money," *Papers and
Proceedings of the Royal Society of Tasmania,* 1903–5, pp. xx-xxv. This discus-
sion was part of a long-standing Australian interest, appearing sporadically over
the years, in decimal currency. cf. "Decimal Systems (the report of three ad-
dresses to the Melbourne Social Science Congress)," *Australasian Insurance and
Banking Record,* V (1881), 10; Rustik, "Decimal Coinage," *Journal of the
Bankers' Institute of Australasia,* III (1899–90), 645–47; and "Report from the
Select Committee on Coinage; together with the Proceedings of the Committee,
Minutes of Evidence, and Appendices," *Votes and Proceedings of the House of
Representatives of the Commonwealth of Australia with Copies of Certain Printed
Papers,* 1901–2.

Johnston's publications were regarded highly outside Tasmania, and twice he was elected president of Section G of the Australasian Association for the Advancement of Science. Moncure Conway, a visitor from America, praised the quality of Johnston's scientific method, and he remarked: "His intimacy with the fauna and flora and the charm of his personality revived in me recollections of my beloved teachers, Baird, Thoreau, Agassiz."[97] The relative insignificance of the Tasmanian economy in the eyes of outside observers, the shortage of funds in a small community for statistical assistance, and the wide range of Johnston's own interests prevented his achieving an international reputation equal to that of either Hayter or Coghlan. Nevertheless, Johnston's work on his favorite subjects—federal finance and national income statistics—was continued effectively by L. F. Giblin, his successor as Tasmanian Government Statistician.

The other colonies. After achieving self-government, South Australia, Queensland, and Western Australia all replaced their Blue Books ultimately with statistical registers. However, none appointed full-time government statisticians, and information was collected usually by various government departments and was processed by registrars general.[98] In South Australia, Josiah Boothby was "Government Statist" from 1863 to 1879, but neither he nor his successors held positions analogous to those of Hayter, Coghlan, or Johnston. These three states published special statistical essays from time to time but seldom of a quality approaching that maintained by officials of New South Wales, Victoria, and Tasmania.[99]

97. Moncure Daniel Conway, *My Pilgrimage to the Wise Men of the East* (London, 1906), p. 81. See also a favorable mention of Johnston's statistics in: B. R. Wise, *Industrial Freedom. A Study in Politics* (Melbourne, 1892), p. 278 n.
98. See for example, "First Report by the Registrar General of the Working of the Statistical Office, from its inception on the 1st of July, 1897, to the 31st of December, 1898," *Minutes and Votes and Proceedings of the Parliament of Western Australia*, 1899; and W. Siebenhaar, "The Use and Scope of Statistics," *Report of the Eleventh Meeting of the Australasian Association for the Advancement of Science held at Adelaide*, 1907, pp. 634–41.
99. See for example: Josiah Boothby, *Statistical Sketch of South Australia* (London, 1876); and Sir Arthur Blyth [Agent-General for South Australia], "South Australia: Her Laws Relating to the Alienation of Agricultural Land, and her Recent Industrial Progress," *Proceedings of the Royal Colonial Institute*, XI (1879–80), 181–221.

Inter-colonial Co-operation and the Commonwealth. Statistical co-operation among the colonies was discussed as early as 1860 when all the colonial governments except that of Western Australia were represented at the European International Statistical Congress with delegates "ranked on the same platform with those of foreign states, but not, as one may suppose, without some difference of opinion on the subject, seeing their respective colonies are all parts of one empire, and the colonists the subjects of one common sovereign."[100] The delegates issued a joint report and discussed co-ordination, both of form and date, of statistical collection.[101] A further meeting was held at Melbourne in 1861 between representatives of Victoria, South Australia, New South Wales, and Queensland, and as a tangible result of these gatherings the census was taken simultaneously in 1871 in New South Wales, South Australia, and Victoria.[102] Henry Hayter reported in 1873 that the first serious attempt to gather systematically comparative statistics of the colonies had been made in the previous year by the Governor of New South Wales, Sir Hercules Robinson. Hayter lauded Robinson's initiative, published the results of his enquiries, and promised: "with approval, to continue the publication of statistics similar to those now presented from year to year."[103] Hayter assumed a dominant position in promoting further co-operation, and he was instrumental in arranging a conference of statisticians at Hobart in 1875. Hayter, Nowell, Ward, and Boothby agreed to promote uniformity of the census, prompt publication of results, the principle of compulsory provision of information, and standardization of methods wherever

100. William Westgarth, *Australia: Its Rise, Progress, and Present Condition* (Edinburgh, 1861), p. 42. Proclamations of the need for inter-colonial statistical cooperation were made during the 1850's by William Archer and others. G. H. Knibbs, *Official Year Book of the Commonwealth of Australia,* I (1908), 5.
101. Part of the Australian report was published as "Remarks on the Irregularity of the Statistical Phenomena Observable in the Australian Colonies Since the Gold Discovery of 1851; and Statement of the Production of Gold in Australia to the Close of 1858. From the Report on Statistics of the Australian Colonies, Presented to the International Congress of July, 1860, by the Delegates of those Colonies . . . ," *Journal of the Statistical Society,* XXIV (1861), 198–207.
102. William Henry Archer, *The Progress of Victoria: A Statistical Essay* (Melbourne, 1873), p. 3 n.
103. "Australasian Statistics for the Year 1873, Compiled from Official Returns, with Introductory Report by the Government Statist of Victoria," *Papers Presented to Both Houses of the Parliament of Victoria,* 1874, p. 9.

possible. They communicated their actions to Western Australia, Queensland, and New Zealand, which had not sent representatives.[104]

Efforts to bring about close inter-colonial statistical co-operation continued through the 1870's and 1880's, and another major conference was held in 1890 again at Hobart and with representatives of all governments present except those of Queensland and Western Australia.[105] Further agreement was reached on co-ordination of technique, particularly with regard to the census, even though by this time certain indications of differences between the colonial statisticians had become evident.

At the conference in 1890, unlike that of 1875, Hayter was no longer an overpowering figure. He was joined now by Coghlan and Johnston, two full-time and energetic statisticians with substantial reputations and independent opinions. Between 1875 and 1890, the active rivalry between New South Wales and Victoria had placed the statisticians of these colonies prominently in the public eye, with frequent comparisons of writings and of abilities, and neither Coghlan nor Hayter was prepared readily to surrender precedence. At a meeting of the Australasian Association for the Advancement of Science in 1890, Hayter examined pointedly a study of the potential meat supply in New South Wales, and there he termed Coghlan's results "unheard of" and "in error."[106] Later, rather conspicuously, Hayter nominated Johnston from among "my brother statisticians" for the position of head of the "central statistical department" which would be created in the proposed Commonwealth. Finally, at this meeting, Hayter offered an ill-concealed reprimand to Coghlan in the form of advice on correct behavior for colonial statisticians. He said:

104. "Report of the Conference of Government Statists, held in Tasmania, January, 1875, with an Introductory Letter by the Government Statist of Victoria, also, with Appendices," *Parliamentary Papers of Victoria*, 1875; similar reports were printed in *Journals of the House of Assembly of Tasmania*, 1875, *Proceedings of the Parliament of South Australia*, 1875, and *Journal of the Statistical Society*, XXXVIII (1875), 252–57.

105. "Report of the Conference of Statists held at the Parliamentary Buildings, Hobart, March 3rd to 18th, 1890," *Proceedings of the Parliament of South Australia*, 1890, and also contained in *Journals of the House of Assembly of Tasmania*, 1890, and *Journal of the Royal Statistical Society*, LIII (1890), 309–23.

106. H. H. Hayter, "Our Meat Supply," *Report of the Second Meeting of the Australasian Association for the Advancement of Science held at Melbourne, 1890,* pp. 575–79.

Statisticians should have no petty jealousies or ambitions, no desire to take credit for originality, or to obtain notoriety by unnecessarily making their work different from that of others. The publication of truth in the most useful form possible should be their aim and object, and they should not mind following in the footsteps of others, if what they follow is really good.[107]

Statistical co-operation could hardly have thrived in the charged atmosphere which must have followed statements such as these by Hayter.[108]

After Federation, state statisticians undertook again to achieve uniformity. Two meetings were held at Sydney in 1900 to co-ordinate plans for the first Commonwealth census, and in 1901 Coghlan wrote to Johnston proposing further consultation on broader questions. A conference was held at Hobart in 1902 with Johnston chairman and with all states represented.[109] In the spirit of the times, participants agreed to increase co-operation even though they must have foreseen clearly that their responsibilities soon would be diminished by appointment of a Commonwealth statistician.

Coghlan, while Agent General for New South Wales in London, was asked in 1906 to become first Commonwealth Statistician. However, at the request of the New South Wales government, he declined.[110] George Handley Knibbs, a native Australian trained in surveying, physics, and mathematics, and a lecturer at Sydney University, received the appointment. Immediately Knibbs set about organizing a competent statistical department, and quickly he made clear that he interpreted his functions in the widest possible context to include many tasks currently undertaken by the states. He explained to a conference of state statisticians at Melbourne in 1907 the significance of accurate and uniform economic information to policy makers within Australia and to merchants, capitalists, and prospective immigrants abroad; he concluded: "Obviously, therefore, the

107. H. H. Hayter, "The Coming Census," *ibid.*, p. 584.
108. Hayter stressed the value of statistical coordination again in "Disturbance of the Population Estimates by Defective Records," *Report of the Fourth Meeting of the Australasian Association for the Advancement of Science held at Hobart, 1893*, pp. 537–41.
109. "Conference of Statisticians at Hobart, January, 1902," *Journals and Printed Papers of the Parliament of Tasmania, 1902.*
110. Noel Butlin, *op. cit.*, p. 37.

Commonwealth, as such, is profoundly and instantly concerned, *statistically, at least*, with practically all questions affecting the progress of the individual States therein."[111]

Knibbs had wide interests in statistics and a keen awareness of social problems. He believed that the distinctive feature of modern statistics was an orientation toward improvement of the human condition. He said: "In a democratic country this idea— viz., that the human unit is the element which, indeed, gives significance to all related facts—arises naturally and inevitably, though such an idea was by no means characteristic of the early statistical conceptions."[112] He viewed his own position as substantially more than that of a technician engaged to process social data. He considered the Commonwealth Statistician a "professional expert in statecraft, assisting the administrative statesman with his counsel and advice."[113] On a trip through Europe in 1909 to examine "various statistical and Census Bureaux," Knibbs prepared an extensive report on social insurance schemes then operating in various countries. He outlined insurance "doctrine," provided an extensive bibliography of relevant literature (more than half the items written in French and German), made specific recommendations for welfare measures in Australia, and he even related the general question of public health to "national destiny."[114] Such imagination and enthusiasm in a field unrelated directly to statistics was more than might have been expected from a pioneer government statistician.

Knibbs was familiar with work in many areas of economic statistics, but his own speciality was population study and here

111. "Unification of Australasian Statistical Methods and Co-ordination of the Work of the Commonwealth and State Bureaux. Conference of Statisticians of the Commonwealth and States of Australia and Colony of New Zealand. Melbourne— November and December, 1906," *Papers Presented to the Parliament of the Commonwealth of Australia, 1907–8*, p. 17.

112. G. H. Knibbs, "The Problems of Statistics," *Report of the Twelfth Meeting of the Australasian Association for the Advancement of Science held at Brisbane, 1909*, p. 509.

113. *Ibid.*, p. 525.

114. "Social Insurance. Report by the Commonwealth Statistician, G. H. Knibbs," *Papers Presented to the Parliament of the Commonwealth of Australia, 1910*; and "Workmen's Insurance. Letter from the Commonwealth Statistician, dated 24 January, 1910, to the Minister for Trade and Customs, *Re* Workmen's Insurance in Europe, together with a General Aperçu on the German System," *ibid.*; Knibbs' work was reviewed favorably in *American Economic Review*, II (1912), 939. See above pp. 349–50.

he built an international reputation.[115] A special concern of Knibbs during his tenure as Commonwealth Statistician was with consumer price levels. In this period, arbitration judges set out to fix wages according to the "cost of living" only to find that they did not know with certainty either what this cost was or when it fluctuated. In 1911 Knibbs published results of a preliminary study he carried out on living costs with generally unsatisfactory results. Less than ten per cent of a sample of fifteen hundred families completed questionnaires on family budgets, a proportion far lower than for similar surveys conducted in other countries. Knibbs felt able to "confirm" Engel's law of declining food consumption with increase of income on the basis of this flimsy evidence, but otherwise he was disgruntled with the uncooperative response of Australians. He observed:

The result in those countries where the people respond willingly to inquiries of this nature is that a better knowledge of sociological and economic conditions is acquired, and the possibility of directing national development on scientific lines is enhanced. In the United States and Germany especially, it appears that the masses of the community are beginning to realise that, in so far as sociological knowledge can contribute to national success, that people have the position of advantage whose investigators discover the largest body of scientific truth, and whose practical men are the most prompt in the application of it in social organisation.[116]

In response to the continuing shortage of information concerning prices, wages, and other matters pertaining to worker welfare, Knibbs established a "Labour and Industrial Branch" of his Office. Gerald Lightfoot, a barrister and the new branch's first chief, explained:

The need for statistics of the nature indicated, especially in a country like Australia, which has advanced probably more rapidly in regard to certain forms of social and industrial legislation than any other community, has been felt to an increasing degree in recent years, and

115. See above pp. 448–52.
116. G. H. Knibbs, *Inquiry into the Cost of Living in Australia, 1910–11* (Melbourne, 1911), p. 20; see also *Prices, Prices Indexes, and Cost of Living in Australia* (Melbourne, 1912), with favorable review by Henry J. Harris, *American Economic Review*, III (1913), 408–10.

a point has now been reached when it has been considered necessary to investigate the various subjects on a comprehensive basis.[117]

By the end of World War I, Knibbs had begun to collect price and labor data from "a great variety of sources of information," and his personal interest in the theory of price indices remained strong.[118]

The enormous waste and destruction of a world war made a great impression on Knibbs' thinking. He came to view the most significant component of a statistician's responsibilities as preservation of peace through elimination of ignorance and prejudice and acceleration of economic growth. He confided to an American friend in 1918 his belief that:

the statistician will have to be the guide of governments as he was in the statistisches Reichsamt in Berlin. I hope that legislating in the dark will be soon a thing of the past and that all nations worthy of the name will watch the trend of affairs in the light of the facts which a proper scheme of statistics would systematically record. . . .

Facts brought to light during this great war have revealed the necessity of watching the food supply and the rate at which our industrial raw material is being exploited. I hope to lay the foundations of good practical systems of statistical methodology before I finish my statistical career, as I feel sure that the world will not be able to live in the future in the haphazard way it has in the past. Mankind is moving towards some great cataclysm or towards a higher evolution —one does not know which—but the deviltry of this war has shown that the human race must either recognize its solidarity or be prepared for conflicts compared with which the present war will be a mere circumstance.[119]

Knibbs urged formation of a strong "Institut International de Statistique" under the League of Nations, and when this ambitious scheme seemed unlikely of fulfillment he worked strenu-

117. Gerald Lightfoot, "Labour Statistics," *Report of the Fourteenth Meeting of the Australasian Association for the Advancement of Science held at Melbourne, 1913*, p. 538.

118. George Knibbs, *Prices, Purchasing-Power-of-Money, Wages, Trade-Unions, Unemployment, and General Industrial Conditions, 1919* (Melbourne, 1920); and "The Nature of an Unequivocal Price-Index and Quantity-Index," *Journal of the American Statistical Association*, XIX (1924), 42–60 and 196–205.

119. "Two Letters from G. H. Knibbs, C.M.G., F.S.S., The Commonwealth Statistician of Australia," *Publications of the American Statistical Association*, XVI (1918–19), 220.

.ously for creation of a more limited Imperial statistical bureau.[120]

In 1915, as a contribution to wartime economics, Knibbs prepared a census of Australia's "private wealth."[121] He discussed various methods of analysis and provided an estimate of the aggregate value of private property and the pattern of its ownership. Charles H. Wickens, successor to Knibbs as Commonwealth Statistician, attempted in 1923 to give greater meaning to this wealth inventory, and he provided a parallel estimate of "human capital." Wickens calculated the "cost of production" and "capitalized earnings" of Australian workers at all ages, and he identified the difference in these two amounts as an element of national wealth. For example, he discovered that an average youth by the age of fifteen years had cost the community in food, clothing, education, and other necessities, a total of £436, while his capitalized expected earnings were £1,923; a fifteen-year-old's gross market value to society, therefore, could be placed at almost fifteen hundred pounds. On this basis Wickens arrived at a total capital value of Australian labor to which he added Knibbs' estimates of physical property and concluded: "at the 30th June, 1915, the human capital of Australia had an aggregate value of not less than 6,211 millions of pounds, as compared with 1,620 millions of private material capital and 517 millions of public capital. It thus appears that on the basis of the estimates here prepared the human capital of Australia has a value approximately equal to three times the whole of the material capital, both private and public."[122] In 1924 Wickens revised his wealth esti-

120. G. H. Knibbs, "Statistics in Regard to World and Empire Development," *Report of the Fifteenth Meeting of the Australasian Association for the Advancement of Science held at Melbourne, 1921,* pp. 181–204; "The Organisation of Imperial Statistics," *Journal of the Royal Statistical Society,* LXXXIII (1920), 201–14 and discussion 214–24; and "Statistical Conference (British Empire). Report and Resolutions Accompanied by Explanatory Memorandum and Observations by the Commonwealth Statistician," *Papers Presented to the Parliament of the Commonwealth of Australia,* 1920–21; see also Charles H. Wickens, "Sir George Knibbs," *Economic Record,* V (1929), 334–35.

121. G. H. Knibbs, *The Private Wealth of Australia and its Growth* (Melbourne, 1918); and favorable review by Willford I. King in *American Economic Review,* VIII (1918), 850–52.

122. Charles H. Wickens, "Human Capital," *Report of the Sixteenth Meeting of the Australasian Association for the Advancement of Science held at Wellington, 1923,* p. 554.

mate using population data produced by the 1921 census.[123] The
basic fault with his analysis was the awkwardness and unrealistic
character of the aggregates. The crucial dynamic element in the
calculations was the level of income flowing to productive factors,
and ficticious capitalization of non-marketable assets, although
likely to correct some popular fallacies, was little more than an
academic exercise. It became increasingly more apparent that
R. M. Johnston's objections to estimates of national wealth voiced
in the 1890's were still valid in the 1920's, and the attention of
statisticians returned to analysis of national income alone.

In the 1920's, which like the 1890's contained a period of
financial difficulties after a boom, a growing body of professional
economists expressed concern about the scarcity of statistical
data needed for study of employment and changes in income
shares among factors. J. B. Brigden in 1922 was the first statistician after Coghlan to present, even in rough form, an estimate
of national income.[124] He was followed in 1926 by James T. Sutcliffe who, like Coghlan, recognized two methods of calculating
"the national dividend": "the Aggregate Industry Method" combining total "recorded production" and estimated "unrecorded
production"; and the "Income Method" relating census data and
average incomes adjusted from taxation records.[125] Sutcliffe was
relieved to discover that both methods yielded approximately the
same results, and that his estimate of labor's share, about 58
per cent, was similar to that calculated for the United States by
the National Bureau of Economic Research. However, Sutcliffe's
results on certain points were incomplete, obscure, and inconsistent; and his methodology was not an important advance on that
of Coghlan. His errors were pointed out repeatedly, both abroad
and at home. Sir Alfred Flux accused Sutcliffe of numerous
mistakes, including that of double counting of production during

123. Charles H. Wickens, "The Wealth of Australia—A New Inventory Estimate," *Report of the Seventeenth Meeting of the Australasian Association for the
Advancement of Science held at Adelaide, 1924*, pp. 556–63.
124. J. B. Brigden, *The Economics of Lyell* (Hobart, 1922). Noel G. Butlin
has compared the methodologies and results of Australian national income statisticians in *op. cit.*, pp. 36–49.
125. James T. Sutcliffe, *The National Dividend* (Melbourne, 1926).

a single time-period, for example both of meat and of hay consumed by animals. Flux concluded concerning Sutcliffe's book:
"it leaves a good deal to be desired, and cannot be held to have
forged a new link in the chain of records by which the fluctuations in national production may be traced."[126]

In Australia L. F. Giblin, F. C. Benham, J. A. Aird, and
others, discussed Sutcliffe's study with greater sympathy, and
they suggested improvements.[127] In 1928 Benham built upon
Coghlan's and Sutcliffe's studies of national income, considered
Knibbs' and Wickens' inventories of wealth, and prepared his
own estimates.[128] N. G. Butlin writes: "Here was the first attempt,
in Australia, to explore with some attention to conceptual meaning the various measures and the content of the concepts. In
this sense, Benham's estimate was the first estimate for Australia
which consciously attempted to measure a carefully devised concept approximating the modern idea of national income."[129]

The Commonwealth Bureau of Census and Statistics consoli-
dated the early statistical progress made by Hayter, Coghlan,
and Johnston. Both Knibbs and Wickens were sensitive to matters
of contemporary concern, and they concentrated efforts wisely
in collection of social and economic aggregates, particularly those
related to population and production. They were interested
deeply in maintenance of national economic efficiency, and were
active in promoting development of economic science as a tool
of government and industry.[130]

126. A. W. F. [Alfred W. Flux], "The National Dividend by Jas. T. Sutcliffe,"
Economic Journal, XXXVIII (1928), 296.
127. "The National Dividend—A Symposium," *Economic Record*, III (1927),
189–216; and J. A. Aird, "The Income Method of Estimating the National Income," *ibid.*, IV (1928), 270–78.
128. Frederic C. Benham, *The Prosperity of Australia* (London, 1928), pp.
20–127.
129. *Op. cit.*, p. 39.
130. See Gerald Lightfoot, "Standardization and Simplification: An Approach
to Industrial Efficiency," *Report of the Seventeenth Meeting of the Australasian
Association for the Advancement of Science held at Adelaide, 1924*, pp. 555–56;
C. H. Wickens, "Australian Productive Efficiency," *Economic Record*, III (1927),
175–88; "Some Statistical Aspects of Australian Industry," *ibid.*, V (1929), 54–
74; "Productive Efficiency," *Report of the Eighteenth Meeting of the Australasian
Association for the Advancement of Science held at Perth, 1926*, pp. 584–95.
Henry Bournes Higgins depended heavily on official statistics in his work on the
Arbitration Court. *A New Province for Law and Order* (London, 1922), pp.

Conclusion

Australian economic statistics evolved rapidly during the nineteenth century and gained a permanent position of worldwide esteem. This development took place in response to sustained demand for statistical services, first to publicize the colonies in faraway centers of population, capital, and Imperial control, and second to facilitate analysis of disturbing and enigmatic economic problems. Australian willingness to support the collection of economic statistics of the highest quality reflects a characteristic optimism both as to what the data would reveal and of how detailed information could be used to achieve satisfactory reform. Economic policies differed widely among the colonies but self-confidence was uniformly high.

Given the considerable public support for economic statistics, the high quality of Australian work was still the result in large measure of efforts by a few energetic individuals, in particular: Archer, Hayter, Coghlan, Johnston, Knibbs, and Wickens. These men accepted the challenge offered to them, and performed their responsibilities with uncommon distinction.

29–30. In 1915 both Wickens and Lightfoot, at that time assistants of Knibbs, lectured in economics under the Melbourne University Extension Board. *Extension Work: Aim, Methods, and Syllabus of Lectures* (Melbourne, 1915), p. 13. Wickens and other statisticians were instrumental in formation of the Economic Society of Australia and New Zealand in 1924. L. F. Giblin, "The *Record* and its Editors (1925–46)," *Economic Record*, XXIII (1947), 1–2.

· 14 ·

Two Pioneers of Macro-economics

Alfred De Lissa and the Birth of a Multiplier

The theory of the multiplier as we know it today was conceived and developed in the 1930's by Professors Richard Kahn, Vernon A. Mund, J. M. Clark, J. M. Keynes, L. F. Giblin, and others.[1] A full seventy years ago, however, an economic model containing most of the important features of a multiplier was formulated by Alfred De Lissa, a lawyer living in Sydney.[2] In this chapter the De Lissa model and the circumstances of its creation will be described.

Like the multiplier of the 1930's, Alfred De Lissa's discovery was the product of a boom period and rapid economic expansion followed by collapse. During the relatively prosperous late 1880's

1. Detailed accounts of the history of the multiplier are: A. L. Wright, "The Genesis of the Multiplier Theory," *Oxford Economic Papers*, VIII (1956), 180–93; Hugo Hegeland, *The Multiplier Theory* (Lund, 1954); and G. L. S. Shackle, "Twenty Years On: A Survey of the Theory of the Multiplier," *Economic Journal*, LXI (1951), 241–60.
2. Publications of Alfred De Lissa which contain material relevant to his multiplier theory are: "The Law of the Incomes," *Australian Economist*, II (1890–93), 6–17, and discussion with De Lissa's reply, *ibid.*, pp. 41–44, and 49; *Protection and Federation* (Sydney, 1890, an address at the Granville School of Arts); "Credit, Currency, and a National Bank," *Australian Economist*, II (1890–93), 111–15; "The Labour Problem," *ibid.*, 120–24; "The Organisation of Industry," *Report of the Fourth Meeting of the Australasian Association for the Advancement of Science held at Hobart, 1892*, pp. 487–520, (a paper delivered to Section F, "Economic and Social Science and Statistics"); "Bi-Metallism, or the Silver Question," *Journal of the Institute of Bankers of New South Wales*, I (1892), 222–40; "Federal Finance," *Australian Economist*, IV (1894–97), 44–46; *Production, Distribution, and Quesnay's Tableau Economique* (Sydney, 1896), a lecture delivered to the Institute of Bankers of New South Wales, June 24, 1896, printed in the *Journal*, V (1896), 253–71 and 356–60, but reprinted in pamphlet form; "The Practical Application of Economics. (Illustrated by Diagrams.)," *Report of the Seventh Meeting of the Australasian Association for the Advancement of Science held at Sydney, 1898*, pp. 885–93 (abstract omitting diagrams of a paper delivered to Section G, "Economic Science and Agriculture"); *An Empire League* (*Hoc Vincet Omnia*) (Sydney, 1905).

and early 1890's, he was concerned principally with the question, what is the full impact upon an economy of a change in the output of staple-producing industries? Through these years, as he watched the buoyant markets for Australia's wool and other primary products, he pondered the exact relationship between sales of primary goods and the employment of new capital and labor. In his own words, De Lissa set out to construct "a theory, or at least a working hypothesis" which would explain "the result of any specific or additional production, the measure of its wealth, how far it will benefit and find employment for all classes."[3] After 1893, and during the great depression of the 1890's, De Lissa's attention was drawn from growth to the immediate problems of unemployment and stagnation. His earlier investigations presupposed the existence of unemployed or underemployed resources in the mother country, conditions analogous for purposes of his theory to those of depression in a closed economy. But the presence of unemployment actually within the colony was the distinctive assumption which pervaded his later work. After the operation of De Lissa's multiplier model has been explained, the development of his thought will be outlined.

The De Lissa Multiplier. Proceeding in the same way as later multiplier theorists, De Lissa began his enquiry by splitting national income into two portions: the first an exogenous magnitude initiating an income-generating process, and the second an endogenous quantity to be determined by the working of the system. Given an increase in the first type of income, De Lissa proposed to explain how a total increase could be calculated. He divided the economy into two income sectors which he called "primary" and "secondary."[4] For Australia and other new countries the first included the producers of staple products: "agriculturists and all others employed in procuring the products of the soil, pastoralists or graziers, manufacturers of every kind and character, all en-

3. "The Organisation of Industry," p. 495.
4. De Lissa disagreed with the Physiocratic distinction between "productive" and "unproductive" labor. He wrote: "Any person not actually idle, discharging the most insignificant office, will be a productive worker," *Production, Distribution, and Quesnay's Tableau Economique*, p. 6.

gaged in mining, quarrying, forestry, and fisheries, capitalists, employers and employed." The secondary sector covered "all engaged in commerce and trade, retail dealers of every kind and character, including the purveyors and modifiers of food; carriers of goods, and all others employed in dealing in any way with the produce," construction workers, entertainers, financiers, and even "the criminal and questionable classes."[5] De Lissa regarded the incomes of primary and secondary producers as essentially different in kind; primary production unlike secondary production was fundamental to the health of the economy. "The fortunes and incomes of the whole community depend upon the extent of the incomes of the primary workers. . . . the industries of those workers . . . underlie, they are the foundations of the whole structure of industrial life."[6] The productive capacity of primary staple industry was, at least in the short run, fixed in size, relatively unalterable in character, and unpredictable from year to year because it depended upon the vagaries of natural phenomena, the discoveries of man, and all the other uncertainties familiar to miners, farmers, and fishermen. Although prices of primary goods varied on an international exchange, the demand for them viewed by a single producing country was effectively unlimited. Goods that were not consumed domestically were sold on the world market. In contrast, the productive capacity of secondary industry was easily adjustable. So long as sufficient demand for services existed in the colonies, capital and labor would flow in from the mother country and increase the supply. Most colonial services unlike primary staples, however, had to be sold within the colony, and an overproduction could not be exported. The demand for and price of secondary goods were determined domestically. For borderline cases, De Lissa's distinction between primary and secondary producers was clearly arbitrary, but it is not difficult to appreciate his important differentiation of such extremes as sheep farmers and retail sales clerks.

Because of what he regarded as the unique significance of the

5. "The Organisation of Industry," p. 492.
6. "The Law of the Incomes," p. 13.

primary sector, De Lissa devoted his attention to determining the relation between activity in this sphere and growth of the national economy. Giving a polar case to illustrate his reasoning he explained: "If all the primary productions were to cease there could be no incomes for the secondary, whose earnings must come out of production."[7]

The entire operation of De Lissa's multiplier takes place over a single primary-production period or crop year, lasting from the time of receipt of one amount of income by primary producers as payment for the previous period's product until time for receipt of the next amount of income in payment for current production. He did not explain in detail the origin of funds constituting primary income, called "circulating capital," but it is clear from several of his writings that he regarded the commercial banking system as the most important source of new money in any advanced economy.[8] A step taking place at the beginning of his multiplier process, therefore, was for De Lissa the creation of a sum of new money through the discount of commercial paper by a commercial bank on the security of primary goods already produced and sold to merchants. For purposes of present illustration, initial primary income may be taken as £100. The working of De Lissa's model with an injection of this amount is summarized in Table I.

De Lissa assumed that income receivers spend all their receipts before receiving their next amount of income. He did not envisage cash hoarding, and did not consider a Keynesian savings leakage.[9]

---

7. *Production, Distribution, and Quesnay's Tableau Economique*, p. 12.
8. De Lissa stated in 1896—"in modern times and more particularly in recent years . . . currency is for the most part banking currency, which has been said to represent from 97 to 99 per cent of wholesale transactions." "Bimetallism or the Silver Question," p. 233. In contrast to his position on most subjects De Lissa held very conservative views on monetary matters. He denounced proposals for revival of bimetallism, could see nothing to be gained from formation of a national bank, and was high in his praise of the existing banking system as an instrument of growth. He said: "I take the view that the wealth of England, and of Australia, as compared with many other countries, is due to the greater development of the banking system." "Credit, Currency, and a National Bank," p. 113.
9. De Lissa stated this assumption of an identity of savings and investment thus: "It is apprehended that all the savings after the production has taken place will be applied through the banks in advances on security, and will thus be devoted to the employment of operatives." "The Law of the Incomes," p. 10.

Table I. Operation of De Lissa Multiplier Model Over Single Production Period

Stage	Income			Expenditures			Changes in volume of loans by banking system
	Total	Primary	Secondary	Total	Primary	Secondary	
1	100	100		100	25	75	+100
2	75	75	$\frac{3}{4} \times 100 = 75$	75	18.75	56.25	−25
3	56.25	56.25	$(\frac{3}{4})^2 \times 100 = 56.25$	56.25	$\frac{1}{4}(\frac{3}{4})^2 \times 100$	$(\frac{3}{4})^3 \times 100$	−18.75
.							
.							
n	$100(\frac{3}{4})^{n-1}$	$100(\frac{3}{4})^{n-1}$	$100(\frac{3}{4})^{n-1}$	$100(\frac{3}{4})^n$	$25(\frac{3}{4})^{n-1}$	$100(\frac{3}{4})^n$	$-25(\frac{3}{4})^{n-2}$
Total	400	100	300	400	100	300	0

Assumptions

1. Sale by producers of primary goods valued at 100 takes place at the beginning of Stage 1.
2. The community "ratio of expenditure" is one-fourth.

He suggested, however, that for analytical purposes, total expenditures could be divided as in the case of income into two parts, the proportion depending upon the division of purchases between primary and secondary goods and services. In this way he categorized expenditure according to the employment of income receivers. De Lissa postulated a propensity to spend on the primary component of goods and services both for consumption and investment taken together for the whole economy, and called this the "ratio of expenditure." In the present illustration, the "ratio of expenditure" may be taken as one-fourth, meaning that out of every pound of income received consumers and investors on the average spend one-fourth on primary products or else purchase goods requiring for their manufacture in the same period an expenditure upon primary products of 5s. and upon secondary products of 15s. In the accompanying illustration, out of the original £100 received and spent by primary producers, £25 is given ultimately for primary products and £75 for secondary goods and services.

In most of his writings, De Lissa suggested that the "ratio of expenditure" for contemporary Australia, Great Britain, and the United States was about one-half. He reasoned that generally the "ratio of expenditure" of a country decreased with the progress of national prosperity and that the "ratio" of about three-quarters he calculated for some Continental European countries indicated near subsistence living. De Lissa realized that a national average "ratio of expenditure" obscured diversity among spenders, and he said: "the extent or proportions in which different incomes consume products in amount of primary value, and give off other incomes, varies considerably."[10] Without developing this point in detail, De Lissa pointed out that, with both individuals and nations, "ratios of expenditure" tended to decrease with the increase of wealth. The "ratio of expenditure" in De Lissa's model is strictly analogous to the propensity to save in the Keynesian framework. From these comments of De Lissa, however, the two expenditure functions have different shapes, the Keynesian leak-

10. "The Law of the Incomes," p. 10. De Lissa suggested that a family man might have a higher "ratio" than a bachelor. *Ibid.*

age increasing and the De Lissa leakage decreasing with prosperity.

The "ratio of expenditure"—one-fourth in the present illustration—is the crucial element in the De Lissa model. It is the withdrawal from the expenditure stream which causes a reduction in the overall velocity of circulation and corresponds to the savings leakage of the conventional employment multiplier. In the same way that De Lissa did not explain carefully where the funds came from which were received initially by the primary producers he did not specify the resting place of subsequent expenditures upon primary products. He said simply: "The currency, after passing through the series of secondary workers, returns to its source."[11] But again it may be understood that by "source" De Lissa meant the banking system. In the example, £25 or the portion of the £100 income spent upon the raw material component of goods, passes through the hands of merchants who had originally contracted loans to make the raw material purchases, and thence to a commercial bank (minus the merchants' commission which De Lissa considered a payment for services) where it is effectively removed from circulation. Because banks in his day were accustomed normally to make loans only on the security of commercial paper, these funds could not be reissued until new primary goods had been produced in the next crop year. It is important to note that in De Lissa's simplified model, primary producers receive their incomes in large sums from merchants as intermediaries. Purchases of primary products by consumers are from these merchants and do not result in an immediate addition to the primary producers' income.

The leakage in the De Lissa model, unlike a savings leakage, is a temporary withdrawal of purchasing power from circulation. Expenditures on raw materials and other primary products cause banks gradually to accumulate idle balances over the multiplier period. At the end of the period, in the event of new production, more applications for loans are received, the balances are reduced, and funds are returned to circulation as the second period begins. This seasonally regenerative feature, which is par-

11. *Production, Distribution, and Quesnay's Tableau Economique*, p. 20.

ticularly appropriate for a staples-producing economy, has never been associated with the conventional multiplier. It clearly implies complications, such as fluctuations over the multiplier period, but De Lissa did not develop these corollaries to his theory.

In the second stage of the model the amount spent in stage one by primary workers and received by secondary producers (£75 in the example) is the full amount available for expenditure. On the assumption of a constant "ratio of expenditure" of one-fourth, one quarter of this amount, £18.75 in the example, is spent upon raw materials and £56.25 upon secondary goods and services. In stage two, as in stage one, the amount spent on raw materials is returned by merchants to the banking system, and thus is removed from circulation for the remainder of the multiplier period. Expenditures upon secondary goods become the income of secondary producers in stage three, which is spent again in the usual proportions, and thus the process continues. With ever-diminishing amounts of income available for expenditure in successive stages, the original amount of money borrowed in stage one (£100 in the example) is gradually returned by merchants to the banking system. When the return is complete, all primary goods produced prior to stage one have been purchased and consumed. The process is ready to begin again with primary producers selling new goods to merchants, and merchants effecting new loans. The total amount of income over the production period resulting from a single injection of primary income can be determined, De Lissa explained, "By the law of geometrical progression" given in the formula

$$\frac{\text{"V (value of [raw material] production)}}{\text{R (ratio of expenditure)}} =$$

$$\text{I (total [national] incomes)"}[12]$$

The example described here was one De Lissa used himself, and he concluded that in this instance: "The total production being 100. . . . If the ratio of expenditure should be ¼, then

12. "The Practical Application of Economics," p. 887.

$$\frac{100}{\frac{1}{4}} = 400 \text{ total incomes } = 300 \text{ incomes for services.}[13]$$

When describing the process of income creation, De Lissa sometimes used terminology familiar today. He remarked in 1890: "A feature arresting attention upon first consideration was the manner in which the incomes multiply, or come one out of another."[14] In way of summary it is worth repeating in De Lissa's own words the outline of another example where the initiating action is the production and sale of primary goods valued at £300, and where the "ratio of expenditure" is one-half.

The currency, representing the circulating capital, leaves its source; it flows into the channels of production, promotes one production after another in diminishing numbers, according to the ratio, until all demands are supplied. There is an interchange with the secondary class, a payment for services which promotes a second production, each amount for services being expended for other services in the like ratio, and when the currency will have passed through all the groups, 300 will have been expended in the purchase of the products representing the circulating capital by one class, and 300 by the other, and the currency returns to its source to commence another circuit when the circulating capital, which has been reproduced, is again disposed of.[15]

In earlier papers, De Lissa constructed his multiplier as an internal relationship between primary and total national income, excluding effects of foreign trade. In a later writing, however, he developed the international implications of his theory by a series of observations on the potential national benefits of different types of new industry. For this purpose, he transformed his internal multiplier into an international trade multiplier making the exogenous variable, not a change in domestic staple production as before, but a change in the balance of payments. Before beginning his examination, De Lissa assumed that each new industry would have an annual product valued at £100 and that the community's ratio of expenditure was one-half. At the lowest level of national utility, De Lissa placed the production of a good

13. *Ibid.*
14. "The Law of the Incomes," p. 10.
15. *Production, Distribution, and Quesnay's Tableau Economique*, p. 21.

504   *The Science of Enquiry*

formerly imported and for which the raw material came from
abroad—a "New production in manufacturing industry, previously the subject of international interchange, in which the raw
material is not produced in the country nor any additional
production in exchange for it."[16] In this case, he explained,
because manufacturers have still to import £50 of raw materials,
£100 of new production leads to a net reduction in imports of
only £50. The reduction, nevertheless, results in an injection into
the expenditure stream of £50 in the form of increased receipts in
the secondary sector, and the final multiplied effect upon total
income of this new production is £100. As De Lissa said, "For
every £100 worth of manufactures so produced there will, according to the ratio which I have indicated, be increased earnings
at least to the amount of £50 by primary workers and £50 by
secondary workers."[17]

Next in order of value to a national economy, De Lissa declared, was a new industry making a product, formerly imported
and which required only domestic raw material for its manufacture.

A new production in manufacturing industry, previously the subject of international interchange, in which the raw material or a
new production of raw material to be given in exchange for it is produced in the country. In this case, for every £100 of manufactures so
produced, there will be increased earnings at least to the amount of
£100 by primary workers and £100 by secondary workers.[18]

At the third level of national utility, but of less determinant
effect, was the "production of a new raw material for which
there is a constant market in other countries." He noted that the
manufacture of such a good, in addition to permitting a reduction of imports, might lead to steadily increasing sales abroad.
For illustration, he assumed that the original production of £100
first replaces former imports and is quickly matched by an equivalent quantity for export. The original production of £100, therefore, can be said to have led to an increase in domestic income
of £400.

16. "The Practical Application of Economics," p. 889.
17. *Ibid.*
18. *Ibid.*

Finally, De Lissa examined the implications of a "new production in a country of some article of invention or utility not in use before," and he concluded that in this case the possibilities for expansion of national income could be limitless. In addition to the multiplier effects already mentioned of reduced imports and increased exports, new subsidiary industries might be brought into being, each with its own demands for services. At this point, De Lissa came close to elaborating a theory of the accelerator when he remarked "There might also be an expenditure of capital for the erection of factories, in a new manufacturing industry, of three-fourths of a million, the general estimate for each million of production; with the like results as to an additional production and secondary incomes."[19]

On several occasions De Lissa discussed the effects of foreign interest payments upon the size of total national income. He considered all payments abroad, whether for imports or for interest on borrowed capital, as leakages from the expenditure stream and as causes of a reverse multiplier effect depending in intensity upon the size of the domestic "ratio of expenditure." He emphasized the importance to a nation, apart from simple business principles, of the rule that borrowing abroad should be only for truly reproductive projects.

If the work of construction is not reproductive, every £100 of product sent away for interest, which would have been otherwise employed, represents two incomes of the like amount, which would have been the result of the employment. The cost to the real wealth of the country is double the rate of interest paid. Where the work is reproductive, yielding interest at the same rate as that which is paid, such interest represents the circulating capital employed in the procurement each year of the product which is sent away.[20]

De Lissa's model cannot be judged simply on the accuracy of

19. *Ibid.*, p. 890. In recognizing and attempting to deal theoretically with the introduction of new techniques into a developing colony, De Lissa's interest and approach were similar to those of John Rae writing in Canada sixty years before. The policy conclusions of these two men with regard to the role of the state in the economy were also much alike. See J. J. Spengler, "John Rae on Economic Development: A Note," *Quarterly Journal of Economics*, LXXIII (1959), 393–406; R. Warren James, "The Life and Work of John Rae," *Canadian Journal of Economics and Political Science*, XVII (1951), 141–63 and my *Canadian Economic Thought*, pp. 122–27.

20. *Ibid.*, p. 892.

its portrayal of the Australian economy. As he recognized fully, his model was, like all models, a simplification designed to illustrate significant relationships and based on assumptions that prevented it from being fully realistic. De Lissa explained the importance of a scientific hypothesis thus:

> If political economy is to be of any material service, it should, where possible to do so, establish as in other sciences, a theory, or at least a working hypothesis, as the basis of deduction; and also of such action as can be taken to carry out the objects with which the science is concerned. Until this is accomplished there can be no material progress. There was none in chemistry until the discovery by Dalton of the atomic theory, deduced from the observation of chemical combination in multiple proportions; nor in astronomy, until the discovery of Newton's theory of gravitation, the basis of science.[21]

Although several of De Lissa's assumptions seem unreasonable today, such for example as the single annual receipt of income and expenditure by primary producers, and also loans by banks strictly on the security of primary products, these were fairly realistic statements of conditions in nineteenth century Australia where wool was overwhelmingly the most important staple product, was sold at annual sales, was produced by pastoralists living in isolation who tended to purchase supplies in bulk, and was financed by a banking system dominantly commercial in character. De Lissa's assumptions were certainly not so improbable that they invalidate the usefulness of his model. Others after him might legitimately have questioned aspects of his theories, and after tests could have suggested improvements and more realistic assumptions. But no tests were ever made, and his assumptions must remain as reasonable and valuable first approximations.

In more congenial surroundings De Lissa's multiplier might have become an important addition to the economist's toolbox. He set out to illustrate how the growth and prosperity of a staples-producing economy depends in large measure on the manufacture and sale of primary products, and he accomplished this with brilliant innovations and remarkable depth of insight. De Lissa's multiplier mechanism was put to a different purpose

21. "The Practical Application of Economics," p. 885.

from that for which the multiplier is used most frequently today.[22] But there can be little argument that he anticipated by a full forty years what has been called by Professor Shackle "one of the landmarks of economics."[23]

Development of De Lissa's Thought. Alfred De Lissa was born in London in 1838, may have attended University College, and came to Sydney, as a young man where he entered the legal profession.[24] By middle age he had established a reputation as an imaginative legal heretic, and one critic in 1882 denounced him for a "fatuous suggestion" made a year earlier that in order to safeguard innocent lenders, borrowers be limited by law from borrowing more than a fixed proportion of their assets. De Lissa was ridiculed as a "philosopher" and dreamer, and the reviewer concluded charitably:

Mr. De Lissa is entitled to all the praise that may be bestowed upon a professional man who, instead of devoting all his thoughts and energies to the details of business, employs a portion of his time in philosophical speculation upon the best modes of ameliorating the law and improving the commercial condition of the British nation, for whose especial benefit, judging from the preface, his pamphlet appears to have been written. But beyond this we fear our commendation ought not to extend. His conclusions and recommendations appear to us to be crude and immature, and utterly unpractical.[25]

Apparently in later life, De Lissa gained greater respectability among his legal colleagues, and he is described in his obituary as "a recognised authority on company and mining matters" and "an authority on trade marks."[26]

De Lissa seems to have begun the economic enquiries which led him eventually to a multiplier theory in the late 1880's after

---

22. In form De Lissa's model is an unsophisticated version of the "matrix" multiplier developed by R. M. Goodwin using varying lags in payments flows. "The Multiplier as Matrix," *Economic Journal*, LIX (1949), 537–55.

23. *Op. cit.*, p. 241.

24. The only biographical information about De Lissa I have been able to discover is an obituary notice: *Sydney Morning Herald*, February 26, 1913, p. 12. It is stated here that De Lissa was a student at University College, but a search through the College records kindly performed by the Registrar revealed no trace of his name.

25. *Melbourne Review*, VI (1882), pp. 104–6.

26. *Sydney Morning Herald*, *loc. cit.* Among De Lissa's legal writings are the following: *Bankruptcy and Insolvency Law* (Sydney, 1881); *Companies' Work*

reading accounts of social problems with an economic basis in the works of Henry George and John Hobson.[27] He turned to economic science in the hope that it could provide prescriptions for some of the world's ills, and he asked in 1892:

> Is it possible for economic science to indicate what that action should be—the true remedy, having regard to existing conditions, which shall control the elements of conflict retarding progress, and render the achievements of thought and science conducive to results more worthy of mankind? If it is possible in a new land like Australia to do so by departing from the old grooves of thought, and recognising new modes of action, it is for the exponents of economic science to indicate what they should be.[28]

By his own account, De Lissa in his early work was on the way to explaining the operation of a conventional income multiplier with a savings leakage. He reminisced in 1896:

> Towards the latter end of December, 1889, I was considering this subject of production, and this question occurred to me. We know very well that if there is an increased production in the country it is the same as if there were the employment of so many new workers. Say that there are increased earnings to the amount of one million, that million will be expended in the purchase of all kinds of food and other products, and in payment for services, and there will be a second production and second body of workers employed in supplying the wants of these new workers. *With the exception of some savings*, all the money will pass out of their hands. That second body of workers want food and other products and requirements, and expend the money which has passed out of the hands of the first set of workers, and give employment to a third; and the third set of workers will expend again. To what extent will further production go on, and when will the circulation cease? I could not attempt to solve that problem, nor could anyone else, having regard to existing data.[29]

De Lissa's interests quickly changed, however, and after his later

---

and Mining Law in New South Wales and Victoria (London, 1894); "Codification of Mercantile Law," *Report of the Conference of Australasian Chambers of Commerce, 1897; The Bill of Lading Question and Marine Insurance Policies* (Sydney, 1901).

27. See "The Organisation of Industry," pp. 487 and 489.
28. *Ibid.*, pp. 490–91.
29. *Production, Distribution, and Quesnay's Tableau Economique*, p. 10, italics mine.

discoveries in technique he never returned to this earlier problem. In March, 1890, De Lissa was elected a member of the Australian Economic Association, and for several years this body was his principal inspiration and forum for discussion.[30] De Lissa decided from the beginning that the discovery in economic science most likely to produce solutions of social problems was the determination of a relationship between the incomes of social groups.[31] He appears to have selected primary and secondary producers as the significant income-group divisions after examining the pioneer national accounts of Timothy Coghlan, the New South Wales Statistician, which made possible such a distinction.[32] De Lissa was profoundly influenced, as was Coghlan, by observation of the Australian economy dependent in large measure upon the sale abroad of staple primary products. As justification for his particular studies, De Lissa declared:

I would point out that no writer has hitherto dealt with the question of the actual incomes derived from the production of a country, or from a specific production; that it has never been shown what proportion there is, if any, between the incomes of the so-called producing and non-producing classes; that no law, or tendency to a given result, has ever been predicated on the subject . . . that no rule has been established or means indicated by which it could be ascertained what numbers could find or expect to find employment according to existing production; and that the question has not been raised as to actual wealth being based upon the incomes of the people, and not merely upon production possibly leaving the country.[33]

In his first paper delivered to the Australian Economic Associa-

30. De Lissa remarked correctly in 1897 that the Association's journal, *Australian Economist*, "should in time to come be valued as a record of economic thought in these colonies." *Australian Economist*, V (1897), 1.
31. De Lissa argued that in political economy, as in any other science, an important preliminary task was classification—"if we are to have any science, any kind of science whatever as to the internal economy of a country, and that of course is political economy, you must have recourse to the method of procedure which is adopted in all science—you must analyse and find a natural classification. It is to such analysis and classification that we owe great discoveries in science. You must have a classification of the multifarious workers to be found in every developed country." *Production, Distribution, and Quesnay's Tableau Economique*, p. 7.
32. De Lissa wrote with glowing praise of Coghlan's statistics and of helpful discussions with Coghlan himself. "The Law of the Incomes," p. 8.
33. *Australian Economist*, II (1890–93), p. 49.

tion in 1890, only a month after he had become a member, De Lissa was pre-occupied with the results of investigations he had carried out of income statistics for different countries. After a comparison of Coghlan's Australian figures with those of Giffen, Baxter, Mulhall, and Levi for the United Kingdom and those of Edward Atkinson for the United States, he discovered that, in each of these economies, incomes of workers in the primary sector equaled approximately incomes of workers in the secondary sector. He admitted openly that he was unable to explain the reason for this uniformity, but added that he believed it indicated the existence of an economic "law."

Results under far less varying conditions have been accepted as indications of the highest laws. We may see or know that a law exists without being able to trace the method of its operation, or the reason of its existence.[34]

He speculated that perhaps this law, like certain laws of physics in his time, might be observable but not explicable. "Herschel tells us it is the character of all the higher laws of nature to assume the form of precise quantitative statements. We cannot account for these laws—they are the mathematics of creation."[35] Although De Lissa was not yet able even to begin explaining the operation of his multiplier model, it is clear that his mind was already running in this direction. He wrote: "The apparent perplexity of the augmentation of the incomes appears in the first instance to militate against the predication of any law giving definite results; but it yields to the consideration that the force of multiplication has limits which are likely to assume some proportions."[36]

For several years after beginning his economic enquiries, De Lissa devoted most of his attention to the discovery of similar income distribution patterns in different countries. Any references to theory were incidental. His observations did not startle his associates, and because he never hesitated to subject an audience to the same material on several different occasions, his

34. "The Law of the Incomes," p. 10.
35. *Ibid.*, p. 11.
36. *Ibid.*, p. 10.

papers were greeted with mixed enthusiasm. Richard Teece, the first president of the Australian Economic Association, suggested that De Lissa was going to "enormous trouble and great fatigue" to explain the obvious. A. Duckworth, the Association's editor, questioned whether De Lissa's subject was even worth discussing.[37] More charitible listeners thought his efforts commendable but his conclusions unimportant. Two exceptional expressions of praise came on the one hand from Archibald Forsyth, an active member of the Association who thought De Lissa's first paper one of the most significant presented to the group thus far, and on the other from an anonymous reviewer in the Sydney *Morning Herald* who asked eloquently:

Is it too much to see in the law of income the first step in the discovery of the forces controlling society, and dare we hope that the glimmering of light which we now have will ere long broaden into the glorious day, when these riddles of life will be made plain, when not only the acknowledgement of the duty of "each for all" and "all for each," but the proper method of its application, so as to harmoniously distribute the necessary labour and enjoyments of existence, will be effectively understood.[38]

By 1892, De Lissa's theoretical model had begun to materialize, and he had developed several important features of the relationship between incomes of primary and secondary sectors. He explained to the Australasian Association for the Advancement of Science in that year:

The hypothesis I have formed to account for the operation of the law is this. . . . The incomes of the secondary workers come out of the incomes of the primary workers and out of one another, so much product representing purchasing power in the different hands through which it passes until it is consumed. Thus, a merchant receiving £3000 a year virtually receives the equivalent of product to

37. *Australian Economist*, II (1890–93), 41–44. De Lissa's obvious unpopularity with the authorities of the Australian Economic Association may be explained partly by his unremitting opposition to bimetallism, a panacea very popular with Teece, Duckworth, and Professor Walter Scott. See for example De Lissa's lengthy criticism of a paper by Scott and the ensuing argument, *Australian Economist*, V (1897), 17–20.
38. "The Law of Incomes," *Sydney Morning Herald*, August 21, 1890, p. 3, signed T., and noted *Australian Economist*, II (1890–93), 65. In this account the similarity of De Lissa's work to that of R. M. Johnston is noted. See above pp. 223–26.

that amount. He pays as rent £500 a year. Product to that amount, without his consuming any portion of it, virtually passes into the hands of the landlord. In like manner, he gives incomes to those engaged in personal services, to professional services, to professionals and others; and the amount he pays in the market-place in the purchase of clothing and of food for himself and family, or for the entertainment of friends, represents so much more of the product than its original cost; the difference being the incomes of the dealers and distributors through whose hands the product has passed. The larger incomes give off a number of smaller ones; the smaller ones give off incomes smaller still, until at length the product reaches hands where it is no longer given away for services, and is consumed.[39]

Although by 1892 De Lissa understood the principle of continued circulation after an initial expenditure, he had not yet developed the concept of a leakage. He concluded uncertainly, and in fact incorrectly, that total income resulting from an initial receipt of primary income equaled the summation of an arithmetic progression.[40]

Between 1892 and 1896 two important developments took place in De Lissa's thought. First, the financial collapse of 1893 and subsequent depression led him to shift his attention from problems of long-run growth for the British Empire to methods of providing immediate relief and employment in his own colony. In 1890, De Lissa had asked: "Does not the want of employment presenting itself on the crowded continents shew too large a number employed within a given area? And must not the tendency be to occupy new lands where all classes will find employment in such proportionate numbers as to equalise numbers?" [41] In 1892 he still argued optimistically:

I believe that in a new country like Australia it is possible to set on foot material measures of reform, not for the reconstruction of society, but in the organization of the industrial system; that it is for an Australian community to initiate promising reforms tentatively. As the twig is bent the tree inclines. It may be possible in some instances to promote new growth. There are giant industries in their infancy, or

39. "The Organisation of Industry," p. 500.
40. *Ibid.*, p. 501.
41. "The Law of the Incomes," p. 12.

not yet started, which may be dealt with in the first stages of progress as they could not be dealt with in the older lands.[42]

But in 1896 De Lissa expressed only gloom and an anxious desire for immediate action: "It is not unreasonable to assume, or, at all events, to surmise, that there must be some want of knowledge or of applications of principles to account for the waste of energy, the losses of capital, and the failure to provide the full measure of employment, which are incident to the industrial operations of the age."[43]

The second development in De Lissa's thought in the early 1890's was a significant improvement in his theoretical apparatus. From the beginning of his work in economics, De Lissa was anxious to discover and gain support from other writers working on similar problems. In addition to Hobson, Henry George, and the statisticians mentioned above, he acknowledged use of Henry Sidgwick (on the distinction between primary and secondary sectors), Engel (on consumption patterns), and Helferich (on the creation of bank money). He tried hard but without conspicuous success to construct a diagram which would illustrate his theories using Bastiat's figure for the "Circle of Universal Industry." De Lissa pictured each income receiver as situated in turn at the center of a set of concentric circles of diminishing increase in radius and intended to represent the multiple but declining effects upon total income of an initial expenditure.[44] The resulting illustration did not convey a picture of continuous circulation, and it failed to indicate the nature of his leakage. Obviously unsatisfied with this attempt, De Lissa explained in 1892 that he had looked at length for aid in the exposition of his ideas, but "The relation has never been considered, so far as I am aware, by any writer or economist."[45] He noted wistfully a reference in Adam Smith's *Wealth of Nations* to François Quesnay's *Tableau Économique*, and he reported regretfully:

42. "The Organisation of Industry," p. 491.
43. *Production, Distribution, and Quesnay's Tableau Economique*, p. 2.
44. "The Organisation of Industry," and *Production, Distribution, and Quesnay's Tableau Économique*." Diagrams are attached to both works.
45. "The Organisation of Industry," p. 495.

I find that this work has been lost, or at all events but one or two copies only exist in some European libraries. . . . It is to be regretted that the results of his [Quesnay's] work, whatever they may be, are not given by any of the modern economists.[46]

De Lissa was delighted when in 1895 the British Economic Association published a facsimile of the *Tableau Économique* with comment in the *Economic Journal* by Stephan Bauer.[47] Describing the "Physiocratic School," De Lissa said "Its philosophy struck a chord in the middle of the eighteenth century which is vibrating still."[48] As with Bastiat's diagram, De Lissa attempted unsuccessfully to adapt the *Tableau* to his own theory,[49] and after two years he had become disillusioned with its usefulness. He reported in 1898:

> Upon a first glance at the "Tableau" it appeared to me that it had anticipated the deduction of a law such as that I have stated, and that the formula which I have presented . . . reproduces the table in another form. This is not, however, the case, although the appearance is very deceptive. The "Tableau" does not show any increase of incomes in the so-called non-productive class . . . that is to say, the circulation of the currency for services yielding income among the secondary workers themselves has not, and necessarily could not, have been considered.[50]

Nevertheless, despite his protestations to the contrary, De Lissa was profoundly influenced by the *Tableau*. It made clear to him such fundamental concepts as the circulation of money, and above all stimulated him to continue his investigations at a time when his associates were either disinterested or positively hostile to what they considered his crackbrained pursuits.

Some time between 1896 and 1898, De Lissa took his theoretical problems to the mathematics department of Sydney University, and there, it appears, the core of his model evolved. In 1898 he admitted for the first time that his statistical observations and the supposed "law of incomes" indicating equality between primary and secondary sectors were not crucial to his hypothesis

46. *Ibid.*, p. 495.
47. "Quesnay's *Tableau Économique*, with Unpublished Letters," *Economic Journal*, V (1895), 1–21.
48. *Production, Distribution, and Quesnay's Tableau Economique*, p. 2.
49. *Production, Distribution, and Quesnay's Tableau Economique*, inside cover.
50. "The Practical Application of Economics," p. 889.

regarding the working of the economy. He also outlined clearly his concepts of expenditures on primary products as a leakage and total derivitive income as the summation of a geometric progression.

> . . . the theory or working hypothesis I have in mind, would not depend upon the question whether the statistical data or my deduction of the ratio were correct; because if it should appear that for any particular country the ratio were not 50 per cent, or a sufficiently close approximation thereto, to be so stated, the ratio of expenditure, whatever it might be, would nevertheless be attended with results of a corresponding character. I am indebted to Professor Gurney of the Sydney University for the form of the calculation which would give the result of any progression based upon my hypothesis . . . .[51]

De Lissa gave up work in pure economics in 1898 after he had presented the most complete exposition of his model to a meeting of the Australasian Association for the Advancement of Science. It may have been that consistent failure to evoke any widespread interest was a final discouragement, but it is more probable that, like many other Australian intellectuals in the 1890's, he moved naturally from economic to political problems as the country began to emerge from the trough of depression and faced federation at the turn of the century. De Lissa's only writings after 1900 which touched on economics were pamphlets in support of a British Empire League.[52]

De Lissa was able to draw several policy implications out of his theoretical conclusions. From his illustration of the connection between the income of one group and the expenditures of another, he was led to emphasize the inter-dependence of economic units. With the great labor disputes and depression of the 1890's before him, he concluded: "The interest of any one pro-

51. *Ibid.*, p. 886. Theodore Thomas Gurney came to Sydney as Professor of Mathematics after he had become third wrangler at Cambridge in 1873. He appears to have been well liked and active in university affairs, but at the end of his career university authorities described him to a committee selecting his successor thus: "Mentally equipped with every gift except ambition, he has, as you know, never published a line. . . ." I. S. Turner, "The First Hundred Years of Mathematics in the University of Sydney," *Royal Australian Historical Society Journal and Proceedings*, XLI (1955), 250. It may be hoped that his important assistance to De Lissa will now be remembered to Gurney's credit.

52. *The British Empire League in Australia* (Sydney, 1906); *An Empire League (Hoc Vincit Omnia)* (Sydney, 1905). In the latter work De Lissa included as an appendix a summary of "the law of the incomes."

ducing class is the interest of all. The strike, which paralyses
industry for a time, and impairs a market, is the concern of all."[53]
In general terms he prescribed an active role for the state in the
economy, and in a new country, he said, a wise government
would devote close attention to primary industry. "The importance of the aid which the organisation of government can give
in promoting the development of industry and the increase of
production in new lands, whose resources are greatly undeveloped, must be manifest. . . ."[54] Like many other economists
writing in less-developed areas, De Lissa saw an important place
for public enterprise: "It is not sufficient, as it is considered in
most countries, that the development of industrial pursuit, no
matter what it may be, should be left solely to individual enterprise. There is much which individual enterprise cannot and will
never do."[55] Provision of accurate economic information, he explained, was a particularly critical function. "Much may be done
by the Statistical Department in every country to ascertain requirements, and to control by the intelligence which it can
exercise."[56] He proposed a government "Bureau of Industry"
which among other things might issue licenses to workers and
employers, thereby eliminating "undue competition" and waste
both of capital and labor.[57] In addition:

Such a department should have correspondents in all parts of the
world, take means to ascertain the successful improvements in the
processes both of manufacture and agricultural art, to indicate what
new industries may be established; and should send its messengers to
distant countries, to ascertain what extent new markets are available.
If such a department should be the means of opening up new markets
for Australian productions in the great Eastern lands it would do more
to secure the advancement of Australia, and the fortunes of her people,
than years of inert action.[58]

De Lissa took no doctrinaire position on commercial policy, and
was willing to consider protective tariffs as a developmental tool.

53. "The Practical Application of Economics," p. 892. See also "The Labour
Problem," *passim.*
54. "The Practical Application of Economics," pp. 892–93.
55. "The Law of the Incomes," p. 13.
56. "The Practical Application of Economics," p. 893.
57. "The Organisation of Industry," pp. 510–12.
58. "The Law of the Incomes," p. 13.

He said: "I believe I am correct in saying that the operation of the Protectionist system is not generally understood where it is applied to a young and growing country."[59] He drew attention to the decline in employment which could follow an adverse balance of payments, and regarded such a change as legitimate reason for refusal to reduce tariffs. He postulated a country which suddenly eliminated protection, with the result that imports increased by one million pounds. If the domestic "ratio of expenditure" were one-fourth, and if there were no compensating increase in exports, the resulting diminution in national income could be four million pounds. From this De Lissa concluded:

> The preservation of true liberty, the true welfare of this country, will consist in that moderation which shall have due regard to all existing interests; in the moderation of a protection which shall not destroy commerce and staple production, whilst providing for increased employment in industries which may be enlarged or which do not exist.[60]

Mindful that one country's unfavorable balance of payments could at least be another country's favorable one, De Lissa argued in defense of close British Empire trade. The multiple reduction in employment brought about in one part of the Empire through a deficit balance would be softened by a surplus balance and employment boom in another. He proposed in 1905 that for this reason an Imperial customs union would result in "increased production within the dominions of the Empire. . . ."[61]

The influence of De Lissa's writings on others was probably slight. Archibald Forsyth, a rope manufacturer and member of the New South Wales Legislative Assembly and of the Australian Economic Association, was apparently his only acknowledged disciple. He praised "the law of the incomes" together with a collection of protectionist arguments when advocating higher tariffs for the new Australian Federation.[62] The Melbourne *Age* in 1901 namd De Lissa with Carey and List as protectionist

59. *Protection and Federation*, p. 20.
60. *Ibid.*, p. 32.
61. *An Empire League* (*Hoc Vincet Omnia*) (Sydney, 1905).
62. *The Lines on Which a Federal Tariff Should be Based* (Sydney, c. 1898). Curiously De Lissa was extremely critical of a paper on "Imports and Exports" presented to the Australian Economic Association by Forsyth in December, 1890. The two carried on a heated argument.

authorities. It described De Lissa's "law" in defense of high tariffs, and concluded that if a "farmer's product be sent abroad to purchase articles from foreign markets, the benefit of the farmer's income is deprived of exactly one half of its fructifying power." [63] Several of De Lissa's associates in the Australian Economic Association and the Australasian Association for the Advancement of Science, notably R. M. Johnston, worked on similar problems of national income analysis and must have been aware of his work.[64] It is most reasonable, however, to regard De Lissa as a largely unnoticed member of a long series of amateur and professional Australian economists who have been intrigued by similar subjects.

De Lissa's discoveries appear today far more remarkable than do those of his Australian contemporaries and predecessors. But at the time these innovations were made public, they involved revolutionary concepts and were not presented in such a way that they would attract attention or could be understood quickly and easily. De Lissa's formulation of a multiplier model in such remarkable detail and his subsequent failure to achieve any recognition are an outstanding example of the impact of environment on the development of economic doctrine. They also indicate clearly the importance in new countries of a critical but receptive audience for what De Lissa himself called departures from "the conventional grooves of thought."

Sir Anthony Musgrave: Colonial Administrator and Monetary Economist

Sir Anthony Musgrave (1828–1888) served as a colonial civil servant in such widely separated portions of the British Empire as Canada, the West Indies, South Africa, and Australia.[1] During

63. *A White Man's Land. Australia for the Australians. Free Trade a Failure. Victoria and New South Wales Compared* (Reprinted from *Age* by the Protectionist Association of Victoria, Melbourne, 1901), p. 80.

64. It is an interesting coincidence that after De Lissa one of the first expositions of the multiplier came from L. F. Giblin, Johnston's successor as Tasmanian Statistician.

1. Musgrave held various minor posts in the West Indies before becoming administrator of St. Vincent in 1861 and lieutenant governor in 1862. He was

the course of his long career, he became fascinated by a variety of economic questions and by middle age was convinced firmly that contemporary theory was unsatisfactory as a guide to policy. As he wrote to H. V. Poor, the New England railway historian, in 1874: "In the course of my experience as the administrator of several colonial governments in different quarters of the world, where it has been part of my duty to deal with financial and economical questions, I have repeatedly found that the prevalent theories must be erroneous, though at the time it was difficult to say why."[2] In the 1870's, overcome with grief at the tragic death of a child, Musgrave turned for solace to serious study of economic theory. He found quickly that in the colonies "opportunity is afforded for studying the effects of alleged principles more easily than in larger communities—just as one can see more readily in a model the details and modes of action of the several parts of a large machine."[3] The results of Musgrave's labors in economics were several journal articles, a number of pamphlets, and a volume of essays entitled *Studies in Political Economy*.[4] These few works contained incisive critiques of current economic opinion and precocious insights into the theory of macro-economics. In themselves they constitute important evidence of ways

---

appointed governor of Newfoundland (1864), governor of British Columbia (1869), lieutenant governor of Natal (1872), governor of South Australia (1873), governor in chief and captain general of Jamaica (1877), and governor and commander in chief of Queensland (1883).

2. Letter to H. V. Poor, dated 16 June, 1874. This, and other personal papers of Sir Anthony Musgrave, are contained in the Duke University Library through the generosity of Sir Anthony's grandson, Mr. William Musgrave.

3. *Studies in Political Economy* (London, 1875), p. 26, hereafter *Studies*.

4. Musgrave published several pamphlets in Adelaide in 1874–75 using facilities of the Government Printer, W. C. Cox. These were: *Money, a Function* (Adelaide, 1874); *What is Capital?* (Adelaide, 1874); *Some Thoughts on Value* (Adelaide, 1874); *A Plea for Some Facts* (Adelaide, 1874); *A Review of Mr. Mill's Fundamental Propositions Respecting Capital* (Adelaide, 1874) [republished as "Capital: Mr. Mill's Fundamental Propositions," *Contemporary Review*, XXIV (1874), 728–49]; and *Economic Fallacies; Free Trade v. Protection* (Adelaide, 1875) [republished as "Economic Fallacies. Free Trade v. Protection," *Contemporary Review*, XXIX (1876–77), 310–34]. These works were reorganized and modified as *Studies in Political Economy* (London, 1875). This volume, apparently, was set in type in Adelaide in 1874 by W. C. Cox but was not published until a year later in England. Musgrave's corrected proof sheets are in the Duke University Library. Later writings by Musgrave, advancing little on his earlier works, are: *Jamaica: Now and Fifteen Years Since*, a paper read before the Royal Colonial Institute on April 20, 1880 (London, 1880); *Economic Fallacies; the Functions of Money* (n. p., n. d. [1885?]); and "The Functions of Money: Bimetallism," *Westminster Review*, LXX (1886), 424–47.

in which ideas may be modified and advanced when transferred from one environment to another, and by their reception they illustrate clearly that accepted doctrine is extremely resistant to change.

Musgrave's monetary theory, the kernel of all his economic arguments, will be examined first; his remarks on capital and the growth process will be treated next, followed by discussion of his comments on the theory of international trade. The influence of Musgrave's thought will be described in the final section.

Monetary theory. Musgrave's writings were based upon a conviction that contemporary monetary theory was in some respects inadequate and in other respects false. He maintained that money performed three distinct functions: as a medium of exchange, as a standard of value, and as a store of value. He argued that classical economists and their followers, particularly John Stuart Mill (whose "work may be considered to be the standard textbook on economical science"), overemphasized the first function, confused the second, and ignored the third.[5]

Musgrave's appreciation of the distinction between money as a medium of exchange and as a standard of value developed from experience in British North America, where transactions were expressed in units of account which had no equivalent among the variety of coins used for trade. He chided Mill for describing transactions of primitive African tribes to illustrate that a medium of exchange need not constitute the monetary standard when such a distinction had been established for decades in the British colonies.

But Musgrave chiefly criticized classical economists for failing to appreciate money as a valuable commodity, desired for itself and for the services it could perform. They regarded money, he complained, as a ficticious intermediary between a sale and an anticipated purchase. Musgrave rejected categorically Mill's famous statement that:

5. *Studies,* p. v.

There cannot, in short, be intrinsically a more insignificant thing, in the economy of society, than money; except in the character of a contrivance for sparing time and labour. It is a machine for doing quickly and commodiously, what would be done, though less quickly and commodiously, without it; and like many other kinds of machinery, it only exerts a distinct and independent influence of its own when it gets out of order.[6]

Musgrave began his own book, *Studies in Political Economy,* with a statement of a new fundamental proposition concerning money.

What I conceive to be the root error, from which a plentiful crop of fallacies springs in modern economical doctrines, consists in ignoring the fact—as hard a fact as any in science—that gold and silver are a 'medium of exchange' only in so far as, and because, they are eminently *articles*—and, from their peculiar value and characteristics, pre-eminently *the* articles—of exchange.[7]

Musgrave denied that money should be treated merely as an intermediary in exchange, converting one good into another. Money was desired for its distinctive moneyness and was exchanged with the same transfer of utilities as were other commodities. Musgrave contradicted Mill's and Fawcett's assertions that gold bullion was desired for either one of two distinct reasons: as money, or as an ordinary article of commerce. He said that the two demands were identical in kind: "If gold is at all, and under any circumstances, an article of commerce, so must money be." Sellers accepted money in exchange for goods or services because of its utility, and they were aware fully that this money was not scheduled to pass as an intermediary to other hands at any fixed date. Money was exchanged by its holders for goods or services only when expected increases in utility through purchases exceeded the satisfaction of possessing liquidity. The

6. *Principles of Political Economy,* edited by W. J. Ashley (London, 1929), p. 488. Musgrave listed extracts from Henry Fawcett's *"Manual of Political Economy* (2nd ed., p. 362)," Ricardo's *Principles* and J. S. Mill's *Principles* (Chapter on "Foreign Exchanges") as forming "a concise expression of the error against which I protest." *Studies,* p. 157. A list by Musgrave of his extensive reading during 1874 is contained in the Musgrave papers, Duke University Library.

7. *Studies,* p. 1.

unique character of money as a liquid asset was particularly evident in the colonies.

It would seem as if, by confusion of ideas, the political economists thought that, because bank-notes are money and are, or ought to be, convertible into sovereigns on demand from a particular person, at a specified place, all money is likewise convertible into something else on demand. No doubt Mr. Mill practically found it so in his experience; but he had not lived in new countries. The possession of gold gives no right at all any more than the possession of bales of cotton or pigs of iron.[8]

When money passed from buyer to seller in exchange for goods, Musgrave emphasized, a transfer of utilities took place, and not as implied by Mill a promise of future utilities to the seller for present ones received by the buyer. For example, if a worker received and spent wages, two separate transactions occurred involving three articles: labor, consumer goods, and money.[9] Reality was distorted or obscured when it was argued that labor was exchanged directly for goods through the intermediary of money.

Musgrave agreed with classical economists on reasons why money was a convenience; it was universally acceptable, stable in supply, recognizable, portable, durable, divisible, and readily convertible into other goods. However, he said that because of money's admitted usefulness, people desired to hold it not merely in contemplation of proximate purchases, but for an indefinite period while they enjoyed the safety and mobility of liquid assets. Unlike the demand for most other goods, the demand for money was almost unlimited—"the next best thing to possessing precisely the article which you need, is to have a store of that which, like Aladdin's lamp, will obtain for you whatever you desire. And there does seem to be something almost magical about the action of gold in the affairs of mankind."[10]

Musgrave believed that because money was regarded universally as valuable and did affect a nation's efficiency and produc-

8. *Studies*, pp. 16–17.
9. *Studies*, p. 34.
10. *Studies*, pp. 46–47. cf. the discussion of "liquidity preference" by J. M. Keynes, *The General Theory of Employment, Interest and Money* (London, 1947), pp. 194–209.

tivity by facilitating trade it should be counted an element of capital stock. Failure to accept this principle would prevent reasonable economic analysis and encourage misguided policy bolstered by mistaken authority—"great men are not protected from the possibility of overlooking, and thus aiding to perpetuate, a fallacy which is assumed to be a truth because they failed to detect it."[11] Musgrave admitted readily that "no one would pretend that all the wealth of the world is gold and silver; but they are demonstrably as much part of it as parcels of Manchester goods, Birmingham wares, or Sheffield cutlery."[12] He suggested that when Mill categorized money as a mere "labour-saving machine" he could have described as easily most other goods in the same way.[13]

Economists who ignored the utility attached to money as a good, Musgrave said, might not understand many economic phenomena, including for example the reasons for general price fluctuations. Inflation and deflation might not, as alleged by classicists, be results exclusively of changes in the supply or costs of production of precious metals but might arise also from changes in public demand for money as liquid wealth.

Failure to treat money as a substantive article of exchange, Musgrave wrote, caused contemporary economists to adopt erroneous theories of value, which related price to labor cost or to labor exchange and command. He argued that money cost of production including payments to all factors, not merely labor costs, was the true determinant of long-run value or price. Malthus had been the only classical economist to recognize the vital role played by money in value theory.

Now it is for the reason that profits not only, as Malthus says, must be estimated in money, but do absolutely in the end consist of money and of nothing else, that the theory of value, so far as there can be any natural value at all, depends upon the cost of production in money, and not upon the amount of labour. It matters nothing to the manufacturer, or agriculturist, or proprietor of mines, whether he employs ten labourers or twenty, or whether he pays them ten shillings a week

11. *Studies*, p. viii.
12. *Studies*, p. 2.
13. *Studies*, pp. 43–44.

or twenty shillings; the question for his consideration is, whether the value of the exchangeable property which he will acquire by their labour will be equal to that which he has to give in exchange for the labour and materials necessary to produce it, with a reasonable profit on the business, such as can be obtained from other employment of the exchangeable property which he possesses. And solution of this question does not depend upon the quantity of labour necessary, nor does it upon the amount of future labour in another place which the products may be able to purchase.[14]

Labor was far less satisfactory than money as a standard Musgrave pointed out, even when value was expressed in terms of labor "command." Labor was a heterogeneous and immobile commodity which varied widely in price between locations and types of employment. "Labour may truly be regarded as a commodity, like articles of exchange, which will vary in value relatively to them in different places and at different times, and cannot, therefore, afford us a standard measure of natural or intrinsic value."[15] Reluctance to accept the conventional standard, money, as valuable in itself, Musgrave concluded, had led to formulation of false labor theories of value.

Musgrave described the price determination of products in colonies which he had governed, fish in Newfoundland, gold in British Columbia and Australia, diamonds in South Africa, and wool in Australasia to show that any concept of "natural" value had little meaning. In terms of wool prices:

Although produced for infinitely less than the wool of Europe, the price for Australian wool in England is regulated by the quantity to be obtained and the demand of the manufacturers for it at the time. Who shall say what is the natural value per pound of Australian wool, and the difference between that and the value of South African fleeces?[16]

14. *Studies*, pp. 106–7.
15. *Studies*, p. 130. Musgrave added: "It is a fruitful source of error and perplexity in the problems of economical writers that they habitually treat labour as if it were a material substance, of which a quantity of certain size and weight in one place were always equal to a quantity of the same size and weight in another, as an ounce of gold or a pound of wheat in one country will always be equal to an ounce of gold or a pound of wheat in another, which the labour certainly is not; and yet that the labour will not vary in value relatively to the other things, as the gold and the wheat certainly will." *Studies*, p. 143.
16. *Studies*, p. 114.

With regard to gold: "The value of the gold obtained by the digger is not measured by the labour which it costs him to get it, but by the amount of other property of any kind which he can get for it. In common parlance, the thing is worth what it will fetch."[17] Value and price should never be considered as more than relative concepts expressed most conveniently in terms of money. He wrote: "We can measure values against an adopted standard like gold, as we can measure height or length or bulk by an adopted standard like the metre; but there is no more an inherent quality called value than there is an inherent size in any object."[18]

Like Lord Keynes, sixty years later, Musgrave believed that on monetary questions the classical reaction against Mercantilism went too far. Classical economists should have recognized their own errors which resulted from false assumptions regarding money, both through experience and from the internal illogic of their arguments.[19] Musgrave cited with approval Locke, Hume, and Huskisson on the significance of money in economic analysis. He wrote of Mercantilist theories in general:

Like many other doctrines treated as erroneous, they contain a half-truth. It would be ridiculous to assert that there is no wealth but gold and silver; indeed, wealth in the old sense of well-to-do-ness, comfort, if not luxury, may well exist, and does exist, in many places without the presence of much money, just as large accumulations of precious metals may be found in gold regions where comfort is conspicuous by its absence; but it is quite as childish to pretend that the precious metals are not wealth while the world recognises their exchangeable value. This is all that I contend for.[20]

Hume's analysis of the effects of inflation on entrepreneurial activity, Musgrave concluded, was still the best explanation currently available for the rapid economic growth of the third quarter of the nineteenth century. Worldwide prosperity during those years had been strengthened by gold discoveries which

17. *Studies*, p. 45.
18. *Studies*, p. 133.
19. *Studies*, p. vii. Musgrave said—"it seems to me that Adam Smith, though very inconsistent, does not fall into quite the same depth of error as that in which Mr. Mill and his disciples appear to have floundered in respect to the character of money." *Ibid.*, p. 16.
20. *Studies*, p. 27.

had enlarged national money supplies and increased the volume of expenditures. He rejected claims that changes in the money supply were results rather than causes of fluctuations in economic activity.

Mr. Fawcett assumes that the sudden development of our trade and commerce about the year 1850 created a demand for a greater quantity of money to be brought into circulation. Suppose that we take the converse of this proposition, and ask whether it was not the acquisition of a larger quantity of money—of exchangeable property of value—which caused this sudden expansion of trade and commerce. The effect upon the gold countries themselves cannot be disputed; but after its fertilising influences had been felt there gold flowed out to other countries, where the same effects have been produced, only lessened in degree by the greater diffusion over a larger surface.[21]

For answers to many questions in economics, Musgrave wrote, the total volume of precious metals in existence should be compared with the quantity of other goods being produced: "it is in these facts and these variations that we must look for explanations of many economical problems which are perplexing—and, indeed, are insoluble without recognition of the truth." [22] After challenging thus the classical doctrine that money is merely a veil, concealing and facilitating transactions involving real goods, Musgrave proceeded to question a variety of related dicta in two other areas of economics: analysis of growth and the theory of international trade.

Economic Growth. Musgrave doubted that classical economists had provided a valid explanation of the economic growth process. "There seems," he wrote, "always to be hanging about the doctrine of the economist an unexpressed idea that property can spring from property, as life springs from life by animal generation."[23] The root of the misunderstanding, he thought, lay with confusion as to the meaning of capital. "It has long appeared to me that there is a deeply-seated misconception as to the character of 'capital' which affects many important and interesting

21. *Studies*, p. 167.
22. *Studies*, pp. 4 and 47.
23. *Studies*, p. 153.

questions. Capital is constantly spoken of as if it were a hidden force like electricity, residing in all property. . . ."[24]

Economists, Musgrave said, had devoted too much attention to the concept of a capital fund, in the sense of a stock of consumable goods in existence at one time, and not enough to changes in rates of production. He denied that most increases in productive power resulted from an accumulation of goods saved, in the classical sense; at any one time the world's stock equaled in value only about three years' annual production. From his experience in new countries, Musgrave doubted the overwhelming importance for economic development of increasing tools and inventories, and he stressed instead improvements in technology, stimulation of entrepreneurial fervor, and maintenance of effective demand.

He denied that many goods included in contemporary estimates of capital had any relation to productive potential, and he predicted that, no matter what the state of future development, stocks of items needed for the subsistence of labor would never be a great deal larger per capita. Rates of current production and consumption together with per capita welfare could increase without any corresponding growth in the fund of goods in existence at one instant in time:

we witness no such accumulations—there are no such savings; and as regards the real necessaries of life, mankind as a whole now, as from the beginning, live literally from hand to mouth; the food to support life must be perpetually cultivated, and is not produced in quantity more than sufficient for immediate consumption.[25]

Musgrave criticized explicitly John Stuart Mill's four celebrated "fundamental propositions respecting capital."[26] He rejected Mill's first proposition "that industry is limited by capital," because "capital," in the sense it was used by Mill as the quantity of goods in existence at any given time, did not necessarily bear a

24. *Studies*, p. 183.
25. *Studies*, p. 51.
26. *Principles of Political Economy* (London, 1929), pp. 63–90. For discussion of Mill's growth theory see Joseph J. Spengler, "John Stuart Mill on Economic Development," in Bert F. Hoselitz *et. al.*, *Theories of Economic Growth* (Glencoe, Illinois, 1960), pp. 113–54.

direct relationship to the productive capacity of an economy. A shortage of "machinery or apparatus and raw material" did limit industry in certain instances but in others shortage actually constituted a spur to production—"in the absence of accumulations of food, or commodities which may be exchanged for food, industry is more imperatively enforced to obtain the means of living."[27]

Musgrave agreed with Mill that to some extent accumulations of goods were associated usually with growth, and that large stocks of valuable articles could be found normally in more developed countries. But he denied that "capital" goods in abundance were vital for national advancement. From his experience with colonies in various stages of development, Musgrave had come to attach paramount importance to more complex social preconditions of growth; he viewed accumulated wealth more as a result than a cause of development. He cited examples of startling economic progress in colonies which began with almost no capital in the classical sense. He described the growth of South Australia in the following terms:

The early settlers, of course, needed some food, some clothes, and some shelter; but these were of the simplest, and many privations had to be endured. Little or nothing of previous savings was brought into a country which, when first occupied, was only a savage wilderness, where nothing was to be bought, and there were no labourers to employ; and if anything was to be done or procured, it had to be done or procured by the settlers themselves. But from very small beginnings property was gradually collected—such of it as was perishable exchanged for what was more useful and durable—and, finally, the surplus savings exchanged with other communities for gold, until, for instance, now, in less than forty years, there is scarcely a more wealthy or prosperous community of the same number in the Queen's dominions than the colony in which I write.[28]

Musgrave insisted that the most significant factor in economic growth was the amount and direction of money expenditures. He had observed during a lifetime in the colonies that aggregate production responded miraculously to changes in total demand,

27. *Studies*, p. 63.
28. *Studies*, p. 61.

either for consumption goods or for investment goods. He speculated that the apparent paradox of great physical waste and
booming prosperity during wartime was the result of redirected
and accelerated government spending and borrowing for muni-
tions and supplies. So long as a nation retained a satisfactory
volume of money with which to mobilize production, postwar
recovery from devastation could be startlingly rapid. He wrote:

If industry were limited by capital, and money, that is, gold and
silver, is not capital, then the devastation having destroyed the capital,
industry must cease and nothing further could be done. But the fact
is that the wealth destroyed would, in any case, have perished sooner
or later, and needed to be replaced by other wealth, as Mr. Mill admits;
though he forgets that it cannot be the same wealth, and that this
must always be done by new labour not before applied; and the
real savings of the former labour of the inhabitants embodied by exchange in gold and silver are not destroyed.[29]

During wartime, products of industry were used without increasing consumer satisfaction, but their final destination had little
effect on levels of subsequent production. So long as total expenditures to industry were maintained, industrial productivity could
remain substantially unimpaired.

The attention of economists and particularly of those in new
countries, Musgrave said, should be focused on the volume and
direction of the circulation of money rather than upon the disposition of goods already produced. A growing economy required
foresight rather than hindsight.

. . . there is very little accumulated property of exchangeable value
which can be applied to the employment of labour, except such as
exists in the form of gold and silver. A man may have a splendid house
and furniture, or a magnificent factory and machinery of all kinds, but
he cannot employ labour with these, nor upon these, without money;
or, at all events, without food and clothing to furnish in exchange—
and no capitalist possesses stores of these.[30]

Monetary improvements had been among the most crucial for
the progress of civilization. In addition to sustaining employment,
money was essential for specialization through exchange and for

29. *Studies*, p. 79.
30. *Studies*, p. 8.

a successful process of capital accumulation. Where money had not supplanted barter, individuals had little opportunity to save real goods in anticipation of a major capital purchase. A farmer could not accumulate easily portions of his crops over several years to make payment for a piece of machinery. With money, however, liquid wealth could be accumulated gradually for the eventual acquisition of substantial capital items. The farmer could save money proceeds of harvests and purchase his tools. "If not for the possibility of exchanging things of perishable nature for something else which will keep and can be accumulated, the aggregation of wealth would be impracticable. And hence we should perceive the mistake of regarding money merely as a medium of exchange."[31]

Musgrave suggested that Mill's first proposition could be rendered meaningful by redefining the term "capital" as a fund of total expenditures or aggregate money demand. After this change, it would be correct to argue that industry was truly limited by capital. Money was the crucial element of wealth used to mobilize production, and for this reason it came nearer than the stock of buildings, tools, and equipment to the classical concept of a fund used for the employment of labor. He illustrated this point with a simile:

If there be indeed any occult power known as capital, it must be generated by the action of money upon labour, as electricity is generated in a galvanic battery by the action of one chemical agent upon another; but it operates through the circulating coin, as the electric current through the wire, and its presence is no more to be looked for in the perishable produce of that action than an electric shock may be expected from a telegraphic message delivered by an errand boy.[32]

Musgrave's redefinition was significant for the policy implications of Mill's proposition. Mill had implied that, except by taxing unproductive activities and directing funds into useful work, government was powerless to create capital through fiscal action and was unable to lessen any "limitation" of industry

31. *Studies,* pp. 122–23. John Rae, writing in Canada in 1834, made similar observations about the importance of money on the frontier. See my *Canadian Economic Thought* (Durham, 1961), pp. 92–97.
32. *Studies,* p. 184.

which might exist. Musgrave argued, in contrast, that government could create capital in the sense of effective demand merely by borrowing and returning idle funds to the expenditure stream. Thereby the state might stimulate both consumption and investment and relieve unemployment during recessions.

The amount borrowed is borrowed in money, which is not destroyed, but put into immediate circulation; and if in the possession of the lender to lend, it could not then have been invested in any productive employment. We talk of 'investing' money, and 'locking up' capital, as if some such thing was really done as enclosing it in something else, or hoarding it for a time, whereas there is no more certain mode of passing money from hand to hand than by exchanging it for other property, which is what we call investment.[33]

Only certain types of new government expenditure could reduce unemployment. One policy advocated by Mill of reducing national debt through taxation and bond retirement could actually reduce the level of employment and income. Anticipating the current rationale for large government budgets, Musgrave explained:

It is totally incorrect to say that capital can be created by laying on taxes. Taxes are merely contributions in small quantities of existing savings, to be again distributed among the community; it may be in very different and much more beneficial proportions among the same mass, though this effect will depend upon the character of the taxation and the purposes to which the contributions are applied. . . . If, by the application of the capital so collected, industry is directed into so-called productive employment, any accession to material property previously in existence must be obtained from new labour, which had not been applied at the time of the collection of the taxes; . . . it is a gross fallacy to assume, as is done by Mr. Mill, that laying taxes on income or expenditure, and applying the proceeds towards paying off the public debts, would be equivalent to employing the amount productively.[34]

Musgrave claimed that Mill's second and third propositions respecting capital, which stated that capital is first saved and is then destroyed, contradicted each other. He argued that capital goods as defined by Mill were used up in the same manner as

33. *Studies*, p. 87.
34. *Studies*, p. 64.

consumer products. The only portion of wealth truly saved and constituting a circulating fund of great durability was money. Goods designated by classical economists as "capital" were really only one species of consumption goods. The concept of abstinence from consumption was a distortion of reality. In essence Musgrave was calling attention to the vital investment process which tended to be ignored in the classical framework through excessive emphasis on saving. He wrote:

There is something amusing in the simplicity with which Mr. Mill states that 'to the vulgar it is not at all apparent that what is saved is consumed.' To them, he says, every one who saves appears in the light of one who hoards. He fails to see that no one does, or, in fact, can, hoard to advantage anything but gold; and that, according to his theory, it ought to be totally immaterial whether that is hoarded or not, it being useless for production.[35]

Musgrave admitted that Mill's fourth proposition, which stated that demand for commodities is not demand for labor, was formally correct. But he complained that this proposition obscured the fundamental importance of continuous money flows for the maintenance of employment. In particular, Mill should have identified what elements did constitute the demand for labor. Economists should be concerned, as was Mill, about excessive production of consumer goods, but they should not neglect factors which determined overall levels of economic activity.

Musgrave stressed two points in criticism of Mill's fourth proposition: first, that the demand for commodities *was* in most practical situations an effective demand for labor—"we know that the business and transactions of mankind are in a state of continuous flux, and the consumption of commodities to-day or this year does create an effective demand for labour to produce more for consumption to-morrow or next year."[36] Second, goods which were already produced might as well be consumed. Consumer goods once produced were suitable for that specific use only, and if not used immediately deteriorated rapidly. He warned that immobilities of productive factors should not be underestimated and that abstinence from consumption would never lead

35. *Studies*, p. 71.
36. *Studies*, p. 89.

to accumulations of capital goods unless both investment spending were forthcoming and productive factors could be shifted to the process of capital construction. If willingness to invest or factor mobility were absent, an income receiver would assist the laboring class not by abstaining from consumption and contracting expenditures but by consuming and helping through his purchases to sustain employment.

The economists constantly speak as if 'production' were a single substance, applicable to all kinds of consumption—as if a piece of it might be turned into a coat, another portion used to feed a baby, and, if not wanted for these purposes, could be made into a railway bridge. It seems to be forgotten that abstinence of A from the consumption of velvet will by no means supply B with bread; the velvet cannot be turned into bread or anything else. The bread can only be obtained, if required in greater quantity, by labour specially applied to land; and it does not at all follow that even by withdrawing the whole of the labour now applied to the production of what are called luxuries, and applying it to the cultivation of the soil, any considerably greater quantity of food can be produced, except in places where there are large tracts of unoccupied country; and in these the lack is not of food but of luxuries, for which the inhabitants of such places are ready to exchange their surplus food. It is for this reason that I conceive it to be altogether a fallacy to state, as Mr. Mill does, that a person who buys commodities and consumes them himself does no good to the labouring class.[37]

Musgrave disputed vigorously assertions that economic growth was necessarily accelerated by abstinence from consumption of so-called "luxuries." Luxuries, he argued, were the natural fruits of growth itself and acted as a vital spur to initiative. Mill had observed the stimulus to development afforded by increased consumption in primitive economies but had failed to detect the vital significance of this relationship for more advanced societies.[38] Of great importance was the overriding danger that if the consumption of luxuries was limited unduly with the intention of increasing "capital" stock, sufficient expenditures would not reach industry to sustain production and employment. Combining simple short-run analysis of employment gener-

37. *Studies*, pp. 91–92.
38. *Studies*, p. 154, and J. S. Mill, *Principles of Political Economy*, ed. W. J. Ashley, pp. 581-82.

ation with long-run growth theory, Musgrave saw correctly that if at any time expenditures for goods were inadequate, a magnified reduction in national income and the growth rate would result.[39]

If income receivers were discouraged from consuming on the advice of economists and did not at the same time increase expenditure in another direction, incomes would always decline. Abstinence under these conditions would benefit no one. Musgrave attacked classical economists explicitly on this point, which was also the core of the Keynesian critique.

In order that we may produce we are not to consume. It does not seem to occur to them that in this case it must be decided what we are to produce; that sumptuary laws must be adopted on a very extensive scale to settle what is and what is not a luxury; and that as luxuries are diminished so will be wealth, and all possibility of accumulating it, except in the shape of gold, which will then be lessened in practical value—so little in the way of comfort, not to say luxury, could be got in exchange for it.[40]

Musgrave emphasized that because no more than a limited quantity of new durable tools were required in an economy at a given time, production had inevitably to be of goods destined for immediate consumption. If this consumption should be restricted, definite provision had to be made for employment of the productive factors released thereby. He stated as a principle:

That luxuries, and wealth which is not money, are practically synonymous; and that, if we are to abstain from the consumption, and therefore the production of luxuries, it is essential for economists to define what is the nature of the 'wealth' which is to be the object of 'production.'[41]

Musgrave was truly a pioneer in pointing out the dangers of over-emphasizing saving in the sense of abstinence and in recognizing consumption both as necessary to uninterrupted production and as the true end of economic activity. To illustrate certain potentially ludicrous conclusions of classical growth theory, he offered the following example from the colonies:

39. *Studies*, pp. 95–97.
40. *Studies*, p. 15.
41. *Studies*, p. 28.

if a person does good to the labouring classes only by his abstinence from consumption, surely there never was a community or state of things more injurious to the working classes than that which may be seen in Victoria, for, I suppose, in no part of the world will 200,000 people be found together who consume nearly so much as the population of Melbourne, which is about that number.[42]

International Trade. Mistreatment of money in economic analysis, Musgrave said, led to dangerous absurdities in discussions of international trade. He cited examples used by Fawcett and Mill to illustrate comparative advantage in a barter situation, and he argued that markedly different results would have been reached had purchases and sales been described realistically to involve monetary exchange. "This fallacy, that exchanging two articles directly for one another will produce the same result that is obtained by their being intermediately changed for another third article of intrinsic value, used as money, runs through all of Mr. Mill's elaborate arguments in his chapter on international trade."[43]

Fawcett claimed that bilateral trade would occur naturally between two countries, one of which had lower production costs for all goods, so long as their comparative costs differed.[44] Musgrave admitted this argument to be correct where trade took the form of barter and merchants in each country exchanged goods produced at the lowest relative cost in their own country for goods produced relatively more efficiently in the other. However, world trade simply was not conducted through barter. International purchases and sales were effected by the exchange of national currencies which were convertible universally into precious metals. In this situation, international trade took place only from a country with an absolute advantage to a country with an absolute disadvantage in terms of money cost of production. The existence of a gold standard destroyed much of the practical relevance of comparative advantage theory. He explained:

so long as money is used in commerce, it will never be found that, where one country has a decided advantage in the production of two

42. *Studies*, pp. 14–15.
43. *Studies*, p. 138.
44. Henry Fawcett, *Manual of Political Economy* (London, 1888) p. 382 f.

commodities, it will be beneficial for her to exchange one for the
other with another community, unless where she has more of the one
and less of the other commodity than she requires; and even in that
case she will sell her surplus for money where she gets the largest
price, and supply her deficiencies where she can buy most cheaply.[45]

To understand the course of trade between Britain and Australia,
Musgrave wrote, the comparative advantage principle was of
little assistance.

Australia, from natural advantages, produces both wheat and wool at
much lower cost than they can be produced in England. What would
any Australian merchant think, if told that it would be for his advantage, or that of Australia, to send wool to England, and there
with it purchase wheat to bring back to Australia at a higher rate than
he can get it for in Australia. His doing so would be regarded as not
showing more knowledge or acuteness than was exhibited by Moses
Primrose in the 'Vicar of Wakefield,' when he sold the Vicar's horse
at the fair for a gross of green spectacles.[46]

To emphasize the change wrought in analysis of international
trade by the presence of money, Musgrave introduced a picturesque analogy.

The effect of the introduction of a third article of exchange in the
transaction is something like that of the presence of the goose in the
child's puzzle of 'The Fox, the Goose, and the Corn.' The affair is
simple enough, so long as only the fox and the corn are to be dealt
with. But the attraction of the corn for the goose, and the goose for the
fox, introduces complications of which it is not easy to dispose.[47]

Musgrave argued finally that failure to treat money as a
substantive article of exchange prevented economists from
comprehending fully the international balance of payments. International flows of funds, he said, were not merely balancing
items to equate major transactions involving real goods. Because
all currencies were convertible into precious metals, money was
exchanged across national borders simply when the utility of
purchases exceeded the estimated benefits from liquidity. "Neither the nation nor the individuals composing it will part with
their gold—their money—for other things unless they happen to

45. *Studies*, p. 142.
46. *Studies*, pp. 138–39.
47. *Studies*, pp. 144–45.

want certain things more than money."[48] If economists considered only the demands for goods without analyzing those for liquidity, they would not gain a full understanding of international payments flows. All voluntary international exchanges in which valuable commodities changed hands, whether of money or of real goods, caused both participants to experience reduced utility from the loss of one good and a more than compensatory increase in utility from acquisition of another good. Money, like other articles, tended to become less desirable per unit as holdings increased, but the usefulness of money as a store of wealth gave it value even when its function as a medium of exchange was fulfilled. In specific criticism of the classical balance of payments analysis, Musgrave wrote:

The erroneous hypothesis which we are considering is based upon the assumption that money is nothing more than machinery, through the agency of which exchanges are effected, and of which a greater amount can never be useful than is required for this purpose, and that the remainder is therefore transferred to some other place where it is more needed. But facts do not accord with this theory. We might with as much reason suppose that more than a certain quantity of any other article of exchangeable value, as clothing or food, can never be required. With money, as with them, it could never be found true until every member of a community had so much that it had become so cheap in exchange for other articles as to be nearly valueless.[49]

Musgrave disputed Mill's contention that money values between nations were determined exclusively by costs of production of the precious metal backing the currency; some changes in the price level resulted exclusively from fluctuations in demand for money. It was apparent that when citizens of one nation for any reason suddenly reduced cash holdings and exchanged money abroad for other goods, the money supply of this country was diminished, prices fell, and the value in exchange of the monetary unit increased while its production costs remained unchanged. Financiers facilitated international money flows by bringing liquid assets to areas where they were prized

48. *Studies*, p. 173.
49. *Studies*, p. 174.

most from places where demands were relatively weak.[50] To illustrate how international money flows could be influenced by changes in liquidity demands, Musgrave pointed out that a recent unfavorable British balance of trade with China had been caused not simply by extravagant British demands for tea and other exotic products, but also by a buoyant oriental preference for cash balances.[51] Transfer of gold from Britain to China was not an inherently unstable situation which would reverse itself by changes in price levels, but was rather an adjustment in both countries between holdings of different goods resulting from changed assessments of relative values. So long as the Chinese retained an increasing fondness for gold, the flow could continue without any correctives taking effect.

Musgrave seldom approached directly questions of public policy. He did conclude, however, that apparent fallacies in international trade theory justified careful re-examination of the potential benefits and losses from tariffs. An account of remarks he made to the Adelaide Chamber of Manufactures is as follows:

Both protectionists and free traders, he thought, carried their argument too far, and did not prove so much as they professed to prove. The extent to which economic problems were affected by domestic competition was too much overlooked in the argument. He did not think free trade was so much a benefit as some believed, or that the advantages of protection were so great as some imagined.[52]

Musgrave acknowledged that protection might cause misallocation of resources, but, he pointed out, the more subtle good effects had never been weighed carefully. In criticism of statements in Cairnes' *Some Leading Principles of Political Economy*, he explained that tariffs could limit an outflow of purchasing power during recession, thus sustaining effective demand, and facilitate self-sufficiency, thereby fostering national pride. Anticipating conclusions of the Giblin tariff report in 1929, Musgrave emphasized that restrictive duties could afford subsidized employment for the masses in a staples-producing economy:

50. *Studies*, p. 162.
51. *Studies*, p. 165.
52. John Fairfax Conigrave, *South Australian Manufactures and Industries* (Adelaide, 1875), p. 21.

"Protection will force, to a certain extent, a more equal distribution of the comforts of life."[53]

Musgrave's Influence. Musgrave's influence on the development of economic science was slight. He lived far away from the mainstream of informed discussion, both geographically and professionally, and his writings aroused only peripheral interest. Moreover, Musgrave's main ideas, sensible and important as they were, lay diffused throughout journal articles and buried in a collection of essays replete with dogmatic pronouncements and harsh comment on venerable authorities. For revolutionary concepts, such as Musgrave's monetary theory, to have gained acceptance they would have required balance and clarity of expression. Lacking the criticism of sympathetic colleagues in his position of intellectual isolation, Musgrave never gained these qualities. He was unable to organize his innovations into a conventional treatise on political economy which might have attracted the attention they deserved.

In the first flush of enthusiasm, Musgrave communicated his discoveries to several correspondents.[54] He poured out thoughts repeatedly to his slightly skeptical father-in-law, David Dudley Field of New York, and through Field made contact with Professor Arthur L. Perry of Williams College. With Perry as with others, Musgrave's title and position guaranteed a respectful hearing, but there is little evidence that he made a profound impact. Musgrave guessed correctly when he predicted that by most readers he would be accused of "reviving the absurdities of what is called the mercantile 'system.' "[55] Henry Dunning Macleod expressed interest in Musgrave's writings but without evident comprehension of their implications and in the belief that they imitated his own work. Musgrave sent copies of his publications to Professor W. E. Hearn of Melbourne University, and he kept up "an irregular correspondence" with Charles Henry Pearson.[56]

53. "Economic Fallacies: Free Trade v. Protection," *loc. cit.*, p. 322.
54. Musgrave's correspondence on economic matters is contained in the Duke University Library.
55. *Studies*, p. 184.
56. William Stebbing, ed., *Charles Henry Pearson, Fellow of Oriel and Education Minister in Victoria* (London, 1900), p. 203.

William Stanley Jevons offered the most enthusiastic response of any major economist to Musgrave's publications. Jevons' reactions may have been caused in part by his well known charity toward other writers, and particularly toward other heretics. Upon receipt of an offprint, Jevons sent the following letter to Musgrave in 1875:

24 August 1875
Witlington
Manchester

Dear Sir

The letter with which you have favoured me arrived when I was away from home, during our college vacation, and I trust that you will excuse the delay which has thus arisen in answering it.

I was perfectly aware of the part which you had taken in recent discussions in Political Economy. What I may call your celebrated article in the Contemporary Review excited more attention among economists than you may perhaps have heard. When I was in Cambridge last December engaged in the Several Science tripos exams I heard it discussed, and it even found its way into some examination papers which I have seen somewhere or other. I am bound to say that most who spoke of your ideas objected strongly to them, but, as I suffer under the same inconvenience myself, I do not regard their objections as conclusive.

I cannot pretend myself to accept all your views, but your criticisms on Mill seem to me most proper and well timed, and I hope you will not let the ball of discussion stop now that you have once put it so well in motion.

I beg to thank you for the pamphlet on Economic Fallacies which you have been so kind as to send. I have found it interesting, and like what you say about money, but am not prepared to agree with your discussion of Cairnes criticisms on Alby. I think that Cairnes is in no danger of refutation in that part of his work.

On the subject of money I am glad to find myself apparently quite in agreement with you. When writing my book on Money from 9 to 15 months ago I was not aware of your writings on the subject, or I should have been glad to avail myself of some of your suggestions. My book has now been in the publisher's hands for 7 or 8 months and has been completely in print for some three months. It will now appear I hope in about four weeks.

I have treated gold as one of many commodities which may and have been used for money, and I think I carry out pretty clearly the doctrine you urge that it always remains a commodity or merchandise, though token money, and paper currency obscure the matter. As regards Professor Bonamy Price's opinions which you discuss, I fear I have not paid the attention I ought to have done if they are consistent either with themselves or with fact.

I take the liberty of sending by book post with this letter copies of several of my papers on economical subjects. The one last published on the 'Theory of Political Economy' gives a better description of my proposed way of regarding utility than you will have found in my larger books of which you speak.

It must take some time to test the soundness of what I put forward but I hope to give a much fuller statement of the theory in the course of a little time.

Believe me to be Dear Sir, Yours Faithfully

W. STANLEY JEVONS[57]

Jevons forwarded to Musgrave an extract from a paper he presented to the Manchester Statistical Society in 1874 wherein he stated that Musgrave had shown Mill's fundamental propositions concerning capital "to involve various fallacies and self-contradictions."

Lord Kimberley, Secretary of State for the Colonies, viewed Musgrave's intellectual endeavors with a cold eye. Musgrave had his knuckles rapped for suggesting that free trade might not be the best policy for countries in all stages of growth and for hinting that the mother country had softened its attitude toward protection. Kimberley wrote:

Private   35, Lowndes Square. S.W.

July 19/75

Dear Mr. Musgrave,

I have to thank you for your pamphlet on 'Economic Fallacies.' I am afraid I must say that I am too steady an adherent to the pure Free Trade theory to become a convert to your views. I see you adduce our recent Treaties of Commerce, and the Act authorizing special customs arrangements between Australian colonies, as examples of our readiness to discard our free trade opinions, where it suits our convenience. I think you are fairly entitled to the benefit of the first. It has always seemed to me that the French Treaty was a departure

57. In a letter of 21 February, 1876, Jevons wrote to Musgrave: "I feel sure that your opinions about Mill's philosophy are right, though I have heard your criticism of his pol. econ. rather strongly condemned. Great as my respect for Mill's straightforward and zealous character is, I fear that his intellect if good originally was misused in youth."

from sound principles, and I doubt whether for that reason it will
not in the long run be found to have done more harm than good.
The second example I do not admit. We never pretended for a moment
to believe that the Australian Act was consistent with sound economical
views. We passed it solely on political grounds, considering that having given the Australian colonies full control of their domestic affairs,
even to the point of allowing them as in Victoria to lay protective
duties on our goods, we could not prudently refuse them the further
liberty they asked for. You will forgive a freetrader for regretting that
the Australian protectionists will be able to quote the authority of so
able a governor as yourself, in favour of a policy which is so antagonistic to the policy of the Imperial government. Apart from the mere
commercial question, I look upon the Protectionist tendency of some
of our colonies as peculiarly dangerous to the permanence of their
connexion with this country.

> Believe me
> Very faithfully yrs.
> Kimberley

Musgrave obtained a mixed reputation in Australia. While governor of Queensland, he gained the undying enmity of radicals
for failing to intervene on the advice of the premier in a criminal
sentence.[58] The *Bulletin* commented in its obituary: "The man
as he was was just an average sample of the painfully narrow
and effete social type which a grovelling nation once worshipped
as 'the British gentleman!'"[59] But Musgrave was respected and
appreciated by local economists. The Australian Economic Association made him an honorary member, and at his death the
Australian Economist reprinted eulogies and selections from his
writings.[60]

Musgrave's economic contributions were the response of an
intelligent and creative thinker who noted that accepted theory
did not explain fully economic activity in the colonies where he
lived. He was not an important innovator in economic thought,
but rather was led to revive and elaborate objections to Say's law
of markets which had been implicit in some mercantilist and

58. See I. D. McNaughtan, "The Case of Benjamin Kitt," *Historical Society
of Queensland Journal*, I (1914–19), 140–54.
59. IX (1888), No. 454, p. 5.
60. I (1888–90), 98–99.

physiocratic writings and explicit in the works of Malthus, Lauderdale, Spence, and Sismondi.[61]

Set apart in a position of eminence from some of the worst heat of politics, Musgrave was able to observe and to deal objectively with a variety of economic problems. But, at the same time, he was isolated by his position both from casual intellectual stimulation and from critical discussion. Musgrave's writings reflect his circumstances: they contain overstatement, impatient criticism, lack of organization, and unnecessary repetition. On the question of money, in particular, he was often obscure, failing to distinguish among bank money and credit, bullion, and government notes. But Musgrave's intelligent attention to macroeconomic magnitudes, willingness to challenge revered authority, and sensible insights on a variety of theoretical questions should bring him more attention than he has received thusfar. He provided another example, less brilliant than Alfred De Lissa, of the potentially beneficial impact of a fresh environment on the development of economic doctrine.

61. See Joseph J. Spengler, "The Physiocrats and Say's Law of Markets," *Journal of Political Economy*, LIII (1945), 193–211 and 314–47.

15

Economics in the Universities

The first Australian university began operations at Sydney in 1852, and by World War I, universities had been established in all the states. Throughout the period under examination, these institutions exhibited many features in common: they were all creatures of colonial or state governments and remained heavily dependent on public funds; they were all secular and, in the main, nonresidential; they were all patterned more or less after British models; and they all looked predominantly to Britain for faculty and staff.[1] Although homogeneity of character was typical, differences among the universities also were significant. Universities in the more populous and prosperous states gained an important head-start on the others and exerted consistently a powerful pull on competent scholars. Furthermore, the Universities of Tasmania, Queensland, and Western Australia, founded late in the 19th and early in the 20th centuries, gave greater attention at their inception to the practical training potential of higher education than did their older predecessors which had concentrated on inculcation of culture in the widest sense. The influence of North American experience increasingly was evident in the later shift towards practical training. In Australia, as in other new countries, universities suffered for many years from isolation, poverty, and diseconomies of small-scale operations.

The development of economics teaching in each of the state universities is examined in the following sections.

1. A summary of Australian university history is contained in *Australian Encyclopaedia*, IX, 77-91.

New South Wales

The first lecture course in economics in New South Wales was given not in a Sydney classroom but in the steerage of a leaky immigrant ship in the waters of Bass Strait. In 1831 John Dunmore Lang recruited from Scotland fifty "mechanics" and teachers to build and operate a proposed "Australian College" in Sydney, and he embarked these sturdy folk under the guidance of the Reverend Henry Carmichael, a clergyman of the Scotch Church, on the ship *Sterling Castle*.[2] "Animated by the fervid desire to impart knowledge which must ever influence the mind of the true teacher," Carmichael organized classes of instruction for the crew and passengers, beginning with geometry and algebra but proceeding to political economy, for which thirty voyagers "eagerly" enrolled. Carmichael described his economics course thus:

This class met for the first time on the 9th of September, and continued to meet regularly twice a-week till the vessel arrived in Bass' Straits, when the meetings took place four days consecutively, for the sake of finishing the prescribed course before the termination of the voyage. During these conversations, the whole of the subjects illustrated so copiously in the first two books of the "Wealth of Nations," were brought under discussion; although not precisely in the order observed by Dr. Smith. The topics chiefly dwelt upon were, the laws which regulate the wages of labour, and the price of commodities in general; the origin and nature of rent,—the question of population—the nature of capital,—nature and effects of machinery,— and the importance of extending to all ranks of society such a course of education as shall embrace an exposition of the leading truths of economical science.[3]

2. Lang's reason for selecting Scotch academic staff was a good economic one. He explained—"Presbyterians are generally found to do literary and other clerical work at a cheaper rate than other people; and this is a consideration of importance in a young colony." *An Historical and Statistical Account of New South Wales, both as a Penal Settlement and as a British Colony* (2nd ed.; London, 1837), II, 333 n.
3. Henry Carmichael, *Introductory Lecture, Delivered at the Opening of the Sydney Mechanics' School of Arts, on 3rd of June, 1844* (Sydney, 1844), pp. 4–5; and reprinted with some typographical errors in Mr. Justice Windeyer's

From Jeremy Bentham in England, Lang obtained about thirty volumes of Bentham's writings for his new college, and one of his first professors was charged with classes in a "Mercantile Department."[4] But there is no evidence that teaching ever exceeded the secondary school level, or that Carmichael's nautical example was followed and that regular lectures were given on political economy.[5]

A select committee, which in 1849 recommended the establishment of Sydney University, regarded higher education as an important social responsibility. It noted "to our shame" that whereas Harvard had been founded only twenty years after the settlement of Boston, Sydney had remained without a university throughout its first sixty years. The committee looked askance at study abroad as a substitute for the home product, and complained—"for all beyond the mere rudiments of learning, we have still to send our sons to some British or Foreign University, at the distance of half the Globe from all parental or family control, and, as might be predicted, in most cases, with certain detriment to their morals; in few, with any compensating improvement to their minds."[6] The plan submitted for the new institution contained provision for five professorships, none of which embraced political economy. However, the Committee noted that "as education progresses and a more minute subdivision of knowledge becomes expedient" new fields, including "'Modern History and Political Economy' . . . will soon be found indispensable."[7] The absence of political economy from the original curriculum did not go unnoticed; a critic in the Sydney *Empire*, probably Henry

Commemorative Address on the Celebration of the Fiftieth Anniversary of the Sydney Mechanics' School of Arts, March 22nd, 1883 (Sydney, 1883), pp. 8–9.
4. Rev. J. D. Lang, *Account of the Steps Taken, in England, with a View to the Establishment of an Academical Institution, or College, in New South Wales; and to Demonstrate the Practicability of Effecting an Extensive Emigration of the Industrious Classes from the Mother Country to that Colony* (Sydney, 1831); and *An Historical and Statistical Account. . .*, II, 315–79.
5. In 1844 an unsuccessful scheme for evening classes in several subjects, including political economy, was put forward in Sydney. See Michael Roe, *Society and Thought in Eastern Australia, 1835–1851*, Thesis Submitted for the degree of Doctor of Philosophy in the Australian National University, 1960, p. 466.
6. "Report from the Select Committee on the Sydney University," *Votes and Proceedings of the Legislative Council of New South Wales*, 1849, p. 4. William Charles Wentworth was chairman.
7. *Ibid.*, p. 3.

Parkes the editor, deplored lack of provision for languages and "intellectual sciences," including "the weighty division of Political Economy." He concluded his critique by asking: "Will not the first B.A.'s be as unfitted for their degree by these omissions as they would have been by a less cumbrous machinery for Classics and Mathematics?"[8]

At least two of the first professors at Sydney University, although not responsible academically for lectures on political economy, expressed interest in economic analysis. In mathematics, Professor Morris Birkbeck Pell's pioneer studies of Australian population and "the political economy of railways" have been discussed above.[9] John Woolley, the first principal and successively professor of classical languages and literature and professor of logic, touched on economics in his university work on several occasions. For example, on an examination in 1861 Woolley asked his logic students to criticize the definition "Political Economy is the science of social well-being," and in 1865–66 "Professor Woolley's Medal for Bachelors of Arts" was awarded for the best essay on the topic "The Influence of Political Economy on the Course of History."[10] Some of the keen enthusiasm for and knowledge of economics manifested by Sir Samuel Griffith in later life was acquired during his years at Sydney University where he studied under Pell and Woolley and took his B.A. degree in 1863 with first class honors in classics, mathematics, and natural science.[11]

Despite the unofficial interest of Professors Woolley and Pell, the *Empire* newspaper remained dissatisfied with the University's failure to include social science in the curriculum. One editorial

8. "The University Papers," *Empire*, June 28, 1852, p. 1138. Criticism of Sydney University throughout the first two decades is described thoroughly in: David S. MacMillan, "The University of Sydney—the Pattern and the Public Reactions, 1850–1870," *The Australian University*, I (1963), 27–59.

9. pp. 438–40, and 286–89. For information about Pell's mathematical work see: Cecil W. Salier, "Professor Morris Birkbeck Pell; A Biographical Note," *Royal Australian Historical Society Journal and Proceedings*, XVIII (1932), 246–51; and I. S. Turner, "The First Hundred Years of Mathematics in the University of Sydney," *ibid.*, XLI (1955), 245–66.

10. Sydney University, *Calendar*, 1862, Appendix, pp. 8 and 9; and *ibid.*, 1865, p. vii.

11. See below pp. 597–99, and A. Douglas Graham, *The Life of the Right Honourable Sir Samuel Walker Griffith, G.C.M.G., P.C.* (University of Queensland John Murtagh Macrossan Lecture for 1938, Brisbane, 1939).

548 The Science of Enquiry

critic made an eloquent appeal for "Political Science: The Want of the Time." He said:

Since the founding of the University the conviction we then had has been growing upon us, that no department of study is more imperatively required to be provided for than the whole science of Political Economy. The public is well aware that this branch of knowledge has been entirely overlooked in the arrangements of that Institution. For the present, at least, the omission is complete, and the present is the time which specially requires the study.[12]

The writer hinted darkly that social sciences had been slighted for some sinister reason. He explained:

Indeed, if we are not mistaken, the various omissions were rather designed than inadvertent. However the thing may be accounted for, the omissions are a heavy drawback to the usefulness of the institution. The plea will probably be, that it was impossible to set so much on foot at once, and that the students could not be expected to be prepared for so extensive a range. In reply we say, we should be glad to be informed what plan has been laid down to include these branches at an early period. Our impression is, that there is no such plan. But we could suggest another reply, which we must withhold just now.

We have referred to Political Economy, and the omission of that in the University plan is the thing which concerns us at present. By Political Economy we mean something more extensive than what is usually understood by the phrase. The name is commonly applied to commercial and financial science exclusively. In our opinion it should include the whole range of public and general social relations, duties, and interests as objects of practical concern.[13]

The Empire argued that with the introduction of responsible government, political economy had become a peculiarly important subject of study for all intelligent citizens. "The recent struggle has sadly revealed the fact, that what we mean both by Political Economy and Political Philosophy is almost as foreign a topic to the colonial mind as it would be to a Feejee or a Tonga islander."[14]

12. "Political Science The Want of the Time," Empire, January 2, 1854, p. 4. I am indebted to Dr. Noel McLachlin for drawing my attention to this article.
13. Ibid.
14. Ibid. The author suggested that a professor of political economy be appointed to lecture to non-matriculated students as a form of extension teaching. "Many who will never matriculate, may yet aspire to be legislators and statesmen. What reason can be given why, without binding them to what they can-

The first regular course in political economy was offered at Sydney University in 1866–67. The *Calendar* announced in 1866 that "Lectures are given on . . . Political Economy," and that James Paterson LL.D. (Sydney) had been appointed Reader in Political Economy. Smith's *Wealth of Nations*, Book I, and Mill's *Principles of Political Economy* were listed under "Logic, &c., &c." as "Subjects for the B.A. Degree."[15] Questions on Paterson's examination paper in 1867 suggest that lectures, if any actually were given, did not go beyond a discussion of classical principles or include Australian material. Paterson does not appear to have retained his position after 1867, when the subject disappeared from the *Calendar*.[16]

During the 1870's and 1880's, occasional complaints were voiced about Sydney University's failure to provide teaching in economics. For example, an ardent free-trader denouncing arguments for protection in 1882 remarked: "If a tenth part of the time devoted to Greek verbs and Latin verses could be spared for the study of a few chapters of even that comparatively ancient work 'The Wealth of Nations,' the student would have no difficulty in seeing through this time-honoured bundle of fallacies."[17] A writer in the Sydney *Bulletin* termed the University "a worn-out institution" for teaching Aristotle and Seneca instead of Bentham and Mill.[18]

In the 1880's political economy did return to the curriculum in a modest way. Candidates in 1886 for the Honours M.A. degree in "Logic, Moral, Mental and Political Philosophy" were examined thoroughly on both Adam Smith and Mill.[19] Francis Anderson, appointed lecturer in philosophy in 1888 and named

not take up, they should not be supplied with the requisite knowledge in the branch which it is indispensable for them they should cultivate"

15. Sydney University, *Calendar*, 1866, pp. v-vii, 13, and 19.

16. Paterson was listed as a university "examiner" until 1870. Professor La Nauze reports that a Dr. Aldcorn applied unsuccessfully for a position in political economy in 1867. *Political Economy in Australia: Historical Studies* (Melbourne, 1949), p. 18 n.

17. Edward Pratt, "The Balance of Trade," *Melbourne Review*, VII (1882), 380.

18. "A Worn-out Institution," *Bulletin*, VIII (1887-88), No. 382, p. 4.

19. Apparently in philosophy an attempt was made to illustrate economic principles with Australian examples. One of the twenty examination questions in 1886 was: "Are (1) a knowledge of Greek, (2) Sydney Harbour, (3) the water in Crown Street Reservoir, (4) a good commercial credit, to be regarded as forms of wealth?" Sydney University, *Calendar*, 1887, pp. cviii-cx.

Challis Professor of Logic and Mental Philosophy in 1890, lectured on economics as a branch of "political philosophy."[20] He asked examination questions dealing more with contemporary social problems than with theoretical refinements, and he directed his courses to a study of topical controversy.[21] In 1893 Marshall's *Principles* joined works by Mill and Smith on Anderson's reading list; two sets of lectures were given, and a term essay was required of students.[22] During the 1890's, Anderson lectured occasionally to undergraduates on political economy under the heading "mental philosophy," and in 1902 he listed divisions of the "School of Logic, Mental, Moral and Political Philosophy" as "1. Logic. 2. Psychology. 3. Ethics. 4. Metaphysics. 5. Education. 6. Economics. 7. Politics."[23]

Apart from Anderson, the attitude of early Sydney professors toward political economy was mixed. G. Arnold Wood, Challis Professor of History from 1891, permitted "political economy as prescribed in the school of logic" to be offered after 1895 as an optional subject for the M.A. degree in history.[24] In 1904 political economy was developed as a special subject in the History

20. Anderson feared possible abuse of a single social science if used in isolation from philosophy and other sciences. He wrote in 1907—"the economist of abstract theory too often forgets, that every country has, and must have, a politics of its own—a politics to suit its circumstances. A political policy—even a protectionist policy, whether it be for protection of local manufactures or protection of local labor—may be in some ways expensive; but it is not on that account alone, foolish and damnable. Social science is not purely and simply an application of the laws of the abstract science of economics, any more than it is a direct deduction from the laws of biology." "Liberalism and Socialism," Presidential Address to the Social and Statistical Science Section, *Report of the Eleventh Meeting of the Australasian Association for the Advancement of Science held at Adelaide, 1907*, p. 221.

21. Anderson's examinations covered regularly the impact of innovations and industrialization on labor, the character of land rent, tariff and currency reform, and the desirability of state ownership. For example, he asked in 1888: "On what grounds does Adam Smith say that, in settling the rate of wages, the masters in his time 'had the advantage in the dispute?' In what respects are the circumstances different in Australia at present?" Sydney University, *Calendar*, 1889, p. cxvi.

22. The essay topic was "The Influence of Trades Unions on wages and constancy of employment. Or, The Social effects of the improvements in machinery introduced during the present century." Sydney University, *Calendar*, 1893, p. ccxxiv.

23. *Ibid.*, 1896, pp. cxxxviii and cxxxix; and *ibid.*, 1902, pp. 163–64.
24. Professor Percy Partridge has noted that Anderson's "similarity to Wood, both in method and in his social faith, was striking." "The Contribution of Philosophy and History," in *One Hundred Years of the Faculty of Arts* (Sydney, 1952), p. 76.

School with texts by Smith, Mill, Marshall, Cobden, Carlyle, and Ruskin.[25]

Walter Scott, Professor of Greek from 1885, was a vigorous advocate of economics outside the university.[26] He told the Australian Economic Association: "Political economy, if it is not to fall behind the times, must be a constantly advancing science. . . . And there is much still to be done in the way of adjusting, for application to Australian society, the doctrines of writers who had before their eyes the somewhat different conditions of England or Germany, France or the United States."[27] Scott's interests ranged from commercial policy through demand theory to monetary reform.[28]

Beginning in the 1880's, lectures on political economy were offered by Sydney University in the evenings for students not working toward a degree. In Michaelmas term, 1886, Alexander C. Wylie delivered a series of thirty lectures on economic principles, "the Distribution of Wealth," and "Practical Applications of Political Economy," under terms of a University Extension Act of 1884.[29] Students were permitted to enroll for the whole

25. Works by Ingram, Price, Ricardo, Hobson, Nicholson, Walker, Toynbee, Cunningham, Gibbons, Morley, and Webb were "also recommended." Sydney University, *Calendar*, 1903, pp. 176–78; and 1905, p. 194.

26. Scott's perception of the economist's distinctive analytical function was illustrated in his Presidential Address to the Economic Science Section of the Australasian Association for the Advancement of Science in 1895. In distinguishing the positive from the normative role of the economist he said: "Tell the economist that you propose to check or modify free bargaining for this or that particular group of people, here and now, in this or that particular way, and he may be able to conclude that certain results will probably follow. But his theory contains no rule that will cover all cases alike." "On Fixing a Minimum Wage," *Report of the Sixth Meeting of the Australasian Association for the Advancement of Science held at Brisbane, 1895*, p. 150. Scott was condemned by the Sydney *Bulletin* for his relatively conservative economic views, and particularly for his faith in the importance to worker welfare of increased production rather than altered income distribution. "Professor Scott's Yarn," *Bulletin*, XIII (1893–94), No. 703, p. 4.

27. Walter Scott, "Inaugural Address of the Eighth Session of the Australian Economic Association," *Australian Economist*, II (1890–93), 95.

28. Walter Scott, "A Free-Trade Criticism on Tariff Restrictions," *Australian Economist*, II (1890–93), 247–51; "The Economics of Consumption," *ibid.*, 203–6; "Inaugural Address," *ibid.*, V (1897–98), 9–14.

29. The only published work by Wylie that has been discovered is an emotional discussion of contemporary income distribution, lacking in economic analysis. For example, Wylie wrote of distribution theories: "It is needless to prattle of labour and capital when we take from the first what are its inherent rights, strip it of its independence, and make capital a plus quantity by conceding to it prerogatives to which it has no righteous claim." "The Relations between Capital and Labour," *Victorian Review*, XII (1885), 377.

series and receive a certificate upon successful completion of an examination, or they could attend individual lectures.[30] Wylie's classes, like those of Anderson, were heavily policy oriented and may have helped to inspire formation of the active Australian Economic Association in 1887.[31] The University took an active part in the Association with Vice-Chancellor H. N. MacLaurin its first president and Professor Walter Scott a continuing inspiration.[32]

The Institute of Bankers of New South Wales co-operated with the University in making available extension lectures to its members. J. Russell French outlined benefits of part-time higher education to his fellow bankers in 1893, and he explained that development of a complex Australian economy had made knowledge of political economy particularly valuable. He said:

In the infancy of banking, when its operations were comparatively simple and easy to follow, an acquaintance with such a subject as political economy was no doubt superfluous, or could readily be dispensed with, but, in these modern days, the operations of banking are becoming more and more complicated every day, and to understand and grasp them, with anything like an approach to accuracy, a man has to be imbued with some knowledge, at all events, of the general causes and influences at work in regulating and controlling the vast fabric making up the trade and commerce of the world, the production of the wealth of the nation and its distribution through various and sometimes devious channels, until it reaches its final destination and use.[33]

French did not defend economics merely as a social science important in itself and for the formulation and criticism of public policy, but rather as a "practical" subject useful to bankers in their daily banking chores. He addressed his remarks in part to apprentice bankers:

We do not want men to develop into mere theorists any more than we wish them to become pedantic, but we do think and believe that

30. Students receiving certificates varied between four and ten each term. Sydney University, *Calendar*, 1887, pp. 272–73, and cxlix–cli; 1888, pp. 229, 284, 285, and clxi–clxii.
   31. See below pp. 629–30.
   32. S. J. Butlin, "The Australian Economic Association, 1887–1898," *Economic Record*, XXIII (1947), 21.
   33. "The Educational Function of the Institute of Bankers of New South Wales," *Journal of the Institute of Bankers of New South Wales*, II (1893), 402.

real practical good will accrue from a careful study of the history of
the evolution and growth of the huge structure of the trade and
commerce of the world, and of the laws and influences which control
its operations; all of which is embraced in the study of political economy. And we feel satisfied that such a study will be found an admirable introduction to, and preparation for, the closer study, which,
as men aspiring to rank as bankers, you will have to make of the
theoretical side of the profession; and, when you enter on this study,
you will at once perceive that banking, as developed in these modern
times, is closely interwoven with and dependent for its elucidation, in
many respects, on the wider science of political economy.[34]

Arthur W. Jose, later a prominent historian, delivered the first
political economy extension lectures to the Institute of Bankers,
using Syme's *Principles of Political Economy* and Marshall's
Economics of Industry as texts.[35] Jose's published remarks after
correcting his first set of bankers' examination papers are revealing. He said:

> The answers on Economics evidently suffered from the short time
> given for preparation, but were, when that is taken into account,
> generally very fair. It is, however, necessary that a student should di-
> gest his reading, and not reproduce it in mangled hunks for the
> Examiner's perusal.
> The work in Arithmetic is undoubtedly the blot on this examination.[36]

The standard of extension lectures to bankers remained elementary, and the syllabus changed remarkably little over the years.[37]

In 1903 the Sydney Chamber of Commerce requested the
University Senate to give consideration to establishment of a
faculty or department of commerce. In response to this petition,
a Senate Committee recommended in 1904 improvement of commerce teaching in secondary schools and formalization of evening
lectures at a more advanced level for possible award of a "Commercial Certificate." "Economics" and "Banking and Finance"
were the first two of nine subjects proposed by the Committee
for the commerce course. The Senate took immediate action to

---

34. *Ibid.*, pp. 402–3.
35. The reading list included also books by Bagehot and Walker. Jose announced that "Syme and Marshall will be sufficient, but the student should not
confine his reading." *Journal of the Institute of Bankers of New South Wales*,
III (1894), 51.
36. *Ibid.*, III (1894), 231.
37. *Ibid.*, IV (1895), 39, 41, and 484; VI (1897), 128–30, 209, and 272; XI
(1902), 68.

implement the recommendation and several special lecturers were appointed to conduct classes "in conjunction with the Sydney Chamber of Commerce." Herbert Stanley Jevons, a son of William Stanley Jevons, on a visit from England, delivered lectures in 1904 on economic principles in both Goulburn and Sydney to classes as large as ninety students.[38] Commercial History was discussed in smaller groups by R. C. Teece, R. L. Nash, and H. Y. Braddon.[39]

After this successful beginning, a conference was held in 1906 between representatives of the State government, the Chamber of Commerce, the Teachers' Association, and the University. It resolved that commercial education be extended in scope, that groups such as bankers be encouraged to co-ordinate closely their teaching and examinations with the University, and, of greatest significance, "That it is desirable that a Professorship of Economics be established at the University as soon as possible, and that, in view of the national importance of the subject, Parliament be requested to provide all or part of the necessary funds."[40] In response to the conference recommendations, the Senate made arrangements for junior and senior commercial examinations to be held in schools. Commerce courses at a more advanced level were offered regularly in the evenings beginning in 1907, leading to a diploma in commerce after three years or as optional subjects for the B.A.[41] R. F. Irvine, H. Dunstan Vane, H. Y. Braddon, and T. G. Taylor were appointed lecturers in a new Department of Economics and Commerce.[42] "Commerce I"

38. Two of Jevons' students took short-hand notes of his lectures, making possible their publication as a book entitled *Essays on Economics* (Sydney, 1905). The volume received a devastating review from H. J. Davenport in *Journal of Political Economy*, XIV (1906), 640–41.

39. Writings of Teece and Nash are discussed above pp. 201 and 363. Extension and other lectures by Braddon are reprinted in *Essays and Addresses* (Sydney, 1930).

40. "Report of the Senate of the University of Sydney for the Year Ended 31st December, 1906," Sydney University, *Calendar*, 1907, pp. 433–34.

41. It was reported that "The Senate was assisted in its deliberations by the report of the New South Wales Education Commissioners, and by a report by Mr. E. R. Holme, Lecturer in English, which was prepared after his personal enquiries at various commercial institutions in Europe." *Ibid.*

42. In 1908 W. G. Woolnough, F. A. Russell, and F. B. Guthrie were added to the Department. Sydney University, *Calendar*, 1908, p. 132.

included lectures on economics by Irvine with texts by Marshall, Bonar, and Ely, and it attracted eighty-four students in 1907, sixty-nine in 1908, and eighty-four in 1909.[43] Economics was taught in each of the three years of the Commerce course, with division of material into value and distribution theory, international trade, public finance, industrial organization, economic history, money and banking, and statistics. In addition to the innovation of a department of economics and commerce, during the first few years of the commerce program, economics continued to be taught by Anderson in philosophy and by Wood in history.

In 1912 Robert Francis Irvine, who came to the University in 1907 from the New South Wales Public Service Board, was appointed Professor of Economics, and a new Bachelor of Economics degree was introduced.[44] These changes were brought about as a result of three pressures upon the university. First, businessmen in the community whose activity was partly responsible for establishment of the commerce course were anxious that their subject be given higher status and prestige. Naturally, this anxiety was shared by the lecturers in commerce.[54] Irvin argued in 1914 that although business leaders were not well informed of work done by his department, their influence was substantial. He said: "Although the Chamber of Commerce took an active

43. For 1909 Gide and McVey replaced Bonar and Ely as texts. *Ibid.*, 1909, pp. 133–34.

44. A biographer of Irvine in the University magazine wrote in 1922: "For fifteen years, first as Chief of Staff, and then as member and chairman of the Public Service Board, he inspired and fostered countless reforms in the methods of recruitment and training of officers, and in the organisation of departmental activities. Let anyone call to mind the Public Service as it was in 1895, and he will have some faint appreciation of the work which confronted Robert Francis Irvine. By his tact and outstanding merit he won recognition for University and scientifically trained men, and for modern business methods in a service traditionally suspicious of either new ideas or machinery. Public servants, however, will remember him best as Chairman of the committee appointed by the Government to devise a scheme of superannuation. Despite recent political recriminations the Act stands as a monument to the unremitting labour, conspicuous ability and foresight of Irvine and his colleagues, and within the last few weeks he has had the satisfaction of seeing it copied by the Commonwealth Government. In 1912 he was appointed a Royal Commission of Inquiry into the Housing of Workmen in England and America, and his report is the classic on this subject in Australia." F.A.B., "R. F. Irvine, M.A.," *Hermes: The Magazine of the University of Sydney*, XXVIII (1922), 183–84.

45. "Department of Commerce, Sydney University," *Journal of the Institute of Bankers of New South Wales*, XXIII (1914), 49.

part in securing the establishment of a Department of Economics and Commerce at Sydney University, it is probably true that the business community is to a great extent unaware of the special work undertaken at the school, and of the kind of men who are being trained there for commercial or administrative pursuits."[46] All community support, however, was not without reservation; Irvine reminisced years later:

> On my appointment to the Chair of Economics at the University of Sydney, a very courtly old gentleman expressed the hope that I would confine my teaching to generally accepted doctrines and "authorities," nothing later, say, than John Stuart Mill, though he understood that Marshall was "sound." He particularly warned me against that "damned scoundrel, Henry George." Naturally, the old gentleman was a protectionist, and a large property owner. We found ourselves unable to accept this advice, and pursued our wayward course, which, however, we took to be the path of intellectual honesty.[47]

As a second pressure on the university, Francis Anderson, Irvine, and a few other faculty members repeated with renewed vigor after 1907 their longstanding requests for full inclusion in the curriculum of the social sciences. In 1912 Anderson explained to a meeting of the Australasian Association for the Advancement of Science that it was vital to begin teaching immediately in all branches of "sociology," as he called the social sciences. He said:

> To put it shortly, Sociology is a "mother science," just as the fundamental sciences of physics, chemistry, biology, and psychology may be described as mother sciences. They are general studies, which are capable of subdivision and ramification, inclusive of many special departments, but each dealing with certain general or fundamental facts, and issuing in the discovery of general laws which govern in subordinate and apparently independent departments. In the history of scientific discovery, it often happens that the subordinate department is investigated and attains the dignity and name of science before the mother science itself. Thus botany and zoology were advanced subjects of study before biology, of which they are both special branches, had even been given its name. Economics, in like manner, has been developed for generations, as if it were a separate and independent study, with no filiation to the general science of

46. *Ibid.*
47. *The Midas Delusion* (Adelaide, 1933), p. 5.

society, the science now known as Sociology. This general and fundamental science, the mother science, Sociology, is now in main outline
firmly established.[48]

Anderson suggested that an unfortunate confusion in the public
mind between social sciences and advocacy of specific public
policies was responsible for opposition to teaching of economics,
politics, and sociology. He continued:

It is probable that the emphasis on the political element, while it
served to stimulate party and popular interest, has helped to delay
the admission of Sociology within the serene abodes of academic research, where none is for a party, but all are for the truth. I am told
that the establishment of a Chair of Economics in Sydney University
was blocked for twenty years because it was thought in certain quarters that the Professor of Economics would think it his duty to preach
the doctrine of free trade. To such uses can politics descend! It may
be that similar objections will be made to the establishment of a
Chair of Sociology. It may be urged that it is tampering with socialism,
playing with fire. Better keep to the safe ground of algebra and Latin
prose. Yet such objections proceed from the same lips which utter
laments over the insignificant part played by the national Universities
in the national life, and over the small number of University graduates
who enter the field of politics.[49]

Anderson must have convinced his audience with his arguments
because "a resolution was unanimously passed recommending the
institution of a Chair of Sociology. The resolution was adopted
at the meeting of the General Council of the Association, and
transmitted to the Universities of Australia."[50] R. F. Irvine remarked in 1914: "Students of the University of Sydney owe a
deep debt of gratitude to Professor Francis Anderson, Professor
of Philosophy. I doubt whether anyone in Australia has done
more than he to stimulate an interest in the Social Sciences."[51]

In 1911 Irvine visited universities in the United States and
Europe and returned full of enthusiasm for what he had seen
and criticism of conditions in Australia. He complained to the
Melbourne University Association of Australian failure to keep

48. *Sociology in Australia: A Plea for its Teaching* (Sydney, 1912), pp. 7–8.
49. *Ibid.*, p. 9.
50. *Ibid.*, p. 11.
51. *The Place of the Social Sciences in a Modern University* (Sydney, 1914),
p. 9n.

abreast of worldwide university development and in particular of a lack of interest in the social sciences. He condemned university governing bodies thus:

Indeed, if report may be credited, they have viewed these subjects with suspicion and alarm, as being likely to unsettle youthful minds or to introduce the fury of controversy into the other-worldly calm of academic life. Thus it has been stated that the establishment of a Chair of Economics in one of our Universities was delayed for several decades because it was feared by one party that the professor might be a free-trader; by another that he might be a protectionist; and by all parties that he might be a "socialist of the Chair," which would be a calamity of the first magnitude!

But I do not think such apprehensions have been the only causes of our backwardness. Our Universities have naturally enough been largely modelled on English and Scottish examples, particularly Scottish; but the trouble is that the modelling was done fifty or sixty years ago, and we have in many respects not kept in touch with the newer ideals.[52]

Irvine rejected the argument that social sciences should wait for inclusion in a university curriculum until the community attained affluence. He continued:

I do not believe that lack of funds has anything to do with the matter. If the governing bodies and University men in general knew enough about these subjects or had any profound conviction as to their worth, the money would long since have been forthcoming. But we have not had the knowledge and we have not had the conviction necessary to make the appeal for money successful.[53]

Irvine contended that because of shortage of trained personnel in the social sciences, Australia had been unable usefully to assess the success of its many economic and social experiments. He said: "Nothing strikes visiting economists and sociologists so much as the meagreness of investigation and criticism by Australians of their own social evolution. The admitted excellence of our Statistical Bureaux cannot remove this disgrace."[54] He hoped to emulate, in Australia, American precedents of co-operation among the social sciences: "I want to gather these human sciences to-

52. *Ibid.*, pp. 6–7.
53. *Ibid.*, pp. 7–8.
54. *Ibid.*, p. 8.

gether into a great faculty or institute where they may be properly correlated. Such an institution as one finds at Columbia University in the faculty of Political Science, Sociology, Economics and Public Law."[55] Irvine reported with approval the close ties between teaching and research in American and German universities.

The result in America and elsewhere has been a large and increasingly valuable output of literature on Sociology, Economics, Political Science and allied subjects. The professors are no longer merely glorified high school teachers, but investigators and leaders of thought; and in America, as well as in Germany, it is considered that the professor who is not an investigator is not likely to be a good teacher.[56]

Irvine absolved the Australian community generally from responsibility for failure to develop social sciences, and in conclusion indicted the universities themselves:

Australian democracy is too open-eyed not to recognise the immense practical advantages of the system I have been describing. It wants all the light it can get upon the social processes, and I am sure it is only too willing to subsidise any University movement which aims at bringing scientific thought into vital relation with the problems of the hour. The fault lies with the Universities themselves who are wedded to obsolete systems and, as it seems to me, to narrow ideals of their functions in a modern community.[57]

A third pressure on Sydney University for improvement in the teaching of economics resulted from revival of the university extension movement during the years just prior to the World War I. G. V. Portus, one of the moving spirits in the revival, has described the pioneer years of extension lecturing thus:

The difficulty was to get the lecture regarded as anything more than an evening's entertainment, even by those who liked that sort of thing. The lectures offered were chiefly popularizations of parts of the regular university courses, remote as these were from the needs of the generality of adult citizens. Gradually the instruction offered became less systematic, until the Extension Movement was little more than a means of providing occasional public lectures, under the patron-

55. *Ibid.*, p. 25. Irvine spoke particularly high praise of the library and research facilities at Harvard, and described these in some detail. pp. 31–32.
56. *Ibid.*, p. 33.
57. *Ibid.*, pp. 35–36.

age of the University, in town and country centres. It was in this stage when I first lectured for the Sydney University Extension Board in 1911.[58]

In 1913 Albert Mansbridge, Secretary and founder of the English Workers' Educational Association, came to Sydney and campaigned for establishment of an Australian branch. Mansbridge's most enthusiastic allies and disciples in Sydney were David Stewart, a trade unionist, and Peter Board, Director of Education for New South Wales. Stewart, "convenor" of an "educational committee" of the New South Wales Labor Council and the first general secretary of the New South Wales Workers' Educational Association, differed slightly from Mansbridge in wishing a preponderant emphasis in worker education on social studies rather than culture in a wider sense.[59] Peter Board, as a member of the University Senate, succeeded in 1912 in having plans made and an act passed providing for new extension work in science, economics, history, and sociology.[60]

In 1913, at the urging of Mansbridge, Board, Stewart, Irvine, and Anderson, a joint University–W.E.A. committee was formed to supervise extension tutorial classes, and on Mansbridge's recommendation Meredith Atkinson, an Oxford graduate and tutorial class lecturer in the University of Durham, was appointed Lecturer and Organiser. After his arrival at Sydney in 1914, Atkinson relieved Irvine of a university course in "industrial history" and set about preparations for the first tutorial classes. Partly because of a current vogue for economic study and partly as a result of Atkinson's personal charm, except for a "preparatory class in Biology, all asked for Economics or Industrial History—a sharp break with the tradition of the Extension Board, which had specialised in lectures on literary, linguistic and scientific subjects." The committee reported that "it had not proved easy to secure the services of Australian graduates whose University

58. G. V. Portus, *Happy Highways* (Melbourne, 1953), p. 171.
59. E. M. Higgins, *David Stewart and the W. E. A.* (Sydney, 1957), p. 18.
60. *Ibid.*, p. 19; and A. R. Crane and W. G. Walker, *Peter Board: His Contribution to the Development of Education in New South Wales* (Melbourne, 1957), p. 165. Board visited the United States in 1909 and returned deeply impressed by the extension program of the University of Wisconsin. He was an enthusiastic delegate to the Imperial Education Conference in Britain in 1911.

courses have fitted them for such work."[61] G. V. Portus, Atkinson's successor as Director of Tutorial Classes in 1918, described thus the success of the extension movement during the war:

Atkinson arrived in Sydney in 1914. From the outset he regarded himself as a missionary for the movement, not only in New South Wales, but in Australia at large, with New Zealand thrown in. But Stewart and Board were the real pioneers, and they took Atkinson to their respective bosoms. . . . In season and out Atkinson preached that only widespread enlightenment would prevent war in future. Also up and down the country he lectured on the economics of war, a subject we knew very little about, and in which, it is safe to say, he was only a couple of jumps ahead of his hearers. This impressed the Labour government of the day, and, with the help of Peter Board, the subsidy to the University for tutorial classes was bumped up until it had been quadrupled by the end of the war.[62]

The war years were the period of greatest activity and accomplishment for the New South Wales W.E.A. Atkinson was elected President in 1915 and organized classes both in the city and in small centers. He directed members' attention principally towards economic problems, and in particular the determinants of income distribution; in the process he generated both enthusiasm and controversy. In 1915, with the co-operation of the Economic Research Society of Sydney and the Labor Council of New South Wales, Atkinson organized a conference to consider "Trade Unionism in Australia." Delegates heard papers from government, university, and private authorities which, taken together, constituted the most thorough investigation of the subject to that time.[63] However, the conference topic was highly contentious and Atkinson's intermediate position between labor and management raised opposition from both sides. Certain employers were undoubtedly suspicious of the dignity and respectability accorded unions by systematic academic study, and

61. E. M. Higgins, *op. cit.*, p. 23.
62. *Happy Highways*, p. 172. Portus recounts an anecdote which may reveal part of the motive behind the active extension movement. "A professor in Sydney, after quoting to me the old nineteenth-century slogan, 'Open a school and close a gaol,' immediately paraphrased it as 'Open a tutorial class and stop a strike.' 'For God's sake,' I implored him, 'don't say that in public.' " *Ibid.*, p. 193.
63. Contributions were made by Meredith Atkinson, R. F. Irvine, W. G. Spence, J. T. Sutcliffe, Gerald Lightfoot, F. W. Eggleston, F. A. A. Russell, and others, and were published as *Trade Unionism in Australia* (Sydney, 1916).

doctrinaire radicals were critical of the plentiful and rather patronizing advice to workers by speakers to study, "cooperate," and act in a more "responsible manner."[64]

By the end of the war, Sydney University had become somewhat disenchanted with the extension work of tutorial classes, and the joint sponsoring committee was reconstituted with W.E.A. representatives in a minority. Subsequently the classes lost some of their old character and influence, in part because of the changed University attitude described by Portus thus:

Accustomed to distinguish sharply between the educated and the uneducated by their own criteria of certificates, diplomas, and degrees, the universities tended to regard the whole business of extra-mural education as a gesture to the under-privileged. These poor chaps, who had never had any education since their primary schooling, were going to have a chance to drink at the fountains of the higher learning. Many of the dons added, *sotto voce*: "And we hope they'll be worthy of it."[65]

Under Portus' directorship after 1918, the W.E.A. remained active, but gradually class emphasis shifted again from serious study back to a mixture of instruction and entertainment. Classes were composed more of business and professional persons than "workers," while natural and behavioral sciences, and particularly psychology, displaced social sciences in popularity.[66] Periods of revival occurred, reflecting the activities of outstanding individual lecturers, such as F. R. E. Mauldon in New South Wales "Northern District No. 1" and B. H. Molesworth in Broken Hill.[67] The W.E.A. remained the principal publisher of writings on the

64. Although comments of the delegates were not recorded in detail an official conference "Observer" remarked: "I have often thought what a pity it is that some of the most intellectual socialists give so little attention to the practical problems of economics, which they admit to be worthy of study. Many of the most irrelevant points raised in the discussions seemed to be due to this wrong view of the purpose of the Conference." *Ibid.*, p. 107. Atkinson's criticism of socialist deities also brought him unpopularity with certain labor leaders. After a discussion of Marxian economics at the Sydney Trades Hall in 1920 Atkinson was vigorously refuted by W. H. Emmett in a pamphlet, *Marx's Economics and Professor Meredith Atkinson* (Sydney, 1920).
65. *Happy Highways*, p. 193.
66. It is reported that in 1920 a brewery executive offered extension economics lectures on his business premises, thus perhaps affording mixed motives for class attendance. E. W. Higgins, *op. cit.*, p. 44.
67. *Ibid.*, pp. 49–50.

Australian economy throughout the 1920's, and by 1922 Stewart
was able to report that the W.E.A. Book Service had "as good a
stock of books on social and economic questions as can be found
in Sydney."[68] But by this time the Association had ceased to be
an important stimulus for improvement in the University teaching of economics.

Irvine remained Professor of Economics until 1921, assisted by
a succession of lecturers, including Atkinson and Portus, who
were associated with the W.E.A., and R. C. Mills. In 1920 a
separate Faculty of Economics was established, offering both
bachelors and masters degrees in economics. The curriculum expanded with increases in staff, but Irvine never considered himself strictly an economist and looked with suspicion on pure
economic theory. He argued that contemporary economists had
risen above "The almost hopeless confusion in the minds of the
older Economists between the social and individual points of
view; their tendency to mistake assumptions for facts; their
beautifully simple and logical reasoning which, however, is only
true of a hypothetical world that never did nor could exist; their
numerous false predictions; their championing of causes that have
had to be abandoned" only to become guilty of "continued
neglect of social factors; a new misuse of the dangerous process of
abstraction; the adoption of inappropriate methods borrowed
from Mathematics and Physical Science, which delude by their
very appearance of accuracy, have given to economic theory an
air of unreality, of remoteness and even of pettiness which has
done much to retard its development and to choke the interest
which men naturally have in economic questions."[69]

Irvine condemned academic economists for a preoccupation
with static theory and for minimizing the economic role of the
state. They should devote more attention, he argued, to contemporary social problems and particularly to the character of income distribution. He appealed to an economic science session
of the Australian meeting of the British Association in 1914 for

68. *Ibid.*, p. 54. And see G. V. Portus, *An Introduction to the Study of Industrial Reconstruction* (Sydney, 1919).
69. *The Place of the Social Sciences in a Modern University* (Sydney, 1914),
pp. 11–12.

study of distribution to discover ways whereby both greater public welfare and higher and more stable production could be achieved.[70] In 1933 Irvine listed as "a few of the books which stimulated our interest and thought, and preserved us from the deadening influence of a specialism like Economics, which had, as we came to think, cut itself off unduly from the rest of life, which, after all, is a living entity" works by Ruskin, Hobson, Crozier, Bertrand Russell, Veblen, Graham Wallas, and R. H. Tawney.[71] It is apparent that Irvine regarded his students and other academic disciplines with greater affection than he did the social science he professed. After his retirement from university life and during the depths of the depression, he reflected on his teaching years at Sydney University; his remarks are worth repeating at some length. He wrote:

It was my good fortune, when the lecture halls knew me, to have a succession, year after year, of student comrades who were eager to join with me in exploring the dark and winding passages of the economic labyrinth. Exactly how this fellowship—for such it was—grew into so delightful a thing, I do not know. Perhaps it was just the spirit of the times. Youth was everywhere coming into its own. It was claiming a larger freedom and independence, the right to see for itself and to form its own judgments. It had grown impatient of ancient taboos and of the mouldy wisdom of the elders. These youthful comrades of mine were a cheerful, sociable, keen, and open-minded band, unabashed in the presence of the great God Mumbo Jumbo, and undaunted by the prestige of the traditional *mores*, shibboleths, and ways of thought. . . . We yawned a good deal, it must be confessed, over "Scientific Method," over "Marginal Utility," and a dozen other theories, illustrated by curves and other graphs, which at least served to break the monotony of the text. We plunged manfully into the "mysteries" of Money, Banking, the Exchanges, and Finance, and rather dismal we found these "mysteries" until we began to suspect that here was the very Citadel and Holy of Holies of Mumbo Jumbo. . . . We had encouraged each other to read books other than textbooks, and other than economic books: books that were alive and palpitant with the hopes and fears of men and women to-day. It did not matter particularly what—poetry, novels, belles-lettres, the more hu-

70. R. F. Irvine, "The Influence of Distribution on Production," *Report of the Eighty-Fourth Meeting of the British Association for the Advancement of Science*, 1915, pp. 481–82.
71. *The Midas Delusion* (Adelaide, 1933), pp. 4–5.

manistic philosophy, the new psychology—and anything that was vital, fearless, and sincere in its interpretation of life. Some of these books cast an entirely new light on our "dismal science," opening windows for minds which were in danger of being suffocated in the close atmosphere in which the text-book writers lived and had their being.[72]

Irvine's career at Sydney was marked by episodes of conflict and moments of public notoriety. In 1918, J. R. Butchart, a prominent banker, named Irvine as the intellectual father of the substantial wartime inflation. Butchart explained: "This is the gentleman who soon after the outbreak of war wrote two articles in the Sydney *Morning Herald,* in which he recommended the Fisher Government to throw overboard the views of those 'conservative stalwarts who maintain a masterly inactivity and content themselves with vain repetition of obsolete doctrines,' and to go ahead and issue paper money. The Government was looking for a lead and he gave them one . . . when every man's work shall be tested as by fire proving what is gold and what mere stubble only fit to be burnt up, the Sydney Professor's share in the great inflation should not be forgotten."[73]

Irvine in 1919, with Meredith Atkinson, contributed a strongly protectionist article to the *Australian Tariff Handbook,* thus taking a doctrinaire position in a highly charged area of political controversy and firmly alienating free-traders.[74] When, in 1922, employee representatives proposed that Irvine preside over a

72. *Ibid.,* pp. 2–4. Irvine expressed sympathy with the cynical views on economics of Stephen Leacock, whose career at McGill University in some respects affords an interesting parallel with his own at Sydney. The following lament of a frustrated humanist misplaced in the social sciences was voiced by Irvine but could as well have come from Leacock. "One finds the field broken up into small patches, with countless research scholars at work picking up every grain of sand, classifying, tabulating, working out graphs of this and that, and forming rather paltry generalizations which do not seem to lead anywhere that matters. . . . Now our industrious economic gleaners in every field are assembling masses and masses of facts, and writing countless monographs which no one, even if he had the proverbial nine lives of the cat, could possibly read and digest." *Ibid.,* p. 8. See also my *Canadian Economic Thought,* pp. 167–68, and 191–92.

73. *Money and Its Purchasing Power* (Melbourne, 1918), pp. 4–5. A conservative account of wartime finance by Irvine, including a defense of the gold standard, not mentioned by Butchart was "Australian Finance, Public and Private," in *Australia To-day 1916* (Special number of *The Australian Traveller,* November 1, 1915), pp. 99–113.

74. Irvine stated "I believe that List's argument still holds good." Ambrose Pratt, ed., *The Australian Tariff Handbook 1919* (Sydney, 1919), pp. 25–28, and above p. 34.

Commonwealth Prime Minister's "Industrial Conference," employers "summarily rejected" the suggestion.[75] Irvine himself told of an instance when, after a public utterance, criticism came from both right and left.

I remember on one occasion giving an address to a Labour educational group, on French Syndicalism, I think. My critical summing-up was not appreciated by the more radical members of the audience, and they subjected me in turn to some of the warmest criticism I had ever encountered. Next day, or the day after, I received a letter from the then Premier of the State, in which he informed me that the Cabinet was much disturbed by the report that at this meeting I had announced myself a syndicalist or communist, or something else equally horrifying![76]

Irvine's frequent appearances in the heat of policy debate must have convinced many skeptics of the "danger" in social sciences, and may explain together with problems in his domestic affairs his premature retirement from academic life in 1921.

R. C. Mills succeeded Irvine in the Sydney chair of economics. A native Australian, Mills was a graduate of Melbourne University where he was led to economics from a study of law under Harrison Moore and of history under E. O. G. Shann.[77] At the London School of Economics, he worked with Edwin Cannan and J. A. Hobson, and he wrote a valuable doctor's thesis on *The Colonization of Australia* (1829–42).[78] Under Mills, most of whose career lies beyond the scope of this study, work in economics was extended; F. C. Benham, E. R. Walker, and R. B. Madgwick were all appointed lecturers in economics during the 1920's.[79] Although the economics department did not disappear

75. D. B. Copland, "The Trade Depression in Australia in Relation to Economic Thought," *Report of the Sixteenth Meeting of the Australasian Association for the Advancement of Science held at Wellington, 1923*, p. 556.
76. *The Midas Delusion*, p. 6.
77. See below pp. 573 and 576.
78. London, 1915, and reviewed favorably by Richard T. Ely in *American Economic Review*, VI (1916), 874–76. A biographical note on Mills by "J. F. B." is contained in *Hermes: The Magazine of the University of Sydney*, XXVIII (1922), pp. 182–83.
79. Mills and Benham wrote together a series of *Lectures on the Principles of Money, Banking, and Foreign Exchange and their Application to Australia* (Sydney, 1925). Reviews were in *Journal of Political Economy*, XXXIII (1925), 695–96; and *Economic Journal*, XXXVI (1926), 472–74. Other writings by these men are discussed above pp. 36, 393, 416, 450, and 493.

from the public eye after Irvine's retirement, Mills and his colleagues made fewer attempts to educate students outside the university, and they participated less in inflammable popular controversies.[80] In contrast to Irvine's identification with state interference in the economy, Benham obtained quickly a reputation of being an "uncompromising free trader of the British school."[81]

Economics entered Sydney University through the back door. Although a prediction was made at the institution's inception that soon political economy would be placed on the curriculum, except for a few sporadic lectures, this forecast was not fulfilled for half a century. From the beginning, support for teaching of the subject came from several distinguished professors within the university, and later from a few business leaders and labor spokesmen seeking extension education. Opposition, usually covert and tacit, came from state governments which provided educational grants with a restrained hand and from university administrations which avoided academic innovations fearing antagonism of sensitive friends. In Australia, the frequent appeals to "laws of political economy" by participants in acrimonious policy debates often gave the subject an aura almost of occult religion in the view of persons unfamiliar with its real content. Legislators, facing endemic financial stringency, felt justified in judging that such a suspicious department might well be neglected for the time. Skeptics could always point in conclusion to Sydney's sister institution, Melbourne University, where the first fifty years of political economy were less than an outstanding success.

When forces favoring the teaching of economics finally over-

80. At least two exceptions to this generalization are the published account of a public lecture by Mills on "The Practical Value of the Study of Economics" and an attack on Benham by a doctrinaire protectionist for advocacy of low tariffs. J. Hume Cook, *The Australian Tariff Problem, Protection versus Free Trade* (Melbourne, 1925). An elementary economics text with Australian institutional material, published in 1923 in pamphlet form for use in the Sydney Teachers' College, was prepared probably by Mills or members of his department, and this may reflect the form of the first-year university course. It was entitled: *An Introduction to the Study of Politics, Section I, being Notes on Economic Theory and some of the more important Economic Problems* (Sydney, n. d.).

81. H. Heaton, "Review of F. C. Benham, *The Prosperity of Australia,*" *American Economic Review*, XIX (1929), 101–4.

powered opposition after the turn of the century, Irvine, the first appointee, bore out in part the fears of some critics. He treated economics less as a science than as one aspect of social philosophy, and he assumed an active role in contentious policy debates. Nevertheless, partly because of economics' popularity with workers in the extension movement and with commerce students, the subject became firmly established. Only after appointment of Mills and expansion of the department during the 1920's, however, did economic science gain a respected place in the university community.[82]

Victoria

A Victorian legislative committee in 1852 proposed establishment of the University of Melbourne and expressed desire that higher education might help to counteract uncivilizing aspects of mounting gold fever. The committee ended its report thus:

But they cannot refrain, in conclusion, from expressing their hope that the institution of an University for the education of her youth, will, under Divine Providence, go far to redeem their adopted country from the social and moral evils with which she is threatened; to improve the character of her people; to raise her in the respect and admiration of civilized nations. At a time when the discovery of almost unbounded wealth is drawing upon her the eyes of the world, let her not neglect to shew that she is mindful of duties to her self and her children, other than the mere protection of order, or the preservation of material riches.[83]

Concern of older Melbourne residents with imminent social change explains in part the relatively prominent position assigned to the social sciences at the University's beginning. Auditor

82. A manifestation of non-academic enthusiasm for economics teaching as late as 1929 was the project of a labor leader to establish a workers' college that would teach "the law of Cause and Effect, Economics, and political science—that will instruct the leaders of the Movement as to the best ways and means of overcoming, if not totally abolishing, the economic slavery of the people." The prospectus continued optimistically: "Let us, therefore, train our leaders and their successors in such a college and the emancipation of the people is as assured as the sun will rise." Fred Saidy, *Workers' College Teaching: The Law of Cause and Effect, Economics and Political Science* (Wollongong, 1929), unpaged.
83. "Report from the Select Committee on the University of Melbourne," *Votes and Proceedings of the Legislative Council of Victoria,* 1852–53, p. 777.

General Hugh C. E. Childers, a prominent supporter of the university and later British Chancellor of the Exchequer, was himself a competent economist and at Oxford had read "all which would be of practical use in after life, *e.g.* modern history, political economy, and constitutional law."[84] Childers could recount with pride that he "almost knew by heart the best of Macaulay's Essays, and Adam Smith's 'Wealth of Nations,'" and it was not surprising, therefore, that one of the four first appointees in 1854 was W. E. Hearn, a distinguished graduate of Trinity College, Dublin, as Professor of Modern History, Modern Literature, Logic and Political Economy.[85]

The initial University syllabus, published in 1858, listed political economy as a course in the third year of the B.A. program, and as an option for the M.A. degree. One of the four "Honours" schools was entitled "Social Sciences" and covered both history and political economy. The reading list for political economy indicated that Hearn placed heavy emphasis on classical principles, and he announced that the course would "chiefly consist of Lectures on the General Principles of the Science as contained in Mr. Senior's Treatise on Political Economy and Adam Smith's Wealth of Nations."[86] There is little evidence, either in course outlines or on examination papers, that students were encouraged to examine local Australian problems. However, a few concessions were made to the direction of public controversy, as in the 1850's when, during agitation for government regulation of currency, eight out of ten readings for the M.A. examinations were related to money and banking. Occasionally Hearn discussed some of his own personal interests in economics, for example his dissatisfaction with the term "political economy," and gradually he enlarged his reading lists through inclusion of works by Bastiat, McCulloch, Jevons, Fawcett, Spencer, and his own

84. Spencer Childers, *The Life and Correspondence of the Right Hon. Hugh C. E. Childers 1827–1896* (London, 1901), I, 17.
85. Hearn's writings, his place in the history of economic thought, and his activities in Australia have been discussed in J. A. La Nauze, *Political Economy in Australia: Historical Studies* (Melbourne, 1949), pp. 45–97; and in D. B. Copland, *W. E. Hearn: First Australian Economist* (Melbourne, 1935).
86. University of Melbourne, *Calendar*, 1858–59, p. 56. Approximately fifteen books in the University Library in 1856 might have been used in political economy. *Catalogue of the Library of the University of Melbourne, Victoria* (London, 1856).

Plutology. Non-conformity was not encouraged, and students were asked on examinations to demonstrate fallacies in the writings of such heretics as Henry Carey.

From 1855 until 1873, while Hearn taught exclusively history and political economy, there were fewer than twenty graduates of his honors program, and only ten M.A.'s. His influence, through his students, however, may have been greater than is indicated by these numbers. His classes contained such distinguished future public figures as H. B. Higgins, H. G. Turner, and Alexander Sutherland.[87] Hearn's impact on Australian thought by his teachings and his writings was substantial. In several areas of policy controversy, he was cited often for authority. Land-reformers referred to his work on Aryan history to provide precedents for communal control of property, and he was quoted at length on the desirability of land taxation.[88] Hearn was regarded by Australian protectionists as a foremost exponent of the "English free-trade School," and he came often under their attack.[89]

Plutology was used as a text not only in Melbourne but at other universities in the colonies. An illustrative but rather ridiculous example of the reverence felt for Hearn by some Australian economists is a ficticious conversation described in an article by R. M. Johnston. A capitalist and a laborer are said to be discussing the effects of wage increases on prices, and the worker, to clinch his argument, quotes from memory but intact (with citation) a complete paragraph from *Plutology.*[90] In 1888,

87. The names of honors students were printed in the University *Calendar* in their graduating year. Turner reported that Sutherland "entertained a very high respect" for Hearn. H. G. Turner, *Alexander Sutherland, M.A.: His Life and Work* (Melbourne, 1908), p. 19. Nettie Palmer notes that Higgins did "most of his work at first . . . under Professor Hearn." Hearn's home "Heronswood" was bought by Sutherland and later by Higgins. Nettie Palmer, *Henry Bournes Higgins: A Memoir* (London, 1931), pp. 65 and 184.

88. See for example J. Reid, "Early Aryan Land Laws," *Australian*, II (Sydney, 1879), 283–91; and William Ritchie, *Letters on Fiscal and Land Law Reform* (Launceston, 1884), p. 22.

89. See for example David Syme, *Outlines of an Industrial Science* (London, 1876), p. 5; and Benjamin Hoare, *Preferential Trade. A Study of its Esoteric Meaning* (Melbourne, 1904), p. 195. Bruce Smith, who studied at Melbourne University and possibly under Hearn, was a leading free trader in New South Wales and colonial treasurer under Henry Parkes, 1891–92. Philip Mennell, *op. cit.*, pp. 419–20.

90. R. M. Johnston, "General Increase of Wages Falls Upon Consumers of Products, and in No Way Encroaches upon Rent or Profits of Capitalists," *Papers and Proceedings of the Royal Society of Tasmania*, 1890, p. 194.

the year of Hearn's death, Henry Hayter paid Hearn high praise in his presidential address to the Economic and Social Science and Statistics Section of the inaugural meeting of the Australasian Association for the Advancement of Science. Hayter said that Hearn's "profound learning, strong common sense, sound judgment, and intimate acquaintance with the higher objects aimed at by this Section, would, if he had lived, at once have pointed to him as the most proper person to be its president, and the one best calculated to guide its deliberations to a useful and practical result."[91]

In 1873, after Hearn's appointment as dean of the Faculty of Law, Charles H. Pearson was named lecturer in history and political economy. The interests of Pearson were mainly in history but he lectured to a class of ten in political economy.[92] One of Pearson's most brilliant students was Alfred Deakin, later to become Premier of Victoria and Prime Minister of the Commonwealth.[93] In 1874 Pearson "did not seek re-election" to the post of lecturer, and Hearn "cheerfully undertook" again his former responsibilities in addition to his new legal duties.

In 1876, after a competition in which H. B. Higgins was almost successful,[94] John Simeon Elkington, one of Hearn's own honor graduates in 1866, was appointed Lecturer in History and Political Economy, and was raised to professorial rank in 1878. Elkington appears to have given little attention to his university work, and apart from a few short articles in his early years did not make any contributions to scholarship.[95] As a public speaker, he

91. H. H. Hayter, "On Official Statistics," *Report of the First Meeting of the Australasian Association for the Advancement of Science held at Sydney, 1888*, p. 417. A particularly laudatory obituary of Hearn can be found in *Imperial Review*, July, 1888, pp. 67–68.
92. See J. M. Tregenza, *The Life and Work of C. H. Pearson 1830–1894*, Thesis Submitted for the degree of Doctor of Philosophy in the Australian National University, 1959, pp. 188–90. Pearson's approach in later life to a variety of economic problems is set forth in his *National Life and Character: A Forecast* (London, 1894).
93. Alfred Deakin, *The Crisis in Victorian Politics, 1879–1881: A Personal Retrospect*, edited by J. A. La Nauze and R. M. Crawford (Melbourne, 1957), pp. 3 and 4.
94. Nettie Palmer, *op. cit.*, p. 72.
95. Two articles in the *Melbourne Review* by Elkington were: "An Historical Glance at the Land Question," II (1877), 235–64; and " 'The Aryan Household' and Other Writings of Dr. Hearn," III (1878), 426–49. Elkington was on the Council of the Free Trade League of Victoria with Hearn and may have assisted

was also less than successful. After a lecture by Elkington to the Bankers' Institute of Australasia on "Political Economy," which was reported to have been "delivered almost without notes," the Chairman was moved to suggest that in future all addresses be submitted in advance, be circulated in written form, and be confined to a definite topic.[96]

Elkington related in 1903 that numbers attending his university lectures had steadily decreased over the years, with the exception that "The Ladies seem to be very partial to Political Economy; about half the class consists of ladies."[97] He explained that he relied "principally upon questioning students rather than getting them to take down what falls from my lips," and he dealt sparingly with economic theory. He said: "I think our local requirements are practical rather than academical. There is a great deal as to value theory, and interminable discussions about theories of rent, and a number of other matters that I treat very, very lightly indeed." When quizzed about printed copies of his lecture notes reputedly distributed by enterprising students, Elkington replied: "I have blushed at some of the statements in them which I am credited with having made in the class." In addition to his university work, Elkington practiced at the bar, and he used his busy life to explain his lack of scholarly output.

I think that you will find that a good deal of loose talking prevails on the subject of research. I do not think myself that much in the way of research can be hoped for unless there is, first of all, leisure; in the next place ability; and, in the third place, that the work is gone into with a sense of duty. Then there is a limited field. A man must be able to concentrate himself, which, with regard to economic subjects,

in the publication of the League's rather primitive propaganda. See *Free Trade Papers Addressed to the People of Victoria* (Melbourne, 1877). Elkington was Honorary General Secretary of the Melbourne Social Science Congress in 1880, but there is no evidence that he took part in the deliberations of the Congress. See below p. 621.

96. *Journal of the Bankers' Institute of Australasia*, II (1888–89), 538–41. Elkington's subsequent unpopularity with the bankers is evidenced by a bitter condemnation in the *Journal* of an alleged public ridicule by Elkington of a student's answer to an examination question. "A Little Weakness of University Examiners," *ibid.*, IX (1895–96), 793.

97. "Royal Commission on the University of Melbourne: Minutes of Evidence on Administration, Teaching Work, and Government of the University of Melbourne," *Papers Presented to the Parliament of Victoria*, 1903 (Second Session), p. 83.

is difficult; for he must first of all master the whole field of the literature.[98]

Elkington concluded that he "did the work of about thirteen lecturers and nine professors at some other universities."

Elkington held the Melbourne chair in economics for nearly thrity-five years, and during this period his curriculum changed remarkably little. Hearn's *Plutology*, which Elkington held to be "one of the clearest and most original expositions of economic principles to be found in the English language" remained as text *emeritus*,[99] while the reading list was expanded nominally to include works by Cairnes, Fawcett, Walker, Marshall, Roscher, Macleod, Giffen, Price, and Bagehot. The importance attached to caution and the example of "Home" universities was illustrated in 1881 when the Cobden Club offered the University of Melbourne a silver medal to be awarded annually to the student most proficient in political economy. After immediate consideration, the University Council refused the offer on the ground that the medal did not have an endowment attached. However, "Upon learning afterwards, by means of further correspondence, that the Universities of Oxford and Cambridge have accepted the medals of the Cobden Club on similar conditions, the Council, on reconsideration, agreed to accept the offer."[100]

During Elkington's tenure, the constituent colleges of Melbourne University began some independent teaching in political economy: John Winthrop Hackett was tutor in "Law, Logic and Political Economy" at Trinity College in 1878;[101] T. J. Smith delivered lectures at Ormond College in 1883 on "Logic, Mental and Moral Philosophy, and Political Economy;" and in the 1880's W. H. Irvine, another graduate of Dublin, lectured also at Ormond on "Political Economy, History, and Law."[102] Among a succession of later lecturers, E. O. G. Shann taught at Queen's

98. *Ibid.*, pp. 85–88.
99. " 'The Aryan Household' and Other Writings of Dr. Hearn," *Melbourne Review*, III (1878), 426.
100. University of Melbourne, *Calendar*, 1881–82, p. 236.
101. Hackett's work in economics is discussed above pp. 102, 109–10, 125–26, and 248–49.
102. For a good defense of classical economic principles by Irvine, see "Professor Bonamy Price on the Doctrine of Rent," *Victorian Review*, X (1884), 217–29.

College from 1906.[103] There is no evidence of co-operative effort between Elkington and the college appointees, but rather some indications of friction. In 1877 Elkington attacked viciously an article by Pearson on land reform, and said: "Professor Pearson's historical conclusions may now and then have seemed a little out at elbows with the facts, but his political economy has completely run away with him."[104] Hackett replied to Elkington in Pearson's defense, and remarked: "the learned lecturer on Political Economy [Elkington] has suffered his pen to commit him to half-a-dozen pages of almost unmixed fallacy."[105]

Before World War I, economics did not obtain substantial popularity at Melbourne, as evidenced for example by the complete absence of candidates for the Cobden Club Medal in 1884, 1885, and 1886. A feeling of disgust for university teaching of economics on grounds of its inappropriateness for the colonial economy was voiced by a critic in the *Melbourne Review* in 1880, at the beginning of Elkington's tenure, but might have been expressed as well at any time over the succeeding forty years.[106] At least two early professors, T. G. Tucker and W. Baldwin Spencer, appear to have been critical of the pretensions of economics to be a science. In 1890 they reviewed a satirical book of social comment by a New Zealander, W. F. Howlett, and wrote:

Perhaps . . . sportive and intentional folly in political economy is less harmful, and certainly it is more diverting, than the quasi-scientific and pretentious folly which knows not that it is folly. It remains, of course, for disciples of Ricardo, Fawcett, and other prophets of "the dismal science," to pose Mr. Howlett with a hundred obvious difficulties.[107]

When the Bankers' Institute of Australasia was founded at Melbourne in 1887, it began its own courses in political economy

103. Francis Gould Smith, a doctrinaire protectionist who published in Melbourne during the late nineteenth century, described himself as "Professor of Political Economy." See for example *Danger Ahead! Anti Imperial Federation of Australasia* (Melbourne, 1889). There is no indication, however, of where he professed.

104. "An Historical Glance at the Land Question," *Melbourne Review*, II (1877), 253.

105. J. W. Hackett, "Our Land Policy," *ibid.*, p. 368.

106. C. Wesley Caddy, "The Education of the Educated," *Melbourne Review*, V (1880), 432–39, and particularly p. 434.

107. "Economics in the Motley," *Australasian Critic: A Monthly Review of Literature, Science and Art*, I (1890–91), 79.

leading to the rank of "associate" of the Institute. The syllabus emphasized monetary matters, although Mill's *Principles* was the text, and the reading list included books by Fawcett, Marshall, Walker, Jevons, Bagehot, and naturally Hearn. The Institute collected an adequate economics library, and endeavored "to lend students the more expensive works." Moving spirits of the economics teaching were two of Hearn's graduates from Melbourne University: Henry Gyles Turner, the Institute's first president, and Alexander Sutherland.[108] Thomas Harlin, a Cambridge graduate, was examiner. A propaganda campaign was undertaken to interest bankers in the courses, and successful prize essays dealing with the topic, "On the Advantage of a Theoretical as well as Practical Training for Bankers," were printed in the *Journal.* One representative contestant wrote: "What Coke, Lyttleton, and the common law are to the barrister, Adam Smith, Gilbart, Bell, M'Leod, Byles, Chitty, Grant, and the usages and customs of mercantile and banking law should be to the banker."[109] It is not possible now to assess accurately the popularity or success of the Institute's economics course, but at the time favorable and enthusiastic comments did appear regularly in the *Journal.*[110] For example, a graduate associate's advice to beginning students in 1893 is illuminating. He said:

it is not desired to master one or two text-books, but to obtain a general insight into the principles treated of. Thus many of my friends stew at Mill, only, on political economy, where it would be better to commence, say with Fawcett's Principles, or one of the many rudimentary works to be found in the Institute Library. Similarly with regard to banking literature.[111]

108. For Sutherland's views on the Institute's teaching plans, see "The Institute's Plan for Examination," *Journal of the Bankers' Institute of Australasia,* I (1887), No. 6, pp. 3–10. Turner outlined his hopes for the Institute as a didactic body in "The Scope of the Institute," *ibid.,* II (1888–89), 441–44.

109. C. A. E. Abbott, "3rd Place Prize Essay," *ibid.,* II (1888–89), 206.

110. A contributor wrote in 1889: "The study of political economy is a most fascinating one when fairly entered on, and the student, when the intellectual mine opens before him, soon leaves the sweets of fiction for the strong meat of philosophy, ethics, and science, and his only wonder is how he could so long have neglected the higher education that is now so easy of access to everyone." "The Educational Influence of the Institute," *ibid.,* III (1889–90), 911–13.

111. Examinee, "Reading for the Associate's Examination," *ibid.,* VI (1892–93), 1178. Representative notices of reading lists and examinations for the associate examinations are found: *ibid.,* II (1888–89), 747; VI (1892–93), 1481; VII (1893–94), 394; XI (1897–98), 685–90.

By sustaining community interest in economics, the bankers certainly strengthened demands for improvements in its university teaching.

Other faculty members apart from Elkington and college lecturers had some contact with economics. E. E. Morris, an Oxford graduate and Professor of English, French, and German Languages and Literature from 1883, was appointed an examiner in political economy. Henry Laurie, Professor of Mental and Moral Philosophy, was concerned with social sciences as outgrowths of philosophy.[112] But the most pronounced enthusiasm for economics was exhibited by William Harrison Moore, Professor of Law. At the request of the Melbourne University Professorial Board in 1898, Moore prepared a "Memorandum on Commercial Education" in which he proposed, as preparatory to later university work, teaching through the University Extension Board of courses in "1. Descriptive Economics; 2. Elements of Economic Theory and History of Industry and Commerce; 3. Elements and Theory of Book-keeping and Accounting."[113] Professor Morris, president of the University Extension Board, and several business and professional groups gave support to Moore and helped to establish a committee with T. Harlin as president to co-ordinate extension activities.[114] J. A. Arthur delivered a first course of lectures on "The History of Industry and Commerce," which was such a success that requests began soon to be voiced for establishment of a permanent "center for commercial studies" at the university.[115] However, no immediate alterations of the University cur-

112. For comments on Laurie, see Ernest Scott, *A History of the University of Melbourne* (Melbourne, 1936), p. 131.

113. Moore's "Memorandum" was published in the *Bankers' Magazine and Journal of the Bankers' Institute of Australasia*, XII (1898–99), 704–8. It followed in the *Journal* an historical account by A. T. Dwyer, Secretary of the Accountants and Clerks Association, Ltd., of the development of "Commercial Education" throughout the world. *Ibid.*, 621–27.

114. Groups co-operating in promotion of the extension movement for commercial education were: the Bankers' Institute, Chambers of Commerce and Manufacturers, the Insurance Institute, the Incorporated Institute of Accountants, the Society of Accountants and Auditors, the Federal Institute of Accountants, the Accountants' and Clerks' Association, and the Association for the Promotion of Technical Education. See "Commercial Education," *ibid.*, XII (1898–99), 829–31.

115. *Ibid.*, XIII (1899–1900), 40 and 51–52. F. A. Campbell, Director of the Working Men's College, Melbourne, explained to junior bank officers in particular the benefits they might derive from a university commerce school. *Ibid.*, pp. 146–53.

riculum resulted from this public clamor.

In 1903 a Royal Commission was instructed to examine the administration, teaching, and government of the University of Melbourne, and in its reports discussed, among other matters, possible improvements in commercial education. Elkington announced to the Commission that he was firmly opposed to plans for a commerce school, even after his questioner had emphasized that such plans envisaged "the higher commercial education as including Economics." Elkington said:

From a University stand-point, which is the only one I feel called upon to adopt, I do not think much could be done in the way of improvement. I have all along paid a good deal of attention to that side of the subject. I am familiar with the calendars of other Universities, and I do not think there is much to change. A great deal of the work set down as university work I consider to be technical college work, or business college work; it is not work for a university—it is work for lads.[116]

Harrison Moore was the dominant exponent of economics and commerce before the Royal Commission, as he had been in the 1890's in the University extension movement. Using carefully documented evidence, he described courses at other universities, and particularly in the United States. He was very enthusiastic about the curricula of several German universities, the Center for Higher Commercial Studies in Paris, the Wharton School of the University of Pennsylvania, the social sciences program at Columbia University, and William Ashley's experimental degree course in Commerce at the University of Birmingham. In answer to critics who believed commercial education consisted merely of bookkeeping and office practice, he described the Harvard course thus:

In respect to Economics, at any rate, you have both the theory, and also an attempt, at any rate, to deal with the application of economic theory to such matters as financial administration, public debts, and the like. Even the principles of accounting form part of that course

116. "Royal Commission on the University of Melbourne: Minutes of Evidence on Administration, Teaching Work, and Government of the University of Melbourne," *Papers Presented to the Parliament of Victoria*, 1903 (Second Session), p. 89.

in Economics, and that approaches as nearly as anything Harvard has got to commercial education.[117]

Moore described the teaching in economics at the Melbourne Working Men's College as "distinctly elementary," and the syllabus of Melbourne University as little better. He said: "As to the details of treatment, I am hardly in a position to speak; but it must be fragmentary from the amount of time that is given to it, and from the fact that it forms only a small part of the work of a very extensive Chair. At Harvard you have a number of people engaged in Economics alone."[118] Moore reported that after an initially favorable response, teaching of economics through the extension movement had not been enthusiastically received.[119] The only sensible approach to the subject, he concluded, was rigorous instruction in a full university degree course.

Moore's testimony before the Royal Commission was supported by other influential witnesses. The president of the Incorporated Institute of Accountants recommended provision for a "chair of commerce" to deal with "economics, commercial history, commercial geography, commercial law, banking, currency, and all cognate subjects of that kind."[120] Athanasius T. Dwyer, Secretary of the Accountants' and Clerks' Association, explained that:

A person who has been successful in life, from a money point of view, thinks practice is the whole thing, but theory must go with practice. We think a man is better in every way if he has a theoretical knowledge as well as a practical one—he is able to grasp subjects better. There are various subjects of study connected with commerce that seem to be lost sight of altogether, such as the study of economics and political economy.[121]

117. *Ibid.,* p. 10.
118. *Ibid.*
119. "I do not know that it can be said that the commercial courses have been a very great success. Some of them have been enormously successful, but others have not, and our experience has been the experience of people everywhere who have attempted to cope with the subject of commercial education—that is, that the intensely practical subjects, like accountancy and commercial law, will attract very large audiences, while such subjects as economics and the history of trade, industry, and commercial geography are not very successful." *Ibid.,* p. 14.
120. *Ibid.,* p. 315. The same opinion was expressed by John Sawers, President of the Melbourne Chamber of Commerce. *Ibid.,* p. 370.
121. *Ibid.,* p. 282. Although convinced of the worth of economics to captains of industry, Dwyer was less certain of the subject's value to "the working classes." He said: "If they studied a little political economy, perhaps it would be an advantage, but it depends upon the text-book they take up. I think it

Henry Bournes Higgins, by this time a distinguished jurist and member of the finance committee of the University of Melbourne Council, proposed formation of a "school of civics" modeled after either the Wharton School of Business and Finance of the University of Pennsylvania or the London School of Economics. He elaborated conclusions he had reached after examination of these two institutions, and he reported discussions he had held with Beatrice and Sidney Webb in London which he believed might help to allay fears that economics would be associated inevitably with a single policy position. Higgins said:

I think the true ideal of the University is that all outside activities should be reflected in the highest intellectual development, and all that is best upon any particular subject should be found there. I would extend it to agriculture also. I think we could learn a lot from that splendid School of Economics which Mr. Sidney Webb started in London. He gave me the calendar for the year. I looked into it and found that it was not confined to one particular school of economics alone, but dealt with matters of wide education and economic problems from all points of view.[122]

The Royal Commission in its Final Report recommended improvement in the teaching of "Commercial Education" at the University of Melbourne, including under this designation "Economics and Allied Subjects" and specifically "(a) History of Economics and Trade, (b) Political and Commercial Geography, including Trade Routes, and (c) Study of Statistics."[123] As a preliminary step to instituting a full degree course in commerce,

---

would be no help for them to have an elementary knowledge of some of those things. As a general rule, a working man is a better student than a clerk; the clerk does not study at all. My experience, after eighteen years, is that you cannot get him to study."

122. *Ibid.*, pp. 213–14.

123. The Commission's rather elaborate definition of "Commercial Education" was—"the greater and more general adaptation of our educational system to commercial ends and for the purposes of modern life, the increase of facilities for training for trade, and the fuller recognition of the necessities for special training for the work of commerce and manufacture, without at the same time surrendering that general education which is recognised as a necessary basis of all public instruction, or sacrificing the means of intellectual discipline which most educationists believe can be furnished by almost any subject if properly taught." "Royal Commission on the University of Melbourne: Final Report on Government, Administration, Teaching Work, and Finances of the University of Melbourne, with Appendices," *Papers Presented to the Parliament of Victoria,* 1904, p. 63.

the Commission proposed that a diploma program be introduced with compulsory evening lectures.[124]

Despite the recommendations of the Royal Commission, improvements in the teaching of economics still did not take place immediately. Elkington remained professor for the time, and James Barrett, a physician and member of the University governing body, joined Moore as an outspoken advocate of the need for reform and critic of the status quo. In 1907, to underline the inadequacy of social science teaching at Melbourne, Barrett cited an essay written in 1809 by Sidney Smith, whose arguments he claimed "might well be reproduced to-day." Smith had begun: "When a university has been doing useless things for a long time it appears at first degrading to them to be useful. A set of lectures upon political economy would be discouraged in Oxford, probably despised, probably not permitted. . . ."[125] Several public bodies continued to urge provision of more university work in the social sciences, and even a group of students requested more teaching of political science on the ground that "the ignorance of our legislators regarding the simplest principles of economic science is proverbial."[126] Finally, in 1912 the University Council approached the State government "to provide for an appointment to a new Chair of Economics and Sociology, the desire being to provide instruction in General Sociology, Economic History, and General Economic Theory, and to encourage advanced work by graduates, under the guidance of the Professor, in subjects for which Australian conditions present special advantages."[127] The State Premier, W. A. Watt, and his government are reported to have greeted this request with coolness and to have implied as conditions for their support the appointment of a native Australian "whose views and training accord with Australian traditions and conceptions of economic matters."[128] Perhaps mindful still of

124. *Ibid.*, p. 70.
125. James W. Barrett, "The Classical Superstition" (reprinted from the Melbourne *Argus*, January 12, 1907), in *The Twin Ideals* (London, 1918), I, 63.
126. Cited in Ernest Scott, *A History of the University of Melbourne* (Melbourne, 1936), p. 204.
127. University of Melbourne, *Calendar*, 1914, p. 625.
128. Ernest Scott, *op. cit.*, p. 204. This incident is described fully by Professor Scott.

the career of W. E. Hearn, the Victorian government was reluctant to subsidize a potential critic, or possibly even a political opponent. In any event, the University Council would not accede to the required conditions and official support was not extended. Elkington retired in 1912, and according to Professor Blainey "the bottle dealer must have made a small fortune when he called at the vacated house in the university grounds."[129] His chair was divided, with Ernest Scott receiving a separate appointment as Professor of History. A succession of junior lecturers was engaged to teach political economy, ending with Edwin C. W. Kelly, who remained in this capacity until after World War I.[130]

In 1913, W. Albert Mansbridge, founder and secretary of the Workers' Educational Association of Great Britain, came to Australia on an organizing tour and was received enthusiastically in Melbourne by James Barrett and others.[131] A Victorian branch of an Australian Workers' Educational Association was formed, and the members set out to revive the ailing University of Melbourne extension movement. This work was hindered somewhat by the outbreak of war, but by 1915 the University Extension Board was offering a variety of courses which included one in "Money and Monetary Economics," taught by Charles H. Wickens of the Commonwealth Statistician's Office, a set of lectures on wages and labor by another statistician, Gerald Lightfoot, and classes in economic history, theory, and policy by Kelly.[132]

129. G. Blainey, *A Centenary History of the University of Melbourne* (Melbourne, 1957), p. 100.
130. R. F. Irvine in 1914, after discussing the work of the few social scientists produced by Melbourne University, remarked to the University Association: "You have every reason to be proud of this succession of good work; but the point is that it is the achievement of individual men, that it owes, so far as I know, little to official University encouragement, and that it has not resulted in the creation of properly equipped University Schools for the study of the Social Sciences." *The Place of the Social Sciences in a Modern University* (Sydney, 1914), p. 9.
131. Barrett claimed that he was responsible for persuading Mansbridge to visit Australia. "Proposed Tutorial Classes" (reprinted from the Melbourne *Argus*, September 16, 1913), in *The Twin Ideals* (London, 1918), I, 163.
132. The "Aim" of the extension courses was "to provide teaching which, though limited in its compass, may approach as nearly as possible the scope and standard of that given at the University." The "Character" was described as "distinguished from the ordinary popular lecture in several ways. (1) Their primary object is education; they seek to instruct and to stimulate rather than to

After the war, the extension movement grew steadily, led by Meredith Atkinson, who came to Melbourne from Sydney University as director of tutorial classes.[133] As well as conducting regular extension classes, Kelly and Atkinson took part in a highly successful series of "Mid-day Commercial Lectures" sponsored by the Melbourne Chamber of Commerce.[134] In 1923, J. A. Gunn, from the University of Liverpool, was named Atkinson's successor as director of tutorial classes and lecturer in sociology. Gunn regarded economics as a branch of "sociology," and the second of four basic sciences of social relations. He wrote: "The sociologist must always present society as a complex of four factors, Breed, Livelihood, Government, and Culture. Among these factors and their subdivisions, Livelihood, together with the problems of Breed or Population, is fundamental."[135] Gunn published a deplorable collection of his lectures to the Commonwealth Accountants' Students' Society entitled *Livelihood,* intended as an elementary economics text.[136] Thus by 1923 economics was

---

entertain; at the same time they endeavour to avoid pedantry or dulness. (2) They are not intended to be isolated lectures, but connected courses. They are thus able to treat fairly wide subjects with some approach to thoroughness, and encourage continuous work in a single branch of study. (3) The work is not confined to lectures. Every practicable facility is offered for reading, study, and writing in connection with the course." *Extension Work: Aim, Methods, and Syllabus of Lectures* (Melbourne, 1915), pp. 1, 13, and 14.

133. In addition to encouraging teaching of economics the W. E. A. also sponsored the publication of research monographs. For a list of publications in the W. E. A. Series up to 1927, see the frontispiece to F. R. E. Mauldon, *A Study in Social Economics: The Hunter River Valley New South Wales* (Melbourne, 1927).

134. The Chamber President declared with pride that these lectures, which covered both commerce and economics, came "from the minds of men who are not mere theorists, but who have had practical experience in the matters with which they have dealt." "Foreword," *Mid-day Commercial Lectures: 1919* (Melbourne, 1919), p. 8.

135. J. Alexander Gunn, *Livelihood: Papers in the Study of the Economic Factor for Social Science Students* (Melbourne, 1927), p. 5.

136. The Commonwealth Accountants' Students' Society placed economics on its examination syllabus in 1921. A spokesman explained—"I cannot see how we can expect to make any great progress in our profession unless we are well grounded in the principles of Economics." *Commonwealth Accountants' Students' Society Lectures* (Melbourne, n. d.), p. 31. *Livelihood* was described by H. Sanderson Furniss as "a somewhat curious jumble of subjects . . . decidedly chaotic . . . miserably printed, horridly got up, and expensive—and all it contains is already easily accessible in numerous well-known text-books." *Economic Journal,* XXXVII (1927), 643–44. Herbert Heaton wrote: "The result is a disappointing collection of snippets of theory, with odds and ends of fact drawn from well-known sources and arranged with little sense of order or proportion." *American Economic Review,* XVII (1927), 686.

being taught in Melbourne more outside the University than inside, and under a variety of guises and sponsors.[137]

In a few years before the end of the period under examination, economics at Melbourne University made up rapidly for lost time. In 1923 the state government at last provided for the maintenance of a school of commerce, and a year later D. B. Copland from New Zealand via the University of Tasmania was named Professor of Commerce.[138] In 1925 Copland and G. L. Wood, joined by F. R. E. Mauldon in 1926, took over the teaching of economics from Kelly and introduced a four course syllabus in place of the old classes in principles.[139] The instant success of the commerce program was evidenced by an initial enrollment of more than three hundred students.[140] Also in 1925, economics became a subject in secondary schools for the leaving examination, including in the curriculum both elementary economic history and theory. Copland's enthusiasm for economics was boundless, and in 1924–25 he was responsible in large part both for organization of a new national Economic Society and for foundation of the *Economic Record*.[141]

On a leave of absence in 1927, Copland visited universities in the United States, Canada, Great Britain, France, and Germany, and the report of his tour was published under the title, *Studies in Economics and Social Science*. He was particularly impressed by the work of American graduate schools,[142] and he recom-

137. Sir Keith Hancock has reminisced about his undergraduate years in Melbourne just after World War I: "All in all, I should find it hard to design a course of study better suited to a young man of my type than the course offered to me at Melbourne. It even included some elementary work in economics which gave a fresh stimulus to my historical studies, though I regret that many years went by before I read Adam Smith. What I did not so much relish was the pretentious mumbo jumbo that was called sociology." *Country and Calling* (London, 1954), p. 70.

138. Copland's work in economics is discussed above esp. pp. 179–81 and 243–44. Several appreciative accounts of Sir Douglas Copland's life work, together with a list of his writings, are contained in "Essays in Honour of Sir Douglas Copland," *Economic Record*, XXXVI (1960), 1–178.

139. This period in the development of the Melbourne Commerce School is discussed by Professor Herbert Burton in "F. R. E. Mauldon, 1891–1961," *Economic Record*, XXXVII (1961), 207–12; and by F. R. E. Mauldon, in "Gordon L. Wood: 'An Appreciation'," *ibid.*, XXX (1954), 1–6.

140. University of Melbourne, *Calendar*, 1926, p. 889.

141. D. B. Copland, "Notes. The Economic Society—Its Origin and Constitution," *Economic Record*, I (1925), 140–44.

142. Copland wrote: "It is generally recognised that America has better op-

584 *The Science of Enquiry*

mended several improvements in Australian university organization, including: establishment at every institution of chairs in economics, commerce, and political science and public administration; improved co-operation between departments of law and economics; new courses in industrial psychology, geography, and agricultural economics; graduate programs in the social sciences; investigation of the "case method" and other experimental teaching systems; and official encouragement to students studying abroad. In 1927, Copland became Sidney Myer Professor of Commerce, and in 1929, Lyndhurst Falkiner Giblin was appointed to a new Ritchie Professorship at the University, the first research chair in economics in Australia.[143] In the years which followed, Giblin obtained a position, described by a critic not given to indiscriminant praise, as "in the true sense of the word, the father of Australian economics."[144]

By the end of the 1920's, the University of Melbourne had moved in less than a decade from a rudimentary principles course in economics, which had remained substantially unchanged for more than half a century, to a balanced curriculum taught by a strong lecturing and research department with substantial influence on government and in the community. This rapid process of reform had roots stretching back at least to the 1890's. Teaching of economics at Melbourne began under the very favorable auspices of W. E. Hearn, but suffered subsequently from a succession of unfortunate personalities. Some observers came naturally to associate the subject with arrogant and uncompromising advocacy of laissez faire, and everyone listened in vain for enlightenment from professional economists on the country's economic problems. When the first improvements in teaching came in 1924, they were in answer to demands by a few non-economists within the university for more work in the social

portunity than ever of establishing leadership in the social sciences. Her work will not be judged by the thousands of college graduates that leave her institutions each year, but rather by the work done in the graduate school by both teacher and student." *Studies in Economics and Social Science* (Melbourne University Press Economic Series, No. 2, Melbourne, 1927), p. 15.

143. Giblin's work in economics, much of which lies outside the scope of this study, has been mentioned above *passim*, and in Douglas Copland, ed., *Giblin: The Scholar and the Man* (Melbourne, 1960).

144. Colin Clark, *Australian Hopes and Fears* (London, 1958), p. 153.

sciences and in response to expressions of opinion by non-academics, both businessmen and labor leaders, that the subject was an important and "practical" discipline, vital to intelligent citizenship and national development. For many years the advocates of economics had been thwarted in their attempts at reform by apathetic or hostile government and an unenthusiastic university faculty. When the subject was finally given support and stature under the mantle of commerce, its retarded beginning was quickly overcome. When the University erected stained glass windows representing "the width of culture cultivated by a University," Adam Smith was given a place which might not have been granted in any previous period since the days of Hearn.

Tasmania

Enthusiasm for economics teaching was voiced in Tasmania long before a university came into existence at the end of the nineteenth century. As early as 1835, a "Correspondent" of the *Van Diemen's Land Monthly Magazine* stated that "learning required in a new Country, must, of course, differ in many respects, from that which is pursued in Countries long established. The instruction must be such as is best adapted to the particular wants of the people, and the peculiar circumstances of the Country they inhabit;—must be suited, in short, to the occupations in which the pupil is expected to be engaged in riper years." Colonial education, he wrote, should consist principally of training in scientific agriculture and "the history and present state of commerce—the general principles which determine success or failure in its different branches—a sufficient degree of acquaintance with political economy. . . ."[145]

In 1872, E. C. Nowell, Government Statistician and Clerk of the Legislative Council, recommended political economy as an

---

145. "Education, Adapted to New Countries," *Van Diemen's Land Monthly Magazine*, III (1835), 145–46. As a concession to reality and the primitive character of contemporary Tasmanian education, the writer added: "A portion of the knowledge here recommended, might be acquired, during the hours of relaxation from other studies." *Ibid.*

important training for leaders of government, education, and business. He said: "no branch of knowledge is more necessary for that large class of men whose province it is to direct or to influence the destinies of States by wielding the Executive and Legislative powers, by instructing the people, and by ministering in the way of commerce, to its wants."[146] Nowell cited Cardinal Newman on the need for economics to dispel political quackery, and he argued that the danger of misguided policies gaining acceptance was particularly great in the colonies. He explained:

In the old countries there is a large sprinkling of men whose minds, even if they have had no special training, are yet prepared by high cultivation to appreciate the force of the abstract truths of philosophy; but in the new, the number is much smaller, and the general tendency is to superficiality, the result of very imperfect acquaintance with first principles; and it is therefore far more necessary in the latter that a science of such vital importance in Government and legislation as political economy, should be made a part of the higher studies of youth.[147]

Nowell suggested that examinations in political economy be offered under terms of the Tasmanian Council of Education and Scholarships Act, and he even proposed that knowledge of the subject be required of all legislators.

Our lawyers must study law, our doctors must study medicine and surgery, our clergy must study theology and bibliology, and give proof of competent knowledge of those subjects before they are allowed to enter their several professions, in order that the interests of the public may be protected against the wild work of ignorance. Why then should state-craft be the only profession in which no special preparation—no study of its principles—is demanded?[148]

A Hobart literary periodical, the *Quadrilateral*, castigated Tasmanian schools in 1874 in the same vein as had Nowell for over emphasizing classics and for not including on their curricula "such subjects as the classification of mental phenomena, usually termed moral science, political economy and sociology." Every

146. "Political Economy," *Monthly Notices of Papers and Proceedings of the Royal Society of Tasmania*, 1872, p. 12.
147. *Ibid.*, p. 13.
148. *Ibid.*, p. 14.

citizen, the journal claimed, "may justly be expected to understand the first principles of political economy."[149]

Several of the most able early Australian economists lived in Hobart—notably Robert Mackenzie Johnston and Judge Andrew Inglis Clark—and they were instrumental in formation of the University of Tasmania in the 1890's.[150] However, for some years the new institution suffered difficulties related to small size, and economics did not immediately receive special attention in a separate department. In the first University regulations approved in 1892, political economy was listed as a subject in the last year of the B.A. course and was included within both the "history group" and "psychology group" of subjects. Walker's *Manual of Political Economy* was the text for students in the pass course, and books by Marshall, Bagehot, Fawcett, Mill, Jevons, and Ingram were "additional for honours."[151] Lectures on political economy, if any were offered, were delivered probably by Robert Leslie Dunbabin, an Oxford graduate and lecturer in classics, modern history, and mental and moral philosophy. Examiners were Dunbabin, Mr. Justice Clark, and Professor Mitchell of the University of Adelaide. During the first twenty teaching years of the university (1893–1912), a mere eleven students passed successfully examinations in political economy, and not until 1906 were there two successful students in the same year.

In 1912 the Tasmanian Government increased the University grant, and, in the following year, with part of the proceeds, Edmund Morris Miller, a graduate of the University of Melbourne, was engaged as lecturer in philosophy and economics. Miller enlarged the curriculum to include economic history and history of economic thought, but he was a philosopher first and economist

149. "The Neglect of Science in School Education in Tasmania," *Quadrilateral*, 1874, pp. 87–89.
150. It is reported that Clark "succeeded in passing the legislation for establishing the University of Tasmania and was its successful defender against moves for its abolition during the depression." John Reynolds, "The Clarks of 'Rosebank,'" *Tasmanian Historical Research Association Papers and Proceedings*, IV (1955), 8. N. E. Lewis has written of Johnston, "As a member of the Council of the University of Tasmania from the time of its establishment, he strongly advocated the scientific side of learning, especially those branches in which he himself took so much delight." *The R. M. Johnston Memorial Volume* (Tasmania, 1921), p. 3.
151. University of Tasmania, *Calendar*, 1896, pp. xiii and 23; 1897, pp. xiv and 22.

by pressure of employment. In 1913 Albert Mansbridge visited Tasmania, and as in Victoria and New South Wales, he aroused immediate enthusiasm for worker education. At Mansbridge's urging, a branch of the Workers' Educational Association was established, and the Tasmanian Parliament provided a special grant for "extra-University tuition in History, Economics, and other subjects." During 1914, Herbert Heaton arrived from Britain as director of tutorial classes and lecturer in economics and history, and Miller became lecturer exclusively in philosophy. Heaton made drastic changes in the syllabus, introducing a new course in economic history, modernizing texts, and requiring work in statistics and public finance.[152] In 1916 economics was inaugurated as a secondary school subject, to be "treated from the historical and descriptive rather than from the purely theoretical point of view."[153] The government grant for extension education was increased successively in 1915, 1917, 1918 and 1919; and Bevil Hugh Molesworth, a graduate of the University of Queensland, was appointed tutorial class lecturer in Northern Tasmania. Meredith Atkinson, from Melbourne University, delivered lectures in smaller Tasmanian towns, and William Judd replaced Molesworth in 1919, by which time forty students were enrolled in economics extension classes. A University Extension Board was founded in 1916 to co-ordinate extra-mural activities, and was replaced by a Committee for Tutorial Classes in 1919.

In 1916 Heaton resigned to join the University of Adelaide, and Douglas Berry Copland from New Zealand was appointed his successor. Almost immediately after arrival, Copland began work on plans to inaugurate a commerce course in Tasmania, and in 1917 a conference on the subject was held with representatives from the Hobart Chamber of Commerce and two accountants' institutes. In 1918 a Commerce School was established, and courses in economics were given a dominant place on the curriculum: all commerce students took classes in economic principles, economic history, and economic geography; if working toward honours they enrolled for "higher economics" and wrote a thesis.

152. *Ibid.*, 1913–14, p. 229; 1915–16, p. 243; 1917–18, p. 257.
153. University of Tasmania, *Manual of the Senior Public Examination*, 1916, p. 27.

In 1920 Copland was relieved of responsibilities in history, and was appointed Professor of Economics. Copland brought improvements in economics in the arts course, parallel to those in commerce.

In 1921 James Bristock Brigden, B.A., Oxford, became university lecturer in history and economics and special lecturer to tutorial classes in the west of Tasmania. In 1924 Brigden was promoted to the economics chair when Copland accepted a post at Melbourne University.[154] In 1927, T. Hytten, a local graduate, was appointed lecturer, and in 1928, upon Brigden's resignation, he was named acting professor.

Economics began at the University of Tasmania as an insignificant arts subject, neglected because of short funds and small staff. Just before and during the World War I, the subject experienced rapid growth because of dual pressures on the University: on one side from advocates of adult education and on the other from businessmen seeking distinction for their occupation and commerce training for their children and potential employees. Under the direction of Heaton, Copland, and Brigden, all of whom went on to distinguished careers from Tasmania, teaching of economics was developed and established firmly. However, the University's continued small size and relative poverty limited diversification of the curriculum and caused outstanding teachers to leave for greener academic pastures.

South Australia

At the inauguaration of Adelaide University in 1876, Sir Anthony Musgrave, one of Australia's most competent and enterprising early economists, was colonial governor and the institution's initial "visitor." The first vice-chancellor, Right Reverend Augustus Short, Bishop of Adelaide, hinted in his opening address that although not a foundation subject, economics might be one

154. Some of Brigden's work in economics is discussed above pp. 36 and 393. He expressed sincere faith in the wisdom of observing carefully economic "principles" and laissez faire in his *Pitt Cobbett Essays and Addresses, Second Series* (Hobart, c. 1927). See also University of Tasmania, *Calendar*, 1920, pp. 223, 228; 1923, pp. 226–27.

of the first fields added to the curriculum as a separate department. He said:

I long to see the day when separate Chairs of Natural Philosophy, Anatomy, Botany, History, Law, and Political Economy, as well as of Practical Engineering, shall be founded; and the youth of South Australia, aspiring to eminence in *all* the various branches of human knowledge, shall be able in their own schools and in this Institution to find a mental training fitting them to take their place side by side with the graduates of other Universities.[155]

Despite these good omens, teaching of political economy received relatively little attention in Adelaide for many years.

In 1878, two years after the University opened, regulations were adopted which stated that candidates for the M.A. degree were "required to show a competent acquaintance with one at least of . . . five branches of knowledge," and the fifth of these was "Metaphysics, Logic, and Political Economy." However, the "competent acquaintance" required could not have been profound, because in 1880 the University library contained only two books on economics, both by John Stuart Mill.[156] In 1882 political economy was listed as the fifth of five subjects for the B.A. degree in which "every candidate shall be required to satisfy the Examiners." Lectures were delivered twice weekly, probably by William Roby Fletcher, Hughes Professor of English Literature in 1882, and after 1883 both Vice Chancellor and all-purpose lecturer capable of doing service in several fields.[157] Fletcher lectured the Adelaide Young Men's Society, of which he was President, in 1878 on the theme "An Evening's instruction and amusement in the study of Political Economy." The account of his talk may give some indication of the quality and tone of the university lectures he delivered a few years later. It was reported in part:

He eloquently urged the study of Political Economy on the grounds of its scientific truthfulness, and on account of its intimate connection with every possible branch of our social organisation. . . .

155. *The Adelaide University Addresses Delivered at the Inauguration* (Adelaide, 1876), pp. 11–12.
156. Adelaide University, *Calendar*, 1879, pp. 41 and 61; and *ibid.*, 1880, p. lxxxvi.
157. *Ibid.*, 1882, pp. 4 and 49. Fletcher was reported to have received his M. A. and a gold medal from London University in 1856.

By means of felicitous expressions, humourous anecdotes, and apt illustrations, he showed the various uses of Political Economy—how it assists in explaining and determining all questions of money and labour, teaches the true relationship subsisting between the employer and employed, and that between the different classes of society. He pointed out how as a science it indicates remedies for social evils, treats of land laws, regulates supply and demand, rent, wages, taxation, and shows to us what we can and what we cannot do under given circumstances. . . .

Mr. Fletcher brought his very interesting, instructive, and amusing lecture to a close by giving some important hints as to the way in which to study the science, and the materials to use.[158]

The first undergraduate economics texts were by Jevons, Fawcett, and Hearn. Examination papers suggest that basic principles were applied in a rudimentary way to colonial conditions and contemporary policy debates, particularly to issues of land tenure and rent; some reference also was made to economic history. For example, an examination question in 1884 asked: "What was Wakefield's theory of colonisation? How has it been confirmed by the history of Western Australia? What is meant by the 'unearned increment' of land? What objections may be urged against its appropriation by the state?"[159] It would be interesting to know what answers were expected for the following three questions in 1887:

III. To what causes do you attribute the present 'Hard Times' in South Australia?
IV. If the South Australian gold fields became richly productive for the next fifty years what would be the economic effect (1) on South Australia, (2) on civilised communities generally?
V. State Adam Smith's canons of taxation, and apply them to the taxation system of South Australia at the present time.[160]

After 1887 political economy disappeared completely into the division of "mental and moral science," at least in part because of financial stringency during depression and the continued small university size. Diversification of the curriculum was impossible

158. *Journal of the Adelaide Young Men's Society*, July 15, 1878, pp. 5–6.
159. Adelaide University, *Calendar*, 1883, pp. 15 and 67; and *ibid.*, 1885, p. xcix. A second examiner with Fletcher was Edward V. Boulger, Hughes Professor of English Language and Literature, and of Mental and Moral Philosophy.
160. *Ibid.*, 1887, p. cxix.

so long as it could be reported, as in 1892, that during the previous year "Five students commenced the course for the B.A. degree, and two completed the first, three the second, and three the third year's course." In 1891 one student only was enrolled for study in mental and moral science.[161]

The first economics text for Australian secondary schools was written in Adelaide by Catherine Helen Spence, a local feminist intellectual,[162] and was published in 1880 at the instance of the South Australian Minister of Education. In the tradition of Harriet Martineau, Miss Spence hoped to instruct her readers as much in social morality as in social science, but her little book, entitled *The Laws We Live Under*, was nevertheless a sensible presentation of basic principles and was at times quite imaginative. When she discussed economic growth, she noted the need for invention to keep pace with accumulation, and she mentioned for illustration the discovery of Ridley's stripper which replaced conventional threshing techniques in South Australia: "no one thing," she explained, "ever did them [the people of South Australia] so much good."[163] She examined the nature of money and "wealth," stressed the importance of frugality, discussed land and commercial policies, and emphasized that public expenditures should be "reproductive." The book received favorable reviews both in the Colonies and in Britain.[164]

All South Australians in the late nineteenth century did not hold Miss Spence's veneration for the teachings of political economy. At the other extreme, a radical land-reformer in 1892 castigated the "Mill-Fawcett school" and concluded in disgust: "Economists of the university-professor type are not quick to admit virtue in any original thinker of the outside world. . . ."[165]

William Mitchell (later Sir William Mitchell) replaced E. V. Boulger in 1894 as Hughes Professor of English Language and Literature, and of Mental and Moral Philosophy. In 1896, Mitchell introduced a new "branch" of the M.A. course entitled

161. *Ibid.*, 1892, p. ccl.
162. See above pp. 110 and 124 for discussion of other writings by Catherine Spence.
163. C. H. Spence, *The Laws We Live Under* (2nd ed.; Adelaide, 1881), p. 26.
164. Appended to later editions was a section of reviews entitled "Opinions of the press."
165. Harry S. Taylor, *Tucker Prize Essay on the Single Tax* (Adelaide, 1892), p. 27.

"Philosophy and Economics," of which one subject was "Principles of Economics." There is no evidence that lectures were delivered, and M.A. students were informed merely that "the Examination will comprise the subjects treated in Mill, but candidates should interview the Professor with reference to a concurrent course of reading."[166] In 1900, under new regulations for the B.A. degree, "Economics" was made a separate subject, distinct for the first time from "Mental and Moral Science;" for honours, a department of "History and Economics" was created. Lectures were offered in alternate years, beginning in 1901, with Marshall's *Economics of Industry* and Mill's *Principles* as texts for "pass" students and special readings for honours from books by Smith, Bastable, and Cunningham. Examination questions indicate that in addition to a knowledge of principles and a little economic history, students were expected to have mastered refutations of such heresies as the single tax, bimetallism, and protection. Thirteen students passed successfully the first examination in 1901.[167]

In 1902-3 a program of "Commercial Education" brought new strength and students to economics. Mitchell continued to give the economics lectures, being listed after 1905 as "Lecturer in Economics and Commercial History" as well as "Professor of English and Philosophy." In 1903 a total of thirty-nine students attended his day and evening classes, including several from the Law Faculty.[168] William Neill joined Mitchell as "Lecturer in Banking and Exchange" in 1906, and gradually the syllabus was expanded. The Joseph Fisher Lectures in Commerce were commenced at that time. In 1909 a two year sequence was introduced, and the *Calendar* announced: "Part I. deals with the Theory of Economic Value and its applications, and Part II with Public Policy and Economic History."[169] Mitchell was anxious that teaching and research in the social sciences be expanded, and he reported with approval to a University Royal Commission in 1911 a recommendation of the Australasian Association for the

166. Adelaide University, *Calendar*, 1896, p. 82.
167. *Ibid.*, 1900, pp. 58–59, 63, and 66; 1901, pp. 68 and 73; 1902, pp. 247–48.
168. *Ibid.*, 1904, pp. 343 and 344.
169. *Ibid.*, 1909, pp. 165.

Advancement of Science that "Social questions . . . be central-
ised in the University so far as their investigation is concerned."[170]
Mitchell's title was changed to "Hughes Professor of Philosophy
and Economics," and in 1913 William Ham was appointed his
assistant lecturer. During 1914, G. V. Portus, a lecturer in history
and English, offered a course in economic history.[171] In 1914
economics became a school subject for the "Senior Commercial
Examination."

No economist at Adelaide University before the Great War
made significant contributions to economic literature. Mitchell
kept abreast of contemporary theoretical developments, no mean
accomplishment considering the required range of his knowledge
in many disciplines, and he contributed articles to the *Hastings'
Encyclopaedia of Religion and Ethics* on "Consumption (Economic)," "Distribution (of income)," and "Production (of
wealth)."[172] He was able also to present a sophisticated summary
of Austrian monetary and interest theory;[173] but this seems to
have been the limit of his enterprise in economics. William Neill
held conservative and unimaginative economic views: he regarded with alarm formation of the Commonwealth Bank and
with horror the possibility of an irredeemable note issue.[174]

Herbert Heaton came to Adelaide from Tasmania in 1917 as
"Lecturer in Economics and Director of Tutorial Classes in connection with the Workers' Educational Association." Mitchell was
relieved of work in economics to devote full time to philosophy
and to his job as Vice Chancellor. Heaton enlarged the Arts
curriculum to include two courses in economics and one in economic history; commerce students followed a special economics

170. "First Progress Report of the Royal Commission on the Adelaide University and Higher Education; together with Minutes of Proceedings, Evidence,
and Appendices," *Proceedings of the Parliament of South Australia*, 1911–12, p.
61. When discussing extension lectures Mitchell said: "As the country centres
have never desired me, I can speak frankly." p. 64.
      171. G. V. Portus, *Happy Highways* (Melbourne, 1953), p. 158; and see
above pp. 559–63.
      172. Edinburgh, 1911 (fourth impression, 1959), IV, 81–83 and 773–75;
and X, 376–78. This reference was obtained from J. A. La Nauze, *op. cit.*, p.
21. Mitchell cited the theoretical work of Marshall and J. B. Clark, and the
statistical analysis of Le Play, Booth, Rowntree, and Engel.
      173. *The Rate of Interest*, (a lecture to the Institute of Accountants in South
Australia, Adelaide, 1909). He argued that in this field "American profundity"
had not been "to much advantage."
      174. William Neill, *The Commonwealth Note Issue* (Lecture Delivered be-
fore the University Society of Commerce, Adelaide, 1911).

syllabus and took an additional course in banking and exchange. A succession of assistant lecturers and tutors provided some assistance for coping with a total of approximately one hundred students in all classes in an average year. A glimpse of Heaton's lectures in economic history may be gained from a short text he published in 1922 under the auspices of the Workers' Educational Association. In the preface he explained:

Until the establishment of the W.E.A. in the Commonwealth, Economics was almost the Cinderella of University studies, but since 1914 the subject has grown rapidly in popularity, both among undergraduates and among that wider public which has been drawn into the University tutorial classes. Experience with both kinds of students in Australia suggests: (1) That the best approach to the study of Economics lies in a historical and descriptive survey of modern economic life and organization; (2) that for Australian students it is better to concentrate on developments since about 1760 than to give much time to the fascinating but (to Australia) scarcely relevant movements of earlier economic history; (3) that the range of treatment should be world-wide, with special reference to Great Britain, Germany, the United States, and Australia, rather than confined to any one country.[175]

In 1924 Heaton and his assistant lecturer, A. L. G. Mackay, reported in the *Economic Journal* on "An Experiment in the Teaching of Economics and Kindred Subjects" carried out at Adelaide in the previous year. Rebelling against the conventional lecture, notetaking, and examination sequence, Heaton and Mackay sought "a method of teaching which will render the student active instead of passive, allow him to study at the pace suitable to his mentality, make him a searcher instead of a scribbler, give him the necessary general guidance and then send him out to study and criticise for himself, and allow for co-operation between the student and his fellows on the one hand and between the student and his teacher on the other."[176] They replaced a lecture

175. H. Heaton, *Modern Economic History with Special Reference to Australia* (Adelaide, 1922), p. vi. Reviews were by L. Knowles, *Economic Journal*, XXXII (1922), 88–89; and by H. E. Egerton, *ibid.*, XXXVI (1926), 267–68.
176. A. L. G. Mackay and H. Heaton, "An Experiment in the Teaching of Economics and Kindred Subjects," *Economic Journal*, XXXIV (1924), 221. They told with concern a story of "an Australian lecturer who noticed that one member of his class was sitting, hands in pockets, while other students were writing hard. 'You don't seem to be taking my lecture down, Mr. Smith.' 'No, sir,' came the reply. 'I have my father's notes here.'"

course in economic history with a series of seminars conducted by the student members and merely observed by the lecturer. Extensive reading and numerous essays were required, and each student's performance was assessed both by the lecturer and by his fellows. Mackay and Heaton found that, although demanding of the student and faculty energies, the experiment was on the whole successful. They concluded:

No claim is made that the teaching plan described above is the only road to the educational Rome. . . . But the results of a year's trial, whether tested in the light of recent educational theory, or by the quality of the students' work and the enthusiastic zeal with which the class attempted herculean tasks, suggest that we are not on a wrong track.[177]

In 1925 Heaton resigned, and economics was taught in subsequent years by junior and temporary faculty members, until in 1929 L. G. Melville, Government Actuary of South Australia and a former lecturer in statistics, was appointed to a new Chair of Economics.

Queensland

Agitation in the last years of the nineteenth century for a university in Queensland culminated in appointment of a Royal Commission which reported thus in 1891:

The general literary and historical cultivation of the highest class to be obtained in a university, including as it must the philosophy of history and government, with constitutional law and political and economic science, is essential in preparing our youth for the higher duties of citizenship in the various minor representative bodies, and in the legislature of the Colony.[178]

The Royal Commission recommended establishment of a university with several faculties, one of which would be designated

177. *Ibid.*, p. 226.
178. "Report with Minutes of Evidence taken before the Royal Commission Appointed to Inquire into the Best Means to be Adopted for the Purpose of Establishing and Maintaining a University in Queensland; together with the Proceedings of the Commission, and Appendices," *Votes and Proceedings of the Legislative Assembly of Queensland*, 1891, p. xix.

"Science" and would have a division of "Economic Science and Sociology." In testimony before the Commission, the headmaster of the Brisbane Grammar School suggested an argument for the teaching of economics which probably lost the proposed university more supporters than it gained. He said: "I think it would be a great thing for the leaders of the working classes if they were within reach of good lectures on political economy; and it would not hurt our capitalists if, in the same way, they were within reach of the best thought on social and economic questions."[179] The editor of the Brisbane *Courier* made an indirect appeal to the business community for funds to sponsor economics, and he explained:

after the establishment of the University I would expect large-hearted men who take an interest in education to dispose of some of their wealth in that way. Take, for instance, a chair of political economy and commercial law. That chair in Edinburgh was endowed by the Merchant Company of Edinburgh; and I do not see why the Chamber of Commerce here, or our leading merchants, should not endow a chair of the same stamp here.[180]

The Commission's report was in vain, and during the depressed and politically turbulent 1890's, no action toward university formation was taken.

Beginning in 1893, extension lectures were offered in Brisbane by Sydney University, largely through the efforts of Professor Walter Scott. Sir Samuel Griffith, president of the lecture series in 1895, explained in his presidential address:

The University Extension movement, as you are aware, was introduced into Queensland two years ago, its objects being . . . to provide, within limits, systematic instruction for students working in association and under competent guidance—to provide, in short, such of the advantages of University training as were capable of being provided in the absence of a University. The movement is entirely voluntary, and has no official recognition from the State, but it is carried on with the cognisance and approval of the University of Sydney.[181]

179. *Ibid.,* p. 2.
180. *Ibid.,* p. 110.
181. Sir S. W. Griffith, *University Extension, Presidential Address, The Appreciation of Gold, Local Council of Education* (reprinted from the Brisbane *Courier* of Friday, 24th May, 1895), p. 1.

Griffith was himself an enthusiastic amateur economist, and he worked to have economics included among the extension lectures. In his address, he outlined his views on the significance of the science, and particularly on the need for inductive study. He announced:

the council hope this year to be able to make arrangements for a course of lectures on political economy. Of course all that can be done in a short course will be to direct attention to some general principles, or to the investigation more in detail of some branch of the science. Political economy ought to be, if it is not, a science based upon careful observation of facts. The phenomena of human society are facts, and they are, all of them, the consequences, and the necessary consequences, of existing and discoverable causes. No doubt the causes are many, and the variety of their action and reaction is so infinite that it appears difficult to discover them. Yet I think it is possible that the difficulty, like many others, may be found to diminish with patient application. And what should be more interesting than a study of these phenomena?[182]

Perhaps as a concession to an anti-theoretical and skeptical audience, Griffith criticized the present state of economics, calling for more application of the true scientific method, and he asked repeatedly for empirical studies to test hypotheses. He said:

Unfortunately, the subject has been so elaborated from a priori theories; and the students of it are expected to accept as axioms or self-evident propositions so many statements which to the ordinary mind are by no means self-evident, that the majority of mankind entertain a profound distaste for it. It may be presumptuous to say so, but I believe that the time has come for the whole matter to be dealt with de novo, by which I do not mean that we are to reject the results, many of them of infinite value, of previous investigators. . . . What I mean is that an effort should be made to disentangle the elementary facts from the overlying strata of comment and controversial inferences, and to build upon the foundations laid bare by the laborious work of others, and with the aid of additional facts yet to be discovered by investigation of phenomena, a simpler superstructure. I entertain the hope that within a measurable time there will be formulated and accepted a science of political economy of which the axioms and fundamental principles will be no more open

182. *Ibid.*, p. 6.

to dispute than the principles accepted by the teachers of medical or astronomical science.[183]

As his own contribution to the introduction of economics to the extension lectures, Griffith concluded his address with a discussion of bimetallism, or "the currency question." Despite his enthusiasm, the extension movement was only a qualified success and produced a mere four formal graduates in fourteen years of operation.[184]

By the time the University of Queensland was founded in 1910, economics was beginning to gain acceptance at other Australian universities. The new institution was modeled in part on an "American scheme" with emphasis on "practical training" rather than on classical or other humanistic studies, and in this framework economics was given a place, but not a large one.[185] A department of History and Economics was formed with E. O. G. Shann, a Melbourne graduate, as lecturer. In the single economics course, Shann lectured on economic history with books by Cunningham and Toynbee as texts; George Elton Mayo from the Philosophy Department taught economic theory, or as it was labeled "systematic economics," using works by Marshall (*Economics of Industry*), Barker, Hobson, and Sykes.[186] Only three students are listed as having passed successfully the economics examination in 1912. In 1913, A. C. V. Melbourne replaced Shann, who moved to the University of Western Australia. Henry Alcock succeeded Melbourne in 1914 and was able in 1915 to take over "systematic economics" from Mayo when B. H. Molesworth was appointed assistant lecturer in history and economics.[187]

The University Senate in 1915, influenced by the newly formed

183. *Ibid.*, p. 6.
184. Harrison Bryan, "The Establishment of the University of Queensland," *Historical Society of Queensland Journal*, IV (1948–52), 650.
185. For a discussion of the "practical" orientation of the University of Queensland in its early years, see *ibid.*, pp. 639–61.
186. University of Queensland, *Calendar*, 1913, pp. 101–2; and *The University of Queensland, 1910–1922* (Brisbane, n. d.), pp. 30–31
187. Molesworth received the first M. A. degree in history and economics from the University of Queensland. A contraction of his thesis was published as "Kanaka Labour in Queensland (1863–1871)," *Historical Society of Queensland Journal*, IV (1914–19), 140–54.

The Science of Enquiry

Workers' Educational Association, provided funds for additional economics teaching, and in 1916, A. C. V. Melbourne, invalided from the army, returned as Assistant Lecturer in History and Industrial History. T. C. Witherby, an Oxford graduate, was made Temporary Lecturer in Social Economics, and with Melbourne, devoted half his time to worker tutorial classes. In the postwar years, special short courses in economics were offered both to workers and to students in engineering and applied sciences.[188]

As early as 1911, the University Senate made preliminary plans for a faculty of commerce, and a "senior commercial" school examination was set to determine admittance (for which there were no candidates). However, no further action was taken.[189] In 1915, 1916, 1919, and 1921, the proposal for a commerce faculty was discussed again.[190] In 1922 lectures leading to a commerce certificate within the Arts faculty were introduced, and in 1923 provision was made for a diploma in commerce. As part of the commerce development, Alcock was appointed McCaughey Professor of History and Economics in 1922, and John L. K. Gifford became lecturer in 1923. As the demands of commerce were added to those of the W.E.A., economics was extended into a second year course, although it remained somewhat historical in character. An honours school of economics was established in 1925, and a faculty of commerce in 1926.[191] Economics entered the secondary school curriculum in 1925 with two courses which included, in addition to elementary principles and a little economic history, the recommendation that: "Candidates, especially those seeking Scholarships, should be shown over a dairy or mixed farm, a factory (of any kind), a retail store, and a railway goods-

188. University of Queensland, *Calendar*, various years; and *The University of Queensland, 1910–1935* (n. p., 1935), pp. 31–32.
189. Queensland, *Manual of Public Examination*, 1910.
190. *The University of Queensland, 1910–1935*, p. 46.
191. Texts by Irving Fisher and Charles Gide replaced *Economics of Industry* by Marshall in 1920. In "Economics, Part II," which began in 1924, texts were by Taussig, Bowley, Edie, Spalding, and Sykes. Students performed "Practical Economic Investigations" and took part in "Tutorially conducted visits to Commercial and Industrial Establishments." University of Queensland, *Calendar*, 1924, pp. 123–24.

yard, and have the organisation of these explained in general terms."[192]

As in other Australian universities, economics teaching in Queensland was initially an undernourished outgrowth of history and philosophy, favored by only a few persons with missionary zeal. It gained strength about the time of World War I as a result of new enthusiasm both for adult education and for commercial training. New lecturers were engaged and new courses were added for classes in business and for worker tutorial groups. By the beginning of the Great Depression, economics at Queensland had only begun to emerge from this service role and to take its place as a respected social science in its own right.

Western Australia

An account of economics in the early years of the University of Western Australia is almost entirely the story of one man, Edward Owen Giblin Shann.[193] Appointed from the University of Queensland in 1913 as the foundation professor of history and economics, Shann was alone in economics through most of the period under examination. He began by offering two courses, and he announced: "The first will include a description of the industrial system and an introduction to the theory of value. The second will approach the problems of modern capitalism by way of the history of the industrial revolution."[194] In the first course, he used texts by Chapman, Marshall (*Economics of Industry*), and Gide, and in the second books by Warner, Price, and Toynbee. Extra readings were required for honours. Eight students passed successfully the first course in 1914. In 1920 a "third course" was added covering "recent developments, such as trusts and combines and modern credit systems."[195] An examination in

192. Queensland, *Manual of Public Examination*, 1923–24, p. 51.
193. Obituaries of Shann are: "Professor E. O. G. Shann: an Appreciation," *Economic Record*, XI (1935), 80–83; and D. B. Copland, "Edward Shann," *Economic Journal*, XLV (1935), 599–601.
194. University of Western Australia, *Calendar*, 1915, p. 114.
195. *Ibid.*, 1922, p. 148. Twenty-four students passed the examination in first-year economics, but only three in each of the second and third year courses.

"Industrial History" was required for the school commercial leaving certificate in 1917, and a school economics course was introduced in 1926.[196]

A succession of lecturers assisted Shann in history, beginning with W. K. Hancock in 1921; but not until 1926 was A. J. Reid, a "Correspondence tutor," appointed to aid in economics.[197] By 1929 the three original courses remained intact, with an average enrollment still falling from thirty-five in Economics A to about three in Economics C. It is remarkable that, despite his heavy load, Shann was able during this period to establish firmly his reputation as a scholar. His *Economic History of Australia,* published in 1930, remains a classic in the field, and a collection of essays written in the 1920's indicates his wide interests in many areas of economics.[198] He carried out notable pioneer studies in the agricultural history of Western Australia.[199]

Conclusion

The character of economics teaching in the early years of Australian universities was determined by circumstances. Financial and academic resources were scarce, and few faculty members could be left with responsibility for teaching in one field alone. Throughout the nineteenth century, and later, the subject received part-time attention at best. Teachers of political economy were at the same time historians, lawyers, philosophers, linguists, theologians, mathematicians, or even university administrators;

196. *Manuals of Public Examinations held by the University of Western Australia,* 1917 and 1925, p. 63.

197. Professor Hancock has described Shann's contribution to the University of Western Australia thus: "From the year of its foundation he had belonged to its exiguous professoriate and he took more than one man's share in establishing its organization and fostering its growth. He was professor both of History and Economics and lectured systematically over a wide range in both subjects, without any help at all until I came to join him. I gave him all the help I could—it was little enough but it meant something to a man who had been quite alone in his professional life." *Country and Calling* (London, 1954), pp. 76-77.

198. *Bond or Free? Occasional Economic Essays* (Sydney, 1930).

199. E. O. G. Shann, "Group Settlement of Migrants in Western Australia," *Economic Record,* I (1925), 73-93; "The Western Australian Sinking Fund," *ibid.,* p. 156 f.; and *Cattle Chosen* (London, 1926).

in some instances they were competent and enthusiastic amateurs, but they seldom had special training or interest in the subject. In several institutions informality of instruction in economics had good results. The impact of Hearn, Shann, Heaton, Moore, Anderson, Mitchell, and Scott was increased by their association with other disciplines. In general, however, multiple responsibilities did not lead to strength. Many university teachers, when faced with the need to maintain fundamental allegiance to only one field, chose to abandon economics. So long as financial stringency prevented academic specialization, the gamble on maintaining high quality teaching in any one area was great. Almost all universities examined in this chapter experienced periods of stagnation in economics attributable largely to inertia of the single person responsible for the subject. The marvel may be that under these conditions any distinguished contributions at all were forthcoming.

Economics, like the other social sciences, met substantial resistance both within and without Australian universities. With few exceptions faculty members in the disciplines of longer tradition and standing were unwilling to encourage a subject which they viewed skeptically as a component of a liberal education and jealously as a potentially "popular" rival. The universities depended heavily upon public support for their operations, and governments regarded political economy as neither vital to the inculcation of culture nor particularly important to national development through the production of trained personnel. Professor Hancock remarked as late as 1929:

Since the State has insisted on tackling the most formidable of Australia's problems, one would have imagined that it would have eagerly sought after the most promising Australian brains. Since its activities have been so extensively economic, one would have expected it to search for administrators capable of unravelling economic causes and imagining economic effects. But the Australians have always assumed that economic problems are simple, and have resented those classifications and rewards which suggest that some men have a higher class of intelligence than that of the majority.[200]

200. *Australia* (New York, 1930), p. 141.

Widespread opposititon to economics among politicians was a result in part of partisan activity by early economists, both locally and in Britain, but in part also of misunderstanding as to the distinction between scientific economic enquiry and doctrinaire advocacy of certain policy dictates. Observers with widely different backgrounds could agree that serious perils lay in the teaching of economics: conservatives saw development of the discipline as an important step on the road to socialism, while radicals anticipated dissemination of propaganda to discourage labor unrest.[201] Both extremes of misunderstanding injured the reputation of the subject. Basic misconceptions as to the meaning and purpose of economic science prevailed throughout the nineteenth century, strengthened by aggressive protagonists who took the subject's name in vain with regularity. The renaissance in economics which began in Britain and the United States in the 1890's and was characterized by the endeavors of Alfred Marshall, J. B. Clark, and others had little immediate impact on Australia. It took nearly a generation for revolutionary changes in attitudes and techniques to reach the antipodes.

A distinctive feature of the development of economics in Australian universities was the vital role played by bodies outside the institutions themselves. With the exception of a few heretics such as Francis Anderson at Sydney and Harrison Moore at Melbourne, the universities remained bastions of conservative opinion, opposing tenaciously innovations in curriculum. As early as the 1850's, demands for liberalization of the entrance requirements and syllabus of Sydney University were voiced by such spokesmen for the working classes as Henry Parkes. Later in the century, professional groups, led by the bankers, appealed for extra-mural teaching of the subject. Municipal chambers of commerce voiced repeated demands for business training which would include an economics component. Efforts of the Workers' Educational Association in the years around World War I were decisive in leading to provision of teaching in the social sciences. Mounting pressure from many sides finally became unbearable after intervention by the disciples of Mansbridge, and during the

201. See above pp. 358–59.

1920's economics was given rapid encouragement and strength. The subject quickly found its own powerful champions in such men as Copland, Giblin, and Mills, but through the early period the W.E.A. remained active, encouraging the employment of new staff, organizing extra-mural tutorial classes, and publishing the first series of monographs dealing with the local economy.

By the beginning of the Great Depression, academic economists were taking respected places in their own universities, in the community, and as advisors to government.[202] Through the revitalized Economics Section of the Australasian Association for the Advancement of Science and a new Economic Society, they began to meet together and to publish their own journal.[203] The final birth of academic economics in Australia was protracted and painful, but was also well attended and successful.[204]

202. One of the earliest government inquiries in which academic economists played important parts was the Royal Commission on Taxation in the early 1920's. See "First Report of the Royal Commission on Taxation; together with Appendices," *Papers Presented to the Parliament of the Commonwealth of Australia*, 1920–21; "Second Report," and "Third Report," *ibid.*, 1922; and "Fourth Report," and "Fifth and Final Report," *ibid.*, 1923–24.

203. See below pp. 633–39, and L. F. Giblin, "The Record and Its Editors (1925–46)," *Economic Record*, XXIII (1947), 1–4; and Herbert Heaton, "Progress and Problems of Australian Economics," *American Economic Review*, XVI (1926), 235–48.

204. A description by Professor Wilfred Prest of current "Teaching Economics in Australian Universities" is in *Economic Record*, XXXVI (1960), 131–38.

16

Growth of a Discipline

In this chapter the gradual development of an economic discipline is traced, in part by a survey of the analysis used in the policy debates described in earlier chapters, and in part by an account of the growth of recognition of economics as a legitimate science in discussion, publications, learned societies, and elsewhere.

Colonial Infancy

During the first half of the nineteenth century, mention of "political economy" in the colonies consisted mainly of veneration for principles developed in the home country. W. C. Wentworth began the earliest major work of an economic character with a characteristic humble apology. He said:

For troubling . . . the public with a repetition of principles, of which the truth is so generally known and acknowledged, the only plea he can urge in his justification is a hope that the reiteration of them will not be deemed unnecessary and obtrusive, so long as their application is incomplete; so long as vice and misery prevail in any part of the world, from the want of their adoption and enforcement.[1]

In general, early colonial writers on economic topics treated "the true principles of political economy" respectfully and as a code of morality which could be transgressed only with peril of committing grievous sin. To these missionaries of the economic gospel,

1. W. C. Wentworth, A Statistical, Historical, and Political Description of the Colony of New South Wales, and its Dependent Settlements in Van Diemen's Land (London, 1819), p. xi. The book was given moderate praise in Edinburgh Review, July, 1819, pp. 28–48.

Adam Smith was Messiah, and Ricardo, James Mill, and McCulloch were disciples.[2]

One exception, Andrew Bent in Hobart, rejected excessive dependence on *ex cathedra* doctrine, and emphasized the "Scientific" character of political economy as distinct from the policy implications of particular conclusions. He said: "Political economy, then, we understand to be the science which teaches how to increase the wealth of nations—the most *advantageous* application of national resources, and the true bearings of the balance of power. On the other hand, moral economy teaches these laws and principles, by which popular morality and religion may be best acquired."[3] Unfortunately, Bent was not representative of contemporary writers.

"Principles" of political economy were publicized widely beginning in the 1830's from the pulpit, on the hustings, in pamphlets and the press, and before gatherings of workers. As the likelihood increased of the colonies achieving some measure of legislative autonomy and democratic suffrage, a need was recognized for widespread familiarity with economic doctrine to preserve voters from the paths of error. Clergymen were leaders among the propagandists. Reverend John Dunmore Lang and Reverend Henry Carmichael were particularly well read in the field, and made regular contributions to mechanics' institutes and other worker associations.[4] Archibald Michie described in 1844 some of the difficulties experienced by early lecturers in an account of an address delivered on the topic "political economy." He recounted:

I had gone carefully over its elementary principles, illustrating them here and there by reference to colonial circumstances; being the utmost extent to which a lecturer can venture to proceed with so

2. W. C. Wentworth, *op. cit.*, pp. 404–6; *Murray's Austral-Asiatic Review*, I (Hobart Town, 1828), 23–24; *Van Diemen's Land Monthly Magazine*, III (1835), 145–46.
3. "The Custom's Duties," *Colonial Advocate, and Tasmanian Monthly Review and Register*, April 1, 1828, p. 91; also "The Banking System," *ibid.*, p. 53, and "Colonial Policy," *ibid.*, May 1, 1828, pp. 113–17.
4. See above pp. 545–46, and A. C. Child, "Studies in the Life and Work of John Dunmore Lang," *Royal Australian Historical Society Journal and Proceedings*, XXII (1936), 69–90, 208–28, and 298–311; and George Nadel, *Australia's Colonial Culture* (Melbourne, 1957), pp. 36–37 and 113–14.

The Science of Enquiry

abstruse a science, unless he can behold with indifference the most interesting portion of his audience in a state of comfortable and profound repose, and can hear without discomfort or dismay the creaking of numerous pairs of Wellington boots, as, with their owners, they disappear from the lecture room. True, these little annoyances, which time out of mind have been incidental to what are commonly called dry lectures, I might have avoided, by diluting a few drops of Political Economy, in a large quantity of obvious and superficial illustration,— a course, however, which notwithstanding its success with an audience in keeping them attentive, and winning a few laughs, is almost as painful as indifference to the true lover of a science, who, on such occasions is apt to be afflicted with an uncomfortable sensation, that his subject is degraded, whilst he is applauded.[5]

Colonial libraries were well stocked with classics of political economy. In 1834, after only eight years of operation, the Australian Subscription Library in Sydney contained works by Bentham, Chalmers, Child, Colquhoun, Ganilh, Malthus, Mandeville, McCulloch, Mill, Ricardo, Say, and of course Smith.[6] By 1839 a special section on "Political Economy and Commerce" had been formed with seventy-five items.[7] The Library of the Legislative Council of New South Wales was equally well furnished, boasting even a complete run of the *Journal of the London Statistical Society* and the *Wealth of Nations* in several editions.[8] Mechanics' institutes, which began to flourish in the 1840's, stocked the accepted classics of political economy hoping presumably to keep members from being captivated by false doctrine.[9] Contemporary auction catalogues of private library sales indicate that almost any collection of reasonable size contained works by Malthus, McCulloch, James Mill, and Smith.[10] An indication of the extent of popular interest is given by a remark of John Dunmore Lang in the auction catalogue of his own library in 1846; he noted

5. Sydney *Morning Herald*, June 4, 1844.
6. *Catalogue of the Australian Subscription Library* (Sydney, 1834).
7. *An Arranged Catalogue of the Books in the Australian Subscription Library and Reading Rooms* (Sydney, 1839). Regular additions were made to the section; *Second Addenda to the Arranged Catalogue of the Books in the Australian Subscription Library* (Sydney, 1841).
8. *Index to the Legislative Council Library, 12 May, 1849* (Sydney, 1849).
9. *Annual Report for 1844 from the Committee of Management of the Melbourne Mechanics' Institution and School of Arts* (Melbourne, 1845), p. 18; and "Sydney Mechanics School of Arts," *Empire*, October 4, 1851.
10. Auction catalogues have been preserved in the Mitchell Library, Sydney.

that his best copy of the *Wealth of Nations* "wants the first vol., which has either been stolen or taken without leave." Domestic sales apparently warranted at least local reprints of J. R. Mc-Culloch's *A Discourse on the Science of Political Economy* in pamphlet form,[11] and of Bastiat's "Petition of the Tallow and Wax-Chandlers" in a Melbourne periodical.[12]

Pronouncements by economists were used extensively for the first time as instruments of violent controversy during the depression of the 1840's. During this period, political economy became identified clearly as a powerful weapon in the arsenal of conservatives. Proposed radical reforms such as a high price for land and a usury law were categorized by critics as "in utter defiance of the principles of political economy," and several periodicals including the Sydney *Morning Herald*, Launceston *Examiner*, and Robert Lowe's *Atlas*, came to judge a variety of issues strictly according to conformity with economists' dicta.[13] The Sydney *Weekly Register*, for example, intoned reverently the pronouncements of economic "theorists," and in particular words of McCulloch, Steuart, Whately, Ricardo, Smith ("thus far the greatest writer on political economy that ever lived"), and James Mill ("one of the most perspicuous of modern writers upon the subject"). When in comment upon a suggested usury law, the *Weekly Register* found it necessary to disagree with the apparent views of Smith, readers were assured that "This part of Smith's work, which certainly carries the feelings of the reader along with the author, is most successfully answered by Bentham, in the celebrated tract to which the world is indebted for correct ideas upon this subject."[14] The *New South Wales Magazine*, when

11. Sydney, 1842.
12. *Australasian*, I (1850-51), 476–78.
13. Michael Roe, *Society and Thought in Eastern Australia, 1835–1851*, pp. 56–61, 74, 129–32, and 494; C. M. H. Clark, *Select Documents in Australian History 1788–1850* (Sydney, 1950), p. 260; "Past, Present, and Future Position of Tasmania," *South Briton; or, Tasmanian Literary Journal*, I (1843), 75; "The Usury Bill," *New South Wales Magazine*, 1843, pp. 549–52. In 1876, long after his return to Britain from the colonies, Lowe obtained a place in the history of economics by declaring publicly that political economy was "a completed science" and stimulating thereby an important reaction by Cliffe Leslie and Jevons. *Economic Journal*, II (1892), 573–75.
14. "Another Usury Bill," *Weekly Register of Politics, Facts, and General Literature*, III (1844), 115; and also "Regulations for the Disposal of Land Laws in British North America," reprinted from McCulloch's *Dictionary of*

giving advice to authors, advised colonial political economists to keep didactic purpose always in mind and to make their style "as homely and Cobbettish as a writer of education can make it."[15]

Before the advent of responsible government, writers in the colonies lacked the facilities, the time, and the occasion for independent and imaginative economic enquiry. Libraries were provided with writings on political economy from Great Britain, but these works contained little theory that was applicable directly to the domestic environment and almost no collections of relevant empirical data. During the early years, Australians knew that major economic decisions would be made "at home," and that long-delayed critical comment from the other side of the world would have little impact on the outcome. Awareness of policy impotence had a decided dampening effect on creative effort. In their own primitive circumstances, colonists found a high premium placed on positive action over mere thought. The local press afforded one avenue for expression, but newspapers depended heavily on sales for existence and could not encourage seemingly esoteric scientific contributions for their own sake. The Legislative Council and adult-education oriented workers' associations provided some opportunity for discussion, but seldom with an atmosphere that was conducive to productive debate. A work entitled *The Political Economy of New South Wales* by N. L. Kentish gave promise in 1838 of becoming the exception to the rule; but the book belied its title and consisted mainly of random comment and description.[16] In 1829, Edward Gibbon Wakefield prescribed from London "one good Political Economist at each settlement," but only, he added, "to prevent us from devising an Australasian Tariff."[17] Wakefield's prescription was not filled, and the main impression made by the Australian colonies upon economic science before 1850 was as a subject for occasional notice

---

Commerce, ibid., 290–91; "The Political Register: The District Corporations," *ibid.*, II (1844), 383–84; and "The Prorogation—Defeat of the Proposed Bread Tax—Retrospect," *ibid.*, I (1843), 345–46.

15. "Mr. Patrick Grant's Pamphlet on an Inquiry into the Causes of the Present Monetary Depression of the Colony of New South Wales, with the Suggestion of a Remedy," *New South Wales Magazine*, 1843, p. 399.

16. N. L. Kentish, *The Political Economy of New South Wales* (Sydney, 1838).

17. Edward Gibbon Wakefield, *A Letter from Sydney the Principal Town of Australasia* (Everyman's Library, London, 1929), p. 85.

by such authorities as Jeremy Bentham, Harriet Martineau, and John Stuart Mill.[18]

Stimulus of Gold

During and immediately following the gold rushes of the 1850's, demands upon colonial governments mounted rapidly for ambitious action in a variety of fields. Special problems of currency and banking, land disposal, transport, and immigration called for swift decisions by the new legislatures and executives. Opponents of an active role for the state found some of their strongest critical arguments in the writings of classical economists, and during the 1850's and 1860's, political economy became identified firmly with advocacy of laissez faire.

Statements of economic principles in crude propaganda form appeared with increasing frequency in the press, in pamphlets, in the statements of politicians, and particularly in lectures to groups of workers.[19] As in the 1840's, the general theme of these presentations was that maximum national production and equitable income distribution could be achieved only in a situation where "the great law of supply and demand" was observed, or, in other words, where government was least in evidence. British and French classical economists were cited most often, particu-

18. F. L. W. Wood, "Jeremy Bentham versus New South Wales," *Royal Australian Historical Society Journal and Proceedings*, XIX, 329–51; Harriet Martineau, *Illustrations of Political Economy: No. X. Homes Abroad. A Tale* (London, 1832); and Hugh S. R. Elliot, *The Letters of John Stuart Mill* (London, 1910), I, 19, 188, and 208; II, 27, 58, 66, 116, 149, 154, 200, and 298.

19. The following lectures all contained policy-oriented expositions of economic principles: W. G. Pennington, "Literature of Working Men," *The Operative: A Journal of Progress in the Interest of the Working Classes*, October 14, 1854 (substance of a lecture to the School of Arts); J. Aikenhead, *Principles of Political Economy* (Tasmania, 1856, three lectures to the Launceston Mechanics' Institute "some years" before); Archibald Michie, *Victoria Suffering a Recovery: a Lecture* (Melbourne, 1860); Colin Campbell, *The Land Question: a Lecture Delivered at the Ararat Mechanics' Institute* (Ararat, 1861); G. K. Holden, *An Enquiry into the New Relations between Labour and Capital induced by Co-operative Societies, Labour Partnerships, and Other Forms of Productive Industry in Which Labour is Employed on a Footing More Independent than Common Hire, with Some Reference to Special Features of Colonial Industry* (Sydney, 1867, substance of a lecture delivered to the Sydney Mechanics' School of Arts); see also, D. C. Griffiths, ed., *Documents on the Establishment of Education in New South Wales 1789–1880* (Melbourne, 1957), p. 202, and George Nadel, *op. cit.*, pp. 137 and 150–51.

larly Smith, the two Mills, McCulloch, Quesnay, Say, and Bastiat.[20] An influx of American immigrants accounts for increased reference also to Carey, Hamilton, and Webster. Interpretation of political economy retained a distinct class bias, and writers usually stressed the admonition that no special assistance be rendered the needy or unfortunate, and that all schemes of social amelioration be avoided which would disturb existing income distribution. In justifying a restatement of basic economic principles in 1866, F. A. Bell complained: "Still there is here a great variety of crude and dangerous nostrums permeating society, notwithstanding all that has been written by Smith, Ricardo, McCulloch, Mill, and others; also notwithstanding the continuous attention which has been given to the subject by the most eminent statesmen of the last forty years."[21] Colonial writers on occasion contradicted a recognized old-country economist when a policy recommendation seemed undesirable locally; for intimating that worker organization might under certain conditions be warranted, parts of a book by J. R. McCulloch were labeled in 1854 either "irrelevant or erroneous."[22]

A few early spokesmen for the working class were able to employ political economy for their own ends; in particular, assisted immigration was categorized as "in direct contravention to the law of supply and demand."[23] Generally, however, economic laws were embraced most enthusiastically by owners of property as

20. Publications illustrating heavy dependence on economic authority were: "State Interference," *Melbourne Monthly Magazine of Original Colonial Literature*, I (1855), 76–83; H. L. Lindsay, *The Industrial Resources of Victoria* (Melbourne, 1856); *Our Financial System* (Melbourne, 1858); Edward R. Drury, "Essay on Currency and Banking in New South Wales," *Sydney Magazine of Science and Art*, II (1859), 96–104; J. L. Montefiore, *A Catechism of the Rudiments of Political Economy* (Sydney, 1861); Samuel Davenport, *Some New Industries for South Australia* (Adelaide, 1864); H. J. Wrixon, "The Condition and Prospects of Australia as Compared with Older Lands," in *Four Lectures Published by Direction of the Committee of the Early Closing Association* (Melbourne, 1869); and the numerous tracts issued by the Free Trade and Financial Reform League of Victoria.

21. Frederick A. Bell, *Industry and Commerce Relieved and Increased by Means of Free Trade and Direct Taxation* (Sydney, 1866), p. 39.

22. "Review of *A Treatise on the Circumstances which Determine the Rate of Wages and the Condition of the Labouring Classes*, by J. R. McCulloch," *Tasmanian Athenaeum; or Journal of Science, Literature, and Art*, I (1853–54), 177–81.

23. C. M. H. Clark, *Select Documents in Australian History 1851–1900* (Sydney, 1955), p. 250. Also see *Empire*, I (1851), No. 85, p. 350; No. 190, pp. 78–79; No. 228, p. 230; and *Empire*, June 24, 1852, p. 1126.

affording justification for their success in the competitive struggle. One Melbourne journalist even suggested to employers in the 1850's that an important advantage of shorter working hours might be widespread familiarity among the "working classes" with "true political economy" and a consequent reduction in unrest. "If acquaintance with the best of systems of political economy be essential to the well-being of a state, it follows that each member of the state should become a political economist."[24]

As early as 1831, the eccentric Scandinavian wanderer Jorgen Jorgenson, writing in Hobart, complained that political economy contained a distinct class bias. He charged:

A set of men have started up within latter days, pampering to the avarice of the rich, and introducing "mystery" . . . under the name of science—that of political economy. But what have these writers done for the world? They know that their expensive works are only within the reach of the more opulent; and therefore their doctrines are so framed as to administer to the passions of the wealthy orders.[25]

After discovery of gold, Jorgenson's conclusion was reaffirmed by later reformers, particularly by advocates of a protective tariff designed to create work for the unemployed. In 1860, James Norton identified as the principal opponents of colonial progress "merchant princes" and "would-be political economists."[26] John Dunmore Lang felt called upon even to deplore excessive consideration of economic criteria when framing all aspects of colonial policy. He warned: "Certain it is, that the man who devotes all his energies to the mere concerns of buying and selling will at length come to estimate everything, not according to what it is really worth, but only according to what it will *bring*."[27]

Genuine enquiry into economic problems, in addition to mere parroting of accepted principles, was given impetus by the discovery of gold. Observers in Britain of colonial conditions were

24. J. A. Aldwell, *Eight Hours and Early Closing Questions* (Melbourne, n. d.), pp. 9–10.
25. Jorgen Jorgenson, *Observations on the Funded System* (Hobart Town, 1831), p. vii.
26. James Norton, *The Condition of the Colony of New South Wales* (Sydney, 1860), p. 7; and James Martin, *Speech Delivered in the Legislative Council on Tuesday, the 2nd Day of July, 1850* (Sydney, 1850), pp. 5–6.
27. *An Historical and Statistical Account of New South Wales* (London, 1875), I, 50–51.

quick to detect opportunities for productive investigation and may have helped inspire some of the earliest local studies. One anonymous writer in London remarked in 1853: "There are lessons worth deducing from these changes which are inevitably associated with new settlements; and it may be that we can observe the working of principles both in trade and politics with greater accuracy when applied to small and rising communities than in old and settled countries."[28] Vigorous discussions of pressing policy questions have been described in earlier chapters, and from these it can be seen that disputants often considered such issues as tariffs, banking reform, or transport development largely in terms of conformity with accepted economic doctrine.[29] The distant dream of inter-colonial federation was examined as early as 1870 for its economic implications, which were found to include a widening of competitive markets, economies of scale, greater ease in attracting capital and immigrants, and even development of "that public spirit by whose inspiration dangers are willingly faced and privations cheerfully borne in the sacred name of country."[30] The colonial legislatures contained an impressive proportion of university graduates, ten in the first Victorian Assembly alone. Together with a few pioneer civil servants, educated legislators helped spread the gospel of economic science,[31] and in particular they encouraged regular acquisition of works in political economy for private and public libraries.[32]

28. *South Australia and the Gold Discoveries* (London, 1853), p. 6; and also Robert Torrens, *Political Economy and Representative Government in Australia* (London, 1855), p. 49.

29. See above Chapters 1–12, and particularly James Thomson, ed., *The Financial Statements of the Colonial Treasurers of New South Wales* (Sydney, 1881), *passim*; and Henry Parkes' monumental "Report from the Select Committee on the Condition of the Working Classes of the Metropolis," *Votes and Proceedings of the Legislative Assembly of New South Wales*, 1859–60.

30. "First Report of the Royal Commission Appointed by His Excellency the Governor to Consider and Report upon the Necessity of a Federal Union of the Australian Colonies for Legislative Purposes and the Best Means of Accomplishing such a Union," *Papers Presented to Both Houses of the Parliament of Victoria*, 1870 (Second Session), p. 5.

31. Joy E. Mills, "The Composition of the Victorian Parliament, 1856-1881," *Historical Studies Australia and New Zealand*, II (1942–43), 32; and e.g. Christopher Rolleston, "The Science of Statistics," *Sydney Magazine of Science and Art*, I (1858), 254–58.

32. The following three reports all indicate considerable holdings of writings in economics by legislative libraries: "Report from the Select Committee of the Legislative Council on the Library," *Votes and Proceedings of the Legislative*

During the 1850's and 1860's, papers on economic topics made their first appearance in the proceedings of newly formed "literary" and other semi-learned societies. In 1856, Governor Sir William Denison succeeded in founding at Sydney a "Philosophical Society of New South Wales," the journal of which, the *Sydney Magazine of Science and Art*, contained some of the first significant discussions of banking, railways, and statistics.[33] In 1860 the Royal Society of Victoria prepared an inventory of "The Resources of the Colony," and the Royal Society of New South Wales welcomed its first contribution on "Social Science" in 1868.[34] The Eclectic Association of Melbourne, with Henry Gyles Turner President and Henry Keylock Rusden Secretary, reported that during the session 1869–70 "seven of the twelve debates during the year were on social or politico-economic subjects."[35] An abortive attempt was made at Melbourne in 1866 to establish a journal which, among other things, would have covered "the advance of Social Science generally" with assistance from W. H. Archer, James Smith, and W. E. Hearn.[36]

Confusion of Theory with Policy

During the 1870's and 1880's, political economy became associated closely and firmly in the public mind with doctrinaire positions in several acrimonious policy debates. Economics as a science of enquiry was concealed behind a disguise as a specific code of ethics. Library holdings in economics continued to grow,

Council of Victoria, 1855–56 (it was reported that *two* copies of Ricardo's *Principles of Political Economy and Taxation* had been stolen during the year); "Library of the Legislature," *Proceedings of the Parliament of South Australia*, 1857–58, 1860, and 1862; and "Report of Commissioners on the Parliamentary Library," *Journals of the House of Assembly of Tasmania*, 1869. See also George Nadel, *Australia's Colonial Culture*, p. 89.

33. See above chaps. v, viii, and xiii and Sir William Denison, *Varieties of Vice-Regal Life* (London, 1870), I, 354.

34. *Report on the Resources of the Colony of Victoria* (Melbourne, 1860); and Alfred Roberts, "On Pauperism in New South Wales," *Transactions of the Royal Society of New South Wales*, II (1868), 107–20.

35. *Eclectic Association of Melbourne, President's Address*, 1869–70 (Melbourne, n. d.), p. 5.

36. *Australasian Monthly Review*, I (1866), inside cover. Apparently the periodical collapsed after two issues.

and current and classic works were available in local bookstores.[37] But with the exception of a few part-time university teachers, practitioners of the discipline remained amateurs, and, in the prevailing atmosphere of bitter political conflict, they were unwilling or unable to guard the disinterested character and integrity of the subject.

In some areas of controversy, more than in others, identification of economics with policy dictates was particularly clear. With the exception of a few heretics, most of those who considered themselves versed in political economy favored unqualified international free trade. Tariff opponents deplored somewhat smugly lack of attention by politicians to the literature of political economy; J. Reid complained in 1887: "The men of action will not study, and the students cannot act. Those in whose hands all the real power is placed, abhor the labour of toilsomely collating the teachings of the men of books. It pays better to disclaim than to study."[38] Free-traders even blamed some writers on political economy themselves for failing to make their productions sufficiently appealing to the working man; Edward Pratt wrote in 1882: "If political economy ceased to be an esoteric study, we might hope that these false and disastrous theories would find arrayed against them much of the now dormant common sense of civilized nations."[39] C. M. Smith gave thanks on behalf of free-traders at least for those "readable and attractive" writers Fawcett and Bastiat. He said:

37. The South Australian Institute in 1873, having absorbed the South Australian Library and South Australian Mechanics' Institute, contained 199 volumes listed as "Class AA. Jurisprudence, Political Economy, Commerce &c." An investigating commission, headed by R. D. Hanson, one of the authors of the Durham *Report*, condemned these holdings as "too light." "Report of Commission Appointed to Inquire into the Whole Question of the New Institute and Museum; together with Minutes of Evidence and Appendix," *Proceedings of the Parliament of South Australia*, 1874. The Library of the Parliament of Queensland contained fifty-five works on "political economy" in 1883. D. O'Donovan, *Analytical and Classified Catalogue of the Library of the Parliament of Queensland* (Brisbane, 1883), p. 299. By 1899 this Library contained over 150 works on "Political Economy." Denis O'Donovan, *Analytical and Classified Catalogue of the Library of the Parliament of Queensland* (Brisbane, 1899), II, 166–69. The Geo. Robertson bookstore in Sydney advertised works on economics in the *Australian Economist*, commencing in 1888. The first advertisement listed works by Smith, Bastiat, Mill, George, McCulloch, Elder, Sidgwick, Rogers, Walker, and Macleod. I (1888–90), 72.
38. J. Reid, "Agricultural Protection," *Sydney Quarterly Magazine*, 1887, p. 66.
39. Edward Pratt, "The Balance of Trade," *Melbourne Review*, VII (1882), 379.

To some extent I blame the earlier English School of political economists for rendering their science an unattractive one. No one doubts
the masterful ability of their contributions to it from Adam Smith
down to Stuart Mill. But they have not lighted it up with that readable
attractiveness which in a later generation makes us thankful for the
work done in the same field by men like Sir Thomas Farrer, and the
late Professor Fawcett. More especially has it been reserved for
the Frenchman, Frederic Bastiat, to brighten the whole theme with
the charm of his wit, and to attract one to it almost as one would be
attracted to a readable novel.[40]

From these statements by Reid, Pratt, and Smith, it can be seen
that even these most staunch defenders of political economy
viewed the subject less as an advancing science than as a collection of immutable moral principles.

Protectionists did not react to the statements of free-traders
by rejecting political economy entirely; for their own part they
were able to call on List, Carey, Byles, and even John Stuart
Mill. But in general they deplored the course of development
they considered the science was taking, and in particular they
rejected the validity of an exclusively deductive method. Setting
out in 1873 to show that protection had "benefited" Victoria,
James Mirams regretted the absence of empirical studies which
might have provided him guidance—"although surrounded with
books, none of them are of a character to afford me any assistance
in this work."[41] Protectionists leaned heavily on historical description to buttress their case. David Syme, publisher of the protectionist Melbourne *Age*, was a pioneer in use of the historical
method, and he assured the bountiful presence of descriptive
empirical evidence in Victorian tariff propaganda.[42] He argued
cogently that ignorance of such variables as ease of factor mobility and strength of incentives prevented simple application of
English classical theory to Australia.[43]

---

40. C. M. Smith, *Free Trade and its Influence on National Prosperity* (Townsville, 1888), p. 2.
41. James Mirams, *A Generation of Victorian Politics: Personal Records* (n. p.,
n. d.), p. 24; see also *The Advantages of Protection* (Port Adelaide, 1883).
42. *Protection in Victoria versus Free-Trade in New South Wales*, reprinted
from the *Age* (Melbourne, 1887); Syme's contribution to economics has been
described by Professor La Nauze, *Political Economy in Australia: Historical
Studies* (Melbourne, 1949), pp. 98–135.
43. David Syme, *Outlines of an Industrial Science* (London, 1876), pp. 18
and 106 f.

Merchants and businessmen viewed political economy as a valuable ally in other controversies besides those related to commercial policy. Bankers cited Smith and other economists on the virtues of a competitive banking system, and they turned to Giffen and Fawcett for denunciation of bimetallism.[44] Exponents of general laissez faire considered widespread knowledge of political economy the best defense against "state socialism." George Lacy complained in 1881: "Good legislation is becoming secondary to patronage, and members of Parliament, instead of making a study of political economy and sociology, reserve their talents for the intricacies of lobbying. Nothing else can come of the system, and the more it is extended, the worse it must grow."[45] Reformers of all types were scolded regularly by conservatives for failing to devote sufficient attention to "such dry studies" as economics.[46] Radicals for their part expressed mounting impatience with the restraints imposed upon them by "theorists."[47]

The impact of political economy on discussions of land policy was complex. Land-owners and others cited classical economists on the desirability of commercial freedom in general, and they claimed that proof of the need for unrestricted ownership and exchange of land was a corollary to the wider market rule.[48] Smith's prescriptions for public finance were used also to deny the validity of a tax on land. C. McKay Smith declared: "The taxation of property would simply operate as a flat contradiction to each and every one of these compact and wholesome maxims."[49] The benefits of private enterprise were listed in refutation of schemes for land nationalization.

Unlike advocates of tariffs, national banking, and other radical legislation, however, land-reformers were able to draw as much

44. See above pp. 197–209. Beginning in the 1870's the *Australasian Insurance and Banking Record* gave steady coverage to developments in economic science.
45. "State Socialism, a Warning," *Australian,* V (1881), 100; and also George Lacy, *Co-operation* (Sydney, 1880), p. 5.
46. F. J. Carter, "On Wages: a Reply," *Victorian Review,* II (1880), 861.
47. John Ebenezer Goodwin, *Scientific Legislation* (Melbourne, 1878), pp. 17–18.
48. Charles Fairfield, "Getting and Holding," *Melbourne Review,* IX (1884), 291–311.
49. *The Taxation of Property* (Sydney, 1888), p. 15; and Prideaux Selby, "Thoughts on Taxation," *Melbourne Review,* III (1878), 215–24.

strength as criticism from economics. Ricardo's description of land rent as a return attributable to the bounty of nature, and Mill's qualified approval of rent confiscation provided in themselves substantial excuse for confiscatory action.[50] Moreover, as any clever writer could show, implications of the "maxims" set down by the Physiocrats and Smith were sufficiently vague to permit approval in principal of almost any tax.[51] Land-reformers made extensive use of examples from economic history to illustrate the beneficial effects of changes in tenure or taxation on development. They greeted Henry George's *Progress and Poverty* as a breakthrough in economics, and thereafter were more willing than ever to embrace the science in general.[52]

Acceptance by colonists of dictates imposed by "economic laws" was not always mere rationalization of self-interest. Classical theory provided a model of social co-operation and growth which was appealing both for its elegant simplicity and for its dependence upon the operation of unrestricted personal liberty. Henry Keylock Rusden explained in 1876 the close relationship he saw between political economy and social ethics:

Political economy is also a part of morality, relating to the best means as a means of happiness, in the interest of society, of increasing wealth. The expenditure or distribution of acquired wealth (which is always in the hands of individuals, and not in those of the State, which has no profits or wealth,) is private economy, and outside the province of political economy; though of course included in morality. It has hitherto been accepted that it would not conduce to the happiness or advantage of society to interfere with private economy further than as, by laws, the protection of one individual against any other individual is provided for.[53]

For one concerned with both principles of equity and physical performance it was not easy to discover an overall code of eco-

50. The following publications gave great weight to Mill's views on land reform: *Land Reform League Tracts* (Melbourne, 1870 and 1871); and James Mirams, *The Land Question in Victoria* (Melbourne, 1882).
51. Edward Langton, "On Taxation in Victoria," *Melbourne Review*, II (1877), 221–34; and "The Writer," *The Coalition between the Squatters and the Free Selectors* (Sydney, n. d.).
52. For example: C. H. Spence, "A Californian Political Economist," *Victorian Review*, IV (1881), 129–46; Frederick Cornell, "Progress and Poverty: A Defence," *ibid.*, VIII (1883), 608–21; Percy R. Meggy, "Land Nationalisation—What is it?," *Sydney Quarterly Magazine*, 1889, pp. 311–16.
53. "Labour and Capital," *Melbourne Review*, I (1876), 68.

nomic behavior which could be justified more completely than laissez faire.

Most interest in political economy during the 1870's and 1880's was a derivative of the policy controversies in which the science played a large part. Enthusiasts of the subject believed that right and justice were on their side in each particular contest and that enlightenment only was needed to convert dissenters.[54] A variety of clubs, societies, and institutes gave time to political economy and in some cases published results of their deliberations. The Adelaide Young Men's Society, under the direction of Reverend William Roby Fletcher of Adelaide University, attempted "to provide, if possible, one paper on some aspect of political economy each quarter."[55] The Eclectic Association in Melbourne continued to bring together such ambitious amateur social scientists as Charles H. Pearson, Henry Gyles Turner, Alexander Sutherland, Alfred Deakin, and William Shiels.[56] Several members were instrumental during the 1870's in founding the *Melbourne Review*, devoted largely to consideration of social problems.[57] The Minerva Club in Hobart contained, among others, R. M. Johnston, Alfred J. Taylor, and Andrew Inglis Clark, who "met together to read liberal works and discuss important subjects."[58]

54. Two statements of the importance of political economy as a discipline were: E. C. Nowell, "Political Economy," *Monthly Notices of Papers and Proceedings of the Royal Society of Tasmania*, 1872, pp. 12–20; and T. F. Bird, "The Basis of National Prosperity," *Melbourne Review*, I (1876), 93–104.

55. *Journal of the Adelaide Young Men's Society*, July 15, 1878, p. 6. The society was only moderately successful in fulfilling its intention.

56. Henry Gyles Turner, *Alexander Sutherland, M. A., His Life and Work* (Melbourne, 1908); and J. M. Tregenza, *The Life and Work of C. H. Pearson 1830–1894*, pp. 209–10. Sutherland published in 1898 an attempt to advance on Smith's *Theory of Moral Sentiments* through Darwinian anthropological study. *The Origin and Growth of the Moral Instinct* (London, 1898), two volumes. W. R. Newbold described this latter work as "a comprehensive induction covering the fields of zoology, physiology, sociology, law, psychology and philosophy" but containing "faults inseparable from the work of an amateur, especially a lack of nice discrimination between concepts which are similar but essentially distinct, and a defective acquaintance with the work of other men in the same field. . . ." *Annals of the American Academy of Political and Social Science*, XIII (1899), 91–94. The Eclectic Association is discussed in Henry Mayer, *Marx, Engels and Australia* (Melbourne, 1964), pp. 48–51.

57. Henry Gyles Turner, "The Beginnings of Literature in Victoria," *Victorian Historial Magazine*, IV (1914–15), 89–90. Even A. Patchett Martin, the *Review's* distinguished literary contributor, viewed political economy with interest and respect. See review of *Economic Studies* by Walter Bagehot, *Melbourne Review*, V (1880), 211.

58. Moncure Conway, *My Pilgrimage to the Wise Men of the East* (London, 1906), p. 80; and John Reynolds, "The Clarks of 'Rosebank,'" *Tasmanian Historical Research Association, Papers and Proceedings*, IV (1955), 8.

This group published the periodical *Quadrilateral* and proclaimed "There are few for whom Sociology and Political Economy have any interest, who are content to eliminate reform altogether from their programme."[59]

Colonial economists were often uncertain as to the distinction between political economy and more general enquiry into all aspects of social problems. Their confusion was illustrated well at the Australian Social Science Congress held in Melbourne during 1880 in connection with the International Exhibition. A "Department No. 5" was created with responsibility for "Economy, Trade, Manufactures" but with a list of discussion topics much wider in scope. Thomas Loader, a retired elder statesman of catholic interests, was elected President of the Department. In addition to worthwhile contributions from Turner on banking and from Hayter and Fenton on statistical subjects, delegates were subjected to a succession of pedestrian and tiresome presentations dealing with, among other matters: "The Origin, Progress, and Present Development of the Principles of Life Assurance, and its Moral Influence in those Communities in which it has taken Root," "Nursing," "Decimal Systems," "Fires and Fire Brigades," and "Poverty among the Working Classes, its Causes and Cure."[60] The *Melbourne Punch* may have expressed the sentiments of many of those present when it characterized the gathering as "Perhaps the most absurd, grotesque, and useless excrescence in connection with our Great Exhibition, not even excluding the fountain."[61]

By the 1880's, Australia had made little impact on the development of economic thought outside the colonies. Only the works of Hearn, Syme, and Musgrave were known abroad, and these had little influence.[62] When colonists with an interest in economic theory or description directed their attention to other countries,

59. "Homo et Ager," *Quadrilateral*, 1874, p. 225.
60. Thomas Loader, *Inauguaral Address* (Melbourne, 1880); reports of papers presented to the Congress are contained in *Argus*, November 23, 25, 26, 1880, and in *Australasian Insurance and Banking Record*, IV (1880), 401–4 and 435–37, and V (1881), 10–16, and 26.
61. *Melbourne Punch*, November 18, 1880, p. 207 and December 2, 1880, p. 228.
62. See above, and J. A. La Nauze, *Political Economy in Australia: Historical Studies, passim.*

it was usually for publicity purposes.[63] William Westgarth, an unusually vocal expatriate, was the exception as an extremely prolific contributor on economic subjects to deliberations of the London Chamber of Commerce and the British Association for the Advancement of Science.[64] With long experience as a merchant, he emphasized above all the importance of mercantile or "floating" capital for national development, and he extolled the virtues of free trade.[65] Westgarth even engaged Henry Dunning Macleod in an extended debate on the meaning and purpose of economic science.[66] The few foreign observers of the Australian economy who recorded their comments were concerned usually with collecting selected evidence of particular policies for use in their own domestic situations.[67]

Challenge of Depression

During the 1880's and 1890's, a marked change took place in the character of persons in the colonies interested in economic

63. Sir Charles Nicholson, "The Principles which Ought to Regulate the Determination of the Political and Municipal Boundaries and Division of the Colonies," *Proceedings of the Royal Colonial Institute,* XII (1880–81), 311–42; R. Murray Smith, *The Finances and Public Debt of the Colony of Victoria* (London, 1882); and David S. MacMillan, "The Australians in London, 1857–1880," *Royal Australian Historical Society Journal and Proceedings,* XLIV (1958), 155–81.

64. "Reform of Joint Stock Banking Law," *Chamber of Commerce Journal,* II (1883), 64; "'The Unearned Increment' of Value in Real Estate," *ibid.,* 95–96; "Practical Commerce *versus* Theoretical Political Economy," *ibid.,* 117–18, 155–56, 182–83, 215–17, 288–90, 327–29, 358–60, and III (1884), 6–7. (This series amounted to a short text of economic principles, complete with chapter headings.); "The Bimetallic Argument," *ibid.,* II (1883), 272–74; "The Unearned Increment," *ibid.,* 341–42.

65. "On the Law of Capital," *Report of the Forty-First Meeting of the British Association for the Advancement of Science,* 1871, transactions, pp. 223–25; "On the Science of Capital and Money," *ibid.,* Forty-Fifth Meeting, 1875, transactions, p. 220; "What is Capital? The Contradictory Responses of Economists to this Question from the Ground of Actual Fact and Life," *ibid.,* Fiftieth Meeting, 1880, transactions, pp. 679–81; "The British Empire in North America and in Australasia," *ibid.,* Fifty-Fourth Meeting, 1884, pp. 835–36; "The Battle between Free Trade and Protection in Australia," *ibid.,* Fifty-Seventh Meeting, 1887, transactions, pp. 833–34.

66. Henry Dunning Macleod, "The Modern Science of Economics," *Chamber of Commerce Journal,* II (1883), 371–72, and III (1884), 4–6. The *Australasian Insurance and Banking Record* followed the dispute eagerly and declared Macleod the winner. VIII (1884), 103–4.

67. For example: "Ph. Phog [!]," *De La Colonisation de L'Australie et de son développement economique* (Rochefort-sur-mer, 1886); Fred. Perry Powers, "The Australian Tariff Experiment," *Quarterly Journal of Economics,* III (1888–89), 87–98; and Joseph Lee, "Anti-Chinese Legislation in Australasia," *ibid.,* 218–24.

science. Up to this time, political economy as a mode of enquiry had been viewed largely as a genteel leisure occupation of a few middle class dilettantes and designed to produce a set of rules for social behavior rather than greater understanding of economic processes. Colonists had been willing to cite economic dicta in one policy controversy or another, but seldom to undertake investigations of their own. The change in character had two features. First, leaders in the developing labor movement discovered that economic arguments were powerful weapons in the bitter conflicts of the period; and they found, furthermore, that policy dictates resulting from economic study were not necessarily laissez faire. Discussion by labor spokesmen of economic questions was a distinctive characteristic of this period. Second, an increasing number of persons came to view economics for the first time in the colonies as a subject area for truly disinterested and useful activity. An outstanding manifestation of this second development was formation of the Australian Economic Association at Sydney.

Enthusiasm of workingmen for political economy came mainly in response to economic adversity. In Australia, prosperity and growth were nearly continuous from the discovery of gold in the 1850's until the mid-1880's. Then, suddenly, a succession of devastating strikes threatened the survival of trade unionism, while at the same time unemployment resulting from declining foreign investment, falling wool prices, and drought, threw doubt on the very viability of the economic system. Political economy was embraced as a possible source of solutions to these problems.

Workers were led to economic study through the same bitter policy controversies in which economic argument had had, for several decades, an important part. By the 1880's, land-reformers and their opponents both were making regular use of economic authorities; defenders of unrestricted private ownership propounded classical theory,[68] while radicals called for extension of the historical method. A typical land-taxer insisted in 1891: "Every Historical event should be looked at, as it were, through the

68. For example: Waldemar Bannow, *Australasia's Future: How to Shape it* (Melbourne, 1890); P. J. Gandon, *"Ecce Homo" in Political Economy* (Sydney, 1890); and Economist (R. M. Johnston), *Taxation—Current Popular Fallacies* (Hobart, 1893).

spectacles of Political Economy, and carefully scrutinized in this way, ere it be approved or condemned."[69] The place of economics in monetary controversies was not so clearly defined; as many respected theoretical authorities could be found to support as to attack proposals for a state bank, and the real significance of such sophisticated schemes as bimetallism was shrouded in mystery for the common man.[70] Protagonists in debates over commercial policy were divided along lines similar to those in discussions of land policy; free-traders set forth elaborate statements of classical theory in defense of the free price economy, and protectionists leaned heavily on historical description of sheltered national growth.[71] Commenting on the highly charged economic debates of the 1890's, Benjamin Hoare observed wisely: "The hurly-burly of political conflict does two opposite things. It often stimulates public inquiry into the 'dismal science,' but it necessarily blurs the public judgment through the bias of partisanship."[72]

Despite the apparent ambiguity of political economy on policy issues, discussion of economic topics became frequent and popular at gatherings of workers. By the 1890's speakers and writers were able safely to cite Jevons, Mill, Marx, Spencer, Macleod Hobson, and even Richard T. Ely and Edward Atkinson, confident that their audience was familiar with these names.[73] Several prominent young labor leaders were particularly well read in the literature of economics: W. M. Hughes, a future prime minister, could discuss intelligently at this time the contributions of Mill,

69. T. O'Reilly, *The People's Heritage: A History of English Land Tenure* (Sydney, 1891); see also, J. Medway Day, *Political Economy in a Nutshell for Young Men and Women* (Adelaide, 1893), and James Ashton, *The Great Land Question!* (Narandera, 1894).
70. See chapters 5 and 6 above.
71. See above chapters 1 and 2, and particularly discussion of writings by Pulsford, Fairfield, Wise, O'Sullivan, and the *Age*.
72. Benj. Hoare, *Twenty-Five Years of Protection: How it has Helped Victoria* (Melbourne, 1896), p. 3.
73. George R. Dibbs, *Address to the Trades and Labour Council* (Sydney 1890), p. 4; *The Labour Question* (Melbourne, 1890); B. R. Wise, "What Parliament Can Do for Labour," *Sydney Quarterly Magazine*, 1891, pp. 220–37; *Leaflets for the People* (Brisbane, n. d.); James Gray, *The Labour Problem, or Social Salvation for Victoria* (Brighton, 1895). See also P. J. O'Farrell, "The Australian Socialist League and the Labour Movement, 1887–1891," *Historical Studies Australia and New Zealand*, VIII (1957–59), 154, and 156–59; L. G. Churchward, "The American Influence on the Australian Labour Movement," *ibid.*, V (1951–53), 258–77; and B. Mansfield, "The Background to Radical Republicanism in New South Wales in the Eighteen-Eighties," *ibid.*, pp. 338–48.

Jevons, Cairnes, and Sidgwick.[74] W. A. Holman, later premier of New South Wales, testified in 1892 that he devoted all his "leisure time to the study of economics."[75] Cheap reprints of economics works were available for wide distribution both from abroad and from local presses.[76] An enthusiastic reviewer of Bellamy's *Looking Backward* reported in 1890: "Political economy used to be called 'the dismal science,' but since manhood suffrage has obtained, it has emerged from its dark and dusty corners, put on fascinating forms, and now, in the book under notice, has blossomed into a love-story."[77]

A few radical writers condemned political economy in general for the direction it had taken, and the "Smith-Mill-Fawcett School" in particular, for giving disproportionate support to advocates of laissez-faire social policies. C. Medway Day charged that "the ordinary textbooks . . . constituted more an apology for the existing condition of things than an explanation of them or a suggestion for their permanent improvement."[78] These critics were influenced by the strategic implications of their attacks, but they were aware also of the pessimistic ferment elsewhere, and particularly of the adverse comments on economics by historians, socialists, and skeptics such as John Ruskin. A writer in the Sydney *Bulletin* complained: "When those who own the earth wish to perpetrate some new swindle for their own profit and for the further exploitation of the poor, they are always careful to explain that their actions are directed by the 'unchangeable and

74. *New South Wales Parliamentary Debates*, 1895, pp. 375–79; referred to in L. F. Fitzhardinge, "W. M. Hughes in New South Wales Politics, 1890–1900," *Royal Australian Historical Society Journal and Proceedings*, XXXVII (1951), 146.
75. "Progress Report from the Select Committee on Post Office Savings Bank-National Bank," *Votes and Proceedings of the Legislative Assembly of New South Wales*, 1892–93, p. 62; and see H. V. Evatt, *Australian Labour Leader* (Sydney, 1945), pp. 34, 39, 42, and 60.
76. An occasional column in the Sydney *Bulletin* entitled the *"Bulletin* Book Exchange" provides a useful picture of contemporary reading tastes.
77. *Pacific Quarterly*, I (Melbourne, 1890), 30.
78. *Wages* (A Paper Read before the Society for the Study of Christian Sociology, Adelaide, 1892), p. 2. Similar critiques were contained in: Harry S. Taylor, *Tucker Prize Essay on the Single Tax* (Adelaide, 1892), p. 27; Cinderella, *A Manual of Political Economy for Free Men* (Sydney, 1890), and *Money versus Wealth* (Sydney, 1890); Arthur Griffith, *The Labour Platform: An Exposition* (Sydney, 1893); and A. J. O., *Labour v. Capital* (Hobart, 1895), p 11.

inexorable law of Demand and Supply.'"[79] The *Bulletin* poet
Dyson lamented sarcastically:

> Lost the causes for which you're fighting, futile all your
>   hopes and vain,
>   For the *Lord* has set His face, and marked a way
> And no power on earth can turn it, or can plan a course again,
>   Whilst men hunger, and they thirst, and toil and pray.
> Like the sun, the Law is steadfast, none may change it, none
>   command—
> Man is but the servile creature of supply and of demand![80]

Strengthening the hand of critics of political economy during the
1890's were a variety of meaningless diatribes issued in the name
of economic science.[81] On balance, even despite this strain of
cynicism, economics had gained by acquiring for the first time a
broad base of interest and support.

Together with the growth of labor interest, the beginnings of
professionalization, described in chapters 13 and 15, strengthened the position of economics. In the universities during the
1880's lectures and enrollments increased, and a growing body of
scholars devoted a substantial proportion of their time to the
subject. A group of remarkably able and energetic statisticians
began to provide economic data of high quality for domestic
analysis and undertook pioneer investigations of their own. Statisticians, by the collection of solid evidence, helped to counteract
the characteristic philosophical tone of earlier economic writings.
R. M. Johnston spoke in effect also for his colleagues Hayter and
Coghlan when he explained in 1890:

> Hitherto, to a great extent, the subject has been governed by the
> more or less plausible generalisations of mere literary men; and their
> deserved fame and undoubted ability and skill as such have given
> them a prestige in political matters to which they are not entitled
> from a practical or scientific point of view. That they have done good
> service in arousing and sustaining attention on such important matters
> is readily admitted; but further progress is impossible so long as the

79. "The Law of Demand and Supply," *Bulletin*, XI (1890), No. 554, p. 6.
80. *Bulletin*, XIV (1895), No. 779, p. 7.
81. For example, Alexander Johnston, *Strikes, Labour Questions, and other
Economic Difficulties: A Short Treatise of Political Economy* (London, 1895);
and *Wages and the Sovereign* (Melbourne, n. d.).

inexact methods of the mere literary athlete are employed. In future the progress of Political Economy as a science depends upon demonstrations based upon quantitative analysis, and not as heretofore upon authoritative dogmas based upon the qualitative analysis of any *one* factor of the problem arbitrarily chosen from a compound or complex equation.[82]

Under pressure to provide immediate solutions for the demanding problems of depression, a variety of associations and institutions gave increasing attention to economics. On the one hand the Bishop of Newcastle lectured his flock on "political economy,"[83] while on the other a commentator told the Insurance Institute of New South Wales after a paper on "the Economics of Fire Insurance:" "People as a rule now carry on their business in a mechanical sort of way, and if the paper just read will induce the public to familiarise themselves with those economic laws which have been spoken of, it will be productive of good to the community generally."[84] Bankers became particularly enthusiastic exponents of economics. They supported actively the Melbourne Social Science Congress in 1880,[85] and, when Bankers' Institutes were founded at Melbourne in 1887 and at Sydney in 1892, instruction in political economy was made a primary function.[86] Bankers' Institute libraries were kept well stocked with books on economics, and members were taught special reverence for such classics as the *Wealth of Nations* (by "that author whose work was as heaven-sent an inspiration of its kind as Milton's of his kind").[87] The institutes' journals reprinted appropriate portions of economic works, and they provided critical discussions of such diverse authorities as Turgot, Cournot, Mallock, and Bohm Bawerk.[88] During the depths of depression, bankers in Melbourne

---

82. "Observations on Current Social and Economic Problems," *Report of the Second Meeting of the Australasian Association for the Advancement of Science held at Melbourne, 1890,* p. 135.
83. G. V. Portus, *Happy Highways* (Melbourne, 1953), p. 50.
84. *Australasian Insurance and Banking Record,* XIV (1890), 615.
85. *Ibid.,* III (1879), 305.
86. See above pp. 552–53 and 574–76.
87. *Bankers' Magazine and Journal of the Bankers' Institute of Australasia,* VII (1893–94), 535, and also 512–14.
88. *Ibid.,* VIII (1894–95), 104–7, and X (1896–97), 857–62; *Journal of the Institute of Bankers of New South Wales,* II (1893), 273–93, and V (1896), 98–100.

were reminded that "economic laws are certain and irresistible in their operation, and that when broken the penalty has to be paid."[89] In Sydney, bankers were assured that "the Institute should follow with ceaseless interest the developments of economic thought."[90]

Amateur economists during the 1880's mobilized effectively for discussion and publication of research. Local Royal Societies were persuaded to accept occasional papers on economic topics, and in 1888 the inter-colonial Australasian Association for the Advancement of Science began with a "Section F. Economic and Social Science and Statistics." This section, promoted from "F" to "G" in 1893, underwent frequent changes of title; but over almost forty years it provided a regular opportunity for economists from both Australia and New Zealand, and particularly from the smaller colonies, to meet and to exchange ideas. It was only in the AAAS that such competent amateurs as A. J. Ogilvy and R. M. Johnston from Tasmania, Sir Samuel Griffith from Queensland, and G. W. Cotton from South Australia, could gain the advantages of a large, diverse, and interested audience. Cotton, president of Section F in 1891, was able to greet the prospective birth of the British Economic Association with pride and humility. He said: "That newly-to-be-formed association will scarcely say of this antipodean institution, *Sequamur, sed non aequis passibus.* We hope, when the great British foundation has advanced beyond our more humble achievements, that we shall keep it well in sight."[91] A year later Cotton's successor, Richard Teece, explained the vital role he envisioned for the section:

This section of our Association has an opportunity afforded it of doing useful work in the development of our nascent nation. These young colonies, which have almost sprung into national existence, like Minerva full-panoplied from the brain of Jove, have inherited no legacy of misdeeds from the past, and furnish us with a favourable opportunity to make experiments in economic science. At the same

---

89. *Bankers' Magazine and Journal of the Bankers' Institute of Australasia,* VI (1892–93), 1417.
    90. *Journal of the Institute of Bankers of New South Wales,* VI (1897), 111.
    91. "A State Bank of Issue the only Solution of the Domestic-Currency Question," *Report of the Third Meeting of the Australasian Association for the Advancement of Science held at Christchurch, 1891,* p. 325.

time our position and our opportunities impose on us grave responsibilities. We are now making the last experiments in the responsible government of a young country which the world shall see; there is scarcely any other great unoccupied space on the face of the earth where the experiment can be repeated.[92]

The outstanding organizational development of the period was formation of the Australian Economic Association at Sydney in 1887. The history of this group has been described fully by Professor S. J. Butlin,[93] and contributions by individual members have been discussed by Professor John La Nauze[94] and elsewhere in this study. The work of Alfred De Lissa, the most brilliant innovator, has been examined separately in Chapter 14. Through a monthly periodical, the *Australian Economist,* and various special papers, the Association helped to keep economic problems before the public eye, although its singular passion for publication led the Sydney *Bulletin* to categorize the organization "that refuge of self-satisfied theoretical bores, the N. S. W. Economic Association."[95] Over a twelve-year period the Association performed an important service in bringing together native-born and immigrant economists, businessmen, journalists, clergymen, labor spokesmen, and university personnel. Andrew Garran expressed the eclectic principles of the Association in an account of "Three Systems of Political Economy," which, he claimed, had prevailed hitherto on the basis of selfish class interests. He explained: "The one rests on the assumption of the supreme importance of the land-owners, the next on the supreme importance of the traders, and the third on the supreme importance of the receivers of wages. Is it necessary to say that a complete system of political economy will take cognisance of them all and do justice to each?"[96]

Throughout the 1890's, the prospect of federation was in the

92. "A New Theory of the Relations of Wages and Profits," *Report of the Fourth Meeting of the Australasian Association for the Advancement of Science held at Hobart, 1893,* p. 142.
93. "The Australian Economic Association, 1887–1898," *Economic Record,* XXIII (1947), 20–31.
94. *Political Economy in Australia: Historical Studies,* pp. 22–25.
95. XIII (1893), No. 696, p. 4.
96. *Report of the Sixth Meeting of the Australasian Association for the Advancement of Science held at Brisbane, 1896,* p. 698. This paper was presented before both the Australian Economic Association and Section G.

air. Inter-colonial union was considered widely to be the solution to many prevailing economic difficulties, and other political nostrums such as imperial federation gained little support.[97] In economics as in politics, the period stimulated discussion of federalism, and the federalist literature of other countries became well known. No local contributions of outstanding value, however, were forthcoming.[98] Economic writers were concerned almost exclusively with the effects of federation on government finance. In most works, American, German, Canadian, and Swiss precedents were described, and various possible divisions of powers and responsibilities outlined.[99] As the conclusion of negotiations for federation approached, two fundamental differences of opinion became apparent: one concerned the division between state and federal revenue sources, responsibilities for expenditures, and debts;[100] the other related to special obligations of the larger and more prosperous states for relief of their less fortunate associates. In Sydney and Melbourne, the latter question stimulated considerable dispute, and Timothy Coghlan in particular made

97. Charles S. Blackton, "Australian Nationality and Nationalism: the Imperial Federationist Interlude, 1885–1901," *Historical Studies Australia and New Zealand*, VII (1955–57), 1–16.
98. R. S. Parker, "Australian Federation: the Influence of Economic Interests and Political Pressures," *ibid.*, IV (1949–51), 1–24; Geoff. Blainey, "The Role of Economic Interests in Australian Federation: a Reply to Professor R. S. Parker," *ibid.*, 224–37; Parker's rejoinder is *ibid.*, 238–40. An incomplete bibliography of the literary output during the federation period is Alan Gross, *Attainment, being a Critical Study of the Literature of Federation* (Melbourne, 1948). An excellent bibliography and digest of authorities on federalism prepared in Tasmania in 1891 is Thomas C. Just, "Leading Facts Connected with Federation, Compiled for the Information of the Tasmanian Delegates to the Australasian Federal Convention, 1891, on the Order of the Government of Tasmania," *Journals and Printed Papers of the Parliament of Tasmania*, 1891.
99. Reginald J. Black, "The Finances of Federation," *Australian Economist*, IV (1894–97), 471–78; C. McKay Smith, "Australian Federation from a Heretic's Standpoint," *ibid.*, 528–33; Dr. Fick, "The Connection between the Economical and Political Federation of Germany," *ibid.*, 568–73; R. R. Garran, "The Financial Basis of Federation," *ibid.*, 615–19; Alfred De Lissa, "Federal Finance," *ibid.*, V (1897), 46–47; J. T. Walker, "Federal Finance," *ibid.*, supplement; A. Duckworth, "The Present Position of the Federation Proposals," *ibid.*, VI (1898), 29–32; James J. Fenton, "An Australian Federal Debt," *Report of the Fourth Meeting of the Australasian Association for the Advancement of Science held at Hobart, 1893*, pp. 562–69; and J. T. Walker, "The Federation of British Australasia: a Sketch from a Political and an Economic Point of View," *Report of the Seventh Meeting of the Australasian Association for the Advancement of Science held at Sydney, 1898*, (abstract), pp. 904–7.
100. This issue was debated in: T. Rolin, "Federal Finance—Railways and Debts," *Australian Economist*, V (1897), 25–30; and Richard Teece, "The Financial Problem in Federation," *ibid.*, 49–52.

valiant efforts to clarify the basic issues.[101] In the smaller colonies, near unanimity was achieved, and local economists waxed eloquent on the potential hardships of union. Sir Philip Fysh in Tasmania, aided by R. M. Johnston, presented in 1897 an elaborate set of calculations to show that, under uniform treatment by the Commonwealth, Tasmania and Western Australia both would suffer more under the proposed federation through loss of tariff revenue and other income sources than they would gain from services rendered and special grants.[102]

During the 1880's and 1890's the interest of foreign observers as well as of local residents in the Australian economy quickened. Outsiders had two strong reasons for paying particular attention to Australia: professional economists viewed the colonies as a unique laboratory of social experiment, and private investors experienced mounting concern over the fate of their capital. Arthur Duckworth, secretary of the Australian Economic Association, was correspondent of the British Economic Association in Australia and maintained a steady flow of comment on current events.[103] A number of other early contributors to the *Economic Journal,* including John Rae, W. M. Acworth, H. H. Champion, Charles Gairdner, L. L. Price, and Robert Giffen, examined such special colonial problems as labor legislation, public enterprise, the financial crisis, and commercial and land policy.[104] Harsh indictments of the colonial economic systems by British critics[105] inspired some expatriate Australians to rise in defense of their

101. R. L. Nash, *Federal Finance: An Inquiry into the Probable Influence of Federation on Finance and Trade* (Sydney, 1897); T. A. Coghlan, *Notes on the Financial Aspect of Australian Federation* (Sydney, 1898); and "Report of the Committee on Federal Finance Appointed by the Government of New South Wales on 28th April, 1898," *Votes and Proceedings of the Legislative Assembly of New South Wales,* 1900. Both Nash and Coghlan assisted the committee.

102. See above e.g., pp. 363 n., 394 n., and 448.

103. *Economic Journal,* II (1892), 425–41; III (1893), 148–54; V (1895), 76–80; IX (1899), 322–27.

104. *Economic Journal,* I (1891), 15–42; II (1892), 100–108, 629–36, and 676–81; III (1893), 293–97, 297–307, and 483–87; IV (1894), 114–19; and VIII (1898), 3–16.

105. For example, Q., "The Borrowings of Australasia," *Investors' Review,* I (1892), 189–205; R. G. C. Hamilton, "Lending Money to Australia," *Nineteenth Century,* XXXII (1892), 194–202; J. W. Fortescue, "The New South Sea Bubble," *ibid.,* XXIV (1893), 22–33; and C. Gairdner, "On the Lessons of the Australian Banking Collapse," *Report of the Sixty-Third Meeting of the British Association for the Advancement of Science,* 1893, transactions, p. 853.

homeland, particularly before meetings of the Royal Colonial Institute.[106] Interest in Australia abroad was confined mainly to Great Britain, but a few economists on the Continent and in the United States published observations during the 1890's and after Federation at the turn of the century.[107]

Apart from the work of the statisticians, the only Australian books on economics which received extensive critical attention abroad during this period were: B. R. Wise, *Industrial Freedom* (Melbourne, 1892), Charles H. Pearson, *National Life and Character: A Forecast* (London, 1893), A. J. Ogilvy, *The Third Factor of Production and other Essays* (London, 1898), and Max Hirsch, *Democracy versus Socialism* (London, 1901).[108] These works were all more polemical than scientific in character.

Doldrums and Revival

The years after Federation were a low point in the history of Australian economic thought. Interest in the subject waned, and few works of good quality were published. The explanation for this decline may lie in the competing attraction of political developments, or in the revival of prosperity which removed the urgency from many economic problems. Much economic enquiry in the 1890's had been carried out by enthusiastic amateurs with little sustained support from professionals or the universities, and this type of endeavor was particularly responsive to fluctuations in public enthusiasm.

106. Matthew Macfie, "Aids to Australian Development," *Proceedings of the Royal Colonial Institute*, XXI (1889–90), 53–82; Sir Edward Braddon, "Australasia: a Vindication," *ibid.*, XXIII (1891–92), 50–89; Flora L. Shaw, "Colonial Expansion," *ibid.*, XXVI (1894–95), 3–29; and C. H. Spence, "Social and Intellectual Aspects of Australian Life," *ibid.*, 30–32.

107. Moritz Kandt, *Ueber die Entwickelung der australischen Eisenbahnpolitick* . . . (Berlin, 1894); Helen Page Bates, "Australian Experiments in Industry," *Annals of the American Academy of Political and Social Science*, XII (1898), 193–213; William Hill, "State Railways in Australia," *Journal of Political Economy*, III (1894–95), 1–23; Leopold Katscher, "South Australian State Socialism," *ibid.*, XI (1903–4), 280–90; Pierre Leroy-Beaulieu, *Les Nouvelles sociétés Anglo-Saxonnes* (Paris, 1901); and Albert Métin, *Le Socialisme sans doctrines* (Paris, 1901).

108. Reviews were: *Economic Journal*, II (1892), 676–81; III (1893), 483–87; IX (1899), 74–75; and XI (1901), 549–52; *Annals of the American Academy of Political and Social Science*, III (1892–93), 160–62; V (1894–95), 140–43.

Defenders of fixed policy doctrines continued after Federation, as they had from the 1850's, to use one-sided interpretations of economic analysis to bolster arguments.[109] But imaginative and objective investigation was exceptional. Government statisticians were almost the only remaining champions of the discipline. R. M. Johnston kept up a steady output of writing on economic questions, but with advancing years he was not able easily to accept new techniques. For example, in 1913 he put forth a rather pathetic defense of the Ricardian labor theory of value against supply and demand analysis.[110] G. H. Knibbs, first Commonwealth Statistician, recognized a close link between economics and statistics, and he was a faithful advocate of both.[111] By 1913, however, Knibbs was complaining still of a general lack of interest in economic problems.[112] The most important single work by an economist after Federation was the four volume economic history *Labour and Industry in Australia*, written by Timothy Coghlan from his post in London as Agent-General for New South Wales and published in 1918.

Literary and scientific societies after 1900 relegated economic discussion to a subsidiary position. The title of Section G of the AAAS was altered significantly from "Economic Science" to the broader "Social and Statistical Science," and the type of contribution was modified accordingly. Members of the defunct Australian Economic Association in Sydney formed an "Economic Science" section of the Royal Society of New South Wales, and

109. For example, Benjamin Hoare, *Preferential Trade: A Study in its Esoteric Meaning* (Melbourne, 1904); Edward Pulsford, *Commerce and the Empire* (London, 1917); *Our Country*, 1900–1901, *passim*; Max Hirsch, "The Limit of State Action," *Report of the Twelfth Meeting of the Australasian Association for the Advancement of Science held at Brisbane, 1909*, pp. 527–31.

110. "Observations Regarding the Production and Distribution of 'Consumable Wealth' and 'Economic Capital,' with an Inquiry into the Probable Effect of Arbitrary Regulation of 'Minimum Wage' Standards upon the 'Cost of Living,'" *Report of the Fourteenth Meeting of the Australasian Association for the Advancement of Science held at Melbourne, 1913*, pp. 474–75.

111. "The Problems of Statistics," *Report of the Twelfth Meeting of the Australasian Association for the Advancement of Science held at Brisbane, 1909*, pp. 505–26; and *Inquiry into the Cost of Living in Australia, 1910–11* (Melbourne, 1911), p. 20.

112. "Unemployment: Report on the Conference of the International Association on, Held at Ghent, September, 1913—by Mr. Donald Campbell, Commonwealth Representative; together with Note by the Commonwealth Statistician," *Papers Presented to the Parliament of the Commonwealth of Australia, 1913*.

the Society's President Liversidge reported in 1901: "the new Section will have the sympathy and support of a large number of our members, and we all look forward to its apparently ensured success."[113] However, despite the continued enthusiasm of the old stalwarts Richard Teece, John Plummer, R. L. Nash, Arthur Duckworth, William Pearse, and George Knibbs, the section seems not to have prospered, and reports of "proceedings" gradually petered out. The Joseph Fisher Lectures in Commerce, inaugurated by the University of Adelaide, became one of the few continuing publications on economic matters.

Interest in the Australian economy by foreign observers as well as by local economists was very limited in the period just before World War I. The *Economic Journal* published only an occasional contribution by Duckworth and a few descriptive accounts of developments in wage and land policy.[114] A meeting of the British Association for the Advancement of Science in Australia during 1914 helped to mobilize support for economics. "Section F" heard papers from such longstanding enthusiasts as Duckworth, Knibbs, and Scott, and from newcomers F. W. Eggleston, R. F. Irvine, Gerald Lightfoot, and C. H. Wickens.[115] The immediate commencement of World War I helped to dull the stimulus afforded by this gathering.

With the exception of a few statisticians and university lecturers, no professional practitioners of economics existed before World War I to guard the scientific objectivity of the subject. Accordingly, as in the nineteenth century, the public view of the discipline was distorted by misrepresentations and misconceptions. Economic science came to be associated to such an extent with violent partisan controversy that a Royal Commissioner

113. "President's Address," *Journal and Proceedings of the Royal Society of New South Wales*, 1901, p. 4.

114. W. P. Reeves, "The Minimum Wage Law in Victoria and South Australia," *Economic Journal*, XI (1901), 334–44; Clara E. Collet, "Wages Boards in Victoria," *ibid.*, XI (1901), 557–65; W. P. Reeves, "Mr. Wise's Industrial Arbitration Act," *ibid.*, XII (1902), 320–26; A. F. Dodd, "Taxation of Land Values in Australasia," *ibid.*, XIV (1904), 401–12; George W. Gough, "The Wages Boards of Victoria," *ibid.*, XV (1905), 361–73; W. P. Reeves, "Land Taxes in Australasia," *ibid.*, XXI (1911), 513–26; and Arthur Duckworth, "White Australia: a Study of Australian Vital Statistics," *ibid.*, XXII (1912), 421–35.

115. "Transactions of Section F," *Report of the Eighty-Fourth Meeting of the British Association for the Advancement of Science, Australia, 1914*, pp. 453–89.

charged to investigate the operation of compulsory arbitration and conciliation laws remarked casually in 1901 that he had not "troubled himself with abstract questions of political economy."[116] Radical writers seldom hesitated to cite economic authorities and principles out of context, often with little real comprehension and occasionally with considerable arrogance.[117] For example, Alexander W. Johnston wrote in the preface to a badly garbled "Manual of the Elements of Political Economy for the Use of Statesmen, Teachers and Students," in 1910:

> Beginning many years ago with the definition, "Political Economy is the science of State Government," I applied myself to the task of producing a work which might afford to others the guidance I found myself in need of, and have since occupied my leisure in formulating other definitions and fundamental principles without which the science could never be of any great practical utility.[118]

When apparent conclusions of economic science seemed not to be in accord with a radical's particular preconceptions, he did not necessarily feel dismayed. Like P. J. Mulholland he could write simply: "scientific principles of political economy, as they bear upon the share of production due to the worker, the margin of profit to the employer, and the polity of making a nation greater in wealth and contentment of its people . . . [have never] been satisfactorily determined."[119]

Even during this depression in economic science before World War I, forces were mounting which would bring change. In particular, several universities made their first important appointments in the subject of men whose voices were heard outside the academic walls.[120] Chambers of commerce and professional associations, pioneered by the bankers and accountants in the 1880's and 1890's, expressed continuing interest in the subject,

116. "Report of Royal Commission of Inquiry into the Working of Compulsory Conciliation and Arbitration Laws," *Votes and Proceedings of the Legislative Assembly of New South Wales,* 1901, p. 34.
117. Argyle McCallum, *The Social Unrest of the Present Day and What Causes It* (Yass, n. d.); Charles Eyre, *The Economics of the Eight-Hours' Day* (Sydney, 1907); W. S. McClure, *Socialism* (Sydney, 1907); Alfred McLennan, *The Other Way Round* (Perth, 1908); Thomas Dowling, *Political Economy* (Camperdown, 1910); Norman R. Freeberg, *Socialism: What is it?* (Brisbane, 1919).
118. *Law and Liberty* (Sydney, 1910), pp. v-vi.
119. *Facts of Finance* (Sydney, n. d.), p. 3.
120. See above Chapter 15.

viewing economics as appropriate training for business.[121] The Workers' Educational Association, established in Australia during 1913, gave impetus not only to improvements in university teaching of the social sciences but also to widespread interest among workingmen.[122] By the outbreak of war the backward state of economics had, at least, begun for the first time to receive attention. F. W. Eggleston explained the situation in the following terms:

Australian democracy has never recognised a science which has formulated exact laws dealing with human wealth and welfare, and which limits the divine right of the democracy to achieve its will. It has never consulted professors of economics as to the possible result of its decrees, nor, when it has passed laws, has it carefully investigated and tabulated the results so as to guide future action. The democratic leaders have listened with impatience to the chorus of *non possumus* which came from the lips of economists and have disregarded it.[123]

R. F. Irvine, making a more practical appeal in 1914, deplored the lack of economic research as a check on dangerous innovations in social policy. He said:

When one considers the political and economic evolution of Australia, one cannot but be astonished at the neglect of these studies in Australian Universities. We have the reputation of being the social laboratory of the world, and we are rather proud of the reputation, even if as individuals we distrust the experiments. . . . Certainly, the fact that Governments have done little and Universities nothing at all, to test experiments by accurate investigation, is fairly strong evidence that our policies have been of the hit-or-miss kind.[124]

Problems of war and postwar reconstruction stimulated interest in and writing on economic matters. Two inconveniences became apparent quickly to economists: shortage of publication facilities

121. Representatives of professional groups testified in favor of economics teaching before the Royal Commission on the University of Melbourne. "Report," *Papers Presented to the Parliament of Victoria*, 1903, pp. 281–82, 314–15, and 370.
122. E. M. Higgins, *David Stewart and the W. E. A.* (Sydney, 1957), p. 18; and G. V. Portus, *Happy Highways* (Melbourne, 1953), pp. 162–63.
123. "The Australian Democracy and its Economic Problems," *Economic Journal*, XXV (1915), 347.
124. R. F. Irvine, *The Place of the Social Sciences in a Modern University* (Sydney, 1914), p. 8.

and lack of provision for meetings and discussion. Historical and literary societies continued, as they had for half a century, to open their doors to economists on a limited scale, and the *Economic Journal* still accepted occasional comments on the Australian scene. Publication of collected essays on specific themes, and a series of volumes issued by the W. E. A. also helped partly to relieve the pressure.[125] Such efforts, however, did little to encourage development of a professional spirit or of a distinctive domestic body of doctrine. Economists as such had still to obtain serious recognition. As D. B. Copland complained as late as 1923:

> Economics . . . receives but scant consideration from the public, and is too frequently confused with politics in the narrower sense. Some months ago it was suggested to a leading Australian daily paper that there might be some interest in an economic treatment of the contemporary trade depression. The proposal was rejected: such a treatment was not in keeping with the views of the journal in question, and, in any case, there was little interest in an "academic" discussion of the problem.
> This is typical of the opinion of those who influence public opinion in the Commonwealth, where there are few trained economists in either official or private life. No recognized economist, *per se*, is asked to serve upon Government Committees, and no system of training officials for higher financial and trade duties has been thought necessary. It is not that the country is not interested in economics; it is wildly so, as every news-sheet shows. But there is a tradition that economists are dull and theoretical, and a young democracy can ignore them with impunity.[126]

Agitation for organization of economists came principally from within the universities. Professors Meredith Atkinson, G. V. Portus, and Herbert Heaton were instrumental in mobilizing the W. E. A. and in demonstrating the utility of domestic publications. At a meeting in Adelaide of the Australasian Association for the Advancement of Science, in 1924, Professor Copland, as President of Section G, submitted a scheme for the establishment of an

125. The first important volume of essays was: Meredith Atkinson, ed., *Australia: Economic and Political Studies* (Melbourne, 1920). G. V. Portus was general editor of the W. E. A. series.
126. "The Trade Depression in Australia in Relation to Economic Thought," *Report of the Sixteenth Meeting of the Australasian Association for the Advancement of Science held at Wellington, 1923*, p. 555.

economic society.[127] The plan was adopted, and a committee of academics, businessmen, and public servants, with Copland as president, organized branches in all major cities.[128] The term "Economics" was returned symbolically to the title of Section G in 1928, and the level of discussion at meetings improved dramatically. L. F. Giblin recounted in 1947: "There was almost an evangelical fervour about the Adelaide meeting and the Section became one of the most active and efficient in the Association —qualities which it has maintained up to the present day."[129]

Copland was the first editor of the journal of the Economic Society, the *Economic Record*, which began publication in 1925. The other two Australian members of the editorial board were R. C. Mills and E. C. Dyason. Again in the words of Giblin:

> The *Economic Record*, 1925–46, has been a great achievement. In Economics, Australia started behind scratch in 1925. Yet it is fair to say that in no other branch of studies, literary or scientific, has Australia produced a journal so widely recognized and highly esteemed in other countries as in Economics. This achievement is due in the first place to Copland and secondly to Mills. That they have had important differences of outlook on life and on Economics has made their harmonious co-operation over the years a triumph for both of them and at the same time has given added force and solidity to the results of their collaboration.[130]

Even after foundation of the Economic Society and the *Economic Record*, Copland did not cease his labors as an effective propagandist for economics.[131]

During the 1920's economics moved from the position, as Giblin said, of a "Cinderella" science to a place of influence in universities, in business, in government, and throughout public

127. D. B. Copland, "Monetary Policy and its Reactions upon Australia," *Report of the Seventeenth Meeting of the Australasian Association for the Advancement of Science held at Adelaide, 1924*, p. 497.
128. D. B. Copland, "Notes. The Economic Society—Its Origin and Constitution," *Economic Record*, I (1925), 140–44.
129. "The *Record* and its Editors (1925–46)," *Economic Record*, XXIII (1947), 1.
130. *Ibid.*, p. 4.
131. See for example Copland's "Report" to the Development and Migration Commission in 1928 on "The Control of Business Cycle with Special Reference to Australia," in "Development and Migration Commission, Report on Unemployment and Business Stability in Australia," *Papers Presented to the Parliament of the Commonwealth of Australia, 1926–27–28*, Appendix I.

life. Australians had never been completely ignorant of economics, even in the early years of the colonies. But only under the leadership of Copland, Giblin, Mills, and their colleagues did the subject gain a position of authority and respect.

Index